An Introduction to Chinese Philosophy

AN INTRODUCTION TO

Chinese Philosophy

From Ancient Philosophy to Chinese Buddhism

JeeLoo Liu

Blackwell Publishing

BLACKWELL PUBLISHING
350 Main Street, Malden, MA 02148-5020, USA
9600 Garsington Road, Oxford OX4 2DQ, UK
550 Swanston Street, Carlton, Victoria 3053, Australia

First published 2006 by Blackwell Publishing Ltd

5   2011

Library of Congress Cataloging-in-Publication Data

Liu, JeeLoo.
An introduction to Chinese philosophy : from ancient philosophy to
Chinese Buddhism / JeeLoo Liu.
p. cm.
Includes bibliographical references (p.) and index.
ISBN: 978-1-4051-2949-7 (hard cover : alk. paper)
ISBN: 978-1-4051-2950-3 (pbk. : alk. paper)
1. Philosophy, Chinese. I. Title.
B126.L564 2006
181'.11—dc22
2005034230

A catalogue record for this title is available from the British Library.

Set in 10/12pt Sabon
by Graphicraft Limited, Hong Kong

The publisher's policy is to use permanent paper from mills that operate a sustainable
forestry policy, and which has been manufactured from pulp processed using acid-free
and elementary chlorine-free practices. Furthermore, the publisher ensures that the text
paper and cover board used have met acceptable environmental accreditation standards.

For further information on
Blackwell Publishing, visit our website:
www.blackwellpublishing.com

Contents

Acknowledgments   vii

Preface   ix

Comparative Philosophy Timeline   xiii

Introduction: What Is Chinese Philosophy?   1

Part I   Ancient Chinese Philosophy

    Introduction   15

1   *Yijing* (*I Ching*): The Cosmological Foundation of Chinese Philosophy   26

2   Confucius (Kongzi) in the *Analects*   47

3   Mencius (Mengzi)   65

4   Xunzi (Hsün Tzu)   86

5   Mozi (Mo Tzu)   108

6   Laozi (Lao Tzu)   131

7   Zhuangzi (Chuang Tzu)   152

8   Hanfeizi (Han Fei Tzu)   182

Part II   Chinese Buddhism

    Introduction   209

9   The Consciousness-Only (*Wei-shi*) School   220

Contents

10	The Hua-yan (Hua-yen) School	248
11	The Tian-tai (T'ien-t'ai) School	277
12	The Chan School (Zen Buddhism)	304

Notes	332
References and Further Reading	379
Appendix: Translation Conversion Table	407
Index	414

Acknowledgments

This book would not have been possible without the generous support from the Chiang Ching-kuo Foundation for International Scholarly Exchange, and the sabbatical leave from the State University of New York at Geneseo. I wish to thank Dr Ying-shih Yu (余英時) for his assistance. I am grateful to the staff at the Information Delivery Service Department of SUNY Geneseo for the prompt delivery of all requested materials. Without their service, the research for this book would have taken much longer. I also wish to thank the philosophy editor at Blackwell Publishing, Jeff Dean, for seeing the potential in me and in my book.

I firmly believe that no personal accomplishment is the result simply of one's own efforts. I would not have been able to produce this book without the vast amount of assistance I have received. My first knowledge of Chinese philosophy came in the main from Master Yu (毓老), under whose tutelage, for seven years, I studied most of the classics of Chinese philosophy. My Master's thesis advisor, Zhang Yong-jun (張永儁), taught me everything I knew about Neo-Confucianism. I owe my training in analytic philosophy to all my former teachers who taught me various aspects of analytic philosophy, in particular, Chen Wen-xiu (陳文秀), Lin Zheng-hong (林正弘), Paul Yu (余英華), Richard Feldman, Earl Conee, Robert Holmes, Douglas Dempster, and John Heil. I wish to acknowledge the contributions from all the students who took my Chinese philosophy course at SUNY Geneseo, and students from my Asian philosophy class at California State University at Fullerton, for their inquisitive pursuit inspired me to formulate my ideas.

On a personal level, I wish to thank the following people for their encouragement and support: Paul Yu, Ying-shih Yu, Craig Ihara, Ellen Yu, Shi-ling Hsiang, Amy Steinberg, Ya-yen Yu, and, of course, my brother and sisters. Finally, I wish to dedicate this book to my mother Liu Lin Zhu-wei (劉林祝闈), who instilled intellectual curiosity in me;

Acknowledgments

to my high school teacher Fan Qing-wen (范慶雯), who pointed the way to philosophy for me when I was only 15; to my beloved husband Michael Cranston, without whom I would not have been where I am today, and to my two boys Collin and Dillon, who have given me tremendous joy in life.

Preface

The aim of this book is to introduce two early periods of Chinese philosophy: ancient Chinese philosophy (ca. 600–200 BCE) and Chinese Buddhism (ca. 300–900 AD). My intended readers are people who are interested in learning about Chinese philosophy in a systematic and scholarly way. It is a serious book that a serious layman might enjoy reading; prior knowledge of Chinese is not required. I use Chinese words sparingly and adopt the commonly accepted translations of key notions in Chinese philosophy. This book could be adopted as a textbook for college-level courses in Chinese philosophy or Asian philosophy. For this purpose, I have included further discussion questions at the end of each chapter. This book could also be enjoyed by anyone who wishes to find a reliable entry into the study of Chinese philosophy. Ample supplementary references and recommended readings are supplied to assist further research in Chinese philosophy.

A few things need to be explained before readers get to the content of this book. First, the approach used is analytic and the analysis is often comparative in nature. By "analytic," I mean the philosophical approach that emphasizes the analysis of concepts, the formulation of arguments, the examination of basic assumptions, and the pursuit of clarity in language. When appropriate, I will formulate the arguments the philosopher uses and give a brief discussion. When no argument is clearly employed by the philosopher, I will analyze his basic philosophical assumptions, methodology, and key notions. In emphasizing "analytic," I wish to distinguish my approach from philological, hermeneutic, or sinological approaches to Chinese philosophy.

By "comparative," I mean that I aim to link the study of Chinese philosophy to the study of Western philosophy. My intention is not to introduce these schools of thought merely as something from a distant past, but to encourage further philosophical investigation on the issues these ancient Chinese philosophers worked on. Ancient Chinese philosophers may not have our contemporary philosophical terminology, but many of the issues they dealt with are of common philosophical interest. Furthermore, among contemporary commentators on Chinese philosophy, many have been trained in Western philosophy and their analyses often reflect their thinking modes with such background. In presenting what contemporary commentators argue about in their reading of Chinese philosophy, we cannot avoid using terminology in Western philosophy. Readers with prior knowledge of Western philosophy may find this comparative approach an aid to their understanding, while readers with no such background may wish to skip these discussions.

Second, this book is not meant to serve as a history of Chinese philosophy. For that purpose, we already have Fung Yu-lan's comprehensive *A History of Chinese Philosophy*, translated by Derk Bodde. The content of the present book does not cover all schools in either ancient Chinese philosophy or Chinese Buddhism. I have chosen only the major schools that have shaped the core development of Chinese philosophy. For historical background, as well as for those other philosophers or schools left out in this book, readers should consult Fung Yu-lan's *History*. A comparative chronology of Chinese and Western philosophy is prepared to enable readers to place each philosopher in his or her historical context.

Third, presently there exist two popular Romanization systems for the pronunciation of Chinese terms: the Wade-Giles system and the Pinyin system. For example, "Dao" in the Pinyin system and "Tao" in the Wade-Giles system are different renditions of the same Chinese word, as are "ren" in the Pinyin system and "jen" in the Wade-Giles system. This book employs the Pinyin system, since it is now the more widely adopted one. However, many works on Chinese philosophy in the Western world were done in the Wade-Giles system. Readers may find it confusing to see different Romanizations of the same philosopher's name or of the same concept. In an appendix, I have constructed a translation conversion table, which should help readers relate names in this book to names used in other works.

Last, but not least, even though this book only focuses on the two early periods of Chinese philosophy, I do not want readers to get the wrong impression that Chinese philosophy has only two important periods. The restricted scope of this introduction to Chinese philosophy is purely a result of pragmatic consideration of the length of this book. Neo-Confucianism, dominating Chinese intellectual history between the eleventh and the seventeenth century, is another major part of Chinese philosophy. Contemporary Chinese nineteenth- and twentieth-century philosophy is also a period that demands more attention from the Western world. To understand the totality of Chinese philosophy, one needs to study those two major periods as well. But to do so, we need to start with a good understanding of the two early periods. I hope that readers will be inspired by this book to seek a more comprehensive knowledge of the whole development of Chinese philosophy.

The first part of this book deals with seven ancient philosophers, representing Confucianism, Daoism, Mohism, and Legalism respectively, as well as a major philosophical text, the *Yijing* (*Book of Changes*). The organization of the chapters is partly chronological, partly thematic. This arrangement is made in order better to present each school of thought and to facilitate a more focused analysis of the debates among different schools. Take *Yijing* for example. Part of the complete *Yijing* predates Confucius, while part of it was probably completed after the ancient period. However, its cosmology lays the foundation for both Confucianism and Daoism. Hence, this book begins with *Yijing*. After *Yijing*, I put three major Confucian thinkers (Confucius, Mencius, and Xunzi) together, followed by Mozi. Even though Mozi predated Mencius and Xunzi, his view can be better grasped after we see what he objected to in Confucianism, since it was primarily developed from his dissension with Confucianism. Therefore, we will have a complete grasp of the major theses of Confucianism before we move on to Mozi's challenge of this doctrine. After Confucianism and Mohism, I present Daoism with two representative thinkers: Laozi and Zhuangzi. Their different metaphysical views and their unconventional ethical advice are the focus of these two chapters. Part I ends with Hanfeizi, the founder of Legalism, which became the dominant political ideology in Chinese history.

Part II deals with four representative schools of Chinese Buddhism: the Consciousness-Only school, the Hua-yan school, the Tian-tai school and the Chan school. These chapters form the most groundbreaking part of the entire book, since no one has ever given these Chinese Buddhist schools any clear and comprehensive analysis before. I focus on the anti-realistic tenet dominant in Buddhism, and analyze how these schools differ in their own interpretations of the emptiness of the phenomenal world. By arranging the four schools in a semi-chronological order, I also wish to show how Chinese Buddhism slowly steered away from the anti-realist thinking of Indian Buddhism. The four schools demonstrate the progressively realistic commitment emerging in the thought of Chinese Buddhists.

I aim to present each philosophy with an unbiased attitude – the exposition does not reflect my personal philosophical leaning, but the collective thinking of contemporary commentators on various subject matters. Naturally, my analysis ultimately represents my own interpretation of the philosophy. The primary texts for each philosophy are usually the philosopher's most representative work in its unabridged form in Chinese. The secondary sources include most of the available articles and books written in English. The discussion in each chapter thus aims to reflect the common interests and contested issues among contemporary commentators. When available, every chapter lists several translations of comparable quality and recommends some contemporary articles written in the analytic style. Since Wing-tsit Chan's *A Sourcebook in Chinese Philosophy* is still the most comprehensive anthology to date, it is listed with every chapter. A recent anthology that covers only the ancient period, *Readings in Classical Chinese Philosophy*, edited by Philip J. Ivanhoe and Bryan W. Van Norden, contains excellent translations of seven ancient philosophers. It is listed with all chapters dealing with these ancient philosophers. With each chapter, I consult the Chinese texts first and then compare the available translations to find the best rendition. When I quote from a particular translator, I stress the translator's name. In cases where I end up using my own translation, I simply give the original textual reference.

In the Western world, Chinese philosophy has often been misrepresented as "non-philosophy," as a form of religion. Two leading schools of thought in Chinese philosophy, Confucianism and Daoism, are often taught as part of the curriculum of *World Religion*. But Chinese philosophy is not simply a way of living, a doctrine inviting believers or followers. It has its cosmological speculations, ethical principles, epistemological arguments, and its methodology. It challenges thinkers to build on philosophical assumptions and to engage in philosophical debates. In comparison to Western philosophy, Chinese philosophy is based on different metaphysical assumptions and it takes different approaches to deal with the same social and moral concerns. The study of Chinese philosophy can thus provide philosophers with a fresh perspective on issues dealt with in the Western tradition. By writing a philosophical introduction to Chinese philosophy, I wish to give Chinese philosophy its proper status in the world of philosophy.

Comparative Philosophy Timeline

Chinese Philosophy	*Western Philosophy*
600 BCE Confucius (551–479 BCE) Laozi (?)	Thales (fl. 585 BCE) Anaximander (ca. 612–545 BCE) Anaximenes (fl. 550 BCE) Pythagoras (585–497 BCE) Heraclitus (540–475 BCE)
500 BCE Mozi (ca. 480–392? BCE) Yang Zhu (ca. 440–360? BCE) Liezi (?)	Parmenides (b. 510 BCE) Anaxagoras (500–428 BCE) Empedocles (ca. 495–435 BCE) Protagoras (485–415 BCE) Zeno of Elea (fl. 450 BCE) Democritus (460–370 BCE) Socrates (469–399 BCE)
400 BCE Zhuangzi (ca. 399–285 BCE) Hui Shi (380–305? BCE) Mencius (371–289 BCE) Gongsun Long (b. 380? BCE) Xunzi (ca. 340–245 BCE)	Plato (427–347 BCE) Diogenes (400–325 BCE) Aristotle (384–322 BCE) Epicurus (341–271 BCE)
300 BCE Hanfeizi (ca. 280–233 BCE)	
200 BCE Dung Zhongshu (ca. 179–104 BCE)	

Comparative Philosophy Timeline

Chinese Philosophy	*Western Philosophy*

100 BCE
Huainanzi (d. 122 BCE)
Yang Xiong (53 BCE–18 AD)

Cicero (106–43 BCE)
Lucretius (99–55 BCE)

CE
Wang Chong (27–100?)

Seneca (4 BCE–65 AD)

100 AD

Epictetus (55–135)
Marcus Aurelius (121–180)

200 AD
Wang Bi (226–249)

Sextus Empiricus (ca. 200)
Plotinus (204–270)

300 AD
Guo Xiang (d. 312)
Seng-zhao (384–414) (Three-Treatise)

Augustine (354–430)

400 AD
Bodhidharma (470–534?) (Chan)
Hui-ke (487–593) (Chan)

Boethius (ca. 480–525)

500 AD
Hui-wen (?–577) (Tian-tai)
Hui-si (514–577) (Tian-tai)
Zhi-yi (538–597) (Tian-tai)
Ji-zang (549–623) (Three-Treatise)
Du-shun (557–640) (Hua-yan)
Guan-ding (561–632) (Tian-tai)
Dao-xin (580–636?) (Chan)
Xuan-zang (596–664)
  (Consciousness-Only)

600 AD
Hong-ren (601–674) (Chan)
Zhi-yan (602–668) (Hua-yan)
Fa-zang (643–712) (Hua-yan)
Shen-xiu (ca. 605–706) (Chan)
Hui-neng (638–713) (Chan)
Shen-hui (670–762) (Chan)

700 AD
Cheng-guan (738–839?) (Hua-yan)
Han Yu (768–824)
Li Ao (fl. 798)

Chinese Philosophy	*Western Philosophy*
800 AD	
Lin Ji (ca. 810–866) (Chan)	
Huang Bo (?–ca. 850) (Chan)	
900 AD	
1000 AD	
Shao Yong (1011–1077)	Anselm (1033–1109)
Zhou Dunyi (1017–1073)	
Zhang Zai (1020–1077)	
Cheng Hao (1032–1085)	
Cheng Yi (1033–1107)	
1100 AD	
Zhu Xi (1130–1200)	
Lu Xiangshan (1139–1193)	
1200 AD	
	Bonaventure (ca. 1221–1274)
	Thomas Aquinas (1224–1274)
1300 AD	
	William Ockham (ca. 1285–1347)
1400 AD	
Wang Yangming (1472–1529)	Desiderius Erasmus (1466–1536)
	Niccolò Machiavelli (1469–1527)
	Thomas More (1478–1535)
1500 AD	
Liu Zongzhou (1578–1645)	Michel de Montaigne (1533–1592)
	Francis Bacon (1561–1626)
1600 AD	
Huang Zongxi (1610–1695)	Thomas Hobbes (1588–1679)
Wang Fuzhi (1619–1692)	René Descartes (1596–1650)
	Baruch Spinoza (1632–1677)
	John Locke (1632–1704)
	Gottfried Wilhelm Leibniz
	(1646–1716)
1700 AD	
Dai Zhen (1723–1777)	George Berkeley (1685–1753)
	Montesquieu (1689–1755)

Comparative Philosophy Timeline

Chinese Philosophy	*Western Philosophy*
	Joseph Butler (1692–1752)
	Voltaire (1694–1778)
	Francis Hutcheson (1694–1746)
	Thomas Reid (1710–1796)
	David Hume (1711–1776)
	Jean-Jacques Rousseau (1712–1778)
	Paul-Henri-Dietrich d'Holbach (1723–1789)
	Adam Smith (1723–1790)
	Immanuel Kant (1724–1804)
	Edmund Burke (1729–1979)
	Jeremy Bentham (1748–1832)
	Friederich Schiller (1759–1805)
	Johann Gottlieb Fichte (1762–1814)
1800 AD	
Kang Youwei (1858–1927)	Georg Wilhelm Friedrich Hegel (1770–1831)
Tan Sitong (1865–1898)	Friedrich Wilhelm Joseph von Schelling (1775–1854)
Liang Qichao (1873–1929)	
Wang Guowei (1877–1927)	Arthur Schopenhauer (1788–1860)
	John Stuart Mill (1806–1873)
	Søren Kierkegaard (1813–1855)
	Henry David Thoreau (1817–1862)
	Karl Marx (1818–1883)
	Friedrich Engels (1820–1895)
	Wilhelm Dilthey (1833–1911)
	Henry Sidgwick (1838–1900)
	Ernst Mach (1838–1916)
	Franz Brentano (1838–1917)
	Charles Sanders Peirce (1839–1914)
	William James (1842–1910)
	Friedrich Wilhelm Nietzsche (1844–1900)
	Gottlob Frege (1848–1925)
	Alexius Meinong (1853–1920)
	Edmund Husserl (1859–1938)
	Henri Bergson (1859–1941)
	John Dewey (1859–1952)
	Pierre-Maurice-Marie Duhem (1861–1916)
	Alfred North Whitehead (1861–1947)
	Max Weber (1864–1920)

Chinese Philosophy	Western Philosophy
	Benedetto Croce (1866–1952)
	Bertrand Russell (1872–1970)
	George Edward Moore (1873–1958)
	Arthur Lovejoy (1873–1962)
	Ernst Cassirer (1874–1945)
Early 1900 AD	
Xiong Shili (1885–1968)	Moritz Schlick (1882–1936)
Zhang Dongsun (1886–1973)	Clarence Irvine Lewis (1883–1964)
Zhang Junmai (1887–1969)	Karl Jaspers (1883–1969)
Hu Shi (1891–1962)	Ludwig Wittgenstein (1889–1951)
Liang Shuming (1893–1988)	Gabriel Marcel (1889–1973)
Jin Yuelin (1895–1984)	Martin Heidegger (1889–1976)
Feng Youlan (1895–1990)	Rudolf Carnap (1891–1970)
Fang Dongmei (1899–1977)	Susanne Langer (1895–1985)
He Lin (1902–1992)	Herbert Marcuse (1898–1979)
Xu Fuguan (1903–1982)	Henry H. Price (1899–1984)
Tang Junyi (1909–1978)	Gilbert Ryle (1900–1976)
Mou Zongsan (1909–1995)	Alfred Tarski (1902–1983)
Zhang Dainian (1909–)	Karl Popper (1902–1994)
Feng Qi (1915–1995)	Theodor W. Adorno (1903–1969)
Li Zehou (1931–)	Jean-Paul Sartre (1905–1980)
	Charles Leslie Stevenson (1908–1979)
	Alfred Jules Ayer (1910–1989)
	Albert Camus (1913–1960)

Introduction: What Is Chinese Philosophy?

A Preliminary Explanation

In this introduction, I shall attempt to offer not a *definition of* "Chinese philosophy," but a *description of* some general traits of Chinese philosophy. No definition of any philosophical development can ever be given, since philosophy itself is an organic body that defies definition. However, even when the goal is merely to *describe* Chinese philosophy, the description must still be incomplete. To be complete, the description of Chinese philosophy would have to include a comprehensive explanation of the historical, social, political, and cultural background of China. This introduction cannot do that. What I sketch here are simply some general characteristics of Chinese philosophy that need to be known by anyone who wants to study Chinese philosophy. I shall explain what propelled the development of Chinese philosophy, what the key concepts of Chinese philosophy are, what traditional Chinese pedagogy was, and how ancient philosophical ideas were recorded. This introduction should give readers a sense of how and why the thinking and writing styles of Chinese philosophy are different from those of Western philosophy. However, readers should be cautioned that any such characterization would tend to be oversimplified.

From Religion to Philosophy: The Motivation behind Chinese Philosophy

Even though the prehistoric Chinese did embrace a worldview with a personified Supreme Being, whom they called "*Shang-di*" (the same term is currently used to translate the English word "God"), this folk religion never entered the realm of discourse of Chinese philosophy. The residue of this primitive belief was sometimes seen in such expressions as "the will of Heaven," which was often identified with the people's preferences, or "the mandate of Heaven," which was sometimes used as a political justification for overthrowing the ruling power. However, the sense of a Divine Will, or Divine Intervention, was not taken as literally as it was in the Old Testament. The predominant belief held by ancient Chinese thinkers was that there was no "Creator" of the cosmos, no volitional act of creation, and no personal adjudicator in Nature. Their religion was more a form of Nature worship, though it was different from the ancient Greeks' assignment of personified gods or goddesses to various natural phenomena. Instead, the ancient Chinese believed that there was a spiritual correspondence between the world of Nature and the world of men. The universe was thought to be an organic system, with all parts integrated into an ordered whole. What is above men is Heaven; what is underneath men is Earth. In ancient Chinese usage, "Heaven" (*tian*) is not merely the sky as viewed from earth; nor is it a transcendent realm used in the Christian sense. "Heaven" stands for the totality of heavenly bodies and phenomena; in particular, it is often used to refer to the operation of the sun. "Earth" (*di*), on the other hand, generally refers to the ground on which everything exists. It includes various territories of the ground, but it is most frequently used to cover lowland territories such as valleys, gorges, basins, etc. To the ancient Chinese, the universe is the totality of Heaven, Earth, and all that exists in between. There was no beginning; the world has always existed.

Since the ancient Chinese believed that there was a spiritual correspondence between natural phenomena and human states of affairs, the common explanation for natural disasters was that they were causally related to some adverse human states of affairs. Drought was attributed to Heaven; flood to Earth. Either of these phenomena could bring about famine in human societies. For an agricultural society, famine poses the greatest risk to human survival, and yet in Chinese history it was a recurring threat. Even so, in the ancient Chinese worldview, there was no evil in Nature. Natural disasters were seen as part of the natural development of the world; hence, they did not stand for "evil." Either they were brought about by the natural correspondence between Nature and the human world, or they represented a form of "temporary deflection from the essential harmony of the universe,"[1] not a positive force in itself. When the human world has accumulated sufficient disorder, the original harmonious state of the world is disrupted. Such disruptions bring about disturbances in Nature, which in turn bring disasters to human society. Some other infrequent natural phenomena

2

such as hail, earthquakes, infestation of insects, etc., were seen as fore-warning signs. These signs were also what naturally happened at the time when the cosmic harmony was disturbed. Therefore, Nature corresponds to the human world, just as a bell would chime upon being struck.

The implicit belief behind this cosmic correspondence is that every-thing is interconnected in this cosmic whole, which has a cosmic rhythm shared by all. Max Kaltenmark says: "Conforming to the rhythm of the universe is the prerequisite of wisdom in all Chinese thinking."[2] A way to "tap into" this cosmic rhythm in ancient China was divination – the method of attempting to foretell the future through oracles or special rites. The earliest form of divination that we now know of was the method of tortoise-shell reading. To perform this divination, some encrypted words were first written on a tortoise shell. (These writings were the earliest writing samples found in China, dating back to 1700–1100 BCE.) The shell was then put into a fire until it started to crack at various points. The reader of the sign would decipher the code depend-ing on how those words were separated. To perform this ceremony, one has to purify one's mind and body beforehand, in order to be in a heightened state of awareness of the cosmic spirit. From this divination, the reader could predict the future development of nature, and in turn decide the best course of action. In the Shang Dynasty (1766–1150 BCE), the king often would appeal to the divination performed by spe-cially appointed augurs, in order to decide major affairs such as whether to launch a war or alter an existing policy.

Later, in the Zhou Dynasty (*c.*1122?–256 BCE), the more commonly used divination was based on *Yijing*, the *Book of Changes*. In its origi-nal form, this text was not a complete book. At the earliest stage, it probably contained merely some esoteric graphs and diagrams. From the initial 8 three-line trigrams, it developed into a complicated system of 64 six-line hexagrams. Judgments (interpretations of the divination results) were then attached to these hexagrams as well as to each line within a single hexagram. The method of divination using *Yijing* was not restricted to the royal courts or the high priests; ancient scholars such as Confucius often appealed to it too. The questions being con-sulted through this divination were no longer merely political affairs of the state; they could also be about what an individual should do in a given situation. To know how to make moral decisions is called "wis-dom," and the possession of wisdom, in this ancient context, signified one's spiritual concord with the spirit of the cosmos. In this respect, "wisdom" for the Chinese has not only a practical connotation, but also a religious origination. If "philosophy" is simply "love of wisdom"

3

(etymologically speaking), then Chinese philosophy can be seen as originating in a religious sentiment about the cosmic spirit.

The construction of *Yijing*'s trigrams and hexagrams is based on two elements alone: *yin* and *yang*. In the symbols of *Yijing*, *yang* is represented by a solid line; *yin* is represented by a broken line. Both *yin* and *yang* are part of the cosmic energy or the cosmic force. All trigrams and hexagrams reflect the various distributions and relations between *yin* and *yang*. Implicit in this ideology is the belief that the whole universe, Nature and human world alike, is nothing but the various distributions of, and relations between, *yin* and *yang*. The language of *yin* and *yang* takes on two dimensions: one is a naturalistic description of states of *yin* and *yang*; the other is a symbolic description of states of human relationships. In *Yijing*, these two dimensions are inseparable. This again reflects the ancient Chinese worldview that the world of Nature and the world of humans are indivisible.

In summary, under the ancient Chinese pre-philosophical worldview, the world is an organic whole with order and regularities, not a chaotic conglomerate dominated by chance. The basic constituents of myriad things in the world are not matter, but energy or force of two natures: *yin* and *yang*, the movement of which follows a regulated rhythm. A sage, or one who is adept at deciphering the divination results, can tap into the cosmic rhythm because his mind and the cosmos are unified. This cosmic rhythm runs through Nature and the human world in the same way. Furthermore, the realm of the spiritual and the realm of the material are not sharply divided. The dead and the living are not situated in incommunicable worlds. One's spirit is not bound by one's body. Once the body is dead, the spirit can roam about in different dimensions – above the living, below the living, or even among the living. There is, in addition, no separation of the self from the world. The subjective person and the objective world are not in opposition, but are parts of an integrated whole. How man lives his life is affected by what goes on in the universe; at the same time, how he lives will affect what continues in the universe. Just as the air we breathe joins the cosmic atmosphere, so what we do interacts causally with the world around us. This belief in the unity of Nature and the human world, mind and matter, body and spirit, or man and the universe, became the foundational thesis for Chinese cosmology.

Basic Concepts in Chinese Cosmology:
Dao, *Qi*, *Yin*, and *Yang*

Chinese cosmology is built on belief in the cosmic order or cosmic pattern, which serves not only as the source for all existence, but also as the governing rule for all cosmic developments. This basic assumption of the existence of a cosmic pattern became the core thesis of all major schools in Chinese philosophy.[3] The universe is seen "as a self-contained organism functioning according to its own inherent pattern."[4] This pattern was commonly referred to as "*Dao*" by ancient philosophers. (*Dao* is capitalized when it is used to designate a unique, all-embracing *Dao*; it is not capitalized when it refers to the Chinese word "dao" or to the dao of particular things.) The pursuit of *Dao* would become an ultimate goal shared by all Chinese philosophers. According to Bryan Van Norden's analysis:

> This word [*dao*] has several related senses. (1) The original sense was "way," in the sense of "path" or "road." It came to mean (2) "way," in the sense of "the right way to do something," or "the order that comes from doing things in the right way," (3) a linguistic account of a way to do something, or "to give a linguistic account," (4) a metaphysical entity responsible for the way things act.[5]

In other words, the word *dao* can be used as a common noun designating roads; it can be used as a moral term signifying the right way of doing things; it can be used as a verb meaning "to speak"; and it can be used as an ontological notion suggestive of the origin of the universe. These four senses, although on the surface widely different, are actually interwoven in the philosophical significance of *Dao*.

In the context of Chinese cosmology, *Dao* stands for an "all-embracing entelechy"[6] – it is a life-giving force responsible for the creation of myriad things. This usage is seen in *Yijing*'s *Great Treatise*, and Laozi (the originator of Daoism) seems to interpret *Dao* this way from time to time. *Dao* in this sense also governs the whole universe from its inception. Hence, *Dao* stands for the cosmic order, *the Way* things are. So an appropriate translation for *dao* is "the Way." "The Way," used in the singular, signifies the existence of a single cosmic order or a single cosmic pattern. It can be loosely rendered as *the Truth*, or *the Reality*. It can also be called the cosmic principle, in the same way that later Neo-Confucians used "Heavenly Principle" in place of *Dao*. The two words in Chinese, *dao* (the Way) and *li* (principle), are often used in conjunction to signify *reasons* or *truth*. Under the holistic cosmic picture, the cosmic order also governs human affairs. Consequently, *Dao* takes on a moral connotation, as the *right* way for states of affairs in the human world to be. Since *Dao* is the "right way," it also comes to stand for "*the path (the Way)* one ought to take." In this sense, *Dao* stands for the highest moral precept for human beings. Confucius definitely uses *dao* in this sense, as do other Confucians. Finally, *dao* as "to speak" reveals the assumption that our language depicts the reality as it is, and to speak the truth means to depict the Way. This assumption was common to early Confucians. Laozi's opening remark in the *Daodejing*, "A *dao* that can be spoken of (*dao*) is not a constant *Dao*," could be seen as a direct challenge to this assumption. We would call such a view, which challenges the possibility of our language's accurate depiction of reality, language skepticism.

Another important notion in Chinese cosmology is that of *qi*, in relation to which *Dao* should also be understood, since *Dao* is often seen as the rhythm or pattern of the movement of *qi*. There is no adequate English translation for *qi*, although it has been rendered variously as "energy," "vital energy," "pure energy," "force," "material force," "spirit," "vapor," "air," etc. Many commentators have pointed out the etymological root of the word "*qi*."[7] Originally, it referred to the steam or vapor coming from boiling rice (the Chinese character for *qi* contains the character for rice as a component). It came to represent the nourishing vapor or the moistening mist, both of which encompass the atmosphere, furnishing the bodies of all creatures and becoming the source of life. From this, the philosophical notion of *qi* was developed and came to stand for the ontological basis for all things. Benjamin Schwartz thinks that this notion is "the closest Chinese approximation of the Western concept of 'matter'."[8] But the two concepts are quite different, in that *qi* is dynamic, while matter is inactive; *qi* penetrates everything, while matter is solid; *qi* is constantly changing, while matter is static. Chinese cosmology treats *qi* as existentially prior to matter – the condensation of *qi* constitutes matter. Everything is comprised of *qi*, and the various degrees of purity or impurity determine the levels of existence. Human beings are made out of the purest of *qi*, while lower animals are produced by *qi* with greater impurity. *Qi* is not volitional; hence, our creation is not the result of any intentional production. *Qi* condenses and rarefies, but it never gets exhausted or even diminished. *Qi* pervades the universe; in other words, the universe is simply the totality of *qi* in perpetual motion and constant alteration. In this cosmology, the cosmos is viewed as being composed of a great force (*qi*) that has no mind of its own. This great force permeates everything in the cosmos; as a result, everything is interconnected in this organic whole.

In the Chinese conception, *qi* is divided into two strands: *yin* and *yang*. Both strands seem to manifest at once physical differences as well as symbolic differences. On the physical level, *yin* and *yang* are both competitive and complementary. On the one hand, the *yin qi* and the *yang qi* are competing forces or opposite forms of energy, which constantly work against each other. Since both are part of the totality of *qi*, when *yin* grows, *yang* declines; when *yang* strengthens, *yin* weakens. The competition is constant and the flow of *qi* is always in motion; hence, change ("*yi*") is the constant state of *qi*. On the other hand, *yin* and *yang* complement each other, since everything relies on both of them to exist. In the physical world, nothing can be either purely *yang* or purely *yin*. We can say that the cooperation of *yin* and *yang* is based on their mutual competition. Things can change, grow, decline, and get reborn, exactly because *yin* and *yang* work against each other. The change of seasons is a perfect illustration of the interaction between *yin* and *yang*. Viewed in this way, nothing that we humans deem to have "negative values" can be dispensed with.

Yin and *yang* do not stand for a simplified polarization between good and evil or light and dark. The cosmic whole cannot be bifurcated into opposites, fighting for the eradication of the other. The apparent competition between *yin* and *yang* is actually the motivating force behind their cooperation. Hence, without one, the other could not exist. As Bodde explains this kind of dualism:

> Never . . . is the suggestion made by [all thinkers who adopt the *yin-yang* ideology] that the one can or should wholly displace the other. Hence there is no real analogy with the dualisms based on conflict (light vs. darkness, etc.) so familiar to us in the West. On the contrary, the *yin* and *yang* form a cosmic hierarchy of balanced inequality in which, however, each complements the other and has its own necessary function.[9]

On a metaphorical level, *yin* and *yang* seem to represent symbolic traits, rather than physical differences, among things in the world. *Yin* represents everything that is female; *yang* represents everything that is male. In Chinese symbolization, the sun is *yang*, while the moon is *yin*; the mountain is *yang*, while the lake is *yin*; fire is *yang*, while water is *yin*; and heat is *yang*, while chill is *yin*. The traits of *yang* include being vigorous, firm, aggressive, active, and strong. The traits of *yin* include being docile, yielding, accommodating, passive, and gentle. All things associated with *yang* are thus symbolic representations of *yang* traits; all things associated with *yin* are symbolic representations of *yin* traits.

From the primitive form of Nature worship, the ancient Chinese developed a sense of admiration and affection toward the natural world around them. This religious spirit prompted a philosophical pursuit of the order of the universe and the ontological foundation for all existence. The ancient philosophers called this cosmic order and the ontological foundation for all things "*Dao*," even though different philosophers assigned different connotations to this notion. This pursuit of the cosmic order and the ontological foundation would later become the quest for the metaphysical "Buddha" in Chinese Buddhism, and the study of the Heavenly Principle (*Li*) in Neo-Confucianism.

Primary Concerns of Chinese Philosophers: Human Society, Human Conduct, and Human Nature

Stemming from the religious spirit in pursuit of the welfare of human societies, Chinese philosophy's main focus is on such issues as how to rule the state, how to conduct oneself, how to do the right thing, etc., so that one does not disturb the cosmic order or deviate from *Dao*. There was a strong humanistic tendency even in the early stage of Chinese philosophical development. Humanism is the system of thought that focuses on the interests and well-being of human society. It is based on the values and characteristics that are believed to be best in human beings, rather than on any decrees by a supernatural authority. Ancient Chinese thinkers had an intense desire to find the best way to make the right political decisions, to alleviate social problems, and properly to conduct themselves. Sociopolitical philosophy and ethics are thus the two core areas in Chinese philosophy. In Part I, we shall see that almost all ancient Chinese philosophers attempted to define the best socio-political structure and the best moral guidance for the rulers as well as for the people. At the same time, since social structure, polity, and human conduct should all cohere with the cosmic order, Chinese philosophy is fundamentally rooted in its cosmology. This cosmology is manifested mostly in the philosophy of *Yijing*.

Chinese philosophers were in general not motivated by a purely intellectual pursuit of knowledge for knowledge's sake. Under the belief that it was the same *Dao* or *principle* that governed natural objects as well as human beings, they investigated natural objects as a means to the end of pursuing knowledge of *Dao* or *principle*. As A. C. Graham says:

From the Western viewpoint, pre-Buddhist Chinese philosophy is epistemo-logically naive. For the Chinese however the purpose of seeking the one behind the many is to find, not something more real than what appears to the senses, but a constant Way behind the changing and conflicting ways of life and government claimed by competing schools as the Way of the sage kings.[10]

Under the pursuit of *Dao* (the Way), when Chinese philosophers studied the external world and its objects, they were intent on finding some moral guidance in the way things are in Nature. This motivation propelled a form of *moralistic epistemology*, which is rather unique to Chinese philosophy.

Another issue of common interest for Chinese philosophers is the understanding of our basic nature – the way we naturally are. Under the ancient Chinese worldview, "the universe is actually a natural harmony, and therefore imbued with a principle of goodness which . . . provides the basis for human goodness."[11] A common assumption of authors of the Chinese classics was that humans are fundamentally good by nature, because they have the heavenly endowment of moral attributes. This view is particularly manifested in *Yijing*. Among ancient philosophers covered in Part I, some describe this natural goodness as "natural innocence" (such as Laozi and Zhuangzi); some describe it as the "sprouts of morality" (in particular, Mencius). There are, of course, some exceptions to this general trend. Xunzi, for example, argues that human nature is intrinsically bad. In spite of this, in all ancient philosophers' views, there was no assignment of "the original sin." Birth itself is celebrated as the union of *yin* and *yang*, as the joint creation of Heaven and Earth. Life is unquestionably valuable. Everyone is created through the union of two forces; hence, everyone is a blessed creation of Heaven and Earth.

In summary, we could say that Chinese philosophy was fundamentally developed by an earnest desire of philosophers to alleviate social problems, and to construct a better world for all humans. Chinese philosophers' eyes were not set on an abstract *Realm of the Forms*, intelligible and yet unreachable. They had a purely this-worldly concern; their goal was to improve on the world *given*. By asserting the initial harmony of the cosmos and the intrinsic goodness of humans, they attempted to demonstrate how social reforms are possible. To all of them, any effective social reform must consist in a moral reform of the rulers as well as of the people. To teach others what constitutes virtue and to inspire others to act morally thus constituted the mission ancient Chinese philosophers all took upon themselves – even though some acted positively while some acted passively.

Intellectual Lineage and the Preservation of Philosophical Ideas

For Chinese thinkers, being a member of a school is of utmost importance. Students revere their teachers, addressing them as "masters." (What we today translate as "Confucius," "Mencius," "Laozi," "Mozi," "Zhuangzi," and "Hanfeizi," are addressed by the Chinese as Master Kong, Master Meng, Master Lao, Master Mo, Master Zhuang, and Master Han Fei.) What teachers do is to transmit *Dao*; hence, they are respected as the "transmitters of *Dao*." To go against one's teacher's teaching would be considered a great betrayal.[12] Therefore, Chinese philosophy is built on the continuation and further explication of teachings of their revered predecessors, not on challenging them or constructing new theories from scratch. Most of the works of ancient Chinese philosophy open discussions with "the Master said," showing that these works were very likely students' notes of what their teachers taught. Even where the teachers themselves wrote philosophical treatises, sometimes the authentic works are compiled together with students' works attributed to their teachers. On some occasions, either out of respect for ancient thinkers or to elevate the importance of their own writing, the authors would even attribute their thought to ancient masters. Hence, we have the notorious problem about the authenticity of authorship in early Chinese philosophy. To see how Chinese philosophy was passed on largely through the extension of early teachings and explication of previous texts, we have to understand the academic background of Chinese schooling too.

In Chinese intellectual history, the study of the classics is an integral part of education. The classics include the *Book of Changes* (*Yijing*), the *Book of Odes* (*Shi-jing*), the *Book of History* (*Shu-jing*), the *Book of Rites* (*Li-ji*), and the *Annals of Spring and Autumn* (*Chun-qiu*). Later in history, these books came to be known as the "five classics." They were seen as voicing the authority on truth and morality from as early as in Confucius' time. Confucius says of himself, "I transmit but do not create. I believe in and love the ancients."[13] It is clear that he does not think he is developing a new philosophy. He views himself as someone who transmits the truth conveyed in the classics and continues the tradition of the old. Confucius often refers to the *Book of Odes* in his teaching, while Mencius often cites the *Book of History* as the voice of truth. Other ancient Chinese philosophers also appealed either to the classics, to Confucius, or to Laozi in order to support their own theories. It is not because they were not confident in their own thinking, but because, to Chinese philosophers, to philosophize is to find the best transmissions of *Dao*.

Typically, ancient Chinese students were given private tutorials from the age of 6. A small group of students gathered either at one of their homes, or at the tutor's studio, to receive lectures on the classics.[14] The tutor typically dominated the whole lecture, leaving no room for open discussion. These tutors were often addressed as "master," which underscored their authority and their superiority. Students were expected to *recite* and to *memorize* the content of these classics, so that they could quote them in exams and, later in life, could apply the teachings to their own life. The merit of the student's comprehension would be based on his ability to synthesize and to elaborate on the teachings, not on his ability to challenge or revise the teachings. As young students grew up, they could choose their philosophical associations by joining a particular school to follow a particular "master." Even within academic settings for mature students, teachers normally lecture while students take notes. This tradition still applies today. Sometimes the pedagogy involves questions and answers, but normally teachers were held in the highest esteem and thus were seldom challenged. Later in Chinese history, when official examinations were devised to select the best intellectuals to become state officials, these examinations were also centered on the classics. Typically, the contestants had to write an expository essay on the selected quote from the classics. One can easily see why, under such an education system, students would develop a sense of awe not only of their masters, but also of whatever the masters taught. Orthodox teaching is the norm; following the tradition is the respectable thing to do. A deviant interpretation could be seen as a novel ingenuity, but it also runs the risk of being seen as a *mis*understanding of the original texts. Consequently, the development of Chinese philosophy leaned heavily toward orthodoxy from the start.[15] This is not to say, of course, that there is only one thread in the development of Chinese philosophy. There are often lots of competing schools at any given time. In the ancient period, for example, we have what is commonly called the "Hundred Schools" (*bai-jia*). Between different schools, we often see interesting philosophical debates and exchanges. The disagreements between Confucians and Mohists, between Confucians and Daoists, and between Confucians and Buddhists present us with perfect examples of the philosophical disputes that took place in Chinese intellectual history.

Starting with Confucius, who modestly claimed that he only transmitted the thought of antiquity and never wrote down his own theory or originated his own ideas, Chinese philosophers did not think highly of establishing intellectual fame through writing. The reason for the lack of systematic philosophical works in Chinese philosophy is directly linked to the philosopher's disinterest in establishing a particular doctrine to gratify his intellectual desire. Like their Western counterparts (Socrates, Plato, etc.), ancient Chinese philosophers were indeed interested in finding and defending truth. However, what they deemed *truth* must be what could help the world and the people. Before paper was invented in China (in the first century AD), books had to be carved onto bamboo plates, which were then assembled with the aid of ropes. Writing would thus take too much time away from the philosophers' real goal – to make others listen to them and to bring about immediate social reform. Among their students, some were good at partaking in social or political reforms, while others were good at truthfully recording what the teachers had said. When we read these ancient Chinese philosophical texts, we must recognize this division of labor. When we refer to, for example, Confucius or Mencius, we would be referring, not to the author of those texts, but to the originator of the thoughts preserved in the texts. Since the thoughts were conveyed in various contexts and recorded by different students, the philosophy often appears unsystematic or even inconsistent. A proper understanding of Chinese philosophy must therefore involve the readers' active attempts at sifting through disjointed remarks to find the common themes.

Part I

Ancient Chinese Philosophy

Introduction

What we here call "ancient Chinese philosophy" falls into two historical periods in Chinese history, both of which came about as the result of the decline of the golden age of the Zhou Dynasty (ca. 1122?–256 BCE). After Zhou's royal court lost its prominent status in China and moved away from its central geographic location, many smaller nation-states emerged as independent sovereignties. Initially, these nation-states co-existed peacefully, though secretly they amassed power, competing to become the strongest nation-state under Zhou. This period is called the "Spring-Autumn" period (722–481 BCE). At the time, China was dominated by five powerful nation-states, which came to be known as the "Five Hegemonies." Eventually, these more powerful nation-states gave up their superficial attempts at peaceful coexistence and began to compete bitterly to aggrandize their territories; henceforth began the "Warring States" period (480–222 BCE).

During the Spring-Autumn period, there were already signs of turmoil boiling up in China and there was a prevailing sense of uncertainty and insecurity. During the Warring States period, nation-states were constantly engaged in warfare, either in the name of protecting their satellite nations or for the sake of taking back lost land. Among them, the seven more powerful nations became known as the "Seven Supremacies." They no longer revered the impotent court of Zhou as "the Son of Heaven," and they began to regard themselves as equals to the king of Zhou. They formed shifting coalitions with one another and the diplomatic world was plagued by deceit, ruse, and subterfuge. Eventually, it was the nation-state Qin which, having conquered other nation-states with bloody warfare, brought about China's first reunification (221 BCE). During both the Spring-Autumn and the Warring States periods, the general populace was frequently threatened with death, starvation, and the deprivation of all material possessions.

Ancient Chinese philosophy thus developed in a particularly strenuous political and social atmosphere, with various philosophers suggesting different ideas about how to solve the social and political problems. Diverse schools of thought emerged, which came to be known as the "Hundred Schools." Among the philosophers covered here in Part I, Confucius and the legendary Laozi belonged to the Spring-Autumn period, while Mencius, Xunzi, Mozi, Zhuangzi, and Hanfeizi belonged to the Warring States period.

Confucianism comes about as an attempt to reconstruct social order and to restore wide-reaching peace. Advocated by Confucius and his followers, the theory is that if the ruler could set a good example to his people in his personal behavior and in his family relationships, and if the people could be morally transformed to preserve good personal conduct and to maintain good family relations, then all societal problems, large and small, would dissolve. This theory sounds overly simplified and optimistic, but it is based on a sophisticated social philosophy. Confucian society is founded on family units. Social order begins with family order. As Derk Bodde puts it:

> Society, in Chinese eyes, consists of a large number of small social units (the family, the village, the guild, etc.), each of which consists in turn of individuals varying greatly in their intellectual and physical capacities.... The welfare of the social organism as a whole depends upon harmonious co-operation among all of its units and of the individuals who comprise these units. This means that every individual, however high or low, has the obligation to perform to the best of his abilities those particular functions in which he is expert and which are expected of him by society.[1]

In the Confucian conception, society is like "a magnified family, the members of which, though differing in their status and functions, all work in harmony for the common good."[2] However, Confucianism does not attempt to construct a socialistic communal world, in which everyone *is* indeed related to one another as brothers or sisters. Confucianism stresses natural family relations, and advocates love with distinctions – one always loves one's family first and foremost.

This Confucian project of social reform begins from the top – from the ruling class. Confucius and his followers spent the major part of their adult lives traveling from one nation-state to another, in the hope of convincing the kings to embrace their ideals. The ideal ruler for the Confucians is someone who has perfect virtue (one who obtains sagehood) internally. His internal virtue would then manifest itself externally as the best rulership. The motto representing the Confucian political view is "internally a sage; externally a king." In the *Great Learning*, a representative text of Confucian political philosophy,[3] the ruler is advised to abide by three principles: (1) manifest a clear character, (2) show concern for the people (or: renew the people),[4] and (3) aim for the highest good. Under this mode of thinking, morality and politics are inseparable. Confucians often appealed to ancient sage kings such as Yao and Shun as their paradigms. These sage kings allegedly instituted civilization in primitive society, teaching the people language and morality along with basic skills for self-preservation. Confucians advocated the belief that if the contemporary ruler modeled himself on the sage kings, the whole world would be appeased. The *Great Learning* describes the eight steps needed to establish world peace, starting from personal moral cultivation through regulation of the family, the establishment of national order, and finally the manifestation of worldly order. The cultivation of personal virtue is likened to the root of a tree. "There is never a case when the root is in disorder and yet the branches are in order."[5] At the same time, once the root is well planted, the branches will all grow healthily. Hence, a well-conducted personal life naturally leads to the moral transformation of the world.

Such a worldwide reformation sounds fantastical. However, in terms of political philosophy, Confucians also devised practical means to assist the moral transformation of the people. To begin with, the common folk, whose primary concern is their material subsistence, need to be free of anxiety and trepidation for their livelihood. It is difficult to advocate moral cultivation for the people when the people are preoccupied with the underdevelopment of their crops and the impending death of their family members. In Mencius' advice to the kings, he often emphasized the importance of setting up an effective agricultural plan so that soil could rest through rotation of crops and adequate labor could produce the maximum yield. What devastated the living conditions of the people at that time was nothing more than a long war: young men were drafted and often killed, while the old, the frail, women, and children were left to tend the fields. In the Warring States period, ordinary people dropped dead like flies, and their bodies were simply dumped in the ditch because others had neither the time nor the energy to bury them properly. In view of this, Confucians were generally opposed to wars undertaken for the sake of conquest. However, they do believe that war is morally praiseworthy when it is launched to relieve the suffering of the people in neighboring countries. Confucians' primary concern is the livelihood of the general masses, with no regard to the boundaries of the nation-states at the time. With their humane hearts extended to all people in China, they totally understood that it was not possible to address the people's moral or spiritual transformation unless their livelihood was first taken care of.

Confucians aim to transform the general masses by means of two cultural enhancements: rites and music. "Rites" incorporate a system of ritual codes for particular situations as well as codes of propriety for daily interactions. In formal ceremonies such as weddings and funerals, there are particular codes of proper conduct ranging from the length of the ceremony, the suitability of the attire, the proceeding of the participants, the preparation of foods, to the sacrifice of animals. Confucius even specified different mourning periods appropriate to one's emperor, one's father, or one's relatives. In daily life, Confucians also observe particular codes of conduct, including how one should address one's elders in the family or elders in the neighborhood; how one should interact with someone of the opposite sex; and how one should conduct oneself in various social contexts, etc. Under these social restraints, one is constantly aiming to be "proper" in respect to different interpersonal relations and social contexts. The ideal man is one who has adapted his own natural inclinations to social restraints such that he no longer needs to curb himself – he is naturally inclined to do whatever is proper in each given circumstance. In Confucian thinking, the value of ritual propriety is not in its being a measure of social control, but in its ability to separate a flock of human beings from a flock of beasts. Human society is possible exactly because humans conduct themselves under social codes of propriety. Without a sense of propriety, we would all follow our animal instincts, which would eventually lead to our mutual destruction. With rites, we manifest respect in our conduct for various social contexts as well as for other people. This behavioral manifestation can teach others to cultivate the same respect. In time, a society is *civilized* through its members' adherence to rites. Therefore, for Confucians, the importance of rites in human society cannot be overstated.

Rites can transform the people externally; music, on the other hand, has a transforming power from the inside. "Music" includes both the recitation of fine poetry and the performance of musical instruments. In Chinese, the same character stands for both music and joy, though the pronunciation is different. Music is a natural expression of one's joy; it also brings joy to its listeners. Furthermore, Confucius believed that music has the function of regulating one's emotions and harmonizing one's sentiments. When one of Confucius' best students governed a small city-state, he had the whole city playing music continuously for three months. When people are virtually "living in music," they no longer feel the need to be aggressive, bitter, hostile, jealous, or greedy. Their minds are at ease with the world around them. But not all music can have this effect. Confucians believe that some melodies will pacify listeners, while others have a more rousing effect that could agitate listeners. We now have very little knowledge of the classical music in ancient China, but from the descriptions given, we understand that this kind of music was generally based on the harmony of chords. "Harmony" depicts a state of balance among various elements; it can be applied to music as well as to one's mental states. In the *Doctrine of the Mean*, another important Confucian text,[6] it is said: "Before the feelings of pleasure, anger, sorrow, and joy are aroused it is called equilibrium. When these feelings are aroused and each and all attain due measure and degree, it is called harmony."[7] This comment reflects the common view in the ancient Chinese world of music that music acts as an expression of one's inner state. There are numerous stories about how a skilled listener could judge the musician's frame of mind – be it noble or violent – by listening to the music he plays. Harmonious music is an expression of its composer's or its players' balanced emotions. At the same time, harmonious music gradually pacifies the temperament of the listener through its regulation of unexpressed emotions. If the whole nation could be regulated with the right kind of music, the people would naturally become well-tempered citizens.

Confucianism as a moral philosophy can be summarized as a philosophy of *ideal personhood*. In the Confucian picture of human societies, there is a moral hierarchy of people with the highest moral attributes (the sages), people of superior moral attributes (superior people), people of petty concerns (petty people), and people of vile characters (tyrants and crooks). The goal of Confucians is to become better human beings themselves, and to help others become better human beings. Accomplishing this very goal constitutes what Confucians call the virtue of "humanity." The virtue of humanity can be seen as the defining virtue of Confucian ethics. The ultimate goal in life for a Confucian is never to allow a momentary lapse in the task of self-improvement. By Confucius' standard, to be a superior person is never to forgo the virtue of humanity even "for as short as one meal's time." The *Doctrine of the Mean* describes the superior person as one who is watchful over herself even when she is alone. She does not allow herself to indulge in idle or improper thinking. The reason is that what one harbors in one's mind will inevitably be manifested in one's appearance and one's conduct. What the whole person manifests is what is inwardly cultivated – the truth of a person's inner self will always be outwardly displayed. However, the point of becoming a better person is not just for outward display, but for one's own inner self. Confucians constantly examine themselves to see whether they have been honest with others, whether they have been conscientious in their tasks, and whether they have put into practice what they have learned from their teachers. A Confucian is thus someone who is always vigilant in his or her self-cultivation and self-examination.

The second major school, Mohism, led by Mozi, is an attempt to reform the world morally by totally remodeling people's way of thinking. Mohism advocates loving one another *equally* and benefiting one another *mutually*. Mozi did not deny that human nature tends toward particular love, focusing primarily on self-interest and the interests of one's family. He believes that this particularist way of thinking is the root of all social and political problems plaguing the Warring States period. Therefore, he advocated universal love and love with no distinctions. His theory stands in direct opposition to the Confucian conception of constructing a family-based society. Mozi believed that to completely avert social disorder, everyone must renounce family relations and dispose of egoistic thinking and self-interested conduct. In Mozi's view, humans do many things detrimental to the nation and to the society in the name of family love and familial loyalty. But we should have only one form of loyalty – toward humanity at large. Everything we do must be done for the well-being of mankind. This universalist way of thinking cannot be promoted unless it can be *universalized*; i.e., unless *everyone* thinks and acts this way. Mozi thus set as his goal the re-education of the general masses to adopt this new way of thinking.

To promote universal love and mutual benefits, Mozi brought out the authority of Heaven in support of his teaching. He reinstated religious sentiment into the rational discourse of ancient Chinese philosophy. He argued that Heaven commands all people to love one another equally and to benefit one another mutually. If one disobeys the Will of Heaven, one will incur harsh punishments from Heaven. He cited historical examples to demonstrate that those who fail to obey the Will of Heaven have all been severely punished. Mozi's philosophy of religion serves as a pragmatic means to the promotion of his ideal. It seems that he was trying to "scare" people into following the teaching of Mohism. To Mozi, having the ruler believe in the existence of a willful Heaven and having the people believe in the existence of formidable ghosts and spirits would be far more beneficial to the world than if they did not possess these beliefs. Therefore, one should promote such religious sentiments.

Mohism is highly pragmatic. Mozi rejected the Confucian institutions of rites and rituals, since they are largely formalistic and impractical. The extensive mourning periods accorded by Confucian rites, for example, take young men away from their daily tasks and allow them to pine away by their fathers' tombs. Mozi also condemned music, which, in his view, is a total waste of society's human resources. The time spent on learning, performing, and enjoying music can be better used to tend to farming, weaving, and governing. A modest society in which everyone can be materially sustained is far superior to a culturally stratified society in which some are laborers while others have the leisure to enjoy high culture. On principle, Mohism denounces anything that is extravagant, and all things not necessary to basic survival are considered "extravagant." Hence, Mozi promoted simple clothing that serves as just enough protection from the cold or heat, or simple food that is just enough to feed oneself. He wanted to establish a society that has no frills, no luxury, no sophistication, and no waste.

In contrast to Confucianism and Mohism, both as a form of collective social reform, the third major school, Daoism, emerges as a form of individual deliverance. For Daoists, what matters the most is one's own spiritual elevation. Seeing that the world has gone beyond the point of salvation, Daoists in the ancient period generally chose to become recluses, by hiding their knowledge and their abilities and pretending to be ordinary farmers or fishermen. Among Confucius' contemporaries, many were reclusive Daoists, who simply scoffed at his efforts to futilely promote his ideal. To them, since the world was already in an irredeemable state, a better way to conduct oneself would be to live in isolation from the world. Laozi, the forefather of Daoism, based his political ideal not on antiquity as Confucius did, but on prehistoric primitive society. His theory is full of anti-social, anti-knowledge, and anti-civilization comments. In his utopia, people do not communicate, or exchange goods, with one another. Life is simple and secluded. We could see from this depiction that Daoism seems to have emerged from an escapist mentality, as a rejection of the contemporary world of turmoil. On the positive side, however, Daoism brings people to a higher spiritual realm in search of true freedom. It teaches one to forget worldly distinctions such as fame and wealth in the pursuit of internal tranquility. Under Daoism, one could learn to forget about the world and *roam about in the world beyond*. One could be liberated from the bondage set by one's present surroundings.

Since Daoists do not wish to be bound by their present surroundings, they are more interested in abstract philosophical thinking. Laozi entertained himself with such issues as the nature of *Dao* and the origin of the universe. Laozi took *Dao* in itself to be the source of all life forms as well as the totality of all existence. This *Dao* predates Heaven and Earth; it is *Nonbeing*, from which all beings emerge. *Dao* does not "create," however. All things simply follow naturally from *Dao*. At the same time, *Dao* does not cease to exist after all things have come into existence. *Dao* is eternal and all-encompassing. *Dao* nourishes everything but does not claim to be their master. *Dao* is fundamentally resistant to our conceptual depiction, since to name it is to confine it into our conceptual scheme. *Dao* is silent in itself; hence, we should not even attempt to begin our discourse on *Dao*. We should be silent as well.

Following Laozi's skepticism of language and human conceptualization, Zhuangzi engaged in the philosophical examination of the nature of language and its correspondence with reality. He did not try to explicate the nature of *Dao*; rather, he focused more on demonstrating our narrow conceptions and prejudiced views. Zhuangzi pointed out that while his contemporary philosophers argue against one another to assert their own view as the truth, there is no objective way to settle the dispute. Whenever a judgment is made as to who has won the debate, it merely reflects the third party's view. We all believe that our own view is correct, while others are wrong. But from the perspective of *Dao*, all particular truths present merely partial truths. Hence, no self-acclaimed truth is indeed *true*. Once we saw this as the *Truth*, we would cease all verbal disagreements. Zhuangzi explained that there is no right or wrong with regard to *Dao*. When we make the distinction between right and wrong, we have already deviated from *Dao*. In reality, *Dao* has no limitation, and speech has no finality.

In terms of philosophy of life, Daoism represents the view that one should follow what naturally happens and not meddle with it. Human agency is not appreciated, because taking action is to go against nature. If we take an action to initiate a change, then we are not accepting things as they are. Even when we act merely to continue a state of affairs, we are not appreciating the fact that without our interference, things will go whichever way is the most natural to them. When this view is applied to politics, the doctrine of "inaction" naturally follows. Laozi thought that the best ruler is one who not only does not meddle with people's affairs, but also is not even known by his people. To Laozi, the best way to rule is to give up embellishment, embrace simplicity, cast off selfishness, and temper material desires. If the ruler does nothing to enhance material existence, to increase social wealth, to employ able people or even to promote virtues, then the world will be in order "on its own accord."

To the Daoist, both the Confucian model of social reform and the Mohist model of psychological reform would interfere with the natural flow of *Dao*. Daoists do not embrace the *humanistic* spirit that marks both Confucianism and Mohism. To them, animals and inanimate things are part of the world just as human beings are. To pay singular attention to human affairs is to go against *Dao*, which is impartial to all creatures. The Daoist principle of impartiality would thus go even further than the Mohist principle of universal love. All things have equal value from the perspective of *Dao*. However, Daoism does not advocate the sentiment of love as Mohists do. It does not ask us to *love* all creatures equally; rather, it promotes a rational detachment from all particular love. It teaches us to view our loved ones as being in a mere transient state of the transformation of *Dao*. When Zhuangzi's wife died, instead of mourning, he gleefully celebrated her changing into a different form of existence – to be unified with *Dao* again. From this perspective, Daoism advises us to treat life's happiness and miseries equally, not to desire life or to abhor death. If we can truly obtain this mental state, then all suffering will be eliminated.

In view of the Confucian project of moral transformation of rulers and the common people, Daoists think that it promotes only a second-rate ideal. Both Laozi and Zhuangzi thought that the distinction between good and bad comes after *Dao* has declined. Using the metaphor of fish on dry land, Zhuangzi tells us that when fish are out of the water, they have to moisten one another with their saliva, whereas when they are in the great ocean, they don't even think about the necessity of water. Similarly, when the Confucian sees the need to cultivate morality in his own person as well as in others, it means that people are already living out of *Dao*. Why not set the fish back in the ocean? the Daoist asks. Why not bring the people back to the world of *Dao*?

To return to the natural state of *Dao*, people have to eliminate desires; to eliminate desires, all value distinctions must be renounced. In this respect, Daoism is quite similar to Mohism. Both schools denounce materialistic possessions; both schools disapprove of cultural refinements. Laozi thought that our senses are the culprit of our mind's demise. When we indulge in the senses' delight, we end up wanting more and seeking more because simple things can no longer gratify our senses. Laozi says, "There is no calamity greater than lavish desires. There is no fault greater than constant discontentment. There is no disaster greater than insatiable greed."[8] To Laozi, the ideal state of individual existence is to return to infancy, when we have not learned the pleasures of the senses. By the same token, the ideal state of society is to go back to the state of primitive society, where people did not even know what would be valuable, what should be cherished, or what could be pursued. Ignorance is *bliss*, in a true Daoist sense.

Finally, the fourth major philosophical school examined here is Legalism, formulated by Hanfeizi. Legalism was a school of thought that descended from Mohism, minus the latter's idealism. Hanfeizi argued that Mohism does not go far enough in its emphasis on pragmatism, because the teaching of love is totally ineffectual. To accomplish what Mozi deems to be the best possible world, what we need is not love, but the severity of law and the harshness of punishment. Hanfeizi believed that harshness would bring obedience, while love would bring spoilage. From our empirical observation, he says, we see that in a severe household even the slaves would not rebel, but in a loving family children are often spoiled beyond rectification. He also criticized the Confucian model of moral politics. He argued that the ruler's virtue and kindness are not sufficient to end social unrest, while an awe-inspiring power can prohibit violence and secure social order. Therefore, Hanfeizi concluded, a ruler should devote himself not to love, but to harsh punishment; not to virtue, but to law.

Unlike the other schools, which cherish either antiquity or primitive society, Hanfeizi was a Modernist. He believed that what was ancient had no relevance to the present time. The ancient sages, however ideal they may have been, would not be able to rule his contemporary world. Times had changed; so should policies. Hanfeizi developed many political tactics for the ruler to be effective; among them, punishment and reward are what he called the ruler's "two handles." We can see that he believed, as Mozi did, that people are motivated and easily manipulated by punishment and rewards. Unlike Mozi, however, Hanfeizi placed the ultimate authority not in the invisible Will of Heaven, but in the concrete will of the ruler. The ruler is not even sanctioned by Heaven; the ruler is Heaven.

Both Mozi and Hanfeizi took humans' egoistic nature as a given. But while Mozi tried to alter this nature, Hanfeizi simply constructed a practical political model on the basis of this very assumption. If humans are all egoistic, then they will always do what they deem to be in their best interests, which is almost without exception the opposite of the interests of the nation or of the ruler. Hanfeizi did not acknowledge the possibility that we could be rationally self-interested; that we might identify our own best self-interest with the general welfare of society. He did not even see the need to educate the people. If humans are by nature selfish, then even the best moral educator, such as Confucius himself, can only have limited success. To achieve the comprehensive, thorough, and across the board political reform that is the goal of Confucianism and Mohism, one must be a Legalist.

The above introduction briefly outlines the similarities and differences between all four major schools of ancient Chinese philosophy. Confucianism, as a philosophy of moral politics, moral families, and moral self-cultivation, became the molding ideology of Chinese culture – it dominated the thought and behavior of Chinese intellectuals and general masses alike. It shaped and sustained Chinese family relations and social structures for thousands of years. Daoism, with its spiritual elevation and its teaching of tranquility, became the mental utopia for Chinese intellectuals. A common Chinese attitude is: "Be a Confucian in interactions with the mundane world; be a Daoist when retreating back to one's inner world." Hence, Confucianism and Daoism can be seen as *yang* and *yin*; two complementary elements in Chinese culture and the Chinese mind. Legalism, as a philosophy of pragmatic rulership, became the ideology embraced by Chinese emperors. It underlay the Chinese political structure and helped maintain political stability in Chinese history. Mohism, although an influential school of thought for two to three hundred years, exited the intellectual stage along with the other multifarious ideas of the Hundred Schools. All schools in the ancient period, however dissimilar in their approaches, shared the same commitment to their contemporary world. Their philosophies were all suggested either as ways to solve, or as routes to evade, their contemporary social and political problems. None of these philosophers entertained an "other-worldly" transcendent realm as their intellectual enterprise. Ancient Chinese philosophy is fundamentally a this-worldly *realist* philosophy.

Chapter 1

Yijing (*I Ching*): The Cosmological Foundation of Chinese Philosophy

Introduction

Yijing, commonly translated as the *Book of Change(s)*, is the single most important work in the history of Chinese philosophy. It is not only the source of Chinese cosmology, but also the very foundation of the whole Chinese culture. Both the two leading Chinese philosophical schools, Confucianism and Daoism, drew cosmological and moral ideas from this book, which has been described as "a unique blend of proto-Confucian and proto-[Daoist] ideas."[1] *Yijing* has also penetrated the Chinese mind. Every Chinese person, with or without philosophical training, would be naturally inclined to view the world the way *Yijing* depicts it – a world of possibilities as well as determination; a world dominated by *yin* and *yang* and yet alterable by human efforts. The dating of the compilation of *Yijing* is still a controversial issue among historians; hence, we cannot safely place the whole *Yijing* as either a pre-Confucian or a post-Confucian text. However, Confucius himself alluded to *Yijing*, and he was traditionally regarded as the author of some of the earlier commentaries on the hexagrams. Philosophically, we could also see how ancient Confucian thought was based on the cosmology laid out in *Yijing*. This explains why we open this book with the chapter on *Yijing*.

Yijing, as we currently have it, includes both the core text and the *Ten Wings* (ten supplementary texts).[2] The construction of the core *Yijing* was a cooperative effort spanning 1,500 years, from 2000 BCE to 500 BCE. In the first stage of formation, there was the diagram of eight trigrams, each of which consists of three lines that are either broken (- -) or solid (——). The solid line represents *yang*; the broken line represents *yin*. Allegedly, a legendary ruler, Fu Xi (ca. 2000 BCE), was respons-ible for the construction of this earliest form of *Yijing*. These trigrams represent the eight basic natural elements: heaven, earth, water, fire, wind, thunder, mountain, and lake. They depict how natural elements are formed out of the duality of *yin* and *yang*.

The eight trigrams are as follows:

Qian	Kun	Zhen	Kan	Gen	Shun	Li	Dui
(Heaven)	(Earth)	(Thunder)	(Water)	(Mountain)	(Wind)	(Fire)	(Lake)

On the level of natural representations, these eight trigrams stand for eight basic natural phenomena. However, they also stand for other relations in a metaphorical sense. For instance, in one of the *Ten Wings*, the *Discussion of the Trigrams* (*shuo-gua*), the trigrams are associated with various things such as daughters and sons, different seasons, dir-ections, colors, and various animals, among others. The exact reason behind these associations is lost, even though there have been many speculations by later interpreters. But at least we should see that the trigrams are not just fixed representations of nature. According to Richard Wilhelm's explanation, the eight basic trigrams further depict the con-tinual process of change in the cosmos:

> These eight trigrams were conceived as images of all that happens in heaven and on earth. At the same time, they were held to be in a state of continual transition, one changing into another, just as transition from one phenomenon to another is continually taking place in the physical world. Here we have the fundamental concept of the *Book of Changes*. The eight trigrams are symbols standing for changing transitional stages; they are images that are constantly undergoing change. Attention centers not on things in their state of being, but upon their movements in change. The eight trigrams therefore are not representations of things as such but of their tendencies in movement.[3]

This interpretation gives us an insight into the whole construction of *Yijing*. If the eight basic units of *Yijing* represent not static states but dynamic potential for change, then their connotations cannot be fixed onto any particular natural phenomenon either. This cosmology is about constant flux; it is a philosophy of change. And this cosmology was envisaged as early ago as the first conception of the eight trigrams.

The second development of *Yijing* took place when the eight trigrams were doubled in various combinations to form 64 hexagrams (i.e., a diagram of six lines). According to the orthodox Chinese account, King Wen of the Zhou Dynasty (ca. 1150 BCE) was the person responsible for the creation of 64 hexagrams. Traditional accounts also attributed the terse explanation on the decision of each hexagram ("the Judgment" or *gua-ci*) as well as the explanation on each component line of the hexagram (*yiao-ci*) to King Wen of Zhou, or to his son Duke Zhou (d. 1094 BCE) At this stage, *Yijing* emerged as a philosophy of life. It was no longer just a book for divination. Each situation, symbolically represented by either the hexagram as a whole or a single line in the hexagram, signifies a moral situation in life. The Judgment frequently refers to "the superior man," depicting his possible options in any given situation along with their possible outcomes. We could perhaps say that the ethics of *Yijing* was developed at this point.

Allegedly, the third major development of *Yijing* came from Confucius, who authored further commentary on the explanations given by King Wen of Zhou. This commentary, called *Commentary on the Judgment* (*tuan-zhuan*), further turned the mystical oracle nature of the ancient text into a philosophical exposition of various situations in life. It serves both as an analysis of the various contexts and as a discussion on the moral duties of individuals in these contexts. Another important addition to *Yijing* was the *Commentary on the Images* (*xiang-zhuan*). When the commentary is on the image of the whole hexagram, it is called "the Great Image"; when it is on the image of each line, it is called "the Small Image." These commentaries derive moral significance from the combination of the two trigram images (one above; one below) that make up a hexagram. They fully developed the sense of Nature's *possessing* moral attributes, or Nature's being symbolic *representations of* various moral attributes. The *Commentary on the Judgment* and the *Commentary on the Images* were both either attributed to Confucius and his immediate followers, or at least were seen as representative of the Confucian philosophy in its early development.

Apart from the Judgment, the *Commentary on the Judgment*, and the *Commentary on the Images*, there were some further commentaries added to the whole *Yijing*. Together, these supplementary texts were called the *Ten Wings* of *Yijing*. Among these other commentaries, the most important texts are probably the two expository treatises on the first two hexagrams, *Qian* and *Kun*. These two treatises are called "*wen-yan*", translated as *Commentary on the Words of the Text*. The content of these texts is very much in line with Confucianism; hence, they have been traditionally attributed to Confucius himself. But since in these texts Confucius is often referred to as "the Master" (as in the *Analects*), it is likely that they were either recorded by his students or were even composed by later followers of the Confucian School. The remainder of the *Ten Wings* were probably attached to *Yijing* as late as in the Han Dynasty (206 BCE–AD 220). Of these later works, the *Great Treatise* (*xi-ci-zhuan*) received the most attention from Neo-Confucians. This treatise is divided into two parts. It covers a wide range of topics, including the nature of *Yijing*, the method of divination, the social reforms made by ancient sages, and the history of human civilization. It can be seen as one of the most important philosophical foundations for Neo-Confucianism.

As the end product, *Yijing* consists of 64 hexagrams and the *Ten Wings*. The whole book is rich in metaphysical and ethical symbolism. All affairs of the world are supposedly represented by these hexagrams. In theory, *Yijing* provides a profound cosmological foundation for Chinese philosophy. In practice, *Yijing* was commonly used in divination, a process in which advice is given to a particular person in a particular situation on how to accomplish success and avoid disaster. Thus, it could be called the guidebook of practical wisdom. Today it is often consulted by those seeking guidance with respect to love, career, politics, interpersonal relationships, and inner development. It also serves as the theoretical basis for *Feng Shui*, an art of the rearrangement of one's life and one's surroundings, which has been popularized in the Western world. In this chapter, we will study *Yijing* from the philosophical perspective. Even though *Yijing* may have been the compilation of multiple authors, later commentaries all seemed to build on earlier ones. Overall, there is no obvious discrepancy in the content of *Yijing*. Hence, in our analysis, we shall treat it as a whole text, not dissecting it into various historical fragments.

Yi: A Constantly Changing Universe

The word *yi* means both "change" and "easy," *jing* means "classic." One explanation for the name of this book is that the method of divination used is much easier than the turtle-shell divination method used in an earlier dynasty; hence, the book received the name of "*yi*." But an explanation more commonly endorsed by traditional Chinese scholars is to say that the word *yi* means "change," and it refers to the alteration between *yin* and *yang*. Since *yin* and *yang* are constantly in motion, nothing can stay the same forever. We shall adopt this interpretation here. Under this interpretation, *Yijing* is fittingly translated as the "Book of Change." It is a book about the cosmos and the human world. Since the universe is constantly changing, every condition bears the seed of change to a different condition.

A theoretical motivation for developing a philosophy of change is that the basic element of the universe is taken to be *qi*, not atoms, or matter. Matter has a spatial and temporal stability that is not observed in the movement of *qi*. The constant change in the atmosphere can serve as a good illustration of the movement of *qi*. If the whole universe along with everything within it is composed of *qi*, then change is simply the constant state of affairs. Myriad objects are not individuated as spatially confined *things*, which begin with the aggregation of atoms, ending with the dissolution of atoms. Instead, each object is seen as a *process* of change, with the condensation of *qi* marking its beginning and the rarefaction of *qi* marking its end. Within each process of condensation and rarefaction, there is also the constant alteration between *yin* and *yang*. Therefore, nothing is assigned a fixed nature. Everything constantly grows, changes, matures, and declines. This is the natural process of the universe.

In *Yijing*, such a cosmology of change is applied to the human context. An important aspect of the construction of the hexagram is that each hexagram describes a movement, or a development, from the bottom line to the top line. The six lines are called "changing lines," since they depict various moments of change. When an explanation is given to each line, it describes a temporarily frozen moment in time; thereafter, multiple developments could take place depending on the action taken at that particular moment in time. The development from the first stage to the last stage of the state of affairs represented in the same hexagram, according to the *Great Treatise* on *Yijing*, constitutes a causal relation. Each bottom line of the hexagram (the first line) describes the beginning of a development, and the top line (the sixth line) of the hexagram describes how things develop following the natural course of events. Therefore, "the beginning line is difficult to understand. The top line is easy to understand. For they stand in the relationship of cause and effect. The Judgment on the first line is tentative, but at the last line everything has attained completion."[4] Understood in this way, the 64 hexagrams demonstrate 64 sequences of causal relations. Each of the six lines of the hexagram represents a stage in the causal development; hence, there are minimally 384 possible transitory situations. Under each given situation, the decision one makes, the action one takes, or even the attitude one chooses, can all contribute to the further development of the state of affairs.

The method of divination is also based on elements of change and non-change. Whether one uses the coin method or the yarrow stalk method,[5] one gets four possible numbers for each line: 6, 7, 8, 9. Both 6 and 8 signify *yin* (the broken line), but the former represents the old *yin* while the latter represents the young *yin*. When *yin* gets "old," it necessarily changes into a *yang*. The same is true for the pair of 7 and 9: 9 represents old *yang* and signifies an impending change into *yin*. In the Judgment for each line, only 6 is mentioned for each broken line (*yin*) and only 9 is used to stand for each solid line (*yang*). Hence, each line Judgment depicts a moment *before* change; a transient state of affairs. As Wilhelm explains:

> The hexagrams, consisting of six lines each, are, so to speak, representations of actual conditions in the world, and of the combinations of the light-giving, heavenly power and the dark, earthly power that occur in these situations. Within the hexagrams, however, it is always possible for the individual lines to change and regroup themselves; just as world situations continually change and reconstitute themselves, so out of each hexagram there arises a new one. The process of change is to be observed in the lines that move, and the end result is the new hexagram thus formed.[6]

When such a view is applied to all of life's situations, what *Yijing* teaches is that we need to adapt our conduct in accordance with our changing relations to the environment. Even if we do not change, other people and other things are constantly changing. Therefore, adapting to changes is far superior to ignorant persistence. The things that change around us are our situation in the local environment, our position in the current situation, our relations to others in the same situation, as well as the local environment's relation to the larger environment. In an adverse situation, one takes precautions and conceals one's brilliance; in a favorable situation, but in a low position, one bides one's time for the right moment to arise. If one has correspondence with or support from others, a new direction can be initiated; one who is isolated and mistrusted does not push their way forward. If the local environment is conducive to the well-being of the larger environment, then we can conform to the local environment; if the local environment brings harm to the larger environment, then we should either quit it or alter it. Everything has to do with the right moment, the right situation, the right people, and the right relations. All these elements are summed up in the notion of "time" (*shi*). "Being appropriate to the time" (*shi-zhong*) is the wisdom of life that *Yijing* teaches.

However, even though the major concept in *Yijing* is *change*, the underlying background is *non-change*. Change is not possible without a frame of reference, which is non-change. Wilhelm says:

> In the [*Yijing*] a distinction is made between three kinds of change: nonchange, cyclic change, and sequent change. Nonchange is the background, as it were, against which change is made possible. For in regard to any change there must be a fixed point to which the change can be referred; otherwise there can be no definite order and everything is dissolved in chaotic movement. This point of reference must be established, and this always requires a choice and a decision. It makes possible a system of coordinates into which everything can be fitted. Consequently at the beginning of the world, as at the beginning of thought, there is the decision, the fixing of the point of reference.[7]

In other words, the relation between the whole hexagram and each line within this hexagram is the relation between non-change and change. The Judgment (or Decision) of each hexagram depicts the point of reference for the change of each line. This is why in the process of divination one always needs to consult the hexagram Judgment before assessing the connotation of the line Judgment, which signifies change.

On the cosmic level, the non-changing frame of reference for the movement of *qi* is simply the totality of *qi*. This totality of *qi* is called "*tai-ji*."[8] If the totality of *qi* is unchanging, then each time *yin* expands, *yang* has to decrease; and vice versa. Even though the two forms of cosmic energy compete with each other, they also work in unison. There is thus a principle of harmony governing the competition between *yin* and *yang*. The *Commentary on the Judgment* for the 38th hexagram says: "Heaven and earth are opposites, but their action is concerted. Man and woman are opposites, but they strive for union. All beings stand in opposition to one another: what they do takes on order thereby. Great indeed is the effect of the time of Opposition."[9] The two opposites are governed by the principle of harmonious whole. Under this principle of harmony, the exchange between *yin* and *yang* takes up certain patterns. These patterns can be deemed the laws of the universe. Hence, there are two senses of "non-change." The first is in the universe's constancy, on whose foundation changes are detectable. A second sense is manifested in the laws governing all changes.

According to R. L. Wing, there are two fundamental laws underlying physical changes in the universe:

> One is the law of *polar reversal*. In all things we see the seeds of their opposites: Just as new life carries in its genetic code the signal for its own decomposition, so too in every human affair lies the seed of a subtle but exacting change. The other law of change is *periodicity*. This law manifests in cycles and rhythms, like the changing seasons, the growth cycles in plants, and the stages in the development of the individual's life and character.[10]

Both these laws can easily be manifested in the movement of *yin* and *yang*. Since the totality of *yin* and *yang* is fixed, once *yin* or *yang* reaches its maximal state, the reversal of development is bound to take place. The natural laws governing the universe thus include the law of cyclical development – things that develop to one extreme would necessarily tend toward the opposite. When the time is right, there is a necessity of *return*. Wilhelm explains the 24th hexagram *Return* this way: "The idea of Return is based on the course of nature. The movement is cyclic, and the course completes itself. Therefore it is not necessary to hasten anything artificially. Everything comes of itself at the appointed time."[11] The law of Nature ordains cyclical development because everything in the universe is constantly changing and transforming. Things develop toward harmony, and yet once harmony is achieved, any further development will simply destroy it. "For it is just when perfect equilibrium has been reached that any movement may cause order to revert to disorder."[12]

From the principle of reversal, we derive the principle of periodicity. Each development eventually leads to its reversal; hence, each development has its limit. In this way, the movement of *qi* and the interchange between *yin* and *yang* sets up the regularity of the universe: weather goes through four immutable seasons and living things go through four inevitable stages of life (birth, maturation, degeneration, and death); similarly, events or human organizations go though four natural stages of development: initiation, growth, expansion, and, finally, deterioration.

Knowledge of the inexorable order of things should make one take care when one is in a favorable situation; it should at the same time make one hopeful when one is in a pitfall. Nothing is fixed forever. Neither the good nor the bad will last long. What one needs is a keen perception of the incoming development. If one sees where one is in the whole progression of events, then one can take appropriate action either to enhance the trend when it is auspicious, or to alter it, at least to slow it down, when it is inauspicious. In the final section of this chapter, we shall deal with *Yijing*'s philosophy of action. But before we turn to *Yijing*'s philosophy as applied to life, let us take a look at another aspect of its cosmology.

A Universe with Moral Attributes: The Foundation for Human Morality

Yijing depicts a universe with goodness inherent in it. In *Yijing*, the eight basic trigrams represent heaven, earth, lake, mountain, fire, water, wind, and thunder, each having certain moral attributes. The natural phenomenon that classical Confucians most often alluded to as the moral paradigm was heaven, or the sun. Heaven exemplifies the attributes of creativity, constancy, and steadfastness. As *Yijing* says, "The movement of heaven is full of power. Thus the superior man makes himself strong and untiring."[13] The sun, on the other hand, exemplifies the attributes of warmth, kindness, and impartiality. For example, the 50th hexagram, *Feng*, depicts "the sun at midday" and asks that the ruler be like it. Wilhelm's explanation says that the ruler "must be like the sun at midday, illuminating and gladdening everything under the sun."[14] Aside from ascribing these moral attributes to heaven and the sun, the basic eight trigrams also list other natural phenomena as signifying moral attributes: wind signifies a gentle penetrating power; lake signifies the attribute of joyousness; thunder represents forcefulness and fearfulness; mountain represents steadfastness and stillness; fire has the attributes of radiance and clarity; water has the attributes of humility and continuity. These other phenomena are more often cited as a model for man's behavior, rather than as having moral attributes themselves. But heaven and the sun, in contrast, seem to be ascribed moral attributes.

From our contemporary perspective, we think that such an ascription must be metaphorical, not literal: how could *Nature* be moral when it has no awareness, no intention, and no volition? However, under *Yijing*'s depiction, the universe *is* a universe with moral attributes; it *is* a moral universe. This philosophy of a moral universe is the very foundation of Confucian ethics. Confucians' sense of morality is grounded on their metaphysics of a moral universe. Humans' moral mission is defined in the context of a moral universe. Confucians typically regard the highest moral accomplishment of humans as that of aiding creation and furthering other lives. They regard this task as the ultimate goal of Heaven and Earth. In this sense, Heaven and Earth, as well as the whole cosmos, are rendered *moral* and *intentional*. Human beings are situated between Heaven and Earth; they have a moral commandment to continue the task of Heaven and Earth. This "Trinity" – Heaven, Earth, and Man – not only depicts a moral structure of the universe, but also prescribes an ultimate moral duty (to be equal to Heaven and Earth) to human beings. When one attains the supreme status of being one of the Trinity, one becomes a "counterpart of Heaven."[15] This is how Confucianism defines "the sage"; it is also what the ancient Chinese expected of a true ruler – the Son of Heaven.[16]

Yijing opens with the hexagram of *Qian* and the hexagram of *Kun*. In the construction of the hexagram, *Qian* is made up of six unbroken lines and *Kun* is made of six broken lines. Hence, *Qian* is purely *yang* while *Kun* is purely *yin*. Since no real existence can be without both *yin* and *yang*, what *Qian* and *Kun* stand for must be abstract principles. Wilhelm and Baynes (1977) translate *Qian* as "The Creative," *Kun* as "The Receptive." We can say that *Qian* stands for the Creative Principle, signified by Heaven; *Kun* stands for the Receptive Principle and is signified by Earth. In this cosmic philosophy, Heaven and Earth are seen as principles of generation and sustenance. But they are not mere "stand-ins" for abstract principles. The thinkers behind *Yijing* project moral attributes onto Heaven and Earth. In their view, a moral universe is the source of our moral attributes and the inspiration for our moral conduct. The morally correct thing for humans to do is to "emulate" the moral attributes of Heaven and Earth. As the *Great Treatise* says, "Heaven creates divine things; the holy sage takes them as models. Heaven and Earth change and transform; the holy sage imitates them."[17] That is to say, this philosophy asserts the absolute value of certain moral attributes. These attributes are not "good" in relation to human judgments or human situations; they are good in the absolute sense because they are manifested in Nature. For humans to be moral is for them to possess these virtues within themselves.

What are the moral attributes that have absolute values? We can sum up the most essential ones in *Yijing* as follows.

The four primary virtues

In *Yijing*, there are four primary virtues assigned to each hexagram, though not all hexagrams have all four of them.[18] The one hexagram that has these four primary virtues unqualified by any other restriction is the first hexagram, the *Creative* (*"Qian"*). Wilhelm and Baynes translate these four primary virtues as "sublime success; furthering through perseverance."[19] In this rendition, the four virtues seem to be divided into two sets: [A] (1) sublimity, (2) success; [B] (3) furtherance, (4) perseverance. James Legge translates them as (1) great and originating, (2) penetrating, (3) advantageous, and (4) correct and firm.[20] Alfred Huang translates them as (1) sublime and initiative, (2) prosperous and smooth, (3) favorable and beneficial, and (4) steadfast and upright.[21] The original Chinese words are: *yuan, heng, li, zhen*. The reason why these translators have used more than one term to render each of the four single words in Chinese is that each word carries with it complicated meanings. The first, *yuan*, signifies the origin of life, the source of existence. This primary virtue is the virtue of the Creative Principle, which initiates life forms and turns non-being into being. The second word, *heng*, signifies the penetration of *qi* into all things. This primary virtue is thus the virtue of fostering life and furthering everything's development. *Li* signifies benefit. It represents the virtue of promoting others and aiding the completion of things. Finally, *zhen* signifies correctness. This last primary virtue is thus the virtue of rectifying everything and making all life forms conform to standards appropriate to them. In the other hexagrams, this word often indicates "perseverance" as well. The connection may be that one should never deviate from the right course; hence, one should always persevere in what is correct.

These four primary virtues depict the roots of human morality as manifested in Nature. What Heaven and Earth accomplish together, via the operation of *qi*, is to create, nourish, benefit, and rectify all things in between. The fundamental moral task for humans is to continue what Heaven and Earth commence and bring the task to its completion. All primary virtues are the ideal virtues that human beings should strive to obtain; they embody the supreme moral commandments from Heaven and Earth.

The good (shan)

One remark in the *Great Treatise* was frequently quoted by neo-Confucians as the definition of *dao*. It says: "One cycle of *yin*; one cycle of *yang*, this is called '*dao*.' What continues it, is 'Good.' What completes it, is 'nature.'"[22] Apart from seeing the definition of *dao*, we also see here the concept "Good" defined as the continuer of *Dao*. To continue *Dao* is to aid the creative and nourishing functions of Heaven and Earth, of *yang* and *yin*. This task constitutes the highest moral goodness for humankind. As the *Commentary on the Judgment* on the 27th hexagram *Yi* (Providing Nourishment) says: "Heaven and Earth provide nourishment for all beings. The holy man provides nourishment for men of worth and thus reaches the whole people."[23] Human beings are related to all creatures as their preservers and nurturers; moreover, the sage (the holy man) is related to the rest of humankind as their leader and protector. The "Good" becomes a "Mandate from Heaven" – it depicts our categorical moral duty.

Lik Kuen Tong explains:

> What the *Great [Treatise]* here means by the "Good" must not be confused with the conventional conception of moral good which owes its specific meaning to the objectified and fixated posturality of a moral code or ethical system. The Good as the "continuer" of integrity and flexibility is the *absolute good* of Being itself in the primordial morality of its posturing power, not the "relative good" of our actions judged from the standards of our consequent moralities.[24]

We may say that since *Yijing* defines the "Good" on the basis of *Dao*, which governs the whole universe, this is *Good* in the absolute sense. To aid others in their fulfillment of life's potentials is not relative to individual or cultural perspectives; it is simply *good* in and of itself. This unqualified assertion of the meaning of our moral sense and the content of our moral duty in *Yijing* became the theoretical foundation for Confucian ethics.

Equilibrium (zhong) *and harmony* (he)

Under the principle of *reversal*, once a development reaches its extremity, the opposite development takes shape. *Yijing* describes a natural harmony in the world of Nature, which balances *yin* and *yang* in the state of *equilibrium* – the balance between two extremes. The Chinese word *zhong* is commonly translated either as "equilibrium" or as "the mean," since it connotes both. The mean is not just the strict middle point between two extremes; rather, it is a state of intrinsic harmony. Hence, some elements could be more than others, as long as the inequality does not disturb the harmonious balance. The two notions, *the mean* and *harmony*, are often used in conjunction. *Yijing*'s notion of the mean is not relative to human judgment. It depicts a cosmic state both before, and after, any disturbance in the flow of *qi*. In other words, it is a natural state of the cosmos, to which all other unnatural states will eventually return. As the 24th hexagram *Return* says, "Return. Success. Going out and coming in without error."[25] We can envisage a cosmic pendulum in the constant movement of *yin* and *yang*. The goal of the movement of *qi* is not to keep the pendulum resting still at the middle point, since this eliminates movement. With the constant swing between two ends, the pendulum maintains a consistent flow. This consistent movement is harmony itself. When the mean is understood as equilibrium, the allowance for variance is much greater. A development toward one end or the other is not necessarily violating the principle of the mean, as long as any deviation eventually returns to the mean. Since the flow of *qi* is naturally ordered in accordance with *Dao*, it contains within itself the natural state of equilibrium and harmony. Such is the Truth, or the Way (*Dao*), of the world.

Based on the assumption of a morally ordered universe, *Yijing* takes the goodness of human nature as given. Humans are born with moral attributes. In *Yijing*, it is said that everything receives its true nature from the creative force of *Qian* and keeps being transformed by it until everything "comes into permanent accord with the Great Harmony."[26] Humans have the purest and the most harmonious combination of *yin* and *yang*; hence, we are the most superior of all living things. The thesis that human nature originally possesses *equilibrium* and *harmony* was later elaborated in one of the Confucian classics: the *Doctrine of the Mean*, allegedly written by Confucius' grandson. The *Doctrine of the Mean* opens with this remark:

> What Heaven imparts to man is called human nature. To follow our nature is called the Way [*Dao*]. . . . Before the feelings of pleasure, anger, sorrow, and joy are aroused, it is called equilibrium (*the Mean*). When these feelings are aroused and each and all attain due measure and degree, it is called harmony. Equilibrium is the great foundation of the world, and harmony its universal path. When equilibrium and harmony are realized to the highest degree, heaven and earth will attain their proper order and all things will flourish.[27]

This esoteric remark is much better illuminated in the context of *Yijing*. If human nature comes from Heaven, then it is naturally good. To follow our nature is to "continue" *Dao*; hence, it is naturally good. Moral goodness for human beings is thus to follow our nature. Within our inborn nature are emotions such as pleasure, anger, sorrow, and joy. Before these emotions are aroused, we are in a state of equilibrium, since our nature is equilibrium itself. Once our emotions are aroused, we need to moderate them so that they are in a state of harmony. In this way, moderation (*the mean*) and harmony are closely linked again. When the human world can attain equilibrium and harmony within itself and further extends them to the world of Nature, then the task of

Heaven and Earth is completed. This is the ideal state of the world for all.

We may say that in the philosophy of *Yijing*, there is no distinction between "what is" and "what ought to be." *Yijing* sets up what *is* – the way the world is – as what *ought to be*. "Ought" implies moral duties or an ideal moral situation; it is specifically applied to the human world. But *Yijing* prescribes our highest moral duties in terms of the way the moral universe *is*. In other words, the moral attributes of the universe are what we humans *ought to* emulate. When human morality is grounded on an objective moral reality, it is part of the fabric of the world as well. This is a form of moral realism, which asserts objectivity and reality in moral values. Under this moral philosophy, what is "good" is not what God commands, not what social conventions decide, not even what human reason prescribes. Good is what is seen in Nature; it is what natural phenomena manifest. This philosophical system derives moral standards from observation of the external world, and the world is conceived differently from a mechanic, physicalistic worldview.

Yijing's Moral Philosophy: Contextual Prescriptivism

Not only do natural phenomena provide moral models for human beings, the relationships among natural phenomena also take up multiple symbolic moral connotations in *Yijing*. When the eight trigrams are doubled in various combinations, they form 64 hexagrams. The 64 hexagrams, as well as the six different lines that make up each hexagram, exhaust all possible situations in the natural world. Human contexts in an abstract way are parallel to these natural contexts. *Yijing* prescribes the best way to act for each and every context. For example, the fifth hexagram, *Xu*, has water on top and heaven below, which signifies clouds rising up in the sky and the impending rainfall. There is nothing one can do but wait for the rainfall. This image symbolizes a time of waiting in the human context and the proper attitude is not to be anxious or agitated. "Thus the superior man eats and drinks, is joyous and of good cheer."[28] Its reverse combination – heaven on top and water below – makes up the sixth hexagram, *Song*, which signifies "conflict," since there are two opposing forces in the elements: heaven tends upward while water tends downward. The *Image* of the hexagram says: "Heaven and water go their opposite ways: The image of Conflict. Thus in all his transactions the superior man carefully considers the beginning."[29] In a similar fashion, all other hexagrams represent different contexts for moral decisions that are derived from the symbolic meaning of the different relationships between natural elements.

Even though all contexts are different, there is a common cosmic structure inherent in all arrangements of hexagrams. This cosmic structure is the hierarchy between Heaven and Earth, between *yang* and *yin*. The *Great Commentary on Yi* [*Da Zhuan*] began with the following description: "Heaven is high, the earth is low; thus [*Qian*] and [*Kun*] are determined. In correspondence with this difference between low and high, inferior and superior places are established."[30] The basic structure of the cosmos consists in various levels of the hierarchy. This cosmic order lays the foundation for the social hierarchy in the human world. As Heaven is above and Earth is below, those who are represented by *yang* should be placed higher than those who are represented by *yin* in the social ladder. This moral structure with the dominance of *yang* and the subordination of *yin* corresponds to the political hierarchy with the emperor at the top, the ministers in the middle, and the people at the bottom. It also corresponds to the familial hierarchy of parents' presiding over children, the husband's expecting submission from the wife, and elder brothers' regulating younger ones. In terms of politics, *Yijing* provides a theoretical justification for the Chinese system of monarchy. In terms of society, *Yijing* affirms the hierarchical family relationships that came to be ingrained in Chinese culture. As *Commentary on the Judgment* says about the hexagram *The Family*:

> The correct place of the woman is within; the correct place of the man is without. That man and woman have their proper places is the greatest concept in nature. Among the members of the family there are strict rulers; these are parents. When the father is in truth a father and the son a son, when the elder brother is an elder brother and the younger brother a younger brother, the husband a husband and the wife a wife, then the house is on the right way. When the house is set in order, the world is established in a firm course.[31]

In this manner, *Yijing* assigns distinct roles to everyone in the family. Each person's doing his or her share within the family will ensure a greater harmony than what would be accomplished if each acted on his or her own.

All contexts explicated in *Yijing* have their unique moral qualities, and the general precept is *to act in accordance with the cosmic order* (*Dao*). As the *Image* of the 34th hexagram, *Da Zhuang*, says, "Thus the superior man does not tread upon paths that do not accord with established order."[32] To act according to what the context prescribes is to act in line with the cosmic order. This contextual prescriptivism is not moral absolutism in its crudest form, since it does not proclaim the same moral duty for everyone in all situations. Time – that is, the various elements in one's external environment – brings about different moral duties. Furthermore, this contextual prescriptivism does not even assign the same moral duty to everyone in the *same* situation; since different people have different personality traits (being aggressive or being passive by nature, for example), they should act in accordance with their own strength or weakness. There are times to take up public offices; there are times to seek reclusion. There are times to persevere in one's conduct; there are times to give up trying. There are times to procure fellowship with others; there are times to remain isolated. There are times to take leadership; there are times to remain subordinate. As the *Commentary on the Judgment* for the 41st hexagram says, "There is a time for decreasing the firm, and a time for increasing the yielding. In decreasing and increasing, in being full and being empty, one must go with the time."[33] The element of *time* is prevalent in all hexagrams. *Yijing* often talks about "the demands of the time." "The time" in *Yijing* means more specifically the variables in situations. Hence, the moral precept of going with the time and following one's natural traits is a form of *situational ethics* rather than a dogmatic form of moral absolutism.

In each given situation, there is a natural development of cosmic elements. When the superior person is placed under a human circumstance that *resembles* the cosmic state, there are certain rules of conduct most appropriate to him or her. In this sense, the social context *prescribes* the individual's moral duties. Under each given circumstance, there are *correct* ways to behave oneself. As Wilhelm explains, "Applied to human affairs ... what the hexagram indicates is action in conformity with the situation. ... The superior man lets himself be guided; he does not go ahead blindly, but learns from the situation what is demanded of him and then follows his intimation from fate."[34] In *Yijing*, the moral advice often seems to consist of hypothetical imperatives in the spirit of egoism. The desired consequences seem to be "good fortune," "felicity," or minimally "no blame"; the undesirable consequences seem to be "misfortune," "harm," "danger," "humiliation," etc. The oracles seem to be saying, "Act this way if you want to achieve felicity and success." However, the egoistic reading of the language of the Judgments in *Yijing* is definitely mistaken. According to the *Great Treatise* on *Yijing*, a deeper understanding of *Yijing* will reveal that the pursuit of good fortune or the avoidance of misfortune is not intended solely for the individuals who do the divination. The *Great Treatise* says: "To be able to preserve joyousness of heart and yet to be concerned in thought: in this way we can determine good fortune and misfortune on earth, and bring to perfection everything on earth."[35] What *Yijing* implicitly assumes is that all those who consult it are moral agents, who aspire to do the right thing and who have in mind the welfare of human society. For example, from the *Image* of the hexagram *Xiao Guo*, "the superior man derives an imperative: he must always fix his eyes more closely and more directly on duty than does the ordinary man, even though this might make his behavior seem petty to the outside world. He is exceptionally conscientious in his actions."[36] In each and every hexagram, there is always a moral imperative given to the "superior man." Therefore, authors of *Yijing* intended the Judgments for the superior moral agents, not for the common folks with petty concerns for their self-interest.

Yijing's moral philosophy should be understood in the background of its cosmology – its philosophy of change and its view of the moral, principled universe. There are things that constantly change in our moral contexts; there are also principles governing all changes. One's social roles change, but the larger hierarchy does not. One's relations to others change, but one's moral duties appropriate to each relation do not. One's situations change, but the moral imperative of being appropriate to the time does not. One's outward behaviors may change with circumstances, but one's inner virtues should not do so. In all situations, there is one absolute moral imperative overriding all other contextual moral duties: *Adhering to the Good.*

Yijing's Philosophy of Action: Causal Efficacy or Fatalism?

How does one conduct oneself in a world that is constantly changing? How does one enjoy autonomy in one's action when each action seems to be "demanded" by the situation in which one finds oneself? What kind of philosophy of life does *Yijing* teach us? Is it an optimistic or a pessimistic philosophy? Is it fatalism, or does it grant human efficacy and human freedom?

In *Yijing*, neither is everything completely determined, nor is everything due to haphazard chance. Since human contexts correspond to natural contexts, we could foresee how things might progress from a given point on. An individual's moral decision in a given context directly contributes to the interchange between *yin* and *yang* in the larger environment; hence, it can *bring about* a change in the state of affairs. Since the interchange between *yin* and *yang* is governed by natural laws, there is some predictability concerning further developments. "Here it is shown that the way to success lies in apprehending and giving actuality to the way of the universe [*dao*], which, as a law running through end and beginning, brings about all phenomena in time. Thus, each step attained forthwith becomes a preparation for the next. Time is no longer a hindrance but the means of making actual what is potential."[37] In *Yijing*, each line symbolically represents a human context, and every moral deed or moral attitude one takes in the given context makes the causal contribution to the later development of that state of affairs. Herein lies human's causal efficacy.

However, one's full effort does not always guarantee success. There are too many things beyond one's control. The initial situation in which one finds oneself is beyond one's control; hence, one can only adapt to the situation to find the best way to behave. Whatever is beyond one's control is called "destiny" or "fate," which can be seen as one's moral constraints. In the *Analects*, Confucius himself often lamented that it was due to his fate that he failed to realize his political ideal. In *Yijing*, these moral constraints set limits to our options, but they are not deterministic in nature. *Yijing* does not predict what each moral agent will do; it only predicts what consequences various moral decisions would bring about. Even when the given situation allows only one recommended conduct, the choice still exists whether or not to comply with the recommendation. Acting against the prescribed conduct can bring danger to oneself and to one's environment. One nevertheless has a free choice. Hence, it would be wrong to use the divination in *Yijing* as a way to foresee our future. Our future is uncertain, because our actions have not yet been decided.

Even if one has chosen the recommended conduct, the outcome is still not completely predictable. When one makes a moral deliberation or takes an action, there are many other elements taking place at the same time. For instance, other people's concurrent decisions and conduct could affect the larger state of affairs. One only has direct knowledge of, and control over, one's own undertakings. Hence, even if the whole universe is governed by *Dao* – the law of *yin* and *yang* – this ontological determination does not guarantee epistemic predictability. Given this epistemic limitation, what we should do is to conduct ourselves in the most appropriate way, and hope for the best.

There is optimism in *Yijing*'s philosophy of life, however. What the philosophy of change can guarantee is that nothing is fixed for good.

43

Whether one is in a supremely good condition, or in a bad one, the good as well as the bad will not last long. This perspective cautions us to be wary of things that happen around us when we are content with where we are; however, it also makes us hopeful that the present woeful situation can turn around. Under this philosophy, one has to have a keen perception not only of one's present situation, but also of the possible changes that are coming one's way. If one perceives the beginning of a wrong turn of events, one could terminate the change in time. As the *Commentary on the Words of the Text* says:

> A house that heaps good upon good is sure to have an abundance of blessings. A house that heaps evil upon evil is sure to have an abundance of ills. Where a servant murders his master, where a son murders his father, the causes do not lie between the morning and evening of one day. It took a long time for things to go so far. It came about because things that should have been stopped were not stopped soon enough.[38]

This commentary explains the first line of the hexagram of *Kun*, which symbolizes the formation of the negative force. When the sign of a negative trend first appears, one needs to recognize it as such and find ways to alter the direction of change. Naturally, when the trend is desirable, one would want to take action to encourage its further development. One's causal efficacy, however, is not dependent solely on one's effort. Sometimes a development could be so entrenched that it would be impossible to stop it or even to slow it down. At this point, any resistance to change, however disagreeable the change may be, becomes futile. To act or not to act – that is the question.

Tze-ki Hon calls each situation in life (as depicted by *Yijing*) "a field of action":

> None of us act on our own, but as members of a team. As players in a field of action, the more we realize where we stand and from where to seek assistance, the better our chances of success. In this regard, the degree to which we are capable of controlling our future depends on how well we know our field of action, and how effectively we interact with it.[39]

In other words, there are no absolute moral successes for everyone in all situations, even if everyone is acting in accordance with *Yijing*'s counsel. What *Yijing* portrays is situational confinement as well as situational possibilities. The given situation and its possibilities are the limits of life. We can work within the given limits of life, to find our choices. There is thus freedom of choice, though our options are limited and our freedom is preconditioned by the intended consequences. One thing that needs to be emphasized in the end, however, is that our choice is only between acting and not acting, never between being moral and being immoral. *Yijing* would never advise that we alter ourselves (our inner virtues) to conform to society.

Conclusion

In this chapter, we have covered some of the most essential theses of *Yijing*. But the philosophy of *Yijing* is much more complicated than what could be covered here. The Judgment for each hexagram as well as for each line in the hexagram can all be elaborated into a philosophy on values and realities. The first two hexagrams, *Qian* and *Kun*, for example, encompass the philosophy of *yang* and the philosophy of *yin* respectively. The philosophy of *yang* is also the philosophy of *dragon*; the philosophy of *yin* is also the philosophy of *mare*. The former depicts an aggressive, assertive, adventurous, and active attitude toward life; the latter depicts a receptive, devoted, yielding, and non-competitive attitude toward life. Later, we shall see that Confucianism takes on the philosophy of *Qian*, while Daoism takes on the philosophy of *Kun*. *Yijing* is indeed the archetype of Chinese philosophy. From as early as the Han Dynasty (206 BCE–220 AD), many Chinese intellectuals would devote their whole life to the study of *Yijing*. There are countless commentaries or philosophical treatises written on it in Chinese intellectual history. *Yijing*'s tremendous impact on the development of Chinese thought cannot be underscored enough.

Further discussion questions

1 Can we define any cosmic pattern? Is there any semblance between cosmic patterns and patterns in human affairs?
2 Why must there be only 64 hexagrams and six lines in each hexagram? Do they really exhaust all *possible* situations in the universe or in the human world?
3 Can humans have freedom of will in a universe governed by *qi*? To what extent does the external environment condition one? To what extent can one alter the external environment?
4 How do human acts affect the larger environment? What kind of *causation* is implied in the interchange between *yin* and *yang*?

Primary texts

Alfred Huang. *The Complete I Ching*. Rochester, VT: Inner Traditions, 1998.

Richard John Lynn (trans.) *The Classic of Changes: A New Translation of the I Ching as Interpreted by Wang Bi*. New York: Columbia University Press, 1994.

Richard Wilhelm and Cary F. Baynes (trans.) *The I Ching: Book of Changes*. Princeton, NJ: Princeton University Press, 1977.

Further readings

Chung-ying Cheng. "On Harmony as Transformation: Paradigms from the *I Ching*." *Journal of Chinese Philosophy* 16, 1989: 125–58.

——. "'*Li*' and '*Ch'i*' in the *I Ching*: Reconsideration of Being and Non-being in Chinese Philosophy." *Journal of Chinese Philosophy* 14, 1987: 1–38.

Shu-hsien Liu. "On the Functional Unity of the Four Dimensions of Thought in the *Book of Changes*." *Journal of Chinese Philosophy* 17, 1990: 359–86.

Bo Mou. "An Analysis of the Ideographic Nature and Structure of the Hexagram in *Yijing*: From the Perspective of Philosophy of Language." *Journal of Chinese Philosophy* 25(3), 1998: 305–20.

Hellmut Wilhelm and Richard Wilhelm. *Understanding the I Ching: The Wilhelm Lectures on the Book of Changes*. Princeton, NJ: Princeton University Press, 1979.

Chapter 2

Confucius (Kongzi) in the *Analects*

Introduction

In the Western world, Confucius (551–479 BCE) is generally regarded as the founder of the moral and political philosophy known as *Confucianism*. The connotation is that this philosophy is *his* philosophy. The name "Confucianism" is less commonly used in China. In the Chinese tradition, Confucius is seen as the pioneering leader of a school of intellectuals known as "*Ru*-ists (*ru-jia*)." *Ru*-ism is the product of joint efforts by early "Confucians" including Confucius, Mencius, Xunzi, and the author (or authors) of two classics: the *Doctrine of the Mean* and the *Great Learning*. *Yijing* is also standardly taken to be a foundational text for *Ru*-ism. Confucius himself did not write any systematic philosophical work. His thought is mostly preserved in the collection of his remarks (the *Analects*), supposedly recorded by his students. Some other philosophical documents were historically attributed to Confucius (such as the *Commentary on Yi*). However, the exact authorship of these documents cannot be established. In this chapter, we will only deal with Confucius as portrayed in the *Analects*.

Confucius lived in a time of chaos and corruption, and he spent most of his life traveling from one nation-state to the next in an unsuccessful attempt to morally transform their rulers. His loyal students followed him in his travel so as to receive his teaching. In traditional Chinese society, the completion of education normally leads to political careers, since an intellectual's ultimate goal is to better the world. Some of Confucius' students did manage to obtain official positions and did try to put his political ideal into practice. But in a world where rulers were intent on amassing their power and expanding their territory, the chance of success for a Confucian political program was marginal. Confucius was once described by a contemporary as "the one who knows a thing cannot be done and still wants to do it."[1] This spirit of "persevering in the good" becomes the defining character of all Confucians.

In analyzing Confucius' philosophical concepts, we need to realize that he did not take a definitional approach. As Antonio Cua remarks, "One main difficulty in understanding Confucian ethics lies in the absence of systematic exposition of its basic ideas, such as *ren* (humanity; humaneness), *li* (propriety), and *yi* (rightness)."[2] Confucius did not think that there could be a universal definition for a moral concept, which would be applicable to everyone in every situation. When students asked him to explain an ethical principle, Confucius would give an answer appropriate to each one's particular strengths, shortcomings, or personal background. Hence, we often see him giving different answers to the same question, when such questions were raised by different students, concerning the meaning of a certain ethical concept such as "filial piety." If we try to find a universal definition for a moral concept in his usage, we may end up concluding that he did not have a coherent conception. To understand his moral philosophy, we need to go beyond mere analysis of his moral concepts and look at the whole picture.

Confucius says that there is a single unifying principle linking all his moral teachings.[3] According to one of his leading students, Zengzi, this principle can be explained in terms of two key elements of Confucius' moral philosophy: one is called *zhong*, literally translated as "loyalty"; the other is called *shu*, literally "empathy."[4] Why would loyalty and empathy be regarded as the "single" thread that unifies Confucius' moral philosophy? How are the two concepts related? In this chapter, we shall see that the basis of Confucius' moral philosophy is his construction of a moral/social hierarchical structure, and that both loyalty and empathy must be understood in relation to this structure.

Moral Hierarchy and the Notion of *Zhong* (Loyalty)

The goal of Confucius' moral philosophy is to construct a moral structure for society. Within this structure, individuals are not all equal in relation to one another. This moral structure corresponds to the political hierarchy, with the emperor on the top, the ministers in the middle, and the people at the bottom. It also corresponds to the familial hierarchy of parents and children, husband and wife, and sibling relationships, as shown in the chart.

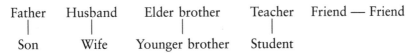

In this moral hierarchy, everyone is assigned a moral role depending on how he or she is related to others. One's moral duties are defined in terms of the roles one plays in the political/social hierarchy. For example, the duty of an emperor is to behave in a kingly fashion and to take care of the people's basic needs. A minister's duty is to assist the emperor in governing the people. The duty of an ordinary citizen is to obey the superiors. In the family, parents have a duty to love their children, while children have a duty to exemplify filial piety toward their parents. The husband's duty is to support the family, while the wife's duty is to manage household affairs. Siblings have a duty to love one another and younger siblings must respect or even obey the elder ones. Such relations can further extend to strangers: seniors should be respected by their juniors; the young should be loved and cared for by the adults. One's moral duties shift as one adopts various roles in life, of which there will always be several in accordance with one's various relationships with different people. However, there is one moral obligation that applies to all roles and all people: the virtue of *zhong* (loyalty).

"Loyalty" is generally understood to be a feeling or an attitude of devotion toward one's superior. In a political context, it is specifically defined as an allegiance to the ruler or the state. However, in the *Analects*, this notion has a broader dimension. For example, Confucius' student Zengzi says: "Everyday I examine myself on three points: whether in counseling others I have not been loyal; whether in intercourse with my friends I have not been faithful; and whether I have not repeated again and again and practiced the instructions of my teacher."[5] Being loyal and being faithful are seen as interrelated virtues and they have a significant place in Confucius' teaching. Confucius is said to teach only four things: culture, conduct, loyalty, and faithfulness.[6] He says: "[The superior person] holds loyalty and faithfulness to be the guiding principle. He would never regard his friends as inferior to himself. He would never be afraid to acknowledge and correct himself when he has made a mistake."[7] In all these quotes we do not see "loyalty" defined as a notion suitable only for a political context. Even in a political context, "loyalty" is defined as an attitude toward a task, not toward a person. When a student asks about politics, Confucius says, "Over daily routine, do not show weariness, and when there is action to be taken, [perform with loyalty]."[8] Loyalty is not a devotion directed specifically toward one's superior; rather, it is directed toward the role one plays – being loyal means doing one's best in whatever one does. In this sense, loyalty can be defined as "doing what one is supposed to do" or "being loyal to one's role." In other words, a social role is not simply a social assignment; it is also a moral assignment. Being loyal to one's role means being able to act in accordance with whatever moral obligations come with the social role. Loyalty is thus being loyal to one's moral obligations and fulfilling the duty that one's role dictates. When asked about how to govern, Confucius replies: "Let the ruler be a ruler, the subject a subject, the father a father, the son a son."[9] This is not a trivial tautology. It compares the actual social role one adopts with the ideal moral role one is supposed to exemplify, and asks everyone to act up to the latter. Being loyal to one's role in relation to others is the meaning of *zhong*.

David Nivison analyzes the notion of *zhong* as merely a relation "directed toward superior, or at most toward equals."[10] A. C. Graham has a similar interpretation of *zhong* as "especially of devoted loyalty to a ruler, but also of wholeheartedness on behalf of inferiors."[11] But this understanding only grasps one aspect of the virtue of *zhong*. Subjects should naturally show respect toward their superiors, since that is what the role of a subject commands. A ruler or a minister, however, should do their best to govern the people so as to command respect from them. Both ways of fulfilling the duty appropriate to one's role are covered under the notion of *zhong*. Confucius once discussed someone who showed no sign of delight when he was three times appointed officer and showed no sign of resentment when he was thrice removed from office. When this man was replaced by someone else, he always made sure that his successor knew how to take over his job smoothly. Confucius thinks that we may not say this person is wise (in that he does not know how to keep his job), but he does have the virtue of *zhong* (loyalty).[12] This loyalty is not targeted toward whoever appointed or dismissed him; it is directed toward his job. At the same time, one should not meddle in any job or social role which is not one's own. Confucius says: "Do not concern yourself with matters of government unless they are the responsibility of your office."[13] This notion can be compared to Socrates' notion of a just city, as expressed in Plato's *Republic*: "A city is just when everyone does his own job." When people meddle in the affairs of others, then chaos and injustice ensue. If everyone does his own job and does it as best as he can, then the social structure will be harmonized and well ordered. As Chad Hansen puts it, it will be a "correct" structure.[14]

The "correctness" of a social structure is obtained when the name of each social role and its actuality correspond. This is what Confucius calls "the rectification of names." Confucius once said that if he were ever offered a governmental position, his first priority would be to rectify names, because,

> [i]f names are not correct, speech will not be in accordance with actuality; when speech is not in accordance with actuality, things will not be successfully accomplished. When things are not successfully accomplished, ritual practice and music will fail to flourish; when ritual and music fail to flourish, punishment and penalties will miss the mark. And when punishment and penalties miss the mark, the people will be at a loss as to what to do with themselves.[15]

It is obvious that he takes the rectification of names to be the first step toward establishing social order. Why is it so important to make *name* and *actuality* correspond with each other? Benjamin Schwartz explains this relationship between social roles and names in this way:

> Thus the language of familial and social roles – words that refer to father, ruler, son, or minister – do not refer simply to bare biological or political facts but . . . every role is the bearer of its own role-norms. The word "father" carries the implication that the father will "act like a father" as well as the assumption that the language will provide information on how to do so.[16]

In other words, the function of "names" in the Confucian language plays not just a descriptive role, but also a prescriptive role – they establish rules of conduct appropriate to each name. In such a moral language, names of social roles do not just pick out the social assignment of various roles; instead, they refer to the ideal categories of "father," "son," "ruler," "minister," etc. Once this language is imposed on human society, it regulates society's relations and its members' behavior. Therefore, the rectification of names is not about language per se; it is about action and ethics.

Using the rectification of names as a means of establishing a correct social structure, Confucius defines universal expectations for each social role. That is to say, there are some general guidelines on how to be a father or a mother, how to be a husband or a wife, how to be a brother or a sister, etc. If everyone follows these guidelines and aims to be loyal to his or her role as a parent, as a spouse, or as a sibling, then social conflicts resulting from anyone overstepping their boundaries would disappear. The notion of *zhong*, as applied in the Confucian moral hierarchy, comprises a moral theory that focuses on moral duties or obligations, rather than on rights or entitlements. It constitutes a basic tenet of Confucianism, which is an ethics built on demands on oneself rather than on others. In contrast to the rights theory, Confucianism is a form of deontology.

Of all moral duties that Confucius advocates, the duty of filial piety is one that has penetrated Chinese culture the most. There is no fitting translation of the Chinese notion "*xiao*" other than the commonly used "filial piety," which stands for a strong sense of respect and loyalty to one's parents. Such a sense of loyalty extends beyond the parents' lifetime. Confucius says: "When a man's father is alive, look at the bent of his will. When his father is dead, look at his conduct. If for three years [of mourning] he does not change from the way of his father, he may be called filial."[17] Confucius stresses the importance of a lengthy mourning period for one's parents – three years is the proper length to mourn for one's father. If a person changes his demeanor as soon as his father has passed away, then it shows how pretentious he had been in the presence of his father. Confucius thinks that we are fully dependent on our parents for survival and nourishment at least in the first three years of our life; hence, it is only natural that after they depart from us, we should spend three years keeping them in constant regard. During our parents' lifetime, Confucius says, we should "never disobey" them. When a student asked him to explain further what he meant by this, he said: "When parents are alive, serve them according to the rules of propriety. When they die, bury them according to the rules of propriety and sacrifice to them according to the rules of propriety."[18] The first comment, "never disobey," has often been taken to mean that parents can demand absolute obedience from their children. In traditional Chinese society, this expectation did prevail among parents. However, from Confucius' elaboration of the first comment, we can see that he does not advocate blind obedience. Filial piety should be checked by "the rules of propriety." Hence, it is a moral duty bound by the role one plays as a son or a daughter, and the rules of propriety should apply to parents and children alike. If parents act *improperly*, then children should be relieved from their duty of filial piety. Confucius further emphasizes the importance of the right mental attitude with regard to filial piety. He says: "Filial piety nowadays means being able to nourish one's parents. But we nourish even those dogs and horses that we raise. If there is no feeling of reverence, wherein lies the difference?"[19] From this remark we can see that in as early as Confucius' times, there was already an expectation that sons should support their parents in their old age.[20] "Supporting one's parents with reverence," in today's context, would probably mean that we should not simply give our parents money or send them to a nursing home and let others perform our duty for us. We should serve them with reverence for as long as they live. This teaching was instrumental to the development of the large multi-generational family structures in traditional Chinese society.

Shu (Empathy): A Confucian Golden Rule

The other half of Confucius' "single thread" is the notion of *shu* (empathy). The importance of this virtue in Confucius' moral philosophy can also be seen in another exchange he had with a student. When asked to give one word that can serve as the guiding principle for one's entire life, Confucius replied that it is *"shu"*, and further elaborated: "Do not impose upon others what you yourself do not desire."[21] This moral guideline is sometimes called the Confucian Golden Rule, in contrast with the Golden Rule in the Christian tradition: "Do unto others as you would have them do unto you."

The Christian Golden Rule commands what one ought to do, whereas the Confucian Golden Rule states what one ought not to do. Are the positive and negative formulations morally significant? If so, which one is a better moral principle? According to Allinson, the positive and the negative Golden Rule are different, and the latter is superior to the former in that (1) it expresses modesty and humility, (2) it does not presume that one necessarily has knowledge of what the good is – what is good for oneself and whether it would be good for other people, and (3) it is less likely to lead to abuse or moral harm to others.[22] Ivanhoe calls the Christian Golden Rule "the principle of reversibility." He says:

> Reversibility might be regarded as a *formal principle* which guides me, in the performance of specific actions, to only proper actions – that is, if before I perform a given action, I first conduct a kind of "thought experiment" and imagine how I would feel if I were in the place of the person or persons who will be affected by my proposed action. If I would be willing to be treated in the way I imagine, then I can act in the proposed way.[23]

But one problem with this moral principle, as Ivanhoe points out, is that "it can end up being a disguised way of advocating the adoption of one's personal preferences. For example, 'the principle of reversibility would seem to urge a masochist to become a sadist – to adopt the motto: 'hurt others as you would have others hurt you'."[24] The Confucian Golden rule, on the other hand, does not seem to have this problem. At first appearance, the negative formulation seems to be a better moral principle. But to see a deeper comparison, we need to consider their applications.

Both the Christian and the Confucian Golden Rules concern actions, not just preferences, in interpersonal interactions. They are not asking others to adopt an individual's maxims or moral preferences; they are simply asking for the individual's sanction of her own behavior. Both principles are stated as a form of *categorical imperative*, that is, they are to be followed not because of some other desired consequences for oneself. Both principles presume that I do not act in a certain way toward others simply because I want them to do the same for me. Both principles are based on the assumption that people's wants and desires are similar and thus we can use ourselves as the measure to gauge other people's minds. Furthermore, any moral consideration formulated in accordance with the Christian Golden Rule can easily be converted into a moral consideration in the spirit of the Confucian Golden Rule, and vice versa. For example, "wanting others to treat us with respect" can be rendered "*not* wanting others to treat us with disrespect"; "not wanting to be robbed by others" can be rendered "wanting others to show consideration for our property." Therefore, a good case can be made that the two formulations are basically identical. But a case can also be made to show that the two principles are slightly different.

If the Golden Rule is to be used as the only moral principle for our action toward others, then there is no universal guideline for us other than our own wishes. Whether our judgment is morally permissible thus depends on what kind of people we are. The positive formulation of the Golden Rule commands us to do unto others what we would have them do unto us. What would we have other people do unto us? At a minimal level, we would want others to respect us, to help us when we are in need, to show us love and concern, etc. It is a reasonable demand on us that we do the same for others. However, if we are of the greedier type, then we might want more from others. We might like it that others give us their money, that others forgive all our shortcomings, that others do us great favors with no strings attached. But at the same time, we find it difficult to do so unto others. In this case, the Christian Golden Rule becomes an impossible command. A reclusive person may simply want to be left alone. Following the Christian Golden Rule, that person would not do anything for anyone else. Other conceivable problems with this moral principle might be the masochist becoming a sadist, a one-directional love turning into a pathetic clinging, etc. Basically, people's desires and wishes are so various that we cannot simply impose on others what we ourselves wish them to do for us.

Would Confucius' notion of *shu*, or the negative Golden Rule, fare better? It commands us not to do unto others what we ourselves do not desire. What don't we want others to do unto us? At a general level, we do not wish others to humiliate us, to laugh at us, to steal from us, to harm us, or simply to mistreat us in any way. It is reasonable that we do not treat others in these ways either. And even if we desire others to act in a certain way toward us, the Confucian Golden Rule does not counsel us to act this way toward others too. It thus avoids the problem of subjective imposition of preferences that we see in the positive formulation. It is arguable whether we know what is undesirable more than we know what is desirable, since people's displeasure can be just as idiosyncratic as their preferences. However, there seems to be more common ground in what people do not desire than in what they do desire. If we gauge others' wishes by checking what we ourselves would not desire, we would have set a reasonable constraint on our action that would affect others. Hence, the Confucian Golden Rule, even if not morally superior to the Christian Golden Rule, is at least more applicable.

How does this notion of *shu* (empathy) fit into Confucius' moral hierarchy, and how does it link up with the notion of *zhong* (loyalty) to constitute his unifying principle? As explained earlier, in this moral hierarchy individuals are interconnected in a social web that includes multilayers of relationships. One needs to be loyal to the different roles one plays relative to the other person. Now with *shu* (empathy), one can also extend oneself to appreciate what the other person in the opposite role would desire. For example, a father can do his best as a father to edify his son. But if he remembers how much he resented his own father's dictatorship, then he should modify his discipline and not impose too much restraint on his son. A student might wish to cheat in her studies. However, once she realizes how disappointed she would be as a teacher, she should understand that her duty is to work honestly instead. The extension of oneself can go beyond the person of an opposite role to reach people of similar roles. For example, if we do not wish our family members to be harmed, then we should not harm any stranger who is also a family member to someone else. If we do not want our children to starve or freeze, then we should give charity to other parents who cannot afford food and clothing for their children. If everyone were to think and act this way, society would have no theft, robbery, rape, murder, or hunger. Loyalty to one's role is not sufficient for securing social harmony unless it is accompanied by everyone's empathetic understanding of other people's wishes. In this way, the two notions, *zhong* and *shu* (loyalty and empathy), are equally essential to the establishment of Confucius' ideal society.

Moral Cultivation and the Establishment of the Moral Ideal: From the Superior Person (*Junzi*), to the Man of Humanity (*Ren*), to the Sage (*Sheng*)

In the Confucian moral society, people are categorized into different groups according to their varying degrees of moral cultivation. One who is morally exemplary is called "the superior person" (*junzi*, sometimes translated as "the gentleman"). Those who not only have superior moral characters themselves, but also help others to cultivate themselves, are men of humanity (men of *ren*); and finally, those who can extend benevolence to all people and bring succor to the multitude, are the sages (*sheng*).[25] The complete moral self-cultivation is a process that one is committed to undertake throughout one's life. Very few people can actually attain the final state of *sheng*. If moral perfection is the end-state of our being, then we are not born perfect. Under Confucius' view, however, we are *perfectible*.

How to define human nature is one of the most vital issues in Confucianism. But unlike later followers, Confucius himself seldom discusses human nature. He focuses more on the pursuit of moral cultivation instead. In other words, Confucius is more interested in *what we can become* than in *what we are born with*. But before we understand our moral goal, we need to have a look at what we are born with. One thing Confucius affirms about human nature is that people are alike by nature. "Men are close to one another by nature. They diverge as a result of habituation."[26] If we are similar by nature, then what is our nature? Confucius holds the view that we are born with righteousness, but we have many desires that can lead us astray. Even he himself could not claim to have all his desires stay within the bounds of propriety until he had reached the age of 70.[27] Therefore, in his view, we are not born perfect, but we can *become* perfect.

Confucius uses "habituation" to explain the varying degrees of goodness and badness in people. Habits are formed through repeated practices. What kind of practice leads to goodness and what kind of practice leads to badness? In Confucius' distinction of *junzi* (the superior person) and *xiaoren* (the petty person) we get a clue: the concern with what is right or virtuous itself leads to superior personhood, while the concern with profit or possession leads to inferior personhood. As Confucius says: "The superior person is concerned with virtue; the petty person is concerned with property. The superior person is concerned with sanctions; the petty person is concerned with personal favors."[28] Confucius is not necessarily against wealth or profit, but he is against wealth accumulated, or profit made, through improper ways. If one wishes morally to cultivate oneself, one needs first to set one's priority on doing the right thing, not on amassing one's own profit. When the priority is on profit, it is tempting to forgo principles just to make a few more bucks. If someone is intent on getting rich, then she may feel ashamed the first time she embezzles money. But through repeated practices, she will eventually become habituated in gaining wealth improperly. Hence, without a secure moral principle, one can easily sink into the category of *the petty people*.

Confucius also says: "The superior [person] seeks the Way and not a mere living. . . . The superior [person] worries about the Way and not about poverty."[29] To learn the Way (*Dao*) is the ultimate goal in life; furthermore, the pursuit of the Way is a never-ending process. If we desire material goods and physical comfort, then we cannot pay full attention to the cultivation of our moral attributes. Confucius says: "A fellow who is ashamed merely of shabby clothing or meager food is not even worth conversing with."[30] To pay full attention to one's moral growth is constantly to examine oneself. Have I failed to cultivate my virtues? Have I failed to delve more deeply into what I have learned? Have I been able to move in the direction of what I just learned to be right? Have I been able to rectify my own misdeeds? A person interested in the pursuit of the Way is thus always diligent and never self-excusing. As Benjamin Schwartz puts it: "The moral cultivation is a long and difficult process, not everyone can accomplish the final goal."[31] Those who aim for the final goal are called *junzi*, the superior person. They are superior not by nature, but by their constant practice of self-examination and self-reform.

Why must we seek to learn the Way and to morally cultivate ourselves? Why can't we rest content with our physical comfort? For Confucius, the goal in life has to do with the meaning of being human. He has an all-embracing moral notion that depicts what it is to be human: *ren* (humanity). It is difficult to find a single moral concept in Western ethics comparable to the notion of *ren*. *Ren* is not a moral principle that gives us specific guidance in life; nor is it accomplishable by a single act.

57

Ren is not about action; rather, it is about a state of being. To be more exact: *ren* represents an ideal state of human being. Ideally, human beings subsist between Heaven and Earth, playing the same roles that Heaven and Earth play. In the Confucian cosmology (as explained in the context of *Yijing*), Heaven and Earth are ascribed many moral attributes, the most prominent of which is *ren*.[32] While Heaven nourishes all living things and Earth sustains them with no discrimination, we should aid our fellow human beings and other creatures in their quest for self-completion. In this context we can understand why Confucius says, "If one sets one's heart on [*ren*], one will be without evil."[33]

Seeing the meaning of "*ren*," we can realize that simply cultivating our own moral attributes is not a sufficient aim in life. We need to help others fulfill their moral personhood as well. This is how Confucius defines "men of humanity": "If one wishes to establish one's moral character, one also establishes the moral characters of others; if one wishes to obtain one's goal, one also helps others obtain their goals."[34] To be a man of humanity is thus the common goal of all superior people. As Confucius says: "The superior person aims to help others fulfill what is good in them; he does not help others carry out what is bad in them."[35] Confucius once explains *ren* as "to love one's fellow men."[36] To love others is not simply to be benevolent or compassionate toward them. One can be benevolent or compassionate by helping others in practical ways: giving them money, providing them with comfort, offering them kind words, etc. The Confucian ideal of *ren*, on the other hand, is to help others to become better people themselves, or, put another way, to help others in their attainment of the state of *ren*. An individual cannot achieve the state of *ren* if he or she does not also try to help others reach that same goal.

The person who can not only help those nearby cultivate themselves but can also spread this effort to the multitude must be more than someone of humanity; that person must be a *sage*. The difference between a person of humanity and a sage could be in the sheer number of people such altruistic efforts can reach. Confucius seems to think that only when the person of humanity also has the status of a king can he be deemed a sage. He regarded ancient kings such as Yao and Shun as sages. His own student, Yan Hui, could not be seen as a sage, however morally perfect he was. Today, the Chinese people regard Confucius as the *Ultimate Sage* (*Zhi-sheng*). This could be seen as testimony to the idea that far-reaching altruistic efforts in helpings others cultivate themselves could also be accomplished through philosophy and education.

All the moral principles discussed so far (being loyal to one's social role, not imposing on others what we ourselves do not desire, helping others establish their characters or obtain their goals) rely heavily on the individual's subjective judgment. An obvious difficulty is this: if we are not born with perfect knowledge of the Way, if the pursuit of the Way is a never-ending process, then we cannot know what we should be doing at any given moment in our life. It seems that we do need some external guidance from time to time. This is where another important Confucian moral concept, *li* (propriety, rituals), comes in. *Li* is about propriety, about what is the right thing to do in a given context. The formalized aspect of *li* is rituals and rites, but there has to be more to it than this. Rituals and rites are a matter of social conventions, and sometimes they can become inflexible and frivolous. Herbert Fingarette wrongly interprets Confucius' notion of *li* to represent some kind of "sacred ceremony" or "holy rites" that have a magical power to shape people's daily behavior.[37] Confucius could not possibly think that we should simply do whatever social conventions prescribe without any personal moral judgment. As Antonio Cua points out, "it is ritual, as comprising customs, conventions, or formal rules of proper conduct, that provides the starting point of individual morality."[38] In fact, textual evidence shows that Confucius does not interpret *li* to consist merely of formal ceremonies, and he does not think that morality simply lies in observing the rites. He says: "The superior person regards righteousness as his essence, and practices it in accordance with propriety."[39] In other words, the observance of propriety has to come from an internal moral sense – righteousness. Confucius only uses rituals as an external amendment to one's subjective state of mind. It is the ideal mental state, *ren*, which bestows value on rituals. Confucius says: "A man who is not *ren* – what has he to do with the ritual?"[40] It is because a person has *ren* as her goal that she would want to do what is proper in each context. She would "refrain from looking at that which is contrary to propriety, from listening in a way that is contrary to propriety, from saying things that are contrary to propriety, and from making any move that is contrary to propriety."[41] For example, it would not be proper to look at what other people do, or listen to what they say, in their private quarters. It is not because we have no means to do so; we should simply choose not to do it. I may have a strong urge to peep or to pry, but I should use self-restraint so that all my actions are in accordance with propriety. The essence of propriety comes from self-restraint. The sense of propriety should be established from within a person, not from a rigid set of public rules and social conventions.

In our society today, many people do not consider propriety as a standard for their conduct. They might use obscene language in public simply because they feel like it. They might insult others for no reason other than that they are in a foul mood. They might act vulgarly simply because they consider it their "right" to do whatever they please. They don't observe social contexts or assess whether their behavior is improper. They regard self-restraint as a restriction on their personal freedom, and they believe that self-expression takes precedence over social etiquette. However, Confucius teaches that to restrain oneself as a way to return to propriety is simply *ren* itself. He says: "To master oneself and return to propriety is humanity (*ren*). If a man (the ruler) can for one day master himself and return to propriety, all under heaven will return to humanity. To practice humanity depends on oneself."[42] Social standards of propriety and social conventions of rites and rituals serve a different function from that of the law. There are many ways in which propriety can be violated. However, for one reason or another we prefer not to establish laws that would ban them altogether. If everyone were concerned with whether or not his or her actions were proper in all situations, there would be less indecent behavior around us. The formalized aspect of propriety – rites and rituals – should serve merely as a reminder of the importance of propriety itself. Through propriety, we preserve human decency – that is how we maintain our humanity (*ren*). Therefore, for Confucius, to establish a society that has all its members fulfilling their moral ideals, an emphasis on propriety would be much more effective than the employment of laws and punishments. Here we turn to the final topic, the political ideal for Confucius.

From the Self to the State: The Confucian Political Ideal

An ideal political state is one that is governed by a ruler who has reached the ultimate goal of moral cultivation. This ideal ruler is called the sage king. In Confucius' opinion, the proper role of government is not just to keep its people materialistically gratified and physically secure, but also morally to cultivate them. Confucius says: "To govern is to rectify."[43] That is to say, the ruler's job is primarily to rectify his people's conduct. To do this, the rulers themselves must first be morally correct. Virtue and rulership are thus inseparable in Confucius' political philosophy. Raymond Dawson describes the Confucian model of government in this way: "[I]t is an agency for ensuring that the influence and example of men of superior moral qualities is brought to bear on the population."[44] Confucius thinks that this ideal of a sage king is not a mere ideal that can never be realized (unlike Plato's "philosopher king") – in ancient times before him, there had been sage kings (Yao and Shun), who had maintained a moral, harmonious state.

From our contemporary perspective, we might ask: how does virtue guarantee political success? To answer this question, we have first to understand that Confucius' political ideal is designed for a small monarchic polity. Within a small nation-state, as those existed in his times, the ruler's virtues were easily observed by the people. Confucius believed that if people respect the ruler, then they will be more likely to follow his rules. He says: "If a ruler sets himself right, he will be followed without his command. If the ruler does not set himself right, he will not be obeyed no matter how many orders he issues."[45] At a time when rulership was not backed by any theory of the divine right of the sovereign, the ruler needed to "earn" the respect of the people. By "setting himself right," Confucius meant not just that the ruler should be correct in his personal conduct, but also that he should be correct in his administrative judgment. Confucius says: "If you promote the straight and set them above the crooked, then the people will be obedient."[46] If the ruler has good judgment on the ministers he chooses to manage the state, then the people will not contest. If the people see that those governing them are all morally upright, then they will be inspired to be righteous themselves. Such an inspired moral transformation is not the result of an ulterior motive: if I *act* in a righteous way, I too could be promoted to a high position. Confucius believes that the people will readily emulate a morally exemplary person, because virtue has the power of moving and transforming people. He says, "Virtue never stands alone. It is bound to have neighbors."[47] This remark gives an interesting portrayal of the power of virtue. If a single person acts with impeccable virtue, then those around him will gradually be inspired to act virtuously. Eventually, the whole neighborhood will be occupied by virtuous people. If a virtuous civilian could have such an impact, then a virtuous sovereign would have an even greater impact on the people. Confucius uses two analogies to describe how effortless such virtuous rulership could be. He once said that the virtuous ruler can be compared to the Pole Star, "which commands the homage of the multitude of stars without leaving its place."[48] He also said that if the ruler himself wishes to be good, his people will be good, because "the character of a ruler is like wind and that of the people is like grass. In whatever direction the wind blows, the grass always bends."[49]

Finally, according to Confucius, law and punishment can only restrain people's behavior; it cannot alter their mind. Under strict laws and punishments, people will simply want to avoid being caught. But if they are taught to observe *li* (propriety), then they will develop their own moral sense and will want to do the right thing of their own accord. Confucius says:

> If you try to lead the common people with governmental regulations and keep them in line with punishments, the law will simply be evaded and the people will have no sense of shame. If, however, you guide them with virtue and keep them in line by means of [propriety], the people will have a sense of shame and will moreover reform themselves.[50]

Confucius' political philosophy can be sharply contrasted with that of Machiavelli. According to Machiavelli, a ruler need only be virtuous when doing so will be to his advantage, and sometimes the ruler must learn how not to be virtuous. Machiavelli also says: "It's far better to be feared than loved if you cannot be both."[51] He argued that the ruler cannot be idealistic and must deal with the actual conditions of the world. People in general are selfish, fickle, forgetful, and greedy. When the ruler's behavior is bound by virtue, he cannot always use the most efficient means to deal with his people. But if he uses harsh law and stiff punishment, then he can at least be sure that they would not dare to violate his rules.

Confucius' political philosophy is exactly the opposite of this kind of Machiavellian politics. He does not see the reality and the ideal as two separate realms. For him, the goal for an individual as well as for a state is always to strive for the ideal. As we saw earlier, this affinity toward the good is innate in us. When properly inspired, everyone will want to be good and to act in the correct way. It is only when we rest content with the present state and concede the impossibility of improvement that we fail to follow the Way. If, under the moral model of a sage king, everyone were constantly to practice self-examination to see if he were truly loyal to his roles (*zhong*), if he were to extend himself to empathize with others (*shu*), if he were to help others attain their moral personhood (*ren*), if he took care to observe propriety in all situations (*li*), then the Way (*Dao*) would prevail and we would have an ideal world.

Conclusion

Confucius depicted a lofty ideal for individuals and for the state. His ideal human being is one who never lapses in the pursuit of self-improvement. Our moral cultivation is like climbing a virtue ladder – we can always become better since there is always room for improvement.

Learning to know the Way (*Dao*) and to lead a life in accordance with the Way are the ultimate goals in life. Knowledge is for the moral growth of the individual learner; education is for building moral character. But at the same time, Confucius also focused on the moral duty to make others better. A Confucian always thinks of himself or herself as a member of human society. To better oneself is not as good as bettering the whole human race; to have a happy life oneself is not as good as making everyone's life happy. The most efficient way to accomplish these ends is to improve the politics of the state. Therefore, the ideal Confucian is one who is inwardly a moral sage, outwardly a *humane* king. By setting up a "moral king" as the ideal, the Confucian political philosophy treats virtue and politics as inseparable from each other.

On the personal level, what Confucius teaches is an adherence to virtue in the way one conducts oneself on a daily basis. A virtuous person does not seek recognition from others. As Confucius says, "Do not worry that you are not known to others; worry rather that you yourself lack ability."[52] Hence, Confucians should scrutinize themselves constantly. What one should care about is only whether one's words and deeds correspond to each other, or whether one's reputation matches the truth. Some people only appear to be virtuous and thus earn the respect from their peers, but Confucius calls such a person "the thief of virtue."[53] Later on, Mencius would give a nice explanation of this phrase:

> If you try to condemn them, there is nothing you can point to; if you try to censure them, there is nothing to censure. They are in agreement with the current customs; they are in harmony with the sordid era in which they live. That in which they dwell seems to be loyalty and [faithfulness]; that which they do seems to be blameless and pure. The multitude delight in them; they regard themselves as right. But you cannot enter into the Way of Yao and Shun with them . . . [Confucius] says, "I hate that which seems but is not."[54]

We can thus conclude that a Confucian is a person who is true to virtue, true to the Way, and true to him- or herself.

Further discussion questions

1 What is the moral justification for a Confucian hierarchy? Is democracy compatible with such a hierarchical structure?
2 What are the different implications between the positive Golden Rule in Christian ethics and the negative Golden Rule in Confucian ethics? Both principles demand that we gauge others' preferences or dislikes on the basis

of our own; hence, both differ from the Kantian moral principle that requires us to think of everyone, including ourselves, as disinterested, purely rational beings. Which approach could generate a more universal application?

3 What virtues does Confucius stress in his moral teaching? How are these virtues different from other virtue ethicists' recommendations?

4 How does Confucius define "filial piety"? How is it different from the common Western expectation of sons or daughters? What is the expectation on children within your own family tradition?

5 Joel Feinberg (1980) discusses an imaginary *Nowhereville*, where people are compassionate, sympathetic, honorable, and are endowed with a strong sense of duty, but the notion of *rights* is lacking. Would a Confucian society be like this *Nowhereville*? What would be missing if a moral society did not have the notion of *rights*?

Primary texts

Wing-tsit Chan (ed.) *A Sourcebook in Chinese Philosophy*, 4th edn. Princeton: Princeton University Press, 1973 (ch. 2; excerpts).

Raymond Dawson. *Confucius: The Analects*. Oxford World's Classics paperback. New York: Oxford University Press, 2000.

Philip J. Ivanhoe and Bryan W. Van Norden (eds.) *Readings in Classical Chinese Philosophy*. Indianapolis, IN: Hackett Publishing Company, Inc., 2003 (ch. 1; excerpts).

D. C. Lau. *Confucius: The Analects*. New York: Penguin Classics, 1979.

Further readings

Robert Allinson. "The Confucian Golden Rule: A Negative Formulation." *Journal of Chinese Philosophy* 12, 1985: 305–15.

Herbert Fingarette. "Following the 'One Thread' of the *Analects*." *Journal of the American Academy of Religion* 47(35), 1979: 375–405.

Philip Ivanhoe. "Reviewing the 'One Thread' of the *Analects*." *Philosophy East & West* 40(1), 1990: 17–33.

Chapter 3

Mencius (Mengzi)

Introduction

Mencius (372–289 BCE) flourished more than 100 years after Confucius. He became the second most important philosopher in the Confucian tradition. Mencius not only defended Confucius' view against other competing schools at the time, he also expanded it into a more systematic theory. The main source of Mencius' thought is in a collection of his remarks, *The Mencius (Mengzi)*.

During his lifetime, Mencius was known to be someone who loved to argue. He wrote:

> Do I really like to argue? I simply have no alternative. . . . If the doctrines of Yang School [Yang Zhu, ca. 440–360 BCE] and Mo School [Mozi, 480–392? BCE] do not subside and the teaching of Confucius is not proclaimed, the people will be misled by heresies and the path of morality will be blocked. When the path of morality is blocked, we are virtually leading animals to devour men. Sooner or later men will start devouring one another. Therefore, I am apprehensive. I wish to safeguard the way of ancient sages to fend off these deviant and extreme doctrines.[1]

Mencius made it his lifelong mission to advocate Confucius' ideals to contemporary rulers and to other intellectuals of his time. Like Confucius, he focused on two aspects of moral cultivation: how to be a good ruler and how to be a good person. Both teachings are based on Confucius' conviction: humans are perfectible. Mencius tried to answer the question: why are we perfectible? The reason given was that we are fundamentally good by nature. Therefore, Mencius' main argument was to establish the claim that human nature is good. This claim would later become the hallmark of Mencius' philosophy.

Mencius often used metaphors and analogies in his debates and lectures. David Wong calls this method "analogical reasoning" or "reasoning by analogy."[2] D. C. Lau wrote:

> It is not unusual for a reader of the *Mencius* to be left with the impression that in argument with his opponents Mencius was a sophist with little respect for logic. Not the least contributory factor to this impression is the type of argument which centers around an analogy. Yet it is difficult to believe that a thinker of Mencius' caliber and reputation could have indulged consistently in what appears to be pointless argument or that his opponents were always effectively silenced by *non sequiturs*. The fault, we suspect, must lie with us.[3]

In other words, if we don't see the *point* of his arguments, then we need to have a better understanding of the *style* of his argument. In this chapter, we will pay close attention to Mencius' argumentation. Argument by analogy is likely to have been a common method of debate at the time, since others used the same method to challenge Mencius. But those challengers often failed to win the argument. Mencius was clearly an expert in forming a persuasive analogy. To judge the success of an analogical argumentation, we have to remember that an analogy can at best be just that: an *analogy*. It shows similarities, but not exact identities, between the fact one wishes to establish and the example one cites. There are always some disanalogies in the two states of affairs being compared. The skill lies in making the similarities intuitively appealing and in reducing the relevance of the dissimilarities. But we should take care not to put too much emphasis on the examples themselves, and thereby lose track of the main claim that Mencius tried to establish.

Finally, in this chapter we will examine Mencius' political philosophy. Mencius had the same political mission as Confucius: to persuade his contemporary rulers to adopt his political ideals. He had limited success in his lifetime, in that he did win the respect and sponsorship of some kings. But ultimately, most of the kings were merely paying lip service to Mencius' teachings. Placing moral hierarchy over political hierarchy, Mencius insisted that as he was the king's moral and political mentor, the king should come and see him and not the other way around. Once, as he was on his way to pay the king a visit, a messenger arrived at his door to deliver a summons from the king. Mencius was offended that the king had treated him like an ordinary citizen, and made the excuse that he was too sick to obey the summons. The next day, he attended a friend's funeral despite his student's concern that the king might find out that he was not sick after all. On that day, the king sent a doctor to check on Mencius' health, and his student sent a messenger to warn Mencius not to return home, but to go to the king's court immediately. Mencius refused to do so; instead, he went to a friend's house to stay overnight. This kind of haughty conduct was politically reckless in such a context, since the king could easily command his death. Mencius regarded proper respect and personal honor to be more important than his own life. But at the same time, however disappointed he was at the king's insincerity, he was still hoping that the king would one day change his attitude. When he finally gave up on the king and left the country, he took three long days to take his departure, hoping in vain that the king might send someone to persuade him to stay. This expectant and yet proud attitude may be a bit hard for contemporary readers to appreciate. But it reveals Mencius' personality and his sincere concern for the realization of his political ideals.

In this chapter, our major interests lie in Mencius' philosophy of human nature, his moral philosophy, and his political philosophy.

What Is Human Nature?

The investigation of human nature[4] has been a shared undertaking by Western and Eastern thinkers alike. By "human nature," we cannot possibly mean simply what we were born with. Infants do not yet have the practice of reasoning, but few thinkers would deny that reason is part of human nature. Infants do not yet have fully developed sexual desire, but few thinkers would deny that sexual desire is innate in humans. Perhaps we could say that "nature" means one's potential, inclinations, or capacities. If that is the case, then the way we are as mature beings is not simply the manifestation of our nature. It is, rather, the outcome of the *fulfillment* of our potential, inclinations, and capacities. In other words, our nature is not an "end-state" of our existence; it is instead a beginning state.

If human nature is a mere beginning state of our existence, then it does not predetermine what we will become. To say that we have a tendency toward good does not mean that we cannot turn bad; to say that we have a tendency toward bad also does not mean that we cannot be made good. Neither tendency can prevent us from turning the other way. What is the point then in arging that humans have a tendency toward good or that they have a tendency toward bad? Shouldn't human nature be called morally neutral instead? A. C. Graham explains the meaning of "nature" in Mencius this way: "the [*xing*] (nature) of an animate thing . . . meant the course on which life completes its

67

development if sufficiently nourished and not obstructed or injured from outside."[5] In other words, nature is not just any tendency or any inclination; rather, it is the *natural* tendency or inclination of a creature. The opposite development not projected in one's original nature is thus not natural, but the result of external conditioning.

"Nature" is often used in opposition to "nurture," which includes all sorts of environmental influences: parental care, family discipline, peer conduct, educational enforcement, social norms, etc. Theoretically speaking, *nature* would be what is present prior to all these results of *nurture*. However, realistically we cannot see how a person behaves until she has been exposed to all sorts of environmental influences. Without nurture, nature cannot begin to be manifested. Therefore, a dichotomy between nature and nurture seems impossible in practice. If we employ empirical observation to gather evidence for the goodness or the badness of human nature, we will never come up with a reliable account. Mature human beings are the mixed results of both nature and nurture, and it is simply not feasible to separate the two factors in all individual cases. What then is the point of the debate over whether human nature is good or bad?

What the debate does is to help settle on issues of nurture: what is the best way to construct a harmonious, moral society? If we believe that humans have tendencies toward the bad, then we would advocate ways to curtail these tendencies: laws and punishments, for example. If we believe that humans have inclinations toward good, then we would advocate ways to enhance these inclinations: education and encouragement, for example. As we shall see, the debate between Mencius, who advocated that human nature is good, and Xunzi, who held the view that human nature is bad, would turn into a debate between Confucian politics, which stresses moral paradigms, and Legalistic politics, which emphasizes stiff laws and harsh punishments. The application of this theoretical debate thus has grave consequences.

Mencius' Assumptions on Human Nature and Human Mind/Heart

To begin with, for Mencius *nature* is a species-specific notion. He quoted from an ancient *Book of Odes*: "Where there is a thing, there is a norm."[6] Different kinds of things would have different norms. These norms define their respective *natures*. The nature of a dog cannot be the same as the nature of a cow, just as the nature of a cow cannot be the same as the nature of a human.[7] Therefore, human nature is what distinguishes humans from all other animals. Mencius further argued that humans are separated from animals exactly because moral virtues are innate to them. Since all humans belong to the same species (Mencius uses the notion *kind*), all humans would have the same nature. Hence, Mencius assumes that human nature is *universal* in all human beings. Taking barley as an example, he says:

> Sow the seeds and cover them. The soil is the same and the time of planting is also the same. They grow rapidly, and by the time of the summer solstice they have all ripened. Although there are some differences, these are due to the richness of the soil, and to unevenness in the rain and in human effort. Hence, in general, things of the same kind are all similar. Why would one have any doubt about this when it comes to humans alone?[8]

Barley is a natural kind. No matter how it grows, it will never turn into rice. Human is also a natural kind. No matter how someone develops, he or she will never become a beast (in the biological sense). From this analogy, we can see Mencius' idea about human similarities and human differences: he would argue that humans are alike by nature, and the differences we see in mature human beings are due to external environment and individual effort.

One could rebut the above claim by arguing that a human's physical and biological attributes may indeed be determined by its biological kind. But when it comes to a human's goodness or badness, we are dealing with a moral attribute that cannot be determined biologically. Mencius' reply would be that the human mind is also a human organ or a capacity that comes with birth.[9] The mind can *learn* to think well just as it can *learn* to have a fully developed moral sense, but the capacities or potential for thinking and morality must be innate in us. He says:

> Mouths have the same preferences in flavors. [The great chef] Yi Ya was the first to discover that which our mouths prefer. . . . The fact that, when it comes to flavors, the whole world looks to Yi Ya is due to the fact that mouths throughout the world are similar. . . . Hence, I say that mouths have the same preferences in flavors, ears have the same preferences in sounds, eyes have the same preferences in attractiveness. When it comes to hearts, are they alone without preferences in common? What is it that hearts prefer in common? I say that it is the fine patterns and righteousness. The sage first discovered what our hearts prefer in common. Hence, fine patterns and righteousness delight our hearts like meat delights our mouth.[10]

69

This argument can be formulated as follows:

1 We humans are alike in our tastes for flavor, our ears for music, and our eyes for beauty such that we would recognize great chefs, great musicians or great beauties.
2 Our minds cannot be so different from our sensory organs that they are not shared by all humans.
3 Therefore, we must all be alike in our minds too.
4 There are sages among human kind. Sages are people whose excellent moral attributes are generally recognized.[11]
5 Therefore, our minds must appreciate morality just as our taste buds appreciate great foods.

In this argument, Mencius compares our mind to our sensory organs, and uses sages as an analogy to those chefs, musicians, or artists who have won the recognition of the populace in terms of their power to please the masses' taste buds, ears, and eyes. If we have a natural liking for the great chefs' culinary production, for example, then we should have a natural liking for the sages' moral conduct. In the context of our contemporary understanding of mental development, Mencius' analogy between the mind and sensory organs seems weak. Even if we grant him the assumption that the mind is a human organ that comes with certain innate capacities, his analogy between sages and great chefs or great musicians is still questionable. The reputation of great chefs or great musicians is often established in a small group of people with similar tastes. A vegetarian would not appreciate the best steak chef; an avid rock and roll fan may not appreciate the best philharmonic orchestra. Even when we go back to infancy, we still cannot establish a universal claim on babies' general liking or dislike in tastes, sounds, and sights. So Mencius' argument cannot rule out the possibility that some people *naturally* prefer morality while some people *naturally* prefer vice.

Mencius' view on human nature is mostly introduced in the context of a refutation of the view presented by his contemporary philosopher Gaozi. Gaozi's theory, as recorded in the *Mencius*, can be summarized as follows:

A The word "nature" simply means *life*, just like the word "white" simply means *white*.[12]
B Human nature is more like a blank slate (like a willow tree that can be made either into wooden cups or into wooden bowls; like a water flow that can be directed either to the east or to the west). Human nature itself is indifferent to good and evil.[13]

C   Desires for food and sex are what come naturally to us. They thus define our nature.[14]

D   Moral virtues such as humanity (*ren*) and righteousness (*yi*) are manufactured by human efforts.[15]

To refute Gaozi's view, Mencius first challenged his analogies. The analogy of the willow tree and cups or bowls is inappropriate, because one has to cut down the tree, disfigure the wood, in order to make wooden cups or wooden bowls. If Gaozi claims that one can be made humane or righteous just as trees can be made into cups or bowls, then he is saying that humanity and righteousness would harm or even maim human nature. This latter claim is something that Gaozi himself would not have accepted. Mencius further pointed out that the analogy of water, on the other hand, is better, but Gaozi has failed to observe a more natural trend of water: that it tends to flow to the low ground. Mencius argued that we could use water as an analogy to human nature: human has a natural tendency just as water has a natural trend. By this analogy, humans do not have a morally neutral nature that can be made to be either good, or bad. As Mencius says:

> There is no man who is not good; there is no water that does not flow downwards. Now in the case of water, by splashing it one can make it shoot up higher than one's forehead, and by forcing it one can make it stay on a hill. How can that be the nature of water? It is the circumstances being what they are. That man can be made bad shows that his nature is no different from that of water in this respect.[16]

Mencius also challenged Gaozi's interpretation of the meaning of the word "nature." He argued that if "nature" simply means life, just as "white" simply means white, then the nature of dog would be no different from the nature of cow, and the nature of cow would be no different from the nature of human, since they all have life. Again, this conclusion would not be acceptable even to Gaozi himself.

   Even had Gaozi accepted Mencius' interpretation of "nature" as one's "natural tendencies," he still would not have agreed with Mencius that humans naturally tend toward goodness. Gaozi noted that humans naturally desire food and sex; hence, the two desires are within human nature. He even conceded that our love for others could be innate in us, but he insisted that our desire to do the right thing is imposed on us from the outside. Here the debate between Mencius and Gaozi becomes intricate. Mencius did not seem to object to Gaozi's claim that the desire for food and the desire for sex are part of human nature, or to the claim that love for family members is innate in us. He focused instead on Gaozi's claim that the desire to do the right thing is imposed on us from outside. This is the famous debate on whether *righteousness* (*yi*) is internal or external. "Being internal" in this context means "coming from one's heart"; "being external" means "being imposed on oneself from outside." The debated issue can be formulated as this: is the standard according to which one does the right thing determined from one's mind/heart, or from external conventions? Gaozi used the example of showing respect to the elderly to demonstrate his view on the externality of righteousness. He argued that if someone is older than I am, then I treat him with respect just because he is older. It does not matter whether this man is a stranger to me, or someone I truly respect. His age alone determines how I should act toward him, just as the whiteness of an object impels me to treat it as white. Therefore, what counts as the right thing to do in this context is truly determined by an external standard.[17] The significance of this debate is that if Gaozi were to succeed in proving that the sense of righteousness was the result of external demands, then the individual on her own could not know how to do the right thing in each context. If the individual does not know what to do on her own, then she does not have moral autonomy. When we judge individuals to be lacking in moral autonomy, we would want to place an indefinite number of external restraints on their behavior. The whole Confucian project of one's moral self-cultivation would thus be aborted. To rebuff this serious claim of Gaozi, Mencius pointed out that in respecting the elderly, the *feeling* of respect ultimately comes from one's own heart. Even if in different contexts we have to consider different conducts accordingly, there is one thing all considerations share in common: we wish to do the right thing in the right context. This wish then, Mencius argues, is the sense of righteousness. Mencius uses the example of toasting an older person on various occasions to demonstrate that even though one's conduct could be modified in accordance with contextual propriety, one's feeling of respect for the elderly is the same in all situations. Therefore, righteousness, or the desire to do the right thing, comes from one's own heart. It is not imposed on the moral agent from outside.

Along with the sense of righteousness, there are other moral sentiments innate in us. Mencius' view is that human nature contains the seeds (or sprouts) of moral virtues; among them, he lists humanity (*ren*), righteousness, propriety, and wisdom. From having the tendency toward goodness to actually being a good person, one needs to cultivate these moral seeds to bring them to maturity. At the same time, man can be made to do evil, when the environment is not conducive to his moral cultivation, or when he does not put in enough effort. After we have examined Mencius' arguments for the existence of the moral tendency in human nature, we will turn to his explanation of moral failures.

Mencius' Arguments for the Goodness of Human Nature

To substantiate the claim that "there is no human who does not tend toward goodness,"[18] Mencius came up with several arguments. He says: "The reason why I say that humans all have hearts that are not unfeeling toward others is this. Suppose someone suddenly saw a child about to fall into a well: everyone in such a situation would have a feeling of alarm and compassion – not because one wanted fame among their neighbors and friends, and not because one would dislike the sound of the child's cries. From this we can see that if one is without the heart of compassion, one is not a human."[19] This remark can be formulated into the following argument (Argument One):

1 Anyone who sees a young child about to fall into a deep well is bound to feel anxiety and commiseration in the heart. He feels this way not to gain friendship with the child's parents, not to seek the praise of others, and not because he detests hearing the child's screaming.
2 This example shows that people cannot bear to see the suffering of others.
3 This very feeling is the beginning of humanity.
4 Therefore, humans have the beginning of humanity in their nature.

It is interesting to note that when Rousseau tried to establish the claim that man is a creature of compassion, he used a similar example of someone's watching "a wild beast tear a child from his mother's breast, crush the child's frail limbs with its murderous teeth and tear out the living entrails with its claws." Rousseau remarked, "What terrible agitation must be felt by this witness of an event in which he has no personal interest! What anguish he must suffer in seeing it and being unable to do anything to help the fainting mother or the dying child!"[20] In the same way, Mencius is here engaged in a kind of thought experiment, in which he asks us to consider the scenario of watching the imminent death of a young child and to draw the same conclusion that he does. With this kind of argument, one could perhaps challenge the first premise: not everyone would naturally commiserate in the given scenario. But Mencius is not making any universal claim on human responses; rather, he is making a general claim, or, as Philip Ivanhoe calls it, a "generic" claim.[21] Hence, a few counterexamples would not have defeated his claim. If it is generally true that most people would have the kind of reaction that Mencius depicts, then it is generally true that most people would naturally have commiseration in the heart. Of course, having this natural sentiment is far from being moral: one could ignore the child and do nothing to save him; one could see the child as the enemy's child and proceed to push the child into the well. As David Wong observes: "An innate compassionate impulse is not compassion in the full sense."[22] Establishing the claim that humans have a natural compassionate impulse, or the beginning of humanity, is merely a first step toward proving that all humans are naturally good.

Mencius next argues:

> Life is something I desire; righteousness is also something I desire. If I cannot have both, I will forsake life and select righteousness. Life is something I desire, but there is something I desire more than life. Hence, I will not do just anything to obtain it. Death is something I hate, but there is something I hate more than death. Hence, there are calamities I do not avoid. . . . From this we can see that there are means of obtaining life that one will not employ. From this we can also see that there are things that would avoid calamity that one will not do. Therefore, there are things one desires more than life and there are also things one hates more than death. It is not the case that only the worthy person has this heart. All humans have it. The worthy person simply never loses it.[23]

1 Everyone desires life and detests death. But if you humiliate someone by giving him food, he would not accept the food even if he needs it for survival.
2 Hence, there is always something that one desires more than life itself, or something that one detests more than death itself.
3 If there is something that one would not do to preserve life and to avoid death, then one is not simply a creature for whom self-survival is the only goal (whereas other animals are).
4 Therefore, we all have our own principle on what to do and what not to do, even when it comes to matters of life and death.
5 A righteous person is simply someone who holds on to his own principle in all matters.
6 Therefore, we all have within ourselves what it takes to be a righteous person.

As stated, this argument (Argument Two) is not even valid. One could perhaps say that from Premise 1 to Premise 2 Mencius is committing a form of *hasty generalization*. One example, even if it is a well-known real-life example, does not warrant the claim that we are not simply creatures driven by our innate desire for survival. However, Mencius is not making such a faulty inference here. His point is rather to use it as an illustration of a general human trait, as stated in Premise 2. If there is *always* something that one would not do even for the sake of survival, then one's existence is more elevated than the basic level of survival (*contra* Gaozi's claim that "nature" simply means life). Having a principle regarding what not to do is in essence the beginning of the virtue of *righteousness*. Hence, the sprout of righteousness is innate in us just as the sprout of humanity is.

Having established the claim that the beginning of humanity and righteousness is prevalent in all of us, Mencius went on to construct his view that human nature contains the beginning of all four essential virtues: humanity, righteousness, propriety, and wisdom. He says:

> Humans all have the heart of compassion. Humans all have the heart of disdain. Humans all have the heart of respect. Humans all have the heart of approval and disapproval. The heart of compassion is [humanity]. The heart of disdain is righteousness. The heart of respect is propriety. The heart of approval and disapproval is wisdom. [Humanity], righteousness, propriety, and wisdom are not welded to us externally. We inherently have them.[24]

We can expand this comment into the following argument (Argument Three):

1 All humans naturally have feelings of commiseration, awareness of shame and dislike, the sentiment of respect and reverence, and a sense of right and wrong.
2 The feeling of commiseration = the sprout of humanity; the awareness of shame and dislike = the sprout of righteousness; the sentiment of respect and reverence = the sprout of propriety; the sense of right and wrong = the sprout of wisdom.
3 Humanity, righteousness, propriety, and wisdom constitute goodness.
4 Therefore, all humans have the sprouts of goodness within their nature.

In the first premise, Mencius is again making a general statement about humans. We sometimes experience pity for someone else's suffering; we sometimes feel ashamed of our own behavior, or we are disdainful of others' conduct; we sometimes have a sense of respect or awe for certain things or certain people; we sometimes make judgments on right and wrong. Mencius called these sentiments the "four sprouts" (or "four beginnings") of morality. In his view, humans and other animals are very similar in many biological aspects, with only these moral sprouts distinguishing humans from other animals. That is why he would call these four moral sprouts or moral inclinations "human nature." Being in possession of them does not guarantee having the fully developed virtues of humanity, righteousness, propriety, and wisdom. But they are nonetheless the common ground for human morality.

From the above arguments, we can see that Mencius believed that morality is rooted in humans' natural sentiments. The origin of morality is not pure human reason, but human emotions. The foundation for ethics is not social conventions, but human nature. According to Mencius, morality gets developed in human societies because the moral sense is *natural* to human beings; in other words, we are born with this moral sense. We can probably call Mencius' ethical theory *the naturalistic view of morality*.

The Explanation for Moral Failures

If humans naturally tend toward goodness and if all humans have the seeds of morality in their mind/heart, then why don't we see sages everywhere? The mere fact that Mencius needed to advocate the presence of moral sprouts, and the importance of moral virtues, demonstrates that even in his times, most people were not acting in the moral way. So, what explains the discrepancy between humans' innate goodness and their manifest badness? If morality is natural to us and yet we are not moral, then there must be some reasons why we fail morally. If people often fail morally, then there has to be a way to teach people to avoid moral failures. Mencius' explanation for moral failures and his pedagogy on moral cultivation are thus closely linked.

Even though Mencius stressed the existence of moral sprouts in human nature, he never denied that the desire for physical comfort and material goods is also part of human nature. He called our sensory organs "the minor part" and the mind/heart "the major part" of our bodies.[25] According to Mencius, the senses would desire food, sex, and other material goods on their own, and these desires seem to be competing with the desire of the mind/heart. Under this view, our mouth desires delicious food, our ears desire pleasing sounds, and our eyes desire beautiful sights, just as our mind/heart desires moral virtues. The mind/heart has four functions: thinking (reflecting); feeling (having emotions and sentiments); willing (*zhi*: that which makes resolution); and the employment as well as the cultivation of the moral *qi*. Moral failures, in most cases, are the result of the mind/heart's not fulfilling its functions.

With the competition between mind/heart and senses, between moral volition and sensory desires, Mencius endeavored to explain why innate moral inclinations do not guarantee mature morality. Sometimes our sensory desires and our moral sense can direct us to different directions; hence, we have moral conflicts. If we go with our sensory desires and deviate from the moral path, then we are paying too much attention to the *minor part*, while neglecting the *major part* of ourselves. For example, someone who is intent on having the most delectable food may spend all her time thinking about ways to obtain it. In Mencius' judgment, this person is enslaving the mind/heart to serve the senses. Furthermore, the mind/heart's not fulfilling its function contributes greatly to our moral failures. The mind's main function is to think or to reflect on one's behavior. If the mind does not think, does not reflect, then it cannot compete with the senses. Secondly, if one's mind does not have a strong will, then even when one wishes to do good, one can easily give up midway. Thirdly, one's heart contains all the natural moral sentiments. If one does not employ these sentiments in one's moral deliberation, then one can easily lose sight of one's intrinsic goodness. Finally, if one's mind does not employ the *qi* properly or if the mind fails to cultivate the right *qi*, then this energy can interfere with the resolution and lead the mind astray.

The notion of *qi* in the *Mencius* is hard to analyze fully.[26] It could be viewed as a form of energy that occupies the whole of the human body, being controlled by the mind/heart, or in particular, by the will. Mencius sometimes used the expression "the flood-like *qi*" to describe it. In response to his student's demand for an explanation of this "flood-like *qi*," Mencius says:

> It is difficult to put into words. It is a *qi* that is supremely great and supremely unyielding. If one cultivates it with uprightness and does not harm it, it will fill up the space between heaven and earth. It is a *qi* that unites righteousness with [*Dao*].... It is produced by accumulated righteousness.... If some of one's actions leave one's heart unsatisfied, it will starve.[27]

If the *qi* is cultivated by one's accumulated righteousness, then it can be viewed as one's moral spirit. But at the same time, this *qi* also seems to have a physical dimension in that one can fix one's resolution (*zhi*) to direct the flow of one's *qi*. With resolution, one can move the *qi* to aid one in overcoming *undesirable* temptations.[28] Mencius thinks that one's moral spirit (*qi*) can be manifested in one's appearance or in one's comportment. He says: "That which a [superior person] follows as his nature, that is to say, [humanity], righteousness, [propriety], and wisdom, is rooted in his heart, and manifests itself in his face, giving it a sleek appearance. It also shows in his back and extends to his limbs, rendering their message intelligible without words."[29] What is within us will naturally be manifested externally. Our eyes, in particular, are the telling mark of our inner world: "Of what is present within a person, nothing is more ingenuous than the pupils of the eyes. The pupils cannot hide one's evil. If, in one's bosom, one is upright, the pupils will be bright. If, in one's bosom, one is not upright, the pupils will be shady."[30] If we want to understand others' intent, therefore, there is no better way than to look at their eyes while listening to their words.

Mencius' explanation for the causes of moral failures can be summarized as follows:

1 *The mind does not think (one lacks reflection on what is good in one's nature).*[31] Mencius quotes Confucius' remark, "Hold it fast and you will preserve it. Let it go and you will lose it."[32] He thinks that this is a perfect description of the mind. If the mind does not perform its function of thinking, then soon it will be lost in one's pursuit of physical pleasures.[33]

2 *One's lost mind/heart is not retrieved.* Mencius says: "A basket of food and a bowl of soup – if one gets them then one will live; if one doesn't get them then one will die. But if they are given with contempt, then even a homeless person will not accept them. If they are trampled upon, then even a beggar won't take them. However, when it comes to a salary of ten thousand bushels of grain, then one doesn't notice propriety and righteousness and accepts them. . . . Is this indeed something that one can't stop doing? This is called losing one's fundamental heart."[34] Some people would not go against their own principles for a small gain; however, they would do just anything in order to aggrandize their wealth and power. In so doing, they are forgetting that initially there was something that they would not have done under any circumstance. Losing the sense of what not to do is losing the sense of righteousness.

3 *One undernurtures one's moral endowment.* Using the analogy of planting, Mencius explains the constant effort needed to develop moral sprouts. Even if there is something very easy to grow, if one exposes it to sunshine for one day and then to coldness for the next ten days, it simply will not survive.[35] Similarly, our moral sprouts cannot mature into moral characters or ethical behavior if we occasionally do one good deed, and then repeat bad acts continually.

4   *One pays too much attention to the minor qualities in their nature (such as the desires for food and sex) or to the minor parts in their bodies (sensory organs such as the palates).* Mencius says, "Those who follow their greater part become great humans. Those who follow their petty part become petty humans."[36] Mencius believed that material desires can often distract one from one's effort in cultivating virtues. Even though he never advocated the elimination of physical desires, he did exhort people to reduce physical desires. He says: "There is nothing better for the nurturing of the heart than to reduce the number of one's desires. When a man has but few desires, even if there is anything [in his original heart that] he fails to retain in himself, it cannot be much; but when he has a great many desires, then even if there is anything [in his original heart that] he manages to retain in himself, it cannot be much."[37]

5   *One maims one's good nature with repeated vile deeds.* Using the analogy of a barren Mount Ox,[38] whose trees had been completely hewn down with axes or hatches and whose newly formed shoots have been constantly grazed by oxen and sheep, Mencius states that if one abuses one's originally good nature with repeated bad deeds, then one will end up being not far from brutes. Those who become tyrants, sociopaths, professional hit men, serial killers, etc., are those who have maimed their initial human nature. Few would believe that there is any trace of goodness left in these people. Bryan Van Norden thinks that the analogy of Mount Ox demonstrates that Mencius held the view that "some humans have no sprouts of morality."[39] However, even with the barren Mount Ox, Mencius points out that it is not in the nature of the mountain not to have any trees. By the same token, it is not that these depraved people do not have moral sprouts or intrinsically good human nature. As soon as the abuse is stopped, a vile person could be morally renewed, just as a barren mountain could grow new trees. Therefore, Mencius' claim on the universality of moral nature is not curtailed even when it comes to extremely vicious people.

6   *Weakness of the will or weakness of the desire to do good.*[40] As the mind can fail to think, so too can it fail to firm up one's initial resolution to do good. For example, we can decide that we will give to charity on a regular basis. But such good resolutions often do not last long. Soon we are back to the old habit of giving in to our own extravagant indulgences, rather than giving money to charities. Such weakness of the will also explains our failure in moral cultivation.

7   *Self-denial or self-abandonment.* Mencius says: "Those who have the four moral sprouts and yet tell themselves that they *cannot* be

moral are ones who deprive themselves."[41] According to Mencius, there are two kinds of acknowledgment of inability: one is genuine inability when the task is beyond one's physical capacity; the other is merely one's inaction when the task is within one's power. Doing the right thing is not beyond one's physical power; thus, one is never justified in denying oneself the ability to do good. Most people, when they claim that they cannot do certain moral deeds, are simply finding excuses for themselves. Mencius seemed to view this problem as the major reason why the rulers of his time were not humane.

With the above explanations, Mencius argued that the absence of good in most people, or the presence of evil in some people, does not disprove his theory that human nature is good. One's heart naturally feels commiseration, shame, reverence, and rightness (the four moral sprouts). But if one does not extend these good feelings, then the moral sentiments remain mere sentiments and do not generate moral behavior. Therefore, the mind has to do a lot in order to transform the moral sprouts in one's nature into fully fledged morality. For Mencius, the debate on human nature was not purely for theoretical interest. Following Confucius' path, he aimed at the actual moral transformation of individuals; and furthermore, of the whole of human society. Therefore, he continued to investigate the most effective ways for moral cultivation.

Moral Education and Methods of Moral Cultivation

To say that human nature is good is not to say that humans are good; to say that there is no one who does not tend toward goodness is not to say that there is no one who is not good. Mencius did not have a naive view of the moral reality of humans. For him, moral cultivation is not at all an easy task. Since there are so many possible routes to moral failure, he has to point to a feasible way to establish one's moral virtues. The one method that he emphasized the most was "extension."[42]

In an example widely discussed by contemporary scholars (*Mencius* 1A:7), Mencius tried to teach the king of his host country to recognize the goodness in his own heart. The king had previously seen an ox being led to be slaughtered for sacrifice, and was moved by its frightened looks. He ordered the ox to be spared but replaced it with a sheep instead, since the ceremony could not be relinquished. From a logical standpoint, the king's behavior is inconsistent – what is the moral difference between killing an ox and killing a sheep? Some people in the king's court thus thought that he replaced the ox with the sheep because the former was more expensive than the sheep. Mencius had a more charitable interpretation of the king's action: the king simply did not see the frightened looks of the sheep. Mencius pointed out that in sparing the ox, the king showed the humane root (the heart of commiseration) in his heart. If he could *extend* this humane root, then he would love his people and become more sympathetic to their suffering.[43]

This method of *extension* can be applied in other cases. A basic teaching of Confucianism is to acknowledge our natural inclination to love our own family more than we would love a stranger. This is the Confucian doctrine of "love with distinction," which was contested by Mozi and his followers.[44] Mencius says that to spread humanity, we do not need to deny these natural inclinations and try to achieve impartiality in our sentiment. We only need to *extend* these natural preferences to others, to empathize with others who have the same feelings toward *their own* family members. Morality is not over and above our partial love; it is simply a demand on us *to take one step further*. Mencius says, "Treat with respect the elders in one's own family, and then extend that respect to include the elders in other families. Treat with tenderness the young in one's own family, and then extend that tenderness to include the young in other families."[45] If one has respect and concern for someone else's parents, then one would not cheat them or rob from them. If one has tenderness toward someone else's children, then one would never want to see them starve or freeze, let alone harm them. Even the most malicious people would have a soft spot for someone or something. If they can recognize this sentiment as the beginning of humanity and work to preserve and enlarge it, they could eventually become sages. On the other hand, if they refuse to extend the humane sprout and keep hardening themselves with cruel thoughts, eventually they will be no different from brutes. Hence, the vast difference between sages and brutes is really formed by an ability to *extend* or not.

The regrettable fact, however, is that even if this method of extension is easy to follow, not many people will heed Mencius' advice. The king who had compassion toward the trembling ox did not succeed in loving his people enough to relinquish warfare, to end his people's suffering, or to gratify their natural desires. After defeating the many excuses that the king offered for his own conduct, Mencius eventually lost hope in the transformation of this king and left the country. What makes a humane king, what constitutes good rulership, thus became a major concern for Mencius.

Mencius' Political Philosophy: Governance with Humanity

Mencius' political philosophy expands on Confucius' moral politics. Whereas Confucius merely discusses the magical power of moral transformation when sages become kings, Mencius is more intent on giving practical guidance and realistic strategies. Almost half of the *Mencius* is devoted to his view on the best ways to govern a nation.

Mencius advocated "governance with humanity." To him, the foundation of humane governance was the maintenance of the people's livelihood. Mencius advised the king:

> Do not interfere with the agricultural seasons, so that there will be enough grain to feed everyone; do not allow nets with too fine a mesh to be used in large ponds, so that there will be enough fish and tortoise for people to eat; do not allow hatches and axes to enter the forests at all time, so that there will be enough timber for people to use.[46]

For the king to practice humane governance, he should also reduce punishment and lessen taxation. If the king pays attention to these details, then the people will all have a comfortable life. Mencius believed that ensuring a comfortable life for the people is really the beginning of truly humane governance.

Of course, the one thing that would definitely destroy the people's comfortable life is warfare. Mencius lived in a time when neighboring countries were constantly attacking one another and all kings were intent on aggrandizing their own power. He believed that if a king is intent only on warfare, his people are bound to suffer. Adult males are drafted, and there is then no one to tend the fields; consequently, old people and young children starve to death, with no one to bury them. If the people cannot even know for sure whether they will make it to the next day, then how could they possibly have the leisure to engage in their moral cultivation? Therefore, the success of moral transformation of the people really lies in the ruler's avoidance of offensive warfare. Not all warfare can be avoided, however. Sometimes there are wars that have to be embarked on because they are "just wars." For Mencius, the criterion of whether a war is just lies not on how the war would benefit the king or his people, but on whether the war will benefit the people of the enemy country. If the people of that country have been starving, freezing, exploited, and abused by their king, then they will welcome the siege. They will not put up any resistance; instead, they will bring food and drink to reward the incoming troops. Therefore, whoever wins the hearts of the people will win the war. As Mencius says, "A humane king has no match."[47]

Mencius likened the role of rulers to that of parents. When parents think about the well-being of their children, the last thing they would want to see is that their children are starving or freezing. A humane king, according to Mencius, should have the same heart. When Mencius uses parenthood as the analogy of rulership, his emphasis is more on parental love than on discipline and regulations. Humanity begins with family love. If the king can extend his love for his own children to his people, then the people will all love him just as they love their own parents. If they love him as their own parents, then they will even die for him when the situation demands it. Clearly, what Mencius taught is the opposite of Machiavelli's teaching – it is far better to be loved than feared if the ruler cannot be both.

One novel idea that Mencius introduced into Chinese political thinking is the idea of revolution. If the king is not humane – i.e., if he abuses the people instead of taking care of their welfare – then he can be legitimately removed. This view may appear contrary to what Confucius teaches: the sociopolitical hierarchy in which the ruler is revered as the ruler, while the subjects always remain subjects. However, Mencius defended his view by pointing out that when the ruler abuses his power, then he is already not a genuine ruler, but a "lone man" loathed by everyone. To remove a lone man from his throne, according to Mencius, is not usurpation. However, even though Mencius argued that the validity of rulership depends on the people's judgment, he does not think that the task of royal replacement should be placed in the people's hands. As A. C. Graham points out, "Mencius is not a defender of popular revolution. . . . Ideally he thinks the tyrant should be removed by his own ministers, and among ministers by those of the old-fashioned kind, those of his own blood."[48] The people will not have the political expertise or the military competence to succeed in this task. A revolution initiated by the people will probably bring the whole nation into complete chaos. Therefore, the task should fall on the shoulders of the ministers who originally assisted the ruler. These ministers themselves have to have some qualifications: they must have the people's well-being in mind and be wise enough to make the right judgment. There is only a very slight margin between legitimate overthrow and illegitimate usurpation, and the margin is set by the ministers' intent. Confucianism has often been charged with supporting Chinese feudalism. But from what Mencius teaches, we should see that he would never support a form of feudalism that does not contain a humane king, prudent ministers, and contented people.

Conclusion

A major difference between Confucius and Mencius is that the former focuses more on individuals while the latter focuses more on the state. Confucius stressed self-discipline; Mencius stressed moral expectations on the king. In turning his emphasis toward rulership, Mencius did not reject Confucius' moral picture that centers on self-cultivation. Rather, he tried to enhance the realizability of the whole Confucian moral ideal. His political philosophy would turn out to play an important role in shaping the history of Chinese politics.

Mencius' philosophy of human nature and human mind also introduced to the forefront of Chinese philosophy a topic on which Confucius did not elaborate. This issue would later become one of the main topics in Neo-Confucianism. In Mencius, moreover, we witness the beginning of philosophical argumentation in Chinese philosophy.

Further discussion questions

1 Is the standard according to which one does the right thing determined by one's heart or by external conventions? Do we have an innate sense of the distinction between right and wrong? Between Mencius and Gaozi, who has the better argument?

2 Do you think that sympathy, or a sense of commiseration, is natural to humans? Can this sentiment be a foundation for morality as Mencius argues? Do we have the "moral sprouts" that Mencius discusses? Are moral propensities biological traits of human beings?

3 Why is the pursuit of physical desires incompatible with the cultivation of moral attributes? Why is the pursuit of profit inferior to the pursuit of knowledge? What is wrong with a life of pure pleasure and sheer profit? Can one justify the moral preferences assumed by both Confucius and Mencius?

4 Can the method of extension be established as a universal moral principle? If we all extend our respect for elders in our family to include the elders in other families, if we all extend our tenderness toward our children to include children in other families, can we bring about a moral society? Is this method of extension *sufficient* to establish morality?

5 Aristotle argues that moral virtues are habits, which can be acquired by doing certain virtuous acts. But these habits could be lost in one's lifetime. They thus need to be sustained by intellectual virtue – reason. In a similar way, Mencius argues that moral character requires constant fostering and maintenance. It can be lost if we do not make constant efforts to preserve the original good. What does Mencius propose as a way to sustain our moral habits? How does his method compare with Aristotle's method?

6 In contrast to the Western ethicists' predominant interest in establishing a universal moral principle on the basis of human reason, Mencius establishes an ethical theory on the basis of human emotions. Can you compare the strengths and weaknesses of each approach? What do you think should be the foundation for human ethics – reason, or emotion?

Primary texts

Wing-tsit Chan, ed. *A Sourcebook in Chinese Philosophy*, 4th edn. Princeton: Princeton University Press, 1973 (ch. 3; excerpts).

Philip J. Ivanhoe and Bryan W. Van Norden (eds.) *Readings in Classical Chinese Philosophy*. Indianapolis, IN: Hackett Publishing Company, Inc. 2003 (ch. 3; excerpts).

D. C. Lau. *Mencius*. London: Penguin Books, 1970.

Further readings

Eric L. Hutton. "Moral Connoisseurship in Mengzi." In Xiusheng Liu and Philip Ivanhoe (eds.), *Essays on the Moral Philosophy of Mengzi*. Indianapolis, IN: Hackett Publishing Company, 2002, pp. 163–86.

D. C. Lau. "On Mencius' Use of the Method of Analogy in Argument." *Asia Major, N. S.*, vol. X, 1963. Reprinted in D. C. Lau. *Mencius*, vols. 1 & 2. Hong Kong: The Chinese University Press, 1984, pp. 334–56.

Kwong-loi Shun. "Moral Reasons in Confucian Ethics." *Journal of Chinese Philosophy* 16, 1989: 317–43.

Bryan W. Van Norden. "Kwong-loi Shun on Moral Reasons in Mencius." *Journal of Chinese Philosophy* 18, 1991: 353–70.

David B. Wong. "Reasons and Analogical Reasoning in *Mengzi*." In Xiusheng Liu and Philip Ivanhoe (eds.), *Essays on the Moral Philosophy of Mengzi*. Indianapolis, IN: Hackett Publishing Company, 2002, pp. 187–220.

Chapter 4

Xunzi (Hsün Tzu)

Introduction

Xunzi (ca. 312–210 BCE) is the third major figure in early Confucianism, but his influence is often deliberately understated by later Confucians. The chief reason is that he opposes the main view of Mencius, widely regarded by Neo-Confucians to be the authentic successor of Confucius. Xunzi's status in Chinese philosophy is also controversial among contemporary scholars. Some take him to be the greatest philosopher, whose writings "constitute the single most sophisticated philosophical explanation and defense of the Confucian point of view,"[1] while some accuse him of being inconsistent, dogmatic, unphilosophical, or even someone who "pandered to the tyrannical passion for punishment."[2] The main text we have of Xunzi is a collection of essays entitled *The Xunzi*. Xunzi himself allegedly wrote most of these essays. His focus is on an individual's scholarship and moral cultivation and the various aspects of rulership, quite in line with the general emphasis of Confucius and Mencius. However, his work is more analytic in that he gives a more systematic analysis of the key notions in ancient Confucianism. His treatises include topics such as the nature of Heaven, the significance of *li* (propriety; rites and rituals), and the function of music. But above all, Xunzi's distinctive claim is his famous slogan: "Human nature is bad; his goodness is the result of man's deliberate effort."[3] In this chapter, as the concluding chapter on ancient Confucianism, we shall discuss three major themes: Xunzi's view on the nature of Heaven, his theory of human nature, and his exposition on the significance of rites and rituals.

A Naturalistic View of Heaven

In contemporary analytic tradition, "naturalism" means the metaphysical view that everything is part of the natural world that natural sciences investigate, or the semantic view that a suitable philosophical analysis of any concept must show it to be amenable to empirical inquiry.[4] Xunzi's view of Heaven (*tian*) is close to the spirit of naturalism, but in Xunzi's times, the power or the credibility of science was not yet an issue of concern. In this context, we shall mean by "naturalism" the simplified view that the only things that exist are natural or physical things and that philosophical inquiry should be backed by empirical investigation. Xunzi's ontology is naturalistic in the sense that it does not posit any supernatural being as the governor of human affairs. It is anti-superstition even if it is not necessarily anti-religion. This ontological view marks an important development in the history of Chinese thought. Xunzi clearly takes a big step away from primitive society's natural worship toward rationality.

Xunzi's notion of Heaven is devoid of anthropocentric connotation, which is closely associated with the folk religion prevalent in ancient China. Xunzi says: "Heaven does not suspend the winter because men dislike cold; earth does not cease being wide because men dislike great distances."[5] As we explained in chapter 1, the ancient Chinese used the term "Heaven" (*tian*) to refer to all natural phenomena associated with the sky, such as the sun, the rain, the cloud, the thunder, etc. In Xunzi's times, the role of a god with personal will was slowly diminishing in Chinese cosmology. However, there was still a prevailing view among the ancient Chinese that these natural phenomena were reflections of states of affairs in the human world. Sometimes these reflections were even interpreted as rewards or punishments, even though the assignment of rewards and punishments was not deemed to be from a willful supernatural being. The implicit moral seems to be that humans should conduct their worldly affairs in agreement with the Way (*dao*), so as to avoid any natural phenomenon that is destructive of their well-being. Neither Confucius nor Mencius encouraged this kind of thinking, but they did not work to dispel such a belief either. Their notion of Heaven has a moralistic connotation in that Heaven does correspond to the goodness and badness in human society, though not always in a way comprehensible to us. Their attitude seems to be that we should simply pay attention to our own conduct in this world, and let Heaven take its own course. What we can accomplish is our own doings; what we cannot control is the fate, or "Heaven's Mandate," which we receive

from Heaven. This view does not promote the superstitious folk practices of praying to Heaven or seeking to please Heaven, but nor does it
denounce the religious attitude toward Heaven. Moreover, both Confucius and Mencius seem to endorse the general belief that "Heaven's
Mandate typically manifested itself in the political arena, where the
righteousness of a ruler earned the sanction of Heaven in the struggle
with his competitors."[6] There is, under this view, a causal connection
between the ruler's moral conduct and the political prosperity that Heaven
invests in him.

Xunzi, on the other hand, argues that Heaven is simply the totality of
natural phenomena and changes of natural phenomena have nothing to
do with human affairs. Order or chaos in the human world also do not
bring about changes in the state of Heaven. Xunzi says: "Heaven's ways
are constant. It does not prevail because of a sage like *Yao*; it does not
cease to prevail because of a tyrant like [*Jie*]."[7] There is simply no
causal connection between natural phenomena and human affairs. Furthermore, by calling Heaven's ways "constant," Xunzi seems to hold
the view that there are lawful regularities in the operations of natural
phenomena. These natural laws do not depend on human cognition or
perception. When humans fail to recognize the law behind occasional
seemingly irregular phenomena, they call those phenomena "anoma-
lies." But Xunzi argues that our failure to perceive the regularities should
not give us a reason to deny the constancy of Heaven's operations. In
ancient times, there were some natural phenomena, such as eclipses of
the sun and moon or the appearance of a meteor shower, which people
could not explain. The common folk took these to be signs of the wrath
of Heaven, and they were apprehensive whenever such phenomena took
place. Xunzi points out that these occasional phenomena, as well as the
regularly observed natural phenomena, are simply "the changes in Heaven
and Earth and the transformations of *yin* and *yang*." He says: "To
marvel at them is alright, but to fear them is not."[8] The change of
attitude from "fear" to "marvel" is a first step away from the superstition of natural worship. It stands for an initial stage toward establishing
a rational investigation of nature.

Xunzi's affirmation of the constancy of Heaven could be seen as a
generalization derived from empirical observation. Based on this postu-
late, he argues against any causal claim between states of affairs in the
natural world and human states of affairs. An unjustified causal claim is
one that connects two things that have no real causal connections. For
example, we now think that astrology unjustifiably connects the positions and aspects of stars and planets with an individual's personality or
daily affairs; that *Feng Shui* unjustifiably connects the success or failure

of a business or a marriage with the location and placement of household objects; that many forms of superstition unjustifiably connect an individual's mishaps with trivial daily events, such as encountering a black cat, etc. In the same vein, Xunzi regards any claim on causal connections between the ruler's conduct and natural events as unwarranted. Drought can happen to a bad ruler just as it can happen to a good one. Heaven operates in its own way; the human world acts out its own course. Even though sometimes the operations of Heaven happen to be favorable to the livelihood of human beings, natural phenomena and human morality are not causally related. However, Xunzi does not therefore think that we should only be concerned with human affairs and pay no attention to the working of Heaven. What we need to study is the operations of Heaven in their own right. Xunzi says:

> The ranks of stars move in progression, the sun and moon shine in turn, the four seasons succeed each other in good order, the *yin* and *yang* go through their great transformations, and the wind and rain pass over the whole land. All things obtain what is congenial to them and grow to life, receive what is nourishing to them and grow to completion.[9]

If we follow the four seasons in planting and harvesting, then we can get the maximum yield for our crops. If we store up water before a foreseeable drought or if we store up food before an impending famine, then even the inevitable drought or flood cannot ruin the order of society. In other words, men should study the regularities of natural phenomena and react accordingly. If we are always prepared, then even when something happens unexpectedly, we will not be devastated. It is not Heaven, but this kind of advanced preparation and good governance, that guarantees prosperity to a great ruler.

Xunzi asserts that the constancy of Heaven can be empirically observed through our senses. He calls our sense organs (eyes, ears, nose, mouth, and body) "the heavenly faculties."[10] Xunzi thinks that our senses can detect the taxonomies of natural objects and properties as they exist in themselves. He asks:

> And how does one go about distinguishing between things that are the same and those that are different? One relies upon the senses. Things which are of the same species and form will be apprehended by the sense as being all the same thing. Therefore, after comparing such things with other things of a similar nature, one may settle upon a common designation. In this way one arrives at a common name for all the things of one class, which everyone agrees to use when the occasion demands.[11]

Apart from the reliability of our sense organs, another dependable source of our knowledge is our mind. Xunzi calls the mind (or the heart in the biological sense) "the heavenly ruler."[12] The mind/heart is a ruler since it is in charge of sensory organs. Its function is to employ the data collected by sensory organs and make its own distinctions. Xunzi says:

> Speech, events, delight, anger, grief, joy, love, hate, and desire are distinguished by the mind. In addition, the mind possesses an overall understanding. Because of this overall understanding, it may rely upon the data of the ear and understand sounds correctly or rely upon the data of the eye and understand forms correctly. But this overall understanding must always wait until it has received new data from the senses and match it with the data already recorded in the mind concerning a particular class of objects, before it can arrive at a correct understanding of the object.[13]

Here Xunzi gives a crude description of his theory of cognition: the mind receives sense data from the senses, on the basis of which the mind forms conceptions. Concepts are the result of the mind's faculty of *understanding*. However, there can be no concepts without sense data. This remark is surprisingly similar to those of modern empiricists.

In these and other remarks made by Xunzi, we see the rudiments of a naturalized epistemology and philosophy of language, which can be summarized as follows:

A Our sense organs and our mind are part of nature just as natural objects and properties are. They correctly perceive the taxonomies of natural objects and properties because they are developed *naturally*.

B The function of the eye is to perceive various shapes, colors, etc.; the function of the ear is to perceive various tones, pitches, etc.; the function of the mouth is to perceive various tastes; the function of the nose is to perceive various smells and odors; the function of the body is to perceive pain, itchiness, cold, heat, smoothness, roughness, etc. No organ can take the place of another to acquire different perceptions proper to the other organ.

C The function of the mind is *to understand*. The mind sorts the various data collected through different senses and organizes them into different categories. After comparing the similarities among similar objects and properties, the mind assigns a common denominator for things of the same nature. Hence, we have the introduction of names and concepts.

D People agree upon the use of names and concepts, because all people (with normal faculties) have the same perceptions and understanding.

E   Therefore, our language and our understanding correctly and uniquely match the natural world.

This view reinforces the basic presupposition of realism in classical Confucianism, which Xunzi further supports with a theoretical explanation.

In addition to refuting the anthropocentric view of Heaven, Xunzi also attacks other forms of irrational beliefs or superstitious practices. For instance, he rejects the belief in the existence of ghosts. He says:

> Always when people [claim to] see ghosts, it is at times when they are aroused and excited, and they make their judgments in moments when their faculties are confused and blinded. At such times they affirm that what exists does not exist, or that what does not exist exists, and then they consider the matter settled.[14]

Our sense organs usually function accurately such that if we do not perceive ghosts, then ghosts simply do not exist. As for the occasional claims of ghost-sighting, Xunzi's analysis is that those who claim to have seen ghosts must be deluded both in vision and in mind. To Xunzi, death is simply the termination of existence. He says, "Birth is the beginning of man, death his end."[15] There is no other form of life that we can call the "afterlife." Therefore, there are no ghosts. Xunzi also attacks the common folk practice of physiognomy, the method of foretelling one's fortune or misfortune by studying one's physical appearance. He lists many examples of historical figures who are either tall or short, large or small, beautiful or ugly, well-proportioned or ill-proportioned to show that there is simply no causal connection between people's accomplishments and their physical appearance. These unjustified causal beliefs are the roots of superstitions.

Even though Xunzi is against superstitions, he is not completely against religion. His view on all religious ceremonies and practices is that they serve a "humane function."[16] When one performs divination as one does with *Yijing*, the purpose is to stress the gravity of the affair to be undertaken. When the ruler performs a certain religious ritual with respect to Heaven or Earth, the function is to demonstrate how he cares about his people's welfare. Xunzi says:

> One performs the rain sacrifice and it rains. Why? I say: There is no special reason why. It is the same as when one does not perform the rain sacrifice and it rains anyway.... One performs divination and only then decides on important affairs. But this is not for the sake of getting what one seeks, but rather to give things proper form. Thus, the gentleman

looks upon this as proper form, but the common people look upon it as connecting with spirits.[17]

With regard to the rites of the dead, Xunzi justifies them by saying, "The rites of the dead can be performed only once for each individual, and never again. They are the last occasion upon which the subject may fully express respect for his ruler, the son may express respect for his parents."[18] In other words, even if there are no gods or ghosts, the performance of a certain religious ceremony in worship of gods or in memory of ancestors can demonstrate respect toward nature or ancestors. Such a demonstration is meant to teach the common people the right attitude, which is to have respect for nature and for ancestors. As Wing-tsit Chan puts it:

> The influence of supernatural forces over man is completely ruled out by [Xunzi]. What he calls spirits is but cosmic change and evolution. To him, in religious sacrifice, whether there are really spiritual beings to receive them does not matter. The important thing is one's attitude, especially sincerity, in the performance. Thus sacrifices are "ornaments," or refined manifestation of an inner attitude.[19]

If religious rituals can accomplish this goal, then they are not harmful to human society. As we shall see later in this chapter, Xunzi thinks that these rituals or ceremonies are actually indispensable exactly because of the humanistic function they serve.

In conclusion, Xunzi's notion of Heaven is quite congenial to our modern view of nature. But his view is different from our modern naturalistic view in that it still preserves the moralistic connotation that Confucius and Mencius associate with Heaven. His view on morality is that our conduct should emulate the attributes we assign to Heaven. He says, "The sage purifies his [heavenly] ruler, rectifies his [heavenly] organs, sufficiently provides for his [heavenly] nourishment, follows the [heavenly] government, and nourishes his [heavenly] feelings so as to bring completion the work of [Heaven]."[20] We can perhaps put Xunzi's ethical thesis into this simple slogan: "To be moral is to be in agreement with Heaven."

On Human Nature

Against Mencius' theory of the goodness of human nature, Xunzi says: "Human nature is bad; his goodness is the result of man's deliberate effort."[21] This debate between Xunzi and Mencius on human nature has captured the interest of many contemporary scholars. On the surface, Mencius and Xunzi seem to hold directly opposite views, but if we study their overall theory of moral cultivation, moral education, and rulership, then we see that their views are actually quite similar. As A. C. Graham says: "It is indeed far from easy to locate any issue of fact on which they disagree. Both recognize the need of learning, the moral acceptability of all fully reconcilable desires, the function of the heart as arbiter between them, and the possibility of anyone becoming a sage."[22] Some scholars argue that there is no genuine disagreement between the two philosophers on the nature of human beings; what they have is simply a terminological dispute on the use of the term "nature."[23] Others argue that the two philosophers disagree more on the nature of morality and the method of moral education, than on the nature of human beings.[24] To see the genuine disagreement between Xunzi and Mencius, we need to take a close look at Xunzi's definition of "nature" versus "deliberate effort," his analysis of the content of human nature and his arguments for the claim that human nature is bad.

To begin with, since Xunzi separates "deliberate effort" and "nature" as the sources of good and evil, let us see how he defines the two concepts. He defines "nature" as "whatever one is born with; whatever comes naturally and not from one's doing."[25] Xunzi thinks that human nature is what one receives from Heaven; and as we saw in the previous section, Heaven for Xunzi is simply the totality of natural phenomena associated with the sky. Therefore, there is no teleological design or moral connotation associated with human nature. What one has at birth are basically one's biological characteristics, which are not so different from those of other animals. Xunzi says: "The basic nature of man is that which he receives from Heaven. The emotions are the substance of the nature and the desires are the responses of the emotions."[26] In other words, he takes the content of human nature to include human desires and human emotions. Desires are related to our sense organs: our eyes prefer pleasing appearances; our ears prefer agreeable music; our mouth prefers delectable tastes; our nose prefers fragrant smells. These desires are *natural* to us. We don't need to learn to have these desires, since all sensory organs naturally prefer things that are agreeable to the senses. At the same time, our mind/heart also has natural emotions, in which Xunzi includes "love, hate, joy, anger, sorrow, or happiness."[27] When the mind/heart loves a certain thing or finds it enjoyable, it generates the corresponding desire. This is why Xunzi calls desires "the responses of the emotions."

Xunzi defines "goodness" and "evil" in this way: "All men in the world, past and present, agree in defining goodness as that which is upright, reasonable, peaceful and orderly, and evil as that which is unbalanced, dangerous, violent and chaotic. This is the distinction between good and evil."[28] If "goodness" is defined as "order and harmony," while "evil" is defined as "chaos and violence," then what we need to find out is whether the world will be peaceful and orderly, or violent and chaotic, when everyone follows his or her inborn nature. Xunzi thinks that humans are all egoists in that they would want to satisfy their own desires first and foremost. If humans follow their natural emotions and desires without any restraint, then the world will be brought to total chaos and eventual ruin. Without proper modifications of the inborn nature, everyone will become a villain. Human nature is bad in the respect that it naturally leads to an evil state.

As for the source of human goodness, Xunzi attributes it to human beings' deliberate effort (*wei*). The original Chinese term "*wei*," meaning literally "man-made" or "artificial," has been translated as "conscious activity" (Watson), "activity" (Chan), "human artifice" (Lau), or "deliberate effort" (Ivanhoe and Van Norden). Xunzi does not associate any negative connotation with the term "artificial"; what he means is simply whatever is mixed with human effort. Since human goodness is the result of people's deliberate effort, this deliberate effort, which forms the basis of human culture, is good. Xunzi defines it as "acting upon the decision of the mind's deliberation; a habit or a routine that is developed after the accumulation of these deliberations and practices."[29] Among human beings' deliberate efforts Xunzi lists rites and righteousness, moral principles and moral teachings, laws and regulations, etc. What deliberate effort accomplishes are all forms of moral conduct and moral sentiments. The whole process of human civilization acts against man's innate desire to aggrandize his possession and gratify his senses. Therefore, Xunzi declares, the goodness of human beings is the result of their deliberate effort. In this sense, human goodness is *man-made*, or *artificial*.

Along with goodness or moral attributes in general, other cultural human attributes, such as being lawful, courteous, etc., are also listed as *artificial* by Xunzi. The distinction between natural attributes and artificial attributes is simply the distinction between nature and effort: between what one is given and what one can work for. Xunzi says:

> Mencius states that man is capable of learning because his nature is good, but I say that this is wrong. It indicates that he has not really understood man's nature nor distinguished properly between the basic nature and conscious activity [*wei*]. The nature is that which is given by heaven; you cannot learn it, you cannot acquire it by effort. Ritual principles, on the

other hand, are created by sages; you can learn to apply them, you can work to bring them to completion. That part of man that cannot be learned or acquired by effort is called the nature; that part of him which can be acquired by learning and brought to completion by effort is called conscious activity. This is the difference between nature and conscious activity.[30]

From this criticism of Mencius, we can see that Xunzi does take "nature" to mean something different. As we explained in chapter 3, what Mencius takes to be "nature" is one's potential or innate inclinations – that which can be cultivated and matured by one's effort. Here we see that what Xunzi means by "nature" is what is given or completed at birth – that which cannot be further advanced by later education or conscious effort. Xunzi lists the eye's ability to see or the ear's ability to hear as part of one's nature, since "you cannot acquire clear sight and keen hearing by study."[31] This view of humans' natural capacities may not be completely accurate by today's standard. However, there does seem to be a distinction between what we have as natural attributes and what we have as cultural attributes.

D. C. Lau summarizes Xunzi's distinction between human nature and human deliberate effort (he calls it "human artifice") in this way:

Human nature is that which (1) is made what it is by heaven, (2) cannot be learned, (3) cannot be improved through application and (4) is not the result of reflection by the mind, while human artifice is that which (1) is invented by the sages, (2) can be learned, (3) can be improved through application, and (4) is the result of reflection by the mind.[32]

We can say that for Xunzi, human nature is what humans share with other animals, while human goodness is what humans develop out of a long process of civilization. Therefore, it is human beings' deliberate effort, rather than human nature, that distinguishes humans from other animals. This is just the opposite of Mencius' claim.

Having examined Xunzi's view on human nature, let us now look at his arguments against Mencius' theory. Xunzi says:

The nature of man is evil; his goodness is the result of his [deliberate effort]. Now, man's inborn nature is to seek for gain. If this tendency is followed, strife and rapacity result and deference and compliance disappear. By inborn nature one is envious and resentful of others. If these tendencies are followed, injury and destruction result and loyalty and faithfulness disappear. By inborn nature one possesses the desires of ear and eye and one likes beautiful sounds and sights. If these tendencies are followed, lewdness and licentiousness result, and the pattern and order of propriety and righteousness disappear. Therefore if a man follows his nature and his feelings, he will inevitably result in strife and rapacity. When such mentality is combined with rebellion against or disregard for social order, he will end in violence. Therefore there must be the civilizing influences of teachers and laws and the guidance of propriety and righteousness. Under such influences, the man will develop the attitude of deference and compliance, which, combined with culture and order, will lead to his being disciplined. From this point of view, it is clear that the nature of man is evil and that his goodness is the result of [deliberate effort].[33]

Let us formulate this argument as follows (Argument One):

1   (i)   By inborn nature, one is fond of profit and gain;
    (ii)   by inborn nature, one has envy and resentment of others;
  (iii)   by inborn nature, one possesses desires for sensory pleasures.
2   (i)   If the tendency to seek profit and gain is followed, then strife and rapacity result while respect and compliance disappear;
  (ii)   if the tendency to have envy and resentment of others is followed, then harm and destruction result while loyalty and faithfulness disappear;
  (iii)   if the tendency to meet one's sensory desires is followed, then lewdness and licentiousness result while propriety and righteousness disappear.
3   Therefore, if one follows one's inborn nature, evil will ensue.
4   The virtues we see in humans such as respect, loyalty, faithfulness, propriety, righteousness, etc. must all be from the influence of teachers and laws.
5   Therefore, man is by nature bad; his goodness is created by deliberate effort.

To examine this argument, we must see if we accept Xunzi's first premise, which is an empirical claim of human emotions. A sweeping empirical claim such as this is hard either to endorse or to refute, since it depends on the stock of evidence one gathers. By this claim alone, Xunzi is not refuting Mencius' observation of the moral inclinations that humans naturally have. He is merely pointing out those *other* inclinations that Mencius does not emphasize. If Mencius could make a sweeping empirical claim about the good human inclinations, Xunzi could also make a sweeping empirical claim about the bad inclinations that humans have. His argument is thus at least as strong, or as weak, as that of Mencius. The second premise in this argument states a conditional claim, with the hidden assumption that the resources in the world are limited. If people want the same things and their desires cannot all be satisfied, then it seems predicable that they will end up fighting for the things they all want. Therefore, if humans all follow their naturally egoistic and antagonistic attitude, then the world will end up in the state of strife and chaos. From this first conclusion, stated as (3), Xunzi introduces premise (4), which does not seem to follow directly from what has been stated so far. We should regard it as a separate supposition. Since Xunzi gives an argument in support of this claim elsewhere, we shall not analyze it here. Aided with this new claim, Xunzi derives his conclusion that human nature is bad.

Xunzi further gives a paradoxical argument. He says:

> Every man who desires to do good does so precisely because his nature is evil. A man whose accomplishments are meager longs for greatness; an ugly man longs for beauty; a man in cramped quarters longs for spaciousness; a poor man longs for wealth; a humble man longs for eminence. Whatever a man lacks in himself he will seek outside. But if a man is already rich, he will not long for wealth, and if he is already eminent, he will not long for greater power. What a man already possesses in himself he will not bother to look for outside. From this we can see that men desire to do good precisely because their nature is evil.[34]

1   A man whose accomplishments are meager longs for greatness; an ugly person longs for beauty; a man in cramped quarters longs for spaciousness; a poor man longs for wealth; a humble man longs for eminence.
2   Hence, whatever a man lacks in himself he will seek outside; what a man already possesses in himself he will not bother to look for outside.
3   Therefore, if people desire to be good, then they do not already have goodness in themselves.

To this argument (Argument Two), A. C. Cua offers a good critique. After considering an objection to the above argument that a scholar can desire to seek learning without being totally unlearned himself, Cua says:

> If it be said that a scholar can desire and seek learning, one can point out that the object that he desires and seeks is *more learning*, and this logically implies that he does not possess what he seeks. . . . The point is that if I desire and seek an object x, assuming that I clearly know x . . . then I cannot be said to desire and seek x unless I do not possess x. But it follows also that a good man can seek and desire goodness, in the sense of

more goodness, without himself lacking in some degree of goodness. There are different degrees of moral goodness. From the conceptual observation about the notion of desire as logically involving the lack of the object desired, [Xunzi] cannot establish the claim that "men desire to do good precisely because their nature is bad."[35]

In other words, we could desire to have *more* money, but this does not mean that we have no money; we could desire to become *better*, but it does not imply that we are not already *good*. Xunzi's argument simply fails to establish his claim.

The next two arguments can be discussed together. Argument Three is based on the assumption that what is *nature* is what cannot be learned or taught. Argument Four is based on the assumption that what is *nature* is what one is born with. First, Argument Three:[36]

1　By human nature we mean the product of Heaven, not something learned or worked for.
2　But we learn to be good and we work hard on making ourselves better.
3　Therefore, the nature of man is bad; his goodness is made by humans' deliberate effort.

Next, Argument Four:[37]

1　Mencius claims that evil comes from the loss of our original nature.
2　But as soon as we are born, we begin to depart from our original state of *naiveté* and simplicity, and thus must inevitably lose what Mencius regards as man's original nature.
3　Therefore, if Mencius is right, then all men inevitably become evil.
4　But the view that all men inevitably become evil is absurd.
5　Therefore, evil cannot come from the loss of our original nature; instead, it must already be part of our original nature.

Both arguments are clearly based on Xunzi's definition of "nature." Mencius certainly would not agree with Xunzi's first premise in Argument Three, or his second premise in Argument Four because for Mencius, human nature is in a developmental state. One can *realize*, *cultivate*, or *edify* one's nature. Hence, it is not true that one's birth state prescribes the totality of one's nature such that one cannot learn to improve on it. As a refutation of Mencius' view, these two arguments are, as A. C. Graham puts it, "a little off target."[38]

Xunzi asks: "If propriety and righteousness are products of accumulated effort and to be regarded as [inherent] in man's nature, then why are Yao and (sage-king) Yu highly honored, and why is the superior man highly honored?" He answers:

> Yao, Yu and the superior man are highly honored because they can transform nature and arouse effort. As effort is aroused, propriety and righteousness are produced. Thus the relation between the sages and propriety and righteousness produced through accumulated effort, is like the potter pounding the clay to produce the pottery. . . . [The tyrant Jie, the bandit Zhi] and the inferior man are despised because they give rein to their nature, follow their feelings, and enjoy indulgence, and lead to the greed for gain, to quarrels and rapacity. It is clear that man's nature is evil and that his goodness is the result of his [deliberate effort].[39]

From this comment we can formulate the following two arguments (Argument Five and Argument Six):

1 If, as Mencius claims, goodness comes from one's inborn nature, then anyone who follows his or her own nature must be good and anyone who receives outside influences is likely to be bad.
2 But what we call "the superior man" is someone who is influenced by teachers and laws, and what we call "the inferior man" is someone who gives rein to his feelings and enjoys indulgence.
3 Therefore, human nature is bad; a person's goodness comes from his or her own deliberate effort (and thus Mencius is wrong).

1 If goodness is natural, then there is no effort involved and sages are just doing what is natural to them.
2 But we praise sages exactly for their accumulated moral efforts in transforming their original nature.
3 Therefore, human nature is bad; a person's goodness comes from his or her own deliberate effort.

Xunzi argues that at birth, man does not already possess propriety and righteousness, the two main virtues constitutive of a civil society. He does, however, acknowledge man's inborn capacities to learn moral principles and to practice moral conduct. He says:

> Any man in the street has the essential faculties needed to understand benevolence, righteousness, and proper standards, and the potential ability to put them into practice. . . . Any man in the street *can* understand the duties required of a father or a son and *can* comprehend the correct relationship between ruler and subject. Therefore, it is obvious that the essential faculties needed to understand such ethical principles and the potential ability to put them into practice must be a part of his make-up.[40]

99

Xunzi grants ordinary people the capacities to understand moral teachings and the potential to practice moral conduct, because otherwise they can never be morally transformed, which is a conclusion he would not accept. Some may argue that this shows that ordinary people do have what Mencius calls "the seeds of morality" within their nature. But what Xunzi emphasizes here are the intellectual aspects, not the moral aspects, of man's inborn capacities. Intellectual capacities are not necessarily moral capacities – a man can learn to swim, to play musical instruments, to learn a second language, etc. These are all capacities that are *amoral*. As Benjamin Schwartz puts it, "The word 'capacity,' which we have used in [Xunzi's] case, does not refer to an immediately available 'intuitive' knowledge. It is a capacity for acquiring experience and reasoning about ex-perience and it demands constant cumulative acts of *mental* exertion."[41] Xunzi never denies that man can learn to be moral, just as he would not deny that man could learn to be immoral. What matters is not whether he has these learning capacities, but the object or the content of his studies. Here Xunzi introduces the importance of scholarship in morality.[42] But even with the right goal, a person can still fail to become moral if he lacks persistence and concentration in his attitude. For an ordinary person, Xunzi says:

> If in his practices and studies day after day for a long time, he concentrates his mind, has unity of purpose, thinks thoroughly and discriminately, and accumulates goodness without stop, he can then be as wise as the gods, and form a trinity with Heaven and Earth. Thus the sage is a man who has reached this state through accumulated effort.[43]

If what separates sages from ordinary people are these deliberate efforts in building morality, then Xunzi seems to have succeeded in arguing his point that moral goodness is the result of human effort.

Finally, Xunzi appeals to the indispensability of external restraints to argue for the badness of human nature. He says:

> Now let someone try doing away with the authority of the ruler, ignoring the transforming power of ritual principles, rejecting the order that comes from laws and standards, and dispensing with the restrictive power of punishments, and then watch and see how the people of the world treat each other. He will find that the powerful impose upon the weak and rob them, the many terrorize the few and extort from them, and in no time the whole world will be given up to chaos and mutual destruction. It is obvious from this, then, that man's nature is evil, and that his goodness is the result of [deliberate effort].[44]

This remark is reorganized into Argument Seven:

1 If goodness is in human nature, then we don't need external restraints for humans.
2 But if we try to remove the authority of the ruler, do away with the transforming influence of principles of propriety and righteousness, discard the regulation of laws and governmental standards, dispense with the restraint of punishment, we will find that the powerful impose upon the weak to rob them, while the majority terrorize the minority and extort from them.
3 Therefore, the nature of man is bad; his goodness comes from his own deliberate effort.

Philosophers arguing for the badness of human nature often employ this form of argument. They tell us to take a look at a society where law and order have been abandoned and we will see that people generally loot, steal, rob, or even kill others. The Greek historian Thucydides, for example, argues that human nature is laid bare in times of plague and civil wars, and what we see are various forms of human conduct of the most despicable form.[45] We cannot trust ourselves, or others, always to do the right thing when no bad consequences will result from our misdeeds. Xunzi says:

> If man's nature is good, sage-kings can be done away with and propriety and righteousness can be stopped. But if his nature is evil, sage-kings are to be followed and propriety and righteousness are to be greatly valued. For bending came into existence because there was crooked wood, the carpenter's square and ruler came into existence because things are not straight, and the authority of rule is instituted and propriety and righteousness are made clear because man's nature is evil.[46]

From the indispensability of rules and regulations, Xunzi concludes that man's nature is bad and that his goodness is the result of external restraints.

Now that we have seen a good sample of Xunzi's argument against Mencius, how should we settle the dispute? Both of them define "nature" in accordance with the common usage of the word; both depict the common conception of human nature. Both of them make sweeping empirical claims that are only partially true about mature human beings, and yet both derive conclusions about human infancy from these partial empirical truths. Both of them employ analogies to natural objects (water in the case of Mencius) or artifacts (clay pots and wooden utensils in the case of Xunzi), and these analogies are merely illustrations, not proofs, of their claims. It is hard to judge which philosopher provides the better argumentation. As we mentioned at the beginning of this section, their overall views on moral education and moral rulership are very similar. Their different assumptions on human nature result from their different cosmology: Mencius' cosmology has a moralistic bent, while Xunzi's is largely naturalistic. Furthermore, because of the fundamental difference in their assumptions on human nature, their views on the nature of morality are drastically different. For Mencius, morality is developed from within a person; for Xunzi, morality is introduced from the outside. Here we turn to Xunzi's exposition of the essential restraining role that rituals and rules of propriety (*li*) play in the moral transformation of man's evil nature.

The Significance of Rituals and Rules of Propriety (*Li*)

If human nature is bad, then where do these moral principles, which we call rituals and rules of propriety, come from? Xunzi's reply is that they were initially invented by ancient sages: "The sages gathered together their ideas and thoughts and became familiar with activity, facts, and principles, and thus produced propriety and righteousness and instituted laws and systems."[47] Xunzi conjectures, semi-historically, that in ancient times, when primitive people operated only on their natural inclinations and instinctive drives, the world was in total chaos. The early sages saw the need to reform humans' emotional nature, to redirect human conduct, and to lead primitive people into a civil society. Therefore, they invented these moral principles and rules of propriety.

The origin of morality is an intriguing issue. Confucius and Mencius seem to view morality as rooted in a moralistic natural world; early Christianity seems to take it to be rooted in the dictates of a supreme God. Now Xunzi says that morality is a human invention; it is rooted in the deliberate creation of ancient sages. But then a question naturally arises for Xunzi: if human nature is bad and is in need of external restraints, then how did the first sage come about? As T. C. Kline puts it: "Xunzi does not . . . explicitly describe how someone growing up in a chaotic society without ritual, teachers, or institutions to guide moral cultivation could possibly become a sage. How did those in the Confucian 'original position' ever manage to transform themselves?" Kline calls this problem "the dilemma of the early sages."[48]

Does Xunzi offer a coherent theory to help us out of this dilemma? In a discourse on the origin of rites, he says:

> The ancient kings hated such disorder, and therefore they established ritual principles in order to curb it, to train men's desires and to provide for their satisfaction. They saw to it that desires did not overextend the means for their satisfaction, and material goods did not fall short of what was desired. Thus both desires and material goods sustained each other over the course of time. This is the origin of rites.[49]

In this analysis, it is the ancient kings, not ancient sages, who first instituted rituals and rites. Their purpose was to use these regulative principles to curtail people's dangerous tendencies to avoid social disorder. The ancient kings' fabrication of moral rules could be merely in order to meet a pragmatic need of social control. Thus, there may not have been any self-taught sage at the initial stage of human society, and Xunzi is not forced to place sages in a species different from that of ordinary people. However, if the ancient kings were not themselves "moral" and yet they invented morality to serve their pragmatic need, then wouldn't the whole creation of moral rules and principles of propriety be what David S. Nivison calls "a noble lie"?[50] Nivison replies:

> No: through their superior intelligence [the ancient kings] understood human nature and the inescapable human situation, and so also saw that the introduction of order was necessary. So seeing, they formulated laws and norms, and then not only promulgated them to other human beings, but also recognized them as binding on themselves. . . . Through their intelligence they moralized themselves as well as us.[51]

In other words, even if the ancient kings did not have morality as part of their original nature, they *became* moral from following the moral guidance that they themselves devised for their people. In other words, morality is the result of an intellectual effort in Xunzi's depiction of the transformation of ancient kings into sages. Sages, or we may say the supremely moral people, come as a result of following moral guidance and eventually appreciating the beauty of morality itself. As Xunzi puts it, "He who knows how to think and to be steadfast, and in addition has a true love for ritual – he is a sage."[52]

Xunzi likens the sages' efforts in transforming people's original nature to the work of craftsmanship. He says:

> A warped piece of wood must wait until it has been laid against the straightening board, steamed, and forced into shape before it can become

straight; a piece of blunt metal must wait until it has been whetted on a grindstone before it can become sharp. Similarly, since man's nature is evil, it must wait for the instructions of a teacher before it can become upright, and for the guidance of ritual principles before it can become orderly.[53]

From this we see that the function of moral teachings and societal rituals of propriety, according to Xunzi, is to *rectify* or *transform* one's original nature. They serve as a regulative force on people's natural inclinations. They are what turn humans from a state of nature into a state of civility.

Kline argues that "[the analogy of craftsman] illustrates that Xunzi conceives of moral cultivation as a process working from the outside in, rather than one of working from the inside out. Teachers, classical texts, rituals, and music become the instruments that shape the person's moral sense from the outside."[54] In chapter 2 we discussed Confucius' notion of propriety, *li*, which is more about a proper mental attitude. The same Chinese word *li*, in the context of *The Xunzi*, takes on the connotation of more rigid, systematized societal rites and rituals.[55] Wing-tsit Chan says: "In the [*Xunzi*], rules of propriety and law are often spoken of together, giving the impression that, unlike Confucius and Mencius who advocated propriety (*li*) as inner control, [Xunzi] advocated it for external control. Thus rules of propriety shifted from being a means of personal moral cultivation to one of social control."[56] However, rules of propriety, for Xunzi, serve as much more than mere social control. He argues that even if the restraints of rites and rituals were initially imposed on us from the outside, they should eventually be internalized by us. The internalization of moral principles and rules of propriety is the process of one's moral cultivation.[57] A cultivated person would need external restraints less and less and would develop his own moral sense, would enjoy doing the right thing in any given situation, would not be easily tempted by his egocentric desires or be compelled by his evil inclinations. Virtue is the accumulation of moral habits that result from repeated efforts in self-restraint. When one has become a cultivated person, one has deviated far from one's original nature. To Xunzi, this is good.

What is the content of these rituals and principles of propriety for them to have such a modifying power on human behavior and such a transforming effect on human minds? According to Xunzi, rites and rituals have three bases: "Heaven and earth are the basis of life, the ancestors are the basis of the family, and rulers and teachers are the basis of order."[58] Ceremonies with regard to Heaven and Earth are sacred. Only rulers of a nation or of a state can perform some of them, and the delineation of differences is clearly marked. Xunzi says: "In this way rites distinguish and make clear that the exalted should serve the exalted and the humble serve the humble, that great corresponds to great and small to small."[59] Ceremonies with regard to ancestors must be handled with careful attention paid to details. Take funerals, for example. There are rules of propriety concerning the number of layers of the coffin, the kind of coffin decoration and ornaments, the amount of food offerings, the length of the mourning period, etc., that should all be considered in correspondence with the social rank of the deceased. Finally, ceremonies with regard to the king must be performed with great reverence. The color of one's attire, the manner of one's speech, etc., must all conform to the proper etiquette specific to the intercourse with the king.

To people outside this cultural tradition, the Confucian advocacy of rites and rituals is often difficult to appreciate. One can easily see them as trivial rules that deal with the form, not the meaning, of important events in life. Xunzi thinks that we naturally have strong emotions, in particular, joy and sorrow, toward significant events in our life. Sometimes when we are driven by these strong emotions, we may go overboard in our expressions of them. Rites or principles of propriety provide us with a guideline as to what is a proper expression of emotion. Xunzi explains the function of rites this way: "Rites trim what is too long and stretch out what is too short, eliminate surplus and repair deficiency, extend the forms of love and reverence, and step by step bring to fulfillment the beauties of proper conduct."[60] In moderating our conduct in a given occasion, rules of rites and propriety allow us to express our emotions fully without being excessive or inappropriate. We thereby get the satisfaction of the need to express our emotions. Thus, instead of suppressing our emotions, Xunzi says, "rites are a means of providing satisfaction."[61] According to Cua, the performance of rites for Xunzi "displays a combination of three different components: (1) a characteristic *form* which exemplifies compliance with a relevant procedure; (2) an attitude or emotion which expresses the actor's feeling deemed as something befitting the occasion; and (3) a joy or satisfaction experienced by the actor in the consummation of the act."[62] He calls this combination "the aesthetic dimension" of rites and rituals.[63]

Naturally, not everyone can achieve a fine balance between these three components. Rites and rituals can become trivialized by people who pay attention only to the form, while lacking genuine emotions of joy or grief. Xunzi does not approve of this kind of pretense. He describes striving deliberately for a distraught and emaciated appearance only for the sake of effect at a funeral as "the way of evil men."[64] Ideally, if one has sincere emotion and wise judgment of situational propriety, one does not need the external restraints laid out as rites and rules of propriety. For the morally cultivated people, in particular the sages, the formality of rites and ritual principles is not essential. They themselves know how to express their emotions "completely and properly, fully and beautifully."[65] However, very few people are able to do this. The gentlemen and the sages thus need to set examples for the common people. Their observance of rites and ritual principles can serve "as a model to ten thousand generations."[66]

Conclusion

From the above discussion, we see that Xunzi offers an interesting perspective on many traditional values. He has enriched ancient Confucianism with his naturalistic theory of Heaven, his anti-superstitious critiques, his contrary view of human nature, his pragmatic view of the origin of morality and the function of rites and rituals. Even though later Neo-Confucians did not pay much attention to his thought, Confucianism would not have been as interesting a school of thought without Xunzi's contribution.

Further discussion questions

1 Between Mencius and Xunzi, who has a more convincing theory of human nature? Who has better arguments? What is your view of the nature of human beings?
2 What is Xunzi's view of nature? How is his view different from the Confucian tradition?
3 Has Xunzi fully explained the origin of morality? Is his solution to "the dilemma of the early sages" successful? Can his view be compared to a social contract theory of morality?
4 Why are ceremonies so important according to Xunzi? Do you see any value in the employment of ceremonies and rites? What social function can they serve?

Primary texts

Wing-tsit Chan (ed.) *A Sourcebook in Chinese Philosophy*, 4th edn. Princeton: Princeton University Press, 1973 (ch. 6; excerpts).

Philip J. Ivanhoe and Bryan W. Van Norden (eds.) *Readings in Classical Chinese Philosophy*. Indianapolis, IN: Hackett Publishing Company, Inc., 2003 (ch. 6; excerpts).

John Knoblock. *Xunzi: A Translation and Study of the Complete Works*, vols. I–III. Stanford, CA: Stanford University Press, 1994.

Burton Watson (trans.) *Hsün Tzu: Basic Writings*. New York: Columbia University Press, 1963.

Further readings

Antonio S. Cua. "The Conceptual Aspect of Hsün Tzu's Philosophy of Human Nature." *Philosophy East & West* 27(4), 1977: 373–89.

——. "Dimensions of *Li* (Propriety): Reflections on an Aspect of Hsün Tzu's Ethics." *Philosophy East & West* 29(4), 1979: 373–94.

——. "The Quasi-empirical Aspect of Hsün-Tzu's Philosophy of Human Nature." *Philosophy East & West* 28(4), 1978: 3–19.

D. C. Lau. "Theories of Human Nature in Mencius and Shyuntzyy [Xunzi]." *Bulletin of the School of Asian and African Studies* 15, 1953: 541–65. Repr. in T. C. Kline III and Philip J. Ivanhoe (eds.), *Virtue, Nature and Moral Agency in the Xunzi*. Indianapolis: Hackett Publishing Company, 2000, pp. 188–219.

Jonathan W. Schofer. "Virtues in Xunzi's Thought: Issues in Comparative Analysis." *The Journal of Religious Ethics* 21, 1993: 117–36. Repr. in T. C. Kline III and Philip J. Ivanhoe (eds.), *Virtue, Nature and Moral Agency in the Xunzi*. Indianapolis: Hackett Publishing Company, 2000, pp. 69–88.

David B. Wong. "Xunzi on Moral Motivation." In Philip Ivanhoe (ed.), *Chinese Language, Thought, and Culture: Nivison and His Critics*. La Salle, Ill: Open Court, 1996: 202–23. Repr. in T. C. Kline III and Philip J. Ivanhoe (eds.), *Virtue, Nature and Moral Agency in the Xunzi*. Indianapolis: Hackett Publishing Company, 2000, pp. 135–54.

Chapter 5

Mozi (Mo Tzu)

Introduction

We know very few positive facts about Mozi (ca. 480–392? BCE), but there do exist a number of unsubstantiated anecdotes about him. He probably flourished shortly after the death of Confucius, and shortly before the birth of Mencius. As rumor has it, he studied under the Confucian School when he was young, but soon turned away from this teaching and launched a severe attack on Confucianism. He was particularly intent on spreading his teaching of universal love and mutual benefits, and he spent a major part of his life forestalling offensive warfare. He was allegedly an expert in constructing defensive apparatus, and trained his students to use them ably. He probably had hundreds of followers in his lifetime; many among them carried out his anti-war ideology and assisted in defensive warfare. He and his followers practiced an austere lifestyle: they wore coarse clothes, eschewed personal possessions, and traveled extensively to help others. Mohism attracted a large following for some hundreds of years. Mohists formed a rigid organization, with authoritative "Grand Masters" acting like military commanders. For some time, Mohism and Confucianism were seen as the two dominant schools in China.

In many respects, what Mozi wanted to accomplish was similar to Confucius' goals: to alleviate social problems, to restore worldly order, and to bring welfare to the common people. Like Confucius, he trained scholars for political careers, so that the kind of political reform he wanted to accomplish could be put into practice by his students. But the audiences for Confucius and Mozi were radically different. According to Wing-tsit Chan, while Confucius' students were the intellectual elite of society, Mozi's followers were mostly from the working class.[1] Their views on the ideal society were also at odds with each other: While

Confucius wanted to rebuild a refined high culture in the paradigm of ancient sage kings such as Yao and Shun, Mozi wanted to reconstruct a modest farming society in the model of another ancient sage king, Yu.[2] Even though both schools shared the common goal of alleviating the suffering of the populace, they vehemently attacked each other's view. Confucius' successor Mencius took Mozi to be his theoretical archenemy. Mencius says:

> Mo advocated universal love, which means a denial of the special relationship with the father. To deny the special relationship with the father and the ruler is to become an animal. . . . If the principles of Yang and Mo are not stopped, and the principles of Confucius are not brought to light, perverse doctrine will delude the people and obstruct the path of humanity and righteousness.[3]

It was because of doctrines such as Mohism, according to Mencius, that he became so argumentative. From this declaration, we could also see that, as early as Mencius' time, Mohism must have already gained wide support among the masses.

What Mozi found to be the major problem with Confucianism was its impracticality; he saw Confucianism as a teaching that promoted wastefulness of human energy as well as of social resources. Many of Mozi's teachings were direct rejections, if not of Confucius' own teachings, at least of the Confucian practices at the time. For example, Mozi condemned the Confucian doctrine of love with distinctions as a form of partiality and advocated universal love in its place. He campaigned for the simplification of funeral rites and the reduction of mourning periods, both of which, in their current format, were taken by Confucius to be necessary manifestations of one's natural emotions toward the deceased. Mozi criticized the study and the enjoyment of music, which was believed by Confucius to be one of the most effective means to transform people's temperament. Finally, even though Confucius himself seldom discussed the issue of fate, Mozi thought that his contemporary Confucians often used "fate" to excuse themselves from entering politics and serving the public. In his harsh judgment, Confucius, as well as the Confucians at the time, were hypocritical, perverse, scheming, self-contradictory, craven, untrustworthy, and vile.[4]

What we have today of Mozi's writing is a book of collected essays, with his name as the title. The essays were most likely his students' records of his remarks, or his followers' extrapolation of his thought. The book contains titles for 71 chapters, 18 of which are missing. Hence, the complete *Mozi* now has only 53 chapters. Of these, 6 that contain the Mohist dialectics are believed to belong to a much later period of the Mohist School. The Mohist dialectics have attracted some attention from modern commentators (such as A. C. Graham), but it played only a small role in the major development of Chinese philosophy. Eleven other chapters contain detailed descriptions of the defensive tactics or apparatus that Mozi and his students devised. They would be of interest to anyone wishing to study ancient Chinese military thought. In this chapter, however, we shall only deal with the core theses of Mozi. We will discuss his doctrine of universal love and mutual benefits, and we will also examine his pragmatic authoritarianism, which laid the foundation for Hanfeizi's Legalist philosophy. Finally, we will analyze his view on the existence of ghosts, spirits, and fate, as Mozi seemed to be the only ancient philosopher who dealt with philosophy of religion.

Universal Love vs. Love with Distinctions

The hallmark thesis of Mozi is his teaching of "universal love," as a direct challenge to the Confucian teaching of love with distinctions. Mozi did not merely advocate that we demonstrate universal concern for all people; he promoted the ideal of treating everyone else just as we would treat ourselves. "Universal love" means loving everyone, family members and strangers alike, *equally*. Mozi says, "Regard others' countries as if they were my own country. Regard others' families as if they were my own family. Regard others' bodies as if they were my own body."[5] Julia Ching calls Mozi's view "radical altruism."[6] Mozi's doctrine of universal love is a preparatory step for his teaching of mutual benefits. "Universal love" demands more from us than the ethical principle of impartiality, which is a demand on our rational moral judgment. The principle of impartiality requires us to eliminate considerations of self-interests and treat others as beings of equal moral worth to ourselves. But it does not ask us to *love* others as we love ourselves. What Mozi hoped to accomplish, then, was not merely behavioral reform, but a psychological transformation of all people.

Mozi thought that the root of all social problems lay in the fact that people do not love one another equally. He says:

> It is the business of the benevolent man to try to promote what is beneficial to the world and to eliminate what is harmful. Now at the present time, what brings the greatest harm to the world? Great states attacking small ones, great families overthrowing small ones, the strong oppressing the weak, the many harrying the few, the cunning deceiving the stupid,

the eminent lording it over the humble – these are harmful to the world. So too are rulers who are not generous, ministers who are not loyal, fathers who are without kindness, and sons who are unfilial, as well as those mean men who, with weapons, knives, poison, fire, and water, seek to injure and undo each other.[7]

The above statements can be formulated into the following argument:

1 The man of humanity has a moral obligation to promote benefits for the world and to remove harm from the world.
2 The harms in the world are: mutual attacks among states, mutual usurpation among families, and mutual injuries among individuals.
3 The cause of these harms is people's lack of universal love.
4 Therefore, the man of humanity must promote the doctrine of universal love and mutual benefits.

The Confucian ideal person is the man of *humanity* (*ren*), someone who helps others become better people. As we saw in chapter 2, Confucius defines "humanity" this way: "If one wishes to establish one's character, one also establishes the characters of others; if one wishes to obtain one's goal, one also helps others obtain their goals."[8] This remark sounds surprisingly similar to what Mozi advocates against the Confucian teaching. What then is the difference between the two theses?

A fundamental difference between the two ethical theories is that for Confucius, being a man of humanity is an ideal state of being; it depicts an internal state of existence. Once one has reached the state of humanity, one will be naturally inclined to help others to become self-fulfilled. Humanity is an altruistic mental frame, but the goal is for others to become better people, to be morally transformed. For Mozi, on the other hand, altruism is entailed by the consequentialist consideration of benefits. The desired goal is the benefit of all, and promoting altruism is a means to that goal. Therefore, Mozi seldom discusses what kind of person "the man of humanity" *is*; rather, he focuses on what the man of humanity *does*. Morality is assessed by one's conduct, not by one's internal virtue. As Benjamin Schwartz points out, "The essence of the matter is that the Mohist truly 'righteous man's' attention is totally and undeviatingly fixed on the world 'out there.' He is totally oriented toward 'doing good' and not preoccupied with 'being good'."[9] Mozi believed that what he was promoting was what the man of humanity should *accomplish* – "to bring benefits to all people; to remove harm from all people."[10] In other words, Mozi's theory is a theory of action.

Mozi often criticized Confucians for being hypocrites or for only speaking but taking no action. He thought that our speech and our action should correspond to each other, such that "there is no speech that is not put into action."[11] We can conclude that Mozi is not rejecting the Confucian ideal of humanity, but he is rejecting the fact that Confucians focus too much on the *internal* ideal person.

Mozi further thought that when Confucius teaches the principle of *empathy* (*shu*) – do not impose on others what we ourselves do not desire – he has not really found the solution to the world's problems. As Mozi pointed out, the root of all worldly troubles is in people's not loving one another. Therefore, the solution must lie in our eliminating the priority of the self, not just in our self-projected considerations for others. He thus advocated love with no distinctions, in contrast to the Confucian teaching of love with distinctions.

What is the origin of our love for others? Is love a natural sentiment, or a socially conditioned one? From the perspective of moral psychology, David Wong argues that love for family members takes "moral priority" over love for strangers. He lists three reasons given by the Confucians for the belief that "caring for others must begin in the family or it will not begin at all":[12]

1   Family is the basic social and political unit. The love for mankind must begin with filial piety and fraternal obedience within the family.
2   We owe our gratitude toward our parents because they have given us life, nurture and sustenance.
3   It is human nature to give greater weight to the welfare of one's parents.

These three points could be seen as the counterargument for Mozi's view from the Confucian perspective.[13] A Confucian would argue that because human society is constituted by atomic family units, and because human beings are reared in the particular family associations, our feelings naturally tend toward our immediate family members first and foremost. This tendency for partial love is within our nature; it is fostered by social conditions and it is further enhanced by our gratitude toward our parents.

However, a Mohist could possibly come up with three rebuttals of the above claims. With regard to human nature, the Mohist would not deny that humans are naturally self-interested; hence, he would argue that self-interest is best served when one is situated in a world where everyone loves one another universally. With regard to social conditions, the Mohist would suggest that we could condition people differently.

Suppose we were not reared in the family unit, would we still love our parents naturally and primarily? In the *Republic*, Plato presented a utopia, in which children are all brought up in a nursing pen with their birth identity suppressed. Parents do not recognize their children; children do not know who their parents were. Plato argued that in such a world, everyone would love one another *as if they were all in the same family*. From this thought experiment we can imagine the kind of universal love possible in a world without family units. Finally, with regard to the point on gratitude, the Mohist would probably point out that if we love and are loved by others universally, then this sense of gratitude would be owed to anyone who is kind to us.

Can a Mohist social reconstruction ever be accomplished? Again, we have to see which form of love is more *natural* to human beings. According to Wong, love does not first begin *universally* and then move toward particularity; instead, loves begins with *particularity* because it is the love which one has received since infanthood that gives one the ability to love or to care for others later in life.[14] From this point of view, human beings naturally form family relations. When we have been born into a particular family, have been taken care of by two particular people, have grown up with a few particular siblings, to renounce love with particularity would be to renounce our natural sentiments toward these people who are the closest to us. To deny this prioritization and to denounce any distinction in our sentiments would turn us into *unloving* creatures. Hence, love with particularity is not just a sub-division of the universal love. Universal love is only possible through the extension of our natural love with particularity.

From this consideration based on our given social environment, we can say that partial love is the more natural sentiment for human beings. However, Mozi was fully aware of the difficulty in teaching people to go against their natural sentiments. Hence, his other strategy was to appeal to humans' natural desire to benefit themselves, to make them see how beneficial it would be if everyone were able to love one another universally. He pointed out that "one who loves will be loved by others, and one who hates will be hated by others."[15] By extension, if we can love others' parents, then others will also love our parents; if we can love others' countries, then people in other nations will also love our country. Ultimately, our own self-interest is best secured when we can love universally.

Mozi says:

> Let us examine for a moment the way in which a filial son plans for the welfare of his parents. When a filial son plans for his parents, does he

wish others to love and benefit them, or does he wish others to hate and injure them? It stands to reason that he wishes others to love and benefit his parents. Now if I am a filial son, how do I go about accomplishing this? . . . Obviously, I must first make it a point to love and benefit other men's parents, so that they in return will love and benefit my parents. So if all of us are to be filial sons, can we set about it any other way than by first making a point of loving and benefiting other men's parents?[16]

Expanding on this comment, we can express Mozi's moral philosophy as being based on the following reasoning:

1 Our primary concern is our self-interest.
2 The most effective way of satisfying our self-interest is when others are all working toward the same goal on our behalf.
3 But others are not going to work toward our self-interest unless they see that we are doing the same for them.
4 Therefore, we ought to benefit one another mutually.
5 But to be able to benefit one another mutually, we must develop mutual love for one another.
6 One who loves others will be loved by others; one who hates others will be hated by others.
7 Therefore, we must develop universal love within ourselves.

We can see that in this reasoning, "universal love" is not the primary goal of Mohism; rather, it is seen as a means to an end. Mozi thought that the maximization of universal benefits can never be accomplished unless everyone is induced to love one another equally. At the same time, even though Mozi's ultimate goal was the overall benefit of the world, he understood that everyone is intrinsically a self-interested creature. Therefore, to induce people to adopt the mental frame of universal love, he appealed to individuals' self-interest to accomplish that goal. As Schwartz says, "Unless men can be induced to love all men universally, the general interests of mankind as a whole will never be realized. In the end, only universal love can enable individuals to identify their own interests with the interests of others."[17] To argue that universal love, as a moral virtue, is *intrinsically good*, and to argue that it is valuable only as a means to an end, are different positions. If universal love only has an "instrumental value"[18] to Mozi's real goal, then once the instrumental value is lost, even Mozi himself would abandon this theory as well. It is thus no wonder that one of Mozi's contemporary philosophers, Yang Zhu, with the same goal, promoted the theory of *selfish love* as a way of obtaining universal benefits. Yang Zhu argued that if everyone is intrinsically self-interested, when they all work toward their own self-interest, society will benefit since society is simply the sum of individuals. In Mencius' time, Mohism and Yangism were the two rivalries that challenged Confucianism from the perspective of *benefits*. It is no wonder that Mencius would often remark: Why does one need to discuss benefits? One should just focus on righteousness.

Next, we turn to Mozi's moral theory based on the consideration of benefits.

Deontological Rightness vs. Utilitarian Benefits

Another major thesis of Mozi is that we should benefit one another mutually. The very notion of *benefit* (*li*) shows a direct challenge to the Confucian ideal.[19] By the term "benefit," Mozi is emphasizing practical advantages such as the restoration of world order, the termination of warfare, the cessation of human conflicts, the sufficiency of social resources, and the security of people's sustenance. He is not even talking about the increase of individuals' profits, wealth, or status; his concern is for the basic level of survival. This concern is not dismissed by Confucians, but they take it a step further: Confucians are concerned with the people's morality, while Mozi was only concerned with their survival; Confucians want to teach people to act in accordance with righteousness, while Mozi wants to teach them to act in keeping with general benefits. This is what separates Mohism from Confucianism.

Mozi's starting assumption was that all humans are naturally egoistic. We may say that he is a *psychological* egoist; he believes that all men are self-interested by nature. However, he is not an *ethical* egoist, since he does not believe that just because we are naturally self-interested, we *ought to* be self-interested. Mozi himself is an ethical altruist. But how could he get other self-interested people to agree with his position? From the assumption of psychological egoism, he tried to promote the idea that the highest self-interest for everyone comes from everyone's benefiting others. In other words, what he promotes is a paradoxical assertion that the best way to promote our self-interest is to *not* promote our self-interest, but to promote others' interests. Herrlee Creel calls this "enlightened self-interest."[20] Mozi says:

> Now if we seek to benefit the world by taking universality as our standard, those with sharp ears and clear eyes will see and hear for others,

those with sturdy limbs will work for others, and those with a knowledge of the Way will endeavor to teach others. Those who are old and without wives or children will find means of support and be able to live out their days; the young and orphaned who have no parents will find someone to care for them and look after their needs. When all these benefits may be secured merely by taking universality as our standard, I cannot understand how the men of the world can hear about this doctrine of universality and still criticize it![21]

Mozi's view is standardly regarded as a version of utilitarianism. The theses of a generic form of utilitarianism can be formulated as follows:

[UT1]   An act is moral if and only if it generates a greater balance of good over bad in its consequences for all people involved, than any other acts available to the agent.
[UT2]   The aim of moral actions is to maximize the greatest happiness for the greatest number of people.
[UT3]   In counting the number of people, each one counts as one. (All individuals are equal in moral considerations.)
[UT4]   Thus, the aim of moral actions is to maximize the greatest happiness for strangers and family members alike.

We can see that all these theses are compatible with Mozi's doctrine of universal love and mutual benefits.

Dennis Ahern challenges this orthodox interpretation of Mozi. He thinks that the standard interpretation of Mozi as a utilitarian "ignores his beliefs about Heaven."[22] When we examine Mozi's assertion about the Will of Heaven, we should interpret him as a Divine Command theorist instead. Ahern argues, from what Mozi says about the Will of Heaven, that we can see that Mozi would endorse the following biconditionals:

[A₁]   "x is a right action" if and only if "x is in accord with the Will of Heaven."
[A₂]   "x is a wrong action" if and only if "x is not in accord with the Will of Heaven."

If Mozi were to judge an act's rightness or wrongness by whether it is in accord with the Will of Heaven, then his ultimate moral principle concerns the Will of Heaven, not utility. Under this kind of moral theory, according to Ahern, one would be morally obligated to obey the Will of Heaven. Hence, Ahern concludes, Mozi was actually advocating a deontological Divine Command theory.

116

In rebuttal, Dirck Vorenkamp argues that Mozi tells us to obey the Will of Heaven not simply because it is Heaven's will, but because "in doing so we will benefit ourselves."[23] Furthermore, the moral rules commanded by Heaven are good "because they are conducive in all cases to both individual and social profit."[24] The justification of a moral rule comes not from its accordance with the Will of Heaven, but from its tendency to generate greater benefits for everyone involved in all individual cases. Therefore, Vorenkamp concludes, Mozi is not only a utilitarian, but also a rule-utilitarian.

The debated issue between the two camps of commentators is whether Mozi takes an action to be right primarily in virtue of the act's being beneficial to the world, or primarily in virtue of its agreement with the Will of Heaven. To settle this debate, let us examine Mozi's comments. The most direct support for the Divine Command interpretation is the following statement by Mozi: "Obedience to the will of Heaven is the standard of righteousness."[25] He seems to be making the following moral precept:

[M1] An act is morally right if and only if it is done in obedience to the Will of Heaven.

But such a moral precept is devoid of content, since we do not know what the Will of Heaven is. In specifying the Will of Heaven, Mozi first argued that Heaven desires righteousness and detests unrighteousness. He goes on to ask: "How do I know that Heaven desires righteousness and hates unrighteousness?" The reason is, according to Mozi:

In the world, where there is righteousness there is life; where there is no righteousness there is death. Where there is righteousness there is wealth; where there is no righteousness there is poverty. Where there is righteousness there is order; where there is no righteousness there is disorder. Now Heaven desires life and hates death, desires wealth and hates poverty, desires order and hates disorder. So I know that Heaven desires righteousness and hates unrighteousness.[26]

From this convoluted argumentation, we seem to find the following reasoning:

[M2] Heaven prefers life to death; order to chaos. Human righteousness would have the consequence of life and order; human unrighteousness would have the consequence of death and chaos. Hence, Heaven desires righteousness and detests unrighteousness.

In the next step of the argument, Mozi attempts to explain how he has derived the conclusion that Heaven desires life and order and hates death and chaos. According to him, we know that Heaven prefers life and order to death and chaos, because we know that Heaven "loves the world universally and seeks to bring mutual benefits to all creatures."[27] This remark clearly shows the following assumption:

[M3]   Heaven loves the world universally and seeks to bring mutual benefits to all creatures.

This thesis gives content to Heaven's will, since now Heaven is seen as a moral agent with volition and intention. Its volition is to love the world universally; its intention is to bring mutual benefits to all creatures. Therefore, the Will of Heaven seems to be simply to love universally and to benefit mutually. A further support for this interpretation comes from the following comment by Mozi. With the attack on the political policy based on partiality, Mozi says: "Examining such a policy, we find that it brought no benefit to Heaven above, to the spirits in the middle realm, or to man below. And because it failed to realize these three types of benefits, it was called an offense against Heaven."[28] We get the following thesis:

[M4]   Disobedience to the Will of Heaven = adopting a policy that brings no benefit to Heaven above, to the spirits in the middle realm, or to the man below.

By inference, we can get the following conclusion:

[M5]   To obey the Will of Heaven = to adopt a policy that brings mutual benefits to all creatures.

In conjunction with [M1], we seem to come back to the following conclusion:

[M6]   An act is morally right if and only if it conforms to the policy that brings mutual benefits to all creatures.

This statement is clearly a thesis of rule-utilitarianism.[29] Under this utilitarian spirit, Mozi argued that the *utility* of obeying the Will of Heaven is that the world will be greatly benefited. As he put it, "Therefore, if one clearly understands how to obey the will of Heaven and puts it into practice in the world at large, then the government will be well ordered, the population harmonious, the state rich, and wealth and goods plentiful."[30] We could perhaps interpret his motivation for advocating the Will of Heaven as an attempt to give his utilitarian theory a further justification. In other words, even his own Divine Command theory falls under his overall utilitarian scheme. We can thus conclude that Mozi is a utilitarian through and through.

Mozi's Political Philosophy: Pragmatic Authoritarianism

Like Confucius, Mozi upheld the system of political hierarchy, with the ruler (the Son of Heaven) at the top. To Mozi, a sound political order must have the ruler's authority revered by everyone below. It is a form of authoritarianism. But the governing principle of this authoritarian polity is not the ruler's dogmatic will or his own personal gain. It is rather the Will of Heaven, which, given to the ruler, would be to love the people universally and to benefit the people collectively.

Mozi's authoritarianism is more radical than other forms of authoritarian systems. He not only advocated strict obedience, but also emphasized a moral, behavioral, and even psychological conformity to one's superior. The common people conform to local officials; local officials conform to ministers and ministers conform to the ruler. But ultimately, Mozi placed Heaven at the apex of this *ideological* hierarchy. He says:

> Subordinates do not decide what is right for their superiors; it is the superiors who decide what is right for their subordinates. Therefore the common people devote their strength to carrying out their tasks, but they cannot decide for themselves what is right. There are [local officials] to do that for them. [Local officials] devote their strength to carrying out their tasks, but they cannot decide for themselves what is right. There are ministers and [state] officials to do that for them. The ministers and [state] officials devote their strength to carrying out their tasks, but they cannot decide for themselves what is right. There are the three high ministers and the feudal lords to do that for them. The three high ministers and the feudal lords devote their strength to managing the affairs of government, but they cannot decide for themselves what is right. There is the Son of Heaven to do that for them. But the Son of Heaven cannot decide what is right. There is Heaven to decide that for him.[31]

Why does Mozi want to eliminate differences in opinions or to establish uniformity of the mind? Again, his reason is that only when everyone is of the same mind and does the same thing, can the whole world get the most benefit. Mozi says:

> In ancient times, when mankind was first born and before there were any laws or government, it may be said that every man's view of things was different. One man had one view, two men had two views, ten men had ten views – the more men, the more views. Moreover, each man believed that his own views were correct and disapproved of those of others, so that people spent their time condemning one another. Within the family fathers and sons, older and younger brothers grew to hate each other and the family split up, unable to live in harmony, while throughout the world people all resorted to water, fire, and poison in an effort to do each other injury. Those with strength to spare refused to help out others, those with surplus wealth would let it rot before they would share it, and those with beneficial doctrines to teach would keep them secret and refuse to impart them. The world was as chaotic as though it were inhabited by birds and beasts alone.[32]

Let us formulate his argument as follows:

1 If each person has his or her own view on what is right, then the more people there are, the more views we get.
2 Each person naturally believes that his or her own view is correct and disapproves of those of others.
3 Therefore, when there are multiple views, there will be multiple disputes.
4 Verbal disputes arouse resentment in the heart.
5 Resentment in the heart reduces harmony in human relationships.
6 When people cannot live harmoniously with one another, what come afterwards are fights, battles, and, eventually, chaos in the world.
7 Therefore, variance in opinions is the root of the world's disorder.

In this argument, Mozi seems to demonstrate his utmost distrust of human rationality. He does not seem to believe that people could settle their differences of opinion through rational discourse. Instead of finding ways to educate the people to be more receptive to others' opinions, he advocates instead the elimination of different opinions. When all other voices are silenced, there has to be one opinion left: the opinion of the superior. In ancient Chinese political hierarchy, the most superior person is the ruler. A. C. Graham points out that the "egalitarian implications of 'Concern for Everyone' did not lead the Mohist in the direction of democracy; like the rest of the philosophers he assumes that government, if one has to have it at all, must be from above."[33] Graham speculates that the reason for the Mohist's not reaching this conclusion of democracy is that "the Mohist, like the Confucian, seeks audience with princes and hopes to be appointed to high office."[34] However, such an interpretation of Mozi's intent seems to assimilate him too much to the Legalist, which he clearly is not. The fundamental reason why Mozi did not come to own conviction in a democratic polity would be that he was highly skeptical of human rationality. Democracy is founded on the assumption that people are of equal rationality; hence, the majority represents a higher degree of rationality than the minority does. In Mozi's time, education was the privilege of the social elite; the majority of people were thus unenlightened. Furthermore, since Mozi believed that the intelligentsia and the common masses alike were self-interested, he would not think that their individual opinions could possibly be in keeping with the general welfare. In Mozi's political picture, the ruler has to be ultimately sanctioned by the Will of Heaven, which has only general welfare in mind. However, the claim that Heaven exists had little persuasiveness even in his time, not to mention in the times of later Mohists. Once this religious spirit is lost, nothing can stop the ruler from taking all decisions into his own hands. Therefore, Mohism, in addition to Legalism, could be used to support Chinese feudal author-itarianism even though Mohism is fundamentally a philosophy for the benefit of the people. Mozi's idea of subordinates' conforming to the superior can also be seen as an encouragement for later emperors' sup-pression of different opinions from below.

Mozi also promoted meritocracy – a sociopolitical system that gives promotion and status to people on the basis of their ability, talents, and virtues. One of the major theses in his political philosophy is "honoring the worthy." Mozi says: "If a government is rich in worthy men, then the administration will be characterized by weight and substance; but if it is poor in such men, then the administration will be a paltry affair."[35] By "the worthy," Mozi means the people with moral virtues, political competence, and genuine effort. He attacked a common mentality of rulers at the time: favoritism. If the rulers favor their own kin, with no regard to the individual's abilities and virtues, then the nation will surely be brought to disorder. What Mozi promoted instead was a form of meritocracy such that "ranks were assigned according to virtue, duties allotted according to the office held, and rewards given according to the effort expended; achievements were weighed and stipends distri-buted accordingly."[36] Under this meritocracy, "no official was necessarily assured of an exalted position for life, nor was any member of the common people necessarily condemned to remain forever humble. Those

121

with ability were promoted; those without it were demoted."[37] In this explanation of meritocracy, we again see his hidden assumption that even the virtuous and the able can be motivated by substantial rewards such as wealth and status. In other words, even those "worthy" people cannot fail to be self-interested.

Another important element in Mozi's political philosophy is his promotion of moderation in expenditures. Every policy or practice should be assessed on the basis of *utility*; i.e., its pragmatic value. Mozi says: "When the sage administers the government, in issuing orders, beginning enterprises, employing the people, or expending wealth, he does not do anything that is not in some way useful. Therefore wealth is not wasted, the strength of the people is not taxed, and yet many benefits are produced."[38] From the perspective of practical utility, Mozi launched his major attacks on Confucianism in terms of the importance of rituals and music.

What Confucius aimed to establish was a civilized society regulated by rituals, rites, and music. What Mozi tried to restore, in contrast, was a much more modest form of a materialistically self-sufficient society. Schwartz points out that in Mozi's times, "there is a much greater sense of urgency – one must almost say desperation – concerning the task of meeting the elemental needs of the people for food, shelter, clothing, security, and peace. Nothing less than a total and sustained concentration of all the energies of the society [is] required to attain this goal."[39] Perhaps it is rather because of this sense of urgency that Mozi launched his attacks on the social practices of elaborate funerals, the production and enjoyment of music or dance, along with his criticism of the manufacture of luxurious goods. He asks: "What is the purpose of making clothing? To keep out the cold in winter and the heat in summer. . . . What is merely decorative and does not contribute to these ends should be avoided."[40] If basic things such as food and clothing should be kept at the minimal level, then other things not crucial to survival must all be even more worthless.

Mozi thought that music may be entertaining, but it does not serve any pragmatic function in people's lives. He says:

> There are three things the people worry about: that when they are hungry they will have no food, when they are cold they will have no clothing, and when they are weary they will have no rest. These are the three great worries of the people. Now let us try sounding the great bells, striking the rolling drums, strumming the zithers, blowing the pipes, and waving the shields and axes in the war dance. Does this do anything to provide food and clothing for the people? I hardly think so.[41]

In Mozi's view, not only can music not provide food and shelter, but also its production and enjoyment are a waste of time, money, and energy. He says that to produce fine music, the rulers have to employ young men and women who are strong and agile. "If they employ young men, then they will be taking them away from their plowing and planting, and if they employ young women, they will be taking them away from their weaving and spinning."[42] Furthermore, for the rulers to enjoy the music, they must not like listening to it by themselves. However, "If they listen in the company of [government officials], then they will be keeping the [officials] from attending to affairs of state, while if they listen in the company of humble men, they will be keeping the humble men from pursuing their tasks."[43] All these activities keep the people away from the production of food and clothing. Therefore, Mozi concludes, "If the rulers, ministers, and [government officials] of the world truly desire to promote what is beneficial to the world and eliminate what is harmful, they must prohibit and put a stop to this thing called music."[44]

Mozi further criticized the Confucian insistence on propriety with respect to funerals. The Confucian teaching on funerals is that they represent the civility of human beings, which elevates us from mere beasts. A proper funeral procedure and the fixed duration of the mourning period enable us to express our sentiments toward the deceased in a socially acceptable manner. But Mozi thought that all these rituals and rules are a waste of social resources such as labor and money. He says:

> [W]e see that in elaborate funerals much wealth is buried, while lengthy mourning prevents people from going about their activities for long periods of time. If the wealth and goods that have already been produced are to be bundled up and buried in the ground, and the means of future production are to be prohibited for long periods of time, and one still hopes in this way to enrich the state, then it is like prohibiting planting and still hoping for a harvest. One could never acquire wealth that way.[45]

If one prepares fine clothing and a quality coffin for the dead, then it is just like burying money underground with no chance of recovery. If one mourns for three months for a relative, or three years for one's parents, then one would be unproductive for that length of time. Therefore, he argues, "If one follows the rules of those who advocate elaborate funerals and lengthy mourning and applies them in government, then the state will become poor, the people few, and the government disordered."[46]

Herrlee Creel says, "[Mozi] conceived of a world at peace, in which a large and orderly population was adequately clothed and fed, as enjoying the best possible state of affairs."[47] But is this state "the best possible state of affairs"? From our contemporary perspective, even after reviewing all the miserable human conditions in history, many still would not embrace such a modest aim. Even in a state of extreme poverty, people still yearn for the pleasure of cultural activities. Even when one does not have the means for a proper burial for one's parents, one would still want to do whatever one could to have the best funeral. These are humans' natural sentiments; they are not merely the teachings of Confucianism. Confucianism merely acknowledges these natural sentiments and institutes socially acceptable means of expression. Mohism, on the other hand, would be denying that ordinary people have any cultural yearnings. At the same time, however, one could also see the persuasion of Mohism. Affluent people do tend to pay too much attention to frivolous details of ceremonies or indulge in extravaganza. Considering how many people are starving or barely surviving, one cannot help sharing Mozi's indignant sentiment toward people's wastefulness. The value of high cultural activities and conventional rites becomes problematic from a purely pragmatic point of view.

A final proposal that Mozi made, not necessarily against Confucianism, was the renunciation of offensive warfare. Again, he took this stand from the point of view of common welfare. He was not a pacifist, however, since he dealt with many defensive tactics in his book, which contains chapters on the fortification of city gates and strategies to employ against an enemy that builds scaling ladders, digs tunnels, causes floods, etc. Mozi would not endorse offensive warfare for the sake of power expansion or territory enlargement. Even if a successful war could in the end bring more profit to the people of the offensive nation, it would never bring *universal* benefit, which is the ultimate justification for all actions.

From the above discussion, we can see that for Mozi, all political considerations were based on utilitarian considerations. His teachings on the authoritarian form of government, the unification of opinions, the prohibition of music, thrift in funerals, moderation of expenditure, the employment of worthy people, and his condemnation of offensive warfare are all theoretical expedients to his goal of benefiting the world.

Philosophy of Religion: Heaven, Ghosts and Spirits, Fate

Mozi seemed to be the most religious among ancient philosophers, but his religious spirit was again prompted by his pragmatism. He argued for the existence of ghosts and spirits and advocated reverence for the Will of Heaven, not because he was superstitious, but because he thought that these beliefs would help promote universal benefit. By the same token, he argued against the existence of fate and the belief that our life is determined by pre-existing destiny, not because he was rational, but because he thought that such beliefs would be detrimental to social welfare.

Mozi listed three criteria for testing whether a theory is acceptable: (1) the origin of the hypothesis; (2) the validity of the hypothesis; (3) the pragmatic results of applying the theory. He says:

> We must set up a standard of judgment. . . . Therefore a theory must be judged by three tests. What are these three tests of a theory? Its origin, its validity, and its applicability. How do we judge its origin? We judge it by comparing the theory with the deeds of the sage kings of antiquity. How do we judge its validity? We judge it by comparing the theory with the evidence of the eyes and ears of the people. And how do we judge its applicability? We judge it by observing whether, when the theory is put into practice in the administration, it brings benefit to the state and the people. This is what is meant by the three tests of a theory.[48]

In other words, the first test of a theory is against historical records. Mozi believed, as did many ancient Chinese thinkers,[49] that the ancient historical records (such as the *Book of Odes* and the *Book of History*) are indisputable records of the thoughts and deeds of ancient sage kings; furthermore, he believed that these ancient sage kings set the standard for truth. Secondly, the test for a theory involves others' testimony. What would count as reliable testimony are people's actual observations and personal experiences. However, Mozi does not suggest any statistical reliability of others' testimony. It seems that as long as a sufficient number of people have reported positively a certain experience, then the negative testimony could be discounted. Thirdly, and most interestingly, Mozi advocated that we judge whether a theory is acceptable by checking to see how pragmatic it would be for us to believe in the theory – how much utility is generated by its acceptance, or its rejection. What is implicit in this view seems to be what we nowadays call a *pragmatic theory of truth*, which is the theory that a belief is true when it is useful to the believer – the believer's acting upon it would yield satisfactory practical results. Under Mozi's pragmatic theory of truth, many philosophical debates would be settled, not on the soundness of the argument or the completeness of the theory, but on each theory's applicability and its practical consequences.

Using these criteria, Mozi argued that ghosts and spirits do exist, that Heaven has its own will, and there is no fate that determines our present or our future. Mozi's view of Heaven seems to follow directly from the ancient religious view, which was downplayed in Confucianism. Many commentators take Mozi to be holding a belief in the existence of a Supreme Being. Burton Watson, for example, says that in Mozi's hierarchical worldview, "heading the hierarchy of the supernatural world he envisions a deity called God, the Lord on High, or Heaven, who creates all beings, loves all beings, and desires their welfare, working toward that end through the earthly representatives of the deity, the Son of Heaven and his officers."[50] If Mozi himself were truly convinced of the existence of such a God, then his view would be quite retrogressive. But Mozi's third test of the validity of theories shows that his motivation for adopting any theory is fundamentally *pragmatic*. He did not have any personal conviction in the existence of Heaven/God or its Divine Will. In his arguments, he often appealed to the benefits of believing in the existence of Heaven and Heaven's will. If the rulers believed that there were Heaven and that Heaven's will were to "promote what is beneficial to the world," then they would not bring harm to the people; if the people truly believed that there were Heaven and "Heaven desires righteousness and hates unrighteousness," then they would not do anything bad.[51] Mozi thus concludes: isn't this a *beneficial* doctrine?

In the same fashion, Mozi tried to convince others that ghosts and spirits supervise our conduct, assigning rewards or punishments accordingly. He says, "If we could only make all the people in the world believe that the ghosts and spirits have the power to reward the worthy and punish the wicked, then how could there be any disorder in the world?"[52] As Vorenkamp explains, for Mozi "the 'belief' in Heaven and ghosts is more important than their actual ontological status."[53] In other words, what Mozi wanted to establish in his philosophy was not the *existence* of ghosts and spirits, but the *utility of the belief in the existence* of ghosts and spirits. Graham thinks that in the Mohist philosophy of religion, "there is little evidence of a spiritual dimension deeper than a guilty fear of ghosts." Hence, "the Mohists are in a sense *less* religious than some they would denounce as skeptics."[54] If we see that Mozi was using Heaven as the ultimate sanction for the rulers' behavior, and ghosts and spirits as the general overseer of the common people's conduct, then we can understand why he was such a calm, detached exponent for the existence of these supernatural beings.

Finally, Mozi rejected fatalism, because it is a belief that gives people excuses for doing nothing. He says:

[I]f we were to accept the theories of the fatalists, then those above would not attend to affairs of state and those below would not pursue their tasks. If those above do not attend to affairs of state, then the government will fall into disorder, while if those below do not pursue their tasks, there will not be enough wealth and goods. There will be no way to provide millet and wine for offerings to the Lord on High and the spirits above, and no way to provide security for the worthy and able men of the world below. There will be no means to entertain and conduct exchanges with the feudal lords who come as guests from abroad, while within the state there will be no means to feed the hungry, clothe the cold, and care for the aged and weak.[55]

From these observations, Mozi concluded: "Hence fatalism brings no benefit to Heaven above, no benefit to the spirits in the middle realm, and no benefit to mankind below. Those who insist upon holding such views are the source of pernicious doctrines, and theirs is the way of evil men."[56] Mozi's criticism of fatalism does not point to the proponent's weakness in reasoning or the paucity of evidence; it points specifically to the bad consequences such a theory will bring. We should not believe that we are determined by our fate, Mozi tells us, because *this belief* does not promote universal benefits for the world. This condemnation of fatalism is clearly an application of his test for the validity of a theory.

We can see that Mozi's philosophy of religion, though superficially affirming the existence of Heaven, ghosts, and spirits, is not really a genuine philosophy of religion. The only philosophical convictions that Mozi had were probably his ethical utilitarianism and his pragmatic conception of truth. The pragmatic conception of truth is simply assumed in his criteria for the test of theories; it is never articulated, let alone defended. It is also interesting to note that even though Mozi's fundamental doctrine is based on a belief in mutual benefits, throughout his entire book there is not a single chapter devoted to the argument for the importance of mutual benefits. This utilitarian moral principle can be seen as his "First Principle." It alone has all the justification within itself. All other theses that Mozi promoted were done so as a means to this end.

Conclusion

While Mozi and his followers were driven by an altruistic concern for the welfare of all people, their extreme pragmatism led them not only to embrace an ascetic lifestyle for themselves, but also to promote an ascetic society. It denies human pleasures; it scorns self-indulgence in the refined and the beautiful, along with the vain and the frivolous. Such asceticism may be necessary for a world greatly deficient in guaranteeing material sustenance; it would not have a lasting appeal to people whose concern was no longer just about survival. This could explain the historical curiosity that even though Mohism was one of the dominant theories in the Warring States period,[57] it soon faded away completely in China after the early Han Dynasty.[58]

Primarily because of its anti-Confucian tenets, Mohism has been seen as a deviant school of thought in the history of Chinese philosophy. It stands out as a unique theory, but it had very little impact on future Chinese philosophers. We should not dismiss Mohism, however, simply because it was not appreciated by the Chinese mind. We should first appreciate its multifaceted coverage. As Alice Lum puts it, "In addition to being called an anti-Confucianist, a utilitarian and a logician, [Mozi] has been identified as being a precursor of the Legalist School, an organizer of China's first religious sect and an advocator for a social welfare state."[59] We should further reflect on its doctrines, and use the theory as a challenge to our received modes of thinking.

Contemporary students of Asian philosophy often find Mohism attractive because it represents a utopia. If all humans could love one another, then there would be no war, no fighting, no quarrels, and no killing. If all humans could forget about the distinction between the self and the others, then there would be no need for possession and no one would starve while others have food. If all humans could treat others as they would treat themselves, then there would be no greed or jealousy and all would be mutually benefited. If all humans could eliminate division, then there would be no strife among countries and no antagonism among races. In short, if the Mohist ideal ever comes true, then the world will be, as John Lennon sings, "as one."

Mozi's utopia is only possible when we can drastically alter human conduct. To accomplish such a total behavioral reform, we have first to change humans' habitual modes of thinking. Such a goal, improbable as it is, is nonetheless not impossible:

> Once an absolute and objective norm of morality was established, [Mozi] states that the condition of society would begin to improve as the people of that society could be taught to use their conscience rightly for the common good of all. With this norm of morality as the basis of his philosophy, [Mozi] proclaimed that all evils such as poverty, war, hunger and political chaos could be eliminated by the conscious working effort of

the people themselves. The Motian 'Work Ethics' could be read as total human production for the benefit of an ongoing working society. In supporting this claim, [Mozi] believed that his teachings were *practicably* capable for attaining the total wellbeing of humanity.[60]

The final judgment on Mohism, therefore, is perhaps its own pragmatic standard: Will it, should it prevail, bring more benefits to the people of the world?

Further discussion questions

1 Are we morally justified in being partial to our loved ones? Are we being selfish in this way? Considering that this kind of partiality is the root of human conflicts (even wars), should moral teachers try to promote universal love?
2 Shouldn't we just love others as members of humankind and love them equally? Does Mozi's theory rest on a higher moral plane than Confucianism?
3 Is it true that the lack of universal love is the reason why the strong overcome the weak, the many oppress the few and the rich insult the poor? Will the promotion of universal love eliminate these harms?
4 How is Mozi's doctrine of universal love different in essence from Confucius' doctrine of the Golden Rule ("Don't do unto others what you would not have them do unto you"), or Mencius' doctrine of "respect others' elders as I would respect mine; love others' youngsters as I would love mine"?
5 Between Confucius' promotion of rituals and music, and Mozi's emphasis on social utility, which one can lead to a better human society? What do you think is the social utility of rituals or music?

Primary texts

Wing-tsit Chan (ed.) *A Sourcebook in Chinese Philosophy*. Princeton: Princeton University Press, 4th edn., 1973 (ch. 9; excerpts).
Philip J. Ivanhoe and Bryan W. Van Norden (eds.) *Readings in Classical Chinese Philosophy*. Indianapolis, IN: Hackett Publishing Company, Inc. 2003 (ch. 2; excerpts).
Burton Watson. *Mo Tzu: Basic Writings*. New York: Columbia University Press, 1963.

Further readings

Dennis M. Ahern. "Is Mo Tzu A Utilitarian?" *Journal of Chinese Philosophy* 3, 1976: 185–93.

Whalen Lai. "The Public Good that Does the Public Good: A New Reading of Mohism." *Asian Philosophy* 3(2), 1993: 125–41.

Dirck Vorenkamp. "Strong Utilitarianism in Mo Tzu's Thought." *Journal of Chinese Philosophy* 19(4), 1992: 423–43.

David Wong. "Universalism versus Love with Distinctions: An Ancient Debate Revived." *Journal of Chinese Philosophy* 16, 1989: 251–72.

Chapter 6

Laozi (Lao Tzu)

Introduction

The interpretation of Laozi's *Daodejing* (*Tao-Te Ching*) is notoriously difficult. To begin with, there may never have been a person named Laozi; secondly, the book was most likely *not* entitled *Daodejing* by its original author. Furthermore, it may not even have been a monograph written by one person. The historical placement of the book is also controversial. The traditional view held that it was written by someone named Lao Dan, who was senior to Confucius (in the sixth century BCE), and that it was written on his exit to the West in response to the request of the gatekeeper. Another popular traditional view placed the work in the fourth or third century BCE, as written by someone named Li Er, who used the name Laozi (meaning "Master Lao" or "the Old Master") to hide his own identity. A more accepted view among contemporary commentators is that this book was a compilation of various sayings of different people, and the present version was completed around the first century AD.

Naturally, the historical placement of the text and the attribution of authorship would affect the interpretation of the text itself, especially since the text contains many apparent inconsistencies both in style and in content. D. C. Lau, for example, argues that "not only is the [*Daodejing*] an anthology but even individual chapters are usually made up of shorter passages whose connexion with one another is at best tenuous."[1] He thus recommends that we deal with shorter sections, rather than the whole chapters, in an attempt to understand the content expressed. Even though Lau acknowledges that there is a general tendency of thought expressed in the *Daodejing*, he does not think that we can expect to find a closely-knit system of thought. Chad Hansen, on the other hand, argues that the *Daodejing* "does have consistent *tone* and develops genuinely Daoist themes."[2] When commentators see the work as largely incoherent, they underscore differences in messages with regard to the nature of *Dao* and the political strategies of rulership. When commentators see the work as largely coherent, on the other hand, they try to explain away the apparent inconsistencies. We therefore get a wide array of translations and interpretations of the *Daodejing*.

There are well over 70 English translations of the *Daodejing* and more than several hundred textual commentaries. Even though commentators disagree widely over the interpretation of the text, they unanimously agree upon its difficulty as well as its philosophical importance.[3] Some of the difficulties in interpretation result from the rhymed style of writing and the lack of punctuation in ancient Chinese texts. With some crucial passages, where to break up the sentence constitutes a major difference in the philosophical import. A prominent example is the very first chapter of *Daodejing*. Diverging commentaries all seem compatible with the original text; thus, we sometimes get contrary interpretations both of which are plausible.

In this chapter, we shall explore the content of *Daodejing* as coherently as possible, without assuming that there is a single author. Following common practice, we shall simply call the collective authorship "Laozi." We will focus on three main philosophical claims that Laozi makes: (1) the nature of *Dao* and the possibility of knowing and representing *Dao*; (2) the ethical advice on virtues, in particular, the virtue of inactivity (*wu-wei*); and (3) the political ideal and the best way to run a government. We shall investigate connections between Laozi's metaphysical view and his practical view on ethics and politics, to show that the latter is actually a natural derivation of the former.

Dao and Language

The most intriguing notion in Laozi's philosophy is that of *Dao* (*Tao*). This notion originally refers to the ultimately correct way of Heaven and of the human world, but it takes on a rich metaphysical meaning in the context of *Daodejing*.[4] It is no wonder that Laozi's *Daodejing* is taken to be the origin of the philosophical school *Daoism*. Presently it is customary to use the phonetic rendition, "*Dao*," of the original Chinese word as used by Laozi to show how difficult it is to find an English counterpart to this notion, even though "the Way" is still a widely used translation for the same word used in discourses on Confucianism.[5] The original Chinese word "*dao*" has multiple meanings. Creel summarizes it well:

Originally meaning "road," it came to mean "way" in general and "method." It was also used to mean "to point out the road," and thus "to tell." And it came to have the sense of "course of conduct," and "principles" in a moral sense, and was used by various philosophers to designate their doctrines.[6]

As we see in this explanation, "*dao*" can be used both as a noun and as a verb. As a noun, it designates either the ultimate and unique metaphysical entity, hence the capitalized "*Dao*", or some general moral principles and doctrines. As a verb, it means either "to follow," which is manifested in one's behavior, or "to tell," which involves the use of language. A daunting task presented to us is that in Laozi's usage, "*dao*" seems to include all the above connotations. We need to look at each particular context to decipher which sense of "*dao*" is being used.

In the opening chapter of *Daodejing*, Laozi says: "A [*Dao*] that can be followed [or: be told of] is not a constant [*Dao*]. A name that can be named is not a constant name.[7] Nameless, it is the beginning of Heaven and Earth; named, it is the mother of the myriad creatures."[8] This remark pinpoints a major concern of Laozi: the relation between *Dao* and language. As mentioned earlier, there are multiple layers of connotations in Laozi's usage of "*Dao*" as a noun. One undeniable layer is his use of "the *Dao*" as denoting the ultimate Reality, or the-reality-as-it-is. This ultimate Reality is *nameless*; in other words, it cannot be depicted by human language. In this sense, *Dao* is "ineffable." As a nameless, ineffable presence, *Dao* is the beginning of Heaven and Earth, which represent the framework of the whole natural world. The introduction of names brings with it the taxonomy of objects. Therefore, it is the mother of myriad creatures. This opening passage of *Daodejing* tells us that *the world as we know it* is thus the result of the combined contribution of the-reality-as-it-is and our human conception manifested in human language.

However, this simple comment contains some of the most difficult metaphysical questions. How does *Dao* generate the universe? Does *Dao* generate the universe temporally, thus serving as the cosmologically primordial source of the world, or does it generate the universe logically, thus serving as the ontological foundation of the world? What is the present relation between *Dao* and the world? Is *Dao* simply the totality of the world, as some commentators argue, or is it an ontologically prior state of the world, as some others claim? Why is *Dao* ineffable? If *Dao* resists any linguistic depiction, how can we ever talk about it? If it is indeed ineffable, is it also cognitively closed to us? Can we ever know what *Dao* is? It is particularly in the attempts to

133

answer these questions that we find a vast array of opinions among commentators.

With respect to the relation between *Dao* and the world, some commentators argue that *Dao* is simply the totality of the world, and thus it is neither prior to, nor independent of, the world as a whole.[9] Some other commentators argue that Laozi clearly assigned a self-subsisting status to *Dao* itself, and that *Dao* is often depicted by Laozi as "the Non-being," which is prior to, and responsible for, the production of the "Being."[10] Among the latter camp, some commentators explain the generative relation between *Dao* and the world as a temporal sequence, such that the world came from Non-being initially.[11] Some others, on the other hand, argue that the generative relation is merely a figurative way of stating the logical priority of *Dao*, since the world has always been and there never was a state of Non-being.[12]

With respect to the relation between *Dao* and language, some commentators point out that *Dao* is fundamentally ineffable for Laozi; that there is no possible way for us to talk about what *Dao* is.[13] If *Dao* is indeed ineffable, then Laozi's whole project of depicting *Dao* in his book is self-defeating. Thus, Laozi's philosophy could be viewed as being paradoxical. Some other commentators argue against this interpretation, and claim that all the passages in which Laozi seems to be making the ineffability assertion could be given a different reading and different interpretation.[14] We may never be able fully to comprehend the intent of the author, or judge the merit of various commentaries. But we can try to do a careful textual analysis to see which view is most supported by what Laozi says.

In Laozi's depictions, we can see different explanations given to the nature of *Dao*, as well as the role *Dao* plays in the origination of the universe. The characteristics of *Dao* are listed as follows (and we shall notice that they do not all cohere):

(1)   *Dao* is Non-being.
Laozi says: "All things in the world came from being. And being comes from non-being."[15] "Being" refers to existence per se, while "things in the world" refers to individual beings with definite shapes and forms. Laozi here makes a clear temporal or logical progression from (1) Non-being, to (2) Being, to (3) things in the world (beings). *Dao*, as the ultimate source of Being per se or beings in general, seems to be identified with pure Non-being. However, Laozi also remarks, "Therefore let there always be non-being so we may see their subtlety, and let there always be being so we may see their outcome.[16] The two are the same, but after they are produced, they have different names. They both can

be called deep and profound."[17] From this passage, we seem to see an equivocation between Being and Non-being, in that the two are taken to be two sides of the same coin. It seems that Non-being and Being are ever-present in the universe, and that they only receive different names *after* they are produced. It is unclear what Laozi takes Non-being to be, but it is at least obvious that in one aspect, *Dao* can be identified with Non-being.

(2) *Dao* is empty and yet its function is inexhaustible.
Laozi says: "[*Dao*] is empty, yet use will not drain it. Deep, it is like the ancestor of the myriad creatures."[18] He also says: "Is not the space between heaven and earth like a bellows? It is empty without being exhausted: The more it works the more comes out."[19] Here a plausible explanation is that Laozi considers *Dao* to be the substance of all things. The production of myriad things is the function of *Dao*. The myriad creatures come into and out of existence; the substance never gets exhausted. The more the substance produces, the more things there are. Since substance itself does not get fixed onto any particular thing, it is empty in nature. If this interpretation is correct, then Laozi is also assigning an ontological status to *Dao*, as the foundation of all things.

(3) *Dao* is constant or eternal.
Laozi says: "Soundless and formless, it depends on nothing and does not change."[20] The constancy of *Dao* is depicted as a non-changing nature. Laozi also says: "To return to destiny is called the eternal [*Dao*]. To know the eternal is called enlightenment."[21] Here *Dao* is described as "eternal." According to Laozi, *Dao* encompasses all things; hence it has no limitations. *Dao* is eternal, in that the totality of all things never terminates even though particular things do. Particular existence does not have constancy, because each existence is confined in time. Laozi says that the *Dao* that can be spoken of is not the constant *Dao*. Once we describe *Dao* in any particular terms, it becomes restricted, confined, and narrowed down to that particular description. Once there is a set limit, we don't have the complete *Dao* in view. From these comments we see that the eternity and constancy of *Dao* come from *Dao*'s all-inclusive nature.

(4) *Dao* exists prior to the whole universe, including Heaven and Earth.
Laozi says: "There was something undifferentiated and yet complete, which existed before heaven and earth. . . . It may be considered the mother of the universe."[22] He also says: "The world had a beginning,

135

and this beginning could be the mother of the world."²³ Both quotes seem to support the interpretation that Laozi is talking about the temporal ordering, rather than *mere* ontological or logical order, between *Dao* and the world. *Dao* is here depicted as "the mother of the universe." As we shall see in the characterization in (11), Laozi attributed a feminine feature to *Dao*. In this respect his understanding of *Dao* was different from the Confucian notion of *Dao*, which is usually taken to be a symbolic paternal presence. Both schools, however, take *Dao* to be the generative and regulating principle of the universe.

(5)   *Dao* generates the world.
Laozi says: "Therefore [*Dao*] produces [the myriad things] and [Virtue] (*de*) fosters them. They rear them and develop them. They give them security and give them peace. They nurture them and protect them. [*Dao*] produces them but does not take possession of them."²⁴ He also says: "[*Dao*] produced the One and the One produced the two. The two produced the three. And the three produced the ten thousand things."²⁵ "The myriad creatures in the world are born from Something, and Something from Nothing."²⁶ "It is [*Dao*] alone that excels in bestowing and in accomplishing."²⁷ In all these quotes, Laozi is talking about *Dao*'s generation or production of myriad things. There is a clear cosmogenesis sense in his notion of *Dao*.

(6)   *Dao* is one and undifferentiated.
Laozi says: "Heaven obtained the One and became clear. Earth obtained the One and became tranquil. The spiritual beings obtained the One and became divine. The valley obtained the One and became full. The myriad things obtained the One and lived and grew. Kings and barons obtained the One and became rulers of the empire. What made them so is the One."²⁸ What he calls "the One" here is clearly *Dao* itself. He also says: "There was something undifferentiated and yet complete, which existed before heaven and earth."²⁹ Since *Dao* is One and undifferentiated, it cannot be carved up by human conception. This One *Dao* existed before the beginning of the universe, and all things need to obtain it to derive their own attributes.

(7)   *Dao* is not perceivable by the senses.
Laozi says: "We look at it and do not see it; its name is The Invisible. We listen to it and do not hear it; its name is The Inaudible. We touch it and do not find it; its name is The Subtle (formless). . . . This is called shape without shape, form without object."³⁰ He also says: "We look at

[*Dao*]; it is imperceptible. We listen to it; it is inaudible. We use it; it is inexhaustible."[31] Here Laozi seems to be emphasizing the inadequacy of our senses as the means to getting acquainted with *Dao*. If *Dao* is imperceptible, then it does not have any observable physical attributes. Furthermore, since we cannot hear *Dao*, there will be no verbal "mandate" or "commandment" from *Dao*. *Dao* does not intervene in human affairs, and its presence can only be felt, but not observed.

(8)   *Dao* is ineffable.

Laozi frequently stressed the difficulty in describing *Dao*. To the extent that all descriptions rely on language, *Dao* is ineffable. All possible descriptions can at best be approximation to the true nature of *Dao*. The descriptions Laozi ended up giving are all very mysterious and vague. For example, he says: "As a thing [*Dao*] is shadowy, indistinct. Indistinct and shadowy, yet within it is a substance. Dim and dark, yet within it is an essence."[32] The reason why *Dao* is difficult to describe is that it cannot fit into our conceptual scheme. Human concept is formed on the basis of detecting similarities and differences among categories of things. But *Dao* transcends all divisions. Hence, it cannot be captured by concepts. Combining (7) and (8), we now see the necessary limitation of human knowledge when it comes to *Dao*. Not only is *Dao* imperceptible to our senses, it is also unknowable by our limited cognition. We can even say that *Dao* is ineffable exactly because it is *cognitively closed* to us.

(9)   *Dao* is nameless.

Because of the imperceptible, undifferentiated, and indescribable nature of *Dao*, we cannot even give it a name. Laozi says: "[*Dao*] is forever nameless. . . . Only when it is cut are there names. As soon as there are names, one ought to know that it is time to stop."[33] In this passage, Laozi presents the impossibility of using our linguistic conventions and our conceptual schemes to depict *Dao*. Names are given to myriad things so that we can mark them apart. The very act of naming is an act of marking boundaries; that is why it is unsuitable for the great *Dao*. Here we see the fundamental dilemma for Laozi: he is talking about something which he calls "*Dao*" and yet this something actually cannot be named "*Dao*" since it simply cannot be named at all. Laozi explains his own dilemma this way: "I do not know its proper name; I have styled it '[*Dao*].' Forced to give it a proper name, I would call it 'Great'."[34] In other words, Laozi's whole project is to give us a full discourse on something which has no name and which he reluctantly calls "*Dao*."

(10) *Dao* models itself after Nature.

Laozi says: "Man models himself after Earth. Earth models itself after Heaven. Heaven models itself after [*Dao*]. And [*Dao*] models itself after Nature."³⁵ What Laozi has called "Nature"³⁶ here cannot be the totality of the natural world as we know it, since this view could contradict his cosmogenesis interpretation of the world from *Dao* itself.³⁷ By Qingjie Wang's interpretation, what Laozi meant by "Nature" was simply "the natural way of everything becoming his/her/itself, i.e., a natural process of self-becoming, self-growing or 'self-so-ing'."³⁸ Lau apparently used the same interpretation when he translated this sentence as "Man models himself on earth, earth on heaven, heaven on [*Dao*], and [*Dao*] on that which is naturally so."³⁹ Yu-lan Fung uses "spontaneity" or "naturalness" to analyze "Nature." He says: "[*Dao*] is not something transcending the world. It is in the world. It is everywhere. It is the whole. The whole of what? The whole of the spontaneity or naturalness of the world."⁴⁰ All these views agree in not taking "Nature" to be a separate entity from *Dao* itself.

It is not exactly clear what Laozi might have meant by the use of "models after" (*fa*). If it means "to take as an example" or "to follow," then the ultimate guidance of human conduct is actually naturalness or spontaneity. Furthermore, the *dao* of Heaven, of Earth, and of Humans are actually one and the same. "*Dao*" in this context seems to be a moral principle, rather than a metaphysical principle. As we will see in the next section, there is a close connection between Laozi's view on *Dao*'s naturalness and Laozi's moral advice on inactivity ("*wu-wei*").

(11) The *Dao* (of Heaven) is the female principle, which represents the
      soft, the passive, the infant, and other similar attributes.

Laozi says: "The gateway of the mysterious female is called the root of heaven and earth."⁴¹ In this depiction, he is giving *Dao* a more specific nature: that of the female principle emphasized in *Yijing* (the *Book of Changes*). Based on this depiction, Kaltenmark argues that Laozi's *Dao* is "an essentially feminine entity."⁴² Laozi gives a self-description in this way: "I alone differ from others, and value drawing sustenance from Mother ([*Dao*])."⁴³ It seems that for Laozi, the fundamental function of *Dao* is to generate life and provide sustenance. This gender-specific anthropomorphic depiction of *Dao* could be derived from the function of the female womb in the process of life production. *Dao* is identified with the maternal force that is responsible for the nourishment and sustenance of life. The description of *Dao* as empty and yet being the source of myriad creatures seems to be a metaphoric association with the female womb.⁴⁴ All the moralistic attributes of *Dao* in relation to human virtue (*"De"*) are also derived from Laozi's (as well as the traditional Chinese) ascription of feminine virtues such as being submissive, passive, yielding, and conforming.

Let us summarize Laozi's view of *Dao* from the above quotations. Laozi appears to have used *"dao"* in several ways, one of which seems to assert a *transcendent* status to *Dao* itself in the sense that *Dao* exceeds the limits of experiences. Under this sense of *"dao,"* there seems to be a *Dao* at the beginning of, if not prior to, the whole universe. We can speculate that in Laozi's view, the experiential world, the world in which we reside, has not always existed. At the beginning there was *Dao,* which generates Being and produces myriad things. *Dao* in this sense seems to be identified with the source of the world. Since it exists prior to our existence, it is beyond our experiential world. Hence, it is transcendent.

In another sense of Laozi's usage of *"dao,"* *Dao* is *immanent* in the world, and it is simply *the way the world naturally is.* We can also view it as the natural pattern of everything in the world. Under this sense, *Dao* does not disappear after the whole universe has come into being; it is the totality of myriad creatures and their natural functions. It can still serve as the generative principle of myriad creatures, since individual things come into and out of existence while new things are constantly being created. Each new creation must take after its previous model, which is part of the whole pattern represented by *Dao.* The generative principle from Non-being to Being *for each individual creature* can also be viewed as *Dao* itself. Therefore, *Dao*'s function never ceases. Individual creatures all eventually perish; *Dao* never dies. In this re-spect, we can see why Laozi says that *Dao* is eternal and inexhaustible.

The transcendent sense and the immanent sense of *Dao* do not necessarily conflict, and thus we don't have to get involved in the debate among commentators on the question: what was it that Laozi truly meant by *"Dao"*? Laozi clearly described *Dao* as the totality of the world, but he also talked about *Dao*'s generation of the world. The transcendent and the immanent *Dao* could just be the two aspects, or the two temporal stages, of *Dao* itself. Ancient Chinese philosophers all seem to embrace the view that the world has always been in existence. Laozi may have been the first Chinese philosopher to speculate on whether the universe had a beginning, whether "something" could come from "nothing." His theory posits Non-being as the source from which Being (existence) is derived, but it appears that Laozi does not view Non-being as nothingness. The notion *"wu,"* which we translate as "non-being" here, is often used by Laozi as a form of negation. For example, "*wu-wei*" means "non-action," "*wu-ming*" means "without names." If "non-being" is taken in the same way, then it is the negation of "being," the absence of existence. It stands for "what is not there." It is not in itself an independent state. Laozi thinks that "what is there" and "what is not there" complement each other. He says:

> Thirty spokes are joined in the hub of a wheel. But only by relying on what is not there, do we have the use of the carriage. By adding and removing clay we form a vessel. But only by relying on what is not there, do we have use of the vessel. By carving out doors and windows we make a room. But only by relying on what is not there, do we have use of the room.[45]

If there is no "*wu*" in a vessel, then it is not even a vessel since it cannot contain anything inside. If there is no "*wu*" in a room, then it is not a room even if all the windows and walls are there. From this we can understand how the "*wu*" (non-being; what is not there) can generate the existence of all things. We can also see how being and non-being are independent of, and complementary to, each other. Non-being generates Being, but it is also immanent in Being.

As for the relation between *Dao* and language, we can say that *Dao* is nameless because it exists prior to the introduction of human conception and human languages. Once our language introduces names to differentiate objects, the myriad creatures are "created." In this analysis, the relation between "the Something that is dim and indistinct" and "the myriad creatures that are all named" is simply that between the world without names/distinctions and the world with names/distinctions. Or we can say, it is a relation between the pre-language world and the post-language world. In an abstract sense then, we humans "produce" myriad things by naming them. *Dao*, on the other hand, had already produced myriad things without naming them. If there is such a pre-language world, to which Laozi assigns the title "*Dao*," then this world is not constructed out of our conceptual schemes. In other words, Laozi did not entertain the possibility that it is *we* who created or constructed *Dao*. *Dao* is the way things "naturally are." We can only copy from it through our observation of the operations of heaven and earth. *The way the world naturally is* exists prior to our own existence and is the source of our conception. Even if there were no humans, no languages, no concepts, there would still be *the way the world naturally is*.

There is, however, a third level of connotation of Laozi's usage of "*Dao*," which is manifested in (10) and (11) above. Under this sense, *Dao* takes on a moral dimension to represent the correct way of human conduct. In this context, Laozi most often used "the Way (*Dao*) of Heaven" rather than just "*Dao*" itself. *Dao* in this sense is the source or the ultimate guideline for human morals. This is where his metaphysics and his ethics meet. We shall engage the discussion of this notion of *Dao* and its connection to *De* (virtue) in the next section.

In some respects, Laozi's metaphysical view can be compared to contemporary metaphysical realism.[46] Metaphysical realism (MR) basically includes the following theses:[47]

[MR1]   The world consists of a mind-independent reality. This reality is external to our conception and our conceptual schemes.

[MR2]   Truth involves some sort of correspondence relationship between thought and the way the world is.

[MR3]   There is exactly one *true* and complete description of the way the world is (though we may never have a language capable of expressing it or may never know it.)[48]

Laozi's view on the nameless *Dao*, the ultimate Non-being or the preconceptual Being itself, is close to [MR1]. In Laozi's metaphysics, there is clearly a reality beyond human conception and linguistic conventions. This reality, which he names "*dao*," is surely "mind-independent." Secondly, Laozi would not reject [MR2] either. He does think that when our thought corresponds to *Dao*, then our thought is considered *true*. However, his notions of truth and correspondence are different from those of metaphysical realists. Metaphysical realists commonly employ a propositional or sentential treatment of knowledge, and a statement is true if and only if it corresponds to states of affairs in the world. But for Laozi, truth is not propositional, and thus the correspondence he seeks is not a relation between our *statements* and *Dao* itself.[49] It is rather a relation between our understanding, as well as our conduct, and *Dao*. We can never expect to give an accurate description of *Dao* by using our concepts and our language, but we can hope to give an approximation to the way the world really is *by thinking and acting properly*.

This approximation of truth is how Laozi viewed his own theory. To Laozi, there is only one true description of the way the world is. All the descriptions Laozi gives to *Dao*, however inadequate they may be, are nonetheless regarded as the only true description of *Dao*. He says:

> My words are very easy to understand and very easy to put into practice, yet no one in the world can understand them or put them into practice. [My] words have an ancestor and [my] affairs have a sovereign. It is because people are ignorant that they fail to understand me. Those who understand me are few; those who imitate me are honored.[50]

From this remark, we see clearly that Laozi did not think that his theory was merely relative to his own conceptual scheme, or that other theories may be equally true. In this respect, Laozi's whole *Daodejing* can be seen as the manifestation of his belief in the thesis [MR3].

According to Hilary Putnam – a major critic of metaphysical realism – metaphysical realism is an untenable theory because of its internal incoherency. He says:

> The reason is that it depends on the assumption that we can conceive of a complete representation of the world which is radically detached from all of our beliefs. In order to conceive of such a representation, our conception of the entities to which our words refer would have to be available independently of all of our beliefs about those entities. But we have already seen that our conception of the entities to which our words refer is not available independently of all of our beliefs about them.[51]

We can see similar problems in Laozi's philosophy: If *Dao* exists prior to language and cannot be spoken of, then how can Laozi even attempt to capture it in words? If *Dao* exists independently of the human mind, then how can Laozi himself comprehend it? If *Dao* is imperceptible and incognizable, then why can Laozi alone see it? If our descriptions and our theories are bound to be inadequate, how can Laozi use such adjectives as "female," "empty," "inactive," "constant," "vast," "dim and dark," "silent and void," etc. to describe *Dao*? We can say that half of Laozi's *Daodejing* is devoted to describing *Dao*. Because of this self-defeating nature of the project, the whole book of *Daodejing* can be viewed as a paradoxical project in itself.

Virtue ("*De*") and Inactivity ("*Wu-wei*")

For Laozi, ethics is built on human conduct's conformity with *Dao*. This correspondence relation comes in a prescriptive form: one *ought to* act in accordance with *Dao*. It demands that all humans conform to *Dao*. Laozi says: "In his every movement a man of great virtue follows [*Dao*] and [*Dao*] only."[52] "A man of [*Dao*] conforms to [*Dao*]. . . . He who conforms to [*Dao*] is gladly accepted by [*Dao*]."[53] "A creature in its prime doing harm to the old is known as going against [*Dao*]. That which goes against [*Dao*] will come to an early end."[54] From these remarks, we see that Laozi embraces the view that an act is good if and only if it corresponds with what naturally is *Dao*. Morality consists in imitating *Dao*, which transcends human conception of the good. Since there is only one good way, ethics is not relative to different opinions or cultures. Laozi would definitely reject ethical relativism, which is often associated with anti-realism. As Schwartz remarks: "[Laozi] had not entirely freed himself from 'value judgment'."[55] To Laozi, there *is* something that is *good* in and of itself.

Laozi's book was later entitled "*Daodejing*," which means "the classic of *Dao* and *De*." The two key notions "*Dao*" and "*De*" are closely related. Laozi says: "The all-embracing quality of the great virtue [*De*] follows alone from the [*Dao*]."[56] Max Kaltenmark explains their relation well. He says:

> The notion of [*De*] always implies a notion of efficacy and specificity. Every creature possessing power of any kind, natural or acquired, is said to have [*De*]. [*Dao*] and [*De*] are thus quite close to each other in meaning, but the former is universal indeterminate Order, and the latter is a virtue or potency enabling a man to accomplish particular actions.[57]

We could perhaps view *De* as the application of *Dao*. When humans apply *Dao* in their conduct, they attain Virtue (*De*). If other creatures manifest *Dao* in their ways of existence, then they also exemplify Virtue (*De*). "Virtue" in this context defines *the way things should be* for all forms of existence.

Those who abide by *Dao* or are well versed in *Dao* are those with the great Virtue (*De*). They are ones considered by Laozi to be "the sages." Under the general term "Virtue" specific to humans, there are many human virtues. For example, since *Dao* is dim and obscure, Laozi says: "[In ancient times,] he who was well versed in [*Dao*] was minutely subtle, mysteriously comprehending, and too profound to be known."[58] He also says: "He who knows the male (active force) and keeps to the female (the passive force or receptive element), becomes the ravine of the world. Being the ravine of the world, he will never depart from eternal virtue, but returns to the state of infancy."[59] In these quotes, we see that what Laozi considered virtues are simply characteristics of *Dao*. These virtues include being subtle, mysterious, yielding, receptive, and self-effacing. Laozi's whole moral philosophy is built on these moral virtues. In this context, his metaphysical *Dao* has a moral dimension since it represents how humans should conduct themselves.

As we said earlier, the function of names is to mark things and attributes into different categories, which stand opposed to one another. Even though the metaphysical *Dao* precedes the categorization, the moral *Dao* seems to be situated within the categories. A. C. Graham describes Laozi's ethical view as showing a preference for the negative in a set of opposites. He says: "The most characteristic gesture of [Laozi] to over-turn accepted descriptions is the reversal of positives in chains of opposites."[60] Of the category of the positives, which Graham lists as category [A], he includes "something," "doing something," "knowledge," "full," etc.; of the category of the negative, which is listed as category [B], Graham includes "nothing," "doing nothing," "ignorance," "empty," etc. Graham says: "In instructing the weak in the strategy of survival, [Laozi] regularly advises him to *prefer* B to A, passive to active...."[61] Chad Hansen, on the other hand, thinks that Laozi's practical advice is the reversal of opposites: "He shows us that we *can* reverse all these conventional *preferences*. They do *not* provide constant guidance. There are cases where opposite guidance (reversing the value assignments) is better."[62] Hansen argues, *pace* Graham, that Laozi's point is *not* to advocate negative values, but to teach people to forget the actual distinction between the positives and the negatives. Along the same line, Max Kaltenmark says: "The [Daoist] considered all social values to be prejudices, and as such, wrong, because they cloud reality and land us in the vicious circle of contradictions. The point is to get out of this circle by transcending it."[63] Here we see two kinds of interpretations: one is to assign a higher status to the negative virtues; the other is to argue for the elimination of, or the transcendence beyond, the distinction between the positive and the negative attributes. In the next chapter, we shall see that Zhuangzi's moral theory is a form of transcendence of all values. But in Laozi, what we see is really the promotion of negative attributes.

The most emphasized negative moral principle in Laozi is that of non-action or inactivity ("*wu-wei*"). According to Wang's summarization, there are at least three existing interpretations of this phrase: (1) literally, "doing nothing"; (2) an agent's "not having intentions/desires" in her actions; and (3) an action which does not force, but yields.[64] The first interpretation concerns action; the other two interpretations concern one's attitude or state of mind. Graham apparently embraces the first interpretation when he suggests that "do nothing" is the proper translation of "*wu-wei*."[65] He thinks that the point of doing nothing is "not to interfere when things are already running well by themselves."[66] Fu also adopts the "non-interference" interpretation. He says: "All things run their courses spontaneously without any interference, and this explains why 'nothing is left undone'."[67] Schwartz's interpretation of "*wu-wei*" seems to belong to the second kind, in that he takes humans' deliberative effort as the opposite of Laozi's ideal.[68] Ahern argues that Laozi's "*wu-wei*" means merely the elimination of "conventional desires," not all desires, since the sage still has the desire to "lead the people in a humble, inobtrusive fashion."⁶⁹ Kasulis seems to adopt the third kind of interpretation in claiming "*wu-wei* to be the name for the non-self-conscious form of responsiveness." He thinks that Laozi's ideal is for the sage to respond to the natural patterns of things and not to impose.⁷⁰ Laozi's comments on the principle of inactivity seem to support all three interpretations. We can perhaps say that Laozi's notion of "*wu-wei*" incorporates all three functions: (1) when things are running well, do nothing to interfere; (2) when the sage has to do something, let him do it with no personal, selfish desire; (3) in all his acts, the sage should conform to *Dao*, the natural pattern of things, and refrain from introducing human intervention.

The virtue of inactivity is assigned to the sage, or the ruler, in particular. From Laozi's emphasis on "Do that which consists in taking no action, and order will prevail,"⁷¹ we can see that the purpose of the ruler's doing nothing is not to let go of worldly affairs, but to ensure worldly peace and order. The problem with *non-action* or *inactivity* as a political principle is: When things are *not* running well by themselves, what can doing nothing accomplish? When the sage sees the world being overtaken by human competitive drives and greedy desires, how can he possibly restore order by eliminating conventional desires? When the sage decides intentionally "not to honor men of worth," "not to value goods," "not to display what is desirable," or when he aims to empty his people's minds, weaken their wills, keep them innocent of knowledge and free from desires, isn't he interfering with the present social state already? From these difficulties, we see that Laozi's principle of inactivity is not meant to "correct" the world. He offers no practical guidance on how to restore worldly order in a world that is already corrupt. What he presents is an ideal instead. The method of inactivity works best when people are in a primitive society with very basic natural needs. If everyone follows their natural needs and the sage makes sure that the crops are well tended to, that animals are well bred, that trees are well planted, etc., then there should be enough natural resources to satisfy everyone's needs. Laozi definitely thought that all unnatural desires are derived from artificial conditioning from society. In his worldview, human nature is basically good and the world of Nature is basically harmonious. Therefore, the less human intervention there is, the better human society will be.

As Schwartz points out, Laozi's emphasis on man's taking no action or having no involvement stands in sharp contrast to Xunzi's emphasis on man's artificial transformation and cultivation. For Xunzi, "man's deliberating, calculating, planning goal-directed mind – his ability to make and fashion (*wei*) – is his glory as man."⁷² Xunzi, as well as other early Confucians, emphasizes the importance of culture and moral cultivation. To them, culture is where human values lie. In contrast, in Laozi's view, culture is the root of human ills. This is why to Laozi, the best possible world is a pre-cultural primitive social state.

Laozi's Political Ideal

Laozi's political ideal is closely associated with his moral ideal. Lau points out that the term "sage" "is almost invariably used for the ruler who understands the [*dao*], and is often used in contrast with . . . the 'common people'."[73] He further argues that "when [Laozi] mentions the way of Heaven, or Heaven and Earth, there is an implicit lesson for the sage, i.e., the ruler."[74] Laozi's moral lessons are indeed intended mostly for the ruler, who, in Laozi's expectation, should be a morally perfected person. In other words, for Laozi politics and morality are inseparable. In this respect, his political view is similar to that of Confucius and Mencius.

However, Laozi's view of the function of government and the moral ideal of the ruler is totally different from the Confucian view. He describes his ideal society this way:

> Reduce the size of the state; lessen the population. Make sure that even though there are labor saving tools, they are never used. Make sure that the people look upon death as a weighty matter and never move to distant places. Even though they have ships and carts, they will have no use for them. Even though they have armor and weapons, they will have no reason to deploy them. Make sure that the people return to the use of the knotted cord. Make their food savory, their clothes fine, their houses comfortable, their lives happy, then even though neighboring states are within sight of each other; even though they can hear the sounds of each other's dogs and chickens, their people will grow old and die without ever having visited one another.[75]

In this political picture, Laozi depicted an ideal state that was small, simple, primitive, anti-technology, self-contained and asocial.

Laozi acknowledged that once the people know what they *could* have, they would not rest content with what they *do* have. Therefore, he promoted ignorance. He says: "Abandon learning and there will be no sorrow."[76] Why is learning detrimental to the world? Isn't Laozi himself preaching his doctrine for people to learn? What Laozi rejected are three kinds of learning in particular: (1) the knowledge of social distinctions (between the good and the bad, the beautiful and the ugly, the valuable and the worthless, the fine and the coarse, the desirable and the undesirable, etc.); (2) the knowledge gained from our senses (such as our ability to make fine discriminations through sense perceptions); and (3) the moral knowledge that Confucians and other moralists teach (in particular, the four cardinal virtues: humaneness, righteousness, propriety, and wisdom). These three forms of knowledge are, in Laozi's eyes, the source of evil.

To begin with, social distinctions divide natural goods into those that humans desire and those they don't. Here we have the major cause of human competition and eventual conflicts. Natural diamonds and natural crystal, for example, may look alike, and yet the former is assigned a much higher value. People are induced to make imitation diamonds that can even fool experts' eyes, and yet the difference in value between the "real" and the "artificial" diamonds is like Heaven and Earth. This value difference can lead to fraud, theft, robbery, and even murder. Social distinctions in values should be blamed for the many human evils. Laozi says:

> When the people of the world all know beauty as beauty, there arises the recognition of ugliness. When they all know the good as good, there arises the recognition of evil. Therefore: being and non-being produce each other; difficult and easy complete each other; long and short contrast each other; high and low distinguish each other.[77]

An imperative Laozi gave to the rulers (the sages) was thus: "Do not exalt the worthy, so that the people shall not compete. Do not value rare treasures, so that the people shall not steal. Do not display objects of desire, so that the people's hearts shall not be disturbed."[78]

Secondly, Laozi blamed sensory stimulations for the disturbance of the mind, which consequently loses its initial tranquility. According to Laozi, an ideal state of mind is that of an infant. "I alone am inert, showing no sign (of desire). Like an infant that has not yet smiled."[79] The mind of early infancy does not know how to make distinctions or to have any preferential treatment. It is, as Laozi describes, "indiscriminate and dull."[80] With sensory stimulation, however, come finer discrimination and more desires that are not innate in us. Laozi says: "The five colors cause one's eyes to be blind. The five tones cause one's ears to be deaf. The five flavors cause one's palate to be spoiled."[81] As an example, we can think about the process of becoming a wine connoisseur. A novice in wine probably could not tell the difference between a Merlot and a Cabernet Sauvignon. With practice, he can learn to pick out the amount of tannin, the balance of sweetness and acidity, the varieties of grapes, the fragrance of oak, the maturity of the wine, etc. The more discriminatory he becomes, the more he will desire better wines. In this way, finer discriminatory ability acquired through constant sensory stimuli is closely linked to the expansion of desires. The palate that is accustomed to strong flavors will not take easily to bland taste; the ear that is habituated to loud sounds will not be quickly attuned to subtle resonance. Someone who becomes astute in all sensory discriminations is far from being the ideal Daoist with an indiscriminate state of mind.

Finally, Laozi rejected learning about moral teachings in general. He says:

> When the great [*Dao*] declined, the doctrine of humanity and righteousness arose. When knowledge and wisdom appeared, there emerged great hypocrisy. When the six family relationships are not in harmony, there will be the advocacy of filial piety and deep love to children. When a country is in disorder, there will be praise of loyal ministers.[82]

One might wonder whether Laozi is reversing the causal order here: is it because of the introduction of morality that the great *Dao* declined, or is it because the great *Dao* declined that morality was introduced? If the decline of *Dao* is not caused by moralists' teachings, then the abandonment of moral teachings is not going to restore the great *Dao*. Perhaps what Laozi wanted to accomplish was not just the abandonment of moral learning, but to do so in conjunction with a return to the primitive social state. This return to the origin, be it infancy or the primordial society, seems to be what Laozi took to be the ultimate goal. To obtain this goal, the method he recommended was slowly to reduce or "unlearn" what an individual or the whole society had acquired through life experiences or cultural development. A major difference between Confucianism and Daoism can be summarized in this remark of Laozi: "The pursuit of learning is to increase day after day. The pursuit of [*Dao*] is to decrease day after day."[83]

A politics built on the people's ignorance can easily become a politics based on manipulation, exploitation, and abuse of the people. But Laozi's political philosophy stressed the virtue of the ruler. Rulers must be sages, ones with the exemplification of *Dao* and the manifestation of *De*. They do not use craft or guile to take advantage of the people. Laozi emphasized the "unselfishness" of the ruler. He advised the sage to model himself on Heaven and Earth which have no self-regard. Therefore, the ruler must first learn to be self-effacing. The ideal ruler is one who is not seen and not heard, not one who is constantly giving speeches, drawing attention to himself, or demanding credit for his acts. If the ruler can always think about his people first, then he can actually preserve himself better. Laozi also says: "The sage has no fixed (personal) ideas. He regards the people's ideas as his own. . . . The sage, in the government of his empire, has no subjective viewpoint. His mind forms a harmonious whole with that of his people."[84] Kirill O. Thompson gives an interesting analysis of this kind of political ideal:

> The [Daoist] view parallels Western anarchist theory in its preference for free association of people and lack of faith in governance by official bodies. . . . Broad-based institutional or legal structures are, to [Daoists], inherently self-defeating, not simply because they are cumbersome and restrictive, but because they seek to impose from above a rigid uniform code on what is inevitably a fluid, multifarious grouping . . . such institutional and legal structures moreover set up grids of artificial concerns which draw people away from their original life tendencies.[85]

Here we see how Laozi's political philosophy is distinguishable from Hanfeizi's Legalist philosophy, even though Hanfeizi's Legalistic philosophy uses many of Laozi's teachings. The two political philosophies are fundamentally different in that the Legalist aims to strengthen institutional control, while Laozi is against the institution as such; the Legalist uses virtue as a means for political success, while Laozi treats virtue as the ultimate basis of politics.

As with Plato's ideal republic, one can ask the same question. Was Laozi serious in promoting this political ideal? How was it ever to be realized? Perhaps half-heartedly, perhaps ironically, Plato at least proposed some practical strategies for the realization of his *kallipolis* through Socrates. Laozi, on the other hand, never even discussed the question of whether this was a realizable ideal. He was against taking over the world to mold it into any particular form. He says: "Those who would gain the world and do something with it, I see that they will fail. For the world is a spiritual vessel and one cannot put it to use."[86] Laozi was against any use of weapon; he rejected all warfare. He says: "Fine weapons are inauspicious instruments. All creatures find them repulsive."[87] "Those who serve their ruler with [*Dao*] will never take the world by force of arms."[88] Mencius approved of just wars; Xunzi discussed means of strengthening the nation's military force. To Laozi, warfare is not just a symptom of the decline of *Dao*; it is also the cause of *Dao*'s deterioration. Whatever the justification is behind warfare, no good can possibly come out of it. From historical reports, we can see that Laozi's political philosophy is a reaction to his time, which was rightly called "the Warring States." He was probably repulsed by what he saw, and did not consider any remedy to the current ills to be effective. To him, culture and civilization were constitutive of current ills. He rejected the Confucian teachings of morals and rituals, because they were part of the civilization process. His call for a *return* to the original state represented his rejection of culture and civilization as a whole.

Conclusion

Whereas ancient Confucians all cherished the contribution of culture and civilization, Laozi advocated going back to Nature or the natural itself. If *Dao* models itself on Nature and humans have to model their conduct on *Dao*, then the less humans take upon themselves to accomplish, the closer they are to *Dao*. From this reasoning, we can see that Laozi's metaphysical view of the nature of *Dao*, his ethical teaching of the principle of inactivity, and his political ideal of returning to the primitives, are all consistent with one another.

Laozi's philosophy makes a significant contribution to the development of Chinese philosophy in that it opens up new directions for inquiry. His discussion on the origin of the universe or the relation between Being and Non-being, in particular, led later Neo-Confucians to an engaged discourse of metaphysics. His teachings on how to live a good life, further developed by Zhuangzi, deeply affected Chinese intellectuals' frame of mind. In Chinese history, it became a common saying that one should deal with worldly affairs with the Confucian attitude while retreating to one's own world with the Daoist attitude. The Chinese intellectual aims to be outwardly a Confucian while inwardly a Daoist. Finally, Laozi's political ideal, though never realized in Chinese history and possibly never realizable in any worldly state, has become an aesthetic prototype in many Chinese paintings. A spiritual ideal captured in Chinese landscape is the kind of Daoist utopia that is simple, peaceful and other-worldly. We can conclude that his philosophy influences the Chinese mind just as much as Confucianism does.

Further discussion questions

1   If *Dao* is unspeakable and cannot be named, how can Laozi himself speak about it and name it as "*dao*"? Does he commit an internal inconsistency by describing *Dao*?

2 Do you think that Laozi's teaching is too pessimistic, too negative and too passive? What can non-competition and non-action accomplish?
3 Do you agree with Laozi that the best moral attitude is doing nothing (*wu-wei*)? Is inactivity the best way to conduct oneself as well as to rule people?
4 Is Laozi correct in his diagnosis of social ills? Can the elimination of discrimination reduce human desires and eventually prevent human conflicts?
5 Is Laozi anti-intellectual and anti-moral? Can such a teaching ever accomplish the high goal that Laozi talks about?

Primary texts

Wing-tsit Chan (ed.) *A Sourcebook in Chinese Philosophy*, 4th edn. Princeton: Princeton University Press, 1973 (ch. 7; in full).
Philip J. Ivanhoe (trans.) *The Daodejing of Laozi*. New York: Seven Bridges Press, 2002. (An updated version of Ivanhoe and Van Norden 2003, ch. 4.)
D. C. Lau, trans. *Lao Tzu: Tao Te Ching*. New York, NY: Penguin Books, 1963.
Philip J. Ivanhoe and Bryan W. Van Norden, eds. *Readings in Classical Chinese Philosophy*. Indianapolis, IN: Hackett Publishing Company, Inc. 2003 (ch. 4; in full).

Further readings

Charles Wei-hsun Fu. "Lao-Tzu's Conception of Tao." *Inquiry* 16, 1973: 367–91.
Chad Hansen. "Linguistic Skepticism in the 'Lao Tzu'." *Philosophy East & West* 31, 1981: 321–36.
D. C. Lau. "The Treatment of Opposites in Lao-Tzu." *Bulletin of the School of Asian and African Studies* 21, 1958: 344–60.
JeeLoo Liu. "A Daoist Conception of Truth: Laozi's Metaphysical Realism vs. Zhuangzi's Internal Realism." In Bo Mou (ed.), *Comparative Approaches to Chinese Philosophy*. Aldershot: Ashgate Publishing Ltd., 2003, pp. 278–93.
Xiaogan Liu. "On the Concept of Naturalness ('Tzu-Jan') in Lao Tzu's Philosophy." *Journal of Chinese Philosophy* 25(4), 1998: 423–46.

Chapter 7

Zhuangzi (Chuang Tzu)

Introduction

If Laozi is hard to understand because he was terse and serious, then Zhuangzi (ca. 399–295 BCE) is even harder to interpret because of his verbosity and his light-heartedness. Zhuangzi expressed his philosophical thinking through fables, fairy tales, parodies, or stories that are mostly fantastic and fanciful. It is not easy to know which of the comments he makes are sincere and which are meant for ironies. As Lee Yearley puts it: "Few books existing anywhere are both as compelling and as mysterious as is the *Zhuangzi*; it simultaneously draws one's attention and eludes one's grasp."[1] Chad Hansen also has a nice description: "Zhuangzi has a unique philosophical style. He wrote philosophical fantasy. . . . This style injects insecurity into interpreters. Yet it attracts us like philosophical honey. His combination of brilliance and elusive statements frustrates, delights, and challenges those who want to interpret him."[2] It is no wonder that Zhuangzi is subject to a wide array of opposing interpretations, with each interpreter able to cite sufficient texts to support his or her view. But it is not to say that the text itself is full of contradictions. Almost no commentator would deny the brilliance of the philosophical thinking hidden behind the text. The task laid out for readers of the *Zhuangzi* is to comprehend the whole picture of Zhuangzi's philosophical outlook, and to reorganize his different strands into a coherent theory.

In the complete works collected in the *Zhuangzi*, there are 33 chapters. The first 7 are grouped as "the Inner Chapters"; the next 15 (8–22) are grouped as "the Outer Chapters" and the remaining 11 (23–33) are grouped as "the Miscellaneous Chapters."[3] An almost unanimous opinion among traditional Chinese as well as contemporary Western commentators is that the Inner Chapters were either written by Zhuangzi or at least are truly representative of his thought, while the Outer Chapters were written by followers of Zhuangzi. The Miscellaneous Chapters were most often discredited, though some commentators think that several passages in them could also be attributed to Zhuangzi himself.[4] Based on this received opinion, our analysis in this chapter will be based primarily on the Inner Chapters.[5] We shall consult the Outer Chapters or the Miscellaneous Chapters when some of those passages can be used to support or illustrate the main ideas expressed in the Inner Chapters. Since all seven of the Inner Chapters were allegedly given a title by their original author, we will treat the disjointed sections in each chapter as expressing the same theme suggested by its title.

In the Inner Chapters, chapter 1, "Free and Easy Wandering," presents a defense of, or an introduction to, Zhuangzi's theory, which was often criticized as being too lofty and useless. Zhuangzi used several stories to illustrate his point that those with narrow vision and little knowledge simply cannot see the grandeur of something extremely big. Chapter 2, "On the Equality of Things and Theories,"[6] discusses the futility of engaging in debates on various theories. It also presents several arguments against the possibility of true knowledge. Some commentators think that this is the most important chapter in the whole *Zhuangzi*. Chapter 3, "The Key to Nourishing Life," presents several ways to preserve one's life and one's spirit, such as avoiding the pursuit of knowledge or fame, following the natural way, and taking one's fate as it comes. Chapter 4, "In the World of Men," compares the Confucian ways of dealing with the contemporary chaotic world (such as volunteering one's service with the hope of rectifying a ruthless king, doing one's duty, etc.) to Zhuangzi's proposal: to be useless. Zhuangzi suggests that if an individual has no knowledge, no virtue, no talent, then he will not be called upon to serve the king. Being useless, as a means of self-preservation, is the only way for one to accomplish one's own grandeur. In the next three chapters, Zhuangzi presents the ideal realm of existence. Chapter 5, "Signs of Virtue Complete," presents his ethical view: morality comes from within; it is not to be judged from one's behavior (or one's appearance). The ultimate moral goal is to be in accord with nature, which means ridding oneself of one's preferences and prejudices. Chapter 6, "The Great and Venerable Teacher," engages in a metaphysical, as well as metaphorical, depiction of *Dao* and those who have truly acquired *Dao*. This is a complicated chapter filled with stories containing esoteric meaning. The linking thread seems to be that the eternal *Dao* embraces all beings and all things. Those who have truly acquired *Dao*, the True Men, are those who recognize that everything in life exemplifies *Dao*. They thus embrace their fate – come what may – with equanimity and contentedness. The final chapter, "The Proper Way for Emperors and Kings," touches upon Zhuangzi's political ideal. The idea linking the several disjointed sections seems to be close to Laozi's idea of "Do Nothing" ("*wu-wei*"). Unlike Laozi, Zhuangzi did not give any detailed strategies for political success.[7] His precept for both emperors and kings (as well as for anyone who aspires to learn *Dao*) is simply this: "Be empty, that is all. The Perfect Man uses his mind like a mirror – going after nothing, welcoming nothing, responding but not storing. Therefore he can win out over things and not hurt himself."[8]

Because many of the issues Zhuangzi dealt with are germane to the concerns of Western philosophy, he has been a favorite subject for comparative philosophy. He has been compared, among others, to Derrida on the deconstructionist view of language and on skepticism of language;[9] to Putnam on the issues of meaning, truth, and reality;[10] to Rorty on anti-representationalism and pluralism;[11] to Sextus Empiricus and Theaetetus on skepticism;[12] to Aristotle on being and identity;[13] to Nietzsche on the philosophy of life and culture;[14] to Wittgenstein on world-making;[15] and to Heidegger on radical concrete particularity.[16] This chapter cannot cover all these issues. Here, we shall focus on three key themes in the Inner Chapters: his view on truth and knowledge, his ethical ideal, and his philosophy of life and death.

Truth, Reality and Knowledge

Zhuangzi's view on truth and reality has been widely branded as "relativism," "skepticism," or even "radical relativism" and "radical skepticism."[17] In this section, we will examine Zhuangzi's views on truth and reality and the possibility of our ever knowing them. To sort out the complicated debates among analytic commentators of Zhuangzi's view, we should first take a look at the various titles that have been assigned to Zhuangzi.[18] (This is a perfect example of how contemporary commentators can engage in philosophical debates on issues dealt with by ancient Chinese philosophers. Readers who are not interested in these debates may wish to skip this part.)

Radical (hard) skepticism or perspectivism

Based on his reading on Zhuangzi's chapter 2, Chad Hansen attributes radical skepticism and what he calls perspectival relativism to Zhuangzi.

Perspectival relativism is the view that all views are from a certain perspective, and that all views are correct within that perspective. Radical skepticism is the view that we can never know the Truth, since there is no truth outside our cognitive enclosures. Hansen says that for Zhuangzi, all the disputing voices are "equally 'right' – at least equally 'natural'," and "all ways are equally valid – none has any special status or warrant from the point of view of the universe."[19] Hansen takes this view because he does not see any metaphysical sense attached to the *Dao* as Daoists use the term. By his interpretation, a *dao* for Zhuangzi is simply a form of discourse or "a scheme of classifications (names)" and is thus a mere linguistic convention. Since there is no mind-independent reality, we can never know the Truth independently of our conceptions.

Soft skepticism or language skepticism

Soft skepticism differs from hard skepticism in that the skeptic is selective in the objects of his doubt. He does not insist that one can never know the truth about anything; he merely suggests that one cannot know the truth in certain realms. Contemporary commentators single out language in particular as Zhuangzi's object of doubt. Mark Berkson explains language skepticism as the claim that "language cannot be seen as a vehicle that can deliver a picture of the world as it actually is. There can be no 'true accounts' of the world in the form of propositional claims."[20] As Philip Ivanhoe puts it: "Such skepticism is a special kind of epistemological skepticism, it does not entail any claim about how things are in the world nor does it in principle preclude other ways of knowing that might help us understand and accord with the things and events in the world."[21] In other words, Ivanhoe thinks that Zhuangzi is a skeptic about the possibility of using human intellect to grasp *Dao* or using human concepts and languages to depict *Dao*, but he does not ascribe radical skepticism to Zhuangzi. He takes Zhuangzi's skeptical arguments to be making epistemological, not metaphysical, claims.

Therapeutic skepticism or methodological skepticism

Therapeutic skepticism is a popular interpretation held among analytic commentators of Zhuangzi.[22] Under this interpretation, Zhuangzi was not even a skeptic in his philosophical conviction. He merely employed skepticism as a method or a therapy for people who are bound by their ignorance of *Dao*. His aim was to dispel people's delusion that they alone know the truth and that others are all wrong. So Zhuangzi's skepticism is used to enlighten ordinary people, to get them to see his real point: the ultimate truth about *Dao*. Similarly, Lisa Raphals separates three kinds of skepticism: skepticism as a thesis; skepticism as a recommendation; skepticism as a method. She argues that (1) Zhuangzi clearly used skepticism as a method to refute existing claims to knowledge; (2) he possibly used skepticism as a recommendation for people to suspend judgment; but (3) he clearly did not endorse it as a thesis that nothing can ever be known.[23] Both therapeutic and methodological skepticism are incompatible with radical skepticism, since their advocate would not deny the very possibility of knowledge. Hence, both interpretations could be seen as attributing to Zhuangzi an even weaker form of skepticism than soft skepticism.

Asymmetrical relativism

This name was suggested by Robert Allinson, who argues that Zhuangzi separated two realms of consciousness: the realm of ignorance, which represents the pre-awakening state of ordinary people, and the realm of knowledge, which represents the awakened state of sages. Truth would be relative to different perspectives in the lower realm but not relative in the higher realm. Allinson says, "Relativism exists only in the dialogical situation of the sage speaking to the aspirant. Once one has achieved the understanding of the sage, the concept of relativism can be understood as having had only a heuristic value."[24] We can see that this interpretation is similar to the previous one, which takes skepticism, rather than relativism, to have a transitional heuristic status. This view is also compatible with a realistic view of the world, as it is at the higher level of knowledge that one sees true reality.

Anti-rationalism or mysticism

A. C. Graham ascribes anti-rationalism to Zhuangzi.[25] In his explanation, Zhuangzi mocked reason and rebuffed any claim to knowledge acquired through reasoning. However, Graham rejects a perspectivist reading of Zhuangzi. He thinks that Zhuangzi does believe that some people's knowledge or skill is better than others, and thus not all forms of knowledge are subject to doubt. One who has true knowledge is one who can let one's heart be like a mirror – it flows with the inevitable mutations of things, "responds but does not retain."[26] Graham thinks this is anti-rationalist because it "plays down or denies the place of reason in becoming aware of objective reality."[27] Jung Lee, among others, concludes that Zhuangzi's view is at bottom mysticism. He thinks that even if Zhuangzi did hold the view that our language and our conceptual schemes are perspectival, he did not believe that reality itself is also perspectival. If one abandons all conceptual schemes and uses a "heightened mode of noesis", then one can apprehend reality "in a direct and unmediated way."[28] Both Graham's anti-rationalistic and Lee's mystic interpretations of Zhuangzi point to a different epistemic mode that Zhuangzi advocates: abandon reason; employ what Graham calls "pure spontaneity" and what Lee calls "a distinct form of numinous knowing, a knowing which is 'the oversight which is seeing things as they are'."[29] According to both commentators, in Zhuangzi's view true knowledge is possible as long as one employs this different epistemic mode.

Realism

Realism, in its simplest form, is the view that there is a fact of the matter with things in the world. Reality is not mind-dependent. We do not construct the world; instead, we ourselves are part of this world. Realism in this form is not incompatible with any form of skepticism. Of the five other interpretations outlined above, the only one that is incompatible with realism is perspectivism. Perspectivism says that there is no single objective reality, or that there are multiple realities relative to multiple perspectives. Realism says just the opposite. As we have seen in earlier chapters, realism is the basic presupposition among all ancient Chinese philosophers. The contemporary commentators who ascribe this view to Zhuangzi include Russell Goodman, Siao-Fang Sun, Mark Berkson, and Philip Ivanhoe.[30]

The above summary manifests the confusing and confused state of our interpretation of Zhuangzi. Our conclusion on his view is a combination of *realism* with respect to *Dao* and the world as a whole, *relativism* with respect to our conceptual schemes and our judgments, and *skepticism* about the possibility of true knowledge.[31] Even though Zhuangzi doubted the function of language in the pursuit of truth, he never doubted the existence of Truth itself, which can be called "*Dao*" or simply "the Reality." Sun makes a distinction that is very helpful to our analysis of Zhuangzi's notion of *truth*. According to Sun, there are two senses of the term as used by philosophers: one is the metaphysical sense in which truth is identical with reality or the real; the other is the

157

semantic sense in which truth is a property of statements.[32] When we apply this distinction to Zhuangzi's theory of truth, we can see that he held realism with respect to truth in the metaphysical sense, but relativism with respect to truth in the semantic sense. Furthermore, because Zhuangzi doubted the possibility of our ever knowing this metaphysical Truth, he held skepticism with regard to our knowledge. In a nutshell, Zhuangzi maintained the following theses:

1 Realism: There is *Dao* existing independently of our perspectives and outside of our conceptual schemes. This *Dao* is the Truth, the Reality, or the way the world is.
2 Conceptual Relativism: All our thought is internal to our conceptual scheme, and our judgments are always reflections of our own perspectives.
3 Knowledge Skepticism: We can never have knowledge about the absolute Truth, nor can we ever describe it with our language. There is no truth in the semantic sense (from A, B).

Here are some arguments Zhuangzi proposed in support of his conceptual relativism (thesis 2). He illustrated this thesis from various angles:

[A]   The Argument for the Relativity of Preferences

> If a man sleeps in a damp place, his back aches and he ends up half paralyzed, but is this true of a loach? If he lives in a tree, he is terrified and shakes with fright, but is this true of a monkey? Of these three creatures, then, which one knows the proper place to live? Men eat the flesh of grass-fed and grain-fed animals, deer eat grass, centipedes find snakes tasty, and hawks and falcons relish mice. Of these four, which knows how food ought to taste?[33]

We can formulate Zhuangzi's argument in this way:

1 Our judgments depend on our natural/physical compositions. For example, men judge dry lands better for living whereas loaches would prefer damp places; men judge animal flesh tasty whereas deer would prefer grass.
2 Different compositions generate different perspectives.
3 Therefore, all judgments are made in accordance with a particular perspective.

158

4   Therefore, there cannot be universal judgments among agents with different compositions.

According to this argument, different species have different physical/biological make-ups. Their judgments are bound to be determined, or affected, by their make-up. What is good according to men is probably bad according to a different species. "Good" and "bad" are thus judgmental terms that are only applicable from within a certain perspective. Since these judgments are relative to perspectives, they cannot be expressions of the objective truth.

Zhuangzi further argued that not only value judgments, but also truth in the semantic sense, or the truth of our judgments, are relative to the speaker's perspective:

[B]   The Argument for the Relativity of Judgments

> There is nothing in the world bigger than the tip of an autumn hair, and Mount [Tai] is little. No one has lived longer than a dead child, and [Pengzu] (a legendary person who lived to over 800 years old) died young.[34]

The seemingly paradoxical statements here are used to show the relativity of our concepts. There is nothing finer than the tip of an autumn hair, and yet from an ant's point of view the tip of a hair may be large. Mount Tai is indeed large, but from a giant's point of view it could be quite small. Similarly, from a moth's point of view the child who died prematurely may have had a long life, but from a tortoise's point of view the longest lived man died prematurely. The way our concepts divide up the world does not reflect any genuine division among things themselves. There is no absolute truth as a property of our judgments.

However, this argument only establishes that our categorization does not reflect reality; it does not establish the further radical relativist view that everything is thus equal. Even if Mount Tai is not "big" in absolute terms, it is at least "bigger" than the tip of an autumn hair. What Zhuangzi wanted to deny was simply the assignment of absolute concepts; he was not denying the possibility of genuine comparisons and actual differences. If we draw the conclusion that because the tip of an autumn hair could be considered "big" from a certain perspective, it is therefore "big," we would be misinterpreting Zhuangzi's argument. In chapter 17 (of the Outer Chapters), when someone asks whether he could judge the hugeness of Heaven as "big," the reply is "No indeed," because "how do we know that heaven and earth can fully encompass the dimensions of the largest thing possible?"[35] In other words, "big" or "small" as our categories of concepts do not apply to things independent of comparison from various perspectives; therefore, they do not carve up the world as it really is.

A better way to understand this argument is to formulate it this way:

1 What is called large or small, young or old, etc. depends on the standard employed.
2 With different standards, the same things can be called both large and small, young and old, etc.
3 But nothing can be both large and small, young and old in itself.
4 Therefore, our categorization of objects and their attributes do not reflect the way things really are.

[C]   The Argument for the Relativity of Perspectives

> Everything has its "that," everything has its "this." From the point of view of "that" you cannot see it, but through understanding you can know it. So I say, "that" comes out of "this" and "this" depends on "that" – which is to say that "this" and "that" give birth to each other. But where there is birth there must be death; where there is death there must be birth. Where there is acceptability there must be unacceptability; where there is unacceptability there must be acceptability. Where there is recognition of right there must be recognition of wrong; where there is recognition of wrong there must be recognition of right.[36]

In this passage Zhuangzi not only pointed out the relativity of perspectives, he also demonstrated the interdependence of perspectives themselves.[37] If there were no "this," there would not be a "that"; if there were no "wrong," there would not be any "right." No statement can possibly be made outside of all conceptual schemes, or from the point of view of *nowhere*. To judge whether a statement is true or false, therefore, we need first to evaluate the conceptual scheme in which this statement is embedded. A statement true to human conception is not necessarily true to another creature's conception. A statement true from one individual's perspective could easily be false from her opponent's perspective. Statements are not determinately true or false independently of our conception; they simply do not have any intrinsic truth-value in and of themselves. The argument can be formulated as follows:

1 Without the opposition of a set of competing concepts, there cannot be any judgment made with either one within the set of opposites.

2   Two opposite concepts are mutually dependent; one cannot be em-
    ployed without the assumption of the other.
3   Therefore, for there to be a judgment made with one of the oppos-
    ing concepts, there would have to be another judgment made with
    the opposite concept.
4   Therefore, no judgment can be made without an opposition; no
    judgment is universally and absolutely true.

Since our ordinary knowledge is relative to perspective, there is no
knowledge that is *the* true knowledge. For Zhuangzi, the Truth that
transcends all perspectives is unattainable and inconceivable by us. Since
Zhuangzi held the view that such a notion of Truth is unavailable to us,
he often made the comment: "How can I really know?"[38] If we say that
knowledge is *true* justified belief, then even when we think our beliefs
are justified (relative to our perspective), we can never obtain knowledge since we cannot know for sure that what we believe *is* true. In this
respect, Zhuangzi can also be called a skeptic concerning human knowledge (thesis 3).

Zhuangzi has several arguments in support of his skepticism about
knowledge:

[D]   The Argument from Dreams

> He who dreams of drinking wine may weep when morning comes; he
> who dreams of weeping may in the morning go off to hunt. While he is
> dreaming he does not know it is a dream, and in his dream he may even
> try to interpret a dream. Only after he wakes does he know it was a
> dream. And someday there will be a great awakening when we know that
> this is all a great dream.[39]

We can formulate his argument as follows:

1   Our dreams seem to us as real as when we are awake.
2   When we are dreaming, we never know that it was just a dream.
3   Therefore, when we think we are awake, we could also be dreaming.
4   Therefore, we can never be sure of our judgment that we are awake.

[E]   The Argument from the Impossibility of Settling Debates

> Suppose you and I had an argument. If you have beaten me instead of my
> beating you, then are you necessarily right and am I necessarily wrong? If

161

I have beaten you instead of your beating me, then am I necessarily right and are you necessarily wrong? Is one of us right and the other wrong? . . . Whom shall we get to decide what is right? Shall we get someone who agrees with you to decide? But if he already agrees with you, how can he decide fairly? Shall we get someone who agrees with me? But if he already agrees with me, how can he decide? Shall we get someone who disagrees with both of us? But if he already disagrees with both of us, then how can he decide? Shall we get someone who agrees with both of us? But if he already agrees with both of us, how can he decide? Obviously, then, neither you nor I nor anyone else can know the answer.[40]

We can reorganize this argument as follows:

1 Different judgments of truth are necessarily relative to different perspectives.
2 Therefore, no two people with different perspectives can determine which judgment is true.
3 If a third party makes a verdict favoring one side, her judgment of truth is also relative to her perspective.
4 If the third party disagrees with both sides, then she is merely proposing a third judgment based on a third perspective.
5 Even if an agreement is reached among different perspectives, that agreement itself is simply relative to that particular perspective of agreement.
6 Therefore, no third party can truly determine which side of the debate is right.
7 Therefore, it is impossible to ever settle a debate.

In [D] Zhuangzi presents a sort of Cartesian argument for the impossibility of knowing that we are not presently in a dream world. If we cannot even know whether we are presently dreaming, then all our judgments that we now hold true could turn out false. An individual simply cannot judge her judgments true. This argument is as compelling as the Cartesian Dream argument. In [E], Zhuangzi expresses the impossibility of obtaining truth on the basis of rational discourse and mutual agreement. We often tend to think that the more people agree on one statement, the more likely it is that that statement is true. But Zhuangzi here pointed out that for any judgment, there is always an opposing judgment. Agreement does not guarantee truth; at most, it demonstrates that the interlocutors share the same perspective. We can contrast Zhuangzi's view with the modern notion of democracy: the majority rules. By extension of Zhuangzi's argument, if "two against one" does not guarantee truth, then neither does ninety-nine people against one. Truth is not determinable by the majority's opinion – the majority simply happens to take one perspective while other perspectives are equally legitimate (or equally illegitimate). Truth cannot depend on opinions, however many people share the same opinion. Both [D] and [E] support the conclusion that *we can never know for sure.* All our knowledge is relative to our understanding and our perspective. The true knowledge that is beyond perspectives is impossible for us. Whatever we claim to know and whatever we claim to be true, is necessarily relative to our conceptual schemes.

Even though Zhuangzi focused on the way our preferences, our concepts, and our judgments are reflections of our own perspectives, his view should be separated from perspectivism. Perspectivism makes the following claim:

[P1] The truth of our judgments is relative to our perspectives. Incompatible statements can both be taken as true as long as they are *true relative to the speaker's perspective.* Therefore, *all* judgments are equally true.

But Zhuangzi merely points out that all our judgments are *made* in accordance with our make-up, our culture or our perspective. He does not say that all our judgments are *made true* by our culture or our perspective. Zhuangzi says:

> Therefore the sage does not proceed in such a way, but illuminates all in the light of Heaven. He too recognizes a "this," but a "this" has both a right and a wrong in it. So, in fact, does he still have a "this" and "that"? Or does he in fact no longer have a "this" and "that"? A state in which "this" and "that" no longer find their opposites is called the hinge of the Way.[41]

What Zhuangzi called "the hinge of the Way" is the standpoint of *Dao*, from which the distinction between "this" and "that" is eliminated. The notion of truth that Zhuangzi advocated relies on the denial of discriminations (of right and wrong, of good and bad, of this and that, etc.). However, he was not eradicating the very distinction between Truth (in the absolute sense) and Falsehood (in the absolute sense). To him, there was a clear Falsehood: to present one's perspective as the only correct one. He says: "But to fail to abide by this mind and still insist upon your rights and wrongs. . . . This is to claim that what doesn't exist exists."[42] To move to the perspectivist level – to view perspective as a determinant of truth, or to claim that all truths are equal – is no better. Zhuangzi says:

163

> [Waiting] for one shifting voice [to pass judgment on] another is the same as waiting for none of them. . . . Right is not right; so is not so. If right were really right, it would differ so clearly from not right that there would be no need for argument. If so were really so, it would differ so clearly from not so that there would be no need for argument.[43]

The paradox he is posing here is that the truly right would have no opposite, and the ultimate "Truth" would actually be the elimination of the distinction between truth and falsehood. What Zhuangzi proposed was a notion of *Truth* that is the synthesis of all perspectives:

[P2]   True knowledge is the knowledge that denies perspectival knowledge. Truth is not relative to perspectives; rather, Truth transcends all perspectives.

In contrast to the perspectivism thesis [P1], Zhuangzi's claims are the following instead:

[P3]   Our judgments are relative to our perspectives.
[P4]   Our judgments are relative to our perspectives, but *Truth* is *not* relative to perspectives. Therefore, *none* of our judgments is true.

In other words, instead of granting all perspectives as equally true, Zhuangzi argued that all perspectives are necessarily false. What he expressed is actually the opposite of perspectivism.

If we separate the two levels of "truth" in Zhuangzi's usage, we may see his view in a better light:[44]

[Truth$_1$]:   This is the notion of truth employed by ordinary people; it is relative to perspectives ("truth" in the semantic sense).
[Truth$_2$]:   This is the notion of truth that is beyond human conception of truth and falsehood; it transcends all human perspectives and it is a clear representation of the Way ("Truth" in the metaphysical sense).

Since Zhuangzi held the view that there is an ultimate notion of Truth$_2$, which is not relative to perspectives, and that this Truth$_2$ is superior to Truth$_1$, he cannot be viewed as embracing perspectivism. This Truth$_2$ is not what *we* could deem as true, because once we call it "true," it is brought back to the cycle of truth/falsehood. What Zhuangzi introduced here is the absence of all discriminations and the cessation of all fact/value judgments. Truth$_2$ is not a correspondence between our conception and the way the world is, because no such correspondence is possible. Things for us or from our point of view are necessarily internal to our conceptual schemes, and different conceptual schemes simply cannot compete for being *the best match* for the world-in-itself.

The claim that our thoughts and our descriptions are all confined to our perspectives and our conceptual schemes does not lead to the conclusion that reality itself is confined to perspectives, or that there is no reality independent of various conceptual schemes. One can argue that there is no such thing as "a view without a viewer" without asserting that there cannot be "a world without a viewer." Zhuangzi certainly did not claim that reality is relative to perspectives or conceptual schemes, or that there is no fact of the matter with regard to the reality in itself. We could probably say that Zhuangzi was skeptical about our linguistic ability to express the truth of reality, but he was not skeptical about the existence of this reality itself. For Zhuangzi, *Dao* is as real as Laozi conceived it to be, but any human description (including his own) is bound to fail to represent it. Zhuangzi says, "As to what is beyond the Six Realms, the sage admits it exists but does not theorize."[45] Therefore, Zhuangzi did not indulge in the effort of explicating *Dao*. No verbal descriptions could possibly do the job of giving us the truth of *Dao* – even his own description would be relative to his conceptual scheme. As an alternative, Zhuangzi resorted to using metaphors, fables, parodies, stories, etc. to give us a mental picture of what the goal ought to be.[46] The statements he made about *Dao* should not be taken to be declarative statements with a definite truth-value. As Sun explains it: "The statement about [*Dao*] is neither true nor false, for we can neither confirm nor deny it; neither prove it nor disprove it."[47]

However, even though Zhuangzi asserted *Dao* or Truth$_2$, he did not think that the knowledge of *Dao* is easily obtainable. First of all, not everyone has the necessary intelligence and aptitude ever to learn this truth. Zhuangzi did not think that the knowledge of *Dao* could be obtained through reason or empirical investigation; instead, people need to cultivate a higher level of intuitive understanding, which he called "illumination" (*ming*), of the whole facet of *Dao*. Once one sees that *Dao* embraces all, one can view all distinctions and particularities with *illumination*. In other words, one's possession of *illumination* comes after one has truly understood *Dao*. But the possession of illumination is not available to everyone. Zhuangzi says: "We can't expect a blind man to appreciate beautiful patterns or a deaf man to listen to bells and drums. And blindness and deafness are not confined to the body alone – the understanding has them too."⁴⁸ In the *Zhuangzi*, there are also many stories of the teachers' dismissal of students' attempt to learn about *Dao*, by telling them that they are not "equipped" to have knowledge of *Dao*. Perhaps it is as Burton Watson puts it: "Most of the philosophers of ancient China are addressed to the political or intellectual elite; [Zhuangzi] is addressed to the spiritual elite."⁴⁹ Furthermore, even if there are people who have truly understood *Dao*, they cannot teach others since no human descriptions would have been adequate. In "Knowledge Wandered North" of the Miscellaneous Chapters it is said, "The Way is not to be asked about, and even if it is asked about, there can be no answer."⁵⁰ In fact, in the whole *Zhuangzi*, the people who have learned *Dao* (or *Truth* in the metaphysical sense) are given descriptions so fanciful that they seem unreal or at least "un-human." Zhuangzi's point is that there is Truth in the metaphysical sense and there is true knowledge, but true knowledge is almost *humanly impossible*. Ordinary human knowledge should all be considered "little knowledge" and "little understanding." They are the proper objects of Zhuangzi's skepticism.

Both Laozi and Zhuangzi considered names and descriptions as those that carve up *Dao*. However, while Laozi focused on explicating this mind-independent reality, Zhuangzi focused on explicating the *impossibility of our knowledge and our description* of this mind-independent reality. If no conceptual framework can correctly capture *Dao*, then certainly the Daoist conceptual framework cannot either. While Laozi lamented that few people could understand his words or follow his way, Zhuangzi never boasted about the correctness of his own view. In this respect, Zhuangzi's whole philosophy is more internally coherent than that of Laozi.

In conclusion, Zhuangzi was a realist with regard to the way the world is, but he was at the same time a relativist with regard to the way we conceive the world. He acknowledged the existence of a mind-independent reality *Dao*, which embraces everything and transcends the empirical world. Zhuangzi says: "whether we discover its reality or not does not affect its being true."⁵¹ His arguments show that we can never have a conception of *the way the world is* independently of our perspective, but he never did go as far as radical relativists in holding that all perspectives are equally right. In our analysis, the incompatibility between the interpretation of Zhuangzi as a skeptic and the interpretation of Zhuangzi as a relativist is dissolved. Zhuangzi was a skeptic with regard to our ability to know Truth₂, and he thought that all other *claims* of truth (Truth₁) are relative to various perspectives.

The Ethically Ideal Condition
and the Perfect Man

With Zhuangzi's ethics, the major debate among contemporary analytic commentators is whether he adhered to ethical relativism, the view that there is no right or wrong independently of one perspective or another. Under such a view, we can never say something is absolutely right or wrong since there is simply no objective standard. Apart from Chad Hansen's branding of Zhuangzi as "perspectival relativism," many contemporary analytic commentators also attribute various forms of relativism to Zhuangzi. David Wong ascribes "moral relativism" to him, in that he denies the possibility of any rational justification for morality.[52] Paul Kjellberg argues that Zhuangzi subscribed to "soft relativism," the belief that "values vary depending on the individual and the situation," but rejected "hard relativism," the view that "what is good for people is whatever they *think* is good for them."[53] By this line of interpretation, in Zhuangzi's view there are no objectively determined values; there is no intrinsic goodness or intrinsic evil, no objectively better or objectively worse conduct.

In the opposite camp of interpreters, there are those who argue that Zhuangzi did not embrace perspectival relativism because he makes a clear distinction between *Dao*'s perspective and our perspectives and he holds that *Dao*'s perspective *is* better than our perspectives. Ivanhoe, for example, argues that Zhuangzi did not reject an ultimate distinction between good and bad, better and worse. There are worse ways for us to lead our lives: to act contrary to our nature or the nature of things; there are better ways for us to be: to be in accord with nature. For textual support, commentators in this camp point to passages in which Zhuangzi emphasizes that *Dao* identifies all things; *Dao* embraces all and rejects none; *Dao* treats everything as equal. The *Dao* that Zhuangzi praises seems to be an ultimate exemplification of the principle of impartiality. From the perspective of *Dao*, or we can say from the Heavenly point of view, all things are equal and there is no distinction between right and wrong, good and bad. But in the world of men, there have to be such distinctions. If *Dao*'s perspective is superior to human perspective, should we, and could we, adopt this perspective? How are we to live among men while adopting the perspective of *Dao* and treat all as equals in value and importance?

Philip Ivanhoe argues that Zhuangzi's depiction of the Heavenly point of view is meant to be "a form of therapy," to "remind us that we are part of the greater pattern within which we are simply one small part."[54]

Therefore, we do not need to abandon our own human perspective; we just need to remember that it is part of a larger scheme. Berkson, on the other hand, argues that we *should* emulate *Dao*'s perspective as employed by the sage. Berkson thinks that once an individual achieves Heaven's point of view, she can treat all states in life (life, death, illness, aging, etc.) in equal manner and not be bothered by any external affairs at all. "One escapes the perspectivism of human-centered points of view trapped within systems by escaping the systems altogether in a Heaven's eye view that illuminates all things to show their relativity and ultimate equality."[55] Yearley thinks that there is a radical as well as a conventional side to Zhuangzi. Under the radical side, Zhuangzi would be advising us to just treat life "as a cinema show, a series of passing frames, a kaleidoscope of ever-changing patterns."[56] We should thus celebrate all life situations in which we find ourselves. By appealing to Zhuangzi's metaphor of the mirror, Yearley continues: "A mirror makes no judgments on rightness or wrongness; it impartially reflects a child killed or a child saved. A mirror possesses no desire to grasp what passes before it; it just lets desirable objects come before it and then pass away."[57] A person with the mirror-like mind, under this interpretation, would have no sorrow about any tragic event in life. Such a person would have no attachment to any person or thing, and would make no judgment on right or wrong. It would seem as if he is not even *human*. Is this Zhuangzi's view? If so, why would he advocate that forgetting moral distinctions and having no emotional attachment is a moral ideal in itself?

To see what Zhuangzi really set up as his moral ideals, we should first separate his depiction of the ethically ideal state and his depiction of the ethically ideal person. And then we can try to see where individuals should place themselves.

The ethically ideal state

Zhuangzi saw the distinction between morality and immorality as an artificial separation introduced by people like Confucius. The ethically ideal state is, according to Zhuangzi, a state where people are naturally moral without even thinking about the notion of morality itself. He gave the following depiction of the difference between his ideal ethical state and the ideal social state that Confucians wished to establish:

> When the springs dry up, the fish are stuck together on the land. They douse each other with spit and spray each other with drool, but it is not

as good as forgetting each other in the rivers and lakes. Praising Yao and condemning Jie is not as good as forgetting them both and transforming with the Way.[58]

When the fish are in the water, they are not aware of the importance of water, nor do they worry about others' survival. But when they are out of water, they have to douse one another with spit to keep everyone alive. When people live in the world of *Dao*, they are not aware of the existence of *Dao* or the morality of other people. But when they are living outside of *Dao*'s world, then they have to teach morality to keep everyone from sinking into the abyss of chaos. The moral of Zhuangzi's story is that it is better for society to *be* moral on its own accord, than for it to be *made moral* by the Confucian moral teachings.

In "Knowledge Wandered North" in the Miscellaneous Chapters, Zhuangzi depicted Laozi telling Confucius: "The Way of the gentlemen [which you preach] is mere superficiality, is it not? But what the ten thousand things all look to for sustenance, what never fails them – is this not the real [*Dao*]?"[59] A contrast between what Confucians envision (a morally transformed world) and what Daoists put on a pedestal (an ideal world of *Dao*) is clearly made in this exchange. According to Laozi (as the spokesperson for Daoism here), human life is but a transitory state of existence, which is nothing but the permutation of *yin* and *yang*. The time in which there is human society is merely a brief moment in the transformation of *Dao*. When Confucius tried to improve human society with his moral teaching, he was looking at *Dao* with a narrow vision. Moral teaching can at best superficially alter people's behavior; it cannot be the true foundation for all beings. Hence, Confucian moral teaching cannot truly represent *Dao*. On the other hand, *Dao* sustains all things inexhaustibly and impartially. The world of *Dao* is eternal and incomprehensible. It cannot be divided into worlds of sages or of tyrants, since either the sage world or the tyrant world is but a fleeting moment in the world of *Dao*. Zhuangzi's point seems to be that things in the world are neither moral nor immoral, because morality is not part of Nature itself. "Morality" is a human conception, which applies only to human conduct. The world of *Dao* transcends the human realm; it is *the realm beyond*. In the world of *Dao*, there is no deficiency or inadequacy; everything is perfectly sustained by *Dao*. Hence, it is a world where moral teaching is *unnecessary*. It is not a state attained through the moral transformation of the people, but it is itself ethically ideal.

To attain this ethically ideal state for Zhuangzi, everyone has to learn the way of *Dao*. If all people could forget distinctions, then there would be no conflicts or contentions. They would have no fear or anger and would accept their condition without complaints or sorrow. They would "forget each other in the arts of [*Dao*]."[60] In this world, the ruler does not have to do anything to govern the people; the best way is to do nothing ("*wu-wei*") and let them be.[61] Everyone will be self-governed and be living in accord with Nature. In other words, the ethically ideal state is when *everyone* becomes the ethically ideal person.

The ethically ideal person

Of the ideal moral persons, whom Zhuangzi called "the perfect people," "the true people," "the pure people," or "the spiritual people," Zhuangzi gave many fanciful descriptions. They are not afraid of height or any other perilous situation; they cannot be harmed by blizzard or fire; they eat nothing but wind and they drink nothing but dew. They can roam about everywhere and never get stuck at any place.[62] To exemplify the great Virtue of *Dao*, the true people have to be totally impartial to what happens to them and be indifferent to their surroundings. "The true people of olden times did not resist poverty. They did not glory in success. They did not plan their affairs. They could miss without regretting it and hit without being pleased. Such people could climb high without shuddering. They could enter water without getting wet and fire without getting burned."[63] In all Zhuangzi's descriptions of these "super" beings, there is no mention of their family or backgrounds. They are depicted as having no human emotions and no human attachments. It seems that these moral ideals are not really humans. They are more like the anthropomorphized version of *Dao* itself.

A reasonable explanation for the nature of these super beings is to take them to be our spirit. Our spirit is not confined by space; hence, it can roam about freely. Our spirit is immaterial; hence, it cannot be harmed by fire or blizzard. Our spirit does not sustain itself on food; hence, it can eat wind and drink dew. Once one reaches the spiritual level, one is no longer restricted by any physical and earthly confinement. Zhuangzi told the story of a great butcher, Cook Ding,[64] who has mastered the way of *Dao* in his craft. Cook Ding explains how he maintains dexterity in butchering an ox:

> When I first began cutting up oxen, I did not see anything but oxen. Three years later, I couldn't see the whole ox. And now, I encounter them with spirit and don't look with my eyes. [My senses and cognition have come to a stop while my spirit moves where it wants.] I rely on the Heavenly patterns, strike in the big gaps, am guided by the large fissures,

and follow what is inherently so. I never touch a ligament or tendon, much less do any heavy wrenching! . . . There are spaces between those joints, and the edge of the blade has no thickness. If you use what has no thickness to go where there is space – oh! There is plenty of extra room to play about in. That's why after nineteen years the blade of my chopper is still as though fresh from the grindstone.[65]

From this story, we get the idea that if we can employ our spirit to have an intuitive grasp of the nature of things, then we will always be able to find room to maneuver our way through life without ever encountering obstruction. We have to use "what has no thickness to go where there is space." In other words, we have to reduce our ego and go with the flow; we have to let go of our insistent attitude and not force our way through. One who can do this will be one who has mastered "the key to nourishing life" (Zhuangzi's title for chapter 3).

In the human world, however, one always encounters obstruction. Not everyone can be the perfect person; not all human affairs can unfold according to the natural pattern of *Dao*. The way of the perfect people is appropriate for the world of *Dao*, where others all live and act in agreement with *Dao*. But the human world is far from the world of *Dao*. Hence, individuals who have learned *Dao* will always be living among men, "in the human realm" (Zhuangzi's title for chapter 4). For such individuals to survive in this world, they would have to either unlearn *Dao*, or accept the ridicule and even the grievance they would receive from their contemporaries. Using Confucius as his voice, Zhuangzi made the following comparison between his ideal persons and Confucius: " 'Such men as they,' said Confucius, 'wander beyond the realm; men like me wander within it. Beyond and within can never meet.' "[66] So, it is clear that Zhuangzi was well aware of the fact that his ethical view would not be suitable for the human world. When one is *in the realm of men*, one has to know how to survive in it. One will be subject to derision and criticisms (as Zhuangzi was from his peers), but one should try one's best to avoid harm and injury. To stand out among one's peers and to show total indifference to human distinctions is to draw attention to oneself and to accumulate either fame or denigration. Therefore, Zhuangzi's ideal personhood is not meant as an ethical ideal for one to conduct oneself in the human world. It is rather an ideal state for one's spirit, which can indeed "wander beyond the realm."[67] In other words, one should let one's spirit *roam freely and easily in the realm of Dao* (the title of chapter 1), so that one is not spiritually confined in the human realm. It would not be good, however, to appeal to the standard of the external realm and lament the flaws of the human realm. The ultimate goal is to be a habitant of the two realms simultaneously and be content in both realms. As Zhuangzi put it, "When neither Heaven nor humanity wins out over the other, this is called being a true person."[68]

On the practical side, Zhuangzi's advice for people conducting themselves in the human realm is threefold:

1   "Be useless." Zhuangzi gave many stories of the various "uses" a thing can have; among these uses "being useless" is a highly valuable, but often discredited, one. Zhuangzi says, "The cinnamon can be eaten so it gets cut down; the lacquer tree can be used so it gets hacked apart. All men know the use of the useful, but nobody knows the use of the useless."[69] To be useless is to hide one's brilliance so as to avoid drawing attention from others, to avoid being called into service for the rulers, and to avoid attracting followers. We can see that this has to be a way of survival in the corrupt and perilous world in which Zhuangzi found himself. As Zhuangzi's mouthpiece, an old oak tree tells a carpenter who deems it "worthless": "I've been trying a long time to be of no use, and though I almost died, I've finally got it. This is of great use to me. If I had been of some use, would I ever have grown this large?"[70] John S. Major puts it well: "An important motif in the [*Zhuangzi*] is based on the proposition that 'uselessness' is the key to survival in man's turbulent and unsatisfactory world, and that, conversely, the possession of qualities or talents conventionally thought to be useful frequently brings injury and grief to the possessor."[71]

2   "Accept fate." "Fate" in the *Zhuangzi* is not a destiny that is determined by some Supreme Being; "fate" simply refers to one's limitations in terms of carrying out one's dreams and ideals. In the Outer Chapters, such comments are put in Confucius' mouth: "For a long time I have tried to stay out of the way of hardship. That I have not managed to escape it is due to fate. For a long time I have tried to achieve success. That I have not been able to do so is due to the times. If it happens to be the age of a Yao or a Shun, then there are no men in the world who face hardship – but this is not because their wisdom saves them. . . . It is time and circumstance that make it so."[72] If the external circumstances are already given as a fixed state of turmoil and yet one still believes one has the ability to alter it, then one would be like "the praying mantis that waved its arms angrily in front of an approaching carriage, unaware that they were incapable of stopping it."[73] Life does not guarantee due rewards for one's effort; many things are beyond one's control. When one sees

the limits of one's ambition, one should just accept one's fate and let it be.

3 "Entertain the perspective of *Dao* and keep on an even keel in all things." Zhuangzi's advice on being useless and accepting fate can be seen as too passive. However, his philosophy is not just about survival. The first two steps are necessary for living out one's natural years so that one may have time to achieve "grandeur." The most essential Daoist teaching lies in possession of *Dao*'s perspective and understanding of *Dao*. One needs a long process of mental preparation to take a leap into the realm of *Dao*; just as the giant bird needs to have the wind piled up deep enough in order to take flight.[74] The kind of mental preparation one needs to have in order to comprehend the truth of *Dao* starts with *forgetting* the teachings of morality, the institutions of rites and music, etc. In other words, one needs first to forget one's bondage in the human realm. One story tells that when Confucius' star student Yen Hui was able finally to "sit down and forget everything," even Confucius wanted to learn from him.[75]

In conclusion, Zhuangzi did not prescribe *Dao*'s perspective, which exemplifies absolute impartiality toward everyone and everything, to individuals in the realm of men as guidance in life. The perspective of *Dao* is used as a mental relief for those who have seen the ideal world and yet know that they are still living in the less than ideal world. In Zhuangzi's view, the Confucian teachings of morality can only be used as a remedy for a world that is already corrupt; they can never build an ethically ideal world from scratch. On the other hand, if everyone can follow *Dao*, if everyone becomes a Perfect Person, then there will be an ethically ideal world realized in the human world. But such may be a mere dream or wishful thinking. One should let one's spirit roam about in this ideal world. But in the meantime, when living among men, one should just accept whatever one is given, resign oneself "to what cannot be avoided," and nourish what is within oneself.[76] In this way, one not only "survives" in the human world, but also "thrives" in the world of *Dao*.

Philosophy of Life and Death

Do death and illness really have an intrinsically negative value? Zhuangzi's many discussions on death and physical deformity may be his most shocking teaching to contemporary readers. He suggests that death is simply a new stage in life, which one should celebrate when it arrives.[77]

He also used many examples of physically deformed people to show that our maladies should not be cause for lamentation; rather, they should simply be accepted with ease.[78] Some commentators think that Zhuangzi's remarks on death and deformity are meant to have a shock value, to liberate the mind from obsessing on the self;[79] while others think that Zhuangzi did believe that our bodies are insignificant and thus both death and physical deformity, which affect only the body, are matters of little concern.[80] Did Zhuangzi really hold the view that life and death are of equal value? And if he did, how much persuasiveness can this view have? As a natural human reaction, we normally cherish life and health, while we abhor death and illness. But do death and illness really have an *intrinsically* negative value?

Zhuangzi discussed the natural value of death extensively. To him, the morally ideal person should be able to treat death indifferently. He says:

> The pure man of old knew neither to love life nor to hate death. He did not rejoice in his birth, nor did he resist death. Without any concern he came and without any concern he went, that was all. He did not forget his beginning nor seek his end. He accepted his body with pleasure, and forgetting life and death, he returned to the natural state. He did not violate [*Dao*] with his mind, and he did not assist Nature with man. This is what is meant by a pure man.[81]

According to one tale recorded in the Outer Chapters, Zhuangzi himself took such an attitude toward his wife's death. After she died, a friend of Zhuangzi went to convey his condolence. He expected to see Zhuangzi mourning; but instead, what he saw was Zhuangzi singing with drumbeats. He scolded Zhuangzi: "You lived with her, she brought up your children and grew old. It should be enough simply not to weep at her death. But pounding on a tub and singing – this is going too far, isn't it?" Zhuangzi's reply was:

> When she first died, do you think I didn't grieve like anyone else? But I looked back to her beginning and the time before she was born. Not only the time before she was born, but the time before she had a body. Not only the time before she had a body, but the time before she had a spirit. In the midst of the jumble of wonder and mystery a change took place and she had a spirit. Another change and she had a body. Another change and she was born. Now there's been another change and she's dead. It's just like the progression of the four seasons, spring, summer, fall, and winter. Now she's going to lie down peacefully in a vast room. If I were to follow after her bawling and sobbing, it would show that I don't understand anything about fate. So I stopped.[82]

Whether this story is true or not, it shows us two things. First, there is a change of attitude, from the ordinary reaction toward the death of the beloved, to the reaction of someone who has learned to view individual lives from a grander perspective. Second, this second attitude is contrary to the social norms and would be considered depraved or eccentric by human standards. No wonder Zhuangzi would say, "the petty man of Heaven is a gentleman among men; the gentleman among men is the petty men of Heaven."[83] It seems that the perspective of *Dao* and the perspective of humans are naturally in conflict. Zhuangzi here clearly recommended *Dao*'s perspective and argued that we should learn to celebrate death just as we do life.

To evaluate Zhuangzi's view on life and death, health and illness, let us see his view presented in arguments:

[F] The Argument from the Ignorance of the Death State

How do I know that loving life is not a mistake? How do I know that hating death is not like a lost child forgetting its way home? Lady Li was the daughter of the border guard of Ai. When the duke of Jin got her, her tears fell until they soaked her collar. But once she reached the royal palace, slept in the king's bed, and ate the meats of his table, she regretted her tears. How do I know that the dead don't regret that they ever longed for life?[84]

Here Zhuangzi used the story of Lady Li to illustrate his point that nobody really knows what death is like. For all we know, we could be having an illusory life while death could be the real life that follows. We fear death, but we really don't have reason to fear it. The shorter our life span is, the longer our death span might be. Death is not a bad thing just as life is not necessarily a good thing. His argument can be formulated this way:

1 When we are alive, we don't know what death is like.
2 We fear death because it is a state different from life.
3 But for all we know, this different state could be better than our present state.
4 To fear an unknown state, which could be better, is not rational.
5 Therefore, we should not fear death.

[G]   The Argument from the Function of Death

> The universe gives me my body so I may be carried, my life so I may toil, my old age so I may repose, and my death so I may rest. To regard life as good is the way to regard death as good.[85]

In this passage, Zhuangzi assumed that there should be different functions for the different states of our life, and he included death as one of the states of life.

1   There are different states of life, which include birth, maturity, aging and death.
2   Each state of life has its own function for us.
3   The function of life gives us toil; the function of death is to give us rest.
4   Without one or the other, life would not be complete.
5   Therefore, if we regard life as good, we should regard death as good too.

Is Zhuangzi successful in convincing us that the fear of death is actually unnatural or irrational? His arguments are based on two metaphysical assumptions. First, there is a form of existence that does not necessarily begin with our life, nor does it end with our death. Zhuangzi's notion of *afterlife*, however, is different from the common Western notion. The kind of existence that can continue after death does not necessarily include a prolonged memory of one's present life or even self-identity. It could be simply a form of dust and matter with no consciousness.[86] From *Dao*'s perspective, such existence is still part of Nature and it is thus no different from the existence that we have had before we die. Life and death should have equal value because there is always *a certain form of existence* that remains. This view on life can be further explained by the comments in chapter 22 of the Miscellaneous Chapters:

> Life is the companion of death, death is the beginning of life. Who understands their workings? Man's life is a coming-together of breath. If it comes together, there is life; if it scatters, there is death. And if life and death are companions to each other, then what is there for us to be anxious about?[87]

From this passage, we see that Zhuangzi's view on life is that it is not just a process from birth to death. Birth and death are simply two stages in the whole transformation of things. The entity of transformation is "breath," or energy ("*qi*") in general. Different material objects are formed when the energy is condensed and their death or disintegration releases the energy back to the universe. Therefore, viewed in the grand picture of things, nothing is gained from an individual's birth and nothing is lost from her death.

Second, the love for life and the fear of death comes from an obsession with the self and the body. If we did not care so much about ourselves, then the fact that after *we* die, *something else* will emerge should be no reason for distress. *We* will no longer exist; *our bodies* will be "eaten by the mole crickets and ants" underground.[88] But our energy (or our spirit) will return to the wind, and our physical stuff will give other creatures nourishments. So, if we can forget about the self and the body, then we really should not be troubled by our own death. Graham says, "It seems . . . that for [Zhuangzi] the ultimate test is to be able to look directly at the facts of one's own physical decomposition without horror, to accept one's dissolution as part of the universal process of transformation."[89]

Under these two assumptions, "Can we do it?" begs the question, since *we* certainly cannot do it. "We" is already a term associated with a self (or selves). For us ever to treat death as of equal value to life is to abandon our self-love, our self-identity, and our human relations. Russell Legge says that the Perfect Person in the *Zhuangzi* is one whose mind "is the group mind." "The only difference between his knowledge and that of others is that his is inclusive and theirs is exclusive. This is the nature of his transcendence. The perfect man has no self-identity apart from others. *His freedom from self makes this possible and in this is his freedom.*"[90] Therefore, Zhuangzi's arguments against the rationality of the fear of death would not be successful *to us* unless we can first learn to abandon our self-insistence. (As we shall see later, abandoning self-insistence is one of the first lessons in Buddhism.)

In this context, we can interpret the famous story of Zhuangzi's dreaming of being a butterfly:

> One night, Zhuangzi dreamed of being a butterfly – a happy butterfly, showing off and doing as he pleased, unaware of being Zhuangzi. Suddenly he awoke, drowsily, Zhuangzi again. And he could not tell whether it was Zhuangzi who had dreamt the butterfly or the butterfly dreaming Zhuangzi. But there must be some difference between them! This is called the transformation of things.[91]

This is not the Cartesian Dream argument once again. In this story, Zhuangzi is explicating his notion of *the transformation of things*. One's self-identity is no longer stable in the perpetual transformation of things. One could be a person at one stage; one could be a butterfly at another.

It is the same elements of *Dao* that get transformed into different shapes. If we can see this point, then we should welcome death, as it opens the door to the next stage of the transformation of things.

Zhuangzi's second task was to rid people of their obsession with their physical appearance. In chapter 5, "Signs of Virtue Complete," he used many examples of people who were born ugly, who suffer from strange illnesses that transform their physical shapes, who receive physical punishment that deprive them of some body parts, etc., to show that appearance really does not matter when it comes to the manifestation of the inner virtue.

Zhuangzi used as an example a story about someone who became physically misshapen by illness to present his own view of the impartial treatment of all physical conditions. When asked by his friends whether he resented the physical mutations, the man replied:

> Suppose my left arm is transformed into a cock. With it I should herald the dawn. Suppose my right arm is transformed into a sling. With it I should look for a dove to roast. Suppose my buttocks were transformed into wheels and my spirit into a horse. I should mount them. What need do I have for a chariot? When we come, it is because it was the occasion to be born. When we go, it is to follow the natural course of things. Those who are contented and at ease when the occasion comes and live in accord with the course of Nature cannot be affected by sorrow or joy. This is what the ancients called release from bondage. Those who cannot release themselves are so because they are bound by material things. That material things cannot overcome Nature, however, has been a fact from time immemorial. Why, then, should I dislike it?[92]

Even though very few people can actually be persuaded by this view, it was not Zhuangzi's point to establish the claim that all physical conditions are really of equal value. A real cock could herald the dawn; a real sling could be used to capture the dove. But a person's body thus transformed would lose the function of the human body. A crippled man cannot run as fast as an ordinary man, a blind person cannot see, and a deaf person cannot hear. These physical impairments do cause inconveniences in life. To interpret Zhuangzi's view as arguing that they are no different from a normal, healthy physical state is to turn him into a sophist, which he clearly is not. What Zhuangzi wanted to show is that when one's physical conditions are given as such, one can only accept one's fate and be content with it. One can amuse oneself with all those fanciful thoughts about the possible functions of one's new body. However, unless one remembers that it is not the body, but the spirit, that is important, one cannot be truly content.

At bottom, Zhuangzi's philosophy of life and of one's conduct or attitude in life is similar to the teaching of the Stoics, which is a philosophical school that also developed during the worst of times. While one cannot change the reality one is given, one can always change one's perception of it. When we stop viewing our life as miserable, our life stops being miserable. Zhuangzi did not develop his view on life and death, on health and deformity, merely as a way to upset the ordinary people's perception of the world in order to establish his theoretical goal. His philosophy actually has a pragmatic goal of helping people deal better with their ill fates. Even with all the talk about "the outer realm," it is still based on a "this-worldly" concern.[93] Under Zhuangzi's teaching, while one must learn to *survive* in the human world and see human distinctions as they are, one can always embrace *Dao*'s perspective that eliminates all human distinctions. One thereby sets one's spirit free, allowing it to roam at ease in the world of *Dao*. The perspective of men enables one to deal with the external world; the perspective of *Dao* enables one to escape into one's inner world. To lose the former would bring harm; to lose the latter would bring sorrow. Therefore, the two perspectives should not obstruct each other.

Conclusion

Zhuangzi stood out among ancient Chinese philosophers in his seemingly carefree attitude toward the turmoil of his time. As we have seen, a shared concern among ancient Chinese philosophers was to find the best way to restore world order, to instill morality in the rulers and the people, and to ensure peace and harmony in human society. Most of them spent the major part of their adult life trying to put their ideals into practice by assiduously seeking employment from lords or kings. Zhuangzi, however, spurned political employment even when the opportunity came to his door. A famous story, recorded by an ancient historian in the second century BCE, tells that when a king sent his messenger with lots of money to entice Zhuangzi to come to his court, Zhuangzi told the messenger:

> Haven't you ever seen an ox used for sacrifice? After it had been fed with fine food for several years, it was clothed in embroidery and brought to the temple to be slaughtered. At that time, even if it wished to go back to its original lone state to be playing in the mud, it could not do it. Away with your money! I'd rather be like the ox playing in the mud than be serving your king. I shall never seek office so that I can always preserve my freedom and happiness.[94]

179

This story and others like it give many commentators the impression that Zhuangzi was egoistic, that he was interested only in his own spiritual freedom and not in the political reform of his world. Some commentators even think that Zhuangzi's whole philosophy spins from his playful attitudes toward life and thus we should not take what he says too seriously.[95] However, there was actually a heavy, serious, and world-oriented side to Zhuangzi that became hidden behind his jesting and teasing. In his time, it was easily possible to incur harsh and unreasonable punishments because of the whims of tyrannical kings. In his stories, Zhuangzi often used examples of people whose legs were amputated, whose foreheads were branded, whose noses were cut off. This shows how difficult it was just to live out one's natural years without harm. Zhuangzi's lesson is about survival in this chaotic world. His favorite contrasting model is Confucius, for whom he seems to have had a great respect as well as mild criticisms. In his lifetime, Confucius was known to be "the one who knows a thing cannot be done and still wants to do it."[96] Zhuangzi thought the glorious past that Confucius longed for could never be brought back; the distant future that Confucius dreamt about could not be brought nearer either. It is better to recognize the fate one is given and see the futility of resisting the inevitable. A passage at the end of chapter 4, "In the World of Men," tells it well: "When the world has the Way, the sage succeeds; when the world is without the Way, the sage survives. In times like the present, we do well to escape penalty."[97] Under this motivation, Zhuangzi launched his attacks on competing schools in his time, and advocated his philosophy of "the use of the uselessness."[98] Zhuangzi's philosophy of life has given mental solace to many intellectuals in Chinese history, as it certainly will to people in the contemporary world as well.

Further discussion questions

1 What is Zhuangzi's view of the universe? What does Zhuangzi mean when he argues that everything in the universe is equal and there is no distinction of values?
2 What does Zhuangzi mean by "the universe is One"? Is Zhuangzi's metaphysical view a version of monism? What is the relation between the One and the Many? Does the One produce the Many according to Zhuangzi?
3 What stands in the way of our knowing *Dao*? What are the fundamental epistemic limitations we have? Can we ever eliminate these limitations?
4 What do you think Zhuangzi is telling us about how we should act in a universe of equal values? What kind of attitude is he teaching people? Do you find Zhuangzi's view too radical?

5 What does Zhuangzi mean by "nature"? If humans naturally desire life and fear death, would it be in accordance with *nature* to prefer life to death?
6 How is Zhuangzi's moral teaching different from the moral teaching of Confucianism? Which one appeals to you more? Why?

Primary texts

Wing-tsit Chan (ed.) *A Sourcebook in Chinese Philosophy*. Princeton: Princeton University Press, 4th edn., 1973 (ch. 8; selections).
A. C. Graham. *Chuang-tzu: the Inner Chapters*. Indianapolis, IN: Hackett Publishing Company, Inc. 2001.
Philip J. Ivanhoe and Bryan W. Van Norden (eds.) *Readings in Classical Chinese Philosophy*. Indianapolis, IN: Hackett Publishing Company, Inc. 2003 (ch. 5; selections).
Burton Watson (trans.) *Chuang Tzu: Basic Writings*, New York: Columbia University Press, 1964; repr. 1996.
—— (trans.) *The Complete Works of Chuang Tzu*. New York: Columbia University Press, 1968.

Further readings

Mark Berkson. "Language: The Guest of Reality – Zhuangzi and Derrida on Language, Reality, and Skillfulness." In Paul Kjellberg and Philip J. Ivanhoe (eds.), *Essays on Skepticism, Relativism, and Ethics in the Zhuangzi*. Albany, NY: State University of New York Press, 1996, pp. 97–126.
Chung-Ying Cheng. "Nature and Function of Skepticism in Chinese Philosophy." *Philosophy East & West* 27(2), April 1977: 137–54.
Russell B. Goodman. "Skepticism and Realism in the *Chuang Tzu*." *Philosophy East & West* 35(3), 1985: 231–7.
Jung H. Lee. "Disputers of the Tao: Putnam and Chuang tzu on Meaning, Truth, and Reality." *Journal of Chinese Philosophy* 25(4), 1998: 447–70.
Deborah H. Soles and David E. Soles. "Fish Traps and Rabbit Snare: Zhuangzi on Judgment, Truth and Knowledge." *Asian Philosophy* 8(3), November 1998: 149–64.
Wenyu Xie. "Approaching the Dao: From Lao Zi to Zhuang Zi." *Journal of Chinese Philosophy* 27(4), 2000: 469–88.

Chapter 8

Hanfeizi (Han Fei Tzu)

Introduction

Hanfeizi (ca. 280–233 BCE) has often been called the synthesizer of Legalism, a school of political thought prominent in the Warring States period of China (403–221 BCE).[1] The Warring States period was a time when multiple nation-states in China competed against one another for more land and power; among them, the king of Qin had the most potency and ambition to unify China. Hanfeizi came from a royal family in the state of Han. He was allegedly a student of Xunzi, but felt dissatisfied with Confucian political philosophy. After studying some of the founding Legalists' thought, he decided to promote a Legalist rulership first to his own king of Han, and later to the king of Qin. According to a reliable historical record (Si-ma Qian's *Historical Records*, second–first centuries BCE), Hanfeizi had a stammer. He thus devoted his energy to writing and became one of the most prolific philosophers in ancient China. The king of Han could not abide by his suggestions on rulership, so Hanfeizi started to promote his ideal elsewhere. The king of Qin read some of his writings and was highly impressed. He invited Hanfeizi to his state with the intention of making him one of his advisory ministers. But unfortunately, Hanfeizi's former classmate Li Si, another of Xunzi's students, was at that time the king's advisory minister. He was well aware of Hanfeizi's intelligence and feared that his own position would be threatened. By accusing Hanfeizi of being a Han loyalist, Li Si managed to incite doubt about Hanfeizi's true intent in the king's mind and Hanfeizi was imprisoned. Before the king had a change of heart (which he later did), Hanfeizi drank the poison supposedly sent by Li Si and ended his life. On the basis of Hanfeizi's teachings, however, the king of Qin later conquered all other nation-states and became the first emperor of China. The main spirit of China's government structure was built on Hanfeizi's philosophy; furthermore, his advice on rulership was the model on which Chinese political culture was based.

Hanfeizi's many articles were later compiled into *Hanfeizi*, a big collection of 55 chapters. Even though some commentators dispute the authenticity of some of these chapters, a consensus among them seems to be that the whole work displays unity and coherence both in thought and in style. We now only have one translation of the complete work,[2] and this is currently out of print. Burton Watson's *Han Fei Tzu: Basic Writings* contains just 12, albeit essential, chapters, while other anthologies have even fewer excerpts. In the intellectual history of China, Hanfeizi's thought has often been neglected, probably because he deals more with the pragmatics of rulership than with profound philosophical thinking. In the minds of historical Chinese scholars (especially Neo-Confucians), Hanfeizi is frequently slighted because he speaks from the ruler's perspective and not from that of the people. Among contemporary scholars on Chinese philosophy, Hanfeizi's thought has also not been given due attention. The only exception was when mainland China renewed its interest in Legalism from the Marxist and Maoist point of view in the late 1970s and early 1980s.[3]

As K. K. Lee puts it, the School of Legalism was not inspired by any particular ideology. Legalists were concerned primarily with establishing political order and administrative efficiency.[4] The main bulk of Hanfeizi's writings are indeed on practical guidance for rulership. He lists many historical events to back up his assertions and to make his recommendations. His political theory is based on empirical studies; it is not constructed from an idealist perspective. Implicit in his practical political guidance is his view on human nature, human society and the function of government. This chapter will be based on the entire work of *Hanfeizi*. We will focus on his philosophy of human nature as well as his political philosophy based on such a view of human nature.

Human Nature and Social Control

Hanfeizi's basic assumption is that humans are by nature self-interested.[5] Unlike his teacher Xunzi, Hanfeizi was not interested in philosophical discussion on the original natural state of human beings; rather, he made the assertion on the basis of empirical studies. In Hanfeizi's usage, human nature consists simply of "the natural tendencies in human conduct." One primary tendency in human conduct is that we all seek to maximize benefits for ourselves and we all try to avoid harm to ourselves. Hanfeizi does not regard this self-interested tendency as "evil";

he merely takes it as a matter of fact and tries to explain how best to achieve social order on the foundation of human nature. However, he shares his teacher's view that civil conduct and moral thinking are "artificial" – they are the result of social conditioning. In Xunzi's view, social conditioning is accomplished through the social institution of rites and rituals; in Hanfeizi's opinion, it can only be achieved through law and punishment.

Hanfeizi says:

> A physician will often suck men's wounds clean and hold the bad blood in his mouth, not because he is bound to them by any tie of kinship but because he knows there is profit in it. The carriage maker . . . hopes that men will grow rich and eminent; the carpenter fashioning coffins hopes that men will die prematurely. It is not that the carriage maker is kindhearted and the carpenter a knave. It is only that if men do not become rich and eminent, the carriage will never sell, and if men do not die, there will be no market for coffins. The carpenter has no feeling of hatred towards others; he merely stands to profit by their death.[6]

With these examples, Hanfeizi shows that human society is an interlocked network of profits and interests. One man's loss may be another man's gain; one profession's success may be completely based on others' demise. Everyone naturally aims for the maximization of his self-interest; therefore, it is only natural that some people should wish for others' loss or demise. Hanfeizi does not place any value judgment on such a mentality. All people are naturally egoistic.

One's mindset is affected not only by one's profession, but also by one's external environment. Hanfeizi says:

> In the spring following a famine year even the little boys of the family get no food; in the fall of a year of plenty even casual visitors are feasted. It is not that men are indifferent to their own flesh and blood and generous to passing visitors; it is because of the difference in the amount of food to be had. Hence, when men of ancient times made light of material goods, it was not because they were benevolent, but because there was a surplus of goods; and when men quarrel and snatch today, it is not because they are vicious, but because goods have grown scarce.[7]

Hanfeizi seems to think that people generally share such moral attributes as kindness and generosity (or their opposites such as callousness and parsimony), but they exemplify different traits because of their various external circumstances. If this is so, then these moral attributes are not part of humans' intrinsic nature. Humans are more or less the product of their socio-economic environment. Moral traits such as generosity and kindness could be promoted when times are good, but they will soon disappear when times are bad.

Hanfeizi also argues that people by nature detest hard work and prefer leisure. If they lead their lives in a relaxed and lazy manner, then their jobs are neglected; if their jobs are neglected, then the government cannot maintain control over the people. Once the government loses control, society would turn into chaos.[8] Therefore, to have a proper working society, one cannot possibly rely on people's self-motivation. It is the job of the ruler to set up an effective system to motivate people to work hard.

Hanfeizi uses the etymological comparison between the Chinese characters for "public" and for "private" to show that even when the two words were first coined, their creator, Cang Jie, must already have understood that *public* and *private* are mutually opposed. The Chinese word for "public" is composed of the Chinese word for "private" and a symbol for "opposed to."[9] If public interest and private interest naturally oppose each other, then people's aggrandizing their self-interest necessarily interferes with society's public interest. In other words, if people are allowed to act according to their natural inclinations, then society will only be hurt by it. If humans are naturally selfish and lazy, rulers need to use drastic means in order to get them to act for the public good. Simply letting them do what they are wont to do will bring disorder and corruption. This is why Hanfeizi thinks that to identify maximizing individuals' self-interest with the enlargement of public interest will only lead to disasters.

Hanfeizi rejects Confucian moral teachings as a means of social control. He argues that even if there are a few genuinely virtuous people who would act morally without external incentives, most people only act in a way to benefit themselves and to avoid bad consequences for themselves. Only laws and punishments could effectively prevent socially disruptive behavior of the general masses. Humans have a universal preference for benefits and a universal aversion to harm; therefore, the way to effectively control them is to employ rewards that would greatly benefit people and punishments that would severely harm people. As Yu-lan Fung puts it, human's self-interested calculation is what makes the system of rewards and punishment possible.[10]

Using an example, Hanfeizi argues his point this way:

Now here is a young man of bad character. His parents rail at him but he does not reform; the neighbors scold him but he is unmoved; his teachers instruct him but he refuses to change his ways. Thus, although three fine influences are brought to bear on him – the love of his parents, the efforts of the neighbors, the wisdom of his teachers – yet he remains unmoved and refuses to change so much as a hair on his shin. But let the local magistrate send out the government soldiers to enforce the law and search for evil-doers, and then he is filled with terror, reforms his conduct, and changes his ways. Thus the love of parents is not enough to make children learn what is right, but must be backed up by the strict penalties of local officials; for people by nature grow proud on love, but they listen to authority.[11]

One could of course object to this argument by pointing out that the conclusion generalizes from one particular example. Even if Hanfeizi's point is valid in this case, it does not prove his point that only law and punishment are effective in general. However, Hanfeizi's conviction is that everyone is like this young man of bad character. There will always be times when people are unmoved by the love of their parents, when they are not amenable to their neighbors' condemnation, and when they are incorrigible in the face of their teachers' admonition. Therefore, law and authority are the only means of social control that will guarantee success.

In summary, what common folk generally prefer are material gains, physical well-being, leisure, eminence, glory, and fame; what they generally detest are poverty, physical injuries (including death), hard work, low status, humiliation, and disrepute. To be a successful ruler, one has to understand the people's preferences and distastes and manipulate them successfully to one's advantage. Rulership is a form of social control, and social control comes from understanding the people's minds. Hanfeizi emphasizes the indispensability of rewards and punishments in social control. Various forms of rewards can motivate the people to act in a certain way – they can even inspire soldiers to fight to their death on the battlefield. Harsh punishment, especially corporal punishment, can intimidate the people into refraining from acting in a certain way – they can even make people ignore gold that is left on the ground. Ultimately, the goal of law and punishment is social order. Hanfeizi says:

> Stiff penalty is what the people dread; harsh punishment is what the people detest. Consequently, the enlightened ruler sets up what the people dread to prohibit their misconduct; he devises what they detest to prevent their evil doing. The nation is in peace and riots or disorder do not arise. From this I see that benevolence, righteousness, love, and favor do not suffice, while stiff penalty and harsh punishment alone can govern the whole nation.[12]

From this remark, we see that Hanfeizi believed stiff penalty and harsh punishment to be the only effective means of social control. We should compare his view to that of Confucius, who says:

> Lead the people with governmental measures and regulate them by law and punishment, and they will avoid wrongdoing but will have no sense of honor and shame. Lead them with virtue and regulate them by the rules of propriety, and they will have a sense of shame and, moreover, set themselves right.[13]

The contrast between Legalism and Confucianism on law versus virtue is our next topic.

Morality and Politics: Legalism *contra* Confucianism

A major difference between Legalism and Confucianism lies in their positions on the relation between politics and morality. Confucians believe that morality is an indispensable element in politics: the ideal ruler should be a sage king; the ideal function of government is to morally transform its people. Under the Confucian view, the ideal society is achieved when the sage king, by setting an example, influences all his people to become morally self-motivated. Legalism, on the other hand, separates politics from morality. Politics is about governing men, not about morally transforming them. Moral transformation should be left to moralists and educators. In this respect, Legalists view politics as *amoral* – not concerned with moral judgment or moral behavior.

Confucians modeled their ideal society on ancient times. Both Confucius and Mencius frequently cited the ancient sage kings Yao and Shun as paradigms of ideal rulership. Hanfeizi, on the other hand, does not think that the ancient world can serve as a prototype to later societies. He has a progressive view of human history: when times have changed, laws and practices must also change. He argues that in the ancient world where resources were plentiful while the population was scarce, it was easier to promote generosity, kindness, and honesty. People were more naive and they knew fewer temptations. In Hanfeizi's times, the world had become much more complicated, and social interactions had become much more complex. One can no longer expect to rule the people as Yao and Shun once did. Hanfeizi says:

> Past and present have different customs; new and old adopt different measures. To try to use the ways of a generous and lenient government to rule the people of a critical age is like trying to drive a runaway horse without using reins or whip. This is the misfortune that ignorance invites.[14]

From a historian's perspective, Fung explains that in ancient society, when the state was smaller, the relationship between the ruler and the subjects was a personal one. Hence, a code of social etiquette (*li*) was a sufficient means of social control. As the state expanded, however, the ruler and his people became more remotely related. It would be difficult to continue to try to maintain social order through personal moral codes. This is when promulgated law becomes necessary.[15] While Confucius, as well as Laozi, wished to revert back to the ancient times, Hanfeizi wanted to move along with the times. While Confucianism and Daoism focus on the *ideal*, Legalism is founded on the *real*. While Confucianism and Daoism build on *potentiality*, Legalism is constructed on *necessity*.

Also contrary to the Confucian teaching of the "sage king," Hanfeizi argues that in terms of governing the people, it is neither the virtue of the ruler nor his love for the people that counts. He says

> When a sage governs a state, he does not wait for people to be good in deference to him. Instead, he creates a situation in which people find it impossible to do wrong. If you wait for people to be good in deference to you, you will find that there are no more than ten good people within the borders of your state. But if you create a situation in which people find it impossible to do wrong, the entire state can be brought into compliance. In governing, one must use what is numerous and abandon what is scarce. Therefore, the sage does not work on his virtue; he works on his laws.[16]

There are indeed exceptionally virtuous people, and when these virtuous people become kings, they could have the overpowering moral impact on the people that Confucianism depicts. But, as K. K. Lee puts it, "Exceptional men are few and far between, and it is ludicrous to hinge such a vital matter on the occasional and chancy appearance of a sage or messiah."[17] If we have to wait for generations for one sage king to appear, if stories of sage kings only occur in ancient myths, then the political model based on the moral power of sage kings cannot be the most suitable format for all nations at all times. "Charisma is too ephemeral and mediocrity is too endemic in man. The law, impersonal, enduring, immanent, yet capable of modification, should be the framework of civil/political order."[18] In this respect, we could say that while

Confucianism's emphasis on sage kings and moral influences may be more ideal, Legalism offers a more practical political model that is built on law rather than personality.

With regard to the ruler's kindness and love, Hanfeizi would have agreed with Machiavelli who claims that in the matter of rulership it is better to be feared than loved. Hanfeizi says:

> Now those who do not understand the art of governing always say, "One must win the hearts of the people." If one could bring about order simply by seeking to win the hearts of the people, there would be no need for great counselors. . . . All one would have to do is listen to the people. But the wisdom of the people cannot be used because their minds are like the minds of infants.[19]

His opinion of the people's judgment shows a deeper distrust for human rationality than Mozi does. Hanfeizi does not even think that humans are rationally self-interested. Just like an infant who would "scream and cry endlessly because it does not understand that enduring [a] tiny bit of discomfort will bring about a great benefit,"[20] humans often do not see that long-term benefits would come from their ignoring any immediate gain. Therefore, the ruler cannot count on having his policies welcomed and willingly obeyed by his people, even when such policies are to the people's benefit.

The right way to enforce any policy, according to Hanfeizi, is to appeal to law and penalty. Hanfeizi argues:

> The severe household has no fierce slaves, but it is the affectionate mother who has spoiled sons. From this I know that awe-inspiring power can prohibit violence and that virtue and kindness are insufficient to end disorder. When the sage rules the state, he does not depend on people to do good for him, but utilizes their inability to do wrong. If he depends on people to do good for him, we cannot even count ten within the state, but if he utilizes the people's inability to do wrong, the whole country may be regulated. A ruler makes use of the majority and neglects the minority, and so he does not devote himself to virtue but to law.[21]

Even if the ruler is genuinely loved by his people, he cannot count on them to put his interest above their own. Love and mercy of the ruler will of course please the people, but most will simply take advantage of the ruler's kindness and become unruly. Even if some are devoted to the ruler because of his virtue or his love, he cannot expect that *everyone* will thus abide by his decrees. Rulership should not be based on chancy successes; it must be guaranteed to succeed in order to be effective.

189

Hanfeizi does not deny that there are exceptions to the rule: not everyone is governed by stringent restraints or motivated by hefty rewards. There are those who have received moral training and are genuinely virtuous. The moral education advocated by the Confucians is not a total waste of effort since it can transform some people to be internally motivated by their good will. But such an education has limited success: even the great moral educator Confucius only obtained 72 devoted followers. Hanfeizi thinks that to control society, we need to find what works for the majority, not just what the ideal way would be according to the moral minority. Confucius may have been right that laws only restrain people from misdeeds and that only virtue can prompt people to act honorably. But most people only do things to gain benefits and to avoid harm. Therefore, it is law, not moral training, that is required in governing the people. Hanfeizi calls this a "necessity" in rulership. He says:

> [T]he enlightened ruler does not value people who are naturally good and who do not depend on reward and punishment. Why? Because the laws of the state must not be neglected and government is not for only one man. Therefore the ruler who has the technique does not follow the good that happens by chance but practices the way of necessity.[22]

Furthermore, according to Hanfeizi, the ultimate aim of rulership is for the ruler to have *absolute* control over his ministers and his subjects. Under this aim, individual moralists can only be viewed as "vermin," most harmful to society. Those who are virtuous cannot be motivated by rewards or be intimidated by punishments; they are thus dangerous to the ruler who aims to get his people to do whatever he wants. Hanfeizi not only thinks that Confucian moral training is ineffective in transforming the whole nation; he also thinks that it poses a great threat to the ruler. What the ruler should want in his people is not that they are virtuous and self-motivated, but that they are lawful and obedient. Hanfeizi stresses many times that "private virtues might very well be public vices."[23] He says:

> The presence of kind-hearted men [leads to] the existence of culprits among the magistrates; the presence of benevolent men, the losses of public funds; the presence of superior men, the difficulty in employing the people; the presence of virtuous men, the violation of laws and statutes; the appearance of chivalrous men, vacancies of official posts; the appearance of lofty men, the people's neglect of their proper duties; the emergence of unyielding heroes, the inefficacy of orders; and the appearance of popular idols, the isolation of the sovereign from the subjects.[24]

For closer examination, we can formulate Hanfeizi's arguments as follows:[25]

Hanfeizi's Argument #1[26]

1 According to human nature, none are more affectionate than parents who love their children, and yet not all children are necessarily orderly.
2 Rulers cannot possibly love their subjects more than parents love their children.
3 Therefore, there are bound to be unruly people even under a loving, humane ruler.
4 Therefore, neither love nor humanity is the way to run a government.

Hanfeizi's Argument #2[27]

1 Arrows are not naturally straight and wood is not naturally round, but skilled workmen can use straightening and bending methods to make arrows and wheels.
2 People are not naturally good, but rulers can use punishment and reward to make them behave.
3 Even if there is a single arrow straight by nature or a single piece of wood round by nature, it is a product of chance and is not valued by skilled workmen.
4 Similarly, even if there are some people who are good by nature and do not depend on punishment and reward, they are rare incidents.
5 One should practice the way of necessity and not act on the principle of chance.
6 Therefore, rulers should appeal to punishment and reward, not to the natural goodness in some people.

Hanfeizi's Argument #3[28]

1 Even with Confucius' moral example of, and his moral teachings on, humanity and righteousness, only 70 people followed him.
2 On the other hand, an inferior ruler with sovereignty of the state would have none in the whole state daring to rebel.
3 Therefore, most people are submissive to power while few men can be influenced by the doctrines of humanity and righteousness.

4 Therefore, using the teaching of humanity and righteousness as the art of rulership is impractical and impossible.

Hanfeizi's Argument #4[29]

1 Teaching virtue can exhort people to do good, while using law can prohibit people's doing wrong.
2 Virtuous people are the minority in any given society, while the majority are only concerned with consequences of breaking the law.
3 In ruling the nation, the goal should be to prohibit wrongdoings of *all* people rather than to promote good deeds in the minority of people.
4 Therefore, a ruler must devote himself not to moral teaching but to law.

What Hanfeizi advocates is that politics and morality are unrelated issues. This would naturally follow from his view on the natural tendencies in human conduct. If the majority of the people were naturally to tend to their self-interest and seek opportunities to violate the law without being caught, then there has to be an effective means to govern the majority. However, his arguments are faulty. With his first argument, we can see that the first premise oversimplifies family relations. It is not true that unruly children all come from families with abundant parental love. From our contemporary experience, children raised by abusive parents are more likely to become disruptive to society than those from loving families. With the second argument, we can point out first that the analogy does not work. Humans are not wood; hence, even if naturally straight wood is accidental, it does not show that naturally good people are exceptions to the rule. Secondly, the conclusion does not follow. For lack of empirical counterexamples, we could grant Hanfeizi that humans are not naturally good. But this does not prove that methods of punishment and rewards are therefore the "necessary means" of control. Other methods could be equally, if not more, effective. With the third argument, we should point out that his contrast of an inferior ruler to Confucius is not adequate. It is indeed true that in the world of politics, one's power of persuasion comes from one's political status. But this does not show that political status in conjunction with Confucius' moral teaching would not be far more powerful than the law instituted by an inferior ruler. Finally, with the fourth argument, we should note the unjustified exclusive disjunction. Even if it is true that moral teaching can exhort people to do good while law can prohibit them from doing wrong, there is no need to choose one over the other. Both moral teaching and law can be essential to rulership, such that most people are taught to be good while the recalcitrant few are restrained by law from committing improper acts. Hanfeizi's Legalist conclusion that *only* law and punishment are necessary to rulership simply does not follow from his claims.

If Hanfeizi's point were merely that moral education should be left to other agencies, which can more effectively promote the moral caliber of the people, then his political philosophy is at most incomplete, not amoral. However, his skepticism and criticism of moralists and intellectuals alike are widely expressed in his writings. He condemns those who are self-motivated to be moral and intellectual and argues that they are useless to the ruler and dangerous to society, for the simple reason that punishments and rewards are ineffectual on them. Hanfeizi's political philosophy aims to establish absolute control for the ruler, not for society itself and the people at large. He is not merely saying that moral education is inept in politics; he is arguing that morality should be rejected in political affairs. His view on morality and politics is not just that politics should be *amoral*, but also that it should be *anti*-moral.

From a Confucian standpoint, a polity that employs only law and punishment as a means of social control is ultimately anti-moral. As K. K. Lee explains:

> The very notion of a scale of punishments smacked of the spirit of utility, as if it was meant to encourage the would-be offender to calculate rationally the profits and the losses incurred in violating the rule, on the basis of which he would decide whether it paid to do so. This would be corruption of morality itself, since the Confucian-deontological view of morality enjoined doing what was right irrespective of the consequences involved.[30]

As critique, we should examine the shortcomings of Hanfeizi's rejection of morality as an element of politics. Theoretically, if one believes that human nature is self-interested and self-interest is opposed to public interests, then everyone is potentially an enemy of the state. The function of law is merely to restrain people and to pre-empt all sorts of socially pernicious acts – this is *law in the negative sense*. At the same time, if people's mindset is to weigh possible gains from wrongdoings against possible harms from punishments, then punishments for undesirable deeds have to be as severe as possible. This theory, when put into practice, would result in harsh corporal punishment, including all forms of mutilation and torture, and lead to cruel and vicious executions. Legalism creates a cruel and ruthless political structure. Government intimidates its people into complete obedience while no other voice is allowed. Such absolutism can easily lead to tyranny, since no one would be there to check the ruler's conduct should he become irrational. Unfortunately, Legalism became the *de facto* ideology for ancient Chinese rulers. Many Legalists in history suffered the consequences of their own teaching. Hanfeizi's predecessor Shang Yang ended up being torn to pieces by five horses; Hanfeizi's fellow student Li Si was cut in half at the waist. In comparison, Hanfeizi's own death from drinking poison could be considered "merciful."

Practical Guidelines for Rulership: Law, Statecraft, and Power

Being a "synthesizer," Hanfeizi combines the three things his predecessors emphasized in their works: law (*fa*), statecraft (*shu*), and political clout (*shi*). "Law" refers to a set of published codes of conduct, which include specific penal codes. According to Hsiao-po Wang's analysis, Hanfeizi's notion of law, in a positive sense, should be authoritative so as to command respect and voluntary compliance, while in a negative sense, it should effectively deter the occurrence of crime by certainty of sanction against the individual responsible for crimes.[31] The emphasis on *public* laws is an important contribution of the Legalists. Instead of making up laws and punishments as the situation arises, Hanfeizi's predecessor Shang Yang (died 338 BCE) inscribed his laws on stone tablets and placed them in the marketplace. All citizens in his state knew the dire consequences of violating these laws. Society was in perfect order during that time. Hanfeizi explains that the important feature of law is that it be publicly known. "The law is codified in books, kept in governmental offices, and promulgated among the hundred surnames [namely, the people]. The law wants nothing more than publicity... when the enlightened sovereign speaks on law, high and low within the boundaries will hear and know it."[32] Once the law is published, it is no longer subject to the whims of the ruler or the administrative officials. In this respect, the publication of laws provides some protection for the people. However, as Benjamin Schwartz points out, "It would... certainly be quite misleading to think of the 'publication' of the penal laws as in any sense a move toward 'democracy' or to fancy that the Legalists would themselves not believe in a highly authoritarian ruling class."[33] Under a Legalist regime, law does not need to be sanctioned by the people. The primary function of law is to control society and to regulate citizens.

Hanfeizi does not think that law itself is sufficient in rulership. Law is for the general public; to govern those close to him – ministers or those in the internal court (such as wives and sons) – the ruler needs to master statecraft. People will always try to find ways to advance themselves, and those closest to the ruler could most easily usurp the ruler's power. 'Statecraft' refers to various techniques or methods in the manipulation and control of others. Yu-lan Fung calls it "the art of conducting affairs and handling men."[34] In Hanfeizi's usage, statecraft is not exercised on society at large; rather, it is specifically geared toward ministers and close family members. Hanfeizi argues that the ruler and his ministers necessarily have conflicts of interests. "What benefits the ruler is employing the able; what benefits ministers is getting employed even when they are impotent. What benefits the ruler is rewarding those who accomplish much; what benefits ministers is getting rewards even when they have done nothing."[35] These ministers will try their best to deceive the ruler, to reap undeserved rewards and to avoid due punishments. Therefore, ministers, when unchecked, are the ruler's worst enemies. In ancient Chinese royal courts, the ruler usually had numerous wives and hence numerous descendants. These wives and sons often plotted against one another, and sometimes against the ruler himself, to secure their status as the rightful heir:

> When consorts, concubines, and heirs apparent have organized their cliques, they long for the ruler's death for, unless he dies, their position will never be really strong. They have no feeling of hatred toward the ruler; they merely stand to profit by his death. The ruler therefore must not fail to keep close watch on those who might profit by his death.[36]

Family relations in royal families are different from those in ordinary families in that there is much more at stake. This is why the ruler must employ statecraft among his family members as well. Since ministers and family members are close to the ruler and can quickly detect the ruler's mind, the ruler needs to be very discreet in his employment of statecraft. Hanfeizi says:

> A law is that which is enacted into the statute books, kept in government offices, and proclaimed to the people. Statecraft is that which is harbored in the ruler's own mind so as to fit all situations and control all ministers. Therefore for law there is nothing better than publicity, whereas in statecraft, secrecy is desired.[37]

The third element, "political clout," refers to the power and authority of the person of higher rank.[38] It is closely related to the manipulation of statecraft. Hanfeizi says, "Statecraft involves appointing officials according to their abilities and demanding that actualities correspond to names. It holds the power of life and death and inquiries into the ability of all ministers. These are powers held by the ruler."[39] In other words, the ruler can secure his political clout by the proper employment of statecraft. The two most important means of control are punishment and favor. Hanfeizi calls them the "two handles" of rulership. He explains:

> What do I mean by punishment and favor? To inflict mutilation and death on men is called punishment; to bestow honor and reward is called favor. Those who act as ministers fear the penalties and hope to profit by the rewards. Hence, if the ruler wields his punishments and favors, the ministers will fear his sternness and flock to receive his benefits. . . . Now if the ruler of men does not insist upon reserving to himself the right to dispense profit in the form of rewards and show his sternness in punishments, but instead hands them out on the advice of his ministers, then the people of the state will all fear the ministers and hold the ruler in contempt, will flock to the ministers and desert the ruler. This is the danger that arises when the ruler loses control of punishments and favors.[40]

In other words, the way to secure political clout is to be the one in charge of the assignment of punishment and rewards. If the ruler gives up this role, then he will soon lose his power to the person actually assigning punishments and rewards. Political clout does not automatically come from one's political status; it comes from the control of punishments and rewards. On the other hand, political clout cannot be established if one is not in the proper political position. It has nothing to do with one's virtue or one's reputation. As we explained earlier, Hanfeizi points out that Confucius was widely respected for his wisdom and virtues, but the people did not obey his words. On the other hand, a person who is inferior in all respects can command obedience from everyone within his sovereignty once he is on the throne. The difference between the effectiveness of the two in demanding obedience is in their political clout.

To keep a close watch on his ministers, the ruler needs to check their behavior against their claims. Hanfeizi gives this method of statecraft a special name: "actuality and name." "Actuality" refers to what one manifests in one's conduct or one's performance. "Name" refers to one's title, position, and one's claim. He says:

> Whenever a ruler wants to suppress treachery, he must examine the correspondence between actuality and names. Actuality and names refer to

ministers' words and deeds. When a minister presents his words, the ruler assigns him a task in accordance with his words and demands accomplishments specifically from that work. If the results correspond to the task and the task to the words, he should be rewarded. If the accomplishments do not correspond to the task or the task not to the words, he will be punished.[41]

In demanding correspondence between actuality and name, or, we may say, deeds and words, Hanfeizi stresses that even if the minister outdoes his words or performs something superfluous to his role assignment, he should still be punished. The aim of this statecraft is to make sure that ministers are true to their claims and their positions, so that no one can boast about what he cannot do or assume someone else's role. To emphasize the correspondence between actualities and names is to caution rulers not to rely on reputations or political factions. If the ruler employs officers according to others' recommendations or praise, then his subordinates will work for appearances and not for essence; they will form cliques and exchange favors. To prevent this, the ruler has to appeal to harsh punishments and generous rewards. Hanfeizi says:

> The Way of an enlightened ruler is to make it so that no minister may make a proposal and then fail to match it with actions and results. For this reason, when an enlightened ruler hands out rewards it is generous, like the fall of timely rain, and the hundred surnames all benefit from his bounty. When he hands out penalties, it is terrifying, like thunder and lightening, and even spirits and sages cannot undo his work. Thus, an enlightened ruler does not skimp on rewards or forgive penalties.[42]

By using the method of punishment and reward, the ruler enforces his insistence on the correspondence between actuality and name of his ministers' performance. This is the art of statecraft.

If the ruler wants to have an accurate grasp of his ministers' intent and conduct, then he cannot let them know what he desires or what would displease him. If his ministers were able to guess the ruler's preferences, then they would simply put on a façade to impress him. Hanfeizi says that the ruler must therefore appear to be free of emotions or desires:

> Remain empty, still, and without concern, so that you may secretly observe the defects of others. See others but do not allow yourself to be seen; hear others but do not allow yourself to be heard; know others but do not allow yourself to be known. Once you understand someone's words, do not alter or change them, but check them using the comparison

of form and name. If you put one person in every office, and do not allow them to speak with one another, then the ten thousand things will all be completed. Cover your tracks, conceal your starting points, and your subordinates will not be able to see where you are coming from. Get rid of wisdom, dispense with ability, and your subordinates will not be able to guess your intentions. Hold on to what people have said before, and look to see if they match it with results. Carefully take hold of the handles of punishment and reward and maintain firm control of them. Cut off all hope of using them, smash all intentions to take them, and do not allow people to covet them.[43]

These practical guidelines for rulership are meant for a monarchical political structure. Simply law alone may be sufficient in a democratic republic, where there is a system of checks and balances that functions to secure its operation. When the system is sound, it will not have severe and lasting tribulations even with a mediocre leader or scheming ministers. In a monarchy, where power is centered on one person alone, the king's position is quite precarious. Not only can power corrupt, the intense desire for power can also corrupt. Those surrounding the king – not just his ministers, but also his wives, sons, brothers, and even servants – will all try to find the opportunity to remove him. Law itself is not adequate to prevent usurpation from the inner circle. Therefore, the king has to be constantly on his guard; he cannot trust anyone. He must not listen solely to one person; he must not confide in anyone. He cannot reveal his true emotions, but must keep others constantly on their toes. He must not allow others the chance to take over his power of control, even though he should not release others from their duties and do everything on his own. He must delegate everything to his ministers; with one exception: he must *never* give up the practice of checking to make sure that their behavior corresponds to their position and their claim. By using this form of statecraft, the ruler can exercise his power and maintain his political clout. These two elements are essential supplements to law in rulership. Hanfeizi thinks that the art of statecraft and rulership are ultimately derived from Laozi's thought.

Hanfeizi and Laozi: *Dao* and *Wu-wei*

No matter how dissimilar Hanfeizi's political view may be to that of Laozi, he did credit Laozi for his philosophical inspiration. In the two chapters where Hanfeizi gives his exposition of Laozi and Daoism, he goes beyond applied political philosophy and engages in metaphysics.[44]

Following the Daoist tradition, he gives *dao* an ontological status. Hanfeizi defines *"Dao"* as the reason for existence for all things and as the origin of the universe. He says, "[*Dao*] is that by which all things become what they are. It is that with which all principles are commensurable."[45] In this comment, Hanfeizi also introduces the notion *principle* (*li*) in contrast to *dao*. He was the first person to give a philosophical analysis of this notion, which later became a key concept in the metaphysics of the Hua-yan School and Neo-Confucianism. He distinguishes *"dao"* and "principle" this way: *Dao* is eternal and universal; principle is the particular principle inherent in each thing. Principle is the order of existence for each particular thing, while *Dao* has no fixed content; it exemplifies itself in all individual things and all particular principles:

> Principles are patterns according to which all things come into being, and [*Dao*] is the cause of their being. Therefore it is said that [*Dao*] puts things in order (*li*). Things have their respective principles and cannot interfere with each other. Since things have their respective principles and cannot interfere with each other . . . principles are controlling factors in things. Everything has its own principle different from that of others, and [*Dao*] is commensurate with all of them [as one].[46]

Everything has its own principle, which separates one thing from another. We can probably call it "the principle of discernibility." Hanfeizi says, "In all cases principle is that which distinguishes the square from the round, the short from the long, the coarse from the refined, and the hard from the brittle."[47] He also thinks that the eternal *Dao* needs particular principles to realize itself; hence, there is no metaphysically dangling *Dao* persisting above the existing world. Nevertheless, even if all particular things disintegrate and all principles lose their material grounds, *Dao* will persist beyond time:

> According to definite principles, there are existence and destruction, life and death, flourish and decline. Now, a thing which first exists and then becomes extinct, now lives and then dies, or flourishes at first and declines afterward cannot be called eternal. Only that which exists from the very beginning of the universe and neither dies nor declines until heaven and earth disintegrate can be called eternal. What is eternal has neither change nor any definite particular principle itself. Since it has no definite principle itself, it is not bound in any particular locality.[48]

Hanfeizi depicts a one-layered ontology, in which *Dao* is not over and above the physical even though it is not confined in time and space. In other words, *Dao* encompasses every particular principle; hence, it cannot be identified with any single principle. Particular things have their spatial and temporal limitations, but *Dao* itself is unbounded by space and time. Particular principles cannot apply to other things of different kinds, whereas *Dao* applies to all things. *Dao* is the *One* when principles are many. The notion of *Dao* in Hanfeizi's understanding is indeed similar to that of Laozi.

In his philosophy of rulership, Hanfeizi also borrows many concepts from Laozi – but with a Legalist twist. He argues that the ruler is to his people as *Dao* is to all things in the universe. In the same way that *Dao* does nothing but accomplishes everything, the ruler should abide by the principle of non-action (*wu-wei*) in his management of the whole nation. Hanfeizi says:

> [*Dao*] is the beginning of the ten thousand things and the guiding thread of truth and falsity. For this reason, an enlightened ruler holds to the beginning so that he may know the source of the ten thousand things, and regulates the guiding thread so that he may understand the starting points of excellence and failure. Thus, empty and still he waits, allowing names to define themselves and affairs to determine themselves. Being empty, he grasps the essence of phenomena; being still, he understands the correctness of movements.[49]

The ruler sets up the bureaucratic system up front such that each minister has his own duties and assignments that come with his title. The ruler should then step back and observe the whole operation quietly and discreetly. As Roger Ames explains this notion, the ruler is "the human embodiment of the authority of the governmental machinery as a whole." The machinery has many individual parts, each running according to its due course. If the ruler intervenes with any part of the system, he will introduce "an arbitrary element into an otherwise automatically functioning system" and ultimately disrupt its operation.[50]

With all the manipulation of statecraft that Hanfeizi discusses, he still insists that the basic principle is non-interference and non-action. According to Laozi, while the sage does nothing, nothing is left undone. Hanfeizi interprets *"wu-wei"* this way:

> An enlightened ruler has wisdom, but he does not use it to make plans. He allows the ten thousand things to know their place. He has worthiness, but he does not use it to conduct his own affairs. He observes what his ministers and subordinates base their actions on. He has courage, but he does not use it to express anger. He allows the assembled ministers to fully extend their martial feelings. Thus, by getting rid of wisdom he

achieves clarity; by getting rid of worthiness he enjoys achievement; by getting rid of courage he possesses strength. When the assembled ministers keep to their duties, the hundred offices follow a uniform standard, and the ruler employs them based on their abilities, this is called "exercising the constant." Thus it is said, "Tranquil, he has no position to occupy. Isolated, no one knows his place."[51]

What he means is that the whole government should be based on the work of ministers and the institution of law. Ministers devise the law and execute it. The people understand and obey the law. The ruler should work as an overseer, whose job is merely to watch over his ministers' work. When every minister does his job properly, there is nothing for the ruler to do. Hence, the ruler has no position within the bureaucratic system; he is over and above it. Using the method of "actualities and names," the ruler checks to ensure that the system runs properly. "When a proposal is made, it itself serves to name the objectives. When an affair is carried out, it itself serves to form the results. When [actuality] and name are matched and found to be identical, there is nothing for the ruler to do, and everything returns to what is essential."[52] As K. K. Lee explains, "From the point of view of the ruler, once he set in motion the mechanism of the law, he could then leave it to run smoothly and uniformly without further direct interference."[53] When the ruler achieves this goal, he exemplifies the virtue of "non-action" of the overseeing *Dao*.

Fleshing out Laozi's anti-intellectualistic ideology into his Legalistic government, Hanfeizi says that in the state of the enlightened ruler, "there is no literature of books and records but the laws serve as the teaching. There are no sayings of ancient kings but the officials act as teachers."[54] It seems that the people only need to know the law and the ruler's decrees; they do not need to acquire erudition. There is no need for moral or intellectual educators; ancient classics or contemporary literature are dispensable. This view later led to the notorious book burning decreed by the First Emperor of Qin. Hanfeizi also had a low opinion of the wandering scholars of his times. In his judgment, these people are non-productive and useless. They don't farm; they can't lift heavy machinery and they are too incompetent to fight on the battlefield. If the people see how these scholars can profit from being idle, then they will all want to become scholars and the nation will be left with few people to till the land or fight the wars. Therefore, a ruler should not encourage scholarship; rather, he should punish scholars so that the people will see that such behavior has bad consequences. A carefree Daoist such as Zhuangzi would also be one of the enemies of the ruler. Zhuangzi himself refused the king's employment offer because he preferred to stay poor but free. People like him will not be motivated by fame or wealth, and thus the ruler will have a hard time manipulating them. In this respect, we see the fundamental difference between Daoism and Legalism: Daoism stresses nature and autonomy, while Legalism is all about manipulation and control.

Under the Daoist model, the ruler not only should not reveal his personal emotions and preferences, but also should have none. He should truly be an impartial observer, letting things run their due course while placing no value judgment on the outcome. In contrast, under the Legalist model, the ruler has his personal agenda: to gain absolute control of his subjects and his subordinates. He merely uses the appearance of having no emotions or preferences as a form of statecraft to accomplish that goal. He is a schemer, not an observer. As Hanfeizi explains the power of "non-action," he says: "When an enlightened ruler practices non-action above, the assembled ministers will be anxious and fearful below."[55] This menacing political atmosphere is clearly not akin to the kind of peaceful laissez-faire rulership that Laozi presents.

Conclusion

In conclusion, in Hanfeizi's sociopolitical design, there is no room for individuality and autonomy. The political theory that he advocates ultimately pays court to the ruler and to the order of the nation. His society would be a collective one; his government would be totalitarian. Even though his ruler may not be a tyrant, who rules by his whims, there would be no guarantee that a tyrannical ruler would not make use of the manipulative techniques Hanfeizi teaches to aggrandize his personal power. As Moody summarizes it:

> In Confucianism the ruler is held to be subject to absolute moral standards which he may never justly violate, and the legitimacy of his rule depends upon his adherence to those standards. In Legalism the only standard is expediency, and, of course, strictly speaking there is not even any *obligation* to do the expedient. There is nothing the ruler may not decree, provided he has the will to make the decree and the will and power to enforce it; and there is nothing the ruler *must* decree, either.[56]

In other words, even though Hanfeizi does not promote totalitarianism itself, his theory gives no defense against that direction of development for rulership.

Secondly, in Hanfeizi's political worldview there is no room for individual opinion and self-governance. In the Legalist society, everyone must obey decrees from above. No individual is allowed to challenge the existing system or ideology. This political system is in total opposition to democracy, which is based on confidence in both the intellect and the virtue of the people. We should note that education of the people is essential to the success of democracy, while suppression of knowledge is vital to the security of a Legalist government. Knowledge and thinking enable people to seek different points of view and alternative systems. When a nation aims to unify its people, diversity is a totally unwelcome phenomenon. Therefore, a Legalist world envisioned by Hanfeizi would simply be a stifled society where humans are herded under a single ruler. This is the major reason why later Confucians all reject Legalism and scorn Hanfeizi.

Thirdly, many historical examples after Hanfeizi's time have demonstrated that Legalism cannot guard against tyranny. We should note that the Legalists' main mistake is that law cannot be given absolute power in social control, and politics should not be separated from morality. Social order should be accomplished by moral education, so that the majority of the people do not contemplate obstructing public interests. Law should be used as a safety net to catch those falling through the cracks of moral training. At the same time, moral attributes should be expected in the ruler, so that he does not abuse his power and bring the whole nation under his personal exploitation.

In all fairness, we should also understand that Hanfeizi himself does not totally neglect the people's welfare. He believes that a fixed totalitarian polity regulated by public law is far superior to the political pendulum between enlightened despots and abominable tyrants as seen in ancient history. He also believes that a unified nation under one supreme power is preferable to constant warfare between multiple nation-states. In his opinion, the lofty idealism of Confucianism is responsible for the contemporary chaos. Only Legalism in its pure form could end the turmoil and restore national peace and social order. The people's interests lie in prosperity and longevity, which can only be obtained under a Legalist rulership. As Hanfeizi himself defends this view:

> The enlightened ruler is the one who scrutinizes the facts of right and wrong and investigates the conditions of order and chaos. Therefore, when governing the state, he rectifies [the law] clearly and establishes punishment severely in order to rescue all living beings from chaos, rid [the whole world] of misfortune, prohibit the strong from exploiting the weak, [forbid the majority from violating the minority], enable the old

and the infirm to die in peace and the young and the orphaned to grow [up], and see to it that [the nation's] frontiers be not invaded, that the ruler and minister be intimate with each other, that father and son support each other, and that there be no worry about being killed in war or taken prisoner. Such is one of the greatest achievements.[57]

In this passage, Hanfeizi depicts his utopia, which is not very different in spirit from that of Confucius and Mencius. Therefore, there may indeed be a "humanistic purpose" behind Hanfeizi's political philosophy.[58]

Further discussion questions

1　Is Hanfeizi right in claiming that politics should be amoral? Do you agree that morality is at best an ineffective, at worst a dangerous, means of social control?

2　Between a Legalist political model based on the distrust of the people and a democratic political model based on the confidence of the general masses, which one is more empirically supported?

3　Do you agree that for the sake of social order, individual liberty should be curtailed to the maximal extent? Do you think that many of our present social problems arise from too much individual liberty? Is order more important than liberty?

4　In view of the constant terrorist attacks in various nations, do you think that a government that enforces tighter control of its people and harsher punishments on enemies of the society should be our new direction?

Primary texts

Wing-tsit Chan (ed.) *A Sourcebook in Chinese Philosophy*, 4th edn. Princeton: Princeton University Press, 1973 (ch. 12; short excerpts).

Philip J. Ivanhoe and Bryan W. Van Norden (eds.) *Readings in Classical Chinese Philosophy*. Indianapolis, IN: Hackett Publishing Company, Inc. 2003 (ch. 7; excerpts).

Burton Watson (trans.) *Han Fei Tzu: Basic Writings*. New York: Columbia University Press, 1964.

Further readings

Chung-ying Cheng. "Legalism Versus Confucianism: A Philosophical Appraisal." *Journal of Chinese Philosophy* 8, 1981: 271–302.

K. K. Lee. "The Legalist School and Legal Positivism." *Journal of Chinese Philosophy* 3, 1975: 23–56.

Peter R. Moody Jr. "The Legalism of Han Fei Tzu and Its Affinities with Modern Political Thought." *International Philosophical Quarterly* 19, 1979: 317–30.

Benjamin Schwartz. *The World of Thought in Ancient China*. Cambridge, MA: Belknap Press, 1985, ch. 8, pp. 321–49.

Hsiao-po Wang. "The Significance of the Concept of 'Fa' in Han Fei's Thought System" (trans. L. S. Chang). *Philosophy East & West* 27(1), 1977: 35–52.

Part II
Chinese Buddhism

Introduction

The introduction of Indian Buddhism into Chinese philosophy was a unique as well as a peculiar phenomenon in the history of Chinese philosophy. It was unique because no other outside philosophy has had such a tremendous impact on the whole development of Chinese philosophy. At the same time, it was peculiar that Indian Buddhism could have had such an impact since the whole religious background, metaphysical assumptions, ethical beliefs, and life concerns of the Indian culture were not only alien, but also contrary, to those of Chinese culture.[1] While Chinese thinkers absorbed the basic tenets of Indian Buddhism, they also reinvented it by placing different emphasis on some of the major themes. Hence, Chinese Buddhism evolved from Indian Buddhism and gradually acquired its own characteristics.

Arthur Wright separates the assimilation of Indian Buddhism to Chinese philosophy into four stages:[2]

Phase I   The Period of Preparation (ca. 65–317 AD)
Phase II   The Period of Domestication (ca. 317–589 AD)
Phase III The Period of Acceptance and Independent Growth (ca. 589–900 AD)
Phase IV   The Period of Appropriation (ca. 900–1900 AD)

According to Yu-lan Fung's *A History of Chinese Philosophy*, Indian Buddhism, through the efforts of non-Chinese Buddhist missionaries, first entered China in the first century AD. Initially, the introduction of Buddhist thinking and Buddhist concepts was made through a "method of analogy" to Daoist thinking and many of the Daoist concepts. This is not only because Daoism, or, properly speaking, a degenerate form of Daoism that places more emphasis on escapism and transcendentalism, was popular among intellectuals of that time, but also because there are indeed some affinities between the two schools of thought. Laozi's notion of *non-being* (*wu*) or Zhuangzi's notion of *forgetting the self*, for example, were appealed to in an attempt to explicate the Buddhist's notion of *emptiness* (*kong*) and *selflessness*. But this method of analogy has the danger of focusing on apparent similarities while neglecting the widely different underlying assumptions. Also, with this method of analogy, the goal was to familiarize people with the alien thinking of Indian Buddhism, not to challenge or to modify it. During the initial phase of introduction and domestication, Buddhism could not yet be viewed as a new school of thought in the history of Chinese philosophy. It was not until the sixth century AD that Chinese Buddhism began to emerge.

Throughout the development of Chinese Buddhism, there have been innumerable Chinese Buddhist schools, differing from one another in their religious methods and their philosophical tenets. In Part II of this book, we shall examine four major schools that are the most philosophically noteworthy:[3] the Consciousness-Only (*Wei-shi*) School, the Hua-yan School, the Tian-tai School, and the Chan (Zen) School. We should bear in mind that Buddhism is fundamentally a religious thinking; thus, it involves both practice and philosophy. My analysis of these schools will focus on their philosophical imports; for the most part I will leave out discussion of their practices.

Before we analyze these schools, however, we should first get a sense of the basic tenets of Buddhism as it was originally founded in India by Siddhartha Gautama (called "Shakyamuni" by the Chinese people) in the sixth century BCE.[4] After he had reached enlightenment, he was revered as *the Buddha*, meaning "the honored one" or "the enlightened one"; hence, the school's name is "Buddhism." According to Masao Abe's explanation: "The term 'Buddha' is not a proper noun, but a common noun. It means 'an Enlightened One' or 'an Awakened One.' . . . The term 'Buddha' is thus a common noun which can be applied not only to Siddhartha Gautama but to anyone who is enlightened by or who awakens to the Dharma, i.e., the truth."[5] In contrast to the prevalent subscription to commonsense realism among ancient Chinese philosophers, the Buddha teaches that the world we live in and its objects are not "real." Because of this teaching, Buddhism can be characterized as the thesis of *Emptiness* (*Sunyata*).[6] Everything we perceive around us is empty, hence unreal. We live in a delusion or a dream-like state in which we believe that things are real. Once we wake up from this delusion or dream, we will realize that nothing, and no one, is what we take it to be. We will then terminate our attachment, our discernment, our perception, our conception, and enter the realm of *Emptiness*. This realm is called *nirvana*. One thing we should emphasize here is that this denial of the perceived world is not a result of skepticism. Buddhism is not based on an epistemological concern for whether or how we can know the Truth. It is, on the contrary, based on a dogmatic conviction that only the "Enlightened Ones" (the Buddhas) know the Truth, and that the Truth is simply not what we as sentient beings come to believe as true through our sense perception and our cognition.

To teach the thesis of emptiness, the Buddha's philosophy begins by emphasizing that the essence of life is suffering.[7] It is not to say that nothing in life can give us pleasure; rather, the point is that nothing in life can give us permanent pleasure. The nature of pleasure is that it is transient. We can perhaps say that pleasure derives from suffering since it merely is the temporary cessation of suffering. Suffering, on the other hand, underlies all life's experiences. According to a contemporary Chinese scholar's explanation, in Buddhism suffering is "the constant" while pleasure is "the variable":

> It is to say that the essence of life is suffering, and pleasure is merely a temporary state of satisfaction of a certain desire in one's whole life process. For example, one derives pleasure from eating when one is extremely hungry. But if one eats more after one is full, it leads to suffering. . . . Only when one eats the proper amount can one feel pleasure. However, even this pleasure cannot last long. In five hours when the food has been digested, one is again back to the state of hunger and suffering.[8]

During one's lifetime, one is bound to have many attachments to things and people one loves. Such attachments are bound to bring pain and agony eventually. Anything one desires will always become the source of one's suffering, whether one's desire is gratified at the time or not. If one does not obtain what one desires, naturally one suffers. But even if one does obtain what one desires, one will eventually suffer from loss since nothing lasts forever. The more one desires something, the more pain that thing will bring to one. Hence, the Buddha concludes:

> Birth is suffering; old age is suffering; sickness is suffering; death is suffering. Sorrow, lamentation, and dejection are suffering. Contact with what is unpleasant and separation from the pleasant are suffering. Not getting what one wishes is suffering. In brief, clinging to the five aggregates of the personality – body (material form), feeling, perception, disposition, and consciousness – as possessions of "my self" is suffering.[9]

An important teaching of the Buddha is that there is no "self." By "no self," the Buddha is denouncing not only the phenomenal self, but

211

also the assumed immortal substance (the soul) that goes through the transmigrations of life. The notion of reincarnation is deeply rooted in the Indian culture. The prevailing Indian belief of the Buddha's time was Brahmanism's teaching that once a life has been completed, the soul re-enters the cycle of different beings, which include the levels of gods, of semi-gods (asuras), of humans, of animals, of hungry ghosts, and finally of hell beings. Existence is conceived as an endless cycle from birth to birth and from life to life, with no permanent joy obtainable while each life is burdened with all kinds of suffering. A person's recent life conditions are affected by what deeds he committed in the previous life. To better one's condition, therefore, one needs to perform the right deeds in order to enter a higher level of existence in the next life. The Buddha, on the other hand, rejects the belief in an immutable substance such as the "soul" that is recycled through lives. Even though the Buddha does conceive human existence as revolving within the wheel of life and death, he does not think that there is one permanent entity that persists through these transitions. Furthermore, in the Buddha's view, it is not the transmigrations into lower levels that are fearful. Birth itself is the root of suffering. Once one is born, the whole process of aging, sickness, and death becomes inevitable. One has to go again through the whole process of dealing with disappointments of unfulfilled desires, pain from the loss of loved ones, suffering derived from one's cravings, attachments, obsessions, resentments, etc. Therefore, to be reborn is not something joyful. The ultimate goal of salvation is to end the cycle of life and death, and never to enter this world again.

To end the cycle of reincarnation, one has to be totally free of desires; in particular, one should not desire life itself, nor should one desire death. Once one has reached the state of enlightenment through realizing that nothing in life, including life itself, is desirable, one can be free of sorrow and enter the realm of "nirvana." Nirvana literally means the extinction of sorrow, the state of complete quietude and tranquility. Having reached this realm, one no longer re-enters the cycle of reincarnation and one thereby gains eternal salvation. An individual who has gained eternal salvation can be called a "Buddha" – the enlightened one. This basic teaching of the Buddha can be summarized as "the Four Noble Truths":

The Truth of Suffering

Suffering marks all existence in the world. Suffering is the essence of existence: birth, old age, sickness, and death are all causes of suffering since the one inevitably leads to the other. Being separated from what one loves causes suffering; being united with what one detests causes suffering; having ungratified desires is suffering; finally, being the sheer result of "Five Aggregates" (body or material form, feeling, perception, disposition, and consciousness) is suffering, since owing to these mental/physical activities we are conditioned to be reborn again.

The Truth of the Origin of Suffering

Our craving for things that are impermanent in nature is the cause of our suffering. Such craving is the result of our ignorance that everything, including ourselves, merely has a dependent nature – everything is the aggregate of the twelve causal links. Nothing is permanent and self-subsisting.

The Truth of the Cessation of Suffering (Nirvana)

The ultimate goal, a state of peace and quietude, totally free from suffering, is possible.

The Truth of the Path to Nirvana

The Path to Nirvana refers to the methods that lead to the eradication of cravings. This "path" is also called the eightfold noble path, which consists of having the right view, right intention, right speech, right action, right livelihood, right effort, right mindfulness, right concentration.

An important mental preparation for understanding the Four Noble Truths is to recognize the non-existence of the self, so that one can be free from desire, craving, anger, and other negative emotions arising from the insistence of one's self. In addition to advocating "no self," the Buddha also advocates "no dharmas." The elements of the universe, spiritual as well as physical, are called "dharmas." This word also means "the Truth," and in that case, it is used as a singular designator *Dharma*. From the etymological connection between the two words "Dharma" and "dharmas," we can see the implied ontological assumption on the nature of worldly elements. In a nutshell, the assumption is that all things and events are simply part of the One – Dharma itself. The multiplicity we observe in worldly elements is the illusory result of our perception.

The Buddha's "no dharma" thesis points out that dharmas do not exist independently; hence, they are unreal. The most fundamental metaphysical assertion of the Buddha is that all dharmas are composed of a relationship called "dependent co-arising."[10] Under this view, there is nothing that can exist on its own. The whole state of being of any particular thing, from its inception to its final decay, depends on various other factors in the world. Without any of the major factors, the thing would not have come into existence; with the alteration of any other factor, the thing would have had a different development. The affecting factor is called a "cause," which can be either a primary cause or an auxiliary cause. For example, for a plant to grow, we may say that the seed is the primary condition, while air, water, etc. are the auxiliary conditions. Without this set of causes as necessary and sufficient conditions, the thing could not have come into existence. The affected thing, on the other hand, is called an "effect," which can further be a cause for yet another state of affairs. The causal connections between various causes and effects are two-dimensional: there exist both a diachronic and a synchronic interconnectedness. In other words, not only is the present state of affairs caused by previous states of affairs in the world, but also it is causally connected to its contemporary states of affairs. This synchronic causal relation further constitutes a form of *mereological* (part-whole) interdependence. Moreover, the causal relation is two-directional: depending on the aspect (or perspective) of the causation, two things can be both cause and effect to each other. According to the Consciousness-Only School's interpretation, for example, the eighth consciousness is the cause of all other forms of consciousness since it is through the transformation of the eighth consciousness that the other consciousnesses are derived. At the same time, the other seven forms of consciousness are the cause for the eighth consciousness, since they "perfume" the eighth consciousness while the latter is merely "the perfumed."[11] There is thus an intricate causal web linking every phenomenon in the universe, from time immemorial to the eternal future. This view can be called "causal holism," since it presents a holistic picture of causality according to which no single event can be isolated from the whole system. Accordingly, everything is dependent on something else; nothing can be said to have inherent subsistence independent of anything. In this sense, nothing is "real" in the sense of having an independent substance; everything is "empty" in the sense of being empty of real substance.

Under such a causal view, scientific prediction becomes impossible. The causal power of each cause cannot be measured, since there is not a single cause for any given event. Even were we able to identify *all* the primary and auxiliary causes, we would still not be able to measure their effects, since this kind of causation is loosely defined as a form of "perfuming." The notion of "perfume" is unique to the Buddhist theory of causality. Being in a room with bouquets, one's hair will slowly take on the fragrance; walking in the mist, one's clothes will gradually become damp. Analogously, anything that takes place will slowly but surely have a perfuming effect on its agent or later events. The perfuming causation cannot be analyzed in physical terms; it cannot be measured in quantity or in quality. It is not necessarily a direct causation, since its effect can be carried through many intermediary means. Sometimes the effect can even take a whole lifetime or several generations to be seen. In addition, the perfuming causation does not have to take place within an individual's life – one agent's activities can have a perfuming effect on another agent. The perfuming causation does not presuppose the temporal priority of the cause, since the cause and the effect can simultaneously exist. Furthermore, the perfuming causation does not have to be one-directional: both cause and effect can mutually perfume each other.[12] In some cases, the perfuming causation also carries a moral connotation, since good deeds and bad deeds have different perfuming effects on one's character.

This perfuming causation is applied specifically to sentient beings, beings that are capable of volitional action. One is thus literally speaking the *product* of one's past "*karma*." "*Karma*" refers to one's past volitional choices, intentional deeds, and relationships, either in one's present life or in one's past lives. One's karma includes mental acts, verbal acts, and behavioral acts. Its effect can be shown in one's physical conditions as well as in one's mental conditions. In Robert Zeuschner's analysis, there are at least six ways in which "karmic choices are supposed to produce their effects":

by creating psychological states which modify subsequent choices, as guilt, and psychological pain (or joy);

by creating latent psychological tendencies or habits;

by creating stronger psychological states which would lead to compulsive behavior;

by creating physical circumstances that are retributive on one's past deeds or by determining the length and states of one's life;

by determining the social status, wealth, family conditions, mental capacities, etc. of one's next life;

by determining which life form one will inhabit in the next life.[13]

The karmic law is not deterministic, since in every step of the causal chain the agent's volitional act or choice would have the potential to produce various consequences. According to the Buddha, the one receiving the karmic effects is not a self-persisting entity, but a cluster of mental functions of a stream of consciousness. However, even though the Buddha rejects the traditional Indian notion of the self and of the soul, the folk Chinese Buddhists typically inherit the Indian notion of a soul persisting through lives. Since they believe that life conditions are affected by past deeds (in one's life or in one's past lives), their attitude is quite "fatalistic" with respect to their present state. But they are not fatalistic with respect to their future states. On the basis of perfuming causation and karmic laws, they believe that a better future can be created as long as they perform the right deeds, have the right thought *now*. This conviction of a system of impersonal (i.e., not given by a Supreme Being) rewards and punishments is prevalent among Chinese Buddhists. The hidden assumption could be the traditional Chinese belief in an invisible cosmic order, which regulates morality with bliss and immorality with misery.

The Buddha emphasizes "dependent co-arising" and the interconnectedness of causality to show that there is nothing permanently fixed underlying the phenomenal world. Everything is made up of all these causal conditions. Once the conditions alter, the thing ceases to exist. Therefore, nothing is *real*. To appreciate this point, we could conceive of ourselves as a "house of cards" – once a card is removed, the whole house would simply collapse. Our very existence is built on myriad relations and chance happenings prior to our birth. If any of those relations or accidents had not occurred, we would not have come into existence. We take our existence for granted, and we think that we own our lives. But we should realize that there are very many things beyond our control, very many people who are not related to us, and yet our existence depends entirely on those things and those people in a fundamental way. The Buddha teaches that ordinary people commit two common mistakes, "insisting on dharmas" and "insisting on the self," because they do not understand that the true nature of existence lies in causality. They cling to objects and to their self, treating them as *really* existent. As a result, they are forever caught in the bondage of existence. To be free from this bondage, the individual needs to gain insight into the nature of his own existence, to recognize it as the mere effect of twelvefold causal links: ignorance, volitional activities, consciousness, name-and-form (one's mental and physical activities), six "gateways" (six sense organs), contact, experience, craving (or passion), grasping (or attachment), becoming (of individual self), birth, and aging and death.

These twelve causal links penetrate our past, present, and future lives. Our former ignorance, craving, attachments, etc. have led to our present life; our present ignorance, craving, attachments, etc., will lead to our future rebirth. Unless we can divest ourselves of our ignorance, terminate all our craving and grasping, we can never be liberated from the cycle of birth and death. This understanding brings enlightenment, which leads to true salvation. As Kalupahana puts it:

> Through understanding this process, a person is able to pacify his dispositions and develop his personality in such a way that, freed from grasping, he can lead a life that not only avoids suffering and unhappiness for himself but contributes to the welfare of others as well. Getting rid of *passion* and developing a *dispassionate* attitude in life, the freed one is able to cultivate *compassion* for himself as well as others. At the time of death, with ignorance gone and dispositions annihilated, his consciousness will cease without establishing itself in another psychophysical personality.[14]

Ending the wheel of life and death, and being free from this causally determined phenomenal world, is the ultimate goal of Buddhism.

Since the Buddha's teaching was conveyed orally, the main sources of his thinking were the compiled notes taken by several of his main disciples. Later generations of Indian Buddhists rendered different interpretations of these terse and esoteric original classics ("sutra"), from which various schools within Buddhism itself were formed. By as early as the fifth century BCE, there were already at least 18 different major Buddhist schools contesting one another's theories. One major dispute is whether the Buddha really denies the existence of the experiential world, even though all schools accept the thesis of emptiness of the ultimate reality. There are two major schools, each comprising many divisions. One school, the School of Being, argues that external objects do exist in the sense of dependent co-arising. Among this school, some divisions advocate that dharmas are real but the self is not; some argue that the self is real while dharmas are not; some even argue that both dharmas and the self are real. The other school, the School of Emptiness, argues that what the Buddha teaches is the emptiness of the external world. This school advocates that there is no substantial existence belonging either to physical stuff or to the mind. The whole universe is empty, and reality itself is the absolute Emptiness. There are also many schools that take the moderate view as a conciliation of the two extreme views. This moderate view, represented by the Madhyamaka School, is also called "the Middle School." This school presents *being* and *emptiness* as "neither one nor other" – all dharmas are real in the form of dependent existence; at the same time they are empty because they do not have their independent self-nature. Because of various schools' different interpretations of the notion *emptiness*, they also preach different methods of reaching nirvana – one needs to quit the cycle of life and death, one needs to reach the extinction of senses and conceptions, one needs gradually to attain the extinction of afflictions, or, simply, one can reach nirvana in a single moment of thought. All these schools claim to represent the Buddha's *true* teaching. Hence, we shall see that in the history of Chinese Buddhism, there are several attempts, most notably by the Hua-yan School and by the Tian-tai School, to rank these teachings by a method called the "judgment on the classification of teachings" (*pan-jiao*).

In terms of the ultimate goal of enlightenment, there was also a split between two major schools: Mahayana (the "Great Vehicle" School) and Hinayana (the "Small Vehicle" School). The opposition of "great" to "small" is evaluative, with clear partiality toward Mahayana. Contemporary scholars prefer using "Theravada" (meaning "the Doctrine of the Elders") instead of "Hinayana." Here we shall follow contemporary practices, even though in Chinese history these schools were called "Hinayana." The Mahayana School aims to spread the Buddha's teaching to the general public who may not have the capacity to gain enlightenment on their own; the Theravada School focuses on individual salvation among the ones who have the intelligence to understand the Buddha's teaching, and the emphasis is on one's own efforts. The ideal person of the Theravada School is called "the arahat" (or "arhat"), one who has reached the state of ultimate enlightenment; one who is thus forever free of sorrow and suffering and can remain in the realm of nirvana. On the other hand, the ideal person of the Mahayana School is called "the bodhisattva," one who vows to help all sentient beings reach enlightenment and salvation. Bodhisattvas have also reached the state of enlightenment, but they are not willing to be totally free of sorrow and thus be out of the cycle of life. They choose not to enter the realm of nirvana so that they can stay in this world to help other sentient beings. Therefore, for the Mahayanists, reaching nirvana is not the ultimate goal. Their goal is rather to be a great vehicle to carry as many people as possible over to the other realm. Although both the state of *arhat* and the state of *bodhisattva* are attainable, there is an ultimate goal – becoming a Buddha – that is superior even to these two levels. Another distinguishing thesis between the two schools is that the Theravada teaches that only a special group of sentient beings have the potential to become a Buddha, while the Mahayana School teaches that all sentient beings could potentially become Buddhas. The former way of thinking is rooted in the caste system in Indian society. But since Chinese philosophy is based on the fundamental acknowledgment of everyone's possible attainment of sagehood, it is the latter way of thinking, Mahayana, which took root in China.[15]

While early Buddhism is set in a philosophical tradition that builds on the "other-worldly" concern, Chinese Buddhism is based on a philosophical tradition with a "this-worldly" concern. Derk Bodde says: "[The] distinctions between Mahayana and [Theravada] doctrine perhaps in part reflect the differences between the 'this-worldliness' of Chinese thought and 'other-worldliness' of that of India."[16] It is no wonder that Chinese Buddhism belongs to the Mahayana schools and further disseminates its ideals and its teachings. However, Chinese Buddhism goes one step further in its *ideal being* than the *arhat* of Theravada and the *bodhisattva* of Mahayana; it is more interested in the attainment of Buddhahood itself. A shared pursuit for Chinese Buddhist schools is the concern with *whether* everyone has the potential for Buddhahood, and *how* one can actually become a Buddha. This pursuit led them to the issue of "Buddha-nature," which can be viewed as a continuation of the assertion of the goodness of human nature as seen in ancient Chinese philosophy. The consensus of all major Chinese Buddhist schools is that everyone can potentially become a Buddha exactly because *everyone has Buddha-nature*. Buddha-nature is not an actualized state; rather, it represents the potential for the ideal state: Buddhahood. In this sense, Chinese Buddhism is based on the assertion that human nature (understood as *potentials*, as in Mencius' view) is intrinsically good.

Chapter 9

The Consciousness-Only (*Wei-shi*) School

Introduction

The great pilgrim and translator Xuan-zang (Hsüan Tsang) (596–664 AD) played a significant role in the development of Buddhism in China. Under his introduction, the Consciousness-Only School[1] (the *Wei-shi* School) was founded in China. Xuan-zang was a legendary person in Chinese history, because he took on a nearly impossible pilgrimage, at the age of 33, through the deserts and mountains of Central Asia to go to India for the purpose of learning Indian Buddhism first hand. The travel took four years, during which he encountered many hardships that nearly cost him his life.[2] After he arrived in India, he spent more than 10 years traveling and studying with various Buddhist masters. When he went back to China, he brought back with him 657 Buddhist texts. He then devoted the rest of his life to the translation of these Sanskrit texts into Chinese. He founded a translation school and, with the help of his many disciples, completed the translation of 75 texts by the time he died.

The Consciousness-Only School was originally founded by two brothers of the Yogacara school in India: Asanga and Vasubandhu (fourth to fifth century AD). The thought of the Chinese Consciousness-Only School originated in the teachings of Vasubandhu, on whose works Xuan-zang wrote his commentary. Vasubandhu wrote many important treatises that became the major texts of various schools in Indian Buddhism. What serve as the foundation for the Consciousness-Only School are two major treatises by Vasubandhu: *The Twenty Stanzas of Consciousness-Only*, and *The Thirty Stanzas of Consciousness-Only*. The *Twenty Stanzas* is mainly a refutation of different opposing schools; it serves as a good introduction to the thought of the Consciousness-Only School. The *Thirty Stanzas*, on the other hand, constructs the basic doctrine for the school. Typically, a Buddhist treatise consists of short verses and the author's commentary on each verse. The *Thirty Stanzas* was completed in the last years of Vasubandhu and it thus represents his most mature thought. However, he did not have time to write a commentary before he died and the work was left to his disciples. There were ten major commentaries on this work, all different in their interpretations on what Vasubandhu meant by each verse. In compliance with his student Kuiji's request, Xuan-zang compiled these commentaries, adhering mostly to Vasubandhu's major disciple Dharmapâla's (ca. 439–507) view. Xuan-zang combined the approved commentary with his translation of the original *Thirty Stanzas*, and came up with his *Cheng Wei-shi Lun* (*A Treatise on the Establishment of Consciousness-Only*).[3] This book is not simply a translation of Vasubandhu's verses, but a selective understanding of the Consciousness-Only thought, and in Xuan-zang's translation he sometimes uses Chinese words with slightly different connotations to subtly supplement the original theory. As a result, this book represents Xuan-zang's view rather than that of Vasubandhu.[4]

Xuan-zang's *Cheng Wei-Shi Lun* (*A Treatise on the Establishment of Consciousness-Only*) is divided into ten volumes. After demolishing the ordinary people's insistence on the self and on the substantiality of dharmas, it develops a detailed analysis of the eight forms of consciousness – their significance, functions, and interrelations. It then moves on to answer many objections raised by outsiders to further explicate the doctrine. Finally, it points to multiple methods of cultivation of the ultimate wisdom to reach enlightenment. Xuan-zang thus claims that this book is a treatise on the *establishment* or the *completion* of Consciousness-Only.[5] It has now become the representation of the thought of the Chinese Consciousness-Only School.

The exposition in this chapter will be based on Xuan-zang's translation of the *Twenty Stanzas*, and his *Cheng Wei-Shi Lun* (*A Treatise on the Establishment of Consciousness-Only*).[6] Both the *Twenty Stanzas* and the *Thirty Stanzas* (on which *Cheng Wei-Shi Lun* is based) contain the refutations of the views of competing philosophical schools at the time or the incorrect views of the common people, in addition to the construction of the doctrine of Consciousness-Only. In this chapter I will first explain the school's basic doctrine, and then analyze their arguments against opposing views. The first section explains the various theses of the Consciousness-Only School. The next two sections contain its founders' arguments against competing philosophical schools in India. These arguments demonstrate the brilliant logical reasoning behind the assertions of the school. Readers who are not interested in these arguments, however, may wish to skip these two sections. The final section deals with specific arguments in support of the doctrine of the Consciousness-Only School. These arguments should be of special interest to readers with a background in Western philosophy.

The Basic Doctrine of the Consciousness-Only School

This school is named "Consciousness-Only" because it emphasizes that from time immemorial there has only been consciousness. The most fundamental form of consciousness is called the "storehouse consciousness" ("Alaya"). It is so called because it stores all the seeds for all the phenomena ("dharmas") of the world. The storehouse consciousness is not restricted to one consciousness. Every sentient being (including humans and animals) has its own storehouse consciousness. Furthermore, no sentient being's storehouse consciousness begins with birth. In the cycle of lives, the storehouse consciousness does not ever perish; it continues from one life to the next eternally. As it goes through an individual's life, it picks up various impacts from the different life experiences of the individual, as well as influences from other consciousnesses. Such an impact is called "perfuming."[7] At the beginning of each life, therefore, the sentient being is endowed with a storehouse consciousness, which has been perfumed to various degrees. Perfuming brings the seeds that are stored in the storehouse consciousness into reality. Therefore, all sentient beings are different from one another. It is through the transformations of multiple storehouse consciousnesses that the whole world becomes existent.[8]

The external world is dependent on consciousness

The Consciousness-Only School denies the *real* existence of the external world. What is meant by "real existence" here is "independent existence." This school claims that external objects do exist in a sense – in the sense of being different from illusory images as in dreams and in one's imagination. But it denies the existence of the external world in realism's sense – in the sense of being existent independently of mental activities (perception, cognition, intellect, and consciousness) of sentient beings. It also denies the permanence of the external world, since consciousness itself is constantly in transformation. As the manifestation of consciousness, the world cannot exist on its own. Everything is the outcome of the transformation of someone's consciousness. Nothing can exist independently of the mind.[9] As Xuan-zang's *A Treatise on the Establishment of Consciousness-Only* explains, "The word 'only' is intended to deny that there are real things separated from consciousness, but not to deny that there are mental qualities, dharmas, and so forth inseparable from consciousness."[10] The external world exists inseparably from consciousness because it exists as the result of the transformation of consciousness.

There are two ways to understand the thesis, "The world is the result of the transformation of consciousness." One is to say that the world as it presently exists was originally "created" by our consciousness; the other is to say that the world as we now perceive it cannot remain this way without the intervention of our consciousness. Perhaps we can say that the former explains the world's dependence on our mind from an ontological point of view, while the latter makes the world dependent on our mind in an epistemological sense. Both views are plausible interpretations of the claim of "consciousness-only."

In contrast to a solipsistic view, according to which the whole world could be the mental imagery of a lone mind, the Consciousness-Only School's teaching is that there are as many consciousnesses as there are sentient beings (humans and animals alike). In other words, "consciousness-only" does not mean "only my consciousness." As one person's consciousness generates a world according to the readiness of her storehouse consciousness, another person's consciousness generates another world according to the readiness of his storehouse consciousness. Even though each storehouse consciousness is unique, all storehouse consciousnesses are largely similar because they have been perfumed in largely the same way. One person's creation is thus not greatly different from that of another person. Furthermore, since the world is the combined creation of all storehouse consciousnesses of all sentient beings, it does not come to be because of one person and it does not cease to be because of one person. This explains why the world has a certain degree of observable regularity and consistency. From this we see that this school can be more closely assimilated to Objective Idealism, which claims that the world is the creation of *intersubjective* minds.

Dependent co-arising and the true nature of the world

The Consciousness-Only School's metaphysical theory is built on the Buddha's fundamental teaching of "dependent co-arising." As explained in Part II's Introduction above, dependent co-arising can be viewed as a causal web, in which everything – past, present, and future – is interrelated. For a thing to exist in the present time, there have to have been many pre-existing conditions that serve as the necessary and sufficient conditions for its existence.

The causal dependence applies not just to external objects and events; it applies to the activities of our mind and consciousness as well. The Consciousness-Only School discusses in particular the perfuming of the storehouse consciousness. Every deed a person performs leaves a trace in his or her storehouse consciousness: a good deed leaves a trace of goodness and a bad deed leaves a trace of evil. The storehouse consciousness is thereby "perfumed" to different states, according to which the person's next life in the transmigration will be determined. In this sense it is the "seed" for future existence. In addition, the storehouse consciousness also accepts seeds from other consciousnesses. It ultimately contains seeds for all elements (dharmas) of the world.

The Consciousness-Only School emphasizes the "threefold nature of existence," namely:

- the nature of being imagined or conceived to be really existent;
- the nature of being dependent on others for its production;
- the nature of the perfect, accomplished reality.[11]

These natures are not three separate natures of all existence; they are, rather, three aspects (hence, "threefold" nature) of existence shared by both the self and the dharmas. One common interpretation of the three aspects is to say that they are derived from the various degrees of understanding of different people. Ignorant people mistakenly think that the self and the dharmas really exist; thus, all existence is ascribed this character of being misconceived to be really existent. What the Buddha (as well as the Consciousness-Only School) teaches is that everything is dependent on other things to exist; hence, all existence is endowed with the nature of dependent co-arising. Finally, the ones with true enlightenment can see that there is no substance underlying the interrelations of dependent co-arising; all existence is thus empty in nature.[12] If this interpretation is correct, then what the "threefold nature of existence" introduces is not the nature of existence per se, but the nature of existence as conceived by different intelligence. We can say that external objects exist (adhering to the thinking of the common masses); we can say that external objects exist as a form of dependent co-arising (adhering to the teaching of the Buddha and of Consciousness-Only); we can also say that external objects are empty (adhering to the wisdom of the ones who have reached nirvana). These claims do not necessarily contradict each other, as long as we see their contexts of discourse. Xuan-zang's *Treatise* appeals to the famous "Two Levels of Truth" to explain how each dharma can have all three seemingly incompatible natures. The two levels of truth include (1) the level of worldly relative truth and (2) the level of Absolute Truth. They are uttered in different contexts as rejoinders to different levels of intelligence. Xuan-zang wrote:

> *We say dharmas are empty* because the [so-called] real dharmas erroneously conceived on the basis of transformations of consciousness are contrary to reason. *We do not say dharmas are empty* because there is no nature of consciousness-only realized by correct and indescribable wisdom. If there were no such consciousness, there would be no worldly (relative) truth, and if there were no worldly truth, there would be no absolute truth, for the two Levels of Truth are established on the basis of each other. To reject the Two Levels of Truth is to have evil ideas of Emptiness, a disease the Buddha considers to be incurable.[13]

According to this comment, both truths are true, and neither truth can hold without the other. There is thus no need to insist either that external objects exist or that they are empty. The self and dharmas can be both existent (as a form of dependent co-arising) and empty (as being without substance). The two aspects are actually the two sides of the same coin. As Vasubandhu's Verse 22 explains, "The Perfect Reality and the dependent are neither the same nor different."[14] Xuan-zang's *Treatise* concludes the chapter on "the Proofs of Consciousness-Only" in this way: "Self and dharmas are not existent. Emptiness and consciousness are not inexistent. Neither existent nor inexistent, hence, corresponding to the Middle Way."[15] Under this view, the debate between the School of Being and the School of Emptiness is rendered insignificant. In this way, the Consciousness-Only School can be viewed as taking a "middle way."[16]

Three stages of the transformation of consciousness

The defining feature of the Consciousness-Only School is its detailed analysis of the transformation of consciousness. According to this, what is responsible for the generation of the whole external world are eight forms of consciousness: the storehouse consciousness (the eighth), the intellective consciousness (the seventh), the sense-coordinative consciousness (the sixth), and the consciousnesses associated with sight, hearing, smell, taste, and touch (the first five consciousnesses). With respect to their characters, these eight forms of consciousness can be further divided into three categories:

1 The kind that contains a multitude of seeds for future development and is therefore the source of worldly phenomena.[17] Only the eighth (storehouse) consciousness belongs to this kind.
2 The kind that is constantly in the process of deliberation. Only the seventh (intellective) consciousness belongs to this category.
3 The kind that discriminates gross spheres of objects. All the first six forms of consciousness belong to this category.

Of all these consciousnesses, only the eighth (storehouse) consciousness is the ontological basis for the whole world; i.e., it alone contains the potentials (the "seeds") for everything's existence and future development. The "stages of transformation" are thus the stages of the transformation of the storehouse consciousness, corresponding to the way in which the other seven forms of consciousness are generated from it.

By "transformation," the Consciousness-Only School means the process of outward manifestations of something internal. If the word "internal" means "internal to consciousness," then nothing would be considered *external* since according to their theory, nothing exists outside of consciousness. Therefore, the distinction between "internal" and "external" should be understood as drawing a line between a sentient being's mind and *what it considers* to be outside its mind (its body would be external in this sense). *A Treatise on the Establishment of Consciousness-Only* says: "The word 'transform' means that the various inner consciousnesses transform and manifest the characters which *seem to be* the external spheres of the self and the dharmas."[18] In this sense, the Consciousness-Only School claims that the *external* world is the mere result of the transformations of the eight forms of consciousness. The world is not really "external" to consciousness.

However, when we come to the three stages of transformation among the eight forms of consciousnesses themselves, we see that the distinction between the internal and the external no longer applies, since all eight forms of consciousnesses are supposed to be "internal" in the above sense. There is actually another sense of "transformation" defined in *A Treatise on the Establishment of Consciousness-Only*: "By 'transformation' is meant that this consciousness, from time immemorial, comes into existence and goes out of existence every moment and changes both before and after."[19] Under this sense, "transformation" means the process of turning a static state into activities, a progression from coming into existence to going out of existence, and a process of continual change. Activities can be generated from a static state because the seeds or potentials for these activities are already contained in the static state. The static state can remain the same permanently; activities, on the other hand, are constantly changing, terminating, and renewing. Once the static form of consciousness is transformed into an active consciousness, it becomes a "consciousness flow" or a "stream of consciousness" in which a previous consciousness generates the present one, which in turn generates the next consciousness. As *A Treatise on the Establishment of Consciousness-Only* puts it: "while [this consciousness] goes out of existence as a cause, it comes into existence as effect, and is thus neither permanent nor one. In this way it can be perfumed by the other transforming consciousness and produce seeds."[20] It is in this sense of "transformation" that we should understand the "three stages of transformation."

An important feature of the Consciousness-Only School is that the transformation of consciousness is taken not as a linear order, but as cyclical. The cyclical process of the transformation of consciousness is seen in the context of the Buddhist cyclical worldview. There is no absolute beginning for *the* world; worlds constantly come into and go out of existence. From world to world, there is no temporal priority or posteriority. Similarly, the storehouse consciousness does not exist prior to, or subsequent to, the other forms of consciousness. On the one hand, the storehouse consciousness is the one that generates the other seven forms of consciousness; on the other hand, it also receives the perfuming effects of those other forms of consciousness so that it could *store* more *seeds* for further transformation. The mutual cause/effect transaction takes place constantly between the storehouse consciousness and the other seven forms of consciousness. Therefore, if we can say that the storehouse exists prior to the other forms of consciousness, the priority must be taken to be in the logical sense, not in the temporal sense. Temporally, the storehouse and the other seven forms of consciousness exist simultaneously and interact continually such that there is no definite moment in time for each single transformation to take place.

By this theory, at the primordial stage of each world cycle, the storehouse consciousness must be in a totally static state – with no activity, no awareness, and no function. The first stage of transformation brings this static storehouse consciousness into a consciousness that is actively turning the seeds it contains from time immemorial into fruition. That is why the first transformation simply generates the storehouse consciousness itself. The second transformation generates the deliberative kind of consciousness, which is the seventh consciousness whose character is intellective. The third transformation brings about the discriminative kind of consciousnesses, which are the first six forms of consciousness associated with sense perception. The eight forms of consciousness should not be considered as separate entities, since each consciousness represents simply a function. Vasubandhu uses the analogy between waves and water to depict the connection between the five sense consciousnesses and the storehouse consciousness.[21] From this analogy, we see that every form of consciousness is really part of the storehouse consciousness; each of them emerges as the storehouse is activated to manifest a particular function. Perhaps this is why Vasubandhu also called the storehouse consciousness "the root consciousness." Based on the root consciousness, various mental functions emerge and become the eight forms of consciousness. These eight forms of consciousness then interact among one another to transform (in the first sense) the whole external world.

According to the Consciousness-Only School, it is not perception that secures the existence of perceptible objects. What the first six sense consciousnesses perceive and discriminate are nothing but what is already contained in the eighth (storehouse) consciousness; namely, the seeds for the dharmas. Iso Kern, in his analysis of Xuan-zang's theory of consciousness, calls the seeds for objective phenomena "the part, or element, of the objective phenomena" within consciousness itself. He quotes from Xuan-zang:

> If the mind and all that belongs to it did not have the character of its objective base (the intended object), it would either be incapable of intentionally holding its own object, or every consciousness would hold everything as its object, since its own object would be like the others and the others like its own.[22] As explained earlier, each storehouse consciousness goes through generations of perfuming in the transmigration of lives. It thus accumulates multiple seeds perfumed through past experiences. The six sense consciousnesses, with the aid of the seventh (intellective), act upon the storehouse consciousness to create the appearance of the external world. Since everything is the outcome of the interaction of these eight forms of consciousness, nothing exists outside, or independently of, consciousness. There is thus no genuinely *external* world. That is why the school claims that everything is consciousness only.

If there is a distinction between the active storehouse consciousness and the static state from which it is transformed, which, then, is the ontological foundation of the universe? *A Treatise on the Establishment of Consciousness-Only* says:

[The storehouse consciousness] neither comes to an end nor is it eternal, for it is in perpetual transformation. By "perpetual" is meant that this consciousness, from time immemorial, had continued in the same way without any interruption. For it is the basis of the construction in the [four] realms [which form the substance of existence] ...[23]

In other words, it is the storehouse consciousness, once transformed, which is the foundation of the universe. One could perhaps raise the question that if the storehouse consciousness has existed "from time immemorial," then how can there be a state *before* the first transformation? What, if anything, is going through the first transformation? If there is something that goes through the first transformation and generates the active flow of the consciousness, then should that *something* be viewed as the ultimate foundation for the universe? The Consciousness-Only School does not deal with this question. To pursue this question further, one would be committing the same mistake as the non-Buddhist Indian schools in the pursuit of the "ultimate substance." However, we can perhaps answer for them. The storehouse consciousness has existed "from time immemorial" because even time itself (as well as space) is generated by the storehouse consciousness. Under their cyclical worldview, the whole universe is a continuum that transcends space and time. For each world-stage, there is a beginning and an end. The cycle itself is not situated in a linear timeline or in a vast space. If even time and space are both the result of the transformation of consciousness, then the storehouse consciousness is rightfully the foundation of the world-stage. What may have existed prior (not temporally, but logically) to the first transformation belongs to a totally different realm, which can no longer be measured temporally or spatially. This is how we should understand the realm of nirvana in this theory: not as a separate "place" in the universe, but as a separate realm from the whole universe itself.[24] And to the Consciousness-Only School, reaching that other realm is the ultimate goal.

The ultimate goal: transforming consciousness into wisdom (zhuan shi cheng zhi)

Ultimately, the transformation of consciousness is viewed in a negative way by the Consciousness-Only School. When the other seven forms of consciousness act upon (or perfume) the storehouse consciousness to bring into fruition the multiple seeds it contains, the perfuming effects are called "defilements." The defilements that come from the interaction with the seventh (intellective) consciousness cause the mistaken attitudes associated with the insistence of the self: self-delusion (lacking understanding of the character of the self); self-view (clinging to the view that the self exists); self-conceit (possessing the feeling of self-importance and superciliousness); self-love (keeping a deep attachment to what is clung to as the self). The defilements coming from the other six sense consciousnesses cause the illusion that the external world really exists and that external objects can be the objects of our desires. The implication of this defilement theory is then that the original state of the storehouse consciousness was pure and clean, but it has been contaminated by all sorts of mental activities, which then generate the appearance of the self and of the external world. "Because of this, sentient beings are bound to the cycle of life and death and transmigration and cannot be free from them. Hence they are called defilements."[25]

Once the first transformation begins, the whole process that eventually leads to the generation of the external world and one's entanglement in this world becomes inevitable. Since entanglement in this world is the root of all suffering, in order to end suffering, one has to prevent the transformation from the start. In other words, one has to prevent the static storehouse consciousness from becoming active; one has to "renounce" the storehouse consciousness itself.

According to *A Treatise on the Establishment of Consciousness-Only*:

> [The storehouse consciousness] has been in perpetual transformation like a torrent from time immemorial. In what state will it be finally renounced? Only in the state of *arhat* (one who has reached the state of ultimate enlightenment and has entered nirvana) will it be finally renounced. It means that the saints are called arhats when they completely cut off all obstacles of defilement. At that time all seeds of defilement in this consciousness are forever eliminated.[26]

When one has achieved the true understanding of the nature of the self and of all dharmas, one can finally abandon all insistence and attachments, be rid of all emotions, and enter into the realm of nirvana; a realm of pure joy. This enlightened understanding or awakening is called "wisdom." Hence, the goal of the Consciousness-Only School is to *transform consciousness into wisdom.*[27]

What kind of wisdom is required for one to reach nirvana? At the end of *A Treatise on the Establishment of Consciousness-Only*, Xuanzang presents Four Transcendental Wisdoms:[28]

The Great Mirror Wisdom (*da yuan jing zhi*)
The Universal Equality Wisdom (*ping deng xing zhi*)
The Profound Contemplation Wisdom (*miao guan cha zhi*)
The Perfect Achievement Wisdom (*cheng suo zuo zhi*)

The Great Mirror Wisdom is a mental state in which all discriminations are terminated. It is likened to a perfectly clean mirror, which contains no impurity and hence reflects the true nature of everything. The Universal Equality Wisdom is a mental state in which everything (including the self and others) is treated as identical. It is full of compassion toward all beings. The Profound Contemplation Wisdom is a mental state in which the mind observes all the unique as well as common characteristics of everything. It is doubt-free and worry-free. The Perfect Achievement Wisdom is a mental state in which the mind desires to help all beings "achieve" their happiness and salvation. It is "perfect achievement" since it brings about the achievement of everything, not just the self. From these descriptions, we can see that the ideal person for the Consciousness-Only School is ultimately the bodhisattva of the Mahayana school – one who is full of compassion for all sentient beings and refuses to enjoy his own salvation unless all other sentient beings have already achieved that goal. To become a bodhisattva, the first step is to eliminate the distinction between the self and others, to be non-selfish, to be all-embracing. A second step is to renounce the distinction between the desirable and the undesirable, so that one can be rid of the greed that makes one "grasp" onto objects or people. Once the mind is totally nondiscriminatory, it can be elevated into the state of perfect wisdom and terminate the transformations of consciousness. This is what the Consciousness-Only School means by "the transformation of consciousness into perfect wisdom."

The transformation of consciousness into wisdom is possible because the four wisdoms are already contained in all sentient beings as "seeds." These seeds are "pure," as distinguished from other impure seeds stored a posteriori from past perfuming. But at the same time, these pure seeds also need proper *perfuming* to be brought into fruition. This is why practices of correct morals and the cultivation of correct understanding are essential.[29] Once one has accumulated sufficient correct thoughts and deeds, one can begin the transformation process. The transformation from consciousness into wisdom is a fourfold transformation of all eight forms of consciousness. Upon the cessation of contamination from the other seven consciousnesses, the eighth consciousness (storehouse) is transformed into the Great Mirror Wisdom. When the seventh intellective consciousness becomes pure, it is transformed into the Universal

231

Equality Wisdom. When the sixth sense-coordinative consciousness is no longer defiled, it is transformed into the Profound Contemplation Wisdom. When the first five sense consciousnesses are no longer defiled, they are transformed into the Perfect Achievement Wisdom. Once all consciousnesses are transformed into wisdoms, they remain in this state "till the end of all ages."[30] Wisdom brings about the eternal cessation of consciousness. The Consciousness-Only School explains that this state is what the Buddha means by the description of "True Thusness" (*Tathata*).[31] When one reaches this state, one has become a "Buddha" (the honorable one). Since all four transcendental wisdoms (in the form of pure seeds) are innate to all sentient beings, all sentient beings have the potential to become a Buddha. This acknowledgement of equality of all sentient beings is again a characteristic trait of the Mahayana School.

As Vasubandhu concludes his *Thirty Stanzas*, he says:

> When in the [spheres of] objects, there is nothing for the wisdom [which no longer discriminates] to grasp, the state of consciousness-only is realized, since the six sense organs and their objects are no longer present. Without grasping, mysterious, and indescribable, this is supramundane wisdom. Because of the abandonment of the force of habits of various previous deeds and the six organs as well as their objects, the transformation [of the seeds of defilement] into the abiding with [perfect wisdom] will be realized. This is the realm of the absence of afflictions (end of transmigration), which is beyond description, is good, and is eternal, where one is in the state of emancipation, peace and joy. This is the Law of "Great Silence."[32]

What Vasubandhu describes here as the eternal realm in which one remains forever in a peaceful, joyous state, free of afflictions and emancipated from the cycle of transmigration, is exactly *nirvana*.

To conclude this section, we see that what the Consciousness-Only School takes as the ultimate reality is actually the eternal cessation of consciousness and the annihilation of the phenomenal world. Even though it claims that the phenomenal world is generated by consciousness and consciousness is the foundation of the world, it eventually aims to denounce consciousness as well as the phenomenal world. Lusthaus argues that for this reason, it is wrong to assimilate the thesis of Consciousness-Only to any form of metaphysical idealism. He says that metaphysical idealism is "the claim that mind alone is real and that everything else is created by mind." "However, the Yogacarin writings themselves argue something very different. Consciousness is not the ultimate reality or solution, but rather the root problem. This problem emerges in ordinary mental operations, and it can only be solved by bringing those operations to an end."[33] Perhaps we can say that the Consciousness-Only thesis can be understood on two levels: on the level of the mundane world, all dharmas are dependent on consciousness and only consciousness is real; on the level of True Thusness or the ultimate reality, however, even consciousness itself does not exist. On the first level, Consciousness-Only can be assimilated to idealism; on the second level it is actually denouncing idealism. This double level of truth constitutes an intriguing and complicated philosophy.

Arguments against the Real Existence of Dharmas (the External World)[34]

"Dharmas" means a variety of things in Sanskrit. In this context, it means broadly all the phenomena in the universe, including objects and events, mental and physical alike. Chan's *Sourcebook* translates it as "elements." Here we shall use "dharmas" to include "elements," "phenomena," "objects," "events," etc. What the Consciousness-Only School establishes is the elaboration of the Buddha's rejection of the view that there is an immutable "substance" underlying what we observe as dharmas, that this substance is beyond human perception and is like what Kant calls the "thing-in-itself."

In the *Twenty Stanzas*, Vasubandhu constructed several arguments in refutation of the various ontological claims about the ultimate reality of atoms or about the real existence of the external world.[35] We shall list them as follows.

A1 Materialism

One major ontological view refuted by the Buddha is the materialism of India (also known as "the Cârvâkas"[36]), according to which the ultimate fact of the universe is matter, and all things are made up of some indestructible atoms. What the Indian Materialists claim to be the substance underlying the dharmas is thus "atom." The way the conception of atom was derived by Indian Materialists is similar to the way Democritus in ancient Greece came up with the notion of atom: things cannot be infinitely divisible; the ultimately fundamental unit of all things is called "atom" – that which cannot be further divided. The Materialists acknowledge four kinds of atoms: earth, water, fire, and air. With various combinations, atoms make up different things and phenomena in the universe. Even consciousness, or any other spiritual phenomenon, is the result of the activities of atoms. There is nothing that cannot be reduced to physical matter. When elements combine into a particular thing, that thing comes into existence; when these elements dissolve, it brings the death or annihilation of the particular object. Material objects and phenomena are constantly in flux, while atoms never change. Therefore, the ultimate reality of the universe is these atoms themselves.

Against this theory, the Consciousness-Only School has the following claim:

To prove: The whole assumption about the existence of a single, indivisible atom is not plausible.

1 If a single atom is to be combined with other atoms to form objects, then it must have surfaces of contact with other atoms.
2 There are six sides of contacts: up, down, left, right, front, back.
3 Therefore, every basic unit is already a unit of six parts.
4 Therefore, there cannot be a single unit that is not further divisible (that has no parts).
5 Therefore, the very concept of *atom* is unintelligible.[37]

A2 *Pluralism*

Another school of thought, the Vaisesika School, proclaims that the world is caused by the combinations of atoms; objects are simply the aggregates or agglomerations of singular atoms. This school is often called pluralism, because of its belief in many substances. It is also called pluralistic realism, since it concedes the existence of the external world.

The pluralistic metaphysics of this school is that there are many substances underlying many qualities we observe through our senses. Qualities do not have permanent existence; they adhere to substances. The two defining characteristics of a substance is that it is "the substrate of qualities" and they are the only kind of entities that "come into contact" with one another.[38] The material objects that we observe are formed out of the combination of various substances. These substances can be divided into nine categories: earth, water, fire, air, ether, time, space, atman (self), and mind. They are called basic elements and, except for ether, consist of atoms (that which is indivisible). Like the Materialists, the Vaisesika School also sees atoms as the ultimate reality. But they also argue that atoms have no spatial extension, because if they did, then they could be further divided.

Vasubandhu saw this as the major difficulty of the theory: how can objects with spatial extension be made up of atoms that have no spatiality? Against this theory, he has the following arguments:

To prove: The theory that material objects are mere "agglomerations" of many (indivisible) atoms is not tenable.

The Argument from Indivisibility
1 If atoms are indivisible, then they have no spatial extension.
2 If single atoms have no spatial extension, then multiple atoms also do not have spatial extension.
3 If the aggregate of multiple atoms does not have any spatial extension, then all the multiple atoms would take up the same space.
4 If the aggregate takes up the same space as a single atom, then it is no different from the single atom – which is ridiculous.
5 Therefore, the theory that material objects are mere "agglomerations" of many (indivisible) atoms is not tenable.[39]

The Argument from the Lack of Solidity
1 Atoms do not have spatial extension; thus, they should be similar to the void[40] and have no solidity.
2 Things with no solidity do not form shadows and do not obstruct each other.
3 What is true of the parts should also be true of the whole; there is no feature emergent in the whole system when the system is made up of the parts of identical nature.
4 Therefore, the aggregates of atoms must also possess no solidity, not form shadows and not constitute obstruction.
5 If the aggregate does not have any solidity, then all atoms would collapse into one single atom and the result is equally ridiculous.[41]

A3 Monism

Another major opponent of Buddhism is the monistic philosophy of the Vedanta School. Vedanta philosophy is derived from the traditional Indian philosophy Brahmanism, which is recorded in the sacred scriptures, the Vedas. One of the major texts for the Vedanta School is the famous Upanisads, part of the Vedas.[42] The basic issue examined in the Vedas is: what is the ultimate reality? The answer common to all schools of Brahmanism is that the ultimate reality is called "Brahman." "The word Brahman always means the Supreme Spirit, and literally means the 'ever-growing,' the 'ever-expanding.' It corresponds to the Western concept of the Absolute."[43] But various schools dispute the nature of Brahman and its relation to the Self ("atman," which means "spirit," "soul" or "the self"). Some hold the view that the Brahman and the Self are two entities, and this view is called dualism. Some others, on the other hand, hold the view that the Self and the Brahman are absolutely identical. Therefore, the world is ultimately One, which is Brahman itself. What we experience as the phenomenal world are the illusory imageries created by the magical powers (called "Maya") of Brahman. To gain knowledge of the Truth, we must see beyond the multiplicity of the phenomenal world and recognize the oneness of the ultimate reality. This view is called monism. To refute this theory, Vasubandhu has the following argument:

To prove: The view that the whole world is *One* is untenable.

1 If, according to this theory, the whole outer world of sense objects is just *One*, then there would be no spatial differentiation or object discrimination.
2 But if the whole world is just one unity and there is no spatial differentiation, then it cannot be possible to walk progressively from one place to another: one step taken reaches everywhere. This is absurd.
3 If the whole world is just one unity and there is no object discrimination, then a single space would contain various objects such as elephants and horses and there would be no demarcation (empty spaces) between them (since each occupying object must fill the whole space occupied). This is also absurd.
4 Therefore, the theory that the whole world is just *One* is impossible.[44]

Arguments Against the Substantiality of the Self[45]

Even though the Consciousness-Only School grants the existence of consciousness, it does not treat consciousness as a subsisting entity. In their view, consciousness is a flow of activities, which do not belong to any particular "self." To insist that there is a self that underlies all these mental activities is against the Buddha's basic teaching of no-self. What is denied by the Consciousness-Only School is not just the substantiality of the self, but also the permanence of the self. The nature of consciousness is that it is in continual transition: once a thought or a perception comes into consciousness, it immediately gets replaced by a new thought or perception. As explained earlier, in the stream of consciousness, the previous state of consciousness causes the present state of consciousness, which in turn causes the next state of consciousness. Furthermore, since the transmission of causation and the continuation of the stream is not restricted to a single life, it is ridiculous to insist that there is an "I," with the present personality traits, feelings, thoughts, interpersonal relationships, etc., which serves as the *subject* of this stream of consciousness. Therefore, the Consciousness-Only School claims that consciousness is real (from time immemorial), but the self (or the *I*) does not exist.

Dan Lusthaus uses the term "alterity" to explicate the idea of perpetual change within the stream of consciousness. He says:

> The momentariness of causes and effects insures that alterity, i.e., "becoming otherwise," is perpetual. Each moment is an intersection of cause and effect, in which, for causes to be causes and effects to be effects, the cause *must be different from* the effect. In the very same moment that something arises and ceases (and, according to Buddhism, that lasts only a moment), there is a "becoming otherwise" into which "self-appropriation" insinuates itself.[46]

In other words, the nature of consciousness is perpetual alteration, going from one state into another. There is thus nothing permanent and subsisting that can be deemed as the true self. Common people's insistence of self-identity comes from a false illusion and a futile attempt to hold on to something that isn't there. As Lusthaus puts it:

> There is an attempt to seize, to grasp, and hold on to that moment, in order to install upon it a stable self, an identity. But the moment itself is simply a moment of "becoming otherwise," an identity that is always already inscribed as alterity. . . . In fact, Buddhist alterity requires a "self" so radically lacking in stable, invariant identity that it can never be a self.[47]

From this explanation, we can see why the Consciousness-Only School confirms consciousness and mind but denies the self or the soul.

The refutation of the real existence of the self can again be separated into various arguments against different theories on the substance of the self. These other non-Buddhist schools (aside from Materialism, which rejects the possibility of soul) recognize the existence of a spiritual entity different from the physical body. Following the Indian Brahmanism tradition, they commonly call this spiritual entity "atman." In their view, atman is eternal, immutable, and indestructible. But the various schools differ in their explanation of the relation between atman and the physical body. The first view is that atman is as extensive as empty space itself; the second view is that atman takes up the same space as the body (in which it resides); the third view holds that atman is as tiny as an atom. Xuan-zang's *Treatise* rejects all three views as being "contrary to reason." These three views will be presented as B1, B2, and B3, as follows.

B1 Atman (the substance of the self) is eternal, universal, and as extensive as the empty space itself. It can act upon the body and can be the subject of happiness and sorrow.

According to Xuan-zang's disciple Kuiji's notation, this theory is held by the dualistic Samkhyas School and the pluralistic Vaisesika School. Against this theory, Xuan-zang's *Treatise* has the following argument:

Argument against [B1]
1 If the self were eternal, universal, and as extensive as empty space itself, then all different selves would simply collapse into one self since they are all as extensive as the empty space itself.
2 Therefore, all sentient beings must share the same self.
3 But if it is the same self that all sentient beings share, then when one being acts and receives the fruits of its action, or when one being achieves salvation, all beings would do the same. This is absurd.
4 Therefore, the theory that the self is eternal, universal, and as extensive as empty space itself is contrary to reason.[48]

B2 Atman (the substance of the self) is eternal and one, but its extension is the same as the body.

Kuiji attributes this theory to the Nirgrantha School and the Jainism school. Against this theory, Xuan-zang's *Treatise* has the following argument:

Argument against [B2]
1 If the self has the same extension as the body, then it would be divisible.
2 If the self is divisible, then it is no longer one.
3 Therefore, the theory that there is one single self that takes up the whole body is contrary to reason.[49]

B3 Atman (the substance of the self) is eternal and one, but it is infinitesimal like an atom, moving within the body and performing acts of all kinds.

Kuiji attributes this theory to the Pasupata School (which worships Animal-Lord) and the Recluses. Against this theory, Xuan-zang's *Treatise* has the following argument:

Argument against [B3]

1   If the atman is as infinitesimal as an atom, then it is too tiny to cause the whole body to move.
2   If the movement of the body is explained by the movements of the atman, then the atman itself must come and go in various parts of the body.
3   If the atman comes and goes, then it is neither eternal nor one, since what is eternal and one cannot go through movements or changes.
4   Therefore, the theory does not have a coherent view of atman.[50]

The *Treatise* further attacks three other views held by different Buddhist schools concerning the nature of the self. These schools base their theories on their different interpretations of the Buddha's teaching of the "five aggregates." The Buddha denies the existence of any permanent, subsisting self; instead, he analyzes what ordinary people conceive to be their selves as the aggregates of five functions: the material form (the bodily organs), sensation, thought, disposition, and consciousness. These schools differ in their analysis of the relation between the self and the five aggregates. One school, in particular, holds that the self is identical to the five aggregates. Kuiji attributes this view to the Yogacara school.[51] Their doctrine can be encapsulated as follows:

B4   The substance of the self is identical with the five aggregates that make up a person (body, sensation, thought, disposition, and consciousness).

Against this theory, Xuan-zang's *Treatise* has the following argument:

Argument against [B4]

1   The theory claims that the self is identical with the five aggregates, which include the senses and other mental activities such as thought and consciousness.
2   But the five senses are parts of the body and are thus physically obstructed.
3   Physically obstructed things are not eternal.
4   Furthermore, mental activities are constantly in transition.
5   Things that are constantly in transition are not eternal.
6   Therefore, the theory that the self, as aggregates, can be eternal is untenable.[52]

From this argument, we can see how the Consciousness-Only School distinguishes itself from its philosophical origin, the Yogacara School. It argues that there is only consciousness, and thus the other four elements in the five aggregates are actually the result of the transformation of consciousness. Of these four elements, body, as well as the five sense organs, is of a physical nature. The Consciousness-Only School denies the existence of the material world. Therefore, it would not consider body and sensation as truly existent. Furthermore, the Consciousness-Only School rejects the very notion of the self, and any adherence to the notion of an eternal self. To the Consciousness-Only School, there is no eternity. Even consciousness itself is not eternal, since there is no permanent entity underlying the constantly changing stream of consciousness. Any form of fixation, whether it is onto the world of dharmas or onto the self, would be totally against the *true* teaching of the Buddha.[53]

Arguments for Consciousness-Only[54]

In Xuan-zang's *A Treatise on the Establishment of Consciousness-Only*, the objector says: "You have refuted my thesis, but the refutation of another person's thesis is not sufficient to establish your own principle."[55] In response, Xuan-zang presented proofs of the theses of Consciousness-Only. His arguments are based on Vasubandhu's original arguments. In both the *Twenty Stanzas* and the *Thirty Stanzas*, Vasubandhu answers other questions raised against the Consciousness-Only thesis. These answers can be considered as further defense of the school. We shall look at two of his arguments as explicated by Xuan-zang. The first deals with the nature of the external world; the second deals with the possibility of our knowledge of other minds. From these two arguments, we can gain more understanding of the theory of the Consciousness-Only School.

The problem of the four characteristics of the external world[56]

A major puzzle entertained by anyone who is a commonsense realist concerning the doctrine of consciousness-only would be this: If the whole world is created by consciousness, then why doesn't it appear in whatever way I imagine it to be? Why doesn't it disappear when I stop imagining? Based on this puzzlement, the objector raises four questions. First of all, if everything is within my mind, why do I have to travel to a particular place to see a particular thing? Secondly, if every event is determined by my consciousness, then why does it occur only in a specific time and not at other times according to my will? Thirdly, if people with problems in the eyes could be seeing tiny threads or little flies in their visual field,[57] then why aren't there tiny threads and little flies for others to see? Why can't a singular consciousness determine the external world? Finally, if everything is caused by consciousness, then how could there be any real function of anything (for example, food can relieve hunger, drinks can quench thirst, knives can wound while clothing can keep one warm, medicine can heal while poison can kill, etc.)? Furthermore, how could we ever hold anyone responsible for his or her act since all events and actions are mere constructions of the underlying consciousness of someone? Vasubandhu listed these objections as *objections from the four characteristics of the external world (and of external objects)*. These four characteristics are:

1 Spatial determination
2 Temporal determination
3 The indeterminacy of singular consciousness
4 The possession of real functions

His rebuttal of the above objections can be formulated as follows:

1 It is said that the world cannot be dependent on consciousness only because it possesses four characteristics: being spatially determined, being temporally determined, not being determinable by a single consciousness, and having real functions.
2 But objects in our dreams can also have the first two and the last characteristics (e.g., in dreams, the objects we see are also fixed in space and time, and sometimes they can have real functions such as one's reaching orgasm in a dream).
3 Furthermore, in the transmigration of lives, different creatures, in virtue of their common past deeds, would perceive the same realm of existence even though those realms do not really exist.[58]
4 Objects of dreams and of illusory imaginations do not exist independently of our consciousness.
5 Therefore, it is not true that external objects cannot exist independently of our consciousness simply because they possess the above four characteristics.

The Consciousness-Only School often uses dream as an analogy to life. When we are dreaming, we cannot tell that we are dreaming. Only when we awaken will we realize that what we previously experienced was a dream. By the same token, when we are going through life's experiences, we would not know that these experiences are not real. Only after we have gained enlightenment can we truly understand how the whole external world is merely the creation of consciousness. Objects in our dreams depend on our imagination; objects in the external world depend on our consciousness. Neither is *real* in the sense of having independent existence. According to Xuan-zang, there is nonetheless a difference between them. He says, "We should realize that some dharmas [which are imagined] are empty and some [which depend on something else, i.e., cause, to complete] are not."[59] That is to say, objects of dreams are both not real and empty; objects that have dependent co-arising as their nature are not real, and not empty. This comment reaffirms the middle-way position that the Consciousness-Only School takes on the debate on whether dharmas are existent, or are empty.

Another difficulty pointed out in this objection is that while dreams, illusions, and imaginations are specific to individuals, the external world is not. Someone with a faulty vision could be seeing tiny threads and flies in their visual field, but other people cannot see them. Therefore, the world exists independently of one's imagination. Vasubandhu's reply points out that the world is dependent, not on a singular consciousness, but on all consciousnesses. Creatures of the same kind must have had their storehouse consciousnesses perfumed in the same way, and thus their consciousnesses jointly generate a world that is largely consistent and universal.[60] Being situated in a world created by all consciousnesses together, an individual cannot simply alter the appearance of the world by will (or by misperception). Therefore, the objections raised do not defeat the thesis of consciousness-only. From this reply, we again see how the Consciousness-Only thesis is different from solipsism.

The problem of other minds[61]

The Consciousness-Only School denies the existence of external objects, but it does not deny the existence of other minds since they too are consciousnesses. Furthermore, it acknowledges the possibility of one mind's knowing other minds. A question is thus raised by the objector: if there is only inner consciousness and no external world, then how can we say that other minds exist? If other minds do exist, on the other hand, then they exist outside of our own minds, are distinct from our own spheres of objects, and are thus part of the external world. Then how can the Consciousness-Only School deny that there is an external world?[62]

To rebuff this line of reasoning, Xuan-zang pointed out the difference between other minds and other objects. The "other" here denotes what is separable from the (imagined) self; in this sense, there are other minds – minds that the individual self does not take as its own. But the "external" here takes on an extended meaning; it denotes what is external to consciousness – any form of consciousness. In this sense, nothing is external since nothing is external to consciousness. That is to say, there are other minds, but they do not constitute an external realm. Therefore, the existence of other minds, or we should say, other forms of consciousness, does not refute the claim that there is only consciousness and that there is nothing external to consciousness. There are multiple consciousnesses, and these consciousnesses are "other minds," but they do not constitute a world independent of all mental activities.

To establish the claim that there is more than one form of consciousness, Xuan-zang's *Treatise* has the following remark:

> If there were only one individual consciousness, how is that there is a variety of ordinary people, saints, the honored ones and lowly ones, and causes and effects in the ten cardinal directions? Who would then expound teachings to whom? What dharmas would there be? And what goal is there to seek? Therefore there is a deep purpose in saying there is consciousness only. . . . Because consciousnesses are their own characters, because consciousnesses are associated with mental qualities, because of the transformation of the perceiving portion and perceived portion [which are products of the transformation], because of the three categories of dharmas, and because of the four true realities, all dharmas are inseparable from consciousness and the general term "consciousness" has been set up. The word "only" is employed merely to deny what ordinary people take to be real matter definitely separated from the various consciousnesses.[63]

Here Xuan-zang seems to acknowledge the differences among people and their respective worlds. Since each world is the product of some consciousnesses, various forms of consciousness produce an assortment of worlds. The Consciousness-Only School holds the view that different forms of consciousness could actually *perceive*, or even *create*, different phenomenal worlds. One example given is that what ordinary people perceive as a river of water could be perceived as a river of pus by hungry ghosts. The nature of the world is thus determined by the nature of the consciousnesses that collectively produce it. Since phenomenal worlds are perceived and thereby created differently by different forms of consciousness, we must acknowledge that there are different consciousnesses. Therefore, other consciousnesses, as well as my own consciousness, exist. As Xuan-zang emphasized, the "only" here does not mean "only mine." The word is used simply to dispel the illusion of the existence of a mind-independent world.

Of course, the problem of other minds is not this easily resolved. Even if the Consciousness-Only School is consistent in its doctrine of the coexistence of multiple consciousnesses, it still needs to explain the interactions among different minds (or different consciousnesses). In other words, even if the ontological problem of other minds can be resolved, the epistemological problem of other minds still needs to be addressed. Each consciousness is involved in its internal cycle of three-fold transformation, from storehouse to self-consciousness to the six sense consciousnesses of external objects, and back to the storehouse consciousness. How then does it ever go out of its internal cycle to cognize another mind? The perception of other objects is explained by the theory that these objects are the mere results of the transformation of one's consciousness. But the knowledge of other minds cannot be so explained, since they are *not* the mere results of the transformation of one's consciousness. Furthermore, the phenomenal worlds as generated by the transformations of other people's consciousnesses are also not available to me, since they are not part of my consciousness. The phenomenal *I* thus exists within its own mental creations, having no direct contact with other minds or other phenomenal worlds. In this way, the Consciousness-Only School's intersubjective idealism seems to collapse into solipsism.

In his attempt to answer this challenge, Xuan-zang uses the analogy of a mirror. *A Treatise on the Establishment of Consciousness-Only* says:

> The consciousness is merely like a mirror, in which what seems to be an external sphere appears. It is in this sense that it is called the mind that discriminates another. But it cannot discriminate [another mind] immediately and directly. What it discriminates immediately and directly are its own transformations.[64]

If we employ this analogy, then we can say the phenomenal world created by each mind is like the image within each mirror, while multiple minds interact among one another just like different mirrors reflecting

244

one another's image. This mirror analogy could illustrate the Consciousness-Only School's point that nothing is real; everything is mere imagery. But ultimately this analogy is unsatisfactory on various counts. First, a mirror does not generate imagery; it reflects something external. Therefore, it is not a proper analogy to consciousness. Secondly, when multiple mirrors reflect one another's image, they cannot avoid duplicating what are already reflected in the other mirrors. Therefore, the analogy fails to relate to the claim of the coexistence of different phenomenal worlds perceived by different beings. Finally, a mirror is always passively receiving, never actively perceiving. It does not *interact* with any other mirror in any epistemic way. Therefore, on the analogy of the mirror, there is no possibility of the knowledge of other minds. In this way, the attempt to explain the possibility of knowing other minds ends up being a concession that such knowledge is not possible.

Vasubandhu's *Twenty Stanzas* ends with the discussion on the possibility of knowing other minds. His reply is that the knowledge of another's mind is just like the knowledge of one's own mind – one has neither. When the objector asks why one cannot have either knowledge of another's mind or knowledge of one's own mind, he replies, "Because of ignorance. Both knowledge of the object, because each is covered and darkened by ignorance, do not know [it] as the ineffable object reached by the pure knowledge of a Buddha."[65] What Vasubandhu claims here is that it is impossible to know other minds; hence, when the Buddha talked about the knowledge of other minds, he was merely speaking to the ignorant ones (who falsely believe that there are other minds). But if this is the view, then he is conceding that because the Consciousness-Only School cannot answer the epistemological problem of other minds, it is forced to deny the ontological status of other minds. This concession may show that the problem of other minds remains the irresolvable difficulty for the Consciousness-Only School.

Conclusion

In this chapter, we have seen how novel this mode of thinking is to the development of Chinese philosophy up to then. The Consciousness-Only School employs many arguments, paying close attention to the form of logical syllogism, which was seldom the way ancient Chinese philosophers would present their thoughts. It examines many issues, such as the existence of substance and the connection between substance and the phenomenal world, which had not been the primary focus of Chinese philosophy until then. It embraces the belief that the essence of life is suffering, which was an ingrained belief of the Indian culture, but not of the Chinese culture. It is based on the "other-worldly" concern rooted in the Indian tradition, and it teaches annihilation of human emotions, desires, family ties, and human bonds. Its ultimate goal is to reach nirvana, which is understood by this school to denote a realm separated from the human world. Chinese philosophy, on the other hand, is based on humanism – the thesis of the primacy of the human world. The whole spirit of this school was so contrary to the basic "this-worldly" love of the Chinese people that it was not to have a lasting effect in Chinese society. As a result, the Consciousness-Only School declined in China around the eighth century AD. Other teachings that were more compatible with the Chinese way of thinking took its place.

Further discussion questions

1 If we did not have *any* form of sense perception and physical sensation – no sight, no sound, no sense of cold or hot, hungry or full, would the world still exist for us? If all sentient beings were not "sentient," would there still be a world?
2 If we were brought up with only a group consciousness or a collective identity such that we would only think in terms of "we," would we still have a sense of the self? What is the foundation for our self-awareness?
3 Do you agree with the Buddha's teaching that the sense of the self is the root of our suffering? Do you think that if we can eliminate our desires and our clinging toward external things, then we will attain true tranquility of the mind?
4 What does the Consciousness-Only School mean by the nonexistence of the self and the nonexistence of dharma?

Primary texts

Wing-tsit Chan (ed.) *A Sourcebook in Chinese Philosophy*, 4th edn. Princeton: Princeton University Press, 1973 (ch. 23; selections of Xuan-zang's *Cheng Wei-Shi Lun* along with all of Vasubandhu's *Thirty Stanzas*).
Clarence H. Hamilton (trans.) Vasubandhu, *Wei shih er shih lun* (*The Treatise in Twenty Stanzas on Representation-only*). Translated from the Chinese version of [Xuan-zang]. New Haven, CT: American Oriental Society, 1938.
Tat Wei (trans.) *Ch'eng Wei-Shih Lun: Doctrine of Mere-Consciousness* by [Xuan-zang]. Hong Kong: The Ch'eng Wei-Shih Lun Publication Committee, 1973.

Further readings

Yu-lan Fung. *A History of Chinese Philosophy*, vol. II, trans. Derk Bodde. Princeton, NJ: Princeton University Press, 1983 (ch. 8: "Buddhism during the Sui and T'ang Dynasties (Part I)," pp. 299–338).

Clarence H. Hamilton. "Introduction" to his translation of Vasubandhu's *Wei shih er shih lun* (*The Treatise in Twenty Stanzas on Representation-only*). Translated from the Chinese version of [Xuan-zang]. New Haven, CT: American Oriental Society, 1938.

Dan Lusthaus. *Buddhist Phenomenology: A Philosophical Investigation of Yogacara Buddhism and the Ch'eng Wei-shih lun.* New York: Routledge Curzon, 2002 (in particular, Parts IV and V).

Chapter 10

The Hua-yan
(Hua-yen) School

Introduction

Hua-yan Buddhism derived its name from the *Hua-yan Sutra*, translated as "The Flower Ornament Scripture" or as "The Flowery Splendor Scripture."[1] This extensive Buddhist text gives a very "flowery" description of the various stages of enlightenment; it also expounds the correct worldview, the correct ethical conduct, among other things. It probably was not composed by a single author, but was a compilation of various works circulating in India and its neighboring regions around the first and the second centuries AD. As far as we know no Indian Buddhist school was ever founded on the basis of this scripture.

The Hua-yan School, like its contemporary Tian-tai School, is indisputably a Chinese Buddhist school. Wing-tsit Chan says that it "represents the highest development of Chinese Buddhist thought."[2] The founder of the Hua-yan School was a Chinese monk named Du-shun (557–640). Though Hua-yan's major sutra came from abroad, Du-shun established Hua-yan Buddhism by introducing new terminology to replace some key Indian notions. He introduced the term "*li*" (principle) to stand for the ultim-ate realm of reality. This notion would prove to be one of the most important in Chinese philosophy.[3] Du-shun used "*shi*" (things or events) to replace the term "form" in traditional Buddhist texts.[4] This substitution manifests a more intense interest in the affairs of the phenomenal world. With this substitution, Hua-yan's first patriarch took a subtle step away from the strong negation of the phenomenal world manifested in the *Hua-yan Sutra*. Du-shun also introduced the theory of the non-interference (or non-obstruction) of principle and things. Future patriarchs of the Hua-yan School would further develop his ingenious idea.

The second patriarch of Hua-yan was Zhi-yan (602–68), who studied with Du-shun. However, it is generally acknowledged that the real founder of Hua-yan Buddhism was its third patriarch, Fa-zang (643–712). Fa-zang systematized Hua-yan philosophy by setting up different categories of existence and different doctrines on the nature of existence. He divided the realm of reality into "the Realm of Principle" and "the Realm of Things" and emphasized that these two realms "interpenetrate" and "interidentify." His theory of the *Ten Mysterious Gates* gives a detailed account of the Ultimate Truth.[5] His teaching was continued by Cheng-guan (738–839?), known as the fourth patriarch of the Hua-yan School. Following Fa-zang's division, Cheng-guan came up with the famous "four dharma realms": the Realm of Principle, the Realm of Things,[6] the Realm of the Non-interference between Principle and Things, and the Realm of the Non-interference of All Things. This theory of four dharma realms would turn out to be the defining thesis for the Hua-yan School.

For English translations of the original Hua-yan works, we have Cleary's translation of the entire *Hua-yan Sutra* (*The Flower Ornament Scripture*),[7] as well as his translations of various works by the four patriarchs. This chapter will be based on the *Hua-yan Sutra*, translated by Cleary, as well as Du-shun's "Cessation and Contemplation in the Five Teachings," his "Contemplation of the Realm of Reality" with Cheng-guan's commentary (entitled "Mirror of the Mysteries of the Universe of the Hua-yan"), Zhi-yan's "Ten Mysterious Gates of the Unitary Vehicle," Fa-zang's "Cultivation of Contemplation of the Inner Meaning of the [Hua-yan]: The Ending of Delusion and Return to the Source";[8] Fa-zang's "A Treatise on the Gold Lion" and his commentary on the *Hua-yan Sutra*.[9]

In some sense, it is oxymoronic to analyze Hua-yan philosophy. Hua-yan philosophy is basically "anti-analysis" and "anti-philosophy." For its practical goal or its religious attainment, Hua-yan Buddhism advocates an immediate understanding that is beyond any doctrine and even beyond the use of words and concepts. As the *Hua-yan Sutra* says: "All philosophies in the world are mental fabrications. There has never been a single doctrine, by which one could enter the true essence of things."[10] Fa-zang also remarks, "[The complete teaching] goes beyond the horizons of speech and thought. It penetrates the trap of words and concepts."[11] However, since our goal in this chapter is to introduce Hua-yan Buddhism as a form of philosophy, not as a form of religious practice, we shall do our best to analyze its teaching in words.

We will focus primarily on the worldview of the Hua-yan School. The chapter is divided into three sections. First, we will look at Hua-yan's interpretation of the nature of the world and its objects. We will then move on to Hua-yan's analysis of the possibility of our gaining knowledge about the world. In particular, we will examine the intrinsic difficulty in employing language and conception to depict reality. The final section deals with Hua-yan's division of moral agents and analyzes its basic moral/religious doctrines. We shall find that even though Hua-yan Buddhism is based on the *Hua-yan Sutra*, some of the themes in the original scripture were not carried on in the works by Hua-yan patriarchs; some of the themes developed by the Hua-yan patriarchs were not originally seen in the *Hua-yan Sutra*. In our analysis, we shall try to mark the authors of these different ideas. But ultimately, Hua-yan Buddhism should be considered as a coherent theory created by the joint efforts of all authors.

Hua-yan Metaphysics

Hua-yan Buddhism has a most fascinating metaphysics, which directly opposes materialism or physicalism – that is, the prevailing worldview of our times. It can best be characterized as a form of subjective idealism, the view that the physical world is not real, but exists merely as the projection of the individual mind. In the previous chapter we saw how the Consciousness-Only School upholds a form of objective idealism. Hua-yan's metaphysical view is different from the Consciousness-Only School in that it not only denies the realness of our present world, but also rejects the commonality among different mental constructions. In this section, we shall analyze five major theses that make up Hua-yan's metaphysics.

The world is a fabrication of the mind

The *Hua-yan Sutra* denies that the phenomenal world really exists. The phenomenal world means the world we, as human beings, presently experience. In the *Hua-yan Sutra*, this world is likened to dream, illusion, phantom, echo, the magician's conjuring, and the reflection in the mirror.[12] Everything we perceive around us is also like a reflection or an illusion. As reflections, objects "have no location" and "no substantial nature."[13] As illusions, objects do not have a real beginning or end, nor do they have a definite origin or a final exit. In one synopsis, the *Sutra* says that all things "have no true reality."[14]

   Another way to say that things have no true reality is to say that they are "empty." A common tenet of all Buddhist schools is the *emptiness* of the mundane world, but different schools give the term different interpretations. We can encapsulate the following connotations for "emptiness":

"Emptiness$_1$" = being devoid of inherent self-nature and of independent existence
"Emptiness$_2$" = being unreal; being illusory; being non-existent
"Emptiness$_3$" = being devoid of any phenomenal characteristics and perceptual qualities
"Emptiness$_4$" = void; nothingness; null[15]

In Tian-tai Buddhism, phenomenal objects are empty in the sense of *emptiness$_1$*, but not in the sense of *emptiness$_2$*. In Hua-yan Buddhism, on the other hand, the whole phenomenal world is empty both in the sense of *emptiness$_1$* and in the sense of *emptiness$_2$*. In the *Hua-yan Sutra*, we see a consistent usage of "empty" in conjunction with "null" or standing for "having no real existence." As the *Sutra* says, "The nature of things is fundamentally empty and null. . . . Things have no true reality."[16] The reason why Hua-yan Buddhists understand "emptiness" in the sense of *emptiness$_2$* is that they make the following identifications:

1 Being empty = being born from conditions (being dependent on other factors for origination)
2 Being born from conditions (being dependent on other factors for origination) = having no inherent nature
3 Having no inherent nature = non-existent
4 Non-existent = unreal[17]

But for the Tian-tai school, (3) is not true. Tian-tai Buddhists do not define "existence" as "self-sufficient existence" or "perpetual existence." Thus, the two schools can agree on their definition of "emptiness" and on their view of the nature of things, and yet come to different assessments on the realness of things.

When "emptiness" (*Sunyata*; *kong*) is used as a synonym for the ultimate reality (the noumenon – something beyond the tangible experiential world), it also has different connotations. Tian-tai Buddhism assigns only *emptiness$_3$* to the noumenon, since it is beyond our perception as well as our conception. But Tian-tai denies that the noumenon itself is a void with nothing inside. Hua-yan Buddhism, on the other hand, seems to assign both *emptiness$_3$* and *emptiness$_4$* to this ultimate reality. As the

251

Sutra says: "All in the worlds is void."[18] It also frequently uses space to be a metaphor for the noumenon. If phenomena are likened to what are enclosed in space while the noumenon is likened to space itself, then this notion of noumenon does seem to connote the void and the null.

The *Sutra* says:

> Living beings and lands, all things there are in all times, in the same way, without exception, are all illusory. Making illusory forms of men and women, elephants, horses, cattle, and sheep, houses, ponds, springs, and such, gardens, groves, flowers and fruits, illusory things have no awareness and also have no abode. Ultimately of the character of nullity, they only appear according to imagination.[19]

According to this remark, worldly phenomena are formed because of the mind's imagination. If the phenomenal world is like the magician's conjuring or the artist's painting, then the magician or the painter is simply the mind itself. "Mind is like an artist, able to paint the worlds. The five clusters all are born thence. There is nothing it doesn't make."[20] In the respect that it regards the world as being dependent on the mind for its existence/appearance, this metaphysical view is clearly that of idealism.

This idealistic theme is emphasized in all Hua-yan patriarchs' commentaries on the *Sutra*. For example, the second patriarch Zhi-yan says:

> Since there is no separate objective realm outside of mind, we say "only mind." If it operates harmoniously, it is called nirvana; therefore the [*Sutra*] says, "Mind makes the Buddhas." If it operates perversely, it is birth-and-death; therefore the [*Sutra*] says, "The triple world is illusory – it is only made by one mind."[21]

The third patriarch Fa-zang also says:

> [W]hatever there is in the world is only the creation of one mind; outside of mind there is not a single thing that can be apprehended. . . . It means that all discriminations come only from one's own mind. There has never been any environment outside the mind which could be an object of mind.[22]

Fa-zang further denies the warranty of sense perception and claims that "sense data have no existence."[23] In other words, the mind's discerning abilities create myriad things in the world. Reality itself does not have all these discriminations; all things we perceive are thus the mind's fabrication.

To say that the phenomenal world is the result of the mind's fabrication is not to say that the mind really "creates" a genuine world. As the *Sutra* says: "All things have no provenance, and no one can create them."[24] It also says: "Mental phenomena are like phantoms, and so indeed is the world. The world does not make itself, nor is it made by another."[25] The world is like the trickery of the magician or the phantoms generated by the deluded mind – the imagery suddenly appears before the eye, but one cannot say that the imagined object comes to be in the real time. Since it does not "come to be," one also cannot say that it "ceases to exist" at any moment.

Hence, we could perhaps say that Hua-yan Buddhism is based on an anti-realistic attitude toward this mundane world. This feature of subjective idealism and anti-realism seems to have been overlooked by many Hua-yan commentators.[26] Both Yu-lan Fung and Wing-tsit Chan take Hua-yan philosophy to be the exemplification of objective idealism. From the above explication of the theory expounded in the *Hua-yan Sutra*, we see that Hua-yan philosophy is clearly idealism of the subjective form. Fung thinks that Hua-yan's idealism "approaches realism more closely than does an idealism which is purely subjective."[27] Francis Cook also says that Fa-zang was "a realist in the Chinese tradition of realism."[28] The realism they have in mind is a kind of commonsense realism – the belief that the world in which we live is real. Cook argues that for the Hua-yan School, "the emptiness doctrine should not be understood as a naive rejection of the material world as pure illusion; it indeed recognizes the existence of the natural world but denies that it has any duration or independent being. In fact, being is rejected in favor of a constant, never-fully-completed becoming."[29] Under this interpretation, the world we live in is an organic whole constantly evolving and transforming. What is denied is simply the self-subsistence of individual entities, not the whole system. Did Fa-zang revolutionize Hua-yan Buddhism so much as to turn its spirit of idealism into realism? Let us turn to Fa-zang's view in particular.

Fa-zang explains the metaphor of dream in the *Hua-yan Sutra* this way:

> [The metaphor of] comprehending a dream's illusion means that the physical manifestations which our deluded minds consider to exist are under examination seen to be as unreal as a man conjured up by magic. The case is indeed like awaking from a night dream to the realization that everything in it was non-existent.[30]

If everything we experience is like a dream, from which we can one day wake up and denounce as "unreal," then the world we live in is certainly *unreal*.

Fa-zang uses the phrase "the Realm of Things" to denote our experiential world. This world depends on what he calls "the Realm of Principle" as its ontological basis. In the sense that the Realm of Principle is real, we could perhaps say that the phenomenal world "exists." Ultimately, however, Fa-zang denies the reality of our experiential world. He says, "Whether spoken of as [thing] or Principle, there is the way (the mind) by which they are formed and exist."[31] So, even though he separates the Realm of Principle and the Realm of Things, both realms are, according to him, productions of the mind. Fa-zang also refers to things in the world (dharmas) as "dharmas of the mind" and says, "There is no dharma outside the mind."[32] Taking a tiny thing such as dust and a huge thing such as a mountain for examples, Fa-zang says that neither comes into nor goes out of existence, since they "turn on and on in accordance with the mind."[33] There is no real beginning or end to the mountain's or the dust's existence. They appear to us and then vanish in front of our eyes, just like a magician's conjured images; neither can be said to exist or to perish. By the same token, motion is only an appearance; there is no real motion in the world. We could think of the motion seen in animation films: even though we perceive it, in reality there is only a chain of still frames succeeding one another. The mind is the artist who draws the picture; with each moment of thought, the mind draws anew. No external thing can have duration from moment to moment.[34]

Fa-zang further denies the reality of all perceptual qualities, which he calls "characters." He says:

> For example, the characters of this small and round particle of dust arise from the transformations of one's own mind. They are false constructions without reality. Now that one cannot be attached to them, we know that they are unreal and non-existent. They are produced by the mind and have no self-nature at all.[35]

If our perception cannot be trusted to give us the truth of the nature of things, then all qualities we assign to things are not their own properties. The world with which we are familiar, the world that contains earth, sky, trees, flowers, people, objects, etc. is nothing but our mental construction. In this sense, nothing is really outside our mind. Nothing really exists independently of us. This view is clearly a form of idealism.

Therefore, we can conclude that Hua-yan Buddhism, whether it is expounded in the original Indian scripture, or by its Chinese advocates, is indeed a form of idealism rather than realism. In fact, for Hua-yan Buddhists, commonsense realism is the root of afflictions and suffering. To attain enlightenment, one needs first to rid oneself of the assumption behind commonsense realism – that the world around us, and all objects within it, are *real*.

The plurality of phenomenal worlds

According to the *Sutra*'s teaching, various minds have various mental activities that lead to various acts. Since worlds are created by mental acts, worlds manufactured by different minds must all be different. The *Sutra* says: "Just as when seeds are different, so are the fruits they produce. Because of differences in the force of acts, living beings' lands are not the same."[36] From the claim that there are infinitely many minds, it concludes that there are infinitely many worlds, differing from one another. "By the individual acts of beings, these worlds are infinite in kind."[37] Hua-yan Buddhism uses individualistic mental patterns as the foundation of individually constructed phenomenal worlds. These mental patterns are not fixed a priori; nor are they constant in each mind. Worlds and objects are created and *recreated* from moment to moment – nothing endures through time. As the *Sutra* says, "By the power of perceiver and perceived, all kinds of things are born. They soon pass away, not staying, dying out instant to instant."[38] Mind's mental patterns can also fabricate worlds of different qualities. In a single moment, the sentient being could see the world as hell, or as heaven.[39]

With the Consciousness-Only School, there are as many minds as there are sentient beings. The mind's various forms of consciousness produce the phenomenal world. In particular, the eighth consciousness, *Alaya* or the storehouse consciousness, contains the seeds for all worldly phenomena. However, even though there are various minds and variously "perfumed" storehouse consciousnesses, the Consciousness-Only School asserts that a common world will be transformed out of sentient beings because they are *perfumed* similarly. In this respect, what it advocates is a form of *objective* idealism. The difference between objective idealism, to which we assimilate the Consciousness-Only Buddhism, and subjective idealism, with which we now compare Hua-yan Buddhism, is that for the former, there is still an objective world shared by different minds whereas for the latter, worlds are different inasmuch as minds are. The *Hua-yan Sutra* stresses that phenomenal worlds are the results of different minds' cognition and discrimination. Sentient beings see worlds differently "according to their mental patterns."[40] The multiple worlds constructed by multiple minds are thus not derived from the mind's perception through sense organs, but from the mind's insight and understanding.[41]

What is distinctive in the *Hua-yan Sutra* is its view of the plurality of worlds. When the *Hua-yan Sutra* describes phenomenal worlds, it often uses exaggerated numbers. For example, it says there are as many world systems as there are "atoms in an ocean of worlds";[42] it says that there are "a hundred billion worlds, a trillion worlds, a hundred trillion worlds, a quadrillion worlds, a hundred quadrillion worlds, a quintillion worlds, a hundred quintillion worlds";[43] finally, it says that there are "countless, unquantifiable, boundless, incomparable, immeasurable, unspeakable numbers of worlds."[44]

Since phenomenal worlds result from various mental activities of sentient beings, there are as many phenomenal worlds as there are sentient beings. As the *Sutra* describes, "Their numbers infinite, equal to beings."[45] At the same time, "Each world system also contains an equal number of worlds."[46] Perhaps we can say that each world system is a world that contains coexisting sentient beings, each of which conjures up its own world. In this respect, we have not only the plurality of world systems, but also the plurality of worlds within each world system.

These multiple worlds are constantly changing and transforming. The *Sutra* says: "In each of the systems of worlds, the worlds are inconceivably many. Some forming, some decaying; some have already crumbled away."[47] All worlds are dependent on individual minds' activities. Since our thoughts are constantly changing, the worlds we manufacture are constantly transforming as well. The duration of a world could be as short as one instant; hence, nothing is fixed and stable.

The multiple phenomenal worlds exist on the same plane as noumenon. To use an analogy, we can picture multiple holograms projected onto the same plane. Each hologram picture contains a whole world, while multiple holograms interpenetrate in the same space. The space itself is identical to the totality of multiple holograms, and yet it is not the same as any one of the holograms. The *Sutra* says, "One world system enters all, and all completely enter one. Their substances and characteristics remain as before, immeasurable, they all pervade everywhere."[48] In other words, all multiple worlds are enclosed in the same space and all mutually merge as one. Therefore, even though the *Sutra* talks about multiple worlds, it also presents the interpenetrated multiple worlds as *one* world.

It says, "The multiplicity of the worlds does not destroy this one world, and the singleness of this world does not destroy the multiplicity of those worlds."[49]

Our minds are also creations of the one mind

If the mundane world is nothing but the creation of our mental fabrications and the outcomes of our actions, then our minds must be the substantial entities behind all appearances; our minds must be real. But Hua-yan Buddhism does not assign more reality to the existence of individual minds than to the physical world. The unreal mundane world is not simply the experiential world external to us; we are part of it as well. In other words, our sensation, perception, and consciousness are all part of this unreal phenomenal world;[50] furthermore, our self-identity and even our very existence are not real. As the *Hua-yan Sutra* says, "Living beings, too, are not other than illusion – on comprehending illusion, there are no 'living beings'."[51] Even though it is the individual's actions that create the world, "in truth action has no agent"[52] and "the doer has no existence."[53] The *Sutra* further denies the functions of individual minds: "Eye, ear, nose, tongue, body, mind, intellect, the faculties of sense, all are void and essenceless, the deluded mind conceives them to exist."[54]

Fa-zang explains that minds are not "really existent" because they too have no self-nature, they too are dependent on material objects. He says, "Matter is the manifestation of mind. But having been thus manifested, it becomes the contributing cause of mind. There must first be this causation before any mental thing can arise."[55] From the set of identifications explained earlier concerning the connotation of "emptiness," we see that "being dependent on other factors for origination" and "non-existent" or "being unreal" turn out to mean the same thing for the Hua-yan School.

In addition to asserting the unreality of multiple individual minds, Hua-yan's theory of mind also assumes that there is one true Mind. This one Mind creates all other minds. As the *Hua-yan Sutra* suggests, the only real mind is the Buddha's Mind, and it is "the power of one mind" that produces various minds.[56] This one Mind is eternal, absolute, and all-embracing. Fa-zang also says, "All things and events of the phenomenal world are manifestations of the absolute mind in its totality, or, to reverse the equation, mind embraces all things."[57] This one Mind is ultimately responsible for the myriad things in and beyond the phenomenal world.

The correlation between the One Mind and multiple minds, and their connections to the noumenon and the phenomenal world, can be illustrated as such:

Multiple Minds	fabricate	Phenomenal Worlds
One Mind	*contemplates* (is identical to)	Noumenon

$\rightarrow$

Under the One Mind's contemplation, there is no arising and disintegration; no forms and appearances; no motion or change. The world contemplated is the noumenon (the Realm of Principle) itself. Under the multiple minds' deluded discriminations are generated birth and death as well as all sorts of forms, movements, and changes. Multiple minds can be identified with the One True Mind as long as they can be free from delusions and discriminations. Once they accomplish this goal, all minds will be identified and united as one. As a result, all phenomenal worlds will be reduced to the one noumenon. This "returning to the One Mind" and "reducing all appearances to the One Noumenon" is the ultimate teaching of the Hua-yan School.

Holism: Fa-zang's "interconnectedness of things" and Cheng-guan's "non-interference of things"

Fa-zang builds up from the interpenetration of multiple worlds to expound his view of the interconnectedness of multiple things within each world. He uses the gold lion example to illustrate that the whole phenomenal world, the Realm of Things, is like one single object, each part of which is inseparable from the other parts. Without any of the multiple parts of the lion, the whole lion cannot exist; without the whole lion, no part of the lion could possibly exist. By the same token, with any single thing lacking in the phenomenal world, the whole world would not exist; without the whole world, no single thing can exist. There is thus mutual entailment between the whole and its parts. This kind of view is now considered a form of holism, the thesis that any single item within a particular system is part of the whole system and cannot be considered independently of the whole.[58] Through Fa-zang's elaboration, Hua-yan Buddhism is known for its holistic worldview.[59] Thomas Cleary explains this view this way:

> The Hua-yan doctrine shows that the entire cosmos is one single nexus of conditions in which everything simultaneously depends on, and is depended

on by, everything else. . . . In seeking to understand individuals and groups, therefore, Hua-yan thought considers the manifold as an integral part of the unit and the unit as an integral part of the manifold; one individual is considered in terms of relationships to other individuals as well as to the whole nexus, while the whole nexus is considered in terms of its relation to such individual as well as to all individuals.[60]

Fa-zang says:

I speak of parts because they are parts on the basis of their identification with the whole. If whole and part are not identical, the whole world would exist without parts, but then how could you have a building without parts? The parts would also then exist outside the whole, but then they would not be parts.[61]

This seemingly paradoxical argument can be laid out as follows:

1   If the whole and parts of the whole are not *identical*, then the whole would exist without the parts and the parts would exist without the whole.
2   But if the whole exists without the parts, then it is not the whole consisting of its parts; if the parts exist without the whole, then they are not parts of a whole.
3   Therefore, the whole and its parts must be *identical*.

If we want to properly understand this argument, we need to add a first premise to the argument:

P1. Being identical means being coexistent.

If we see that the identity relation is not numerical identity – the identity of self-same object – but merely necessary coexistence, we can accept the argument as "valid."

Other than the interconnectedness between parts and whole, Fa-zang also presents the interconnectedness among parts themselves. To the extent that each part is a part of the whole, all parts entail the whole that entails all parts. Therefore, all parts manifest one another because of their mutual entailment. Du-shun calls this mutual containment and interpenetration "one in one; one in all; all in one; all in all."[62] To illustrate the inter-manifestation of multiple parts, Fa-zang uses the metaphor of "the Net of Indra," which is a net of jewels that belongs to King Indra:

Each loop of this net is decorated with a jewel, in such a way that each jewel not only reflects the image of every other jewel, but also all the multiple images reflected in each of those other jewels. In this way the doubling and redoubling of reflections continues without end.[63]

Another famous method that Hua-yan masters used was the "ten mirrors" demonstration. They arrange ten mirrors in a circle with a candle in the middle of the circle. In this way the reflection of one mirror enters those of the other nine mirrors, and the ten mirrors each includes in them the reflections of nine mirrors. The generation of reflections goes on non-stop in this manner.

In Cheng-guan's theory of "four dharma realms" (*si-fa-jie*), the interdependence between the whole and parts is called "the realm of non-interference of principle and things," while the interpenetration of parts is called "the realm of non-interference of all things." The former depicts the harmony between the noumenon and phenomena; the latter depicts the collaboration and mutual dependence of all phenomena. The non-interference among *phenomena* (or things) is the most revolutionary thesis of the Hua-yan School. It goes beyond the shared concern among all Buddhist schools for the relationship between the noumenon and phenomena, and deals with elements of the phenomenal world themselves. It can be viewed as a direct affirmation of the value of phenomena.[64] When asked why all things (phenomena) would coexist harmoniously with one another, Cheng-guan listed ten reasons, the first being that they are all manifestations of the same Mind.[65] Cheng-guan's reasoning is that if all things ultimately have the same origin, then they cannot stand opposed to one another. If all things are manifestations of the One Mind, if everything is the function of the same substance and share the same nature, then there should not be any interference or obstruction among them. We can say that Cheng-guan's "non-interference among phenomena" is a further elaboration of Fa-zang's holistic theory. If everything relates to one another as units of the same web, then they must be mutually dependent and mutually supportive.

Another thesis that explains the holistic relationship is the "six aspects in harmony" (*liu-xiang-yuan-rong*) theory. Fa-zang illustrates this thesis with his "gold lion" example: When we view the lion as a whole, we see its *totality*; when we view each part of the lion, we see their *individuality*; when we see that all parts are parts of the same lion, we see their *similarity*; when we see that each part is nonetheless different from one another, we see their *differences*; when we see the various parts coming together to form the lion, we see the *integration*; when we see that the lion eventually breaks down to individual parts, we see the *disintegration*. In all objects as well as in the whole phenomenal world, these six aspects (totality, individuality, similarity, difference, integration, and disintegration) are present. Manifesting one aspect does not prevent the thing from manifesting all other aspects. In this respect, the six aspects are harmoniously contemplated. The point of this theory is again to emphasize that things do not have inherent self-nature. The way things are – their characteristics, their natures – are nothing but the way they are contemplated by the mind. Different perspectives generate different characteristics; the real perspective is the one that encompasses all perspectives and sees them as harmoniously compatible with one another.

Even though Hua-yan Buddhism views all objects and events in the whole universe as mutually causally dependent and as ontologically interconnected, it does not posit a real causal network among them. To assume that there are any real causal connections among things is to assume that causality itself is real and that causal agents are real. Both claims are denied by Hua-yan philosophers. The only real causal agent should be the Mind only, which produces multiple minds, which in turn through their delusions create multiple things. Even though from our perception there are primary and subsidiary causes that can be discerned in each effect, ultimately both causes and effects are only "epiphenomena" superimposed by the real cause – the Mind.

The noumenon: "True Thusness" or "the Realm of Principle"

We have seen how in Hua-yan philosophy, there is a division of two levels of existence (two dharma realms).[66] On the level of the essence or the essential nature of the world, we have what can be called "noumenon," to use the Buddhist's term, "the True Thusness" (*zhen-ru*), or what Fa-zang calls "the Realm of Principle" or "substance." On the level of phenomena, we have either multiple phenomenal worlds or our single mundane world. According to the *Hua-yan Sutra*, there are multiple phenomenal worlds; therefore, the relation of phenomenal worlds to this noumenon is that of many-to-one. However, in Fa-zang's treatment, there seems to be only a one-one relation between the Realm of Reality and the Realm of Things. We shall now compare the two views on the division of two dharma realms.

In the *Hua-yan Sutra*, sometimes this noumenon is likened to the mirror, while phenomena or multiple phenomenal worlds are compared to reflections in the mirror. The *Hua-yan Sutra* says: "Like a clear mirror, according to what comes before it, reflecting forms, each different."⁶⁷ Just as different people coming before a mirror receive different reflections while the mirror itself remains the same, different phenomenal worlds are created by different mental activities while the noumenon itself remains the same. Just as reflections do not alter the clarity of the mirror, so also the defilements of various mundane worlds would not contaminate the purity of the noumenon itself.

Sometimes this noumenon is referred to as space itself, which is where all phenomena and phenomenal worlds are manifested. Cheng-guan explains the metaphor of space this way:

> We take in general two senses of *space*; one is the sense of complete pervasion as it universally pervades all places, material and immaterial; the other is the sense of inclusion – in principle it contains all with nothing outside, there being not a single thing which goes outside of space.

He further explains that the noumenon is likened to space "because it is all-pervasive and all-inclusive."⁶⁸ From this interpretation, we see that the noumenon is something that encloses all phenomena and penetrates into each one of them.

With these metaphors, the noumenon seems to be something *other than* the totality of phenomena. The mirror contains all its reflections, but without reflections there would still be the mirror that is by nature clear and pure. Space encloses all objects, but without objects there would still be space itself. The *Hua-yan Sutra* denies that the totality of phenomena is identical to noumenon itself. Phenomena and noumenon are by nature contrary: it is only through the elimination of all phenomena (all reflections, all objects) that one can see the original nature of the noumenon (the clear mirror, the empty space).

Fa-zang's view on the relation between the noumenon and phenomena is different. The metaphor Fa-zang employs in explicating the connection between the Realm of Principle and the Realm of Things is the gold lion. Gold is like the Principle, whereas the lion made by gold is like the Thing. There is no real lion; all its characteristics are mere appearances. What really exists is only gold itself. Thus, the lion relies on gold to be formed. But gold as the substance cannot be manifested other than by the appearance of the lion (or other gold objects); hence, gold relies on the lion as well.⁶⁹ The mutual dependence between gold and the lion illustrates how the phenomenal world and the noumenon are interdependent in Fa-zang's view. With this metaphor, noumenon is regarded as the substance, while the objects manifested by noumenon are functions of this substance. There is no function without the substance, but without function, the substance is not manifested. Function is nothing other than the function of the substance, though it cannot be identified as substance per se. Under this view, the correlation between the noumenon and phenomena is much tighter than the one presented in the *Hua-yan Sutra*: without phenomena, there would not be noumenon, and vice versa. Since everything in the Realm of Things is constituted out of the same substance, the totality of things in the phenomenal world is simply this substance. Therefore, noumenon is nothing other than the totality of phenomena.

Sometimes this noumenon is compared to the ocean, while phenomena or multiple phenomenal worlds are like ocean waves. Hua-yan's first patriarch Du-shun frequently uses this metaphor, so does Fa-zang. Whether it is in the gold/lion or the water/waves analogy, the Realm of Principle and the Realm of Things do not appear to be really separable or distinguishable.[70] Gold is what makes up the lion; water is what underlies waves. Without the totality of the gold lion, there is no gold; without the totality of waves, ocean does not exist. As Du-shun says:

> The waves are waves which are none other than water – the waves themselves show the water. The water is water, which is no different from waves – the water makes the waves. Waves and water are one, yet that does not hinder their difference. Water and waves are different, yet that does not hinder their unity.[71]

Thus we see that in Du-shun's philosophy, noumenon and phenomena are merely different states of the same world. Du-shun puts it this way: "Noumenon and phenomena are relative to each other; they are neither one nor different."[72]

Cheng-guan takes this view even further. In his explication, Principle is sometimes identified as "the principle of emptiness"; sometimes as "the principle of absence of inherent nature" and sometimes as "the principle of having no self-nature and inherent identity." In other words, Principle is nothing but the true nature of all phenomena; it is the *Truth* of all things. According to Cheng-guan:

> Since [this Principle] is the principle of things having no self or inherent identity, how could this Principle, or noumenon, exist outside of phenomena? Therefore noumenon is empty and without substance – taking phenomena as a whole, their fundamental emptiness is simply the real noumenon. . . . Therefore noumenon is simply identical to phenomena.[73]

Table 10.1 The One and the Many

Noumenon (The One)	Phenomenal worlds (The Many)
Pure	Defilements
Non-origination and non-disintegration	Birth and death
Equality of all	Discriminations
Atemporal (outside of time)	Separated by past, present, and future
Eternal	Limited existence
Void	Multiple lands
Beyond motion and stillness	Motion and action
Signless	Signs and names
Indescribable (beyond words)	Describable (language)
Non-conceptual	Divided by conceptions
Imperceptible	Perceived by senses
Beyond logic and philosophy	Logic and philosophy

If this explanation truly represents Hua-yan philosophy, then what Fa-zang calls "the Realm of Principle" is really not another realm of existence, but merely a different view (what he calls "contemplation") under which one regards the true nature of things to be without self-nature, without inherent identity and "empty." When one gains this contemplation, one's mind is in the realm of nirvana. All false appearances cease to exist because the deluded mind is eliminated, just as all waves cease to be stirred when the wind has died down. Cheng-guan sometimes calls the two realms "noumenon vis-à-vis phenomena," or "phenomena vis-à-vis noumenon."[74] Since noumenon and phenomena are different aspects of the same thing, noumenon is not a realm separated from the phenomenal world. In this respect, the Chinese founders of the school do see the relationship between noumenon and the phenomenal world differently from that expounded in the *Hua-yan Sutra*. Noumenon is no longer *that which reflects phenomena* or *that which encloses phenomena*. It is just the totality of phenomena seen in their true aspect.[75]

We can use two charts to contrast the two views. Under the explication of the *Hua-yan Sutra*, the differentiating characteristics of the two realms can be summarized as shown in table 10.1. In Fa-zang's view, the relation between the Realm of Principle and the Realm of Things can be summarized as shown in table 10.2.

In summary, Hua-yan's metaphysics denies the reality of our mundane world and attributes the cause of all phenomena to mental fabrications. It rejects the warranty of sensory perception and mental conception,

Table 10.2 Substance and Function

The Realm of Principle (Substance)	*The Realm of Things (Function)*
Unchanged	Constantly changing
Non-origination and non-disintegration	Formation and disintegration
Eternal	Limited existence
One and the same	Multiple forms and functions
Self-complete and self-sufficient	Dependent arising (from causes)
Absence of characters	Illusory characters (appearances)
Contemplated by the pure mind	Delusions of multiple minds

and identifies these mental operations as the root of the generation of phenomena. The *Hua-yan Sutra* treats the noumenon as a boundless void, in which all things appear as illusions. Hua-yan patriarchs regard the noumenon either as a substance that has no motion, no size, no perceptible qualities and no characters; or as an abstract principle of the empty nature of things. What all Hua-yan philosophers seem to agree upon is that the only thing that exists outside of minds' delusions and discriminations is this eternal, atemporal, all-equal, all-characterless *True Thusness*.

If the ultimate reality or Truth-in-itself does not correspond to human perception and conceptual schemes, then what is the possibility of our ever knowing the truth of this ultimate reality? If we cannot employ our concepts and cannot trust our senses, then what should we use to get to the Truth? In the next section, we will turn to the issue of the knowledge of this *True Thusness*.

Hua-yan Epistemology: Language and Reality

Hua-yan Buddhists endorse a form of language skepticism, the view that "language cannot be seen as a vehicle that can deliver a picture of the world as it actually is."[76] As the *Sutra* says: "In all worlds there only exists verbal expression and verbal expression has no basis in facts."[77] It also says: "Things expressed in words cannot disclose the character of reality."[78] Under this view, there is no correspondence between our statements and genuine states of affairs in the world; there is no possible match between our conceptual scheme and the true nature of things.

265

In this section, we shall summarize their arguments for such a view and explain what they take to be a better form of knowledge.

To Hua-yan Buddhists, Truth is "inconceivable." The inconceivability comes from its indescribability, and the indescribability of Truth comes from the limitations of our language. Our language fails to capture the way things really are, because it is based on our perception of the world. We have our sense organs and our sensory inputs. But through these organs we can only perceive that which is perceivable by senses. *True Thusness* transcends our perception and our conception. Hence, it can never be what our language can depict.[79]

In Robert M. Gimello's analysis, another reason why Truth is ineffable for Hua-yan Buddhists (and for almost all Buddhist schools) is that our words do not have any referential content. Since all things are without determinate identity, our words fail to refer to any particular category of things. As Gimello puts it:

> The Buddhist ultimate truth of emptiness is ineffable, then, but in a special sense – not because our words fall short of describing some transcendent absolute reality called "emptiness," but because all words are such that they lack referential content or are "empty" of substantive meaning. This holds despite appearances and the common usage of words. As there are really no determinate entities to be referred to, so words do not actually refer. Their indexical function is illusory, indeed it is one of the major fabricators of illusion."[80]

A third implicit argument that we can find in Hua-yan Buddhism for the inconceivability of Truth or reality per se can be derived from this statement: "By their suchness, the essence of things is beyond thought."[81] Calling the ultimate reality "*ru*" ("Thusness" or "Suchness") is a common practice among Chinese Buddhist schools. What this term signifies is that the ultimate reality or the true essence of things is simply *the way it is*, independent of any description. For lack of any suitable name, Buddhists tentatively name it "Thusness" or "Suchness." As we analyzed in the first section, for the Hua-yan School this "Thusness" or "Suchness" is without discrimination, without differences, and without demarcations. All is identified as One. But human minds cannot avoid making all sorts of discriminations. Our descriptions are based on our discriminatory capacities. Thus, our descriptions can never capture the *True Thusness*.

The argument can be summarized this way:

1   The essence of things is simply their "suchness" – the way they are on their own.

2   When we employ our thought and conception, we are giving things *our own* descriptions.
3   Things on their own are all identical; when we describe things, we necessarily discriminate them.
4   Therefore, our thought and conception cannot capture the way things are.
5   Therefore, the essence of things is beyond thought and conception.

What is discrimination and what is wrong with discrimination? According to the Hua-yan School, discrimination does not necessarily involve differences in attitudes or evaluations; it could be as evaluatively neutral as conceptualization – separating things into different categories for understanding. This kind of epistemic discrimination is the basis for all sciences. In fact, to operate in our mundane world, we rely on our discriminatory capacities. And yet, the Hua-yan School rejects any form of epistemic discrimination. What it advocates is an attitude that can truly wipe out all discriminations. Under Hua-yan's anti-realistic attitude, the anti-discrimination thesis is not simply a moral imperative to treat all things equally, but rather a call to denounce sensory perception and to forgo all mental cognition.

The *Hua-yan Sutra* says, "Things expressed by words, those of lesser wisdom wrongly discriminate. . . . This is because such people cannot yet have the pure objective eye."[82] From this quote we see that there are two epistemic routes asserted by the Hua-yan School: one is the way ordinary people discriminate objects in accordance with their conceptual schemes and mental patterns; the other is what is called "the pure objective eye" which does not discriminate. The *Sutra* further says, "Things spoken of in conventional terms, people wrongly conceptualize. . . . If one sees they are equal, not different, one won't discriminate among things."[83] "If one dwells on discrimination, one ruins the eye of purity."[84] We see that "the eye of purity" is contrary to "the eye of discrimination." Employing the eye of purity will be the way one can get to know Truth.

How does one obtain the epistemic route of the purely objective eye? Hua-yan Buddhists generally think that learning cannot come from teaching or studying. Teachings and doctrines rely on words, and since words necessarily demarcate things, teachings and doctrines cannot really tell us the Truth. How should one learn then? Du-shun's answer is: actual experience helps. He says, "Only by experiential realization will you know it for yourself. Therefore the *Sutra* says, 'It is like someone drinking cold water – only he himself knows how cold it is.' The meaning of this is outside words. Do not cling to words to think about the Principle."[85]

If one has ever experienced the mental realm in which all discriminations and distinctions are wiped out, then one has learned the Truth. Such an experience cannot be taught through words – it is purely an individual experience.

In Hua-yan's emphasis on experience as the only reliable epistemic route, its theory of knowledge is very different from that of the Western philosophical tradition. If true knowledge is only acquired through personal experience, then it is not sharable, not generalizable, and not verifiable. Whether or not one has gained true knowledge is not something others can pass judgment on. What one deems as *true* knowledge may be different from what another deems true. What one has learned cannot be conveyed in words to another, unless the other has also reached the required level of understanding through her own experience. In all these respects, true knowledge becomes private – unsharable and incommunicable.

In its skepticism of the correspondence between language and reality, Hua-yan Buddhism is very similar to early Daoism. If there is an ultimate reality that is independent of human perception, then this reality will be forever beyond our language which reflects the categories we made on the basis of our discriminatory senses. However, human perception is not the only epistemic route. Both early Daoism and Hua-yan Buddhism acknowledge a different mode of knowledge which relies on a different mental attitude: the attitude that eliminates all discriminations and identifies all as *one*. To understand the true reality, one must take a different perspective, which Zhuangzi calls "the perspective of *Dao*," while the Hua-yan School calls it "the pure objective eye." Later we shall see that the Chan School would further develop Hua-yan's rejection of language and teaching, to advocate abandoning doctrines and theories in pursuit of "immediate enlightenment." Finally, Hua-yan's promotion of the epistemic advantages of learning through actual experiences, in contrast to learning through studying, would be taken up later by Neo-Confucians, especially by Wang Yangming.

Hua-yan Ethics: Buddhas, Bodhisattvas (Enlightening Beings), and Sentient Beings

The term "Buddha" in Hua-yan discourses has multiple meanings. On the one hand, it could refer to the historical Buddha; on the other hand, it could refer to multiple others who have attained the highest level of existence. In some contexts, it is used to signify the fundamental principle of the universe; in some other contexts, it is used to represent the ultimate reality itself. As Cleary points out in his translation of the *Hua-yan Sutra*, "'The Buddha' shifts from an individual to a cosmic principle and manifestations of that cosmic principle; the 'Buddha' in one line might be 'the Buddhas' in the next, representing enlightenment itself, the scope of enlightenment, or those who have realized enlightenment."[86] It would be an incorrect understanding by the Hua-yan standard, however, to claim that the term "Buddha" is ambiguous. The Hua-yan School identifies the one Buddha with the millions of Buddhas in the million phenomenal worlds. In some contexts, the term seems to denote the one ultimate being who, out of compassion for sentient beings, manifests himself in multiple worlds without ever leaving his seat of enlightenment.[87] In some other contexts, however, the Buddha is objectified to be the universe itself.

Tian-tai Buddhism acknowledges that there can be an infinite number of Buddhas. Every sentient being is potentially a Buddha in the making. Hua-yan Buddhism, on the other hand, insists that there is only one Buddha. According to Hua-yan's teaching, as the Buddha appears in multiple worlds and multiple lands, we come to think that there is an infinite number of Buddhas. But these Buddhas are all actually the one Buddha's manifestations. The *Sutra* says: "Just as the clear full moon appears in all bodies of water, and while the reflections are numberless, the real moon is not two. So does the one of unimpeded knowledge with perfect true enlightenment universally appear in all lands, yet the Buddha-body is non-dual."[88] It also argues that when the Buddha is in one world, it is neither really in that world, nor outside the world, "[j]ust as reflections in water are not inside or outside."[89] Therefore, even as we read about the birth and death of the historical Buddha (Siddhartha Gautama) in our world, we should understand that the true Buddha was never born into, and never departed from, our world. The life story of the historical Buddha serves as a device for teaching enlightenment. The Buddha should not be identified only with this historical Buddha. The *Sutra* also says: "In each Buddha-field, a Buddha appears in the world, spending billions of years, expounding unexcelled truths."[90] Since this one Buddha appears in multiple worlds, each one of the Buddhas that appears should be viewed as a "reflection" of the One True Buddha. In this sense, the Buddha is a Supreme Being that is beyond time and beyond worlds.

On a more abstract level, the Buddha is also identified with the universe in its totality. In the *Sutra*, this objectified Buddha is called "Vairocana." It says about Vairocana: "The Buddha body extends throughout all the great assemblies. It fills the cosmos, without end.

Quiescent, without essence, it cannot be grasped. It appears just to save all beings."[91] This Buddha-body is identified with space, penetrating all phenomena. Like space, the Buddha-body persists outside the three time frames (past, present, future); it is atemporal. In the *Sutra*, "the Buddha," "space," and "the noumenon" all refer to the same thing. The ultimate reality is simply the Buddha itself, whose body, as space, fills the whole cosmos. All things are manifestations of the Buddha.[92] As the *Sutra* says, "The Buddha-body is infinite, yet can manifest finite bodies."[93] Cook calls this view "a species of pan-Buddhism."[94] He says, "Hua-[yan] is thus a form of pan-Buddhism if by that term we understand that 'Buddha' is not a substance in things, nor the material and sufficient cause of a material universe which emanated from him. Everything is the Buddha because there is nothing which is not empty."[95] When Hua-yan Buddhism is viewed as a form of religion or moral teaching, it presents a *personified* Buddha as the ultimate goal of attainment. When Hua-yan Buddhism is viewed as a philosophical view of the world, it presents an *objectified* Buddha as the ultimate nature of reality. The two views are not incompatible within Hua-yan's system.

For most other Chinese Buddhist schools, such as Tian-tai, the highest state of attainment is Buddhahood. Everyone has inherent Buddha-nature and everyone should strive to become a Buddha. For the Hua-yan School, however, the most praiseworthy level of moral cultivation is that of bodhisattvas. Bodhisattvas' realm is between those of Buddhas and of sentient beings; bodhisattvas can enter nirvana just as those who have accomplished Buddhahood do. But bodhisattvas, out of their compassion for all sentient beings, take the vow to remain in the world of afflictions until everyone has entered nirvana.[96] Fa-zang says: "The experiencing of the Buddha-realm means the emptiness of matter, absence of personal ego, and absence of phenomenal quality. . . . However, after experiencing entry into this realm, one may not dwell forever after in calm extinction, for this would be contrary to the teaching of the Buddhas."[97] In other words, what the Buddha teaches is not the way of reaching final extinction for oneself, but the way of helping others reach that goal. This kind of moral teaching reflects a fundamental *humanistic* spirit ingrained in Chinese philosophy.

For Hua-yan Buddhism, nirvana is not a separate realm of existence, but a different mental realm. In other words, it does not advocate an individual's being "lifted" or "getting entry into" a different realm of existence. It advocates a different realization, a different mental state. The *Sutra* calls this mental state "the other shore of form, and of sensation, perception, patterning and consciousness."[98] This mental state is devoid of all sensory and cognitive activities. It would thus seem that one wouldn't be able to reach this state during one's lifetime, or at least one couldn't stay in this state if one is to function in this world. Fazang, on the other hand, says that the state of nirvana is reached once one is free from afflictions: "[The] mind is as calm as the sea. Erroneous thoughts all cease, and there are no compulsions. One gets out of bondage and is free from hindrance, and forever cuts off the source of suffering. This is called entry into nirvana."[99] According to this interpretation, to be in nirvana, one does not have to be in a state of total non-cognition and non-consciousness. One needs merely a different moral attitude; a mental cleansing of desires and grasping.

Bodhisattvas have experienced the realm of nirvana that is eternally quiescent, and yet they do not stay in nirvana eternally. Du-shun explains the paradoxical mental state of bodhisattvas this way:

1 Because existence is emptiness, you do not abide in birth-and-death.
2 Because emptiness is existence, you do not dwell in nirvana.
3 Because emptiness and existence are one whole, both being there, you dwell both in birth-and-death and in nirvana.
4 Because emptiness and existence cancel each other out and neither remains, you dwell neither in birth-and-death nor in nirvana.[100]

If bodhisattvas want to remain in the world of afflictions, then they themselves cannot be totally free of all humanly afflictions. The difference between bodhisattvas and sentient beings, both residing in the Realm of Things, is that bodhisattvas do not suffer afflictions on their own account. Bodhisattvas remain in the mundane world along with sentient beings, but they do not view mundane things the way sentient beings do. Their minds are as clear as those of Buddhas; their voluntary afflictions do not bring them suffering. Their mental state is full of glorious joy, imbued however with sorrow and compassion for others' suffering.

The greatest virtue of bodhisattvas is compassion. They are willing to put others' interests ahead of their own, even to the point of self-sacrifice. According to the *Sutra*, bodhisattvas think to themselves:

> I should accept all sufferings for the sake of all sentient beings, and enable them to escape from the abyss of immensurable woes of birth and death. I should accept all suffering for the sake of all sentient beings in all worlds, in all states of misery, for ever and ever, and still always cultivate foundations of goodness for the sake of enlightening beings.[101]

Out of this compassion for all sentient beings, bodhisattvas take on an ascetic lifestyle. They do not seek physical comfort or worldly pleasure; they only seek "supreme knowledge."[102]

"Supreme knowledge" is important for moral cultivation because it is a particular form of knowledge, through which one understands that the true nature of things is emptiness:

> Thus knowing the nature of things is like this, they don't wrongly grasp acts or results. There are no things without form, nor formless things. . . . They realize all are ungraspable. All things are born of causes and conditions – their essential nature is neither existent nor non-existent. And in causes and conditions, what they produce, they ultimately have no attachment at all.[103]

This "non-attachment to things in the world" is one of the basic teachings of the Buddha: there are no dharmas. True knowledge of the empty nature of all things necessarily leads to non-attachment to things. This is thus an essential step toward the state of bodhisattvas.

Bodhisattvas are freed from thought and cognition; they do not discriminate between large and small, good and evil, or anything whatsoever. For Hua-yan Buddhists, forgoing conception and cognitive discrimination is the first step toward the elimination of desires and value judgments. The *Sutra* says:

> Name and form are born together, inseparable, and by the development of name and form, the assembly of six sense mediums takes place; once the mediums are formed, from their mutual contact sensation comes to be; and that sensation being enjoyed and sought more and more, the operation of craving grows; craving being developed, existence comes to be; once there is existence, birth, death, sorrow, lamentation, suffering, sadness, and anxiety appear. Thus does the mass of suffering of sentient beings arise.[104]

It is difficult for us to comprehend how one can completely abandon names and renounce senses, because we need our sensory apparatus to function in this world. What Hua-yan is teaching here is perhaps a different cognitive mode on the basis of our understanding of the true nature of all things. Once we see that all things are fundamentally dependent on the mind and are thus empty in their self-nature, we may be able to transcend the categorization that comes from our senses and our conceptions.

A further moral objective for those aiming to become enlightened is to abandon the notion of *self*. Self-love and the fulfillment of self-interests are often deemed as part of human nature. Many ethical theories are based on egoism – even the ethical theories of the Theravada schools are founded on egoism.[105] Hence, having a self is not necessarily immoral or unethical. However, Mahayana Buddhists, Hua-yan in particular, treat the notion of *self* as the root of evil as well as the cause of suffering. The *Sutra* says: "The origins of worldly ways are all due to attachment to self. In those who have no attachment to self the development of worldly ways do not take place."[106] Therefore, the insistence on one's self is the root of all sufferings, since it keeps humans within this world.

What seals the fate for sentient beings is their own doing: attachment to the self, falsely discriminating between things that are by nature identical, grasping and desiring things that are in essence empty, and indulging in worldly pleasures that are actually the same as suffering itself.[107] For these reasons, "sentient beings bob and sink in the ocean of existence. Their troubles are boundless; they have no place to rest."[108] To end their suffering, sentient beings need to extract themselves from this world. They need to discard conception, perception, cognition, and discrimination; they need to terminate their attachment to their self, to their beloved ones, to the society and to the nation. Ultimately, they need to see the world as illusion; see all their life experiences as dreams.

A philosophical problem that may exist for Hua-yan's view on sentient beings is whether freedom of will is possible. As analyzed earlier, under Hua-yan's view even sentient beings are not real. Everything is ultimately caused by the Buddha; all minds are the manifestations of the One Mind. In that case, all human beings' decisions and actions seem to have the same illusory status. There is in truth no agency, no causation. If a person "vows" to follow the right path, her decision will not be *her own*. The *Hua-yan Sutra* sometimes seems to imply that no sentient beings' moral deeds are of their own doings. It says: "The Buddha causes their minds to develop faith and resolution."[109] But sometimes it also attributes a "will" to sentient beings as, for example, when it says: "If any have the will, they see Buddha everywhere."[110] It thus seems to be inconsistent in its treatment of free will and determinism. In the Chinese Hua-yan patriarchs' "one in all; all in one," "interidentify," "non-interference," and "all harmonized" theories, the individual agent does not even exist independently of others. All beings mutually reflect one another's doings; all acts are causally dependent on infinitely many acts done by others. If sentient beings are not causal agents and do not initiate their own moral improvement, then they are not morally responsible for all their good deeds. The ethical assignment of reward and punishment for the accumulation of good and bad deeds (i.e., the notion of perfuming) that is fundamental to the traditional Buddhist teaching cannot be maintained in this holistic system. This theoretical inconsistency seems to be an irresolvable problem for the Hua-yan School.

Conclusion

It is generally acknowledged that Hua-yan philosophy had a great impact on further developments of Chinese philosophy. As Wing-tsit Chan says: "The main concepts of Neo-Confucianism, those of principle and material force, were derived through, if not from, those of principle and [things] in Hua-[yan]. Its one-is-all and all-is-one philosophy shows unmistakable Hua-[yan] imprints."[111] Of all the contributions that the Hua-yan School makes to the development of Chinese philosophy, its notion of Principle (*li*) is the most important one.[112] As Whalen Lai remarked:

> The use of *li* (Principle) in the [Hua-yan] school, probably the most sophisticated Sinitic Mahayana school, demonstrates . . . a synthesis of the Dharma and [*Dao*] – both symbols of Transcendence – and articulates their structural inter-relationships in a manner previously unknown in either India or China. *Li* provided a new insight into an eternal Truth.[113]

In Gimello's analysis, the Chinese patriarchs' choice of the word "*li*" to express the Indian notion of *Emptiness* makes a significant change in the spirit of the philosophy. He says:

> Principles have noetic, not ontic, significance. They suggest regularity and truth but do not imply either substantive existence or its opposite, non-existence. . . . It clearly does not prompt a search for an ontological some-thing (even an ineffable something) called emptiness or the indeterminate.[114]

When the ultimate reality is defined as "the Realm of Principle," it takes on a more abstract dimension than its accompanying notions such as nirvana or substance. Is there One Principle governing the whole universe? Does the Principle "create" or "support" the phenomenal world? Does each worldly thing manifest or partake in this Principle? Do all things share the same Principle or does each thing have its own individualized principle? Does Principle exist logically prior or temporally prior to the myriad things in the phenomenal world? Since the Hua-yan School also posits the One Mind (the Buddha's Mind) as the final substance, the question concerning the relation between Principle and Mind also ensues. These are all questions generated by Hua-yan philosophy, and yet one cannot find all the answers within Hua-yan philosophy. The ongoing pursuit of ways to analyze the relations between Principle and Things, between Principle and Mind, etc., dominates the next era of Chinese philosophy.

Further discussion questions

1 What is the Hua-yan School's view on reality? How do they interpret the world (worlds)? How is the view different from the Consciousness-Only School's worldview?
2 Does the Hua-yan School have a coherent metaphysical view? How do you apprehend the theory that there is no real world and no real mind?
3 What is the metaphor of the gold lion? How does this metaphor signify the essential teachings of Hua-yan?
4 Does *Reality* defy human cognition and conception? If we cannot know what *Reality* is, can we still operate in this world?
5 Altruism seems to be the ethical principle advocated by Hua-yan Buddhism. Do you think that we have an ultimate moral responsibility to aid other beings before we can enjoy our own salvation?

Primary texts

Wing-tsit Chan (ed.) *A Sourcebook in Chinese Philosophy*, 4th edn. Princeton: Princeton University Press, 1973 (ch. 25; translation of Fa-zang's "A Treatise on the Golden Lion" in completion, and part of his *Hundred Gates to the Sea of Ideas of the Flowery Splendor Scripture*).
Thomas Cleary (trans.) *The Flower Ornament Scripture: A Translation of the Avatamsaka Sutra*. Boston, MA: Shambhala Publications, Inc. 1993. (The size of this book is enormous. For those interested in Hua-yan's philosophical import, I recommend chs. 2, 4, 5, 9, 10, 14, 20, 24, 26, 29, and 37. For those interested in Hua-yan's practices, I recommend chs. 8, 11, 12, 15–18, 21, 25–9, 36, and 38. Ch. 39, "Entry into the Realm of Reality," stands on its own as an essential introduction to Hua-yan Buddhism.)
—— (trans.) *Entry into the Inconceivable: An Introduction to Hua-yen Buddhism*. Honolulu: University of Hawaii Press, 1983. (This book includes the translations of Du-shun's "Cessation and Contemplation in the Five Teachings," his "Contemplation of the Realm of Reality" with Cheng-guan's commentary, Zhi-yan's "Ten Mysterious Gates of the Unitary Vehicle," and Fa-zang's "Cultivation of Contemplation of the Inner Meaning of the Hua-yan: The Ending of Delusion and Return to the Source.")

Further readings

Garma C. C. Chang. *The Buddhist Teaching of Totality: The Philosophy of Hwa Yen Buddhism*. University Park, PA: The Pennsylvania State University Press, 1971.

Thomas Cleary. "Introduction" to *Entry into the Inconceivable: An Introduction to Hua-yen Buddhism*. Honolulu: University of Hawaii Press, 1983, pp. 1–42.

Francis H. Cook. "Causation in the Chinese Hua-yen Tradition." *Journal of Chinese Philosophy* 6, 1979: 367–85.

Robert M. Gimello. "Apophatic and Kataphatic Discourse in Mahayana: A Chinese View." *Philosophy East & West* 26, April 1976: 117–36.

Whalen Lai. "The *I Ching* and the Formation of the Hua-yen Philosophy." *Journal of Chinese Philosophy* 7, 1980: 245–58.

Chapter 11

The Tian-tai (T'ien-t'ai) School

Introduction

The Tian-tai School was founded by Zhi-yi (Chih-i) (538–97). It derived its name from the Tian-tai Mountain in China, because Zhi-yi lived and taught there for many years. From its name, we can see that the intention was for this school to be genuinely Chinese, rather than just a further development of Indian Buddhism. The major Buddhist text endorsed by the Tian-tai School is the *Lotus Sutra*, short for "the Sutra of the Lotus Blossom of the Subtle Dharma" (*Miao-fa-lian-hua Jing*, commonly abbreviated as "*Fahua Jing*"). Zhi-yi regards this scripture as having the highest status of all Buddhist doctrines, preaching the most perfect teachings of the Buddha. David Chappell calls the *Lotus Sutra* the "definitive sacred text" for the Tian-tai tradition,[1] and Burton Watson says that it is "one of the most important and influential of all the sutras or sacred scriptures of Mahayana Buddhism."[2] To understand Tian-tai philosophy, therefore, we must begin with the *Lotus Sutra*.

Zhi-yi has two major works on *the Lotus Sutra*. One is *Fa-hua-xuan-yi* (*The Esoteric Meaning of the Lotus Sutra*), which explicates the hidden meaning behind the sutra. The other is *Fa-hua-wen-ju* (*The Words and Phrases of the Lotus Sutra*), which gives a phrase-by-phrase explanation of the sutra. He also has another work on the methods of practice, entitled *Mo-he-zhi-guan* (*The Great Calming and Contemplation*). All three works consist of lecture notes compiled by his chief student Guan-ding. They have been viewed as "the three great texts of Tian-tai."[3] Of these three works, *The Esoteric Meaning of the Lotus Sutra* and *The Great Calming and Contemplation* are especially important, because, according to Yu-kwan Ng, "they reflect comprehensively [Zhi-yi's] most mature thought and cover nearly all of the key concepts and philosophical methods involved in the study of our basic questions."[4]

A major difficulty for an English reader wishing to do research on Tian-tai philosophy is the sheer number of original works, in conjunction with the limitation of partial translations and interpretations of only a small number of these original texts. Aside from the many later works in the Tian-tai tradition, there are at least 20 major works attributed to Zhi-yi himself, either with him as the author or with his lecture notes as the content. Different interpreters of Tian-tai philosophy have adopted different texts as their basis for interpretation. For example, Donner and Stevenson focus on *Mo-he-zhi-guan*, but they only translated the first chapter of this book. Swanson uses *Fahua xuanyi* to explain the "foundations" of Tian-tai philosophy, but he too only translated the middle part of this book. In his explication of Tian-tai Buddhism, Chappell chooses *The Fourfold Teachings*, which was written by a Korean Chinese monk Chegwan in the tenth century. Finally, both Wing-tsit Chan in his *Sourcebook* and Fung Yu-lan in his *History of Chinese Philosophy* quote from *The Method of Cessation and Contemplation in Mahayana* to explicate Tian-tai philosophy, even though they acknowledge that its authorship (allegedly Zhi-yi's teacher Hui-si) is contestable.[5] Probably the most comprehensive study in English of Zhi-yi's philosophy is undertaken in Yu-kwan Ng's *T'ien-t'ai Buddhism and Early Madhyamika*, in which he consulted all the works mentioned above and some others. This chapter will be based on Chinese texts and Chinese commentaries, supplemented by current English translations. Because of the limited availability of English translations, we will use the *Lotus Sutra*, part of Zhi-yi's *The Esoteric Meaning of the Lotus Sutra* and part of his *Great Calming and Contemplation* as primary sources in English. We will also consult Hui-si's *The Method of Cessation and Contemplation in Mahayana* as translated by Fung and Chan, with the caution that his philosophy is not quite the same as that of Zhi-yi.

Zhi-yi's philosophical training can be traced back to the thought of Nagarjuna, the founder of the Indian Madhyamika School.[6] He often referred to some of Nagarjuna's major works, and it is clear that he was deeply influenced by Madhyamika philosophy. But unlike Xuan-zang's Consciousness-Only School, the Tian-tai School is not just another extension of an Indian Buddhist school. Zhi-yi greatly modified the basic tenets of the Madhyamika School to formulate the main tenets of Tian-tai philosophy. In Swanson's assessment, the key to Tian-tai Buddhism is Zhi-yi's concept of the "Threefold Truth."[7] Most Tian-tai scholars adopt the same view. However, Yu-kwan Ng challenges this widely accepted view and argues it is rather Zhi-yi's notion of *Buddha-*

nature that stands as the core of Tian-tai philosophy. Ng says that the Threefold Truth concerns the method of understanding Truth, while Buddha-nature "is an issue of the Truth itself." "Logically speaking, the conception of the Truth precedes the way through which the Truth is to be realized."[8] In this chapter, we will analyze these two key notions of Tian-tai and examine their theoretical connections. Both notions deal with the issue of truth. Following a distinction introduced by Siao Fang Sun,[9] we shall separate the notion of truth into the metaphysical sense and the semantic sense: the former refers to "truth" understood as external reality itself, or as Ng puts it, "the authentic nature of the phenomenal world";[10] the latter refers to "truth" understood as a property of our descriptions of reality. When truth is used in the metaphysical sense, we shall use "Truth" (capitalized) to signify its uniqueness. When it is used in the semantic sense, we shall simply use "truth." As we shall see, Tian-tai's notion of truth is complicated in that it allows different interpretations in different contexts.

Tian-tai's Notion of Truth in the Metaphysical Sense: The Ultimate Reality

The most distinctive trait of the Tian-tai worldview is that there is only one reality, which is both the phenomenal world and nirvana. Zhi-yi tries to explain away the apparent incompatibility between this view and the two-world view that marks early Buddhism. He formulated many famous phrases and slogans of Tian-tai philosophy, such as "Ten dharma realms," "Ten suchnesses," "Ten realms mutually contained," and "One thought contains three thousand worlds." Even though Tian-tai Buddhism is based on the *Lotus Sutra*, none of these descriptions appears in the *Lotus Sutra* itself. These phrases constitute the core theses of Tian-tai philosophy. We shall explain each of them in turn.

Ten dharma realms and oneness of reality

When early Buddhism divides the phenomenal world and nirvana, the two realms of existence are mutually exclusive. The phenomenal world is marked by the cycle of transmigration. Nirvana is the cessation of transmigration. What early Buddhism means by the "phenomenal world" is not just the physical world that we sentient beings experience. It includes six realms of existence (called "six destinies" or "six dharma

Table 11.1 The phenomenal world and nirvana

Cycle of Life and Death	
1 Hell beings	
2 Hungry ghosts	*Nirvana*
3 Beasts or beings of animal nature	
4 Asuras (demons)[12]	
5 Human beings	
6 Gods or heavenly creatures	

realms") that range from hell beings to gods, with beasts and men as the middle realms.[11] Therefore, what we call the spiritual realm or the afterlife, such as hell and heaven, is also included in the phenomenal world. One's existence is not defined as starting from the birth, and ending in the death, of an individual being; rather, it is a continuous cycle of life and death. To reach nirvana is to be completely free of this recycling of life and death, to exit the whole phenomenal world. In early Buddhism, nirvana is the ultimate reality. The phenomenal world is not *real*. Earlier in the Consciousness-Only School, we also saw that even though the storehouse consciousness is responsible for the generation of the phenomenal world, it is not the ultimate reality. The ultimate reality, the "True Thusness" (*Tathata*), is the annihilation of all activities of consciousness. It is reached when one's consciousness is no longer contaminated and is turned into "Wisdom." Therefore, the phenomenal world and the "True Thusness" cannot coexist.

A simple diagram can illustrate the polarity of the two worlds conceived in early Buddhism (see table 11.1). A major thesis of the Tian-tai school, on the other hand, is to claim that the phenomenal world *is* nirvana and nirvana *is* the phenomenal world. There is only one reality, not two. As Zhi-yi puts it, "A single, unalloyed reality is all there is – no entities whatever exist outside of it."[13] His student Guan-ding also explains the worldview of Tian-tai this way: "There is no duality, no difference between them; the phenomenal, as it stands, is the real."[14] This one reality is divided into ten dharma realms, the last four of which are additions to the six dharma realms of early Buddhism (see table 11.2). The first four realms are called "the evil path." They represent the lowest and the most painful states of existence. The next two realms, human beings and gods, are placed in the same category, in that both existences are mortal and are mixtures of happiness and misery. The last four additional realms are called "the holy path." They include

Table 11.2 The ten dharma realms

1	Hell beings	→ Cycle of Life and Death
2	Hungry ghosts	→ Cycle of Life and Death
3	Beasts or beings of animal nature	→ Cycle of Life and Death
4	Asuras (demons)	→ Cycle of Life and Death
5	Human beings	→ Cycle of Life and Death
6	Gods or heavenly creatures	→ Cycle of Life and Death
7	Skravakas ("Voice-hearers")	→ Nirvana
8	Pratyekabuddhas ("Self-enlightened Ones")	→ Nirvana
9	Bodhisattvas	→ Cycle of Life and Death/Nirvana
10	Buddha	→ Nirvana

the highest form of attainment for the Hinayana school, arahats, which are divided into Voice-hearers and Self-enlightened Ones. "Voice-hearers" refers to those who listened to the Buddha's early teachings and followed the doctrines of early Buddhism. "Self-enlightened Ones" refers to those who gained understanding on their own. Both forms of arahats have accomplished the goal of extinction and they regard nirvana as the negation of the phenomenal world. They are not interested in helping others reach the same goal. At the next level, we have the highest form of attainment for the Mahayana school: bodhisattvas. Bodhisattvas also regard nirvana as the ultimate goal of attainment; however, they choose not to enter nirvana out of compassion for all sentient beings that have not entered nirvana. Finally, the utmost highest form of existence is called Buddha. According to the *Lotus Sutra*, Buddhas can move between nirvana and the phenomenal world as they wish. Tian-tai's teaching is that everyone should aim to become a Buddha.

According to Zhi-yi, "All reality is included within these ten dharmas."[15] Nothing exists outside the ten dharma realms. They are distinguished because of their different causes and conditions, but they are not sharply divided as separate realms. One notable tenet of the Tian-tai school is that "the ten dharma realms are mutually contained." This mutual containment is difficult to understand, however. The most direct analysis is to say that in each of the ten dharma realms, there is a further subdivision into ten sub-dharma realms. Another analysis is to say that each realm contains the "potential" (or "seed") of all ten realms, but it only "manifests" the one that characterizes itself.[16] A third interpretation is to say that each single realm is at the same time the totality of all ten: all is one and one is all. This last interpretation is the one most consistent with Zhi-yi's "one reality" theory. In other words, when Zhi-yi divides the world into ten dharma realms, he does not think that they exist apart from one another. The nirvana in which Buddhas reside is the same world as the hell in which hell beings reside; it is also the same world as the physical world which present sentient beings inhabit. As Zhi-yi says, "All of reality is included in hell and does not transcend this destiny. . . . The same is true for all destinies up to and including the Buddha realm."[17] Accordingly, these ten dharma realms are mutually contained since they are all part of the whole world, with no boundaries setting them apart.

In both early Buddhism's picture of six dharma realms and Tian-tai Buddhism's picture of ten dharma realms, we see that their shared worldview can be regarded as "anti-physicalism." The physical world is not the only reality – it is merely part of the whole reality we experience through our various forms of existence. Furthermore, the identity we establish since birth is not our true identity – it is rather a state in the whole process of life cycles. In this sense the "experiential world" is not just what we experience after we are born. It is the totality of our experiences as hell beings, as beasts, as human beings, as gods, and for the Tian-tai School, it even includes our experiences as arahats, bodhisattvas, or even Buddhas.

The fundamental difference between early Buddhism and Tian-tai Buddhism (as well as other major schools of Chinese Buddhism) is that according to the former, the ultimate goal is to exit this world and enter a totally different realm of existence, while according to the latter, there is no this world/other world distinction. Contrary to early Buddhism's setting of the ultimate goal as terminating the cycle of life and death, the *Lotus Sutra* says: "There is no ebb or flow of birth and death, and there is no existing in this world and later entering extinction."[18] When the four realms of the "noble path" are included in the same world as the cycle of life and death, one no longer needs to deny one's present experiences, negate one's present emotions, and renounce one's present life in order to reach nirvana. As Zhi-yi says: "Since cyclic birth and death itself is identical with emptiness, how could it ever be discarded? Since nirvana itself is identical with emptiness, how could it ever be attained?"[19]

The mind and the world

Zhi-yi says: "One thought contains the ten dharma realms. Each dharma realm also contains the ten dharma realms, [so there are] one hundred dharma realms. Each dharma realm contains thirty worlds; so one hundred dharma realms contain three thousand worlds. These three thousand worlds are contained in one thought."[20] This is the famous Tian-tai thesis: "one thought contains three thousand worlds" (*yi nien san qian*), or as Hurvitz translates it, "the Trishiliocosm in a moment of consciousness."[21]

What does the word "contain" mean in this context?[22] How can one thought contain all of reality? We can say that there are at least three plausible interpretations:

1 "Capable of producing" – in this way the claim is close to idealism which treats the world as a mere figment of the mind's imagination.
2 "Capable of perceiving" – in this way the claim is still compatible with commonsense realism and places more emphasis on the function of sense organs.
3 "Capable of conceiving" – in this way the claim is at least not incompatible with realism and stresses more the mind's cognitive function.

Sometimes Zhi-yi's remark inclines us to take the first interpretation. He says, "There are no distinct dharmas in the three realms; all are but the product of one single mind. Mind is like a skilled painter, producing all sorts of forms. It constructs the six destinies, introducing innumerable distinctions in appearance and value [among them]."[23] If "contain" really means "produce," then the world as the product of the mind's creation becomes illusory and unreal. This interpretation would make Tian-tai's worldview close to idealism as seen in the Consciousness-Only School and in the Hua-yan School.

However, Zhi-yi is not an idealist. To associate Tian-tai's claim that "one thought contains three thousand worlds" with the Consciousness-Only School's claim that "*Alaya* is the storehouse for all seeds of worldly phenomena" is to greatly misconstrue Tian-tai's worldview. Zhi-yi does not claim that the only thing real is Mind and that the world is dependent on Mind's activities. The world is not a by-product of the Buddha's mind, or of any mind whatsoever. As Zhi-yi puts it, "The objects of the [true] aspects of reality are not something produced by Buddhas, gods, or men. They exist inherently on their own and have no beginning."[24] From this quote, we can see that Tian-tai philosophy is fundamentally a realist philosophy. Its world is an objective world, not a creation of the Buddha or the Mind. "One thought contains three thousand worlds," but this one thought is not therefore the *substance* of the three thousand worlds. To Zhi-yi, the world is as real as the mind is, and the mind is as empty as the world is. He explains, "In what way is [this thought] identical with emptiness? Because [all factors of its arising] come into being through conditions: whatever originates conditionally lacks subjective own-being, and to lack own-being is to be empty."[25] The mind does not exist substantially, since it relies on the world to generate its cognitive content. At the same time, the world relies on the mind's cognition to contain all dharmas. According to Zhi-yi, neither the mind nor dharma has the power to arise spontaneously on its own. Since each one is the condition for the other's arising, each one depends on the other for its existence. "When they are separate they do not arise at all."[26] Because of their ontological interdependence, the mind and the world are logically coexistent – one is not prior to the other. As Zhi-yi puts it, "We do not say that the mind exists first and dharmas come to be later; nor do we say that dharmas exist first while the mind comes to be later."[27]

Under this mind–world relationship, we see how the first interpretation is not acceptable. Of the two remaining interpretations of "contain," "capable of conceiving" gives a reading that has a broader scope than "capable of perceiving" does. If "perception" is taken to refer to the function of sense organs, then it is questionable whether the mind is really capable of perceiving the totality of reality (the three thousand worlds). To say that the mind is capable of conceiving the totality of reality, on the other hand, poses no difficulty. The minds of sentient beings conceive all dharmas to be objects of craving and attachment, or resentment and rejection. These sentient beings are thus caught in the cycle of life and death and can never be totally free of suffering. The minds of Voice-hearers, Self-enlightened Ones, and Bodhisattvas conceive all dharmas to be provisionally existent and empty in self-nature. These beings therefore separate the phenomenal world and nirvana into two distinct realms. Finally, the minds of Buddhas conceive all dharmas to realize their true dharma nature – all are provisionally existent, empty, *and* all manifest the Middle Way. They can therefore recognize that all dharmas and dharma realms are in one unified reality. Therefore, the creation of ten dharma realms depends on sentient beings' mental power. A single thought could bring one down to the realm of hell; a single thought could also elevate one to the realm of the Buddhas. As Zhi-yi elaborates on his painter analogy, he says: "By going back and over-turning this [deluded] mind, one produces understanding – just as the painter first washes away the previous forms, applies white plaster, [and is then able to] paint anew."[28] We can see that it is the same canvas, the same world; what changes is simply how we paint, or conceive, it. It is in this sense that we should understand the connection between mind and the world.

The true nature of things (dharmas): the Threefold Truth

Zhi-yi's Threefold Truth (*san-di*) is the defining thesis for the Tian-tai school. Zhi-yi himself does not take the credit for being the initiator of the notion of Threefold Truth. He does not think that it is a novel idea specific to the Tian-tai teaching either. He says, "Many Sutras contain the meaning [of the Threefold Truth] in detail, but the terms come from the [*Ying Luo Jing*] and the [*Ren Wang Jing*]."[29] Zhi-yi's idea of the Threefold Truth is derived from Nagarjuna's statement: "Whatever dharma arises through causes and conditions, that I declare to be identical to emptiness. It is also a provisional designation. This, furthermore, is the meaning of the Middle Way."[30] However, Zhi-yi's Threefold Truth and Nagarjuna's statement are quite different in spirit. Nagarjuna himself advocates the Two Truths theory: one is the supreme truth, the other is the mundane truth. The mundane truth takes all dharmas in the phenomenal world to be dependently existent, while the supreme truth illuminates their empty nature. On the level of the mundane world, we can say that things exist; on the level of the ultimate reality, however, we must say that things are all empty in nature. For Nagarjuna, emptiness means "devoid of self-nature" and "devoid of manifold." Things cannot be said to exist or not exist; they are simply *empty*.

While Nagarjuna stresses the aspect of "emptiness," Zhi-yi emphasizes the aspect of "existence." The former thesis is called "true emptiness" (*zhen-kong*), while the latter thesis is called "subtle existence" (*miao-you*). The *true emptiness* signifies both not-being and not-nonbeing; hence, it is based on double negation. The *subtle existence* signifies both being and nonbeing. For Nagarjuna, things are empty because they do not have independent self-nature. For Tian-tai, things do exist in the sense of provisional dependence. Though "lacking self-nature" expresses the same idea as "being dependent co-arising," the two schools' emphases are slightly different. Hence, there is a subtle difference between Nagarjuna's "middle-way" and Tian-tai's "middle-way." Tian-tai's *subtle existence* notion became the dominant idea in Chinese Buddhism. The introduction of this notion marked a further step away from early Buddhism's emphasis on purely non-existent *emptiness*. Zhi-yi says: "The highest truth concerns the character of reality. The character of reality is that no character is not a character (an appearance). Adhering to this character of reality, however, all Buddhas can obtain the truth. Hence, this character of reality is called 'subtle existence'."[31] Here he seems to affirm the reality of the phenomenal world. Buddhas do not need to denounce the character of reality in order to reach nirvana.

Zhi-yi's Threefold Truth includes:

1   The truth of provisional existence (*jia-di*)[32]
2   The truth of emptiness (*kong-di*)
3   The truth of the Middle Way (*zhong-di*)

The truth of provisional existence states that all dharmas depend on many causal factors to exist. Without these causal factors, things would not have existed. Therefore, dharmas exist, but they exist provisionally, temporally, and dependently. The emphasis of this truth is on existence, and thus it represents the acknowledgement of this phenomenal world. *The truth of emptiness* states that all dharmas are empty in the sense that they do not have self-nature or substance. From this truth we see that the term "empty" in Tian-tai's usage does not mean void or nothingness, but "empty of substance." Finally, the term "middle" in this context does not mean the mid-point of two poles, but the avoidance, or the transcendence, of extremes. To transcend the insistence on existence (the School of Being) as well as the insistence on emptiness (the School of Emptiness) is the Middle. Leon Hurvitz explains it as "the complete lack of contradiction" between the two extremes.[33] According to Zhi-yi, "The reality of non-duality is called the Middle."[34] "The Middle" and "the Real" are thus interchangeable in his usage. The word "way" is translated from the Chinese word "*dao*," which stands for the highest principle of the universe. Therefore, "the Middle Way" is simply another name for the ultimate reality or the highest principle of the universe itself. *The truth of the Middle Way* states that the Reality itself is simply thus: all dharmas are both provisionally existent and empty.[35]

From these three truths, we can see the true nature of all dharmas and of the Reality itself. There is no other realm outside the provisionally existent phenomenal world. The world manifesting emptiness (nirvana) is simply the provisionally existent phenomenal world. Since this world has both provisional existence and emptiness, it is the world of the Middle Way. With the introduction of the Middle Way, Zhi-yi eliminates the polarity between the phenomenal world and nirvana. The Threefold Truth describes the one unified Reality (called "the Middle Way"), which is the phenomenal world *and* nirvana at the same time.

The three Truths can be seen as the three aspects of the same reality. As Zhi-yi puts it: "Though these [three aspects of reality] are an integrated unity, they are called threefold; though they are threefold, they are called a unity."[36] This is Tian-tai's famous "threefold truth in unity" (*san-di-yuan-rong*) thesis.

Zhi-yi thinks that ten dharma realms themselves also manifest the Threefold Truth. Even though reality is conventionally divided into ten realms, the division should not be seen as absolute. All ten dharma realms are at the same time empty, provisionally existing, and manifesting the Middle Way. Following his teacher Hui-si, Zhi-yi describes this integration of the three aspects of ten dharma realms simply as "suchness" (*ru*) or "such-like characteristics" (*ru-shi-xiang*). He says that the ten dharma realms have "Ten Suchnesses":[37] such-like appearance, such-like nature, such-like essence, such-like power, such-like function, such-like causes, such-like conditions, such-like results, such-like retributions, and such-like ultimate identity of beginning and end.[38] Without going into detail about what each of the "Suchnesses" means, we can say that "Ten Suchnesses" simply means that what we want to investigate as *the ultimate reality*, is simply *as such* – as what we see around us in the phenomenal world. Earlier we saw how the Consciousness-Only School distinguishes "True Thusness" from the phenomenal world transformed by consciousness, and the Hua-yan School posits *Suchness* as the ultimate reality with no discrimination or division. Now we see that the Tian-tai School simply calls *this phenomenal world's suchness* the "True Thusness." There is no need to find a reality beyond this reality – there is no other reality.

Buddhahood, Buddha-realm and Buddha-dharma

In some contexts, the *Lotus Sutra* describes the Buddha as an eternal being, ever present in the world. All the past, present, future Buddhas are all the personifications of this one eternal Buddha. As the Buddha himself explains in the *Lotus Sutra*:

> After this Buddha had finished bringing great benefit to living beings, he passed into extinction. After his correct law and counterfeit law had ended, another Buddha appeared in the same land. . . . This process continued until twenty thousand million Buddhas had appeared one after the other, all bearing the same name.[39]

This quote seems to present the Buddha as an immortal "God," who is all-knowing and all-loving, and who goes in and out of the human world as he pleases. Watson says: "From this we see that in the *Lotus Sutra* the Buddha, who had earlier been viewed as a historical personality, is now conceived as a being who transcends all boundaries of time and space, an ever-abiding principle of truth and compassion that exists everywhere and within all beings."[40]

In Tian-tai's interpretation of the *Lotus Sutra*, however, the Buddha exists not as a personified God, but as the objective underlying principle of the universe. The ever-presence of the Buddha is not just manifested in the *realized* Buddhas of all ages, but also in all beings, sentient and inanimate alike. Zhi-yi emphasizes that one of the correct understandings of the essence of Buddhahood is that "the essence [of true reality] pervades all places."[41] Even though he occasionally follows the *Lotus Sutra* in regarding the Buddha as a Supreme Being with compassion and will power, more often than not he uses the term "Buddha" to signify the objective reality. Zhi-yi also uses the notion Buddhahood to represent the essence of the objective reality itself, and sometimes he calls reality-as-it-is "Buddha-dharma" (*fo-fa*) or "Buddha-realm" (*fo-jie*). The notion of Buddha in these contexts is identified with the universal principle itself (or we can call it "Principle"). Strictly speaking, Buddha-realm is the tenth of all dharma realms, the realm in which only Buddhas reside. But since ten dharma realms are "mutually contained," Buddha-realm and the other nine realms are one and the same reality. In other words, "Buddha realm" and "Dharma realm" (*fa-jie*) are different designators for the same realm. Zhi-yi says, "Various terms name one ultimate [reality]. Only one ultimate reality is given many names."[42] Thus, other names such as "True Thusness," "*Tathata*," etc., which are the focus of meticulous analysis for other Buddhist schools, are all treated by Zhi-yi as "co-designators."

If "the Buddha" is understood as the underlying principle of the universe, and "Buddhahood" simply means "the essence of reality," then the religious undertone of Tian-tai Buddhism is greatly reduced. The Buddha does not create the world; nor is it a particular individual being. Tian-tai Buddhism purges mysticism out of its philosophy, and focuses more on the practical aspect of improving one's conception of the present world. The Consciousness-Only School calls the basis of this phenomenal world "the storehouse consciousness," which can be taken to refer to the Buddha's consciousness or everyone's consciousnesses. The world seems to be physically contained within this storehouse consciousness as multiple seeds. The Hua-yan School calls multiple phenomenal worlds "the fabrications of multiple minds," and multiple minds are "the creations of the One True Mind." The Tian-tai School also views the world as being contained in the Buddha's Mind. However, when they treat "Buddha realm" as identified with "Dharma realm" and "Buddhahood" as identified with "the essence of Reality," Tian-tai's notion of Mind becomes objectified and externalized. Tian-tai's philosophy is no longer any form of idealism.

In summary, Tian-tai identifies the ultimate reality with the phenomenal world; hence, it does not posit a "noumenon" or substance beyond the phenomenal world. The world as we know it is the only world there is. While Hua-yan emphasizes that the world in which we live is nothing real outside of the empty noumenon, Tian-tai's emphasis is that the realm of noumenon or the state of nirvana is nothing beyond the world in which we live and our present existence. The former assigns the "emptiness" of noumenon to the phenomenal world as a whole; the latter assigns the "realness" of the phenomenal world to noumenon itself. Under Tian-tai's philosophy, there is no need to find another realm of higher existence. As Zhi-yi says: "To keep away from the mundane dharmas and yet seek the ultimate Truth [elsewhere] is similar to avoiding this Emptiness and seeking Emptiness elsewhere. The mundane dharmas are themselves the ultimate Dharma [i.e., the Truth]. There is no need to forsake the mundane and adhere to the sacred."[43] This remark clearly asserts that nirvana does not exist in another realm.

Even though Zhi-yi views ordinary people's knowledge of the world as partial or erroneous, Tian-tai philosophy is not epistemic skepticism. It does not question our ability to know the ultimate reality. The Threefold Truth is the Truth of this reality. Here we turn to the issue of knowledge, or truth in the semantic sense.

Tian-tai's Notion of Truth in the Semantic Sense

Tian-tai's notion of truth as a property of our statements or our descriptions has multiple dimensions. In some contexts, Zhi-yi seems to think that it is possible to grant multiple truths, even though they are mutually contradictory. In some other contexts, Zhi-yi seems to think that multiple partial truths are mutually supplementary in jointly providing a true picture of the world. In some contexts, Zhi-yi argues that there is only one truth; while in some others, Zhi-yi argues that there is no truth. In what follows, we shall separate these different comments on the notion of truth into several categories.

Truth as correspondence with reality or with the true nature of things

In Zhi-yi's explication of the Threefold Truth, we see that he takes all three statements to be true for the reason that they all correspond with the true nature of things. All dharmas are provisionally existent; are empty (devoid of self-nature), and are part of the Middle Way (the True Reality). Therefore, all three truths are *truth*. But how are the three truths related to one another? Do they represent three different aspects of reality? Do they jointly express one single truth (hence the translation "threefold truth" instead of "three truths")? Is one truth better (or "more true") than the others?

There are at least three possible interpretations of the relationship between the three truths, all of which seem to be supported by what Zhi-yi says at one time or another. First, they represent three levels of truth depending on the different levels of understanding; each one is better than the previous one:

The Middle Way:	The understanding of Mahayana
Emptiness:	The understanding of Hinayana (Theravada)
Provisional Existence:	The understanding of ordinary people

Second, they are divided into two levels, with the Middle Way better than the other two extreme views:[44]

The Middle Way
[Synthesis]

Provisional Existence	Emptiness
[Thesis]	[Antithesis]

Third, they stand on the same level because they are identical:

Provisional Existence	=	Emptiness	=	The Middle Way

In support of the first interpretation, we can quote from Zhi-yi:

> "The truth of existence" refers to reality as perceived in the mind of [ordinary] worldly people; this is called "the truth of existence," and is

also called "the mundane truth." "The truth of [emptiness]" refers to reality as perceived in the mind of people who have transcended the world; this is called "the truth of non-being," and is also called "the real truth." "The supreme truth of the Middle [Way]" refers to reality as perceived by all Buddhas and bodhisattvas; this is called "the supreme truth of the Middle [Way]," and is called "the one real truth."[45]

From this quote we can see that the truth of emptiness is higher than the truth of provisional existence, while the truth of the Middle Way is even higher than the truth of emptiness. In the end, only the truth of the Middle Way can be said truly to correspond to the nature of things. It is thus the one ultimate truth.

However, another quote from Zhi-yi seems to support the second interpretation, which takes the truth of emptiness and the truth of provisional existence as equally "not true." Zhi-yi says:

Now, if one knows that the mundane is not mundane, then the extreme [view] of the mundane is put to rest, and if one realizes the non-mundane [nature of conventional (provisional) existence], then the extreme [view] of emptiness is put to rest. This is called "cessation as an end to both extremes."[46]

In this quote, we see that the truth of emptiness is regarded as an extreme view of nihilism, and is equally wrong as the truth of provisional existence. Only the truth of the Middle Way remains to be the one ultimate truth.

Even though both interpretations can be supported by Zhi-yi's remarks, what he really means by the Threefold Truth is that all three truths are ultimately identical. Zhi-yi's famous slogan, "emptiness is identical to [provisional] existence and the Middle Way,"[47] supports this identity interpretation. Standing alone, each of the three truths expresses a partial truth (hence none of them is wrong or expresses false understanding); taken together, they jointly depict the one ultimate reality. That is why they are not "three truths" but one "threefold" truth. As Zhi-yi says, "This threefold truth is perfectly integrated; one-in-three and three-in-one."[48] In *the Great Calming and Contemplation*, he also says, "All three [statements] are empty because the path of speech and discursive thought is cut off. All three are provisional because they are names only. All three are the middle because they are identical with ultimate reality."[49] When one takes up this interpretation of the identity of the three statements of truth, one has gained what Zhi-yi calls "the perfect understanding" of the Threefold Truth. The other two interpretations of the Threefold Truth are not wrong, but they are not the best understanding.

Truth as relative to understanding and intelligence

Tian-tai philosophy is most renowned for its classification of the various doctrines of Buddhism. The classification of Buddhist doctrines did not originate with Zhi-yi, but his system is regarded as being the most comprehensive and consistent. Ever since Indian Buddhism was introduced into China, Chinese Buddhists were troubled by the vast doctrinal differences in the various scriptures. Instead of arguing which ones are right or wrong, they try to synthesize all doctrines into a coherent system. With the classification of doctrines, Chinese Buddhists suggest that incompatible teachings are simply the various expedient means that the Buddha employed to enlighten people of different levels of intelligence.[50] Zhi-yi says: "Teachings are [taught] basically as responses to capabilities. There are distinctions and differences in the scriptures because the capabilities [of sentient beings] are not the same."[51] In this sense, we can say that a doctrine is true as long as it is appropriate to the listener's level of understanding.

In this respect, we can analyze the notion of *truth* relativistically:

P is true$_a$ for audience$_A$
Q is true$_b$ for audience$_B$
R is true$_c$ for audience$_C$

when P, Q, R, each expresses a different truth.

Using the method of classification of doctrines, the Tian-tai school distinguishes four major branches of Buddhist teachings. Each of these branches has its own "truth." Tian-tai's classification of doctrines begins with Zhi-yi, who divides all Buddhist teachings (sutras or treatises) into four kinds; this is his famous "Fourfold Teachings" (*si-jiao*):[52]

1   The Tripitaka Teaching (*zang-jiao*): the Theravada teaching that renounces the experiential world and emphasizes the distinct realm of nirvana. It is meant for people who have little intelligence and low ambition; who are entrenched in the experiential world and are only interested in their own salvation. Its truth is that the world is *empty* in the sense of being illusions. According to this teaching, the way (the right path) to nirvana is the renunciation of the world of suffering

and aggregation. The mundane world and nirvana thus stand opposed to each other.

2   The Common Teaching (*tong-jiao*): the teaching shared by both the Theravada and the Mahayana Schools. It is meant for people who can understand the truth of emptiness and recognize that dharmas have no real self-subsisting nature. Its truth is still about *emptiness*, except that the notion *emptiness* means nothing other than dependent co-arising. Thus, these schools do not necessarily advocate exiting the mundane world to reach nirvana. Madhyamaka is a representative of this teaching.

3   The Special Teaching (*bie-jiao*): the special teaching of the Mahayana School, which is meant for people with compassion for other sentient beings. The preached goal of attainment is that of bodhisattvas, who vow to help all sentient beings reach nirvana before they themselves do. These schools emphasize that everyone is born with Buddha-nature, which enables one to become a Buddha. Truth for this branch of Buddhist schools is the Middle Way (the Ultimate Truth). These schools identify the Middle Way with Buddha-nature. To obtain Truth, therefore, one needs to realize one's intrinsic Buddha-nature. To realize one's Buddha-nature, furthermore, one needs to gradually get rid of one's afflictions. "Nirvana" is interpreted as the extinction of all afflictions. Hua-yan is a representative of this teaching.

4   The Perfect Teaching (*yuan-jiao*): the teaching of the ultimate reality, which is the Middle Way itself. The Middle Way identifies nirvana with the phenomenal world. One does not need to leave the phenomenal world to enter nirvana. Only those with perfect understanding can listen to this teaching. Tian-tai puts its own teaching into this group. As the Special Teaching, it too presents the Middle Way as the ultimate truth; it too upholds Buddha-nature in every sentient being. It is different from the Special Teaching in that it advocates sudden enlightenment. Under this teaching, afflictions are not necessarily bad, and the path to nirvana does not even require the extinction of afflictions. One can gain enlightenment even in the midst of afflictions. One only needs to attain perfect wisdom that the phenomenal world and our afflictions are not an obstacle to our enlightenment.[53]

All four branches teach truths, and yet what they teach are different from one another. Truth is thus relative to the intended audience or readers. This notion of *truth* is closely related to the next one: truth as a means to an end.

Truth as a pragmatic notion: "expedient means"

In the *Lotus Sutra*, the Buddha tells a story about a rich old man who tried to save his young children's lives. Upon seeing his house on fire, the old man was very concerned for the safety of his children, who were at the time engrossed in the games they were playing and refused to heed to their father's warning to get out of the house. The old man thus informed them: "I have marvelous toy carts drawn by goats, deer and oxen waiting outside for you. You must come outside right now to get them." After his sons had reached safety, however, the old man did not give them the toy carts as he had promised, but offered them real carts filled with jewels instead. The Buddha explains that the world is like the house on fire, and sentient beings are like the ignorant children unaware of their perils. He taught them ways of attaining extinction so as to lure them out of their misery, but ultimately what he offers them is not extinction, but Buddha wisdom.[54]

Based on this story, Zhi-yi offers another explanation for the existence of contradicting teachings of the Buddha: they are all used as "expedient means" to enable people with different capacities and intelligences to gain true enlightenment. If a statement can serve the pragmatic purpose of enabling enlightenment, then it is *true* even if it expresses falsehood. In other words, the notion of *truth* can be interpreted as a pragmatic notion. It is not what the statement *says*, but what it *does* (i.e., what it accomplishes), that makes the statement true. If this is the case, then it is futile for us to debate which of the contradicting statements is really true. As long as they accomplish the pragmatic goal of enlightenment, they are all *true*.

According to the *Lotus Sutra*, the whole teaching about nirvana as the state of extinction is such an "expedient means." The Buddha says of ordinary people: "such living beings have never in the past cultivated good roots, but have stubbornly clung to the five desires, and their folly and craving have given rise to affliction."[55] He continues: "I have for their sake established expedient means, preaching the way that ends all suffering, and showing them nirvana. But although I preach nirvana, this is not a true extinction. All phenomena from the very first have of themselves constantly borne the marks of tranquil extinction."[56] From this quote, we see that the *Lotus Sutra* rejects the whole belief of a separate realm of nirvana that is rooted in early Buddhism. Zhi-yi interprets this "expedient means" as yet another form of truth. All things uttered by the Buddha are "truths"; some are true in virtue of their correspondence with reality; some are true in virtue of being expedient means to enlighten people of little intelligence.

Truth in Tian-tai philosophy is thus not merely a semantic notion, but also a pragmatic notion. This pragmatic twist of the notion of truth is possibly the inspiration for the Chan School's using all kinds of non-verbal means to accomplish the goal of enlightenment. If a false statement or a partial truth can be regarded as truth from a pragmatic standpoint, then the act of hitting on the head, throwing a rock, yelling at the student, etc., can all be regarded as truth as long as they serve the same pragmatic function.

Truth as hierarchical: "one truth"

While "truth" is defined relativistically, it does not mean that all relative truths would have to be granted the same status. Even as we see

P is true$_a$ for audience$_A$
Q is true$_b$ for audience$_B$
R is true$_c$ for audience$_C$

when P, Q, and R each expresses a different truth, we can still have the following distinctions between the levels of intelligence and understanding of audience A, B, and C:

C is better than B, and B than A.

Therefore, we can get:

R is better than Q, and Q than P.

In other words, we can still place different "acknowledged truths" into a hierarchy of truths. This is also where Zhi-yi's judgment of the classification of Buddhist doctrines (*pan jiao*) comes in. According to Zhi-yi, the Tripitaka Teaching stands at the lowest level in the hierarchy of all Buddhist doctrines, while the Perfect Teaching stands at the highest level. He puts the *Lotus Sutra* in the group of the Perfect Teaching. Hence, in his judgment, the Tian-tai school's truth of the Middle Way represents the highest form of truth. It is meant for people who are Buddhas.[57] This shows that Zhi-yi's notion of truth is ultimately a hierarchical system of various truths – the ones at the bottom are called "truth" either because they are the expedient means for people with low levels of understanding or because they serve the pragmatic goal of enabling enlightenment. "Truth" in this sense is relative and functional. However, at the top of the hierarchy of truths, there is only one ultimate truth, which is the truth of the Middle Way itself. That is why even though Zhi-yi talks about multiple truths, he ends up by claiming that there is only "One Truth."

Zhi-yi's "one-truth" theory could be seen as deriving from the Buddha's claim in the *Lotus Sutra* that even though he preaches "three vehicles" (three paths to obtaining Buddhahood), there is ultimately only one "Great Buddha Vehicle."[58] These three other vehicles can be seen as the three paths of Voice-hearers, of Self-enlightened Ones, and of Bodhisattvas respectively; they can also be seen as the doctrines taught in the Tripitaka Teaching, the Common Teaching, and the Special Teaching. They are like the toy carts in the Buddha's story about the old man and his sons – they are employed as expedient means, but they are not really true. Therefore, in Tian-tai's usage, there is only one truth, not just in the metaphysical sense (one reality), but also in the semantic sense (one ultimately true description of reality). The Tian-tai school certainly does not embrace relativism when it comes to the notion of truth.

Truth as "subtle": "No Truth"

Even with all these discussions on truth, ultimately Zhi-yi claims that the real truth is unspeakable, indescribable, and beyond human understanding. The complete title for the *Lotus Sutra* is *"the Sutra of the Lotus Blossom of the Subtle Dharma,"* and Zhi-yi explains that " 'subtle' means 'beyond conceptual thought'."[59] Watson points out that this inexplicability is a common trait of Mahayana Buddhism: "Mahayana Buddhism has always insisted that its highest truth can never in the end be expressed in words, since words immediately create the kind of distinctions that violate the unity of Emptiness."[60] We have seen how Hua-yan pays special attention to proving the limitations of language and conception; we shall see that the Chan School goes even further in rejecting the possibility of the verbal transmission of truth.

Zhi-yi introduces the notion of "No Truth" as such: "The one truth is [actually] No Truth; all truth is at rest. Each and every [truth] is ultimately inexpressible."[61] Truth is inexpressible because verbal expression has its limits – reality itself is not a verbal construct. However, Zhi-yi is not denying our capacity to know or to understand the truth of

Reality. For those who have attained Buddhahood (those Buddhas themselves), the One Truth is simply the Threefold Truth. His theory of "No Truth" is a way to reject other Buddhist schools' engaging in verbal debates on what the Buddha really meant or what the essence of Reality is. When people engage in verbal speculation, they lose sight of the real goal – Buddha wisdom. Therefore, Zhi-yi feels the need to advocate "No Truth" to bring Buddhists back to the pursuit of mental elevation. He says, "It is necessary to say 'No Truth' for the sake of those who have not fulfilled attainment, and in their attachments give rise to delusions. For those who have real attainment, there is [a positive truth]; for those [lost] in vain speculation, there is none."[62] The "No Truth" can be seen as yet another "expedient means" – this time as employed by Zhi-yi himself.

Tian-tai's Notions of Buddhahood, Buddha-nature and Pure Mind

Tian-Tai's interpretation of the existence of the Buddha is quite contrary to the tradition of Indian Buddhism. The orthodox legend of the Buddha is that he was a prince who left the royal court to search for the true meaning of life. After multiple trials, he finally gained enlightenment and started preaching to the masses. The different sutras are supposedly all notes of his lectures. The term "Buddha" is always used in the singular definite designator as "the Buddha." But in the *Lotus Sutra*, the term is often used in the plural. There are actually tens of thousands of Buddhas, or, as the *Lotus Sutra* says, "The Buddhas of the present and future, whose numbers are beyond calculations."[63] The number of Buddhas is incalculable, since they include all those who have attained Buddhahood in the past, present, and future. They are no different from the rest of us, and they reside in the same reality as we do. The moment they gain true enlightenment, they turn the phenomenal world into nirvana.

If what we call the phenomenal world is the same reality that the Buddhas call nirvana, then our emancipation from this phenomenal world does not mean that we enter a different reality, but rather that we have altered our perception of the self-same reality. Therefore, the difference between being in the mundane world and entering nirvana is nothing more than our internal perception and our understanding of this reality, not the reality itself. It is open to all of us to alter our mistaken views and delusions to gain true insights; it is open to all of us to obtain salvation and reach nirvana. This very possibility lies in the fact that we all possess "Buddha-nature" from time immemorial. The universality of Buddha-nature is what makes it possible for everyone to attain Buddhahood and enter nirvana. Zhi-yi says, "[The teaching of the *Lotus Sutra* concerning] the essence [of Buddhahood] is that one is endowed with all virtues and is completely endowed with all good qualities."[64] The phrase "Buddha-nature" simply means these inborn virtues and good qualities that we all share.

Zhi-yi defines "nature" as "that which has its point of reference internally" and "Buddha-nature" as "the inherent wisdom of the Buddha."[65] We can say that "Buddha-nature" signifies the potential for attaining Buddhahood. It is what is innate in everyone. If everyone has innate Buddha-nature, then why doesn't everyone already possess Buddhahood and become a Buddha? Tian-tai's explanation is not different from that of early Buddhism: ignorance prevents people from attaining Buddhahood. But whereas early Buddhism puts ignorance at the beginning of the *Twelve Causal Links* that define our existence, the Tian-tai School does not treat ignorance as the original state of our existence. Zhi-yi gives an analogy of a pauper to explain his view that we all have Buddha-nature within ourselves:

> Suppose there is a pauper with a cache of treasure around her house of which she is totally unaware. A friend shows her where it is buried, whereupon she comes to know of its existence. She clears away the weeds and trash and begins to dig it out. Gradually she gets closer and closer, until, on reaching it, she opens the cache of treasure, takes it all out, and puts it to use.[66]

From this analogy, we can see that for Zhi-yi, our Buddha-nature is actually the original state of our existence, and all we need to do is simply to clear away our delusions and mistaken views, so that we may *regain* access to this precious Buddha-nature.

However, in Tian-tai's established theory, human nature is not simply good and pure; it is also evil and defiled.[67] Zhi-yi emphasizes that the defiled human nature is no different from the pure Buddha-nature. He says, "It is like water when it freezes to form ice – there is no ice apart from the water."[68] There is only one human nature, which is identical to Buddha-nature, universal to all human beings. In general terms, all dharmas have this pure "Dharma Nature." According to Ng, "[Zhi-yi] does not confine the Buddha-nature to sentient beings, but broadens its dimension to cover the non-sentient. This is done by identifying the Buddha-nature with the Dharma Nature, which means the true nature of dharmas or entities."[69] If all things inherently contain the nature of the Buddha, then all things ultimately merge with the Buddha itself. Nirvana is not to be sought outside of oneself or one's existence; nirvana is merely a state of mind. And the mind is initially "pure." Zhi-yi says: "The instant one realizes that suffering and the origin of suffering are inherently devoid of suffering and any arising of suffering, one comes to merge with the dharma-nature."[70]

Since the phenomenal world is the same as nirvana and since our minds are the same as the Buddhas' minds, the origin of our sufferings is also the basis for our salvation. What makes us good and what makes us bad have one and the same source: the mind. As Zhi-yi puts it, "Nescience when turned around itself transforms into illumination, just as ice becomes water when it melts. [Enlightenment] is not something distantly removed, nor does it come from some other place. It is completely present in each and every moment of thought."[71] A shocking implication of the claim is that contrary to the teaching of early Buddhism, in particular the Four Noble Truths (Suffering, Craving, Cessation, and Path) taught by the Buddha, we do not need to renounce our cravings or afflictions. Furthermore, we do not need to wait until this present life is over to attain nirvana so that we will not be reborn again. In our present life, in a single present thought of ours, we can immediately enter nirvana. Zhi-yi says, "If beings are already identical with enlightenment, then there is nothing further to obtain. If beings are already identical with nirvana, then there is nothing further to annihilate. This being the case for a single thought, it is the case for all thoughts and for all dharmas as well."[72]

Since the phenomenal world is identified with nirvana, our suffering and our salvation are thereby inseparable. Zhi-yi treats defilements or contamination not as things to be extirpated, but as things to be overcome. If there were no contamination, there would not be decontamination; if there were no ignorance, there would be no enlightenment. This idea leads to an interesting thesis that evil not only is present in our nature, but also is indispensable. Zhi-yi says:

> In evil there is good; apart from evil there is no good. It is the overturning of various evils upon which the tenability of good is based. This potency is like the bamboo in possession of the potency of fire. . . . [Likewise], evil is [the potency of] good, though it has not yet become actually [good]. When it meets subsidiary causes and is actualized, it can overturn evil.[73]

Zhi-yi's theory of human nature thus affirms both that human nature is pure (*jing*), and that human nature is contaminated (*ran*).

Zhi-yi's theory of human nature is called the theory of "containment in nature" (*xing ju*) by contemporary Chinese commentators. Earlier, we have seen that for Tian-tai, the ten dharma realms are mutually contained, and ultimately the mind contains all ten realms. If this is the case, then the mind includes the realm of demons, beasts, hungry ghosts, and hell beings. In other words, what we have in mind – our negative emotions, our vile thoughts, and any other affliction we have – can bring us down to the realm of hell. These evil paths are thus "contained" in our nature, just as the holy paths are contained in our nature. The potential for enlightenment is rooted in our nature, so is the chance for our eternal downfall. According to a contemporary Chinese monk, Master Sheng-yan, Zhi-yi's theory treats "nature" as the nature, or the substance, of the mind. Hence, for Zhi-yi, if a single mind can contain three thousand worlds (*xin ju san qian*), then all three thousand worlds are already contained in the nature (*xing ju san qian*).[74] Furthermore, according to Zhi-yi, evil is intrinsic to us – it is part of our *nature*. He says: "Even when a Buddha cuts off all evils and all contaminations, evil is still in his or her nature."[75] The reason why even Buddhas cannot be without evil nature is that they need to know what evil is or how to overcome evil in order to help other sentient beings. In other words, Buddhas need to experience evil first hand so that they can be truly compassionate to others – not just in a condescending way from a detached, superior position.

Zhi-yi says, "The goodness and the evil of nature is the gateway to good and evil. Nature cannot be altered. Even if one goes through multiple generations, one cannot destroy one's nature."[76] Evil is like the material upon which good can be built. By the same token, we can say that the phenomenal world is the foundation upon which nirvana can be realized. Neither our evil nature nor the phenomenal world needs to be completely wiped out. What makes enlightenment, or the realization of one's Buddhahood, possible, is the mind. It is important to realize that for Zhi-yi, the process of turning oneself into a Buddha is not a process of transformation through outside influences, but a process of internal realization. Leon Hurvitz explains it well: "When one has done this, one will realize that nothing has changed. I have not become Buddha; I am Buddha, and always have been. The difference between then and now is that then I was not aware of it, while now I am."[77] This internal realization is accomplished by the mind.

As Zhi-yi explains the term "mind," it is the function of "cognitive reflection";[78] it is "the sentient awareness of objects that distinguishes us from trees and stones."[79] He further explains, "the power of mind to make discursive evaluation [with respect to these objects] is called 'thought' or 'cognitive activity'."[80] Since the mind's main function is "thought" or "cognitive reflection," ignorance and enlightenment are two possible states of the mind. We have explained earlier that the mind, or what Zhi-yi calls "one thought," contains three thousand worlds, in the sense that it takes the totality of reality as its object of cognition. Zhi-yi emphasizes that Buddhas are not fundamentally different from ordinary people. He says: "know . . . that your own mind here and now contains replete within it the whole of the Buddha's dharmas."[81] Furthermore, one should understand that one's mind "is equal to the mind of the Buddha."[82] The Buddha differs from ordinary folks simply by his turning away erroneous thoughts and gaining perfect insights into the essence of reality. Zhi-yi says, "It should be known that the Buddha's knowledge and insights dwell [inherently] within sentient beings."[83] He calls our minds "the inherently pure mind."[84] Zhi-yi's theory of Pure Mind seems to be derived from that of his teacher Hui-si. Hui-si holds that we all have an inborn pure mind, and this pure mind is never lost within us. We do not see our pure mind because it is covered by all sorts of contamination. Hui-si says: "Although this mind has been obscured from time immemorial by contaminating dharmas based on ignorance, yet its nature of purity has never changed."[85] Therefore, we do not need to go elsewhere for enlightenment. We are all potentially Buddhas and our minds are the same as the Buddha's mind (or Buddhas' minds). All we need to do is simply rediscover our original purity and retrieve our innate knowledge. As we shall see in the next chapter, this teaching has a great affinity to the Chan School.

When the mind attains enlightenment, it is in the state of "calming and contemplation," as Zhi-yi calls it. He explains: "Contemplation is the unaroused yet unimpeded [vision of this thought of enlightenment]. Calming is the quiescent extinction that is its essential nature. Calming and contemplation are themselves identical to enlightenment, and enlightenment is identical to calming and contemplation."[86] What Tian-tai teaches as the method of moral cultivation is fundamentally a method of self-help – one needs to rediscover one's innate purity and inborn knowledge. External restraints do not accomplish moral training; doctrines and theories do not teach wisdom. One needs to realize that one's innate Buddha-nature alone is sufficient to bring about one's becoming a Buddha, or, as Zhi-yi puts it, it is "the complete cause of Buddhahood."[87]

Conclusion

In Tian-tai philosophy, we see the germane characteristics of Chinese Buddhism. By making "Buddha" a pluralistic designator, it reduces the mono-theological aspect of Indian Buddhism. By advocating ten dharma realms instead of six dharma realms, it merges the world of ordinary people and the world of Buddhahood. By identifying nirvana with the phenomenal world, it abolishes the polarity between this world and "the other world" as present in the Indian culture. By recognizing the universality of Buddha-nature, it rejects any caste system that was endorsed in early Theravada schools. By emphasizing that the real truth is "subtle" and beyond description, it guides Chinese Buddhists to steer away from the meticulous study of Indian sutras. Its teaching leads to the establishment of a genuinely Chinese Buddhist school: the Chan School.

Furthermore, Tian-tai philosophy not only links up with traditional Chinese philosophy, but also sets off new directions for its development. Its acknowledgment of the original goodness of human nature and the original purity of the human mind can be traced back to Mencius' theory of human nature and human mind. Its concession of the innate evil in human nature, on the other hand, reflects the teaching of Xunzi. Its discussion on the connection between Buddha-nature and Pure Mind, in particular, paves the way for the centuries-long debate between the School of Nature and the School of Mind among Neo-Confucians. Tian-Tai philosophy can be rightfully seen as the bridge between classic Confucianism and modern Neo-Confucianism.

Further discussion questions

1 What is the Tian-tai School's view on reality? How do they interpret the world? How is it different from the Hua-yan School's worldview?
2 What does Tian-tai mean by this slogan: "One thought contains three thousand worlds" or "The Trishiliocosm in a moment of consciousness"?
3 What are the three levels of truth according to Tian-tai? How should we understand Tian-tai's notion of truth? Can we accept a notion of truth that is merely functional and pragmatic?
4 Do you agree that we could be intrinsically good, that we could have Buddha-nature inherent in us? If so, why can't many people rediscover their inner goodness? How can the Tian-tai School explain our moral deficiencies?

Primary texts

Wing-tsit Chan (ed.) *A Sourcebook in Chinese Philosophy*, 4th edn. Princeton: Princeton University Press, 1973 (ch. 2; excerpts from *The Method of Cessation and Contemplation in Mahayana*).

Burton Watson (trans.) *The Essential Lotus: Selections from the Lotus Sutra*. New York: Columbia University Press, 2002.

Zhi-yi (Chih-i). *Fa-hua-xuan-yi*, trans. Paul L. Swanson. In Paul L. Swanson, *Foundations of T'ien-T'ai Philosophy: The Flowering of the Two Truths Theory in Chinese Buddhism*. Asian Humanities Press, 1989.

Zhi-yi (Chih-i). *Mo-Ho Cessation and Contemplation*. In Neal Donner and Daniel B. Stevenson, *The Great Calming and Contemplation: A Study and Annotated Translation of the First Chapter of Chih-i's Mo-ho chih-kuan*. Honolulu: University of Hawaii Press, 1993.

Further readings

Yu-kwan Ng. (Ru-jun Wu) *T'ien-t'ai Buddhism and Early Madhyamika*. Honolulu: University of Hawaii Press, 1993.

Paul Swanson, "Truth in T'ien-T'ai Philosophy." In his *Foundations of T'ien-T'ai Philosophy: The Flowering of the Two Truths Theory in Chinese Buddhism*. California: Asian Humanities Press, 1989, ch. 1, pp. 1–17.

Chapter 12

The Chan School (Zen Buddhism)

Introduction

The Chan School, developed in China between the sixth and the eighth century, is generally regarded as a genuinely Chinese Buddhist school. It was later taken to Japan where it became prominent. Because Chan was first introduced to the Western world in the twentieth century through its Japanese branch (most notably through the interpretations of a Japanese scholar Daisetz Teitaro Suzuki), it is more commonly known by its Japanese pronunciation, "Zen." The word "chan" is the Chinese translation of the Sanskrit *dhyana*, which means meditation.[1] Chan's Indian heritage was not clearly established, even though according to the legend within the Chan School, the teaching of Chan originated in India with the historical Buddha. Legend has it that the Buddha transmitted his esoteric teaching in private to a disciple, and this teaching was different from what the Buddha preached to the general assembly. This teaching did not rely on written sutras, and was orally passed on from one patriarch to another. The twenty-eighth patriarch Bodhidharma (470–543) brought the teaching to China in the sixth century, so the legend goes, and the Chan School revered him as the First Patriarch. The lineage continued with Hui-ke (487–593), Seng-can (dates unknown), Dao-xin (580–636) and to Hong-ren (601–74). Within the Chan tradition, they were regarded as the second, the third, the fourth, and the fifth patriarch respectively.[2] But the school split into the Northern Chan and the Southern Chan after Hong-ren. Each of the two schools claimed that their leader, Shen-xiu (ca. 605–706) for the Northern School and Hui-neng (638–713) for the Southern School, was the authentic sixth patriarch.

According to the *Platform Sutra of the Sixth Patriarch*, the fifth patriarch Hong-ren held a contest among his disciples for the verse that best expounded the teaching of Chan, so that he could choose the disciple to become his successor. Shen-xiu was the head disciple at the time, while Hui-neng was an illiterate, low-class laborer at the temple. After Shen-xiu had written his verse, all disciples thought that he would surely inherit the sacred robe as well as the title. But Hui-neng came up with another verse, which was judged by Hong-ren to be superior. For fear that other disciples might impose harm on Hui-neng out of jealousy or contempt for his low class, Hong-ren passed on the sacred robe secretly to Hui-neng in the middle of the night and sent him away. Hui-neng went back to the southern part of China, where he originally came from. After Hong-ren's death, followers of Shen-xiu put him forward as the sixth patriarch. Years later Hui-neng also amassed a sufficient following and a separate Chan School was formed in the South. The rivalry between the Northern School and the Southern School lasted for about 100 years, and initially the Northern School had the upper hand. Eventually, however, largely through the efforts of Hui-neng's major disciple Shen-hui (670–762), the Southern School was recognized by the Chinese royal court to be the genuine Chan. Hui-neng thus became the generally acclaimed "sixth patriarch" of the Chan School.

There is now a consensus among commentators that this story, as told in the *Platform Sutra*, was probably fabricated by Hui-neng's followers, in particular by Shen-hui. We thus cannot be sure whether the fifth patriarch Hong-ren really passed on the robe to Hui-neng. Some scholars argue that it was actually Shen-xiu, not Hui-neng, who inherited the true spirit of Chan's tradition descended from the first patriarch.[3] Nevertheless, it was Hui-neng's teachings, especially the ones revealed in the *Platform Sutra* (sometimes translated as the *Altar Sutra*) that got passed on to later generations and became the core teaching of the Chan School.[4] In D. T. Suzuki's praise: "The development of [Chan] thought in China until the day of Hui-neng followed more or less the Indian pattern, but after him its course began to run characteristically along the Chinese channel."[5] To understand Chan's thought as a form of Chinese Buddhism, we should study Hui-neng's rather than Shen-xiu's teaching. Therefore, our analysis of the Chan School will focus on the Southern School originated in Hui-neng. Whenever we use "the Chan School" or "Chan" without qualification, we refer specifically to the Southern Chan School. We will treat the *Platform Sutra of the Sixth Patriarch* as the theoretical foundation of the Chan School.

The *Platform Sutra of the Sixth Patriarch* is a work of great philosophical significance. As Philip Yampolsky says: "This work marks a shift in emphasis in Chinese Buddhism, a move from an abstract Nirvana to an individual enlightenment, available to anyone who seeks to realize through meditation the Buddha nature inherent within him."[6]

There are different versions of the *Platform Sutra*, but two of them stand out. One is the more elaborated version compiled in the thirteenth century. It thenceforth became the standard text for the Chan School. Another was a much older, shorter, but error-packed version, which was unearthed in the caves of Dun-huang at the turn of the twentieth century.[7] The primary sources for this chapter include these two versions of the *Platform Sutra*, as well as Hui-neng's commentary on the *Diamond Sutra*. We will also consult works by two leading Southern Chan masters: Huang Bo [Huang Po] (?–ca. 850) and Lin Ji (Lin-Chi) (ca. 810–66), since both were instrumental in the further development and transformation of the Chan School.

In a nutshell, the essence of Chan's philosophy could be described as a philosophy of pure mind.[8] The Chan School preaches the retrieval of one's original mind. Hong-ren describes the heritage of Chan as the teachers' intimately imparting the original mind from one to another.[9] The passage of mind-transmission does not rely on verbal communication. Therefore, Chan masters play down the importance of language. Their view on mind and their view on language are closely related. In this chapter, we shall explicate the Chan School's philosophy of mind and philosophy of language. But before we begin, a careful comparison between the Northern Chan and the Southern Chan is in order. We should note that it was through the transformation that the Southern School made to the original heritage that the characteristics of the Chinese Chan School were established. This school does not posit any transcendental realm over our mundane world; it does not represent the Buddha as a supreme being. It is a philosophy about ordinary people and ordinary things. But it is in their ordinariness that the Chan School places the highest value.

Theoretical Divergences between the Northern School and the Southern School

Even if the story about the competition between Shen-xiu's verse and Hui-neng's verse is unfounded, it is a historical fact that there were two schools with different teachings and practices. The Northern School taught gradual enlightenment; the Southern School taught immediate enlightenment. The Northern School emphasized the method of "sitting in meditation," in the process of which one contemplates one's mind; the Southern School disputed the practice of sitting in meditation and proclaimed that enlightenment could be reached in the midst of any daily activity, such as drinking tea or chopping wood.[10] Furthermore, according to several Chan scholars, the theoretical foundation of the Northern School is the *Lankavatara Sutra*, while the Southern School expounds primarily the *Diamond Sutra*.[11] In this section, we will begin by analyzing the two verses by Shen-xiu and Hui-neng, to see how the two schools differ philosophically.

Two verses

Shen-xiu's verse says:

> The body is the tree of enlightenment [the Bodhi tree][12]
> The mind is like a clear mirror-stand.
> Polish it diligently time and again,
> Not letting it gather dust.[13]

Hui-neng's verse says,[14]

> Enlightenment [Bodhi] originally has no tree,
> And a clear mirror is not a stand.
> Originally there's not a single thing –
> Where can dust be attracted?[15]

In the verse of Shen-xiu, the assumption is that we have an originally pure mind, but it is being constantly defiled by greed, anger, and confusion (the so-called "Three Poisons" of the mind). Therefore, we need to keep a vigilant watch over our mind, to get rid of all defilements. The mind mentioned in this verse seems to be an inactive entity, which can "gather dust" from time to time. As Whalen Lai notes: "The mind as mirror is passive, a receptacle of external data. It is vulnerable to the distortion by defilements (dust)."[16] The real agent seems to be our "self" – the one doing the monitoring, cleansing, and polishing. There is thus a duality between the inborn pure mind and the watchful mind. Furthermore, the initial purity of our mind cannot be preserved without the assiduous effort of the watchful mind. It is therefore a tireless process to attain enlightenment. Nirvana is the end result of one's vigilance: if one manages to wipe away all dust, *eventually* one will get there. But the verse does not mention that an obtainable goal is in sight. This verse supports the Southern School's accusation that the Northern School teaches *gradual* enlightenment.

In Hui-neng's verse, on the other hand, there is no duality between the inborn mind and the active mind or between purity and defilement.

There was not even a "One" to begin with – there was originally *nothing*. The motto "Originally there's not a single thing" became a fundamental precept of the Chan School.[17] Hui-neng's verse points out Shen-xiu's mistake in treating Mind as a substance or an entity that needs to be preserved and cleaned all the time. Hui-neng's teaching is that there was no Mind, no thing. Since there was no entity, no substance, there can be no defilement. The mind is originally clean and pure and it remains clean and pure at all times.[18] There is no need to be troubled by worldly trivialities, since nothing could possibly obstruct the mind. Once one can see this point, one *immediately* gains enlightenment. "Enlightenment is only the mind (lamp) allowed to shine forth by itself (light). The mind is none other than its own enlightenment."[19] This realization is the foundation for the Southern Chan's method of immediate enlightenment. Instead of using the metaphor of a mirror-stand gathering dust, Hui-neng often uses the metaphor of the sun's being covered by clouds. If our mind is like the mirror-stand which has gathered dust, then it is no longer clean and pure. If, on the other hand, it is like the sun temporarily covered by clouds, then even if we don't see it, it is still brilliant and clear. Clouds do not change the brilliant nature of the sun; false views and erroneous habits do not alter the purity of the mind either.

Another subtle criticism Hui-neng's verse makes of Shen-xiu is that in the latter's depiction there is an element of conscious effort to attain something in the latter's depiction.[20] Shen-xiu's verse speaks of constantly wiping away dust to preserve the mind's purity, but in Hui-neng's view, this is to *fixate* on purity. He says: "If you arouse the mind to fixate on purity, you create the delusion of purity."[21] Hui-neng says of the Buddha: "it is because the notion of attaining something does not occur that he realizes enlightenment."[22] If one consciously engages in the task of cleansing, polishing, and achieving, then one has already violated the first teaching of the Buddha: do not grasp, do not fixate. Therefore, Hui-neng's verse is meant to point out how Shen-xiu does not understand the true spirit of Buddhism.

The underlying theoretical differences between these two verses could be traced back to the two main texts: the *Lankavatara Sutra* adhered to by the Northern School and the *Diamond Sutra* taught by the Southern School. What are the differences in the two texts' teachings? According to Wing-tsit Chan's summary, the emphasis of the *Lankavatara Sutra* is Ultimate Reality, while the focus of the *Diamond Sutra* is the Mind.[23] However, for the *Lankavatara Sutra*, the Mind *is* Ultimate Reality. A more fitting description is to say that the *Lankavatara Sutra* has a metaphysical interest in Mind as Ultimate Reality, while the *Diamond*

Sutra has primarily an ethical concern with individual minds as the foundation for self-realization.

Mind-Only

The *Lankavatara Sutra* expounds the theme of "Mind-Only."[24] The *Mind* (with a capital letter) is not the same as *minds* of sentient beings. This Mind is called "the Pure Mind" or "the One Mind." An ordinary person's mind is called "a defiled mind," which is many steps away from the One Pure Mind. In Robert Zeuschner's explanation, "the so-called defiled mind is the activity of mind which conceptualizes, judges, distinguishes subject from object, hates, craves, and constructs the conceptual framework within which we categorize our perceptions and experiences."[25] If this interpretation is correct, then the defiled mind is simply humans' (as well as other sentient beings') cognitive activities, through which the world-as-we-know-it comes into existence. Only the Pure Mind has the status of being reality-as-such, being the *True Thusness*. There are thus two senses of "mind": the one metaphysical, pure, and ultimate; the other experiential, defiled, and phenomenal. The *Lankavatara Sutra*'s teaching of the two senses of "mind" is in agreement with the general theme in Mahayana Buddhism. The *Treatise on the Awakening of Faith in the Mahayana*, for example, presents the two aspects of "mind" as follows: "One is the aspect of Mind in terms of the Absolute (Suchness), and the other is the aspect of Mind in terms of phenomena (birth and death). Each of these two aspects embraces all states of existence."[26] Relying on these teachings, Shen-xiu also talks about the two functions of mind this way: "The first is the pure mind. The second is the defiled mind. . . . From the very beginning, both exist."[27] The theory of "Two Minds" in the Northern Chan School is thus established.

The *Lankavatara Sutra*'s "Mind-Only" thesis is also a reassertion of the anti-realist tenet of Buddhism in general. In the *Sutra*, it is constantly repeated that only Mind is real; the external world does not exist outside of Mind. In its worldview, there is no dualism between Mind and the world. What the *Lankavatara Sutra* means by non-duality is that all things are reflections of Mind, and thus "all things have no reality." It says: "When it is recognized that the visible world is no more than Mind itself, external objects cease to be realities, and there is nothing but what is discriminated by the mind and perceived [as external]."[28] As we have seen in the Consciousness-Only School and the Hua-yan School, a correlated thesis of Mind-Only is that of anti-realism. In the *Lankavatara Sutra*, the Buddha denies that he has fallen "into a realistic view by upholding the noble doctrine of self-existing reality."[29] Reality does not exist without Mind, and what we take to be external objects are in reality *not* external to us.

According to the *Lankavatara Sutra*, furthermore, to say that all things are reflections of Mind does not give credence to the existence of things, because these "reflections" were brought about by the discrimination of deluded individual minds. The *Lankavatara Sutra* says: "People grasping their own shadows of discrimination uphold the discrimination of dharma and [no-dharma] and, failing to carry out the abandonment of the dualism, they go on discriminating and never attain tranquility."[30] The causal process between discrimination and external things, as depicted in the *Lankavatara Sutra*, is very similar to the one given by the Consciousness-Only School. At the basis is the Alaya consciousness, from which "the whole psychic system evolves mutually conditioning."[31]

Various forms of consciousness discriminate shapes and sounds, etc., thereby producing various characteristics and objects. The cessation of all consciousnesses, on the other hand, is the attainment of "noble wisdom" or the enlightenment itself. It is only "when the [consciousness] which is caused by discrimination ceases," that one can "enter into Nirvana."[32] "By Nirvana . . . is meant the looking into the abode of reality as it really is in itself."[33] This realization can only be obtained through the transformation of one's consciousness into *wisdom*.

In contrast to the *Lankavatara Sutra*'s teaching of Oneness, the *Diamond Sutra*'s teaching seems to be about "nothingness." However, it also rejects all conceptual distinctions such as "One" and "many" or "being" and "non-being." The *Diamond Sutra*'s basic doctrine is that one should not adhere to anything, including the very notion of "nothingness." The *Sutra* says: "The Tathagata[34] teaches that all ideas are no-ideas, and again that all beings are no-beings."[35] In the text, the Buddha advises people to rid themselves of ideas of *dharma* and *no-dharma*. He says, "Why? Because if . . . they cherish the idea of a dharma, they are attached to an ego, a person, a being, or a soul. . . . If they cherish the idea of a no-dharma, they are attached to an ego, a person, a being, or a soul. Therefore, do not cherish the idea of a dharma, nor that of a no-dharma."[36] From these quotes we can see where Hui-neng's assertion "there was originally nothing" comes from.

In summary, both the Northern and the Southern Schools can be grouped under the general "Mind-Only" school, but they have different interpretations of "Mind-Only." The Northern Chan's Mind-Only thesis is close to the "Consciousness-Only" thesis of the Consciousness-

Only School and the "Mind-Only" thesis of the Hua-yan School: The world is unreal; external objects are productions of transforming consciousnesses or deluded minds. Thus, the world can be ontologically reduced to the Mind. The Southern Chan places less emphasis on the unreality of our world. Hui-neng's interpretation of "Mind-Only" is that "all truths are in our own minds."[37] In other words, it is not that the whole world exists only in our minds, but that if we see our minds' pure essence, then we see all the truths about the world. By the same token, once we see that the mind and the world are identical, we will see that the understanding of truths about the world leads to knowledge of the mind. The world thus becomes an epistemic route to our knowledge of the ultimate truth of the mind. The mind–world identity becomes an epistemic claim, rather than a claim of the ontological reduction of the world to the mind.

Beholding the mind vs. seeing one's nature

Following the *Lankavatara Sutra*, Shen-xiu's teaching focuses on "beholding the mind"; "beholding purity."[38] To "behold" means to watch; in this case, it is to watch with the mind's eye during solitary meditation. Mind and purity are one and the same: it is also called the "Pure Mind." Shen-xiu says: "Of the myriad dharmas, mind is the most basic. All the various dharmas are simply the products of the mind. If one can comprehend the mind, then the myriad practices will all be accomplished."[39] By keeping the original Mind and original purity in view, one can spot all sorts of defilements. One thus needs to be particularly diligent in extirpating attachments and obscurations that defile the mind. According to Robert Zeuschner, this purifying process begins with controlling "the activities of the senses," since defilements are rooted in sense perceptions.[40] For example, our taste buds get more sophisticated as we mature and our desire increases with our more discriminatory senses. As a result, we lose the infant's simple enjoyment of food. Our mind makes further discrimination which sometimes eludes the senses. For instance, our eyes may not be able to detect any difference between natural and artificial diamonds. But because we call the former "real" diamond and the latter "fake", we crave one but not the other. These discriminations are the root of our cravings and discontents. When the defiled mind is cleansed of all obscurations that come from conception and perception, one *beholds* purity.

Hui-neng takes the *Diamond Sutra* to be about "seeing one's essential nature." In his *Commentary on the Diamond Sutra*, he says: "It was just because people of the world do not see their essential nature that the teaching of seeing essential nature was established."[41] There are at least two differences between Hui-neng's "seeing essential nature" and Shen-xiu's "beholding the mind." First, "to see" (*jian*) depicts a more alert mental state than "to behold" (*guan*) does: the former implies comprehension and awareness; the latter could refer to an act of passive watching or looking.[42] Second, "nature" has the connotation of "essence" that the term "mind" does not. As Suzuki puts it: "[Nature] means something without which no existence is possible, or thinkable as such."[43] In other words, we could never lose our nature, but we could someday lose our mind. Hui-neng does not give up the use of the term "mind"; rather, he interprets "mind" in the way "nature" is normally understood. For example, he explains the view of mind in the *Diamond Sutra* this way: "Clear, free, empty, and silent, perception and action equally enlightened, mirrorlike awareness unobstructed – this is truly the liberated Buddha-nature."[44] This shows that the clear, free mind is simply the inherent Buddha-nature itself. Since it is our individual minds that sustain Buddha-nature, Hui-neng's interest is in the minds of sentient beings, not in some abstract *Mind*. Neither in the *Diamond Sutra*, nor in Hui-neng's *Platform Sutra*, was there strong emphasis on the defiled mind. Our minds are not just *originally* clean and pure; they are *intrinsically* clean and pure. That is to say, our pure minds are never lost within us; their essential nature *is* forever clean and pure. By shifting attention from "mind" to "nature," or by identifying "pure mind" with "essential nature," Hui-neng establishes a new school of Chan. The Southern Chan thus separates itself from the Northern Chan in its rejection of the "two minds" theory. Instead, it focuses on the essential Buddha-nature and the intrinsic pure mind, with which everyone is endowed at the root of his existence. Furthermore, our essential nature is Buddha-nature, which enables us to become Buddhas ourselves. Hui-neng clearly states: "All beings are originally themselves Buddhas."[45] If so, then there is no unbridgeable gap between the Buddha and us: all we need to do is to see *this*. If we can see that we ourselves are Buddhas, then we would understand that there is no need to seek teachings from sutras or masters. We should be our own teachers.

Meditation

The *Lankavatara Sutra* advocates meditation (the original meaning of the word *chan*) as the method for ceasing discrimination and entering nirvana. According to the Buddha's teaching in the *Lankavatara Sutra*, there are four kinds of meditation: (1) meditation as practiced by the ignorant; (2) meditation as devoted to the examination of meaning; (3) meditation with True Thusness (*Tathata*[46]); and (4) meditation with all beings as its objects. The first kind of meditation is done by beginners, who, after recognizing the unreality of worldly things, aim for the cessation of thought. They examine each of their thoughts, casting them away until they reach the mental state where there is no thought. The second kind of meditation is performed by those who have gone beyond the first level and proceeded to the investigation of the true meaning of Reality. These people have a deeper understanding of the egolessness of things. The third kind of meditation enables one to eliminate all discrimination. It is accomplished by people who have entered nirvana. The final kind of meditation is the pure form performed by the Tathagata. In this meditative mode, one contemplates all sentient beings and devotes oneself to the relief of their suffering.[47]

The Northern School's teaching of gradual enlightenment could be seen as a natural outcome of its teaching of the purity of the Mind and its practice of meditation. Since ordinary people's minds are all defiled, they need to sit in meditation when they examine their thoughts one by one and cast away the erroneous ones. The more that dust is wiped away, the cleaner the mirror becomes; the more that erroneous thoughts are eradicated, the purer the mind gets to be. This process requires accumulated efforts, and thus it is "gradual."[48] When one engages in meditation, one needs to shun the outside world and confine oneself in a quiet solitude. In the *Lankavatara Sutra,* the Buddha says to his disciple, "This discrimination must be discarded by you, and having discarded this, you should declare the truth of solitude."[49] The method of solitary "sitting meditation" seems to be the original teaching of the Chan School as expounded in the *Lankavatara Sutra.*[50] Only through this method can one reach the state of tranquility. "By tranquility is meant oneness, and oneness gives birth to the highest [concentration], which is gained by entering into the womb of Tathagatahood, which is the realm of noble wisdom realized in one's inmost self."[51] In other words, the *Lankavatara Sutra* advocates "a quietistic contemplation of one's self-nature or self-being."[52] This becomes the basis for the practice of the Northern Chan.

Hui-neng often criticizes the method of "sitting meditation" that characterizes the Northern Chan. He says: "Stopping the mind and contemplating quietude is pathological; it is not *chan*. Sitting all the time constricts the body – how does it help toward truth?"[53] He explicitly criticizes followers of Shen-xiu this way: "There are also deluded people who sit quietly with empty minds, not thinking of anything whatsoever, and claim this is greatness. This sort of person is not worth talking to, because theirs is a wrong view."⁵⁴ To Hui-neng, *chan* or meditation is not about sitting in quietude and emptying one's mind. It is rather the practice of not letting the mind get "aroused over any good or bad objects in the external world"; it is seeing "the immutability of your own essential nature inwardly."⁵⁵ Such a practice does not require solitude or isolation from worldly affairs. It can be accomplished at any time in doing anything. At any moment of one's daily life, once one sees the importance of a pure mind and drops all trivial concerns, one gains sudden enlightenment. Whenever one can understand that one's true nature is essentially clean and pure, one stops fighting against oneself and enters nirvana instantaneously. In Suzuki's explanation, the *chan* or meditation that Hui-neng preaches "is not quietism, nor is it tranquillization; it is rather acting, moving, performing deeds, seeing, hearing, thinking, remembering." In fact, this kind of meditation "is attained where there is, so to speak, no [meditation] practiced."⁵⁶

Enlightenment and self-realization

Both the Northern School and the Southern School preach "self-realization." They call nirvana "the realm of self-realization." Self-realization is possible because one is endowed with the pure self-nature. If one can rediscover this innate pure nature, then one can realize oneself. We have seen that the Northern Chan emphasizes self-purification, which is an accumulated effort. Hence, enlightenment has to be a gradual process.⁵⁷ For the Southern Chan, self-realization requires one to employ inborn wisdom. Hui-neng says: "When you are not obstructed by the characters of things, that is called realization."⁵⁸ Using the metaphor of mining gold in the mountain, Hui-neng says:

> The body is like the world, personal self is like the mountain, afflictions are like the ore, Buddha-nature is like the gold, wisdom is like the master craftsman, intensity of diligence is like digging. In the world of the body is the mountain of personal self; in the mountain of personal self is the ore of affliction; in the ore of affliction is the jewel of Buddha-nature. Within the jewel of Buddha-nature is the master craftsman of wisdom.⁵⁹

This quote reveals a process of going inward into one's mind, to uncover one's innately pure nature. In another context, Hui-neng also says: "Those who aspire to enlightenment should see all beings as having Buddha-nature, should see all beings as inherently endowed with uncontaminated all-knowledge."[60] Sometimes our inborn wisdom is also described as our "teacher." Hui-neng says: "There is a teacher within one's own mind that understands spontaneously."[61] Because all we need to do is to see our own mind, our own nature, to find our own teacher and to realize our own Buddhahood, the enlightenment process is immediate, sudden, and spontaneous.

Huang Bo makes it even more clear that enlightenment (or awakening) is not something to be acquired; it is innate to us. He says, "Bodhi [Awakening, Enlightenment] is not a state. The Buddha did not attain to it. Sentient beings do not lack it. It cannot be reached with the body nor sought with the mind. All sentient beings ARE ALREADY of one form with Bodhi."[62] According to Huang Bo, since Buddhahood is our essential nature, it is within us at all times. He says: "Your true nature is something never lost to you even in moments of delusion, not is it gained at the moment of Enlightenment."[63] If that is the case, then there is no "effort" required. Huang Bo's student Lin Ji also says:

> Followers of the Way, the Dharma [True Teaching] of the Buddhas calls for no special undertakings. Just act ordinary, without trying to do anything particular. Move your bowels, piss, get dressed, eat your rice, and if you get tired, then lie down. Fools may laugh at me, but wise men will know what I mean.[64]

This remark is close in spirit to Zhuangzi's famous motto: "*Dao* lies in excrement and urine." The Southern Chan distinguishes itself from the Northern Chan in its emphasis on being at ease, taking it naturally. In this respect, it is more similar to the attitude of early Daoists; in particular, to that of Zhuangzi. In contrast, we could perhaps say that the Northern Chan's watchful diligent examination of one's mind is closer to the spirit of Confucianism.

The Southern Chan's teaching of "immediate" or "sudden" enlightenment is not just aimed at refuting the Northern Chan's teaching of "gradual enlightenment"; it is also directed against the traditional Indian Buddhist teaching of self-cultivation through many lives. As Lin Ji says, "You followers of the Way fail to realize that this journey to enlightenment that takes three [immeasurably long periods of time] to accomplish is meaningless."[65] Enlightenment does not take any measurement of time; what counts is only the present moment. "Everything I say to you is for the moment only, medicine to cure the disease."[66] According to Hui-neng, what it takes is only a moment of thought. He says: "When your own nature produces a single thought of good, it can achieve the ending of countless evils, all the way to unsurpassed enlight-enment."[67] One good thought can wipe out all past evil deeds; one bad deed can also stamp out all past good deeds. From thought to thought, one can either get into nirvana or quit nirvana. Therefore, the nirvana as the Southern Chan teaches it is not some realm other than this world. It is a mental state in which one is free from obsession and attachment. One is still in this world, yet one's thought transcends the world. This is nirvana. At the same time, reaching nirvana does not guarantee eternal bliss. The next moment, one could be plagued by negative thoughts and emotions again and be brought back to the mundane world. Human drama inevitably sets in and one is constantly afflicted with disappoint-ment, jealousy, despair, resentment, disquietude, and anguish. From nirvana to living hell, it all depends on one's single thought. This is the essential teaching of Southern Chan's sudden enlightenment.

Summary of theoretical differences between the two schools

In conclusion, we can say that the Northern Chan holds a thesis about the world that is very similar to those of the Consciousness-Only School and the Hua-yan School: the world is not real. Along with the Hua-yan School, the Northern Chan upholds the view that only Mind is real. Furthermore, the Northern Chan teaches solitary meditation as the means for entering nirvana. The Southern Chan, in comparison, holds a view closer to that of the Tian-tai School.[68] The world we live in is the only world there is. To seek nirvana, one does not need to shun the world, cease thought, and regard all things as illusions. Secondly, the Northern Chan's theory of mind is based on the "Pure Mind/defiled mind" division that is prevalent in Mahayana Buddhism. Its method of purifi-cation is closer to the Confucian spirit of daily self-examination. By contrast, the Southern Chan's notion of mind is closer to the Daoist conception. As Whalen Lai puts it: "The Southern [Chan] school seems to follow more faithfully the notion of mind discovered by [Zhuangzi]: an innately pure, vacuous, radiant mind without any defilements, shin-ing forth like the light from a candle."[69] The method advocated by the Southern Chan is also in the spirit of Daoism: appreciate *Dao* in the trivialities of daily affairs. Do not strive to "attain" since *Dao* is simply in everything we do.

In the following sections, we shall use the Southern Chan as our representative of the Chan School, to further analyze Chan's views on reality, on mind and nature, on self-knowledge and language.

Metaphysics: Chan's View on Reality

The Chan School does not posit an ontologically independent realm separate from this world. Hui-neng states clearly: "Buddhism is in the world. It is not realized apart from the world. Seeking enlightenment apart from the world, is like looking for horns on a hare."[70] When asked about the *Nirvana Sutra*'s teaching of "quiescent extinction," Hui-neng accused the student of resorting to "heretical, perverted views of nihilism and externalism."[71] In his explication, nirvana is not "the cessation of the cycle of life and death" taken literally. "Extinction of life and death" means "the extinction of grasping and rejecting." In a nutshell, Hui-neng's view of reality is that there is only one reality – our world.

Hui-neng tries to explain away the separation of the two realms – one ultimate; the other worldly – in many Buddhist texts. For instance, he says that when the *Diamond Sutra* discusses an enlightened person leaving behind the mundane world of life and death and "never returning," it does not mean that he or she is thus entering a different world. It is simply that such people have abandoned their desires. "They certainly do not take on life in the realm of desire, so they are referred to as not coming back; yet in reality there is no coming, so they are also called non-returners."[72] He also denies that terminology such as "the other shore," "the Pure Land," or "True Thusness" designates a separate ontological realm. Hui-neng says: "When the mind is confused, it is 'this shore.' When the mind is enlightened, it is 'the other shore.' When the mind is distorted, it is 'this shore.' When the mind is sound, it is 'the other shore'."[73] Hui-neng describes the "pure land," the land inhabited by the Buddha, as simply "the emergence of the pure mind."[74] The pure land was traditionally taken to be a transcendent realm, where those who are free from the cycle of life and death could enter and reside forever. But under Hui-neng's interpretation, it is nothing but the mental state of purity. The "True Thusness," the Ultimate Reality that Budd-hists seek to enter, to Hui-neng, is simply a state of mind. He explains, "Reality does not change, suchness does not differ, when the mind does not change or differ in any situation, that is called reality as such."[75] Therefore, our goal is not to exit this world of life and death, but to let our minds be liberated from obsessions about life and death.

Even where the *Diamond Sutra* appears to be denying the realness of our world, Hui-neng turns the statement into a discourse on the various states of our mind. The *Diamond Sutra* says: "All created things[76] are like dreams, illusions, bubbles, shadows; like dew, and like lightning.

They should be viewed this way." Hui-neng's commentary explains: "The dreams are bodies astray, the illusions are wandering thoughts, the bubbles are afflictions, the shadows are the barriers created by past actions. These are called created things. As for uncreated truth, it is reality, apart from labels and appearances."[77] In other words, it is not that external objects are mere illusions or dreams of the mind; it is rather that our mental conceptions and afflictions are illusions or dreams of the mind. Instead of taking the denial of the existence of worldly things literally, Hui-neng interprets the denial as a metaphorical explanation of the nature of our mental activities.

In this respect, the Chan School's notion of nirvana is very similar to that of the Tian-tai School. To enter nirvana does not mean that we must die and never re-enter the cycle of life and death. The separation between nirvana and the cycle of life and death becomes merely metaphorical: when one can see the true nature of things and stop obsessing about them, one is already in the realm of nirvana. Therefore, in one instant of thought, one can immediately enter nirvana and thereby quit the mundane world.

However, to say that there is no other realm that is the *true* Reality, is not to say that therefore this reality that we are familiar with is real or that we should take things as they appear to be. To Hui-neng, our world is filled with falsehoods that we humans have created, even if it is the *only* world in which we live and die. He says, "When you understand reality is falsehood, you understand that falsehood is reality – reality and falsehood both disappear, and there is nothing else."[78] Discriminations and evaluations, artificially introduced by humans, necessarily distort the true nature of things. If we recognize this fact, then we should refrain from making judgments with various terms of opposites: "beautiful" and "ugly"; "good" and "bad"; "rich" and "poor"; "knowledgeability" and "ignorance"; "just" and "unjust." The Chan School rejects social conventions and societal discriminations. To call Chan's view "realism" can only be done as a meta-philosophy; i.e., a second-level description of its view. It itself would not have characterized its own philosophy as "realism." The very antinomy between the School of Being and the School of Emptiness, according to the Chan School, is founded on an invalid dichotomy between "existence" and "non-existence." Hui-neng says, "You may want to say it is real, yet no defining characteristics can be found; you may want to say it is unreal, yet it functions without interruption. Therefore it cannot be said not to exist, yet cannot be said to exist."[79] Only when we completely forget the distinction between being and non-being, real and unreal, can we have true understanding of Chan's view on reality.

Chan's View on Mind and Nature[80]

A famous Chan motto is: "This mind is the Buddha."[81] What could this possibly mean? In the Buddhist tradition, the term "Buddha" could designate the Ultimate Reality itself; it could also designate the historical Buddha. But in this quote, it is used in neither of these two senses. The term "Buddha" in this context should be taken to be a general term designating the property of being ultimately pure, profoundly wise, immensely compassionate; it is a synonym for "Buddhahood." Since "the Buddha" in this context refers not to a specific person, but to a specific property, the question posed by students of Chan to their masters was often: "What is the Buddha?" and not "Who is the Buddha?" This Buddhahood is the "Buddha-enabling" property; it is what makes one's becoming a Buddha possible. The Chan School teaches that everyone is born with inherent Buddhahood. As a Chan master Huang Bo explains, "The One Mind alone is the Buddha, and there is no distinction between the Buddha and sentient things."[82] Since possessing the property of *Buddha* makes one a Buddha oneself, a second meaning of the term "Buddha" is "one with inborn Buddhahood."

In contrast to Mencius' advocating the innate goodness of human nature, the Chan School does not posit "goodness" in human nature. According to Hui-neng, the essential Buddha-nature is neither good nor bad, since the distinction between good and bad is already a human discrimination. Hence, calling human nature "good" would fall onto the level of duality and relativity. Furthermore, Buddha-nature for the Chan School is not merely a potential, as "human nature" is for Mencius. It is rather an actuality. Everyone is already born a Buddha, but through time and mental development in the experiential world, this original state is not manifest in ordinary people. Therefore, as one gets closer to one's intrinsic nature, one gets closer to being a Buddha oneself. Enlightenment comes through an internal retrieval of the original state of one's mind and one's nature. This is the essence of Chan's teaching.

As we have explained, the Southern Chan is not as interested in the metaphysical *Mind* as it is in individual *minds*. It seldom deals with the Pure Mind as Reality-as-such. There are, however, two different conceptions of the individual mind. One is the inborn "original mind"; the other is the post-development, experiential mind that is sometimes called "the conditioned mind." Even though there are these two conceptions of individual mind, the Southern Chan rejects the two-minds theory of the Northern Chan. It insists that the original mind is not different from the conditioned mind, since we only have one mind, not two. But it also presents the two minds as "not one." How do we understand this "not one; not two" relation between the original mind and the conditioned mind?

What characterizes the conditioned mind is "discrimination." Suzuki explains that "By 'discrimination' . . . is meant analytical knowledge, the relative and discursive understanding which we use in our everyday thinking."[83] The conditioned mind begins with one's various contacts with the *outside* world after one is born. One's eyes perceive different shapes and colors; one's ears perceive different sounds and tones. All these sensory data are categorized through the discriminatory capabilities of sense organs. Names are introduced; concepts are formed. Social conventions begin to take shape and value systems get instigated in the societal conceptual scheme. We are thus biologically and socially *conditioned*. Being conditioned to see differences in qualities and in values, we are deprived of our original, nondiscriminatory mind. The original mind and the conditioned mind are "not one; not two," because there is only one mind, but it is a mind being developed at different stages. Once our mind starts to be discriminatory, it is no longer the original mind.

However, to retrieve the original pure mind, we do not need to go back to the pre-cognitive infant mind. A pure mind can be built on the post-developmental conditioned mind if we find the right way – the right view. This right view is called the "noble wisdom," which simply consists of seeing that everyone and everything has essentially the same Buddha-nature. Differences are appearances only; in essence everything is the same. From seeing equality in all, we thus re-establish a nondiscriminatory mind. This nondiscriminatory mind is not the same as an infant's naive inability to discriminate. It is rather a sophisticated, fully evolved Buddha mind. Because the Chan School does not shun the experiential world, it does not advocate the elimination of all perceptions, which are indispensable in our daily interactions with the world. What it preaches as "nondiscrimination" is rather a mental attitude at a different level – not at the epistemic level but at an ethical level. Hui-neng says: "If you see everyone's bad and good but do not grasp or reject any of it, and do not become affected by it, your mind is like space."[84] "Fixation on objects the moment before was affliction; detachment from objects the moment after is enlightenment."[85] These sayings show that enlightenment comes when one understands that despite apparent differences in objects, all things should be assigned equal value and be given equal treatment.

The Chan School emphatically upholds the universality of Buddha-hood. Buddha-nature is inherent in everyone. There are no degrees or variations of Buddha-nature. Hui-neng says: "You should know that the Buddha-nature is fundamentally no different in ignorant people and in wise people. It is just because of difference in confusion and enlightenment that there is ignorance and wisdom."[86] Hui-neng does not deny that people have different "faculties," and that those with small faculties have a harder time getting enlightened. They cannot awaken to the Truth on their own because "the barriers of their false views are heavy and the roots of their passions are deep."[87] But this barrier is not insurmountable. These people need the right teachers to enlighten them. In a sense the teacher's role would be similar to the role of a midwife: he does not give or add anything to the recipient; he merely aids the recipient in the latter's self-realization.

Hui-neng's famous question "where is Buddha?" is grounded on his assertion that the Buddha is in everyone's mind. He says, "Our minds inherently have Buddha in them; your own inner Buddha is the real Buddha. If there were no Buddha-mind, where would we look for the real Buddha?"[88] He also says, "If you say you take refuge in Buddha, where is Buddha? If you do not see Buddha, where can you take refuge?"[89] Instead of seeking salvation from a Supreme Being from the outside, we need to seek "self-refuge." The way to seek refuge in one's self is simply to be moral and wise – to exemplify Buddhahood. "If you rectify your mind, it will always produce wisdom. Observe your own mind, stop evil, and do good; this is opening the knowledge and wisdom of Buddhahood for yourself."[90] The teaching of "stopping all evil and doing all good" may seem so simple that even a three-year-old could understand, but to practice it faithfully would be hard even for a seventy-year-old who has spent all his or her life following this teaching. In this respect, becoming a Buddha is easier said than done. Ordinary people are simply Buddhas not yet enlightened, while Buddhas are simply enlightened ordinary people.[91]

In its new definition of "Buddha," Chan Buddhism turns against the religious spirit of traditional Buddhism. A later Chan master, Lin Ji (Lin Chi), further denounces the supremacy of the historical Buddha. He criticizes other Buddhists in their promoting the Buddha as the "ultimate goal." He asked, if that Buddha was the ultimate goal, then "where is the Buddha now?" Instead of portraying the Buddha's departure from this world as a temporary exit (as the Hua-yan school does), Lin Ji says that the historical Buddha died too, and "from this we know clearly that he was no different from us in the realm of birth and death."[92] In Lin Ji's Chan, there is no Supreme Being; we are the ultimate beings ourselves. He asks:

When students today fail to make progress, where's the fault? The fault lies in the fact that they don't have faith in themselves! If you don't have faith in yourself, then you'll be forever in a hurry trying to keep up with everything around you, you'll be twisted and turned by whatever environment you're in and you can never move freely. But if you can just stop this mind that goes rushing around moment by moment looking for something, then you'll be no different from the patriarchs and the Buddhas.[93]

From the transmission of these teachings, Chan became very much a self-help practice and a moralistic philosophy.

As we have explained, the teaching of Chan is basically all about "seeing one's nature." This teaching can be called "the principle of realizing Buddhahood by seeing essential nature." Why is seeing one's nature so important? If enlightenment only requires one to see one's nature, then it does not seem unobtainable. In practice, however, seeing one's essential nature is not that easy. This principle obliges us to deny our personal identity, to embrace the principle of impartiality, to eliminate any distinction between others and us: love and hate; good and evil. To see our own essential nature, we must also see that everyone, and everything else, shares this nature with us. In other words, even inanimate things such as grass and stone are Buddhas – noble, supreme, inexhaustibly vast, and yet fundamentally empty. If we can truly adopt this attitude in treating everyone and every object, then according to the Chan School, we have realized Buddhahood.

Chan's ethical teaching is built on knowledge and wisdom – as long as we truly *see* that we are in essence and by nature Buddhas, we can immediately be morally transformed. It thus denies the gap between knowledge and action; all moral ills are attributed to lack of knowledge, to ignorance. It is a most fondly repeated story in the Chan tradition that once a butcher drops his butcher's knife, he is immediately turned into a Buddha. But in our real life experience, it is most often the case that our realization is momentary, while our old habits are hard to kick. After momentary awakening, we can easily slip back to our old way of thinking and acting. Suppose we have understood that those who harbor hostile feelings toward us are people who are worthy of our compassion, and we have made a resolution to forgive them. The minute we are directly insulted by someone, our rage surges and we completely forget our resolution. Suppose we have grasped the truth that external distinctions such as wealth and fame are insignificant, and we have vowed to pay attention only to the purity of our mind. As soon as we lose money or fail to get the promotion we think we deserve, we become so agitated that we allow our mind to lose its tranquility. Our habit-energy can be so ingrained in us that a momentary awareness of our Buddha-nature cannot remove all the negative forms of habit-energy. The knowledge that we have pure Buddha-nature has to become a deeply entrenched "wisdom" in order for us really to alter our past habit-energy.

A method emphasized by Chan masters to preserve our pure, unperturbed mind is to focus on the present. Having a present-awareness can help us weed out unpleasant regrets about the past or disquieting concerns about the future. We can thereby enjoy the present moment more. A story was told about a man who, escaping from a tiger, slipped over a cliff and clung to a vine. He noticed that there was another tiger at the bottom waiting to devour him, and yet he could not climb up since the first tiger was still there. Worse still, there were two mice, one white, the other black (signifying day and night), gnawing on the vine that kept him suspended between two ill fates. At that moment, the man noticed a juicy strawberry on the side of the cliff and decided to enjoy it.[94] This story tells us that what is past is past and what is going to come will come; hence, we should try to enjoy our present moment and be mindful of whatever experience we currently have. If we can truly enjoy the present and not let the past or the future disturb our peace of mind, then we are in nirvana.

A curious phenomenon in the history of the Chinese Chan School is that different Chan masters often each claimed to have seen the true mind, while accusing one another of failing to see it. The dispute between the Northern School and the Southern School is a salient example. The disagreements did not cease with the flourishing of the Southern Chan. Even Lin Ji failed to understand what his teacher Huang Bo tried to convey.[95] If everyone has the same one mind, which everyone should be able to see immediately, then the lack of mutual understanding and agreement among those who have seen the true mind is difficult to explain. Either there is no "one same mind," or it is simply impossible to convey to another person what one sees and knows. The Chan School generally embraces the second answer. Here we turn to its view on the possibility of knowledge and the limitations of language.

Chan's View on Knowledge and Language

The Chan School does not refute the possibility of knowledge, but it advocates a different form of knowledge. The proper objects of knowledge are not external things, but one's own mind. In Chan's theory of knowledge, knowledge about the external world and knowledge about other minds can only be mediated through knowledge about one's own mind. Because one knows one's mind, one thereby knows (i) other minds, since everyone shares the same mind; (ii) the external world, since every object in the world is produced by the mind's conceptualization. Under this epistemology, the object of knowledge is the subject's own mind. Therefore, the distinction between subject and object is eliminated. Furthermore, since one does not need an external medium in order to know one's own mind, descriptions and names become useless in this context. The Chan School clearly teaches that one has direct access to one's mind. This self-knowledge is different from the self-knowledge discussed in contemporary philosophy of mind, because what one directly knows in Chan's teaching is not one's thought, but one's mind in a state of "no-thought." It is not just knowledge about one's mind, but also knowledge about one's *original* mind.

In the *Platform Sutra*, Hong-ren is recorded as saying that direct awareness of one's original mind and nature does not require any thought. "People who have seen essential nature should see it the moment it is mentioned."[96] Suzuki interprets this form of knowledge as "intuitive knowledge."[97] He says:

> [this form of intuition] is not derivative but primitive; not inferential, not rationalistic, nor mediational, but direct, immediate; not analytical but synthetic; not cognitive, but symbolical; not intending but merely expressive; not abstract, but concrete; not processional, not purposive, but factual and ultimate, final and irreducible; not eternally receding, but infinitely inclusive; etc.[98]

These descriptions may not help us understand what kind of knowledge it is, but they do suggest that Chan's epistemology is not about "knowledge" in the ordinary sense. It does not rely on language or conception. It cannot be taught or studied. When one achieves knowledge of one's original mind, one does not gain any information ; one is simply "transformed." In Chan's terminology, one is immediately at one with the reality-as-such. This kind of experiential knowledge has to be personal and private. As a common Chan saying puts it: "It is just like someone drinking water: only he himself would know how cold or hot the water is."

Following the path of early Daoism and Buddhism, the Chan School also rejects the validity of language in its role of reference and description. The Chan School teaches that names and words are merely "temporary setups."[99] Reality in itself has no sign or label. Hui-neng says: "All verbal and literary expressions are like labels, like pointing fingers. Fingers and pointers mean shadows and echoes. You obtain a commodity by its label, and you see the moon by way of the pointing finger –

the moon is not the finger, the label is not the thing itself."[100] In other words, we may use our names and conceptions to depict reality, just as we could use the finger to point at the moon. But we should not mistake our conceptual descriptions of the world for reality-as-it-is, just as we should not think that the finger has anything to do with the moon. The Chan School separates language and the world, and denies that language serves a truth-preserving function of the real aspect of the world.

A fundamental deficiency Chan masters find in language is that it is based on "discrimination." Our concepts mark differences in categories of things; hence, we inescapably see things as different when we use language. Since the Chan School holds the view that everything is the same in their essence (nature), it would naturally reject the taxonomy we introduce though various concepts. The moment we use any basic form of language, we are already committed to the relativistic and divisionary mode of thinking. There is therefore an irreconcilable conflict between language and truth. The more one tries to speak of the truth, the farther removed one is from it; the more one tries to explain the truth, the less successful one is in getting others to see it.

But how do we communicate with each other if we cannot use language? How can Chan masters enlighten others if they do not speak? Speech is unavoidable, and thus the employment of language is a necessary evil. Chung-ying Cheng presents Chan's rejection of language in theory and its reliance on language in practice as a "paradox." He says:

> The doctrine of [Chan] holds that no rational and intellectual doctrine is pertinent and necessary for the realization of the ultimate truth called Buddhahood.... Yet in their search for Enlightenment they produced a vivid and vigorous body of brief and pithy dialogic exchanges named "public cases" or "public documents" [gong-an in Chinese; koan in Japanese], which seem to defy intellectual understanding. One is thereby tempted to ask: Why is there a gap between theoretical training and practical life in [Chan]?[101]

This paradox has captured the interest of many contemporary commentators on Chan. In the final section, we shall take a look at how Chan masters produced a practical means of education in their theoretical commitment to the limitation of language.

Chan's Pedagogy

Over the years, Chan masters developed their mode of verbal communication, often in the form of short dialogues (called *"mondo"* in

Japanese), which is not always comprehensible if taken literally. Many contemporary commentators compare Chan masters' speech acts to what J. L. Austin calls "perlocutionary" speech acts.[102] Perlocutionary acts "are the acts a speaker performs, or desires to perform, *by* saying something."[103] In other words, perlocutionary acts are speeches that serve a special purpose of the speaker to elicit the intended response of the listener. It is a performance; the communication goes beyond the conveyance of information based on the literal meaning of the utterance. The success of such a communication depends not on whether the listener comprehends what the speaker says, but on whether the listener responds in the way the speaker intended. In the context of Chan, the use of language by Chan masters is intended to awaken the listener, to make him or her see the self-nature. Sometimes the perlocutionary goal is simply to "shock" the listener out of his habitual way of thinking. The format could be a riddle, a poem, a piece of nonsense, a shout, or simply silence. If it is true that Chan's language serves merely a perlocutionary function, then to understand it, we should discard semantics and appeal only to pragmatics. Or, as Ha Poong Kim argues, we should see that in Chan masters' utterances, words are *liberated* from the fixed roles they normally play within a particular language, and thus "they cease to *mean* anything – even if they may happen to be used in accordance with the rules of a language game."[104]

The use of language in Chan dialogues is inevitably an "expedient means," but to say that language is therefore a form of non-language or that words are not used as "words" would defy Chan's spirit of taking things naturally. The Chan School does not endorse the role of language in its function to depict reality. If the very nature of language, including all the conceptualizations as the basis of language, is fundamentally relativistic and discriminatory, then it cannot be used to refer to reality-as-such. But to refrain from using language as a normal discourse or to insist on silence would be like going back to the isolationist Chan that Hui-neng criticizes. But why then did many Chan masters refuse to answer questions directly? Their point is that if a student needs to ask someone else, then he or she has already missed the major point of Chan's teaching: one needs to see it for oneself. We should remember that Chan masters do not *always* resort to paradoxical dialogues; they sometimes do expound Chan's essence for students. But if a student insists on receiving a clear analysis of the meaning of certain concepts, then he or she is paying too much attention to language and conceptions themselves and forgetting what Chan is all about. Huang Bo says:

> There is only the One Mind and not a particle of anything else on which to lay hold, for this Mind is the Buddha. If you students of the Way do not awake to this Mind substance, you will overlay Mind with conceptual thought, you will seek the Buddha outside yourselves, and you will remain attached to forms, pious practices and so on, all of which are harmful and not at all the way to supreme knowledge.[105]

So, Chan language is at times performative – in uttering nonsense or in giving irrelevant answers, Chan masters do not convey any information. Instead, their intention is that listeners should see the limit of language itself and try to gain true knowledge on their own. Language is like the finger pointing at the moon: one should see the moon and not just look at the finger. Furthermore, a Chan dialogue usually took place between a master and a student in a particular context, and what the master aimed at was to enlighten that student *at that moment*. The records of *koan* or *mondo* are futile in preserving the teaching of Chan. We do not gain any insight into what the master tried to convey since we are not the student being addressed, and we are no longer in that context. Therefore, we should not *over*analyze the meaning of these paradoxical dialogues.

Some commentators on Chan take it to be a non-doctrinal school. However, the initial Chan School was not founded on a total rejection of doctrines and sutras. Hui-neng himself preached the *Diamond Sutra*, and he did not instruct his disciples not to study sutras.[106] But he clearly criticizes some followers for reciting sutras by heart without ever understanding their true meaning. He thinks that the essence of the Buddha's teaching "has nothing to do with written words."[107] Rather, it concerns "the original mind," and thus, "if one does not discern the original mind, it is of no benefit to study the teaching."[108]

Later Chan masters began to downplay the importance of studying sutras and learning doctrines, because they found words and conception major obstacles to seeing the true mind. Huang Bo says: "If you students of the Way wish to become Buddhas, you need study no doctrines whatever, but learn only how to avoid seeking for and attaching yourselves to anything."[109] The essence of Chan's teaching is all about seeing one's own mind, and this kind of self-knowledge cannot go through secondary conceptualization. This self-knowledge is immediate and direct. Conceptualization turns the mind into an "object" of knowledge, while for the mind to see itself, there is no separation of subject and object. That is why Huang Bo says: "Mind is the Buddha, while the cessation of conceptual thought is the Way."[110] "It is by preventing the rise of conceptual thought that you will realize Bodhi (Enlightenment); and, when you do, you will just be realizing the Buddha who has always existed in your own mind!"[111]

If one cannot pass on the essence of Chan through verbal communication or written discourse, if Chan can only be transmitted "directly from one mind to another," then the pedagogy has to be totally different from the traditional method of lecture and explication. As Huang Bo acknowledged, even though 500 people gathered on the mountain to listen to his sermon, few could fully understand his teaching. "Why? Because my Way is through Mind-awakening. How can it be conveyed in words?"[112] This explains why later Chan masters would resort to various extreme measures in their pedagogy. They do not explain; further, they do not "say things plainly," because words and speech distract the mind away from the true goal of attainment: to see the mind itself.

Huang Bo's follower Lin Ji was noted for "shouting" and "hitting" in answer to his students' questions. To him these are pedagogical means. He says, "I don't have a particle of Dharma [True Teaching] to give to anyone. All I have is cure for sickness, freedom from bondage."[113] He said that no one had ever come to him "alone and free," and what he tried to do was to break everyone's bondage. "If they come with a raised hand, I hit the raised hand; if they come mouthing something, I hit them in the mouth; if they come making motions with their eyes, I hit them in the eye."[114] To those outside the Chan School, these methods often seemed ridiculous and even cruel. But to Chan masters, the method one uses is unimportant – what matters is whether the students understand the point right away.

One hundred and fifty years after Hui-neng's death, the Chan School turned itself into a school known for using *koan*, riddles, shouting, beating, and many other unconventional means of teaching. Suzuki describes the change of Chan's pedagogy this way:

> The scene has almost entirely changed from that which was visible until the time of the Sixth Patriarch. Only what may be called Sutra terminology had been in use in the exposition of Zen. No one had ever thought that beating, kicking, and other rough methods of treatment would be accorded to the students. "Mere seeing" is gone, and acting has taken its place.[115]

But since the nature of the Chan masters' performance is "acting," it is sometimes difficult for outsiders to gauge the real intent behind the acts. When we read records of later generations of Chan masters, we can be quite amazed at the seeming indolence, violence, rudeness, and scorn they demonstrate toward their students or each other. In Suzuki's opinion, these techniques are "so varied, so original, so entirely unconventional, that each time we come across them we feel thoroughly refreshed, and frequently as if resurrected from the grave."[116]

Conclusion

Chan's claim that the Buddha is within us and that all we need to do is to see our essential nature is liberating to those with a religious bent. As a form of religion, it does not posit any Supreme Being who is responsible for our wellbeing; who assigns punishments and rewards for our deeds. It does not ask us to give up our will to obey an external, superior commandment. It does not insist on our studying any sacred text or memorizing any sacrosanct precept. All it teaches is a simple method of recognizing one's self-nature and appreciating the fact that other beings all share the same essential nature that one has. Its teaching reinforces self-confidence and at the same time cautions against arrogance or conceit. The pragmatic goal of this school is very society-friendly.

As a form of philosophy, on the other hand, Chan is less systematic than the other schools of Chinese Buddhism that we have studied. Its philosophy can be encapsulated in a few short aphorisms, but Chan masters seldom defended or put forward arguments for their theses. We have to extrapolate their philosophical presuppositions from their remarks. One of the most important philosophical claims of the Chan School is that we do not need to reject the phenomenal world totally in order to reach nirvana. Even though they place utmost emphasis on the mind, they do not insist that all worldly phenomena are illusions or productions of the mind. In this respect, the Chan School, along with the Tian-tai School, takes Chinese Buddhism farther away from the anti-realistic spirit of traditional Buddhism. Chan asserts reality, but it is not a form of naive realism, which is the common people's view that Buddhism rejects. Dan Lusthaus puts it well: "Chan is not a naive realism; it is a kind of intuitive phenomenology. One should not mistake the rejection of transcendental metaphysics for a naïve realism – that would be to fall to the other pole of the dichotomy Chan seeks to erase."[117]

Another important philosophical thesis of the Chan School is the universality of Buddhahood. Buddhahood is innate to all beings; it defines the essence of everything in the universe. Humans are not superior to other species of animals; rocks and stones are not less significant than cats and dogs. This acknowledgment of the universality of Buddhahood reinstates the traditional Chinese conviction of a harmonious, holistic universe, in which everything and everyone plays a crucial role.

The Chan School stands at the pivotal point between ancient Chinese philosophy and Neo-Confucianism. Whalen Lai thinks that its theory of mind "borrowed a [Daoist] concept of mind," its theory of Buddha-nature "incorporates the mind-nature association made by Mencius," and that it "thereby anticipated the philosophy of Wang Yang-ming."[118] According to Lai, the very choice of the word "nature" (*"xing"* in Chinese) as the translation for the Sanskrit word *"gotra"* (meaning "seed") or *"garbha"* (meaning "womb") "was influenced by the popularity of this term in Chinese philosophical usage."[119] The theory of Buddha-nature thus reflects the Chinese tradition. Later in the history of Chinese philosophy, Wang Yangming, deeply influenced by the Chan School's theory of mind, developed his philosophy of mind to a more sophisticated level.

Further discussion questions

1 Between the Northern School's conception of mind and the Southern School's conception of mind, which view is closer to your understanding of our mind?
2 How can Chan's teachings be applied to today's lifestyle? How can we achieve the nondiscriminatory state of mind? How would this attitude affect human relationships?
3 What does "everyone is a Buddha" mean? How do you assess the truth of this claim?
4 Do you agree that in depicting reality with our languages and in cognizing the world with our conceptions, we inevitably create a world according to human conception and consequently a "world-not-in-itself"? What could reality-in-itself be without human conception?
5 How do you compare Daoism (especially Zhuangzi's philosophy) to Chan? Can this kind of teaching reform society?

Primary texts

John Blofeld [Chu Ch'an] (trans.) *The Zen Teaching of Huang Po on the Transmission of Mind*. New York: Glove Press, 1958.
Wing-tsit Chan (ed.) *A Sourcebook in Chinese Philosophy*, 4th edn. Princeton: Princeton University Press, 1973 (ch. 26).
Thomas Cleary (trans.) *The Sutra of Hui-neng: Grand Master of Zen*. (With Hui-neng's Commentary on the *Diamond Sutra*.) Boston and London: Shambhala, 1998.

Alexander Holstein (trans.) *Pointing at the Moon: 100 Zen Koans from Chinese Masters*. Rutland, Vermont and Tokyo, Japan: Charles E. Tuttle Company, 1993.

D. T. Suzuki (ed.) *Manual of Zen Buddhism*. New York: Grove Press, 1960.

Burton Watson (trans.) *The Zen Teachings of Master Lin-Chi [Lin-chi Lu]*. New York: Columbia University Press, 1999.

Further readings

Chung-ying Cheng. "On Zen (Ch'an) Language and Zen Paradoxes." *Journal of Chinese Philosophy* 1, 1973: 77–99.

Hsueh-li Cheng. "The Roots of Zen Buddhism." *Journal of Chinese Philosophy* 8, 1981: 451–78.

Whalen Lai. "The Meaning of 'Mind-Only' ('Wei-Hsin'): An Analysis of a Sinitic Mahayana Phenomenon." *Philosophy East & West* 27(1), 1977: 65–83.

Alan W. Watts. *The Way of Zen*. New York: Vintage Books, 1957.

Robert B. Zeuschner. "The Understanding of Karma in Early Ch'an Buddhism." *Journal of Chinese Philosophy* 8, 1981: 399–425.

Robert B. Zeuschner. "The Understanding of Mind in the Northern Line of Ch'an (Zen)." *Philosophy East & West* 28(1), 1978: 69–79.

Notes

Introduction: What is Chinese Philosophy?

1 Bodde 1942: 298.
2 Kaltenmark 1969: 46.
3 As Derk Bodde explains it, "Prominent in all these schools is the belief that the universe is in a constant state of flux but that this flux follows a fixed and therefore predictable pattern consisting either of eternal oscillation between two poles or of cyclical movement within a closed circuit; in either case the change involved is relative rather than absolute, since all movement serves in the end only to bring the process back to its starting point" (1953: 21).
4 Ibid. 43.
5 Van Norden 2002: 24.
6 Wilhelm's term (Wilhelm and Baynes 1977: 323).
7 See, for example, Schwartz 1985: 180, and Van Norden 2002: 26.
8 Schwartz 1985: 180.
9 Bodde 1953: 61.
10 Graham 1989: 223.
11 Bodde 1953: 39.
12 There have been many "betrayals" in the intellectual history of China, of course. But once the student challenged the teacher's doctrine, he (or she, in rare cases) would quit the school and find some other teachers more representative of the *Dao*.
13 *Analects*, 7:1 (Chan 1973: 31).
14 We do not know whether Confucius himself went through any private education when young. He describes his childhood as poor and lowly; hence, he learned about many menial tasks. He also says that it was at the age of 15 that he dedicated himself to learning. But Mencius allegedly went to school from as early as 6 years old.
15 In Chinese intellectual history, we have witnessed several major overturnings of previous trends. But such overturnings of doctrines and schools often took hundreds of years to develop.

Part I   Introduction

1   Bodde 1953: 46–7. He gives the examples that "the ruler should rule benevolently, his ministers should be loyal yet at the same time ready to offer if need be their frank criticism, and farmers should produce the maximum of food, the artisans should take pride in their manufactures, the merchants should be honest in their dealings."

2   Ibid.

3   This short text, *Da-xue* (the *Great Learning*), was originally a chapter in *Li-ji* (the *Book of Rites*). Its author is unknown. Organized by Zhu Xi, a Neo-Confucian scholar, this chapter, as well as another chapter of the *Book of Rites*, "*Zhong-yong*" (the *Doctrine of the Mean*), stands out as a separate treatise. Zhu Xi grouped the *Great Learning*, the *Doctrine of the Mean*, along with the *Analects* and *Mengzi*, as "the Four Books." These four books have been viewed as the Confucian classics ever since.

4   The Chinese word receives two different readings among traditional Chinese scholars. Some said it was *qin*, which means "to be close to" or "to show concern for," while others argued that the text was corrupt and the correct word should be *xin*, which means "to renew." Under the first reading, the king's task is to take care of the people; under the second, the task is to educate or morally transform them.

5   *The Great Learning* (Chan 1973: 87).

6   This short text is also a chapter from the *Book of Rites*. Its author was traditionally taken to be Confucius' grandson, but contemporary scholars generally dispute this attribution and place it in a later period, around 200 BCE.

7   *Doctrine of the Mean* (Chan 1973: 98).

8   *Daodejing*, ch. 46 (my translation).

Chapter 1   *Yijing* (*I Ching*): The Cosmological Foundation of Chinese Philosophy

1   Fleming 1993b: 133.

2   The *Ten Wings* include: (1) Commentary on the Judgment (*tuan-zhuan*), Part I; (2) Commentary on the Judgment (*tuan-zhuan*), Part II; (3) Commentary on the Images (*xiang-zhuan*), Part I; (4) Commentary on the Images (*xiang-zhuan*), Part II; (5) The Great Treatise (*xi-ci-zhuan*), Part I; (6) The Great Treatise (*xi-ci-zhuan*), Part II; (7) Commentary on the Words of the Text (*wen-yan*); (8) Discussion of the Trigrams (*shuo-gua*); (9) The Sequence of the Hexagrams (*xu-gua*); and (10) Miscellaneous Notes on the Hexagrams (*za-gua*). The orthodox Chinese view treats the first seven wings as belonging to the core of *Yijing*. Standard Chinese *Yijing* texts usually place the first four wings in each hexagram, accompanying the original Judgment texts and Images. (Cf. Wilhelm and Baynes 1977: 255–61.)

3   Wilhelm and Baynes 1977: 1.

4   *The Great Treatise* IX (Wilhelm and Baynes 1977: 350).
5   For a detailed explanation of these methods, one could consult any *Yijing* workbook. Most English translations of *Yijing* would also include a brief explanation of the methods.
6   Wilhelm and Baynes 1977: 263.
7   Ibid. 281.
8   See my Introduction to this book for more analysis of the notion of *qi*.
9   Wilhelm and Baynes 1977: 575.
10 Wing 2001: 12.
11 Wilhelm and Baynes 1977: 98.
12 Ibid. 244.
13 This is from the first hexagram, *Qian* ("the Creative") (ibid. 6).
14 Ibid. 213.
15 This phrase comes from the *Doctrine of the Mean* (Chan 1973: 112).
16 Chad Hansen explains this expectation thus: "The king is the liaison between heaven:nature and human society. He sets society on the ritual path necessary to keep it in harmony with nature. Only that path will result in human flourishing. Human flourishing preservers order. Order preserves nature's approval and [Heaven's] mandate remains" (1992: 63).
17 Part I, ch. 11 (Wilhelm and Baynes 1977: 320).
18 Of the 64 hexagrams, only six are assigned all four primary virtues. They are: (1) The Creative; (3) Difficulty at the Beginning; (17) Following; (19) Approach; (25) Innocence; and (49) Molting. Most of them, however, are followed by some precautionary comments about harm or shame.
19 Wilhelm and Baynes 1977: 4.
20 Legge 1964: 57.
21 Huang 1998: 22.
22 *The Great Treatise* I: 5 (my translation).
23 Wilhelm and Baynes 1977: 521.
24 Tong 1990: 331.
25 Wilhelm and Baynes 1977: 97.
26 Ibid. 371.
27 Chan 1973: 98.
28 *Image of Xu* (Wilhelm and Baynes 1977: 25).
29 Ibid. 29.
30 Ibid. 280.
31 Ibid. 570.
32 Ibid. 134.
33 Ibid. 590.
34 Ibid. 12.
35 *The Great Treatise*, II: 12 (Wilhelm and Baynes 1977: 353).
36 Ibid. 241.
37 Ibid. 5.
38 Ibid. 393.
39 Hon 1997: 29.

Chapter 2 Confucius (Kongzi) in the *Analects*

1 The *Analects*, 14:41 (Chan 1973: 43).
2 Cua 1995: 209.
3 The *Analects*, 4:15.
4 There are many different translations of the two notions. For *zhong*, Ivanhoe and Van Norden's translation (2003) is "loyalty," Lau's (1979) is "doing one's best," Dawson's (2000) is "loyalty," and Chan's (1973) is "conscientiousness." For *shu*, Ivanhoe and Van Norden's translation is "sympathetic understanding," Lau's is "using oneself as a measure to gauge others," Dawson's is "reciprocity," and Chan's is "altruism."
5 Chan 1973: 20.
6 The *Analects*, 7:24.
7 Ibid. 1:8 (my translation).
8 Ibid. 12:14 (modification of Lau's translation). Lau's original translation of "loyalty" is "give of your best," which shows that he understands this notion in the same way.
9 Ibid. 12:11 (Lau 1979: 114).
10 Nivison 1996: 65.
11 Graham 1989: 21.
12 The *Analects*, 5:19.
13 Ibid. 8:14 (Lau 1979: 94).
14 Hansen 1992: 62.
15 The *Analects*, 13:3 (Ivanhoe and Van Norden 2003: 34).
16 Schwartz 1985: 92.
17 The *Analects*, 1:11 (Chan 1973: 21).
18 Ibid. 2: 5 (Chan 1973: 23).
19 Ibid. 2: 7 (slight modification of Chan's translation; 1973: 23).
20 In ancient Chinese society, daughters, once married, belong to their husbands' families. The duty to take care of parents in their old age typically does not fall on daughters.
21 The *Analects*, 15:24 (Ivanhoe and Van Norden 2003: 42).
22 Allinson 1985: 306–12.
23 Ivanhoe 1990: 23.
24 Ibid.
25 Zigong said, "If there were one able to universally extend his benevolence to the people and bring succor to the multitude, what would you make of him? Could such a person be called *ren*?" The Master said, "Why stop at *ren*? Such a person should surely be called a sage! . . . Desiring to take his stand, one who is *ren* helps others to take their stand; wanting to realize himself, he helps others to realize themselves. Being able to take what is near at hand as an example could perhaps be called the method of *ren*." The *Analects*, 6:30 (Ivanhoe and Van Norden 2003: 19).
26 Ibid. 17:2 (my translation).

27 Ibid. 2:4. Confucius says, "At seventy I could follow my heart's desire without transgressing moral principles" (Chan 1973: 22).

28 The *Analects*, 4:11 (modification of Chan's translation; 1973: 27). A similar remark is recorded at 4:16.

29 Ibid. 15:31 (Chan 1973: 44).

30 Ibid. 4:9 (Ivanhoe and Van Norden 2003: 10).

31 Schwartz 1985: 96.

32 In later chapters, we will see how Daoists, Laozi in particular, reject this view.

33 The *Analects*, 4:4 (Dawson 2000: 13).

34 Ibid. 6:30.

35 Ibid. 12:16.

36 Ibid. 12:22.

37 Fingarette 1972: 7.

38 Cua 1995: 226.

39 The *Analects*, 15:10.

40 Ibid. 3:3 (Ivanhoe and Van Norden 2003: 7).

41 Ibid. 12:1.

42 Ibid.

43 Ibid. 12:17 (Chan 1973: 40).

44 Dawson 1982: 53.

45 The *Analects*, 13:6 (modification of Chan's translation; 1973: 41).

46 Ibid. 2:19 (Dawson 2000: 8).

47 Ibid. 4:25 (Lau 1979: 75).

48 Ibid. 2:1 (Dawson's translation).

49 Ibid. 12:19 (Chan 1973: 40).

50 Ibid. 2:3 (Ivanhoe and Van Norden 2003: 5).

51 Machiavelli, *The Prince*, ch. 17.

52 The *Analects*, 14:30 (Ivanhoe and Van Norden 2003: 39).

53 Confucius says, "The village worthy is the thief of virtue." The *Analects*, 17:13 (Ivanhoe and Van Norden 2003: 45).

54 *Mencius* 7B:37 (Ivanhoe and Van Norden 2003: 152–3).

Chapter 3   Mencius (Mengzi)

1 *Mencius* 3B:9 (modification of Lau's translation; 1970: 130).

2 Wong 2002.

3 Lau 1963: 334.

4 Roger Ames (1991) has a detailed argument against translating the original Chinese words "*ren xing*" used by Mencius as "human nature." I think the two terms are comparable. For an informative comparison of the two terms, see A. C. Graham 1990: 1–2. Granted that Mencius holds a different view of human nature from others, but conceptual differences should be reflected in philosophical debates, not just on the translation of terms. So I shall simply use "human nature" in this discussion. For further discus-

sion on Ames' view, see Graham 1990; Bloom 1997; Bloom 1994; Shun 1997.

5 Graham 1989: 124.

6 *Mencius* 6A:6 (Lau 1970: 162–3).

7 Cf. ibid. 3.

8 Ibid. 7 (Lau 1970: 164).

9 As Mencius uses it, the Chinese word *xin* stands for a human organ that has both emotive and cognitive capacities. Philip Ivanhoe says: "the early Chinese believed the *xin* 'heart and mind' is an organ that contains cognitive (i.e., rational) faculties, affective (i.e., emotional) faculties – including certain ethical sensibilities – as well as our volitional abilities (something akin to but distinct from our common notion of will" (2002b: 222). The English words "mind" or "heart" alone do not cover all these connotations.

10 *Mencius* 6A:7 (Ivanhoe and Van Norden 2003: 144–5).

11 Eric Hutton has a good description of Mencius' view of sages. Using the comparison to the great connoisseur of tastes, Hutton says: "The sages are above all connoisseurs of the human heart" (2002: 174).

12 Here I am following the translation of the word *"sheng"* in Ivanhoe and Van Norden 2003: 141. Other common translations of *sheng* include "what one is born with" and "the inborn." With this claim, Gaozi is relying on the etymology of the Chinese word *"xing"* (nature) and its connection to the Chinese word *"sheng"* (life; to give life). According to D. C. Lau, "the two words . . . though slightly different in pronunciation, were probably written by the same character in Mencius' time. This would make the statement at least tautological in written form and so parallel to 'white is what is meant by "white"'" (1970: 160–1, n. 1). Under the other two translations, Mencius' challenge of Gaozi's claim would not make sense.

13 *Mencius* 6A:1, 2, 6.

14 Ibid. 4.

15 Ibid. 1.

16 Ibid. 2 (Lau 1970: 160).

17 Cf. ibid. 4.

18 Ibid. 2 (Ivanhoe and Van Norden 2003: 141).

19 Ibid. 2A:6. Ivanhoe and Van Norden 2003: 125.

20 This story is from Jean-Jacques Rousseau's *A Discourse on Inequality*, translated by Maurice Cranston, Penguin Classics. New York: Penguin Books USA Inc., 1984: 100.

21 Ivanhoe 2002b: 222–3. A universal claim binds all cases such that a single counterexample would disprove the claim. A general claim, on the other hand, applies to general cases with some exceptions. As long as it is *generally true* that we humans would be moved by others' distress, Mencius' argument here is sound.

22 Wong 1991: 34.

23 *Mencius* 6A:10. Ivanhoe and Van Norden 2003: 146.

24 Ibid. 6 (Ivanhoe and Van Norden 2003: 143–4). A similar remark is seen in *Mencius* 2A:6.

25 Cf. ibid. 6A:15.

26 The cosmological notion of *qi* is explained in chapter 1. In the *Mencius*, the *qi* is not a purely cosmological notion since it is mostly discussed within the human context. It is not merely a physical energy since it also has a moral dimension. David Nivison calls it "our emotional energies" (1996: 128). Whalen Lai calls it a "moral breath that overflows the individual" (1984: 154).

27 *Mencius* 2A:2 (Ivanhoe and Van Norden 2003: 123).

28 To Mencius, that which we *can* desire is morally acceptable. He says, "The desirable is called 'good'" (7B:25). This statement provokes many discussions among the Neo-Confucians. There could be at least two ways to analyze the relation between desire and goodness. One is to say that we should only desire what is morally acceptable; the other is to say that whatever we can desire without depriving anyone else of their desires is morally acceptable. I think we can make the tentative claim here that Mencius does not advocate the total elimination of desires.

29 Ibid. 7A:21 (Lau 1970: 186).

30 Ibid. 4A:15 (Ivanhoe and Van Norden 2003: 134).

31 Ibid. 6A:6.

32 Ibid. 8 (modification of Chan's translation; 1973: 57).

33 David Nivison explains it in this way: "our 'pro-attitude' toward something we recognize as morally good does not result in active appropriation of or acting out the good unless we 'think.' 'If the mind thinks, it will get it,' Mencius says" (1996: 87).

34 *Mencius* 6A:10 (Ivanhoe and Van Norden 2003: 146–7). See also ibid. 11.

35 Ibid. 9.

36 Ibid. 15 (Ivanhoe and Van Norden 2003: 147).

37 Ibid. 7B:35 (Lau 1970: 201–2).

38 Ibid. 6A:8.

39 Van Norden 1991: 359.

40 David Nivison argues that it is the *acedia*, rather than *akrasia* (weakness of the will), that is the typical concern of early Chinese moral philosophers, including Mencius. He says that "acedia" occurs when "I judge I should do something yet do not, or perhaps cannot, care enough about it to act" (1996: 92).

41 *Mencius* 2A:6 (my translation).

42 The Chinese word that Mencius uses is "*tuei*," which literally means "to push."

43 There are several different interpretations of Mencius' pedagogy in this case. Kwong-loi Shun suggests that what Mencius asks the king to do is to employ a form of "analogical reasoning." He thinks that Mencius asks the king to see that he does have sympathy toward the ox and then extends the same logical consistency to the case of the sheep and further to his people. Shun says, "To extend such reactions and attitudes is to actually come to have similar reactions and attitudes in the appropriate situations and toward the appropriate objects" (1989: 322). Bryan Van Norden challenges

this interpretation and argues that Mencius does not simply aim for theoretical consistency. He says: "If Mencius' argument is what Shun claims that it is, then it would be open to Mencius' opponents to escape the dilemma he creates for them by eliminating within themselves all traces of benevolence that they possess" (1991: 355). Van Norden's own interpretation suggests that Mencius is trying to bring the king's attention to the suffering of his people, so as to induce the king to generate a similar moral judgment on the need to spare his people (ibid. 364–5). David Nivison also focuses on logical consistency in interpreting Mencius' method here. He says: "Without forcing more logic into Mencius' persuasion than is there, we might represent [Mencius] as urging the king to think as follows: (1) I ought to be compassionate toward my people if I can be; but I just can't. But, (2) it is easier to be compassionate toward human beings than toward animals. And (3) here I am, compassionate toward this animal. Thus, (4) I can be compassionate toward animals. Thus, (5) I can be compassionate toward my people. Thus, (6) I ought to be compassionate toward my people. I have no excuse for not being" (1996: 97–8). David Wong argues that Nivison "errs in interpreting Mencius as trying to change the king through logical argument – as trying to convince him that he ought to feel compassionate toward his people because he would be inconsistent if he did not in the case of his people and yet in the case of the ox" (1991: 38). Wong's own interpretation sees Mencius as trying to get the king to recognize "a reason to act." He says, "Mencius is giving the king a way for the motive force of the instinctually compassionate response to enter into practical deliberation. The suffering of sentient beings, not just of the ox, now can become a consideration in the king's deliberation over what to do" (ibid. 39). Philip Ivanhoe refutes this interpretation by pointing out that "Mengzi is not trying to get the king to accept a view about moral reasons, and such views do not play any direct role in achieving his primary goal" (2002b: 230). Instead of teaching analogical reasoning, Ivanhoe argues, Mencius is teaching the king a form of "analogical resonance." It is a method to teach someone "to identify, focus upon, and appreciate his nascent moral sense" (ibid. 234).

44 For a detailed comparison of the two doctrines, go to chapter 5 on Mozi.
45 *Mencius* 1A:7 (modification of Chan's translation; 1973: 61).
46 Ibid. 3 (modification of Lau's translation; 1970: 51).
47 Ibid. 5 (my translation).
48 Graham 1989: 116.

Chapter 4   Xunzi (Hsün Tzu)

1 Kline III and Ivanhoe 2000: ix.
2 Hansen 1992: 309.
3 As we shall see, there are several slightly different translations of this famous slogan. One key difference lies in the rendition of Xunzi's view on

human nature as "evil" or "bad." I think that the word "evil" has a strong Christian association, and thus "bad" is a better rendition. But in some contexts where the word "evil" is more appropriate, I will use that word instead. The choice of the two words does not reflect a difference in the original Chinese text. The other key difference lies in the rendition of his view on human goodness as a result of human's effort. The various choices of translation will be explained later in this chapter.

4   This description is a summary of various authors' explication of "naturalism"; in particular, Terry Horgan and Mark Timmons, "Metaphysical Naturalism, Semantic Normativity, and Meta-Semantic Irrealism," and Jaegwon Kim, "Naturalism and Semantic Normativity," both in Enrique Villanueva, ed., *Naturalism and Normativity* (Atascadero, CA: Ridgeview Publishing Company, 1993), pp. 180–204 and 205–10, respectively; Brian Leiter, "Naturalism in Legal Philosophy," online in the *Stanford Encyclopedia of Philosophy*; and Fredrick F. Schmitt, "Naturalism," in Jaegwon Kim and Ernest Sosa, eds., *A Companion to Metaphysics* (Oxford: Blackwell Publishers, 1995), pp. 343–5.

5   "A Discussion on Heaven," *The Xunzi*, ch. 17 (Watson 1963: 82).

6   Goldin 1999: 42.

7   "A Discussion on Heaven," *The Xunzi*, ch. 17 (Watson 1963: 79).

8   Ibid. (Ivanhoe and Van Norden 2003: 262).

9   Ibid. (Watson 1963: 80).

10 Ibid.

11 "Rectifying Names," *The Xunzi*, ch. 22 (Watson 1963: 142).

12 "A Discussion on Heaven," *The Xunzi*, ch. 17 (my translation).

13 "Rectifying Names," *The Xunzi*, ch. 22 (Watson 1963: 142).

14 "Dispelling Obsessions," *The Xunzi*, ch. 21 (modification of Watson's translation, 1963: 135).

15 "A Discussion of Rites," *The Xunzi*, ch. 19 (Watson 1963: 96).

16 Machle's term (1976: 451).

17 "A Discussion on Heaven," *The Xunzi*, ch. 17 (Ivanhoe and Van Norden 2003: 263).

18 "A Discussion of Rites," *The Xunzi*, ch. 19 (Watson 1963: 97).

19 Chan 1973: 121.

20 "A Discussion on Heaven," *The Xunzi*, ch. 17 (Chan's translation, with the replacement of his terms "Nature" with "Heaven" and "natural" with "heavenly").

21 "Human Nature is Bad," *The Xunzi*, ch. 23 (my translation).

22 Graham 1989: 250.

23 For example, Graham says, "If we look at [Xunzi's] very careful definitions, it is clear that his argument starts from a conception of human nature quite different from Mencius'. . . . Mencius thinks in terms of a natural tendency to goodness as to long life, actualized only if nourished by education as the healthy body is nourished by food. For [Xunzi] on the other hand, whatever has been affected by education is by definition *not* man's nature,

which consists of the inclinations born as his energies first respond to external stimulation, before the beginnings of thought" (1989: 246).

24 D. C. Lau says: "It is more illuminating to consider the two from the point of view of disagreement over the nature of, or, if one prefers, the way of looking at, morality, which leads in turn to a difference in the method of moral education" (1953: 545). David Soles (1999) also thinks that the two philosophers disagree not over the empirical facts of human nature, but over the nature of morality; in particular, he argues that Mencius holds a virtue theory of morality while Xunzi holds a rule-based theory of morality.

25 "Rectifying Names," *The Xunzi*, ch. 22 (my translation).

26 Ibid. (Watson 1963: 151).

27 Ibid. (my translation).

28 "Human Nature is Bad," *The Xunzi*, ch. 23 (modification of Watson's translation, 1963: 162).

29 "Rectifying Names," *The Xunzi*, ch. 22 (my translation).

30 "Human Nature is Bad," *The Xunzi*, ch. 23 (Watson 1963: 158–9).

31 Ibid.

32 Lau 1953: 559.

33 "Human Nature is Bad," *The Xunzi*, ch. 23 (modification of Chan's translation, 1973: 128).

34 "Human Nature is Bad," *The Xunzi*, ch. 23 (Watson 1963: 161–2).

35 Cua 1978: 4.

36 The complete quote was already given above, in the context of Xunzi's distinction between "nature" and "deliberate effort."

37 Xunzi says: "Mencius states that man's nature is good, and that all evil arises because he loses his original nature. Such a view, I believe, is erroneous. It is the way with man's nature that as soon as he is born he begins to depart from his original naiveté and simplicity, and therefore he must inevitably lose what Mencius regards as his original nature. It is obvious from this, then, that the nature of man is evil" ("Human Nature is Bad," *The Xunzi*, ch. 23; Watson 1963: 159).

38 Graham 1989: 246.

39 "Human Nature is Bad," *The Xunzi*, ch. 23 (Chan 1973: 133).

40 Ibid. (Watson 1963: 166–7).

41 Schwartz 1985: 293.

42 For Xunzi's view on this subject, see his "Encouraging Learning," *The Xunzi*, ch. 1, and his "Cultivating Oneself," *The Xunzi*, ch. 2.

43 "Human Nature is Bad," *The Xunzi*, ch. 23 (Chan 1973: 134).

44 "Human Nature is Bad," *The Xunzi*, ch. 23 (Watson 1963: 163).

45 In Thucydides' *The History of the Peloponnesian War*, he gives a detailed description of human conduct in times of the plague in Athens and the civil wars at Corcyra. His conclusion is exactly that without law and order, what is manifested by people's conduct is human beings' evil nature.

46 "Human Nature is Bad," *The Xunzi*, ch. 23 (Chan 1973: 132).

47 Ibid. (Chan 1973: 130).
48 Kline 2000: 155–6.
49 "A Discussion on Rites," *The Xunzi*, ch. 19 (modification of Watson's translation, 1963: 89).
50 Nivison 2000: 186.
51 Ibid.
52 "A Discussion of Rites," *The Xunzi*, ch. 19 (Watson 1963: 95).
53 "Human Nature is Bad," *The Xunzi*, ch. 23 (Watson 1963: 164).
54 Kline 2000: 157.
55 A. S. Cua gives a detailed explication of the notion of *li*. He says: "In general, the notion of *li* refers to a normative domain consisting of rites, ceremonies, decorum, courtesy, and civility, which may conveniently be labeled 'the domain of propriety.' It is a domain consisting of specific requirements or rules for proper conduct for different types of occasions in personal and social intercourse" (1979: 373) This shows that *li* in the Confucian discourse is a rich concept. However, Cua thinks that when the notion of *li* is taken to include so many things, then there might be a problem of conceptual unity in this notion.
56 Chan 1973: 129.
57 As Kline points out, "These factors, external to the self and one's nature, socialize a person by developing moral perceptions and dispositions and eventually shaping one into a cultivated Confucian" (2000: 157).
58 "A Discussion of Rites" (Watson 1963: 91).
59 Ibid.
60 Ibid. (Watson 1963: 100).
61 Ibid.
62 Cua 1979: 382.
63 The other two dimensions listed by Cua (1979) are "moral" and "religious."
64 "A Discussion of Rites" (Watson 1963: 101).
65 Ibid. (Watson 1963: 102).
66 Ibid. (Watson's translation).

Chapter 5   Mozi (Mo Tzu)

1 Chan 1973: 212.
2 Yu (r. 2205–2198? BCE) was the founder of the Xia Dynasty (2205–1766? BCE). In the account given by Mencius, Yu was so devoted to solving the problem of flooding at the time that during the many years working on constructing dikes and waterways, he thrice went by his own home without entering it.
3 Chan 1973: 72.
4 These criticisms are mostly in Mozi's "Against Confucianism," Part II, *Mozi*, ch. 39. Part I of this essay is lost.
5 "Universal Love," Part II, *Mozi*, ch. 15 (my translation).
6 Ching 1978: 163.

7   "Universal Love," Part III, *Mozi*, ch. 16 (Watson 1963: 39).
8   The *Analects*, 6:30 (my translation).
9   Schwartz 1985: 146.
10 "Universal Love," Part II, *Mozi*, ch. 15 (my translation).
11 Ibid.
12 Wong 1989: 254.
13 Wong does not rest his ethical theory completely on the Confucian model of love with distinctions, however. He thinks that a proper ethic must both recognize the human nature of loving one's family members first and foremost and at the same time recognize "the universalist perception of the moral worth of all" (ibid. 267). He therefore recommends combining the Confucian particularist view and the Mohist universalist view.
14 Wong says, "Even if we do perceive the equal moral worth of human beings, we must recognize the power of the motivation that moves us to give priority to those particular people who stand in special relations to us. An ethic that cannot accommodate this motivation risks irrelevance as an ethic for *human beings*" (1989: 260).
15 "Universal Love," Part III, *Mozi*, ch. 16 (Watson 1963: 47).
16 Ibid. (Watson 1963: 46–7).
17 Schwartz 1985: 147.
18 This phrase comes from a Chinese historian of philosophy, Lao Si-guang. See his *History of Chinese Philosophy*, vol. I (Hong Kong: Chong-ji Books, 1985), p. 239 (in Chinese).
19 As Benjamin Schwartz points out, "In the *Analects* [the word 'benefit'] means a concern with personal interest and it is the opposite of the motive of . . . righteousness. [Mozi's] use of the term in his own way thus almost suggests a gesture of defiance" (1985: 145).
20 Creel 1953: 5.
21 "Universal Love," Part III, *Mozi*, ch. 16 (Watson 1963: 41).
22 Ahern 1976: 188.
23 Vorenkamp 1992: 430.
24 Ibid. 431.
25 "The Will of Heaven," Part II, *Mozi*, ch. 27 (Watson 1963: 92–3).
26 Ibid., Part I, *Mozi*, ch. 26 (Watson 1963: 79).
27 Ibid., Part II, *Mozi*, ch. 27 (Watson 1963: 88).
28 Ibid. (Watson 1963: 91).
29 Those who interpret Mozi as a rule-utilitarian include Dirck Vorenkamp (1992) and Christian Jochim (1980).
30 "The Will of Heaven," Part II, *Mozi*, ch. 27 (Watson 1963: 86).
31 Ibid., Part I, *Mozi*, ch. 26 (Watson 1963: 79–80). Here the phrase "local officials" is used to replace the original translation, "gentlemen." In this context, the original Chinese "*junzi*" seems to be better understood as "local officials." See later for a slightly different rendition of "*junzi*."
32 "Identifying with One's Superior," Part I, *Mozi*, ch. 11 (Watson 1963: 34).
33 Graham 1989: 45.
34 Ibid.

35 "Honoring the Worthy," Part I, *Mozi*, ch. 8 (Watson 1963: 18).
36 Ibid. (Watson 1963: 20).
37 Ibid. (Watson 1963: 20–1).
38 "Moderation in Expenditure," Part I, *Mozi*, ch. 20 (Watson 1963: 62).
39 Schwartz 1985: 151.
40 "Moderation in Expenditure," Part I, *Mozi*, ch. 20 (Watson 1963: 62).
41 "Against Music," Part I, *Mozi*, ch. 32 (Watson 1963: 111).
42 Ibid. 112.
43 Ibid. 113. Here "government officials" is used to replace Watson's original translation, "gentlemen." The original Chinese is "*junzi*," which in the Confucian context is translated as "the superior people." In this passage, Mozi clearly meant the officials governing stately affairs.
44 "Against Music," Part I, *Mozi*, ch. 32 (Watson 1963: 116).
45 "Moderation in Funerals," Part III, *Mozi*, ch. 25 (Watson 1963: 68–9).
46 Ibid. (Watson 1963, 70).
47 Creel 1953: 66.
48 "Against Fatalism," Part I, *Mozi*, ch. 35 (Watson 1963: 118).
49 As Watson points out, "By making such an appeal [to historical records of ancient sage kings], he was following the approved practice of the thinkers of his age, and we may suppose that, if his listeners accepted the validly of his account of antiquity, they must have felt strongly compelled to accept this conclusion" (1963: 4).
50 Ibid. 8.
51 "The Will of Heaven," Part I, *Mozi*, ch. 26 (Watson, 79).
52 "Explaining Ghosts," Part III, *Mozi*, ch. 31 (Watson, 94).
53 Vorenkamp 1992: 436.
54 Graham 1989: 48.
55 "Against Fatalism," Part I, *Mozi*, ch. 35 (Watson 1963: 123).
56 Ibid.
57 Chan says, "In ancient China, up to the beginning of the Han dynasty (206 BC–220 AD), the greatest schools were Confucianism and [Mohism]. They dominated the intellectual scene from the fifth to at least the third century BC. And they vigorously attacked each other" (1973: 211).
58 Cf. Schwartz 1985: 168.
59 Lum 1977: 187.
60 Ibid. 188.

Chapter 6   Laozi (Lao Tzu)

1 Lau 1963: xiii–xiv.
2 Hansen 1992: 210.
3 Benjamin Schwartz calls it "one of the most difficult and problematic texts in all of Chinese literature" (1985: 192); Charles Fu says that the book "is probably the most puzzling, controversial, and yet metaphysically important work" (1973: 367); Lau points out that this book "has had an influence on

Chinese thought through the ages out of all proportion to its length" (1963: vii); A. C. Graham calls it "the masterpiece of a kind of intelligence at the opposite pole from the logical" (1989: 218).

4 As Schwartz asks: "How does a term which seems to refer in Confucianism mainly to social and natural *order* come to refer to a mystic reality?" (1985: 194).

5 By Herrlee G. Creel's account (1983: 304–11), the word has also been translated as "God" or "the great everlasting infinite First Cause from whom all things in heaven and earth proceed" by G. G. Alexander; it is translated as "the Reason" by Paul Carus and Jean Pierre Abel Rémusat, and it is translated as the German word "Sinn" ("meaning," "intellect," or "mind") by Richard Wilhelm.

6 Creel 1983: 302.

7 Most translations render the first *Dao* as uniquely designated, "the *Dao*" or "the Way." However, since there is no distinction between the singular and the plural form of nouns in Chinese, it is not clear why Laozi did not use an indefinite designation of "*dao*," since he wasn't referring to one singularly designated name, "the name." For the first two lines to be stylistically consistent, it seems that "the *Dao*" should be rendered as "a *Dao*" just as "the name" is rendered "a name." I therefore adopt Ivanhoe's translation. This translation does not beg the question on whether there is one unique *Dao*. However, by my interpretation Laozi does posit such a unique *Dao* as the ultimate Reality.

8 *Daodejing*, ch. 1 (Ivanhoe 2002: 1). The second half of this quote is a typical example of how the different punctuation could affect the reading. A different reading of these two lines would be: "*Nothingness* names the beginning of Heaven and Earth; *Being* names the mother of myriad creatures." This other reading takes the word "name" to be a verb. I think both readings are acceptable; however, I shall follow the more common translation in rendering the distinction as one between nameless and named.

9 For example, Fu adopts this explanation. He says: "[Laozi's] metaphysical attention is essentially focused on Nature as such or (the totality of) things-as-they-are, without positing or speculating upon what possibly exists behind or beyond Nature" (1973: 369).

10 Sung-peng Hsu argues that in Laozi's conception of *Dao* as the ultimate reality, there is a separate existence of *Dao* itself, which is the essence of *Dao*. The world is merely the "function" or "manifestations" of this essence. Hsu says: "[*Dao*] as the ultimately real is *wu*, nonbeing, not-having-anything, or empty" (1976: 203). Max Kaltenmark says what Laozi calls *Dao* is a kind of an "absolute void," which is unseen and imperceptible, that comes anterior to the One (1969: 40). If so, then in his view *Dao* does exist as a separate entity from the world as a whole. Bo Mou also seems to adopt this interpretation, as well in claiming that *Dao* has a "transcendental character" (2000: 429). T. P. Kasulis argues that the word "*Dao*" has two meanings, one of which represents "the ultimate, ineffable absolute . . . the term 'absolute' indicating that this [*Dao*] is beyond all

oppositions and contradiction" (1977: 383–4). Kasulis further identifies Laozi's notion of *Dao* in its absolute respect with "Non-being," and argues that Non-being "is, in fact, prior to Being and is the ultimate source of all things" (ibid. 386).

11   Graham seems to take this position. He says: "Using the language in which the Way is itself a thing with a name and 'mother of the myriad things,' it converts a logical into a generative sequence" (1989: 222). In Lau's translation of chapter I, he uses the past tense ("was") in the description of the nameless and the named as being the beginning of the universe and the mother of the myriad creatures. So he seems to take the generation to be a temporal sequence too. Zhu points out that later Daoists all take Laozi's depiction of the generation of Being from Non-being to be a process of "cosmogenesis" (1998: 55). Zhu himself also interprets Laozi's philosophy as belonging to cosmology (concerning the generation of the universe), not ontology (concerning the logical order of the universe) (ibid. 49).

12   Yu-lan Fung at one time advocates this view. He says: "This saying of [Laozi] does not mean that there was a time when there was only Non-being, and that then came a time when Being came into being from Non-being. It simply means that if we analyze the existence of things, we see there must first be Being before there can be any things. . . . What is here said belongs to ontology, not to cosmology. It has nothing to do with time and actuality" (as quoted in Fu, 1973: 379). Schwartz also seems to take this position in calling *Dao* the "principle of unity," the "dynamic order," or the "total organic pattern" of things in the world. He thinks that elements and relations may change, but the principle of unity will remain (1985: 194–5). In this sense, *Dao* may be logically prior, but not temporally prior, to things in the world.

13   This is the more popular interpretation. For example, Graham says: "The trouble with words is not that they do not fit at all but that they always fit imperfectly" (1989: 219); Schwartz also says: "Here . . . we find the constant paradoxical effort to speak about the unspeakable" (1985: 198). Arthur Danto first asserts that *Dao* is ineffable, and then tries to define the mode of the ineffability of *Dao*. He offers his speculation, but does not defend it, that *Dao* is ineffable because it is "the innominable space between name [the language] and nominatum [the world]" (1973: 54). Creel's explanation for the ineffability of *Dao* is that since *Dao* is "an indivisible whole," we cannot possibly find any eternal name to designate it (1983: 320). Kaltenmark's explanation for the ineffability of *Dao* is that names are personal and intimate, thus not suitable for the Supreme Principle like *Dao* (1969: 28).

14   For example, Dennis Ahern says: "D. C. Lau . . . says that no name or description can appropriately be attached to the [*Dao*]. If this were true, then it would seem that the book is trying (at least in part) to do the impossible. . . . I shall argue . . . that there is very little evidence to support a claim of ineffability" (1977: 357). His main argument is that all those passages in question can be reinterpreted to "be understood as focusing

attention on the need for special kinds of words to talk about the [*dao*]" (Ibid. 381). Bo Mou also seems to argue against the ineffability of *Dao*. He thinks that "because the eternal *Dao* goes on forever and keeps changing to transcend its own finite dimension, anything that has so far been (descriptively) characterized in language about the *Dao* only captures the finite part of the *Dao* that presents itself in a finite way" (2000: 435). But Mou argues, it is not the case that any language engagement with the ultimate concern will absolutely fail.

15   *Daodejing*, ch. 40 (Chan 1973: 160).
16   Another common translation is to break up the sentence differently to render it as making a distinction between "always eliminate desires" and "always have desires." Lau, Ivanhoe, and many others use that kind of translation. However, I don't think that Laozi would counsel people constantly to have desires. Also, when he persists in saying "the two are the same," he cannot possibly be identifying the elimination of desires and the possession of desires. Hence, here I adopt Chan's translation.
17   *Daodejing*, ch. 1 (Chan 1973: 139).
18   Ibid. ch. 4 (Lau 1963: 8).
19   Ibid. ch. 5 (Lau 1963: 9).
20   Ibid. ch. 25 (Chan 1973: 152).
21   Ibid. ch. 16 (Chan 1973: 147).
22   Ibid. ch. 25 (Chan 1973: 152).
23   Ibid. ch. 52 (Lau 1963: 59). Chinese does not have any distinction in the tenses of the verb. All the commonly used English translations employ the past tense in this sentence, such as Chan's "there was a beginning of the universe," Ivanhoe's "the world had a beginning" and James Legge's "the [*Dao*] which originated the world," etc. This use of past tense implies the temporal ordering of *Dao* and the world.
24   Ibid. ch. 51 (Chan 1973: 163).
25   Ibid. ch. 42 (Chan 1973: 160). There are many interpretations of what Laozi might have meant by "the One," "the two," and "the three." I shall not go into a detailed analysis here. Let it suffice to say that in the same chapter Laozi talks about "yin" and "yang"; so, "the two" could very likely designate *yin* and *yang*.
26   Ibid. ch. 40 (Lau 1963: 47).
27   Ibid. ch. 41 (Lau 1963: 48).
28   Ibid. ch. 39 (Chan 1973: 159).
29   Ibid. ch. 25 (Chan 1973: 152).
30   Ibid. ch. 14 (Chan 1973: 146).
31   Ibid. ch. 35 (Chan 1973: 157).
32   Ibid. ch. 21 (Lau 1963: 26).
33   Ibid. ch. 32 (Lau 1963: 37).
34   Ibid. ch. 25 (Ivanhoe 2000: 25). In Chinese philosophy, *Dao* is often called "the Great *Dao*." The difference between one's proper name and one's styled name is that the former is more often used among close family members, while the latter is the one used in public. As Ivanhoe explains it,

"There is a play here on the difference between one's *ming*, 'proper name,' and one's *zi*, 'style.' In traditional Chinese society, one does not use the former, personal name in public. And so the author can be understood as saying he is not intimately familiar with the *dao* and so knows only its style, or perhaps that it would be unseemly to speak its true and proper name to those unfamiliar with it" (2000: 89, n. 53).

35 Daodejing, ch. 25 (Chan 1973: 153).

36 The Chinese term used here is "*zi-ran (tzu-jan)*," which can be translated as "Nature" or "naturalness." Most commentators agree that the latter translation is better.

37 Xiaogan Liu also says: "by no means does [*zi-ran*] mean 'nature' in our sense as the natural world. Even when [*zi-ran*] is used as a noun, the meaning of the word is still primarily adjectival, indicating 'natural' instead of 'nature,' and it is thus far better to translate the noun [*zi-ran*] as 'natural-ness' or 'spontaneity'" (1998: 424).

38 Wang 1997: 291.

39 *Daodejing*, ch. 25 (Lau 1963: 30).

40 Quoted in Creel (1983: 312).

41 *Daodejing*, ch. 6 (Chan 1973: 142).

42 Kaltenmark 1969: 37.

43 *Daodejing*, ch. 20 (Chan 1973: 150).

44 As Kaltenmark puts it: "In [Laozi], the idea of mother, female, mystical womb is closely associated with that of emptiness" (1969: 43).

45 *Daodejing*, ch. 11 (Ivanhoe 2002: 11).

46 In contemporary analytic discourse, "metaphysical realism" and "scientific realism" are often used interchangeably or at least jointly. But the two views make separate claims, which do not have to be endorsed together. Scientific realism emphasizes the validity of science, claiming that successive scientific theories can often be viewed as better approximation to the truth. Under this view, there may eventually be a "finished science" that gives us the "one true and complete description of the way the world is." Laozi would not accept scientific realism even if he were to live in a world of modern science. To him, science, as part of human's projection of the world, is bound to fall short of capturing the way the world is.

47 This summary of theses is a paraphrase of Hilary Putnam's remarks in *Reason, Truth and History* (Cambridge: Cambridge University Press, 1981, p. 49), and from Ernest LePore and Barry Loewer's formulation of Putnam's characterization of metaphysical realism in "A Putnam's Progress" (*Midwest Studies in Philosophy* XII, 1988: 459–73, p. 460). But I deliberately changed some of the wording. What Putnam calls "the fixed totality of mind-independent objects," I change to "mind-independent reality." What Putnam calls "words or thought-signs," I change to "thought." I don't think the rewording alters the spirit of metaphysical realism, but it does allow us to see Laozi's view more in the light of metaphysical realism. Laozi thinks that reality exists independently of our conception, but distinctions of objects come from the conventions of language/signs. So, he

would not call this ultimate reality "the totality of objects," though he does embrace its mind-independence.

48 The parenthesis is added by LePore and Loewer (1988: 460).

49 Chad Hansen, in his analysis of Laozi's view on knowledge, points out that "where Western or Indian analyses of knowledge focus on propositional knowledge (knowing-that), Chinese, especially Taoist, critical theory focuses on practical knowledge *cum* skill (knowing-to or knowing-how-to.)" (1981: 322). In the same way, I argue that Laozi's notion of truth is also not to be viewed as expressing a relation between some proposition/ sentence and some states of affairs in the world.

50 *Daodejing*, ch. 70 (Lau 1963: 77).

51 This quote is from Gary Ebbs's interpretation of Putnam's argument (in "Realism and Rational Inquiry," *Philosophical Topics* 20(1), 1992: 1–33, p. 17).

52 *Daodejing*, ch. 21 (Lau 1963: 26).

53 Ibid. ch. 33 (Lau 1963: 28).

54 Ibid. ch. 30 (Lau 1963: 35); also ch. 60 (Lau 1963: 62).

55 Schwartz 1985: 204.

56 *Daodejing*, ch. 21 (Chan 1973: 150).

57 Kaltenmark 1969: 27.

58 *Daodejing*, ch. 15 (modification of Lau 1963: 19).

59 Ibid. ch. 28 (Chan 1973: 154).

60 Graham 1989: 223.

61 Ibid.

62 Hansen 1992: 223.

63 Kaltenmark 1969: 48.

64 Wang 1997: 302–3.

65 Graham 1989: 232.

66 Ibid.

67 Fu 1973: 384.

68 Schwartz 1985: 309.

69 Ahern 1977: 367.

70 Kasulis 1977: 391.

71 *Daodejing*, ch. 3 (Lau 1963: 7).

72 Schwartz 1985: 309.

73 Lau 1958: 357.

74 Ibid. 358.

75 *Daodejing*, ch. 80 (Ivanhoe 2000: 83).

76 Ibid. ch. 20 (Chan 1973: 149).

77 Ibid. ch. 2 (Chan 1973: 140).

78 Ibid. ch. 3 (Chan 1973: 140).

79 Ibid. ch. 20 (Chan 1973: 150).

80 Ibid.

81 Ibid. ch. 12 (Chan 1973: 145).

82 Ibid. ch. 18 (Chan 1973: 148).

83 Ibid. ch. 48 (Chan 1973: 162).

84 Ibid. ch. 49 (Chan 1973: 162–3).
85 Thompson 1990: 176–8. Laozi's political view is often compared to West-ern anarchistic theories. However, Roger Ames points out that "[a]n im-portant difference between [Daoist] political thought and Western anarchist theory is that [Daoism], with its conception of the correlativity between person and state, does not reject the state as an *artificial* structure, but rather sees the state as a *natural* institution, analogous perhaps to the family. The [*Laozi*] certainly rejects coercive rule and authoritarian government, but importantly, devotes considerable attention to non-coercive and non-authoritarian organization under the aegis of the *Sage-King*" (1983: 35; italics in the original].
86 *Daodejing*, ch. 29 (Ivanhoe 2000: 29).
87 Ibid. ch. 31 (Ivanhoe 2000: 31).
88 Ibid. ch. 30 (Ivanhoe 2000: 30).

Chapter 7   Zhuangzi (Chuang Tzu)

1 Yearley 1996: 152.
2 Hansen 1992: 265.
3 The grouping has been established since as early as in the fourth century AD. See Watson 1968: 13–14.
4 For example, A. C. Graham attributes chapters 23–7 and chapter 32 to Zhuangzi; see Graham 1983: 4.
5 Commentators who based their interpretations on the whole *Zhuangzi* tend to find more metaphysical discussion on the transcendent *Dao*, which, however, is not a major concern in the Inner Chapters.
6 The meaning of this title has been debated since the ancient time. The more accepted interpretation is to render the title as "A Discourse on the Equal-ity of Things." Most commonly used English translations follow this tradi-tion. However, a contesting view suggests that the title is really about different "theories of things" and the author's intent is to equalize the various theories. Commentators of this camp argue that the whole chapter is aimed at refuting theories and discourses, and thus Zhuangzi would not describe his own chapter as a "discourse." They suggest rendering the title as "Equalizing Theories of Things" instead. However, commentators of the other camp argue that "theories of things," as a term in Chinese, was introduced long after Zhuangzi's times. I think that the best rendition of the title is "On the Equality of Things and Theories," which I have seen only in Kuang-ming Wu's writings. This rendition avoids the difficulty the other two renditions encounter and fits best with the content of the whole chapter.
7 As Herrlee G. Creel puts it, while Laozi "gives a great deal of advice to kings and feudal lords and ministers on how to get and hold power," Zhuangzi "is in the main politically indifferent or even anarchistic" (1970: 6).

8   *Zhuangzi,* ch. 7 (Watson 1964: 95).
9   Yeh 1983; Berkson 1996.
10 Lee, J. H. 1998.
11 Lee, K. S. 1996.
12 Kjellberg 1994, 1996; Raphals 1996.
13 Li 1993.
14 Parkes 1983; Hall 1984.
15 Wu, L. C. 1986.
16 Owens 1990.
17 Even though contemporary analytic commentators commonly associate various forms of skepticism with Zhuangzi, a few people argue that he is not a skeptic at all. See, for example, Sun 1953; Cheng 1977.
18 Some other interpretations are left out here for the sake of brevity. One of these is epistemic nihilism, suggested by Deborah and David Soles. They argue that Zhuangzi is an epistemological nihilist "who rejects, as meaningless, any talk of knowledge" (1998: 161). They say, "It is not that knowledge is something that perhaps we could have had but happen to lack; rather there is no such meaningful concept or category that might or might have instances" (ibid.). Epistemological nihilism is different from radical skepticism, according to the Soles, in that a skeptic is still interested in eventually gaining true knowledge, while an epistemological nihilist simply declares the whole pursuit meaningless. They think that for Zhuangzi, there is no "perspective-free" knowledge; there is no "God's-eye view perspective." All forms of knowledge are equally limited and therefore unsatisfactory. However, in attributing this ultimately negative view to Zhuangzi, the Soles seem to leave out Zhuangzi's extensive portrayal of "the True Man" and "the Perfect Man" who have gained true knowledge of *Dao.*
19 Hansen 1983: 35–9.
20 Berkson 1996: 98.
21 Ivanhoe 1996: 199.
22 See Berkson 1996; Chinn 1997; Kjellberg 1996; Schwitzgebel 1996 and Van Norden 1996.
23 Raphals 1996: 26–49.
24 Allinson 1989: 23.
25 There are others who accept Graham's anti-rationalism interpretation. David Loy (1996) and Mark Berkson (1996) are two examples.
26 Graham 1983: 9.
27 Graham 1989: 194.
28 Lee, J. H. 1998: 458–9.
29 Ibid. 463.
30 Goodman 1985; Sun 1953; Berkson 1996; Ivanhoe 1996. Berkson and Ivanhoe did not specifically attribute "realism" to Zhuangzi. But Berkson says: "there is a way the world really is, a true reality, an underlying *Dao*" (1996: 118). Ivanhoe says: "The *Dao* is a metaphysical concept; it is the deep structure of the pattern and processes of the world" (1996: 201). Both of these comments seem to me to be giving a realist interpretation of *Dao.*

31   In my article "A Daoist Conception of Truth: Laozi's Metaphysical Realism vs. Zhuangzi's Internal Realism" (2003) I argue that the combination of these views constitutes *internal realism* as defined by Hilary Putnam. I shall not repeat the argument here.

32   Sun 1953: 138.

33   *Zhuangzi*, ch. 2 (Watson 1964: 41).

34   Ibid. (Watson 1964: 38).

35   Ibid. ch. 17 (Watson 1964: 99).

36   Ibid. ch. 2 (Watson 1964: 35).

37   Jung Lee offers an interesting analysis of this passage. He says, "For [Zhuangzi], the indexicality of demonstratives, the basis of all judgments, undergirds his conceptual relativity" (1998: 456). So, he takes this discussion of "this" and "that" to be a discussion on indexicals.

38   As Christoph Harbsmeier points out, "Zhuangzi nowhere directly and dogmatically states that we cannot know. He only persists in asking 'How do we know?' He is not an adherent of the dogma that we cannot know anything" (1993: 25).

39   *Zhuangzi*, ch. 2 (Watson 1964: 43).

40   Ibid. (Watson 1964: 43–4).

41   Ibid. (Watson 1964: 35).

42   Ibid. (Watson 1964: 34).

43   Ibid. (Watson 1964: 44).

44   Chung-ying Cheng also separates two levels of truth. He thinks that Zhuangzi's skepticism and his metaphysics of [*dao*] "reinforce each other and form a dialectical process of establishing a theory of distinction between lower level (limited) truth and higher level (unlimited) truth" (1977: 141).

45   *Zhuangzi*, ch. 2 (Watson 1964: 39).

46   The closest Zhuangzi gets to describing *Dao* is the following seemingly paradoxical remark: "The Way has its reality and its signs but is without action or form. You can hand it down but you cannot receive it; you can get it but you cannot see it. Before Heaven and earth existed it was there, firm from ancient times. It gave spirituality to the spirits and to God; it gave birth to Heaven and to earth. It exists beyond the highest point, and yet you cannot call it lofty; it exists beneath the limit of the six directions, and yet you cannot call it deep. It was born before heaven and earth, and yet you cannot say it has been there for long; it is earlier than the ancient times, and yet you cannot call it old" (chapter 6: Watson 1964: 77).

47   Sun 1953: 145.

48   *Zhuangzi*, ch. 1 (Watson 1964: 27).

49   Watson 1964: 5.

50   *Zhuangzi*, ch. 22 (Watson 1968: 244).

51   Ibid. ch. 2 (Chan 1973: 182).

52   See Ivanhoe's explication and critique of Wong's position (1996: 202–9).

53   Kjellberg 1996: 14.

54   Ivanhoe 1996: 200.

55   Berkson 1996: 108.

56   Yearley 1983: 130.
57   Ibid. 133.
58   *Zhuangzi,* ch. 6 (Ivanhoe and Van Norden 2003: 231).
59   Ibid. ch. 22 (Watson 1968: 239).
60   Ibid. ch. 6 (Watson 1964: 84).
61   Using Confucius as his spokesperson, Zhuangzi says, "For those who thrive in the Way, don't bother about them and their lives will be secure" (ibid. Watson 1964: 84).
62   "Their skin is like frost, and they are gentle and restrained like virgins. They don't eat the five grains but sip wind and drink dew. They chariot the cloudy mists, ride the flying dragons, and wander beyond the four seas. By concentrating on their spirit, they keep things from harm and ripen the harvest" (ibid. ch. 1: Ivanhoe and Van Norden 2003: 207).
63   Ibid. ch. 6 (Ivanhoe and Van Norden 2003: 230).
64   "Cook Ding" is the translation for "*pao-ding,*" which in Chinese either means "someone who manages the kitchen," or "some cook named 'Ding'." Here I adopt the second interpretation.
65   *Zhuangzi,* ch. 3 (Ivanhoe and Van Norden 2003: 220). This quote contains a slight modification of the original translation.
66   Ibid. ch. 6 (Watson 1964: 83).
67   As John C. H. Wu puts it, "[Zhuangzi] did not believe, as later degenerate [Daoists] came to believe, in the cult of physical immortality. . . . When he spoke of the 'True Man' whom water would not drown, nor fire burn, nor death kill, he was really speaking of the spirit or soul of man, which is not something physical and is therefore beyond the realm of time and space" (1963: 19).
68   *Zhuangzi,* ch. 6 (Ivanhoe and Van Norden 2003: 231).
69   Ibid. ch. 4 (Watson 1964: 63).
70   Ibid. (Watson 1964, 60–1).
71   Major 1975: 265.
72   *Zhuangzi,* ch. 17 (Watson 1964: 106).
73   Ibid. ch. 4 (Watson 1964: 59).
74   Ibid. ch. 1 (Watson 1964: 24).
75   Ibid. ch. 6 (Watson 1964: 87).
76   Ibid. ch. 4 (Watson 1964: 58).
77   Even though Zhuangzi emphasizes "survival" as an important goal of life, he does not advise fear of natural death. As Major puts it, "[Zhuangzi] saw no reason to fear a natural death in nature's good time, but an untimely death at the hands of a cruel and unnatural world was very much to be avoided" (1975: 275).
78   As Graham points out: "The 'Inner Chapters' show a remarkable interest, not shared by later [Daoists] even in [*Zhuangzi*] itself, in cripples, freaks, mutilated criminals, who are able to accept and remain inwardly unaltered by their condition" (1989: 202).
79   This is the "therapeutic" view again. See Ivanhoe 1996; Van Norden 1996; Graham 1989.

80 David Loy says: "Daoism and Buddhism agree that there is no such personal identity or continuity [as the self], which means that we are, in effect, depreciating everything that exists in order to cherish something illusory" (1996: 53).

81 *Zhuangzi*, ch. 6 (Chan 1973: 192).

82 Ibid. ch. 18 (Watson 1964: 113).

83 Ibid. ch. 6 (Watson 1964: 84).

84 Ibid. ch. 2 (Ivanhoe and Van Norden 2003: 217–18).

85 Ibid. ch. 6 (Chan 1973: 194).

86 Whether in the afterlife there is any awareness of the present life is left an open question. As we have seen, the story of Lady Li is based on the possibility that we are simply transported to a different world and we can still remember our previous regret about dying. Zhuangzi would not assert either form of afterlife, since his attitude would be: "How can I ever know?"

87 *Zhuangzi*, ch. 22 (Watson 1968: 235).

88 In ch. 32 in the Miscellaneous Chapters, the story of Zhuangzi's imminent death is told. Zhuangzi instructs his students not to prepare a sumptuous burial for him. He says, "I will have heaven and earth for my coffin." When students express the concern that the crows and kites will eat his corpse, Zhuangzi replies that it is either the crows and kites above ground or the mole crickets and ants underground who will devour his body, "Wouldn't it be rather bigoted to deprive one group in order to supply the other?" (Watson 1968: 361).

89 Graham 1989: 203.

90 Legge 1979: 18; italics in original.

91 *Zhuangzi*, ch. 2 (Ivanhoe and Van Norden 2003: 219).

92 Ibid. ch. 6 (Chan 1973: 197).

93 Wenyu Xie puts it well: "It becomes clear that what Zhuangzi wants to analyze is not cosmology, as he clearly rejects the feasibility of investigating the origin of all things in his criticism of the *Daodejing*. Rather, he wants to penetrate into human existence" (2000: 484–5).

94 The same story is also recorded in chapter 32 in the Miscellaneous Chapters. See Watson 1968: 360–1.

95 Eric Schwitzgebel, for instance, seems to suggest such an interpretive attitude. He says, "Zhuangzi is setting himself up to have what *he* says taken less seriously . . . I doubt, then, that Zhuangzi would be too bothered if the reader did not place much credence in his words" (1996: 72).

96 The *Analects*, 14: 41 (Chan 1973: 43).

97 *Zhuangzi*, ch. 4 (Watson 1964: 63).

98 Ibid.

Chapter 8   Hanfeizi (Han Fei Tzu)

1 "Legalism" is a term derived from "'law." The school of thought represented by Hanfeizi was originally called the School of *fa* – the School of

Law. Therefore, "legalism" seems a fitting rendition and has been adopted by almost all translators. Arthur Waley, however, opts to call this school "the Realists," for the reason that the major principle behind this school is that government must be based on "the actual facts of the world as it now exists" (1982: 151).

2 Liao 1939.

3 See, for example, Liang, E. 1976; Liang, L. 1976; Ti 1978; Tong 1982/83; Yang 1978. The opening paragraph of Chung-ying Cheng's "Legalism versus Confucianism: A Philosophical Appraisal" (1981) gives the political background of this movement.

4 Lee 1975: 31.

5 Several commentators have made the same observation. Yih-jing Lin (1989) calls Hanfeizi's theory of human nature "psychological egoism," which is the claim that humans are by nature self-interested. See also Wang 1977; Ho 1988; Goldin 2001.

6 *Hanfeizi*, ch. 17 (Watson 1964: 86).

7 Ibid. ch. 49 (Watson 1964: 98).

8 Cf. ibid. ch. 54.

9 Hanfeizi says, "In ancient times when [Cang Jie] created the system of writing, he used the character for 'private' to express the idea of self-centeredness, and combined the elements for 'private' and 'opposed to' to form the character for 'public.' The fact that public and private are mutually opposed was already well understood at the time of [Cang Jie]. To regard the two as being identical in interest is a disaster which comes from lack of consideration" (ibid. ch. 49; Watson 1964: 106).

10 Fung 1983: 327.

11 *Hanfeizi*, ch. 49 (Watson 1964: 103).

12 Ibid. ch. 14 (my translation).

13 *Analects* 2:3 (Chan 1973: 22).

14 *Hanfeizi*, ch. 49 (Watson 1964: 101).

15 Fung 1983: 313.

16 *Hanfeizi*, ch. 50 (Ivanhoe and Van Norden 2003: 341).

17 Lee 1975: 45.

18 Ibid. 45.

19 *Hanfeizi*, ch. 50 (Ivanhoe and Van Norden 2003: 341).

20 Ibid. (Ivanhoe and Van Norden 2003: 341).

21 Ibid. (Chan 1973: 253).

22 Ibid. (Chan 1973: 254).

23 Lee 1975: 41.

24 *Hanfeizi*, ch. 47 (Liao 1939, vol. 2: 248).

25 These arguments are paraphrased from Hanfeizi's own remarks. They do not exhaust all the arguments that he has made, but they are representatives of his general line of reasoning.

26 Hanfeizi says, "According to human nature, none are more affectionate than parents who love all children, and yet not all children are necessarily orderly. Although the parents' love is deep, why should they cease to be

disorderly? Now the love of ancient kings for their people could not have surpassed that of parents for their children. Since children do [not] necessarily cease to be disorderly, then why should people be orderly? Furthermore, if the ruler sheds tears when punishment is carried out according to law, that is a way to show humanity but not the way to conduct a government. For it is humanity that causes one to shed tears and wish for no punishment, but it is law that punishment cannot be avoided. Ancient kings relied on laws and paid no heed to tears. It is clear that humanity is not adequate for a government" (*Hanfeizi*, ch. 49; Chan 1973: 257–8).

27 Hanfeizi says, "If we had to depend on an arrow being absolutely straight by nature, there would be no arrow in a hundred generations. If we had to depend on a piece of wood being perfectly round by nature, there would not be any wheel in a thousand generations. There is not one naturally straight arrow or naturally round piece of wood in a hundred generations, and yet in every generation people ride carriages and shoot birds. Why? Because of the application of the methods of straightening and bending. Although there is a naturally straight arrow or a naturally round piece of wood [once in a hundred generations] which does not depend on any straightening or bending, the skilled workman does not value it. Why? Because it is not just one person who wishes to ride and not just one shot that the archer wishes to shoot. Similarly, the enlightened ruler does not value people who are naturally good and who do not depend on reward and punishment. Why? Because the laws of the state must not be neglected and government is not for only one man. Therefore the ruler who has the technique does not follow the good that happens by chance but practices the way of necessity" (ibid. ch. 50; Chan 1973: 253–4).

28 Hanfeizi says, "Confucius was a sage known throughout the empire. He cultivated his own character and elucidated his doctrines and traveled extensively within the four seas (China). People within the four seas loved his doctrine of humanity and praised his doctrine of righteousness. And yet only seventy people became his devoted pupils. The reason is that few people value humanity and it is difficult to practice righteousness. . . . On the other hand, Duke Ai of Lu was an inferior ruler. When he sat on the throne as the sovereign of the state, none within the borders of the state dared refuse to submit. For people are originally submissive to power and it is truly easy to subdue people with power. Therefore Confucius turned out to be a subordinate and Duke Ai, contrary to one's expectation, became a ruler. . . . Nowadays in trying to persuade rulers, scholars do not advocate the use of power which is sure to win, but say that if one is devoted to the practice of humanity and righteousness, one will become a true king. This is to expect that every ruler must be equal to Confucius and that all people in the world are equal to his [seventy-odd] followers. This is absolutely impossible" (ibid. ch. 49: Chan 1973: 258).

29 Hanfeizi says, "When the sage rules the state, he does not depend on people to do good for him, but utilizes their inability to do wrong. If he depends on people to do good for him, we cannot even count ten within

the state, but if he utilizes the people's inability to do wrong, the whole country may be regulated. A ruler makes use of the majority and neglects the minority, and so he does not devote himself to virtue but to law" (ibid. ch. 50: Chan 1973: 253).

30 Lee 1975: 40.
31 Wang 1977: 39.
32 *Hanfeizi*, ch. 38 (my translation).
33 Schwartz 1985: 327.
34 Fung 1983: 318.
35 *Hanfeizi*, ch. 11 (my translation).
36 Ibid. ch. 17 (Watson 1964: 86).
37 Ibid. ch. 38 (Chan 1973: 256).
38 This notion is more complicated than the notion of power or authority in the political context. As Arthur Waley points out, the Chinese word for "power," "potency," or "force" and the Chinese word for "position," "circumstance," or "situation," are one and the same (1982: 181). In Hanfeizi's usage, one possesses power *in virtue of* one's political position or surrounding circumstances. Outside of political context, the word also signifies a necessary tendency in the natural development of affairs. Peter R. Moody aptly calls it "the sum of the determining conditions" (1979: 320). Here I am following the common practice in emphasizing the political dimension of this notion.
39 *Hanfeizi*, ch. 43 (Chan 1973: 255).
40 Ibid. ch. 7 (Watson 1964: 30).
41 Ibid. (Chan 1973: 256–7).
42 Ibid. ch. 5 (Ivanhoe and Van Norden 2003: 301).
43 Ibid. (Ivanhoe and Van Norden 2003: 299).
44 These two chapters are "Explicating the *Laozi*" (ch. 20) and "Metaphors for the *Laozi*" (ch. 21). These chapters express the most abstract philosophical thinking that is distinguishable from the rest of the book. Naturally, many commentators doubt their authenticity. Burton Watson's *Han Fei Tzu: Basic Writings*, for example, does not include them. However, Hanfeizi makes similar remarks, though in a less abstract context, in other chapters. See, for example, ch. 8, where he also gives his exposition of "*Dao*." It is reasonable to conclude that he did derive philosophical inspiration for his practical political theory from the abstract philosophy of Laozi.
45 *Hanfeizi*, ch. 20 (Chan 1973: 261).
46 Ibid.
47 Ibid.
48 Ibid.
49 Ibid. ch. 5 (Ivanhoe and Van Norden 2003: 298).
50 Ames 1994: 51.
51 *Hanfeizi*, ch. 5 (Ivanhoe and Van Norden 2003: 298–9).
52 Ibid. (Ivanhoe and Van Norden 2003: 298).
53 Lee 1975: 34.

54 *Hanfeizi*, ch. 49 (Chan 1973: 260).
55 Ibid. ch. 5 (Ivanhoe and Van Norden 2003: 298–9).
56 Moody 1979: 323.
57 *Hanfeizi*, ch. 14 (Liso 1939, vol. 1: 124; my modifications in square brackets).
58 Wang 1977: 48.

Part II   Introduction

1 Litian Fang (1989) gives a good explanation of the social and intellectual setting of China at the time, which rendered the acceptance of Indian Buddhism possible.
2 Wright 1959.
3 Pure Land Buddhism (*jing-tu-zong*), although probably the most popular form of Buddhism in China, focuses more on religious practices. Hence, we shall not deal with this school.
4 "Shakyamuni" means "the sage from the tribe of the Shakyas." See Masao Abe's "Zen and Buddhism," *Journal of Chinese Philosophy* 3, 1976: 236.
5 Ibid.
6 *Sunyata* is usually translated as "emptiness" or "void." In Buddhism, it is also a designator for the Truth, the Ultimate Reality, or the Substance.
7 The Buddha apparently was not the inventor of the view that the essence of life is suffering. According to Radhakrishnan, "That life is suffering and the object of the world only lures and torments, seemed to be the heritage from the *Upanishads*" (1962: 277).
8 This quote is my translation from the Chinese text, *The Contemporary Interpretation of Indian Buddhism*, written by a scholar in Hong Kong, Ru-jun Wu.
9 Kalupahana 1992: 86.
10 According to Kalupahana, the central conception of Buddhism is the "theory of dependent arising" (1992: x). This notion is expressed as "dependent origination" by the Dalai Lama. Here I use "dependent co-arising," which is also a common translation for this notion.
11 More on this in chapter 9.
12 For example, the tree is the effect of the seed while, at the same time, the form of the tree is the cause of the seed.
13 Cf. Zeuschner 1981: 401–2.
14 Kalupahana 1992: 77; italics in original.
15 According to Derk Bodde's note: "Hinayana Buddhism, which is closer to the tenets of original Buddhism, has to this day remained dominant among the Buddhist countries of Southeast Asia. Mahayana Buddhism, which is an enormously elaborated and sophisticated development of primitive Buddhism, received its chief growth in the countries north and northeast of India: Central Asia, China, and Japan, especially China" (Fung 1983, vol. II: 238).
16 Ibid.

Chapter 9 The Consciousness-Only (*Wei-Shi*) School

1 There are other existing translations for the name of this school, such as the "Representation-Only School" (see Hamilton 1938), the "Mere Ideation School" (see Bodde's translation of Fung 1983), the "Mere Consciousness School" (see Wei 1973; Kern 1988), or the "Mere Conception School" (Kalupahana 1992). Here I follow Chan's translation in his *Sourcebook* (1973).

2 The story of his pilgrimage inspired later writers to come up with various versions of the trip, the most notable of which is Wu Cheng-en's *The Journey to the West*, first published in 1592. It became one of the four classic works in Chinese literature.

3 The background of Xuan-zang's writing of this book and the selection of Dharmapâla's commentary over the rest was told by Kuiji, in his annotation to *Cheng Wei-Shi Lun*. This story has been treated as authentic by most scholars historically. Recently, however, Dan Lusthaus challenged Kuiji's story. He questions the existence of ten commentaries or even the fact that Dharmapala wrote a commentary. He speculates that the whole story of the transmission of *Cheng Wei-Shi Lun* could have been invented by Kuiji to secure his own status within the school. See Lusthaus 2002: ch. 15.

4 According to Hamilton and La Vallée Poussin's comparative study, Xuan-zang's text often contains words whose equivalents are not found in the other Tibetan or Sanskrit texts or even in the other Chinese translations (see Hamilton 1938.) Dan Lusthaus's comparative studies of the original text, Xuan-zang's translation, and another Chinese translation of the *Thirty Stanzas* also shows how Xuan-zang took liberties with his translation. See Lusthaus 2002: ch. 12.

5 Cf. Wei 1973: 80–9.

6 There are, unfortunately, very limited resources for studying the thought of this school. Of the *Twenty Stanzas*, the only English translation is by Clarence Hamilton (1938); of *Cheng Wei-Shi Lun*, the only complete English translation is by Tat Wei (1973), who based his translation on the French translation by Louis de La Vallée Poussin (1928). Both of these English translations are presently out of print, and only a limited number of libraries have a copy of these books. Hamilton's translation is largely readable, and it includes a lot of footnotes based on Xuan-zang's student Kuiji's commentary. Tat Wei's translation retains most of the Sanskrit terms and is thus difficult to read. For an alternative, we also have the excerpt in Chan's *Sourcebook* (1973: ch. 23), which contains most of the important discussion of the original book. I therefore recommend it. Dan Lusthaus's *Buddhist Phenomenology* (2002: 273–350) also contains a comparative translation of Vasubandhu's *Thirty Stanzas*.

7 See Part II's Introduction for the explanation of this notion.

8 The details of the transformations will be discussed later in this chapter.

9   In the Chinese Consciousness-Only School, the words "consciousness" and "mind," along with "thought" and "cognition," are used interchangeably. According to Kalupahana's interpretation of Vasubandhu's philosophy, however, such a conflation constitutes a gross misunderstanding of Vasubandhu's metaphysical view. Kalupahana argues that Vasubandhu "was no metaphysical idealist." He thinks it is unfortunate that in the Chinese translations, all these four terms are "lumped together and defined as synonyms" (1992: 186). Since we are dealing with the Chinese (Xuan-zang's) modification of Vasubandhu's philosophy, we will use the two terms interchangeably and elaborate on the idealistic theme in Xuan-zang's own philosophy.

10   Chan 1973: 386.

11   There are many other plausible interpretations of these three phrases.

12   Cf. Fung 1983: 329–30.

13   Chan 1973: 389; my italics.

14   Ibid. 393.

15   Lusthaus 2002: 459.

16   "The Middle Way," sometimes translated as "the middle path," is the translation for Sanskrit *Mādhyamaka*. It is the name of a branch of the Mahayana School, whose main doctrine is that things are neither existent nor nonexistent. It stands as the middle way between the School of Being and the School of Non-Being (the School of Emptiness). See Part II Introduction.

17   According to Xuan-zang's *A Treatise on the Establishment of Consciousness-Only*, this is the consciousness "whose fruits ripen at a later time . . . because it possesses in abundance the nature to ripen at later times" (Chan 1973: 380).

18   Ibid. 386; italics mine.

19   Ibid. 382.

20   Ibid.

21   *Thirty Stanzas*, verse 17.

22   Kern 1988: 284.

23   Chan 1973: 382 (square brackets in original).

24   Different Buddhist schools interpret "nirvana" differently. That the term denotes a separate realm is the consensus of the Theravada Schools. In this respect, the Consciousness-Only School's teaching is closer to Theravada than to Mahayana. See Part II's Introduction, where the differences between the two branches are explained.

25   Chan 1973: 383.

26   Ibid. 382 (parenthesis mine).

27   The *transformation* here should be taken in a different sense. When consciousness is transformed into wisdom, it is not engaging in the threefold transformation that result from defilement or perfuming. Consciousness is actually being eliminated or terminated in this process. Derk Bodde uses "turned over" to supplement the connotation of "transformation" in this context. He translates Fung's comments this way: "At this time the eight kinds of consciousness are all 'turned over' or transformed into . . . true Wisdom, and become untainted, i.e., devoid of all tainted seeds" (Fung

1983: 338). Dan Lusthaus also uses "Overturning the Basis" to explain the process of turning consciousness into *wisdom* (which he translates as "enlightened cognitive abilities"; 2002: 511).

28 Wei 1973: 767–9.

29 The detailed explanation of the methods of cultivation and the stages of attainment is given in Book IX of Xuan-zang's *A Treatise on the Establishment of Consciousness-Only*. In this Book, Xuan-zang describes the "five stages" in the "Holy Path of Attainment," which are: (i) the stage of moral provisioning; (ii) the stage of intensified effort; (iii) the stage of unimpeded penetrating understanding; (iv) the stage of exercising cultivation; (v) the stage of ultimate realization. See Wei 1973: 669–809.

30 Ibid. 769.

31 According to Lusthaus, "Tathata" means "seeing everything, including so-called appearance, just as it is." He says: "Claming that nirvana is a cognitive object is problematic. More commonly Buddhists, especially in Mahayana, use the term tathata to denote the object of Awakened cognition" (2002: 255). In this sense, nirvana is an ontological state, while *tathata* is a cognitive (epistemic) state.

32 *Thirty Stanzas*, verses 28–30 (Chan 1973: 394–5); brackets and parenthesis in original.

33 Lusthaus 2002: 533.

34 The discussion on the insistence on dharmas first appears in Vasubandhu's Commentary on his own *Twenty Stanzas*. The same discussion is recorded in Xuan-zang's *A Treatise on the Establishment of Consciousness-Only*, though the original *Thirty Stanzas*, on which *A Treatise on the Establishment of Consciousness-Only* comments, does not contain this discussion.

35 These claims were all made by Vasubandhu's contemporary schools of thought. Xuan-zang's major disciple Kuiji identified each of these theories in his commentary. Hamilton (1938) lists these annotations in his footnotes. My interpretation of what these schools say is primarily based on the following introductions to Indian philosophy: Chatterjee and Datta 1968; Banerjee 1974; Raju 1971.

36 According to Chatterjee and Datta, "'Cârvâka' is the word that generally stands for 'materialist.' But the original meaning of this word is shrouded in mystery. According to one view, 'Cârvâka' was originally the name of a sage who propounded materialism. The common name 'Cârvâka' is derived from this proper name and means the followers of that sage, i.e., a materialist. According to another view, 'Cârvâka' was even originally a common descriptive name given to a materialist, either because he preaches the doctrine of 'eat, drink and be merry' (*carv* – eat, chew), or because his words are pleasant and nice (*câru* – nice, *vâk* – word)" (1968: 55–6).

37 Cf. *Twenty Stanzas*, Stanza XI and Commentary (Hamilton 1938: 47).

38 Raju 1971: 144.

39 Cf. *Twenty Stanzas*, Stanza XI and Commentary (Hamilton 1938: 47).

40 This interpretation follows the commentary of Xuan-zang's major disciple Kuiji. See Hamilton 1938: 51, n. 85.

41 Cf. *Twenty Stanzas*, Stanza XIII and Commentary (Hamilton 1938: 51–3).

42 According to Raju, "the word Vedanta means the end of Veda, because the Upanisads form its last part, and it also means the final teaching of the Vedas. The Vedas are supposed to teach different philosophies to different men with different levels of maturity, and the Vedanta is meant, it is said, for those men whose minds are the most mature" (1971: 49).

43 Ibid.

44 Cf. *Twenty Stanzas*, Stanza XIV and Commentary (Hamilton 1938: 55–7).

45 The discussion on the insistence of the self appears only in Xuan-zang's *A Treatise on the Establishment of Consciousness-Only*. It is not in the original *Thirty Stanzas* by Vasubandhu.

46 Lusthaus 2002: 428.

47 Ibid.

48 Cf. *A Treatise on the Establishment of Consciousness-Only* (Chan 1973: 375; Wei 1973: 15–17).

49 Cf. ibid.

50 Cf. ibid. (Chan 1973: 376; Wei 1973: 17).

51 There are two other variations of this theory; one claims that the self is separate from the five aggregates, the other claims that the self is neither identical with nor separate from the five aggregates. Since the latter two theses do not contribute any new view of the self, and the refutations simply point out their incoherence, I shall skip those two theories here.

52 Cf. *A Treatise on the Establishment of Consciousness-Only* (Chan 1973: 376; Wei 1973: 17–19).

53 Different Buddhist schools often interpret the Buddha's teachings differently, and they all have their textual support. It would seem that the Buddha does not have a consistent teaching. According to the Consciousness-Only School, some of the teachings were meant for people with little intelligence or people at the initial stage of their learning. It argues that only the Consciousness-Only is the Buddha's real intent. As we shall see in the next two chapters, both Tian-tai and Hua-yan schools also analyze the various teachings of the Buddha into different stages or levels.

54 The arguments are from Xuan-zang's *A Treatise on the Establishment of Consciousness-Only*, Book V, ch. 2: "Proofs of Consciousness-Only." Cf. Wei 1973: 507–25.

55 Wei 1973: 507.

56 This problem is dealt with in Verses and Commentaries 1–2 of the *Twenty Stanzas*.

57 What is described here could be what we now call the "eye floaters syndrome," which is when people see tiny black lines floating in their visual fields. These floaters are probably caused by tiny bits of vitreous gel or cells casting shadows on the retina.

58 This is an extended translation of the original text. The original text uses "hungry ghosts" and the "pus river" as the illustration. To understand the point, one has to know the whole story about the transmigration of different life forms and the hellish creatures discussed in Buddhism.

59 Chan 1973: 389.
60 As Chan explains: "This school treats regularity [consistency and continu-
    ity of ideas] as simply characters of dharmas and as such, to be explained
    in terms of cause and effect. In this process of mutual cause and effect,
    certain seeds regularly perfume in a certain way, and therefore people with
    similar seeds in them are perfumed in the same way" (ibid. 390).
61 This problem is introduced in Verses and Commentaries 19–20 of the
    Twenty Stanzas. But Vasubandhu's answer to the objector's question is not
    satisfactory. Xuan-zang takes up further discussion in his *Treatise*. The
    following discussion is based on Xuan-zang's Commentary on Stanza 17,
    in his *A Treatise on the Establishment of Consciousness-Only* (see Chan
    1973: 391–2).
62 The original objection is: "If external matter is really nonexistent, it may
    be granted that it is not a sphere of objects for one's inner consciousness.
    But the mind of another person really exists. Why is it not an object of
    one's own consciousness?" (ibid. 391).
63 Ibid. 392.
64 Ibid. 391.
65 Hamilton 1938: 77.

Chapter 10   The Hua-yan (Hua-yen) School

1 The Sanskrit title for this scripture is *Avatamsaka*. Thomas Cleary (1993)
   translates it as "The Flower Ornament Scripture," while Wing-tsit Chan
   (1973) translates it as "The Flowery Splendor Scripture."
2 Chan 1973: 406.
3 According to Garma C. C. Chang's analysis, "*Li*, in different contexts,
   can mean 'principle,' 'universal truth,' 'reason,' 'the abstract,' the 'law,'
   'noumenon,' 'judgment,' 'knowledge,' and so forth" (1971: 142).
4 Chang says: "[Shi] can mean a 'thing,' an 'event,' the 'particular,' the
   'concrete,' 'phenomenon,' 'matter,' and so on" (ibid.).
5 These ten gates (theories) describe the ten fundamental aspects of the
   nature of existence. They include the nature of dependent arising, the
   nature of characterless non-generation, the entry into nirvana, etc. In this
   chapter, we will not discuss them separately from the general analysis of
   Fa-zang's metaphysical theory. For their names and descriptions, see for
   example Fa-zang's "A Treatise on the Gold Lion" (Chan 1973: 411–13),
   and Yu-lan Fung's explanation (Fung 1983: 341).
6 Chan translates this as "the realm of facts," and Cleary translates it as
   "the realm of phenomena." But I think Yu-lan Fung's "the realm of
   things" is a better translation since it preserves the literal meaning of the
   original Chinese phrase.
7 There are various Chinese translations of the *Hua-yan Sutra*, differing in
   length (most notably the following three versions: 60 scrolls, dated 420 AD;
   80 scrolls, dated 699 AD; 40 scrolls, dated 798 AD). Cleary's translation

(1993) is based on the longest version, 80 scrolls, which was produced by a monk named Shikshananda (652–710). This text is divided into 39 books (chapters). In the first entry of the suggested primary text at the end of this chapter, I list the chapters I would recommend for various reader interests.

8   These are all selected in Cleary 1983.

9   In Chan 1973.

10 *Hua-yan Sutra*, ch. 10: 300 (page references here and in subsequent such notes are from Cleary 1993).

11 Cleary 1983: 157.

12 *Hua-yan Sutra*, ch. 29: 880–6.

13 Ibid. ch. 2: 175.

14 Ibid. ch. 5: 248.

15 There is another sense of "emptiness" which all Buddhist schools reject: the sense of *annihilation* or *extinction*. The difference between "void" or "nil," and "annihilation" or "extinction," is that the former set depicts a constant state while the latter set depicts the negation of a previously existing state – the state of *being*. As Chang explains, "The common sense notion of death is a typical example of emptiness of annihilation: life exists for a period, then it is annihilated by external or natural causes and is reduced to nothingness" (1971: 63). Since for Buddhists phenomena are *by nature* empty and noumenon is *eternally* empty, their notion of *emptiness* cannot be taken to mean this temporary state of annihilation.

16 *Hua-yan Sutra*, ch. 14: 375.

17 Cf. Cheng-guan, "Mirror of the Mysteries of the Universe of the Hua-yan" (Cleary 1983: 105).

18 *Hua-yan Sutra*, ch. 14: 382.

19 Ibid. ch. 29: 880.

20 Ibid. ch. 20: 452.

21 "The Mysterious Gates of the Unitary Vehicle of the Hua-yan" (Cleary 1983: 145).

22 "Cultivation of Contemplation of the Inner Meaning of the Hua-yan" (Cleary 1983: 165).

23 Ibid.

24 *Hua-yan Sutra*, ch. 20: 445.

25 Ibid. 449.

26 There are, of course, a few commentators who also point out the idealistic spirit of Hua-yan Buddhism. See, for example, Chang 1971 and Lai 1986.

27 Fung 1983: 359.

28 Cook 1979: 380.

29 Ibid. 369.

30 *Hundred Gates to the Sea of Ideas of the Hua-yan Sutra* (Fung 1983: 356).

31 "A Treatise on the Gold Lion" (Chan 1973: 413; parentheses in original).

32 *Hundred Gates to the Sea of Ideas of the Hua-yan Sutra* (Chan 1973: 414).

33 Ibid. 421.
34 Chang calls this view the radical "momentarilism" of Buddhism (1971: 73).
35 *Hundred Gates to the Sea of Ideas of the Hua-yan Sutra* (Chan 1973: 416).
36 *Hua-yan Sutra*, ch. 5: 243.
37 Ibid. 246.
38 Ibid. ch. 10: 301.
39 In this respect, the Ten Reality Realms from Hell to the Realm of Buddha are marked by each sentient being's conception of the world. In reality, there are not ten distinguishable realms – what we see is merely a figment of our imagination.
40 *Hua-yan Sutra*, ch. 5: 244.
41 In this respect, Hua-yan Buddhism is very different from Berkeley's idealism, which uses perception and perceptual qualities as the foundation of the perceptible world ("To be is to be perceived"). It is also separable from Berkeley's objective idealism, which posits some Supreme Being as the basis of the experiential world. Even though Hua-yan Buddhism also embraces the view of the One Mind, it does not see the One Mind as the ontological foundation of phenomenal worlds.
42 *Hua-yan Sutra*, ch. 5: 213.
43 Ibid. ch. 9: 296.
44 Ibid.
45 Ibid. ch. 4: 188.
46 Ibid. ch. 5: 213.
47 Ibid. 243.
48 Ibid. 215.
49 Ibid. ch. 27: 821. This plurality of worlds view, however, does not seem to be preserved in the thinking of Hua-yan patriarchs. Fa-zang only presents the phenomenal world as "the Realm of Things," and he seems to be concerned with only one realm as such. It could be interpreted that *the Realm of Things*, as Fa-zang interprets it, is the coexistence and interpenetration of the multiple phenomenal worlds. The relationship of harmonious interpenetration and mutual identification of multiple worlds is not emphasized.
50 The *Sutra* says, "What are mundane phenomena? Material form, sensation, perception, conditioning and consciousness" (ch. 22: 488).
51 Ibid. ch. 29: 880.
52 Ibid. ch. 26: 751.
53 Ibid. ch. 10: 301.
54 Ibid. 300.
55 *Hundred Gates to the Sea of Ideas of the Hua-yan Sutra* (Fung 1983: 345).
56 Ibid. ch. 24: 522.
57 *Hundred Gates to the Sea of Ideas of the Hua-yan Sutra* (Fung 1983: 353).

58 The opposite of holism is atomism. In contemporary philosophy of language and philosophy of mind, holism has been associated with the truth or meaning of sentences and with thought or belief ascription. It is called "meaning holism" or "mental holism" respectively.

59 Francis Cook thinks that what Fa-zang advocates is close to a form of organic holism, the thesis that the whole world is an organic whole system in which every part is an indispensable part. He says: "there is no whole apart from parts and no part separate from the whole. Consequently, the parts that conjunctively make up the whole are not independently existing individuals at all; they are empty of independent being. The individual is simply a function of the whole environment and at the same time *is* the whole" (1979: 378). I think to call Fa-zang's theory "organic" holism is to imbue too much realism into his worldview. Organic holism regards the world as an organic whole because the world was presumably evolved as a whole. Fa-zang's holism, on the other hand, bases the interconnectedness of parts and whole on the reasoning that it is the same Mind, the same noumenon and the same principle that encompasses the whole *Realm of Things*. The world as a whole is not an independently self-arising organic whole. Its very nature is illusory. One argument in support of this interpretation is to point to the fact that Fa-zang's example of the world is a *gold* lion, not a real lion. The whole lion body is constructed out of the same substance; it is not an organic body.

60 Cleary 1983: 2.

61 Cook 1979: 379.

62 "Contemplation of the Realm of Reality" (Cleary 1983: 113).

63 *Hundred Gates to the Sea of Ideas of the Hua-yan Sutra* (Fung 1983: 353).

64 Charles Wei-Hsün Fu explains that seeing all things harmoniously coexist is the highest stage of spiritual progress, in which "the enlightened man . . . reaches a thoroughly naturalistic and humanistic understanding of the relational origination of all things in the world as the true Dharma-realm itself" (1984: 241–2).

65 For the complete list of other reasons, see Chang 1971: 25.

66 The Hua-yan School emphasizes the "nonduality" or the identity of the two levels, however.

67 *Hua-yan Sutra*, ch. 20: 301.

68 "Mirror of the Mysteries of the Universe of Hua-yan" (Cleary 1983: 111).

69 "A Treatise on the Gold Lion" (Chan 1973: 409).

70 As Whalen Lai remarks, with the metaphor of water and waves, "it makes sense . . . to speak of nirvanic suchness participating in the creation of the samsaric waves – and, in such a way, that the latter . . . is in essence (in 'wetness') no different from the original body of water (or from one another)" (1986: 3).

71 "Cessation and Contemplation in the Five Teachings" (Cleary 1983: 58).

72 "Contemplation of the Realm of Reality" (Cleary 1983: 95).

73　"Mirror of the Mysteries of the Universe of the Hua-yan" (Cleary 1983: 104–5).

74　Cleary 1983: 107.

75　By identifying the phenomenal world with the noumenon, Hua-yan patriarchs do not thereby assert the reality of the phenomenal world. Rather, their emphasis is that the world in which we live is nothing but the empty noumenon. In other words, what they assert is not that the noumenon is *as real as* the phenomenal world, but that the phenomenal world is *as empty as* the noumenon.

76　The various forms of "skepticism" were discussed in chapter 7, in the context of Zhuangzi's philosophical view. This quote is from Berkson 1996: 98.

77　*Hua-yan Sutra*, ch. 21: 462.

78　Ibid. ch. 14: 379.

79　Thomas Cleary explains the position this way: "The nature of mental construction is the conceptual order (including perceptual order) which we learn to accept as 'the world.' The relative nature is the conditional existence of the world of experience as a relationship of sense faculties, sense consciousness, and sense data. Thus we can see that the order is a mental projection or construction rather than an inherently fixed property of an objective world as conceived" (1983: 22).

80　Gimello 1976: 120–1.

81　*Hua-yan Sutra*, ch. 26: 744.

82　Ibid. ch. 14: 375.

83　Ibid. 377.

84　Ibid. 377.

85　"Cessation and Contemplation in the Five Teachings" (Cleary 1983: 61). Du-shun explains the significance of experiential realization in the context of his explication of the fourth teaching: the end of words and views. In his explication of the fifth teaching, the Rounded Teaching, which is exemplified by the *Hua-yan Sutra*, he also says that it is necessary to "strike down conceptual attachments."

86　Cleary 1993: 1.

87　The *Sutra* says, "In each atom the Buddhas of all times appear, according to inclinations. While their essential nature neither comes nor goes, by their vow power they pervade the world" (ch. 4: 201).

88　Ibid. ch. 24: 523.

89　Ibid. ch. 29: 884.

90　Ibid. ch. 5: 250.

91　Ibid. ch. 1: 65.

92　According to the *Sutra*, the manifestations vary in nature from one sentient being to another. It says: "Buddha manifests all bodies according to sentient beings' minds" (Ibid. ch. 24: 527). Therefore, even though Hua-yan claims that all phenomena are manifestations of one Buddha, this view is not the same as the Consciousness-Only School's objective idealism.

93 Ibid. 525.
94 Cook 1972: 404.
95 Ibid. 414.
96 Since bodhisattvas have already entered the realm of reality that is beyond time, they are regarded as "immortal" in a sense. They enter the mundane world through each birth, and they go through the same process of birth, aging, illness, and death as ordinary people do. But they can re-enter the world with all memories of their multiple past lives intact. So, they are "trans-world" beings.
97 *Hundred Gates to the Sea of Ideas of the Hua-yan Sutra* (Fung 1983: 358).
98 *Hua-yan Sutra*, ch. 25: 625.
99 "A Treatise on the Gold Lion" (Chan 1973: 414).
100 "Cessation and Contemplation in the Five Teachings" (Cleary 1983: 58).
101 *Hua-yan Sutra*, ch. 25: 534.
102 Ibid. 539.
103 Ibid. 565.
104 Ibid. ch. 26: 708.
105 One basic teaching of the Buddha is "no self." However, for the Theravada schools, one's goal is one's own final release from the mundane world. Chinese Mahayana Buddhists therefore criticize what they called "Hinayana" (small-vehicle) Buddhists for the latter's attachment to the self and their implicit self-love.
106 *Hua-yan Sutra*, ch. 26: 745.
107 According to the *Hua-yan Sutra*, it is not just that worldly pleasures will eventually lead to pain and suffering; it is rather that "mundane pleasures are all suffering" (ibid. ch. 25: 535).
108 *Hua-yan Sutra*, ch. 9: 295.
109 Ibid. ch. 1: 66.
110 Ibid. ch. 5: 250.
111 Chan 1973: 408.
112 The notion of *li* (principle) originated in *Yijing* (*The Book of Changes*).
113 Lai 1980: 245.
114 Gimello 1976: 125–6.

Chapter 11   The Tian-tai (T'ien-t'ai) School

1 David Chappell in his Foreword to Paul Swanson's *Foundations of T'ien-T'ai Philosophy* (1989: viii).
2 In his Introduction to his translation of the *Lotus Sutra* (2002: xvii).
3 Donner and Stevenson 1993: 5.
4 Ng 1993: 10.
5 Zhi-yi's thought is actually quite different from that of his teacher Hui-si in many respects. In particular, Hui-si continues the idealistic tradition of Indian Buddhism and treats the Mind as the substance of this world, while

Zhi-yi clearly denies that the Mind is the substance. Hui-si claims that worldly phenomena "are merely products of mind, and are thereby false in appearance and without reality" (Fung 1983: 367), but Zhi-yi clearly states that the world is not the product of the Buddha or of any mind. I do not think that Hui-si's *The Method of Cessation and Contemplation in Mahayana* is representative of Tian-tai philosophy. In this chapter, the main tenets of Tian-tai are explained according to Zhi-yi's view. My interpretation of Tian-tai philosophy is thus different from the one given by Fung.

6   According to Guan-ding's account in his introduction to *The Great Calming and Contemplation*, Zhi-yi studied with Hui-si, who studied with Hui-wen, and Hui-wen was a student of Nagarjuna's philosophy.

7   Swanson 1989: ix.

8   Ng 1993: x.

9   See ch. 7.

10 Ng 1993: 4.

11 The Indian notion of gods and hell beings are unlike their Western counterparts in that Indian gods and hell beings are not eternal beings – they too can die and re-enter the cycle of transmigration.

12 *Asura* (in Sanskrit) is "one of the six modes of existence, sometimes reckoned among the higher modes and sometimes among the lower. In the sense of a higher or good mode of existence, *asura* refers to the lower gods who dwell on the slopes or summit of the world mountain Sumeru or in castles of air. Seen as a lower or evil mode of existence, the *asuras* are the enemies of the gods. They belong to the sensual desire realm" (*The Shambhala Dictionary of Buddhism and Zen*, trans. Michael H. Kohn. Boston: Shambhala Publications, 1991: 13).

13 *The Great Calming and Contemplation* (Donner and Stevenson 1993: 114).

14 Ibid. 127.

15 *The Esoteric Meaning* (Swanson 1989: 181).

16 This analysis was given by a Chinese monk in the sixteenth century. See Jui-Liang Chang (*Rei-liang Zhang*), 'The Philosophical Method of Chih-I (*zhi zhe zhi zhe xue fang fa*)." *National Taiwan University Philosophical Commentary* 14, 1988: 181 (in Chinese).

17 *The Esoteric Meaning* (Swanson 1989: 182).

18 Ch. 16 (Watson 2002: 102).

19 *The Great Calming and Contemplation* (Donner and Stevenson 1993: 188).

20 Swanson 1989: 13.

21 Hurvitz 1962: 275.

22 The original Chinese phrase does not have a verb. The literal translation would be "one thought three thousand worlds." The word "contain" is added in English.

23 *The Great Calming and Contemplation* (Donner and Stevenson 1993: 189–90).

24 *The Esoteric Meaning* (Swanson 1989: 210).

25 *The Great Calming and Contemplation* (Donner and Stevenson 1993: 194).

26 *The Esoteric Meaning* (Swanson 1989: 198).

27 *The Great Calming and Contemplation*, vol. 5 (my translation).

28 Ibid. (Donner and Stevenson 1993: 190).

29 *The Esoteric Meaning* (Swanson 1989: 252).

30 Guan-ding's Introduction to *The Great Calming and Contemplation* (Donner and Stevenson 1993: 107).

31 This passage comes from *Fahua xuanyi* (*The Esoteric Meaning of the Lotus Sutra*). In *Da-zheng-zang*, vol. 33: 783 (my translation).

32 The Chinese word for this truth literally means "falsehood," and has been translated either as "provisional existence" or as "conventional existence." Using the term "conventional" assumes the intervention of human activities such as languages and descriptions, but the Buddha's teaching is not about how human conventions introduce the demarcation of objects. The nature of things is such that they all depend on other factors (natural as well as artificial) to exist. Therefore, I opt for "provisional existence."

33 Hurvitz 1962: 274.

34 Swanson 1989: 153.

35 Some commentators take the truth of the Middle Way to be a mere restatement of the first two truths. But under that interpretation, the truth of the Middle Way adds nothing new to the original Two Truths of the Madhyamika school. I think the truth of the Middle Way is a statement of the ultimate reality itself, explaining how this reality is both the phenomenal world and nirvana. This new truth reintroduces the realist tenet back to Chinese Buddhism.

36 *The Esoteric Meaning* (Swanson 1989: 176).

37 Tian-tai's theory of "suchnesses" is much more complicated than what I can explain here. Zhi-yi not only talks about "Ten Suchnesses," he also discusses how "one hundred suchnesses" and "one thousand suchnesses" are generated. He says, "Each one of these ten dharma realms contains the ten suchlike [characteristics]. The ten dharma realms [therefore] contain one hundred suchlike [characteristics]. Also, one dharma realm contains the [other] nine dharma realms, therefore there are one hundred dharma realms and one thousand suchlike [characteristics]." [*The Esoteric Meaning* (Swanson 1989: 182).

38 Ibid. (Swanson 1989: 180).

39 Ch. 20 (Watson 2002: 110).

40 Watson 2002: xxvii.

41 *The Esoteric Meaning* (Swanson 1989: 176).

42 Ibid. (Swanson 1989: 167).

43 *The Great Calming and Contemplation* (quoted and translated by Ng 1993: 166).

44 Donner and Stevenson seem to adopt this interpretation. They say: "For Tian-tai thinkers, it is the Middle that is ultimately real and fundamental. The two truths of emptiness and provisionality are secondary derivations – false or, at best, provisional constructs devised to convey the ultimate reality of the Middle in a language consistent with the conventions of

deluded experience" (Donner and Stevenson 1993: 12). Paul Swanson appears to adopt the same interpretation.

45 Swanson 1989: 13.
46 Ibid. 118.
47 *The Esoteric Meaning* (Swanson 1989: 182).
48 Ibid. (Swanson 1989: 253).
49 *The Great Calming and Contemplation* (Donner and Stevenson 1993: 178).
50 As David Chappell explains it: "A major problem in the development of Buddhism in China was the need to reconcile and integrate the widely disparate doctrines and practices which arrived from India. From the first to the sixth century AD, more and more monks and scriptures arrived representing different schools of Indian Buddhism and offering various messages about the true teachings of the Buddha. It became increasingly obvious to the Chinese that these different teachings would not all be equally true. Rather than discard any doctrine or practice, the Chinese finally adopted a convenient theory developed within Mahayana, namely that the Buddha had given different teachings and adopted different methods of instruction on different occasions in order to accommodate the different capacities of his listeners" (1983: 21–2).
51 *The Esoteric Meaning* (Swanson 1989: 165).
52 The following summary is based primarily on Chappell, 1983, supplemented by discussions in Yu-Kwan Ng's book on Chinese Buddhism, *zhong-gua fo-xue de xian-dai quan-shi*. Taipei, Taiwan: *wen-jin* Publishing, 1998, pp. 48–53.
53 As is said in the *Lotus Sutra*, "This *Lotus Sutra* is preached for those with profound wisdom" (ch. 3; Watson 2002: 51).
54 Ch. 3 (Watson 2002: 43–50).
55 Ch. 2 (Watson 2002: 14).
56 Ibid. 15.
57 Zhi-yi's evaluation of the *Lotus Sutra* is based on the text itself. In the *Lotus Sutra*, it is written that the subtle Buddha Law expressed in the *Sutra* "is not something that can be understood through pondering or analysis. Only those who are Buddhas can understand it" (ch. 2; Watson 2002: 9).
58 Ibid.
59 *The Esoteric Meaning* (Swanson 1989: 203).
60 Watson 2002: xxviii.
61 *The Esoteric Meaning* (Swanson 1989: 255).
62 Ibid. 256.
63 Ch. 3 (Watson 2002: 28).
64 *The Esoteric Meaning* (Swanson 1989: 169).
65 Ibid. (Swanson 1989: 190).
66 *The Great Calming and Contemplation* (Donner and Stevenson 1993: 214).
67 The theory of evil nature is not seen in the three major Tian-tai texts written by Zhi-yi. It was first introduced in his later work, *guan-yin xuan-yi*. His major follower Zan-ran turned this theory into a main doctrine of the Tian-tai philosophy. So the theory of evil nature is usually attributed to Zan-ran.

68 *The Great Calming and Contemplation* (Donner and Stevenson 1993: 165).
66 Ng 1993: 78.
70 Ibid.
71 *The Great Calming and Contemplation* (Donner and Stevenson 1993: 198).
72 Ibid. (Donner and Stevenson 1993: 196).
73 *The Esoteric Meaning* (quoted by Ng 1993: 171–2).
74 Sheng-yan Fa-shi, *Da-sheng-zhi-guan-fa-men-zhi-yan-jiou* (Research on *Mahayana Gates for Contemplation*). Taipei, Taiwan: *fa-gu-wen-hua* Publishing, 1997, p. 195.
75 Zhi-yi's remark quoted by Master Sheng-yan, 200 (my translation).
76 Ibid.
77 Hurvitz 1962: 273.
78 *The Great Calming and Contemplation* (Donner and Stevenson 1993: 140).
79 Ibid. 272.
80 Ibid. Besides defining "mind" and "thought," Zhi-yi also defines "consciousness" as "full discriminative identification." However, he immediately adds this warning: "Whoever [clings to] such distinctions as absolute falls into perverted mind, perverted thoughts, and perverted views" (ibid.). When we deal with the analysis of Tian-tai's terminology, we should keep this warning in mind.
81 Ibid. (Donner and Stevenson 1993: 195).
82 *The Esoteric Meaning* (Swanson 1989: 177).
83 Ibid. 178.
84 Ibid. 190.
85 *The Method of Cessation and Contemplation in Mahayana* (Chan 1973: 399).
86 *The Great Calming and Contemplation* (Donner and Stevenson 1993: 204).
87 *The Esoteric Meaning* (Swanson 1989: 190).

Chapter 12   The Chan School (Zen Buddhism)

1 According to Alan Watts, the Sanskrit word *dhyana* is best left untranslated: "'Meditation' in the common sense of 'thinking things over' or 'musing' is a most misleading translation. But such alternatives as 'trance' or 'absorption' are even worse, since they suggest states of hypnotic fascination. The best solution seems to be to leave *dhyana* untranslated and add it to the English language as we have added Nirvana and Tao. As used in Buddhism, the term *dhyana* comprises both recollectedness (*smritti*) and [contemplation] *samadhi*, and can best be described as the state of unified or one-pointed awareness. On the one hand, it is one-pointed in the sense of being focused on the present, since to clear awareness there is neither past nor future, but just this one moment . . . which Western mystics have called the Eternal Now. On the other hand, it is one-pointed in the sense of being a state of consciousness without differentiation of the knower,

the knowing, and the known" (1957: 54–5). However, unlike "nirvana," and perhaps "Tao [Dao]," *dhyana* has not become part of the common English vocabulary. Here I am following the general practice in translating *dhyana* into "meditation."

2   Many contemporary historians have challenged the verity of this legend. Some argue that Bodhidharma's identity was questionable, and some argue that the third patriarch Shen-can probably did not exist. See for example Hu 1953; Fung 1983; and Yampolsky 1990.

3   For example, Huei-nan Yang argues that Shen-xiu's view follows "the orthodox teachings" of Hong-ren and Dao-xin, while Hui-neng's view deviates from such a tradition ("Shen Hsiu and Tao Hsin's Way of Zen: A Comparison" (in Chinese), 1988, pp. 205–25).

4   The *Platform Sutra* records Hui-neng's biography, anecdotes of his encounters with other disciples, and his teachings. It was probably written by one of his followers. Over the years, the text expanded and more stories were added. It may not be a reliable historical text, but its doctrinal content is what is important in our study.

5   Suzuki 1964: 85.

6   Yampolsky 1990: 249.

7   Yampolsky dates the Dun-huang manuscript to sometime between 830 and 860 (ibid. 90).

8   Many Chan practitioners will probably deny that there is a "philosophy" of mind in the Chan School. They are likely to point out that one of Chan's fundamental teachings is that we should discard philosophizing and conceptualization. It is indeed true that the essential spirit of Chan is practice, not theory. But again, as with other Chinese Buddhist schools, the goal of this chapter is to analyze the theoretical foundations of this religious/ethical teaching.

9   *Platform Sutra* (Cleary 1998: 11).

10   As Richard Garner puts it, "the fundamental tendency of the southern school is to avoid both the transcendent and the phenomenological, and to focus attention on the world of everyday experience" (1985: 162).

11   There seems to be consensus among contemporary scholars that what was passed on from Bodhidharma to Hong-ren was the *Lankavatara Sutra*, but what was emphasized from Hui-neng to later Chan masters was the *Diamond Sutra*. According to some documents recovered in the caves of Dun-huang, Bodhidharma handed over the *Lankavatara Sutra* to the second patriarch Hui-ke, saying: "I have observed in this land of China there is only this sutra. If you depend upon this sutra, you will be able to save the world" (see Heinrich Dumoulin's "The Northern School of Chinese Zen" in his 1994: 308). In an epitaph for Shen-xiu, it is also suggested that he "held the *Lankavatara Sutra* in special reverence and recommended it to his disciples" (ibid. 322). In the *Platform Sutra of the Sixth Patriarch*, on the other hand, Hui-neng was described as having reached enlightenment when he heard someone reciting the *Diamond Sutra*. It was further alleged that when Hong-ren passed on the sacred robe to Hui-

neng, he also expounded the essence of the *Diamond Sutra* as his method of transmitting the True Teaching.

12 The Chinese version contains the Chinese phonetic rendition of "Bodhi," which means "enlightenment." The legend has it that the historical Buddha obtained enlightenment under a Bodhi tree.

13 Cleary 1998: 8.

14 There was another version recorded in the Dun-huang text, which reads: "The mind is the Bodhi tree. The body is the mirror stand. The mirror is originally clean and pure. Where can it be stained by dust?" (Yampolsky 1967: 132). It is not clear why there were two versions. Some commentators speculate that the author of the *Platform Sutra* was trying out different formulations of basically the same idea.

15 Cleary 1998: 10.

16 Lai 1979: 250.

17 According to Suzuki: "When Hui-neng declared, 'From the first not a thing is,' the keynote of his Zen thought was struck, and from it we recognize the extent of difference there is between him and his predecessors and contemporaries" (1964: 24). This statement is thus revolutionary on Hui-neng's part.

18 In Steven W. Laycock's analysis: "Shen-[xiu], believing the mind to be analogous to a mirror, advocates a *procedure*: wipe away the dust. Hui-neng's iconoclasm will not, however, permit the analogy. . . . The mind is *already* enlightened, Self Nature is *already* self-transparent, and no procedure which simply leaves us where it found us is of any avail in *realizing* the already-enlightened character of mind" (1985: 192).

19 Lai 1979: 250.

20 Interestingly enough, Chan master Huang Bo later spelt out this criticism. When asked why Shen-xiu did not receive the sacred robe, Huang Bo replied, "Because he still indulged in conceptual thought – in a dharma of activity. To him 'as you practice, so shall you attain' was a reality" (Blofeld 1958: 64).

21 *Platform Sutra* (Cleary 1998: 35).

22 *Hui-neng's Commentary of the Diamond Sutra* (Cleary 1998: 127).

23 Chan 1973: 426.

24 In contrast to the *Flower Ornament Sutra* (the *Hua-yan Sutra*), the *Lankavatara Sutra* rejects the assumption of the existence of atoms. It says: "Analyzed down to atoms, there is indeed no form to be discriminated as such; what can be established is the [truth of] Mind-Only" (*Lankavatara Sutra*, ch. 2; Suzuki 1932: 49).

25 Zeuschner 1978: 69.

26 Quoted in ibid. 71.

27 Ibid.

28 *Lankavatara Sutra*, ch. 2 (Suzuki 1932: 106).

29 Ibid. 143.

30 Ibid. 20.

31 Ibid. 109.

32 Ibid.

33 Ibid. 172.

34 Cleary translates "Tathagata" in Hui-neng's Commentary on the *Diamond Sutra* as "the Realized One" (1998). According to Nyanatiloka's *Buddhist Dictionary*, Tathagata means "the 'Perfect One' . . . the One who has 'thus gone,' or 'thus come.' [It] is an epithet of the Buddha used by him when speaking of himself" (San Francisco, CA: Chinese Materials Center, Inc. 1977, p. 133).

35 *Diamond Sutra* (Suzuki 1960: 46).

36 Suzuki 1960: 41.

37 *Platform Sutra* (Cleary 1998: 20).

38 See Huei-nan Yang "Shen Hsiu and Tao Hsin's Way of Zen: A Comparison" (in Chinese), 1988, pp. 205–25.

39 Dumoulin 1994: 323.

40 Zeuschner 1978: 74.

41 Cleary 1998: 85.

42 The Chinese words "*guan*" (to behold) and "*jian*" (to see) reflect these distinctions. The translations "to behold" and "to see" are meant to capture the differences in the connotations of the original Chinese words.

43 Suzuki 1964: 39.

44 Ibid. 103.

45 Ibid. 137. In the *Platform Sutra* he also states: "Ordinary mortals are themselves buddhas. . . . Deluded the moment before, you were an ordinary mortal; enlightenment the moment after, you are a buddha" (see Cleary 1998: 18).

46 "Tathata" means "suchness" or "Thusness." See chapter 9 for related reference.

47 *Lankavatara Sutra*, ch. 2 (Suzuki 1932: 85).

48 Ivan Strenski argues that the term "gradual" can be taken to mean something temporal, like "slow," but it may also mean "graded," and the graded method is not necessarily slower (1980: 4). Whichever sense we use in "gradual," it is clear that in Shen-xiu's teaching, the preparation for enlightenment has to be a gradual process, even though the final leap may take only a moment.

49 Suzuki 1932: 108.

50 In the history of Chan, there were stories about how the First Patriarch Bodhidharma sat in a cave facing the wall for many years before he started preaching.

51 *Lankavatara Sutra*, ch. 1 (Suzuki 1932: 20–1).

52 Suzuki 1969: 25.

53 *Platform Sutra* (Cleary 1998: 6).

54 Ibid. 17.

55 Ibid. 35.

56 Suzuki 1964: 50.

57 However, the *Lankavatara Sutra* actually teaches both gradual and instantaneous purification. See the *Lankavatara Sutra*, ch. 2, sect. XIV

(Suzuki 1932: 49–50). Some commentators also argue that Shen-xiu never taught only gradual enlightenment, and that the characterization of the Northern Chan as "the school of gradual enlightenment" was actually the false accusation made by Shen-hui.

58 *Hui-neng's Commentary on the Diamond Sutra* (Cleary 1998: 129).

59 Ibid. 87.

60 Ibid. 143.

61 *Platform Sutra* (Cleary 1998: 21).

62 Blofeld 1958: 82; emphasis in original.

63 Ibid. 93.

64 Watson 1993: 31.

65 Ibid. 26.

66 Ibid. 34.

67 *Platform Sutra* (Cleary 1998: 42).

68 In the *Platform Sutra*, there is a record of a Chan master who "was well versed in the Tian-tai teaching." And it says: "The words he spoke spontaneously agreed with the grand master of Chan" (ibid. 56). Hui-neng also appeals to the *Lotus Sutra* a number of times in his teaching. The connection between Chan and Tian-tai is not seen only in the thought of Hui-neng. Dumoulin points out that the fourth patriarch of the Chan School, Dao-xin, had a "proximity" to Tian-tai's teaching (1994: 310).

69 Lai 1977: 79.

70 *Platform Sutra* (Cleary 1998: 23).

71 Ibid. 53.

72 *Hui-neng's Commentary on the Diamond Sutra* (Cleary 1998: 106).

73 Ibid. 88.

74 Ibid. 107.

75 Ibid. 92.

76 Suzuki translates it as "composite things."

77 *Hui-neng's Commentary on the Diamond Sutra* (Cleary 1998: 144).

78 Ibid. 112.

79 Ibid. 119.

80 Within the Chan School, there is no distinction between "nature" and "mind." In fact, if one insists on analyzing the differences between nature and mind, then one is, according to Chan masters, "on the wrong track." The Chan School identifies Buddha with one's original mind and with one's essential nature. Both "mind" and "nature" designate one's inherent state of existence. Later in Neo-Confucianism, the debate between the School of Mind and the School of Nature takes the center stage.

81 Hui-neng's *Platform Sutra* records a student's asking him to expound the meaning of "mind itself is Buddha" (Cleary 1998: 44). This shows that Hui-neng already used this slogan frequently. Many later Chan masters also used this slogan to expound the essence of Chan; for example, Huang Bo's teaching dealt especially with this thesis.

82 Blofeld 1958: 29.

83 Suzuki 1964: 51.

84 *Platform Sutra* (Cleary 1998: 17).
85 Ibid. 18.
86 Ibid. 16.
87 Ibid. 20.
88 Ibid. 78.
89 Ibid. 40.
90 Ibid. 47.
91 This remark is a modification of Hui-neng's remark. See Suzuki 1960: 86.
92 Watson 1993: 48.
93 Ibid. 23.
94 An interesting contrast is the same story told by Tolstoy in his "Confessions." Tolstoy describes the predicament of a traveler who was caught between two beasts waiting to devour him. He could go neither up nor down. In this frightful quandary, the traveler suddenly saw some drops of honey hanging from some leaves. So he decided to stick out his tongue to taste the honey drops. Tolstoy apparently got this story from the same source; however, his reflection on the moral of the story was totally different. He wrote: "Just so I hold on to the branch of life, knowing that the dragon of death is waiting inevitably for me, ready to tear me to pieces, and I cannot understand why I have fallen on such suffering. And I try to lick that honey which used to give me pleasure; but now it no longer gives me joy, and the white and the black mouse day and night nibble at the branch to which I am holding on. I clearly see the dragon, and the honey is no longer sweet to me. I see only the inevitable dragon and the mice, and am unable to turn my glance away from them. That is not a fable, but a veritable, indisputable, comprehensible truth. The former deception of the pleasures of life, which stifled the terror of the dragon, no longer deceives me. No matter how much one should say to me, 'You cannot understand the meaning of life, do not think, live!' I am unable to do so, because I have been doing it too long before. Now I cannot help seeing day and night, which run and lead me to death. I see that alone, because that alone is the truth. Everything else is a lie. The two drops of honey that have longest turned my eyes away from the cruel truth, the love of family and of authorship, which I have called an art, are no longer sweet to me. My family – but my family, my wife and children, they are also human beings. They are in precisely the same condition that I am in: they must either live in the lie or see the terrible truth. . . . Since I love them, I cannot conceal the truth from them, – every step in cognition leads them up to this truth. And the truth is death" (Tolstoy, *Confession*. W. W. Norton & Company, Reissue, 1996). Tolstoy's gloomy reading of the story clearly shows that he had not mastered the teaching of Chan.
95 See Watson 1999: 104–5.
96 Cleary 1998: 7.
97 Suzuki 1953: 33.
98 Ibid. 34.
99 *Hui-neng's Commentary on the Diamond Sutra* (Cleary 1998: 134).

100   Ibid. 106.
101   Chung-ying Cheng 1973: 77. Cheng tries to explain away the paradoxical nature of Chan *koan*. He analyzes it, and concludes that the apparent paradoxes are generated only by those who are not yet enlightened. Once one is enlightened, then one sees that the language of Chan goes beyond "the surface semantic structure" and refers to a "deep ontological structure." This deep ontological structure "is a framework which does not admit any description of things according to a framework of specific categories or paradigms" (ibid. 91). In other words, he thinks that normally our language refers to our mundane world and worldly things, but when it is used by Chan masters in paradoxical dialogues, it refers instead to a different ontological level – the ultimate reality. Cheng's article generated a host of responses. See for example, Bossert 1976; King-Farlow 1983; Levin 1976; and Tucker 1985.
102   See, for example, Cua 1975, Kim 1980–1, Rosemont 1970b, Scharfstein 1976.
103   Rosemont 1970b: 116.
104   Kim 1980–1: 110.
105   Blofeld 1958: 31.
106   Hui-neng says: "Some people who cling to emptiness repudiate the scriptures, simply saying they don't need writings. If they say they don't need writings, then people shouldn't speak either, because speech has the characteristics of writing. . . . Don't slander the scriptures, the obstacles caused by this error are countless" (*Hui-neng's Commentary on the Diamond Sutra*; Cleary 1998: 72).
107   *Platform Sutra* (Cleary 1998: 44).
108   Ibid. 11.
109   Blofeld 1958: 40.
110   Ibid. 67.
111   Ibid. 38.
112   Ibid. 67.
113   Watson 1993: 53.
114   Ibid. 52–3.
115   Suzuki 1964: 102.
116   Ibid. 88–9.
117   Lusthaus 1985: 175.
118   Lai 1977: 66.
119   Ibid. 73.

References and Further Reading

Introduction

Allinson, Robert (ed.) (1995) *Understanding the Chinese Mind: The Philosophical Roots*. New York: Oxford University Press, 6th impression.

Bodde, Derk (1942) "Dominant Ideas in the Formation of Chinese Culture." *Journal of American Oriental Society* 62(4): 293–9.

—— (1953) "Harmony and Conflict in Chinese Philosophy." In Arthur F. Wright (ed.), *The American Anthropologist Studies in Chinese Thought*. The American Anthropological Association, vol. 55, no. 5, part 2, memoir no. 75. December: 19–80.

Chan, Wing-tsit (ed.) (1973) *A Sourcebook in Chinese Philosophy*, 4th edn. Princeton, NJ: Princeton University Press.

Cheng, Chung-ying (1971) "Chinese Philosophy: A Characterization." *Inquiry* 14: 113–37.

—— (1974) "Conscience, Mind and Individuals in Chinese Philosophy." *Journal of Chinese Philosophy* 2: 3–40.

—— (1983) "On the Hierarchical Theory of Time: With Reference to Chinese Philosophy." *Journal of Chinese Philosophy* 10: 357–84.

Creel, Herrlee G. (1953) *Chinese Thought: From Confucius to Mao Tse-Tung*. Chicago: University of Chicago Press.

De Bary, William Theodore and Bloom, Irene (eds.) (1999) *Sources of Chinese Tradition*, 2nd edn. Volume I. *From Earliest Times to 1600*. New York: Columbia University Press.

De Bary, William Theodore and Lufrano, Richard John (eds.) (2001) *Sources of Chinese Tradition*, 2nd edn. Volume II. *From 1600 Through the Twentieth Century*. New York: Columbia University Press.

Feng, Qi (1986/7) "Scientific Method and Logical Categories in Ancient China." *Chinese Studies in Philosophy* 18, Winter: 3–28.

Flew, Antony G. N. (1979) "The Cultural Roots of Analytic Philosophy." *Journal of Chinese Philosophy* 6: 1–14.

Fung, Yu-lan (1966) *A Short History of Chinese Philosophy* (ed. Derk Bodde). New York: The Free Press.

—— (1983) *A History of Chinese Philosophy*, vol. I. (trans. Derk Bodde) Princeton, NJ: Princeton University Press.

Graham, Angus C. (1989) *The Disputers of the Tao: Philosophical Argument in Ancient China*. La Salle, IL: Open Court.

Hansen, Chad (1992) *A Daoist Theory of Chinese Thought*. New York: Oxford University Press.

Kaltenmark, Max (1969) *Lao Tzu and Taoism* (trans. from the French by Roger Greaves). Stanford, CA: Stanford University Press.

Levi, Albert William (1979) "Modern Cultural Roots of Analytic Philosophy." *Journal of Chinese Philosophy* 6: 15–35.

Li, Chenyang (1999) *The Tao Encounters the West: Explorations in Comparative Philosophy*. Albany, NY: SUNY Press.

Liu, Shu-hsien (1974) "Time and Temporality: The Chinese Perspective." *Philosophy East and West* 24: 145–53.

—— (1998) "Background for the Emergence of Confucian Philosophy." In his *Understanding Confucian Philosophy: Classical and Sung-Ming*. Westport, CT: Praeger, ch. 1.

Needham, Joseph (1951) "Human Laws and Laws of Nature in China and the West." *Journal of the History of Ideas*, XII. Part I: 3–30; Part II: 194–230.

Neville, Robert (1980) "From Nothing to Being: The Notion of Creation in Chinese and Western Thought." *Philosophy East & West* 30(1): 21–34.

Schwartz, Benjamin (1985) *The World of Thought in Ancient China*. Cambridge, MA: Belknap Press.

Tang, Chun-I (1962) "The T'ien Ming [Heavenly Ordinance] in Pre-Ch'in China," pts. I and II. *Philosophy East & West* 11: 195–218; 12: 29–50.

Van Norden, Bryan W. (ed.) (2002) *Confucius and the Analects: New Essays*. New York: Oxford University Press.

Wilhelm, Richard and Baynes, Cary F. (trans.) (1977) *The I Ching: Book of Changes*. Princeton, NJ: Princeton University Press.

Zhang, Dainian (2002) *Key Concepts in Chinese Philosophy*. New Haven, CT: Yale University Press.

Part I   Ancient Chinese Philosophy

Introduction

Bodde, Derek (1953) "Harmony and Conflict in Chinese Philosophy." In Arthur F. Wright (ed.), *The American Anthropologist Studies in Chinese Thought*. The American Anthropological Association, vol. 55, no. 5, part 2, memoir no. 75. December: 19–80.

Chan, Wing-tsit (ed.) (1973) *A Sourcebook in Chinese Philosophy*, 4th edn. Princeton, NJ: Princeton University Press.

Cheng, Chung-ying (1995) "Chinese Metaphysics as Non-Metaphysics: Confucian and Daoist Insights into the Nature of Reality." In Robert Allinson (ed.), *Understanding the Chinese Mind: The Philosophical Roots*, 6th impression. New York: Oxford University Press, pp. 167–208.

De Bary, William Theodore and Bloom, Irene (eds.) (1999) *Sources of Chinese Tradition*, 2nd edn. Volume I. *From Earliest Times to 1600*. New York: Columbia University Press.

Graham, Angus C. (1989) *The Disputers of the Tao: Philosophical Argument in Ancient China*. La Salle, IL: Open Court.

Hansen, Chad (1992) *A Daoist Theory of Chinese Thought*. New York: Oxford University Press.

Ivanhoe, Philip (ed.) (1996) *Chinese Language, Thought, and Culture: Nivison and His Critics*. La Salle, IL: Open Court.

Ivanhoe, Philip J. and Van Norden, Bryan W. (eds.) (2003) *Readings in Classical Chinese Philosophy*. Indianapolis, IN: Hackett Publishing Company, Inc.

Schwartz, Benjamin (1985) *The World of Thought in Ancient China*. Cambridge, MA: Belknap Press.

Chapter 1 *Yijing* (*I Ching*): The Cosmological Foundation of Chinese Philosophy

Anderson, Allan W. (1990) "The Seasonal Structure Underlying the Arrangement of the Hexagrams in the *Yijing*." *Journal of Chinese Philosophy*: 275–99.

Anthony, Carol K. (1981) *The Philosophy of the I Ching*. Stow, MA: Anthony Publishing Company.

Baynes, Christopher (1964) "The Concrete Significance of Number with Special Reference to the *Book of Changes*." *Systematics* 2(2): 102–29.

Blofeld, John. (trans.) (1965) *I Ching: The Book of Change*. New York: Penguin Books.

Bodde, Derek (1953) "Harmony and Conflict in Chinese Philosophy." In Arthur F. Wright (ed.), *The American Anthropologist Studies in Chinese Thought*. The American Anthropological Association, vol. 55, no. 5, part 2, memoir no. 75. December: 19–80.

Brown, Chappell (1982) "Inner Truth and the Origin of the Yarrow Stalk Oracle." *Journal of Chinese Philosophy* 9: 197–210.

—— (1982) "The Tetrahedron as an Archetype for the Concept of Change in the *I Ching*." *Journal of Chinese Philosophy* 9: 159–68.

Burr, Ronald (1975) "Chinese Theories of Causation: Commentary." *Philosophy East & West* 25: 23–9.

Cheng, Chung-ying (1976) "Model of Causality in Chinese Philosophy: A Comparative Study." *Philosophy East & West* 26: 3–20.

—— (1977) "Chinese Philosophy and Symbolic Reference." *Philosophy East & West* 27: 307–22.

—— (1987) "'*Li*' and '*Ch'i*' in the *I Ching*: Reconsideration of Being and Non-being in Chinese Philosophy." *Journal of Chinese Philosophy* 14: 1–38.

—— (1989) "On Harmony as Transformation: Paradigms from the *I Ching*." *Journal of Chinese Philosophy* 16: 125–58.

—— (1997) "Reality and Divinity in Chinese Philosophy." In Eliot Deutsch (ed.), *A Companion to World Philosophies*. Oxford: Blackwell Publishing.

Clarke, A. G. (1987) "Probability Theory Applied to the *I Ching*." *Journal of Chinese Philosophy* 14: 65–72.

Cook, Daniel J. and Rosemont Jr., Henry (1981) "The Pre-established Harmony between Leibniz and Chinese Thought." *Journal of the History of Ideas* 42: 253–68.

Dixon, Paul W. (1993) "Classical Taoism, the *I Ching* and our Need for Guidance." *Journal of Chinese Philosophy* 20(2): 147–57.

Doeringer, F. M. (1980) "Oracle and Symbol in the Redaction of the *I Ching*." *Philosophy East & West* 30: 195–209.

Fang, Tung-Mei (1976) "The Creative Spirit of Confucius as Seen in the *Book of Changes*." *Chinese Studies in Philosophy* 7: 78–89.

Feng, Jing-yuan (1985) "'*Qi*' and the Atom: A Comparison of the Concept of Matter in Chinese and Western Philosophy." *Chinese Studies in Philosophy* 17, Fall: 22–44.

Fleming, Jess (1993a) "Categories and Meta-categories in the *I Ching*." *Journal of Chinese Philosophy* 20(4): 425–34.

—— (1993b) "A Set Theory Analysis of the Logic of the *I Ching*." *Journal of Chinese Philosophy* 20(2): 133–46.

—— (1996) "Philosophical Counseling and the *I Ching*." *Journal of Chinese Philosophy* 23(3): 299–320.

Goldenberg, Daniel S. (1975) "The Algebra of the *I Ching* and Its Philosophical Implications." *Journal of Chinese Philosophy* 2: 149–79.

Hacker, Edward A. (1987) "Order in the Textual Sequence of the Hexagrams of the *I Ching*." *Journal of Chinese Philosophy* 14: 59–64.

—— (1983) "A Note on the Formal Properties of the Later Heaven Sequence." *Journal of Chinese Philosophy* 10: 169–72.

Hansen, Chad (1992) *A Daoist Theory of Chinese Thought*. New York: Oxford University Press, ch. 3, pp. 57–94.

Hatton, Russell (1982) "A Comparison of *Chi* and Prime Matter." *Philosophy East & West* 32: 159–74.

Hershock, Peter D. (1991) "The Structure of Change in the *I Ching*." *Journal of Chinese Philosophy* 18: 257–85.

Hon, Tze-ki (1997) *Teaching the Book of Changes. Education about Asia* 2(2), Fall: 26–31.

Huang, Alfred (1998) *The Complete I Ching*. Rochester, VT: Inner Traditions.

—— (2000) *The Numerology of the I Ching: A Sourcebook of Symbols, Structures, and Traditional Wisdom*. Rochester, VT: Inner Traditions.

Joseph, Audrey (1980) "Karman, Self-Knowledge and *I Ching* Divination." *Philosophy East & West* 30: 65–75.

Lee, Jung Young (1972) "Death Is Birth and Birth Is Death." *Systematics* 9: 188–200.

Legge, James (trans.) (1964) *I Ching: Book of Changes*. Edited with Introduction and Study Guide by Ch'u Chai with Winberg Chai. New York: University Books.

Leung, Koon Loon (1982) "An Algebraic Truth in Divination." *Journal of Chinese Philosophy* 9: 243–58.

Liu, Shu-hsien (1990) "On the Functional Unity of the Four Dimensions of Thought in the *Book of Changes*." *Journal of Chinese Philosophy* 17: 359–86.

Liu, Zheng (1993) "The Dilemma Facing Contemporary Research in the *Yijing*." *Chinese Studies in Philosophy* 24(4): 47–64.

Loy, David (1987) "On the Meaning of the *I Ching*." *Journal of Chinese Philosophy* 14: 39–57.

Lynn, Richard John (trans.) (1994) *The Classic of Changes: A New Translation of the I Ching as Interpreted by Wang Bi*. New York: Columbia University Press.

Mair, Victor H. (1979) "A Reordering of the Hexagrams of the *I Ching*." *Philosophy East & West* 29: 421–41.

Mcevilly, Wayne (1968) "Synchronicity and the *I Ching*." *Philosophy East & West* 18: 137–50.

Milcinski, Maja (1997) "The Notion of Feminism in Asian Philosophical Traditions." *Asian Philosophy* 7(3): 195–205.

Mou, Bo (1998) "An Analysis of the Ideographic Nature and Structure of the Hexagram in *Yijing*: From the Perspective of Philosophy of Language." *Journal of Chinese Philosophy* 25(3): 305–20.

Reifler, Sam (1974) *I Ching: A New Interpretation for Modern Times*. New York: Bantam Books.

Schulz, Larry J. (1990) "On the Concept of Freedom in the *I Ching*: A Deconstructionist View of Self-Cultivation." *Journal of Chinese Philosophy*: 301–13.

Shibles, Warren A. (1999) "On Death: The *I Ching* As a Metaphorical Method of Insight." *Journal of Chinese Philosophy* 26(3): 343–76.

Smith, Richard J. (1998) "The Place of the *Yijing* in World Culture: Some Historical and Contemporary Perspectives." *Journal of Chinese Philosophy* 25(4): 391–422.

Stevenson, Frank W. (1993) "Discourse and Disclosure in the *I Ching*." *Journal of Chinese Philosophy* 20(2): 159–79.

Tadashi, Ogawa (1998) "*Qi* and the Phenomenology of Wind." *Continental Philosophy Review* 31(3): 321–35.

Tang, Mingbang (1987) "Recent Developments in Studies of the *Book of Changes*." *Chinese Studies in Philosophy* 19, Fall: 46–63.

Tong, Lik Kuen (1974) "The Concept of Time in Whitehead and the *I Ching*." *Journal of Chinese Philosophy* 1: 373–93.

—— (1990) "The Appropriation of Significance: The Concept of *Kang-Tung* in the *I Ching*." *Journal of Chinese Philosophy*: 315–44.

Walker, Brian Browne (1992) *The I Ching or Book of Changes. A Guide to Life's Turning Points*. New York: St Martin's Press.

Wilhelm, Hellmut (1977) *Heaven, Earth and Man in the Book of Changes*. Seattle: University of Washington Press.

Wilhelm, Richard and Baynes, Cary F. (trans.) (1977) *The I Ching: Book of Changes*. Princeton, NJ: Princeton University Press.

Wilhelm, Hellmut and Wilhelm, Richard (1979) *Understanding the I Ching: The Wilhelm Lectures on the Book of Changes*. Princeton, NJ: Princeton University Press.

Wing, R. L. (2001) *Workbook of I Ching*. New York: Broadway Books.

Wu, Joseph S. (1975) "Causality: Confucianism and Pragmatism." *Philosophy East & West* 25: 13–22.

Zhang, Dainan (1987) "On Heaven, *Dao, Qi, Li,* and *Ze.*" *Chinese Studies in Philosophy* 19, Fall: 3–45.

Chapter 2   Confucius (Kongzi) in the *Analects*

Allinson, Robert (1985) "The Confucian Golden Rule: A Negative Formulation." *Journal of Chinese Philosophy* 12: 305–15.

—— (1992) "The Golden Rule as the Core Value in Confucianism & Christianity: Ethical Similarities and Differences." *Asian Philosophy* 2(2): 173–85.

Chan, Wing-tsit (ed.) (1973) *A Sourcebook in Chinese Philosophy,* 4th edn. Princeton, NJ: Princeton University Press, ch. 2.

Creel, H. G. (1960) *Confucius and the Chinese Way.* New York: Harper & Row.

Cua, Antonio (1995) "The Concept of *Li* in Confucian Moral Theory." In Robert Allinson (ed.), *Understanding the Chinese Mind: The Philosophical Roots.* New York: Oxford University Press, 6th impression, pp. 209–35.

Dawson, Raymond (2000) *Confucius. The Analects.* Oxford World's Classics paperback. New York: Oxford University Press.

Dawson, Miles Menander (1939) *The Basic Thoughts of Confucius: The Conduct of Life.* New York: Garden City Publishing Co., Inc.

De Bary, William Theodore (1991) *The Trouble with Confucianism.* Cambridge, MA: Harvard University Press.

Feinberg, Joel (1980) "The Nature and Value of Rights." In his *Rights, Justice, and the Bounds of Liberty: Essays in Social Philosophy.* Princeton, NJ: Princeton University Press, ch. 7, pp. 143–58.

Fingarette, Herbert (1972) *Confucius: The Secular as Sacred.* New York: Harper and Row.

—— (1979) "Following the 'One Thread' of the *Analects.*" *Journal of the American Academy of Religion* 47(35): 375–405.

Graham, Angus C. (1989) *The Disputers of the Tao: Philosophical Argument in Ancient China.* La Salle, IL: Open Court, Part I, ch. 1, pp. 9–33.

Hall, David L. and Ames, Roger T. (1987) *Thinking Through Confucius.* Albany, NY: State University of New York Press.

Hansen, Chad (1992) *A Daoist Theory of Chinese Thought.* New York: Oxford University Press, ch. 3, pp. 57–94.

Ivanhoe, Philip J. (1990) "Reviewing the 'One Thread' of the *Analects.*" *Philosophy East & West* 40(1): 17–33.

—— (2000) *Confucian Moral Self Cultivation.* 2nd edn. Indianapolis, IN: Hackett Publishing Company, ch. 1.

Ivanhoe, Philip J. and Van Norden, Bryan W. (eds.) (2003) *Readings in Classical Chinese Philosophy.* Indianapolis, IN: Hackett Publishing Company, Inc.

Lau, D. C. (1979) *Confucius: The Analects.* New York: Penguin Classics.

Liu, Shu-hsien (1972) "A Philosophical Analysis of the Confucian Approach to Ethics." *Philosophy East & West* 22: 417–25.

—— (1998) *Understanding Confucian Philosophy: Classical and Sung-Ming.* Westport, Connecticut: Praeger, ch. 2.

Nivison, David (1996) "Golden Rule Arguments in Chinese Philosophy." In Bryan Van Norden (ed.), *The Ways of Confucianism: Investigations in Chinese Philosophy.* La Salle, IL: Open Court, pp. 59–76.

Schwartz, Benjamin (1985) *The World of Thought in Ancient China.* Cambridge, MA: Belknap Press, chs. 2–3.

Slingerland, Edward (trans.) (2003) *Confucius: Analects.* Indianapolis, IN: Hackett Publishing Company.

Trapp, Rainer Werner (1998) "The Golden Rule," *Grazer Philosophische Studien* 54: 139–64.

Van Norden, Bryan W. (ed.) (2002) *Confucius and the Analects: New Essays.* New York: Oxford University Press.

Chapter 3   Mencius (Mengzi)

Ames, Roger (1991) "The Mencian Conception of Ren xing: Does it Mean 'Human Nature'?" In Henry Rosemont, Jr. (ed.), *Chinese Texts and Philosophical Contexts: Essays Dedicated to Angus C. Graham.* La Salle, IL: Open Court, pp. 143–75.

Bloom, Irene T. (1994) "Mengzian Arguments on Human Nature." *Philosophy East & West* 44(1): 19–54. Repr. in Xiusheng Liu and Philip Ivanhoe (eds.), *Essays on the Moral Philosophy of Mengzi.* Indianapolis, IN: Hackett Publishing Company, 2002, pp. 64–100.

—— (1997) "Human Nature and Biological Nature in Mencius." *Philosophy East & West* 47(1), January: 21–32.

Chan, Alan K. L. (ed.) (2002a) *Mencius: Contexts and Interpretations.* Honolulu: University of Hawaii Press.

—— (2002b) "A Matter of Taste: *Qi* (Vital Energy) and the Tending of the Heart (*Xin*) in Mencius 2A2." In Alan K. L. Chan (ed.), *Mencius: Contexts and Interpretations.* Honolulu: University of Hawaii Press, pp. 42–71.

Chan, Wing-tsit (ed.) (1973) *A Sourcebook in Chinese Philosophy,* 4th edn. Princeton, NJ: Princeton University Press, ch. 3.

Chen, Ning (2002) "The Ideological Background of the Mencian Discussion of Human Nature: A Reexamination." In Alan K. L. Chan (ed.), *Mencius: Contexts and Interpretations.* Honolulu: University of Hawaii Press, pp. 17–41.

Chong, Kim-chong (2002) "Mengzi and Gaozi on *Nei* and *Wai.*" In Alan K. L. Chan (ed.), *Mencius: Contexts and Interpretations.* Honolulu: University of Hawaii Press, pp. 103–25.

Cua, Antonio S. (2002) "*Xin* and Moral Failure: Notes on an Aspects of Mencius' Moral Psychology." In Alan K. L. Chan (ed.), *Mencius: Contexts and Interpretations.* Honolulu: University of Hawaii Press, pp. 126–50.

Graham, Angus C. (1989) *The Disputers of the Tao: Philosophical Argument in Ancient China.* La Salle, IL: Open Court, Part II, ch. 1, pp. 107–37.

—— (1990) "The Background of the Mencian Theory of Human Nature." In A. C. Graham, *Studies in Chinese Philosophy and Philosophical Literature.*

Albany, NY: SUNY Press. Repr. in Xiusheng Liu and Philip Ivanhoe (eds.), *Essays on the Moral Philosophy of Mengzi*. Indianapolis, IN: Hackett Publishing Company, 2002, pp. 1–57.

Hansen, Chad (1992) *A Daoist Theory of Chinese Thought*. New York: Oxford University Press, ch. 5, pp. 153–95.

Heng, Jiuan (2002) "Understanding Words and Knowing Men." In Alan K. L. Chan (ed.), *Mencius: Contexts and Interpretations*. Honolulu: University of Hawaii Press, pp. 151–68.

Hutton, Eric L. (2002) "Moral Connoisseurship in Mengzi." In Xiusheng Liu and Philip Ivanhoe (eds.), *Essays on the Moral Philosophy of Mengzi*. Indianapolis, IN: Hackett Publishing Company, pp. 163–86.

Im, Manyul (1999) "Emotional Control and Virtue in the Mencius." *Philosophy East & West* 49(1): 1–27.

—— (2002) "Action, Emotion and Inference in Mencius." *Journal Of Chinese Philosophy* 29(2), June: 227–49.

—— (2004) "Moral Knowledge and Self Control in Mengzi: Rectitude, Courage, and *Qi*." *Asian Philosophy* 14(1), March: 59–77.

Ivanhoe, Philip (2002a) *Ethics in the Confucian Tradition: The Thought of Mengzi and Wang Yangming*. 2nd edn. Indianapolis, IN: Hackett Publishing Company.

—— (2002b) "Confucian Self Cultivation and Mengzi's Notion of Extension." In Xiusheng Liu & Philip Ivanhoe (eds.), *Essays on the Moral Philosophy of Mengzi*. Indianapolis, IN: Hackett Publishing Company, pp. 221–41.

Lai, Whalen (1984) "Kao Tzu and Mencius on Mind: Analyzing a Paradigm Shift in Classical China." *Philosophy East & West* 34: 147–60.

Lau, D. C. (1963) "On Mencius' Use of the Method of Analogy in Argument." *Asia Major, N. S.*, vol. X. Repr. in D. C. Lau. *Mencius*, vols. 1 & 2. Hong Kong: The Chinese University Press, 1984, pp. 334–56.

—— (1970) *Mencius*. London: Penguin Books.

Legge, James (1970) *The Works of Mencius*. New York: Dover Publications, Inc.

Liu, Shu-Hsien (1996) "Some Reflections on Mencius' Views of Mind-Heart and Human Nature." *Philosophy East & West* 46(2), April: 143–64.

—— (1998) *Understanding Confucian Philosophy: Classical and Sung-Ming*. Westport, CT: Praeger, ch. 3.

Liu, Xiusheng (2002) "Mencius, Hume, and Sensibility Theory." *Philosophy East & West* 52(1): 75–97.

Liu, Xiusheng and Ivanhoe, Philip (eds.) (2002) *Essays on the Moral Philosophy of Mengzi*. Indianapolis, IN: Hackett Publishing Company.

Nivison, David (1996) *The Ways of Confucianism: Investigations in Chinese Philosophy*. Ed. Bryan Van Norden, La Salle, IL: Open Court, chs. 6–12.

Richards, I. A. (1964) *Mencius on the Mind: Experiments in Multiple Definition*. London: Routlege & Kegan Paul, ch. 3, pp. 65–85.

Schwartz, Benjamin (1985) *The World of Thought in Ancient China*. Cambridge, MA: Belknap Press, ch. 7.

Shun, Kwong-loi (1989) "Moral Reasons in Confucian Ethics." *Journal of Chinese Philosophy* 16: 317–43.

—— (1991) "Mencius and the Mind-Inherence of Morality: Mencius' Rejection of Kao Tzu Maxim in *Meng Tzu* [*Mengzi*]." *Journal of Chinese Philosophy* 18: 371–86.

—— (1996) "Ideal Motivations and Reflective Understanding." *American Philosophical Quarterly* 33(1), January: 91–104.

—— (1997a) *Mencius and Early Chinese Thought*. Stanford, CA: Stanford University Press.

—— (1997b) "Mencius on Jen-Hsing." *Philosophy East & West* 47(1), January: 1–20.

Tan Sor-hoon, "Between Family and State: Relational Tensions in Confucian Ethics." In Alan K. L. Chan (ed.) (2002) *Mencius: Contexts and Interpretations*. Honolulu: University of Hawaii Press, pp. 169–88.

Tu, Wei-ming (1978) "On the Mencian Perception of Moral Self-Development." *Monist* 61(1): 72–81.

Van Norden, Bryan W. (1991) "Kwong-loi Shun on Moral Reasons in Mencius." *Journal of Chinese Philosophy* 18: 353–70.

Waley, Arthur (1982) *Three Ways of Thought in Ancient China*. Stanford, CA: Stanford University Press (orig. pub. London: Allen & Unwin, 1939).

Wong, David B. (1991) "Is There a Distinction between Reason and Emotion in Mencius?" *Philosophy East & West* 41(1): 31–44.

—— (2002) "Reasons and Analogical Reasoning in *Mengzi*." In Xiusheng Liu and Philip Ivanhoe (eds.), *Essays on the Moral Philosophy of Mengzi*. Indianapolis, IN: Hackett Publishing Company, pp. 187–220.

Chapter 4   Xunzi (Hsün Tzu)

Allinson, Robert E. (1998) "The Debate between Mencius and Hsün-Tzu: Contemporary Applications." *Journal of Chinese Philosophy* 25: 31–49.

Chan, Wing-tsit (ed.) (1973) *A Sourcebook in Chinese Philosophy*, 4th edn. Princeton: Princeton University Press, ch. 6.

Cheung, Leo K. C. (2001) "The Way of the *Xunzi*." *Journal of Chinese Philosophy* 28(3), September: 301–20.

Cua, Antonio S. (1977) "The Conceptual Aspect of Hsün Tzu's Philosophy of Human Nature." *Philosophy East & West* 27(4): 373–89.

—— (1978) "The Quasi-empirical Aspect of Hsün-Tzu's Philosophy of Human Nature." *Philosophy East & West* 28(4): 3–19.

—— (1979) "Dimensions of *Li* (Propriety): Reflections on an Aspect of Hsün Tzu's Ethics." *Philosophy East & West* 29(4): 373–94.

—— (1985a) *Ethical Argumentation: A Study in Hsün Tzu's Moral Epistemology*. Honolulu: University of Hawaii Press.

—— (1985b) "Ethical Uses of the Past in Early Confucianism: The Case of Xunzi." *Philosophy East & West* 35(2): 133–56. Repr. in T. C. Kline III and Philip J. Ivanhoe (eds.), *Virtue, Nature and Moral Agency in the Xunzi*. Indianapolis, IN: Hackett Publishing Company, 2000, pp. 39–68.

—— (2002) "The Ethical and the Religious Dimensions of *Li* (Rites)." *The Review of Metaphysics* 55(3), March: 471–519.

Eno, Robert (1990) "Ritual as a Natural Art: The Nature of T'ien in the *Hsün Tzu*." In his *The Confucian Creation of Heaven: Philosophy and the Defense of Ritual Mastery*. Albany, NY: SUNY Press, pp. 131–69.

Goldin, Paul Rakita (1999) *Rituals of the Way: The Philosophy of Xunzi*. La Salle, IL: Open Court.

Graham, Angus C. (1989) *The Disputers of the Tao: Philosophical Argument in Ancient China*. La Salle, IL: Open Court, Part III, ch. 2, pp. 235–67.

Hagen, Kurtis (2000) "A Critical Review of Ivanhoe on Xunzi." *Journal of Chinese Philosophy* 27(3), September: 361–73.

Hansen, Chad (1992) *A Daoist Theory of Chinese Thought*. New York: Oxford University Press, ch. 9, pp. 307–43.

Hutton, Eric (2000) "Does Xunzi Have a Consistent Theory of Human Nature?" In T. C. Kline III and Philip J. Ivanhoe (eds.), *Virtue, Nature and Moral Agency in the Xunzi*. Indianapolis, IN: Hackett Publishing Company, pp. 220–36.

Ivanhoe, Philip (1994) "Human Nature and Moral Understanding in the *Xunzi*." *International Philosophical Quarterly* 34(2), June: 167–75. Repr. in T. C. Kline III and Philip J. Ivanhoe (eds.), *Virtue, Nature and Moral Agency in the Xunzi*. Indianapolis, IN: Hackett Publishing Company, 2000, pp. 237–49.

Ivanhoe, Philip J. and Van Norden, Bryan W. (eds.) (2003) *Readings in Classical Chinese Philosophy*. Indianapolis, IN: Hackett Publishing Company, Inc.

Kline III, T. C. (2000) "Moral Agency and Motivation in the *Xunzi*." In T. C. Kline III and Philip J. Ivanhoe (eds.), *Virtue, Nature and Moral Agency in the Xunzi*. Indianapolis, IN: Hackett Publishing Company, pp. 155–75.

Kline III, T. C. and Ivanhoe, Philip J. (eds.) (2000) *Virtue, Nature and Moral Agency in the Xunzi*. Indianapolis, IN: Hackett Publishing Company.

Kupperman, Joel J. (2000) "Xunzi: Morality as Psychological Constraint." In T. C. Kline III and Philip J. Ivanhoe (eds.), *Virtue, Nature and Moral Agency in the Xunzi*. Indianapolis, IN: Hackett Publishing Company, pp. 89–102.

Lau, D. C. (1953) "Theories of Human Nature in Mencius and Shyuntzyy [Xunzi]." *Bulletin of the School of Asian and African Studies* 15: 541–65. Repr. in T. C. Kline III and Philip J. Ivanhoe (eds.), *Virtue, Nature and Moral Agency in the Xunzi*. Indianapolis, IN: Hackett Publishing Company, 2000, pp. 188–219.

Machle, Edward J. (1976) "Hsün Tzu as a Religious Philosopher." *Philosophy East & West* 26(4), October: 443–61.

—— (1993) *Nature and Heaven in the Xunzi*. Albany, NY: SUNY Press.

Martin, Michael R. (1995) "Ritual Actions (*Li*) in Confucius and Hsün Tzu." *Australasian Journal of Philosophy* 73(1), March: 13–30.

Munro, Donald J. (1996) "A Villain in the Xunzi." In Philip Ivanhoe (ed.) *Chinese Language, Thought, and Culture: Nivison and His Critics*. La Salle, IL: Open Court, pp. 193–201.

Nivison, David (1991) "Hsün Tzu and Chuang Tzu." In Henry Rosemont, Jr. (ed.), *Chinese Texts and Philosophical Contexts: Essays Dedicated to Angus C. Graham*. La Salle, IL: Open Court, pp. 129–42. Repr. in T. C. Kline III and Philip J. Ivanhoe (eds.), *Virtue, Nature and Moral Agency in the Xunzi*. Indianapolis: Hackett Publishing Company, 2000, pp. 176–87.

—— (1996) "Xunzi on 'Human Nature'." In Bryan Van Norden (ed.), *The Ways of Confucianism: Investigations in Chinese Philosophy.* La Salle, IL: Open Court, pp. 203–13.

Rosemont, Jr., Henry (2000) "State and Society in the *Xunzi:* A Philosophical Commentary." In T. C. Kline III and Philip J. Ivanhoe (eds.), *Virtue, Nature and Moral Agency in the Xunzi.* Indianapolis, IN: Hackett Publishing Company, pp. 1–38.

Schofer, Jonathan W. (1993) "Virtues in Xunzi's Thought: Issues in Comparative Analysis." *The Journal of Religious Ethics* 21: 117–36. Repr. in T. C. Kline III and Philip J. Ivanhoe (eds.), *Virtue, Nature and Moral Agency in the Xunzi.* Indianapolis, IN: Hackett Publishing Company, 2000, pp. 69–88.

Schwartz, Benjamin (1985) *The World of Thought in Ancient China.* Cambridge, MA: Belknap Press, ch. 7.

Soles, David E. (1999) "The Nature and Grounds of Xunzi's Disagreement with Mencius." *Asian Philosophy* 9(2), July: 123–33.

Van Norden, Bryan W. (1992) "Mengzi and Xunzi: Two Views of Human Agency." *International Philosophical Quarterly* 32, June: 161–84. Repr. in T. C. Kline III and Philip J. Ivanhoe (eds.), *Virtue, Nature and Moral Agency in the Xunzi.* Indianapolis, IN: Hackett Publishing Company, 2000, pp. 103–34.

Watson, Burton (trans.) (1963) *Hsün Tzu: Basic Writings.* New York: Columbia University Press.

Wong, David B. (1996) "Xunzi on Moral Motivation." In Philip Ivanhoe (ed.), *Chinese Language, Thought, and Culture: Nivison and His Critics.* La Salle, IL: Open Court, pp. 202–23. Repr. in T. C. Kline III and Philip J. Ivanhoe (eds.), *Virtue, Nature and Moral Agency in the Xunzi.* Indianapolis, IN: Hackett Publishing Company, 2000, pp. 135–54.

Chapter 5   Mozi (Mo Tzu)

Ahern, Dennis M. (1976) "Is Mo Tzu A Utilitarian?" *Journal of Chinese Philosophy* 3: 185–93.

Birdwhistell, Anne D. (1984) "An Approach to Verification Beyond Tradition in Early Chinese Philosophy: Mo Tzu's Concept of Sampling in a Community of Observers." *Philosophy East & West* 34: 175–84.

Brandt, Richard B. (1989) "Comment on Chad Hansen's 'Language Utilitarianism'." *Journal of Chinese Philosophy* 16: 381–5.

Chan, Wing-tsit (ed.) (1973) *A Sourcebook in Chinese Philosophy,* 4th edn. Princeton, NJ: Princeton University Press, ch. 9.

Chang, Li-wien (1979) "A Short Comment on Mo Tzu's Epistemology Based on 'Three Criteria'." *Chinese Studies in Philosophy* 10: 47–54.

Ching, Julia (1978) "Chinese Ethics and Kant." *Philosophy East & West* 28: 161–72.

Creel, Herrlee G. (1953) *Chinese Thought: From Confucius to Mao Tse-Tung.* Chicago: University of Chicago Press, ch. 4, pp. 46–67.

Duda, Kristopher (2001) "Reconsidering Mo Tzu on the Foundations of Morality." *Asian Philosophy* 11(1): 23–31.

Hansen, Chad (1989) "Mo Tzu: Language Utilitarianism." *Journal of Chinese Philosophy* 16: 355–80.

Jenner, Donald (1984) "Mo Tzu and Hobbes: Preliminary Remarks on the Relation of Chinese and Western Politics." *Cogito* 2: 49–72.

Jochim, Christian (1980) "Ethical Analysis of an Ancient Debate: Mohists versus Confucians." *Journal of Religious Ethics* 8: 135–47.

Johnston, Ian (2000) "Choosing the Greater and Choosing the Lesser: A Translation and Analysis of the Daqu and Xiaoqu Chapters of the Mozi." *Journal of Chinese Philosophy* 27(4): 375–407.

Lai, Whalen (1991) "In Defense of Graded Love." *Asian Philosophy*: 51–60.

—— (1993) "The Public Good that Does the Public Good: A New Reading of Mohism." *Asian Philosophy* 3(2): 125–41.

Lau, D. C. (1953) "Some Logical Problems in Ancient China." *Proceedings of the Aristotelian Society* 53: 189–204.

Lum, Alice (1977) "Social Utilitarianism in the Philosophy of Mo Tzu." *Journal of Chinese Philosophy* 4: 187–207.

Scarre, Geoffrey (1996) *Utilitarianism*. New York: Routledge.

Schwartz, Benjamin (1985) *The World of Thought in Ancient China*. Cambridge, MA: Belknap Press, ch. 6, pp. 186–254.

Soles, David E. (1999) "Mo Tzu and the Foundations of Morality." *Journal of Chinese Philosophy* 26(1): 37–48.

T'ang Chun-I. (1962) "The T'ien Ming (Heavenly Ordinance) in Pre-Ch'in China, II." *Philosophy East & West* 12: 29–50.

Taylor, Rodney L. (1979) "Mo Tzu on Spirits and Funerals." *Philosophy East & West* 29: 337–46.

Vorenkamp, Dirck (1992) "Strong Utilitarianism in Mo Tzu's Thought." *Journal of Chinese Philosophy* 19(4): 423–43.

Watson, Burton (1963) *Mo Tzu: Basic Writings*. New York: Columbia University Press.

Watson, Walter (1981) "Principle for Dealing with Disorder." *Journal of Chinese Philosophy* 8: 349–69.

Winance, Eleuthere (1961) "A Forgotten Chinese Thinker: Mo Tzu." *International Philosophical Quarterly* 1: 593–619.

Wong, David (1989) "Universalism versus Love with Distinctions: An Ancient Debate Revived." *Journal of Chinese Philosophy* 16: 251–72.

Chapter 6   Laozi (Lao Tzu)

Ahern, Dennis M. (1977) "Ineffability in the 'Lao Tzu': The Taming of A Dragon." *Journal of Chinese Philosophy* 4: 357–82.

Ames, Roger T. (1983) "Is Political Taoism Anarchism?" *Journal of Chinese Philosophy* 10: 27–47.

Chan, Wing-tsit (ed.) (1973) *A Sourcebook in Chinese Philosophy*, 4th edn. Princeton, NJ: Princeton University Press, ch. 7.

Chang, Chung-yuan (1974) "Tao: A New Way of Thinking." *Journal of Chinese Philosophy* 1: 127–52.

Cheng, Chung-ying (1983) "Metaphysics of 'Tao' and Dialectics of 'Fa'." *Journal of Chinese Philosophy* 10: 251–84.

Creel, Herrlee G. (1970) *What Is Taoism? And Other Studies in Chinese Cultural History*. Chicago, IL: The University of Chicago Press.

—— (1983) "On the Opening Words of the 'Lao-Tzu'." *Journal of Chinese Philosophy* 10: 299–330.

Csikszentmihalyi, Mark and Ivanhoe, Philip J. (eds.) (1999) *Religious and Philosophical Aspects of the Laozi*. Albany, NY: SUNY Press.

Danto, Arthur C. (1973) "Language and the Tao: Some Reflections on Ineffability." *Journal of Chinese Philosophy* 1: 45–55.

Fu, Charles Wei-hsun (1973) "Lao-Tzu's Conception of Tao." *Inquiry* 16: 367–91.

Graham, Angus C. (1989) *The Disputers of the Tao: Philosophical Argument in Ancient China*. La Salle, IL: Open Court, Part III, ch. 1, pp. 215–35.

Hahn, Robert (1981) "Being and Non-being in 'Rig Veda X' in the Writings of the 'Lao-Tzu' and 'Chuang-Tzu' and in the 'Later' Plato." *Journal of Chinese Philosophy* 8: 119–42.

Hang, Thaddeus T'ui Chieh (2000) "Understanding Evil in the Philosophies of Mencius, Hsün Tzu, and Lao Tzu." In Sandra A. Wawrytko (ed.), *The Problem of Evil: An Intercultural Exploration*. Amsterdam and Atlanta, GA: Rodopi, pp. 1–9.

Hansen, Chad (1981) "Linguistic Skepticism in the 'Lao Tzu'." *Philosophy East & West* 31: 321–36.

—— (1992) *A Daoist Theory of Chinese Thought*. New York: Oxford University Press, ch. 6, pp. 196–230.

Hsu, Sung-peng (1976) "Lao Tzu's Conception of Ultimate Reality: A Comparative Study." *International Philosophical Quarterly* 16: 197–218.

—— (1976) "Lao Tzu's Conception of Evil." *Philosophy East & West* 26: 301–16.

Ivanhoe, Philip J. (1999) "The Concept of *de* ('Virtue') in the Laozi." In Mark Csikszentmihalyi and Philip J. Ivanhoe (eds.), *Religious and Philosophical Aspects of the Laozi*. Albany, NY: SUNY Press, pp. 239–57.

Kaltenmark, Max (1969) *Lao Tzu and Taoism* (translated from the French by Roger Greaves). Stanford, CA: Stanford University Press.

Kasulis, T. P. (1977) "The Absolute and the Relative in Taoist Philosophy." *Journal of Chinese Philosophy*, 4: 383–94.

Kato, Joken (1970) "The Origin of the Oriental Idea of Correspondence with Nature." *Philosophical Studies of Japan* 10: 95–114.

Kohn, Livia and LaFargue, Michael (eds.) (1998) *Lao-tzu and the Tao-te-ching*. Albany, NY: SUNY Press.

Lau, D. C. (1958) "The Treatment of Opposites in Lao-Tzu." *Bulletin of the School of Asian and African Studies* 21: 344–60.

—— (1963) *Lao Tzu: Tao Te Ching*. NY: Penguin Books, pp. vii–xlv.

Liu, JeeLoo (2003) "A Daoist Conception of Truth: Laozi's Metaphysical Realism vs. Zhuangzi's Internal Realism." In Bo Mou (ed.), *Comparative Approaches to Chinese Philosophy*. Aldershot: Ashgate Publishing Ltd., pp. 278–93.

Liu, Xiaogan (1998) "On the Concept of Naturalness ('Tzu-Jan') in Lao Tzu's Philosophy." *Journal of Chinese Philosophy* 25(4): 423–46.

—— (1999) "An Inquiry into the Core Value of Laozi's Philosophy." In Mark Csikszentmihalyi and Philip J. Ivanhoe (eds.), *Religious and Philosophical Aspects of the Laozi*. Albany, NY: SUNY Press, pp. 211–37.

Mou, Bo (2000) "Ultimate Concern and Language Engagement: A Reexamination of the Opening Message of the 'Dao-De-Jing'." *Journal of Chinese Philosophy* 27(4): 429–39.

—— (2001) "Moral Rules and Moral Experience: A Comparative Analysis of Dewey and Laozi on Morality." *Asian Philosophy*, 11(3): 161–78.

Schwartz, Benjamin (1985) *The World of Thought in Ancient China*. Cambridge, MA: Belknap Press, ch. 6.

Shien, Gi-ming (1951) "Nothingness in the Philosophy of Lao-Tzu." *Philosophy East & West* 1: 58–63.

Stern, Axel (1949–51) "Remarks of Two Chapters of Laotse's *Tao Teh Ching*." *Synthese* 8: 65–72.

Thompson, Kirill O. (1990) "Taoist Cultural Reality: The Harmony of Aesthetic Order." *Journal of Chinese Philosophy* 17(2): 175–85.

Wang, Qingjie (1997) "On Lao Tzu's Concept of 'Zi Ran'." *Journal of Chinese Philosophy* 24(3): 291–321.

Wawrytko, Sandra A. (2000) "The Problem of the Problem of Evil: A Taoist Response." In Sandra A. Wawrytko (ed.), *The Problem of Evil: An Intercultural Exploration*. Amsterdam and Atlanta, GA: Rodopi, pp. 21–39.

Welch, Holmes (1966) *Taoism. The Parting of the Way*, rev. edn. Boston: Beacon Press.

Xie, Wenyu (2000) "Approaching the Dao: From Lao Zi to Zhuang Zi." *Journal of Chinese Philosophy* 27(4): 469–88.

Zhu, Bokun (1998) "Daoist Patterns of Thought and the Tradition of Chinese Metaphysics." *Contemporary Chinese Thought* 29(3): 13–71.

Chapter 7 Zhuangzi (Chuang Tzu)

Allinson, Robert E. (1986) "Having Your Cake and Eating It, Too: Evaluation and Trans-Evaluation in Chuang Tzu and Nietzsche." *Journal of Chinese Philosophy* 13: 429–43.

—— (1988) "A Logical Reconstruction of the Butterfly Dream: The Case for Internal Textual Transformation." *Journal of Chinese Philosophy* 15: 319–39.

—— (1989) "On the Question of Relativism in the *Chuang Tzu*." *Philosophy East & West* 39(1), January: 13–26.

Ames, Roger T. (ed.) (1998) *Wandering at Ease in the Zhuangzi*. Albany, NY: SUNY Press.

Behuniak, James Jr. (2002) "Disposition and Aspiration in the *Mencius* and *Zhuangzi*." *Journal of Chinese Philosophy* 29(1), March: 65–79.

Berkson, Mark (1996) "Language: The Guest of Reality – Zhuangzi and Derrida on Language, Reality, and Skillfulness." In Paul Kjellberg and Philip J. Ivanhoe (eds.), *Essays on Skepticism, Relativism, and Ethics in the Zhuangzi*. Albany, NY: State University of New York Press, pp. 97–126.

Burneko, Guy C. (1986) "Chuang Tzu's Existential Hermeneutics." *Journal of Chinese Philosophy* 13: 393–409.

Callahan, W. A. (1989) "Discourse and Perspective in Daoism: A Linguistic Interpretation of *Ziran*." *Philosophy East & West* 39(2), April: 171–89.

Chan, Wing-tsit (ed.) (1973) *A Sourcebook in Chinese Philosophy*, 4th edn. Princeton, NJ: Princeton University Press, ch. 8.

Chang, Chung-yuan (1977) "The Philosophy of Taoism According to Chuang Tzu." *Philosophy East & West* 27(4), October: 409–22.

Cheng, Chung-ying (1977) "Nature and Function of Skepticism in Chinese Philosophy." *Philosophy East & West* 27(2), April: 137–54.

Chinn, Ewing Y. (1997) "Zhuangzi and Relativistic Skepticism." *Asian Philosophy* 7(3), November: 207–20.

Coleman, Earle J. (1991) "The Beautiful, the Ugly, and the Tao." *Journal of Chinese Philosophy* 18: 213–26.

Cook, Scott (ed.) (2003) *Hiding the World in the World: Uneven Discourses on the Zhuangzi*. Albany, NY: SUNY Press.

Creel, Herrlee G. (1970) *What Is Taoism? And Other Studies in Chinese Cultural History*. Chicago, IL: The University of Chicago Press.

Cua, Antonio S. (1977) "Forgetting Morality: Reflections on A Theme in *Chuang Tzu*." *Journal of Chinese Philosophy* 4: 305–28.

Fleming, Jesse (1991) "A Response to Kuang-Ming Wu's 'Non-World Making'." *Journal of Chinese Philosophy* 18, March: 51–2.

Fox, Allen (1996) "Reflex and Reflectivity: 'Wu-wei' in the *Zhuangzi*." *Asian Philosophy* 6(1), March: 59–72.

Gaskins, Robert W. (1997) "The Transformation of Things: A Reanalysis of Chuang Tzu's Butterfly Dream." *Journal of Chinese Philosophy* 24(1), March: 107–22.

Girardot, N. J. (1978) "Chaotic 'Order' ('*Hun-Tun*') and Benevolent 'Disorder' ('*Luan*') in the *Chuang Tzu*." *Philosophy East & West* 28, July: 299–321.

Goodman, Russell B. (1985) "Skepticism and Realism in the *Chuang Tzu*." *Philosophy East & West* 35(3), July: 231–7.

Graham, Angus C. (1983) "Taoist Spontaneity and the Dichotomy of 'Is' and 'Ought'." In Victor H. Mair (ed.), *Experimental Essays on Chuang-tzu*. Asian Studies at Hawaii, No. 29. Honolulu: University of Hawaii Press, pp. 3–23.

—— (1985) *Reason and Spontaneity: A New Solution to the Problem of Fact and Value*. London: Curzon Press.

—— (1989) *The Disputers of the Tao: Philosophical Argument in Ancient China*. La Salle, IL: Open Court, Part II, ch. 3, pp. 170–211.

Hall, David (1984) "Nietzsche and Chuang Tzu: Resources for the Transcendence of Culture." *Journal of Chinese Philosophy* 11: 139–52.

Hansen, Chad (1983) "A Tao of Tao in Chuang-tzu." In Victor H. Mair (ed.), *Experimental Essays on Chuang-tzu*. Asian Studies at Hawaii, No. 29. Honolulu: University of Hawaii Press, pp. 24–55.

—— (1992) *A Daoist Theory of Chinese Thought*. New York: Oxford University Press, ch. 8, pp. 265–303.

Hara, Wing Han (1993) "Between Individuality and Universality: An Explication of Chuang Tzu's Theses of *Chien-tu* and *Ch'i-wu*." *Journal of Chinese Philosophy* 20(1), March: 87–99.

Harbsmeier, Christoph (1993) "Conceptions of Knowledge in Ancient China." In Hans Lenk and Gregor Paul (eds.), *Epistemological Issues in Classical Chinese Philosophy*, Albany, NY: SUNY Press, pp. 11–30.

Ivanhoe, Philip J. (1996) "Was Zhuangzi a Relativist?" In Paul Kjellberg and Philip J. Ivanhoe (eds.), *Essays on Skepticism, Relativism, and Ethics in the Zhuangzi*. Albany, NY: State University of New York Press, pp. 196–214.

Ivanhoe, Philip J. and Van Norden, Bryan W. (eds.) (2003) *Readings in Classical Chinese Philosophy*. Indianapolis, IN: Hackett Publishing Company, Inc.

Kjellberg, Paul (1994) "Skepticism, Truth, and the Good Life: A Comparison of Zhuangzi and Sextus Empiricus." *Philosophy East & West* 44(1): 111–33.

—— (1996) "Sextus Empiricus, Zhuangzi, and Xunzi on 'Why be Skeptical?'" In Paul Kjellberg and Philip J. Ivanhoe (eds.), *Essays on Skepticism, Relativism, and Ethics in the Zhuangzi*. Albany, NY: State University of New York Press, pp. 1–25.

Kjellberg, Paul and Ivanhoe, Philip J. (eds.) (1996) *Essays on Skepticism, Relativism, and Ethics in the Zhuangzi*. Albany, NY: State University of New York Press.

Kupperman, Joel J. (1989) "Not in So Many Words: Chuang Tzu's Strategies of Communication." *Philosophy East & West* 39, July: 311–17.

Lee, Jung H. (1998) "Disputers of the Tao: Putnam and Chuang-tzu on Meaning, Truth, and Reality." *Journal of Chinese Philosophy* 25(4): 447–70.

Lee, Kwang-sae (1996) "Rorty and Chuang Tzu: Anti-Representationalism, Pluralism and Conversation." *Journal of Chinese Philosophy* 23(2): 175–92.

Legge, Russel D. (1979) "Chuang Tzu and the Free Man." *Philosophy East & West* 29: 11–20.

Li, Chenyang (1993) "What-Being: Chuang Tzu versus Aristotle." *International Philosophical Quarterly* 33(3): 341–53.

Liu, JeeLoo (2003) "A Daoist Conception of Truth: Laozi's Metaphysical Realism vs. Zhuangzi's Internal Realism." In Bo Mou (ed.), *Comparative Approaches to Chinese Philosophy*. Aldershot: Ashgate Publishing Ltd.

Loy, David (1996) "Zhuangzi and Nagarjuna on the Truth of No Truth." In Paul Kjellberg and Philip J. Ivanhoe (eds.), *Essays on Skepticism, Relativism, and Ethics in the Zhuangzi*. Albany, NY: State University of New York Press, pp. 50–67.

Mair, Victor H. (ed.) (1983) *Experimental Essays on Chuang-tzu*. Asian Studies at Hawaii, No. 29. Honolulu: University of Hawaii Press.

Major, John S. (1975) "The Efficacy of Uselessness: A Chuang-Tzu Motif." *Philosophy East & West* 25, July: 265–79.

Merton, Thomas (1965) *The Way of Chuang Tzu*. New York: New Directions Publishing Corporation.

Möller, Hans-Georg (1999) "Zhuangzi's 'Dream of the Butterfly': A Daoist Interpretation." *Philosophy East & West* 49(4), October: 439–50.

Oshima, Harold H. (1983) "A Metaphorical Analysis of the Concept of Mind in the *Chuang-tzu*." In Victor H. Mair (ed.), *Experimental Essays on Chuang-tzu*. Asian Studies at Hawaii, No. 29. Honolulu: University of Hawaii Press, pp. 63–84.

Owens, Wayne D. (1990) "Radical Concrete Particularity: Heidegger, Lao Tzu and Chuang Tzu." *Journal of Chinese Philosophy* 17(2): 235–55.

Parkes, Graham (1983) "The Wandering Dance: Chuang Tzu and Zarathustra." *Philosophy East & West* 33: 235–50.

Pas, Julian F. (1981) "Chuang Tzu's Essays on 'Free Flight into Transcendence' and 'Responsive Rulership' (chs. 1 and 7) of the *Chuang Tzu*." *Journal of Chinese Philosophy* 8, December: 479–96.

Radice, Thomas (2001) "Clarity and Survival in the *Zhuangzi*." *Asian Philosophy* 11(1): 33–40.

Raphals, Lisa (1994) "Skeptical Strategies in the *Zhuangzi* and *Theaetetus*." *Philosophy East & West* 44(3): 501–26. Repr. in Paul Kjellberg and Philip J. Ivanhoe (eds.), *Essays on Skepticism, Relativism, and Ethics in the Zhuangzi*. Albany, NY: State University of New York Press, 1996, pp. 26–49.

Saso, Michael (1983) "The *Chuang-tzu nei-p'ien*: A Taoist Meditation." In Victor H. Mair (ed.), *Experimental Essays on Chuang-tzu*. Asian Studies at Hawaii, No. 29. Honolulu: University of Hawaii Press, pp. 140–57.

Schwartz, Benjamin (1985) *The World of Thought in Ancient China*. Cambridge, MA: Belknap Press, ch. 6.

Schwitzgebel, Eric (1996) "Zhuangzi's Attitude Toward Language and His Skepticism." In Paul Kjellberg and Philip J. Ivanhoe (eds.), *Essays on Skepticism, Relativism, and Ethics in the Zhuangzi*. Albany, NY: State University of New York Press, 1996, pp. 68–96.

Shen, Vincent (1996) "Confucianism and Taoism in Response to Constructive Realism." *Journal of Chinese Philosophy* 23: 59–78.

Soles, Deborah H. and Soles, David E. (1998) "Fish Traps and Rabbit Snare: Zhuangzi on Judgment, Truth and Knowledge." *Asian Philosophy* 8(3), November: 149–64.

Sun, Siao Fang (1953) "Chuang Tzu's Theory of Truth." *Philosophy East & West* 3, July: 137–46.

Van Norden, Bryan W. (1996) "Competing Interpretations of the Inner Chapters of the 'Zhuangzi'." *Philosophy East & West* 46(2), April: 247–68.

Waley, Arthur (1982) *Three Ways of Thought in Ancient China*. Stanford, CA: Stanford University Press (orig. pub. London: Allen & Unwin, 1939).

Wang, Youru (2000) "Philosophy of Change and the Deconstruction of Self in the 'Zhuangzi'." *Journal of Chinese Philosophy* 27(3): 345–60.

Watson, Burton (trans.) (1964) *Chuang Tzu: Basic Writings*. New York: Columbia University Press (repr. in 1996).

—— (trans.) (1968) *The Complete Works of Chuang Tzu*. New York: Columbia University Press.

Wu, John C. H. (1963) "The Wisdom of Chuang Tzu: A New Appraisal." *International Philosophical Quarterly* 3: 5–36.

Wu, Kuang-ming (1981) "Trying Without Trying: Toward a Taoist Phenomenology of Truth." *Journal of Chinese Philosophy* 8: 143–68.

—— (1990) *The Butterfly as Companion: Meditations on the First Three Chapters of the Chuang Tzu.* Albany, NY: SUNY Press.

—— (1991) "Non-World Making in *Chuang Tzu.*" *Journal of Chinese Philosophy* 18, March: 37–50.

Wu, Laurence C. (1986) "Chuang Tzu and Wittgenstein on World-Making." *Journal of Chinese Philosophy* 13, December: 383–91.

Xie, Wenyu (2000) "Approaching the Dao: From Lao Zi to Zhuang Zi." *Journal of Chinese Philosophy* 27(4): 469–88.

Yan, Beiming (1981) The Reevaluation of Zhuangzi." *Journal of Chinese Philosophy* 12: 63–89.

Yearley, Lee (1983) "The Perfected Person in the Radical Chuang-tzu." In Victor H. Mair (ed.), *Experimental Essays on Chuang-tzu.* Asian Studies at Hawaii, No. 29. Honolulu: University of Hawaii Press, pp. 125–39.

—— (1996) "Zhuangzi's Understanding of Skillfulness and the Ultimate Spiritual State." In Paul Kjellberg and Philip J. Ivanhoe (eds.), *Essays on Skepticism, Relativism, and Ethics in the Zhuangzi.* Albany, NY: State University of New York Press, 1996, pp. 152–82.

Yeh, Michelle (1983) "The Deconstructive Way: A Comparative Study of Derrida and Chuang Tzu." *Journal of Chinese Philosophy* 10: 95–126.

Yukawa, Hideki (1983) "Chuangtse the Happy Fish." In Victor H. Mair (ed.), *Experimental Essays on Chuang-tzu.* Asian Studies at Hawaii, No. 29. Honolulu: University of Hawaii Press, pp. 56–62.

Chapter 8   Hanfeizi (Han Fei Tzu)

Ames, Roger T. (1994) *The Art of Rulership: A Study of Ancient Chinese Political Thought.* Albany, NY: SUNY Press.

Chan, Wing-tsit (ed.) (1973) *A Sourcebook in Chinese Philosophy*, 4th edn. Princeton, NJ: Princeton University Press, ch. 12.

Chang, Leo S. and Wang, Hsiao-po (1986) *The Philosophical Foundations of Han Fei's Political Theory.* Honolulu: University of Hawaii Press.

Cheng, Chung-ying (1981) "Legalism Versus Confucianism: A Philosophical Appraisal." *Journal of Chinese Philosophy* 8: 271–302.

—— (1983) "Metaphysics of 'Tao' and Dialectics of 'Fa'." *Journal of Chinese Philosophy* 10: 251–84.

Fung, Yu-lan (1983) *A History of Chinese Philosophy*, vol. I (trans. Derk Bodde). Princeton, NJ: Princeton University Press, ch. 8, pp. 312–36.

Goldin, Paul R. (1983) "Han Fei's Doctrine of Self-Interest." *Asian Philosophy* 11(3): 151–9.

Graham, Angus C. (1989) *The Disputers of the Tao: Philosophical Argument in Ancient China.* La Salle, IL: Open Court, Part III, ch. 3, pp. 267–92.

Hansen, Chad (1992) *A Daoist Theory of Chinese Thought*. New York: Oxford University Press, ch. 10, pp. 344–76.

—— (1996) "*Fa*: Laws or Standards." In Smart, Ninian (ed.) *East-West Encounters in Philosophy and Religion*, Long Beach, CA: Long Beach Publishing.

Ho, Pao-chung (1988) "An Analysis and Critique of Han-Fei's Thought." *National Taiwan University Philosophical Critique*, No. 11, January, pp. 247–60 (in Chinese).

Ivanhoe, Philip J. and Bryan W. Van Norden (eds.) (2003) *Readings in Classical Chinese Philosophy*. Indianapolis, IN: Hackett Publishing Company, Inc., ch. 7 (excerpts).

Lee, K. K. (1975) "The Legalist School and Legal Positivism." *Journal Of Chinese Philosophy* 3: 23–56.

Liang, Enyuan (1976) "The Legalist School Was the Product of Great Social Change in the Spring and Autumn and Warring States Periods." *Chinese Studies in Philosophy*, Fall: 4–20.

Liang, Ling-i. (1976) "The Crystallization of Pre-Ch'in Legalist Thought." *Chinese Studies in Philosophy* 7, Summer: 35–56.

Liao, W. K. (trans.) (1939) *The Complete Works of Han Fei Tzu*. London: Arthur Probsthain.

Lin, Yih-jing (1989) "A Study of the Pre-Chin Legalist Theory of Human Nature." *National Taiwan University Philosophical Critique* 12, January: 145–73 (in Chinese).

Manicas, Peter T. (1977) "Two Concepts of Justice." *Journal of Chinese Philosophy* 4: 99–121.

Moody Jr., Peter R. (1979) "The Legalism of Han Fei Tzu and Its Affinities with Modern Political Thought." *International Philosophical Quarterly* 19: 317–30.

Schwartz, Benjamin (1985) *The World of Thought in Ancient China*. Cambridge, MA: Belknap Press, ch. 8, pp. 321–49.

Ti, Ch'ing (1978) "A Reading of Han Fei's 'Wu Tu' (Five Vermin)." *Chinese Studies in Philosophy* 10, Fall: 19–33.

Tong, Shuye (1982/3) "A Study of Han Fei's Thought." *Chinese Studies in Philosophy* 14, Winter: 61–98.

Vervoorn, Aat (1981) "Taoism, Legalism and the Quest for Order in Warring States China." *Journal Of Chinese Philosophy* 8: 303–24.

Waley, Arthur (1982) *Three Ways of Thought in Ancient China*. Stanford, CA: Stanford University Press (orig. pub. London: Allen & Unwin, 1939).

Wang, Hsiao-po (1977) "The Significance of the Concept of 'Fa' in Han Fei's Thought System" (trans. by L. S. Chang). *Philosophy East & West* 27(1): 35–52.

Watson, Burton (1964) *Han Fei Tzu: Basic Writings*. New York: Columbia University Press.

Watson, Walter (1981) "Principles for Dealing with Disorder." *Journal Of Chinese Philosophy* 8: 349–70.

Yang, K'uan (1978) "Han Fei's Theory of the 'Rule of Law' Played A Progressive Role." *Chinese Studies in Philosophy* 10, Fall: 4–18.

Part II   Chinese Buddhism

Introduction

Chan, Wing-tsit (ed.) (1958) "Transformation of Buddhism in China." *Philosophy East & West* 7: 107–16.

—— (1973) *A Sourcebook in Chinese Philosophy*, 4th edn. Princeton, NJ: Princeton University Press.

Chatterjee, Satischandra and Datta, Dhirendramohan (1968) *An Introduction to Indian Philosophy*, 7th edn. Calcutta: University of Calcutta Press.

Ch'en, Kenneth K. S. (1964) *Buddhism in China: A Historical Survey*. Princeton, NJ: Princeton University Press.

Cheng, Hsueh-li (1980) "Motion and Rest in the *Middle Treatise*." *Journal of Chinese Philosophy* 7: 229–44.

—— (1981) "Chi-tsang's Treatment of Metaphysical Issues." *Journal of Chinese Philosophy* 8: 371–89.

Dalai Lama (1997) *The Four Noble Truths*. London: Thorsons.

—— (2000) *The Meaning of Life: Buddhist Perspective on Cause and Effect* (trans. Jeffrey Hopkins). Boston: Wisdom Publications.

De Bary, William Theodore and Bloom, Irene (eds.) (1999) *Sources of Chinese Tradition*, second edition. Volume I. *From Earliest Times to 1600*. New York: Columbia University Press.

Fang, Litian (1989) "A Tentative Discussion of the Characteristics of Chinese Buddhism." *Chinese Studies in Philosophy* 20, Summer: 3–71.

Fung, Yu-lan (1983) *A History of Chinese Philosophy*, vol. II. (trans. Derk Bodde). Princeton, NJ: Princeton University Press, ch. 7, pp. 237–92.

Gethin, Rupert (1998) *The Foundations of Buddhism*. Oxford: Oxford University Press.

Hurvitz, Leon (1975) "The First systematizations of Buddhist Thought in China." *Journal of Chinese Philosophy* 2: 361–88.

Inada, Kenneth K. (1979) "Problematics of the Buddhist Nature of Self." *Philosophy East & West* 29(2), April: 141–58.

—— (1985) "Two Strains in Buddhist Causality." *Journal of Chinese Philosophy* 12: 49–56.

Kalupahana, David J. (1975) *Causality: The Central Philosophy of Buddhism*. Honolulu: The University Press of Hawaii.

—— (1992) *A History of Buddhist Philosophy: Continuities and Discontinuities*. Honolulu: University of Hawaii Press.

Kieschnick, John (2003)*The Impact of Buddhism on Chinese Material Culture*. Princeton, NJ: Princeton University Press.

Koller, John M. (1972) "Dharma: An Expression of Universal Order." *Philosophy East & West* 22: 131–44.

Lai, Whalen (1977) "Chinese Buddhist Causation Theories: An Analysis of the Sinitic Mahayana Understanding of *Pratiya-samutpada*." *Philosophy East & West* 27(3): 241–64.

Liu, Ming-wood (1985) "The Yogacara and Madhyamika Interpretations of the Buddha-Nature Concept in Chinese Buddhism." *Philosophy East & West* 35, April: 171–93.

—— (1989) "The Early Development of the Buddha-Nature Doctrine in China." *Journal of Chinese Philosophy* 16: 1–36.

Mitchell, Donald W. (1976) "The Paradox of Buddhism Wisdom." *Philosophy East & West* 26: 55–67.

Potter, Karl H. (1964) "The Naturalistic Principle of *Karma*." *Philosophy East & West* 14: 39–49.

Radhakrishnan (1962) *Indian Philosophy*, vol. I. New York: Macmillan Company (orig. pub. 1923).

Saso, Michael (1977) "Buddhist and Taoist Notions of Transcendence: A Study of Philosophical Contrast." In Michael Saso and David W. Chappell (eds.), *Buddhist and Taoist Studies I*. Honolulu: The University Press of Hawaii, pp. 3–22.

Siderits, Mark (2001) "Buddhism and Techno-Physicalism: Is the Eightfold Path A Program?" *Philosophy East & West* 51(3), July: 307–14.

Streng, Frederick (1975) "Reflections on the Attention Given to Mental Construction in the Indian Buddhist Analysis of Causality." *Philosophy East & West* 25: 71–80.

Ueda, Yoshifumi (1964) "The World and the Individual in Mahayana Buddhist Philosophy." *Philosophy East & West* 14: 157–66.

Varma, V. P. (1963) "The Origins and Sociology of the Early Buddhist Philosophy of Moral Determinism." *Philosophy East & West* 13(1): 25–47.

Wayman, Alex (1974) "Two Traditions of India: Truth and Silence." *Philosophy East & West* 24: 389–403.

Wright, Arthur F. (1959) *Buddhism in Chinese History*. Stanford, CA: Stanford University Press.

—— (1990) *Studies in Chinese Buddhism*, ed. Robert M. Somers. New Haven, CT: Yale University Press.

Zeuschner, Robert B. (1981) "The Understanding of Karma in Early Ch'an Buddhism." *Journal of Chinese Philosophy* 8: 399–425.

Chapter 9   The Consciousness-Only (*Wei-shi*) School

Banerjee, Nikunja Vihari (1974) *The Spirit of Indian Philosophy*. New Delhi, India: Arnold-Heinemann Publishers.

Betty, Stafford L. (1971) "The Buddhist-Humean Parallels: Postmodernism." *Philosophy East & West* 21, July: 237–53.

Chan, Wing-tsit (ed.) (1973) *A Sourcebook in Chinese Philosophy*, 4th edn. Princeton, NJ: Princeton University Press, ch. 23.

Chatterjee, Satischandra and Datta, Dhirendramohan (1968) *An Introduction to Indian Philosophy*, 7th edn. Calcutta: University of Calcutta Press.

Fung, Yu-lan (1983) *A History of Chinese Philosophy*, vol. II. (trans. Derk Bodde). Princeton, NJ: Princeton University Press, ch. 8, pp. 299–338.

Hamilton, Clarence H. (trans.) (1938) Vasubandhu, *Wei shih er shih lun* (*The Treatise in Twenty Stanzas on Representation-only*). Translated from the Chinese version of [Xuanzang]. New Haven, CT: American Oriental Society.

Kalupahana, David J. (1992) *A History of Buddhist Philosophy: Continuities and Discontinuities*. Honolulu: University of Hawaii Press, chs. 19–20, pp. 184–205.

Kern, Iso (1988) "The Structure of Consciousness According to Xuanzang." *Journal of the British Society for Phenomenology* 19(3), October: 282–95.

Lusthaus, Dan (2002) *Buddhist Phenomenology: A Philosophical Investigation of Yogacara Buddhism and the Ch'eng Wei-Shih lun*. New York: RoutledgeCurzon.

Raju, P. T. (1971) *The Philosophical Traditions of India*. Pittsburgh: University of Pittsburgh Press.

Wei, Tat (trans.) (1973) *Ch'eng Wei-shih lun Doctrine of Mere-Consciousness* by Hsüan Tsang, Hong Kong: The Ch'eng Wei-Shih Lun Publication Committee.

Chapter 10   The Hua-yan (Hua-yen) School

Berkson, Mark (1996) "Language: The Guest of Reality – Zhuangzi and Derrida on Language, Reality, and Skillfulness." In Paul Kjellberg and Philip J. Ivanhoe (eds.), *Essays on Skepticism, Relativism, and Ethics in the Zhuangzi*. Albany, NY: State University of New York Press, pp. 97–126.

Chan, Wing-tsit (ed.) (1973) *A Sourcebook in Chinese Philosophy*, 4th edn. Princeton, NJ: Princeton University Press, ch. 25.

Chang, Garma C. C. (1971) *The Buddhist Teaching of Totality: The Philosophy of Hwa Yen Buddhism*. University Park, PA: The Pennsylvania State University Press.

Cheng, Hsueh-fli (1984) "Phenomenology in T'ien-tai and Hua-yen Buddhism." In Anna-Teresa Tymieniecka (ed.), *Phenomenology of Life in A Dialogue between Chinese and Occidental Philosophy*. Dordrecht: Reidel Publishing Company, pp. 215–27.

Cleary, Thomas (trans.) (1983) *Entry into the Inconceivable: An Introduction to Hua-yen Buddhism*. Honolulu: University of Hawaii Press.

—— (1993) *The Flower Ornament Scripture: A Translation of the Avatamsaka Sutra*. Boston, MA: Shambhala Publications, Inc.

Cook, Francis H. (1972) "The Meaning of Vairocana in Hua-yen Buddhism." *Philosophy East & West* 22, October: 403–15.

—— (1977) *Hua-yen Buddhism The Jewel Net of Indra*. University Park, PA: Pennsylvania State University Press.

—— (1979) "Causation in the Chinese Hua-yen Tradition." *Journal of Chinese Philosophy* 6: 367–85.

Fu, Charles Wei-hsün (1984) "Chinese Buddhism and An Existential Phenomenology." In Anna-Teresa Tymieniecka (ed.), *Phenomenology of Life in A Dialogue Between Chinese and Occidental Philosophy*. Dordrecht: Reidel Publishing Company, pp. 229–51.

Fung, Yu-lan (1983) *A History of Chinese Philosophy*, vol. II (trans. Derk Bodde). Princeton, NJ: Princeton University Press, ch. 8, pp. 339–59.

Gimello, Robert M. (1976) "Apophatic and Kataphatic Discourse in Mahayana: A Chinese View." *Philosophy East & West* 26, April: 117–36.

—— (1990) "Li T'ung-hsüan and the Practical Dimensions of Hua-yen." In Robert M. Gimello and Peter N. Gregory (eds.), *Studies in Ch'an and Hua-Yen*. Honolulu: University of Hawaii Press, pp. 321–66.

Gimello, Robert M. and Gregory, Peter N. (eds.) (1990) *Studies in Ch'an and Hua-Yen*. Honolulu: University of Hawaii Press.

Gregory, Peter N. (1990) "The Teaching of Men and Gods: The Doctrinal and Social Basis of Lay Buddhist Practice in the Hua-yen Tradition." In Robert M. Gimello and Peter N. Gregory (eds.), *Studies in Ch'an and Hua-Yen*. Honolulu: University of Hawaii Press, pp. 253–319.

Inada, Kenneth K. (1974) "Time and Temporality: A Buddhist Approach." *Philosophy East & West* 24: 171–9.

—— (1983) "The Metaphysics of Cumulative Penetration Revisited." (A critique of Steve Odin's "A Metaphysics of Cumulative Penetration: Process Theory and Hua-[yan] Buddhism.") *Process Studies* 13, Summer: 154–8.

King, Winston L. (1979) "Hua-yen Mutually Interpenetrative Identity and White-headean Organic Relation." *Journal of Chinese Philosophy* 6: 387–410.

Lai, Whalen (1980) "The *I Ching* and the Formation of the Hua-yen Philosophy." *Journal of Chinese Philosophy* 7: 245–58.

—— (1986) "The Defeat of Vijnâptimatratâ in China: Fa-Tsang on Fa-hsing and Fa-hsiang." *Journal of Chinese Philosophy* 13: 1–19.

Odin, Steve (1981) "Fantasy Variation and the Horizon of Openness: A Phenomenological Interpretation of Tantric Buddhism Enlightenment." *International Philosophical Quarterly* 21, December: 419–36.

—— (1982) *Process Metaphysics and Hua-yen Buddhism: A Critical Study of Cumulative Penetration vs. Interpenetration*. Albany, NY: SUNY Press.

Panikkar, Raimundo (1974) "Toward a Typology of Time and Temporality in the Ancient Indian Tradition." *Philosophy East & West* 24: 161–4.

Puligandla, R. (1974) "Time and History in the Indian Tradition." *Philosophy East & West* 24: 165–70.

Wright, Dale (1982) "The Significance of Paradoxical Language in Hua-yen Buddhism." *Philosophy East & West* 32, July: 325–38.

—— (1986) "Language and Truth in Hua-Yen Buddhism." *Journal of Chinese Philosophy* 13: 21–47.

Chapter 11   The Tian-tai (T'ien-t'ai) School

Chan, Wing-tsit (1990) "The *Lotus Sutra*." In Wm. Theodore de Bary and Irene Bloom (eds.), *Approaches to the Asian Classics*. New York: Columbia University Press, pp. 220–31.

—— (ed.) (1973) *A Sourcebook in Chinese Philosophy*, 4th edn. Princeton, NJ: Princeton University Press, ch. 24.

Chappell, David W. (ed.) (1983) *T'ien-T'ai Buddhism: An Outline of the Four-fold Teachings.* Recorded by Chegwan, trans. by the Buddhist Translation Seminar of Hawaii. Compiled by Masao Ichishima. Tokyo: Daiichi-Shobō. Honolulu: distributed by the University Press of Hawaii.

Cheng, Chung-ying (2001) " 'Unity of Three Truths' and the Three Forms of Creativity: Lotus Sutra and Process Philosophy." *Journal of Chinese Philosophy* 28(4), December: 449–59.

Cheng, Hsueh-fli (1984) "Phenomenology in T'ien-tai and Hua-yen Buddhism." In Anna-Teresa Tymieniecka (ed.), *Phenomenology of Life in A Dialogue between Chinese and Occidental Philosophy.* Dordrecht: Reidel Publishing Company, pp. 215–27.

Donner, Neal and Stevenson, Daniel B. (1993) *The Great Calming and Contemplation : A Study and Annotated Translation of the First Chapter of Chih-i's Mo-ho chih-kuan.* Honolulu: University of Hawaii Press.

Fu, Charles Wei-hsün (1984) "Chinese Buddhism and An Existential Phenomenology." In Anna-Teresa Tymieniecka (ed.), *Phenomenology of Life in A Dialogue between Chinese and Occidental Philosophy.* Dordrecht: Reidel Publishing Company, pp. 229–51.

Fung, Yu-lan (1983) *A History of Chinese Philosophy,* vol. 2 (trans. Derk Bodde). Princeton, NJ: Princeton University Press, ch. 9, pp. 360–86.

Hurvitz, Leon (1962) *Chih-i (538–597): An Introduction to the Life and Ideas of a Chinese Buddhist Monk.* Brussels: L'Institut Belge des Hautes Études Chinoises.

Ikeda, Daisaku, et al. (2000) *The Wisdom of the Lotus Sutra: A Discussion,* vol. 1. Santa Monica, CA: World Tribune Press.

Ng, Yu-kwan (Wu, Ru-jun) (1993) *T'ien-t'ai Buddhism and Early Madhyamika.* Honolulu: University of Hawaii Press.

Swanson, Paul L. (1989) *Foundations of T'ien-T'ai Philosophy: The Flowering of the Two Truths Theory in Chinese Buddhism.* California: Asian Humanities Press.

Watson, Burton (trans.) (1993) *The Lotus Sutra.* New York: Columbia University Press.

—— (2002) *The Essential Lotus: Selections from the Lotus Sutra.* New York: Columbia University Press.

Ziporyn, Brook (2000) "Setup, Punch Line, and the Mind-Body Problem: A Neo-Tiantai Approach." *Philosophy East & West* 50(4), October: 584–613.

—— (2001) "Inherent Entailment (Xingju) and Negative Prehensions: Givenness, The Agency of the Past, and the Presence of the Absent in White-head and the T'ien-t'ai Reading of the Lotus Sutra." *Journal of Chinese Philosophy* 28(4), December: 399–414.

Chapter 12   The Chan School (Zen Buddhism)

Abe, Masao (1976) "Zen and Buddhism." *Journal of Chinese Philosophy* 3: 235–52.

Blofeld, John [*aka* Chu Ch'an] (trans.) (1958) *The Zen Teaching of Huang Po on the Transmission of Mind*. New York: Glove Press.

Bossert, Philip J. (1976) "Paradox and Enlightenment in Zen Dialogue and Phenomenological Description." *Journal of Chinese Philosophy* 3: 269–80.

Brear, A. D. (1974) "The Nature and Status of Moral Behavior in Zen Buddhist Tradition." *Philosophy East & West* 24: 429–41.

Chan, Wing-tsit (ed.) (1973) *A Sourcebook in Chinese Philosophy*, 4th edn. Princeton, NJ: Princeton University Press, ch. 26.

Chang, Chen-chi (1957) "The Nature of Ch'an (Zen) Buddhism." *Philosophy East & West* 6: 333–55.

Cheng, Chung-ying (1973) "On Zen (Ch'an) Language and Zen Paradoxes." *Journal of Chinese Philosophy* 1: 77–99.

—— (1976) "Rejoinder to Michael Levin's 'Comments on the Paradoxicality of the Koans." *Journal of Chinese Philosophy* 3: 291–7.

Cheng, Hsueh-li (1981) "The Roots of Zen Buddhism." *Journal of Chinese Philosophy* 8: 451–78.

—— (1985) "Confucianism and Zen (Ch'an) Philosophy of Education." *Journal of Chinese Philosophy* 12: 197–215.

—— (1986) "Negation, Affirmation and Zen Logic." *International Philosophical Quarterly* 26: 241–51.

—— (1987) "Zen Morality within this World." In Anna-Teresa Tymieniecka (ed.), *Morality within the Life- and Social World*. Dordrecht: Kluwer Publishing, pp. 245–58.

—— (1996) *Exploring Zen*. New York: Lang Publishing.

Cheshier, William L. (1971) "The Term 'Mind' in Huang Po's Text *Huang Po Ch'uan Hsin Fa Yao*." *Inquiry* 14: 102–12.

Chun, Fang Yu (1979) "Ta-hui Tsung-kao and 'Kung-an' Ch'an." *Journal of Chinese Philosophy* 6: 211–35.

Cleary, Thomas (trans.) (1998) *The Sutra of Hui-neng: Grand Master of Zen*. (With Hui-neng's Commentary on the *Diamond Sutra*.) Boston and London: Shambhala.

Cua, Antonio S. (1975) "Uses of Dialogues and Moral Understanding." *Journal of Chinese Philosophy* 2: 131–48.

Davidson, Bruce (1996) "Does Religious Faith Mean Uncritical Thought? Exploration of a False Dilemma." *Inquiry* 16(1), Fall: 55–66.

Dumoulin, Heinrich (1994) *Zen Buddhism: A History*. New York: Simon & Schuster Macmillan.

Faure, Bernard (1993) *Chan Insights and Oversights: An Epistemological Critique of the Chan Tradition*. Princeton, NJ: Princeton University Press.

Fromm, Erich (1960) "Psychoanalysis and Zen Buddhism." In D. T. Suzuki, Erich Fromm, and Richard De Martino (eds.), *Zen Buddhism and Psychoanalysis*. New York: Harper & Brothers, pp. 77–141.

Fung, Yu-lan (1983) *A History of Chinese Philosophy*, vol. II (trans. Derk Bodde). Princeton, NJ: Princeton University Press, ch. 9, pp. 386–406.

Garner, Dick (1977) "Skepticism, Ordinary Language and Zen Buddhism." *Philosophy East & West* 27(2), April: 165–81.

Garner, Richard (1985) "The Deconstruction of the Mirror and other Heresies: Ch'an and Taoism as Abnormal Discourse." *Journal of Chinese Philosophy* 12: 155–68.

Gimello, Robert M. and Gregory, Peter N. (eds.) (1990) *Studies in Ch'an and Hua-Yen*. Honolulu: University of Hawaii Press.

Glass, Newman Robert (1998) "A Logic of the Heart: Re-Reading Taoism and Zen Buddhism." *International Philosophical Quarterly* 38(4), December: 383–92.

Hershock, Peter D. (1994) "Person as Narration: The Dissolution of Self' and Other' in Ch'an Buddhism." *Philosophy East and West* 44(4), October: 685–710.

Holstein, Alexander (trans.) (1993) *Pointing at the Moon: 100 Zen Koans from Chinese Masters*. Rutland, Vermont: Charles E. Tuttle Company.

Hu, Shih (1953) "Ch'an (Zen) Buddhism in China: Its History and Method." *Philosophy East & West* 3(1): 3–24.

Hyers, M. Conrad (1970) "The Ancient Zen Masters as Clown-figure and Comic Midwife." *Philosophy East & West* 20: 3–18.

Inada, Kenneth (1988) "Zen and Taoism: Common and Uncommon Grounds of Discourse." *Journal of Chinese Philosophy* 15: 51–65.

Izutsu, Toshihiko (1977) *Toward a Philosophy of Zen Buddhism*. Tehran, Iran: Imperial Iranian Academy of Philosophy.

Jan, Yün-hua (1977) "Conflict and Harmony in Ch'an and Buddhism." *Journal of Chinese Philosophy* 4: 287–302.

—— (1981) "The Mind As the Buddha-Nature: The Concept of the Absolute in Ch'an Buddhism." *Philosophy East & West* 31(4): 467–77.

Kapleau, Philip (1980) *The Three Pillars of Zen: Teaching, Practice, and Enlightenment*. Garden City, NY: Anchor Press/Doubleday.

Kasulis, Thomas P. (1979) "The Two Strands of Nothingness in Zen Buddhism." *International Philosophical Quarterly* 19: 61–72.

Kim, Ha Poong (1980/1) "What Do Zen Masters Do with Words?" *Philosophical Forum* 12(2), Winter: 101–15.

King-Farlow, John (1983) "Review on 'On Zen Language and Zen Paradoxes': Anglo-Saxon Questions for Chung-ying Cheng." *Journal of Chinese Philosophy* 10: 285–98.

Knaul, Livia (1986) "Chuang-Tzu and the Chinese Ancestry of Ch'an Buddhism." *Journal of Chinese Philosophy* 13: 411–28.

Lai, Whalen (1977) "The Meaning of 'Mind-Only' ('Wei-Hsin'): An Analysis of a Sinitic Mahayana Phenomenon." *Philosophy East & West* 27(1): 65–83.

—— (1979) "Ch'an Metaphors: Waves, Water, Mirror, Lamp." *Philosophy East & West* 29(3), July: 243–53.

Lee, Jung Young (1976) "Zen Enlightenment and the Intellectual Approach." *Journal of Dharma* 1: 211–26.

Laycock, Steven W. (1985) "Hui-neng and the Transcendental Standpoint." *Journal of Chinese Philosophy* 12: 179–96.

Levin, Michael E. (1976) "Comments on the Paradoxicality of Zen Koans." *Journal of Chinese Philosophy* 3: 281–90.

Lusthaus, Dan (1985) "Ch'an and Taoist Mirror: Reflections on Richard Garner's 'Deconstruction of the Mirror'." *Journal of Chinese Philosophy* 12: 169–78.

Milcinski, Maja (1977) "Zen and the Art of Death." *Philosophy East & West* 27: 65–83. (Repr. in *Journal of the History of Ideas* 60(3), July 1999: 385–97.)

Mitchell, Donald W. (1980) "Faith in Zen Buddhism." *International Philosophical Quarterly* 20: 183–98.

Nakamura, Hajime (1985) "The Non-logical Character of Zen." *Journal of Chinese Philosophy* 12: 105–15.

Nishida, Kitaro (1966) *Intelligibility and the Philosophy of Nothingness*. Honolulu: East West Center Press.

Nishitani, Keiji (1981) "Ontology and Utterance." *Philosophy East & West* 31: 29–44.

Nordstrom, Louis (1980) "Zen and Karman." *Philosophy East & West* 30(1): 77–86.

—— (1981) "Mysticism without Transcendence: Reflections on Liberation and Emptiness." *Philosophy East & West* 31: 89–95.

Olson, Carl (2000) *Zen and the Art of Postmodern Philosophy: Two Paths of Liberation from the Representational Mode of Thinking*. Albany, NY: SUNY Press.

Perry, John (1963) "Paradoxical Logic." *Philosophy East & West* 13(2): 155–7.

Ren, Jiyu (1984) "A Brief Discussion of the Philosophical Thought of Chan Buddhism." *Chinese Studies in Philosophy* 15: 3–69.

Riepe, Dale (1966) "The Significance of the Attack upon Rationality by Zen Buddhism." *Philosophy and Phenomenological Research* 26: 434–7.

Rosemont, Jr., Henry (1970a) "The Meaning Is the Use: Koan and Mondo As Linguistic Tools of the Zen Masters." *Philosophy East & West* 20: 109–19.

—— (1970b) "Is Zen Buddhism A Philosophy?" *Philosophy East & West* 20: 63–72.

Scharfstein, Ben-Ami (1976) "Salvation by Paradox: On Zen and Zen-like Thought." *Journal of Chinese Philosophy* 3: 209–34.

Stauffer, Lee (1989) "Is an Ethical Theory Possible Within Zen Buddhism?" *Southwest Philosophical Studies*, Spring: 80–4.

Steffney, John (1975) "Symbolism and Death and Jung and Zen Buddhism." *Philosophy East & West* 25: 175–85.

—— (1977) "Transmetaphysical Thinking in Heidegger and Zen Buddhism." *Philosophy East & West* 27(3): 323–35.

Strenski, Ivan (1980) "Gradual Enlightenment, Sudden Enlightenment and Empiricism." *Philosophy East & West* 30(1): 3–20.

Suzuki, Daisetz Teitaro (1949) *Essays in Zen Buddhism. First Series*. New York: Grove Weidenfeld.

—— (1951) "The Philosophy of Zen." *Philosophy East & West* 1(2): 3–15.

—— (ed.) (1960) *Manual of Zen Buddhism*. New York: Grove Press.

405

References and Further Reading

—— (1964) *The Zen Doctrine of No-Mind.* New York: Grove Press.

—— (trans.) (1966) *The Lankavatara Sutra: A Mahayana Text.* London: Routledge & Kegan Paul Ltd. (orig. pub. 1932).

—— (1972) *An Introduction to Zen Buddhism.* Christmas Humphreys (ed.) York Beach, Maine: Weiser Books.

—— (1996) *Zen Buddhism: Selected Writings of D. T. Suzuki,* ed. William Barrett. New York: Doubleday (orig. pub. 1956).

Tominaga, Thomas T. (1983) "Ch'an, Taoism, and Wittgenstein." *Journal of Chinese Philosophy* 10: 127–45.

Tucker, John (1985) "An Anglo-Saxon Response to John King-Farlow's Questions on Zen Language and Zen Paradoxes." *Journal of Chinese Philosophy* 12: 217–21.

Wang, Youru (2000) "The Pragmatics of 'Never Tell Too Plainly': Indirect Communication in Chan Buddhism." *Asian Philosophy* 10(1), March: 7–31.

Watson, Burton (trans.) (1999) *The Zen Teachings of Master Lin-Chi* [*Lin-chi Lu*]. New York: Columbia University Press.

Watts, Alan W. (1957) *The Way of Zen.* New York: Vintage Books.

Wright, Dale S. (1993) "Emancipation from What? The Concept of Freedom in Classical Ch'an Buddhism." *Asian Philosophy* 3(2): 113–24.

Yampolsky, Philip B. (trans.) (1967) *The Platform Sutra of the Sixth Patriarch* [from the *Tun-huang* manuscript]. New York: Columbia University Press.

—— (1990) "The Platform Sutra of the Sixth Patriarch." In Wm. Theodore de Bary & Irene Bloom (eds.) *Approaches to the Asian Classics.* New York: Columbia University Press, pp. 241–50.

Yi, Wu (1985) "On Chinese Ch'an in Relation to Taoism." *Journal of Chinese Philosophy* 12: 131–54.

Yü, Chün-Fang (1979) "Ta-hui Tsung-kao and Kung-an Ch'an." *Journal of Chinese Philosophy* 6: 211–35.

Zeuschner, Robert B. (1976) "The 'Hsien Tsung Chi' (An Early Ch'an (Zen) Buddhist Text)." *Journal of Chinese Philosophy* 3: 253–68.

—— (1978) "The Understanding of Mind in the Northern Line of Ch'an (Zen)." *Philosophy East & West* 28(1), January: 69–79.

—— (1981) "The Understanding of Karma in Early Ch'an Buddhism." *Journal of Chinese Philosophy* 8: 399–425.

Translation
Conversion Table

(In alphabetic order by the first appearing Romanized word)

English	Pinyin	Wade/Giles	Chinese
Analects	Lun-yu	Lun-yü	論語
Annals of Spring and Autumn	Chun-qiu	Ch'un-ch'iu	春秋
Artificial (artifice; deliberate effort)	wei	wei	偽
Being appropriate to the time	shi-zhong	shih-chung	時中
Benefit	li	li	利
Book of Changes (Book of Change)	Yijing	I Ching	易經
Book of Odes	Shi-jing	Shih Ching	詩經
Book of History	Shu-jing	Shu Ching	書經
Book of Rites	Li-ji	Li Chi	禮記
Buddha	fo	fo	佛
Buddha-dharma	fo-fa	fo-fa	佛法
Buddha-nature	fo-xing	fo-hsing	佛性
Buddha-realm	fo-jie	fo-chieh	佛界
	Cang Jie	Ts'ang Chieh	倉頡
Chan, Wing-tsit			陳榮捷
	Cheng-guan	Ch'eng-kuan	澄觀
	Cheng Hao	Ch'eng Hao	程顥
	Cheng Yi	Ch'eng I	程頤
Commentary on the images	xiang-zhuan	hsiang-chuan	象傳

English	Pinyin	Wade/Giles	Chinese
Commentary on the judgments	tuan-zhuan	t'uan-chuan	彖傳
Confucianism	Ru-jia	Ju Chia	儒家
Confucius	Kongzi	K'ung Tzu	孔子
Consciousness-Only	Wei-shi	Wei-shih	唯識
Contaminated	ran	jan	染
Containment in nature	xing-ju	hsing-chü	性具
Containment of 3,000 worlds in mind	xin ju san qian	hsin chü san ch'ien	心具三千
Containment of 3,000 worlds in nature	xing ju san qian	hsing chü san ch'ien	性具三千
Cook Ding	pao-ding	p'ao-ting	庖丁
Cosmic force (cosmic energy) (material force) (force) (vital force)	qi	ch'i	氣
	Dai Zhen	Tai Chen	戴震
	Daodejing	Tao-te Ching	道德經
	Daoism	Taoism	道家
	Dao-xin	Tao-hsin	道信
	Da-zheng-zang	Ta-cheng-zang	大正藏
Dharma	fa	fa	法
Dharma realm	fa-jie	fa-chieh	法界
Discussion of trigrams	Shuo-gua	Shuo Kua	説卦
Divination	zhan-bu	chan-pu	占卜
Doctrine of the mean	Zhong-yong	Chung-yung	中庸
	Du-shun	Tu-shun	杜順
	Dung Zhongshu	Tung Chung-shu	董仲舒
Earth	di	ti	地
Empathy (sympathy) (sympathetic understanding)	shu	shu	恕
Emptiness	kong	k'ung	空
Esoteric meaning of the Lotus Sutra	Fahua Xuanyi	Fa-hua Hsüan-i	法華玄義
	Fa-zang	Fa-tsang	法藏
	Fang Dongmei	Fang Tung-mei	方東美

English	Pinyin	Wade/Giles	Chinese
	Feng Youlan	Fung Yu-lan	馮友蘭
Filial piety	xiao	hsiao	孝
Flower Ornament (Flowery Splendor) Scripture	Hua-yan Jing	Hua-yen Ching	華嚴經
Four teachings	si-jiao	ssu-chiao	四教
Tripitaka teaching	zang-jiao	tsang-chiao	藏教
Common teaching	tong-jiao	t'ung-chiao	通教
Special teaching	bie-jiao	pieh-chiao	別教
Perfect teaching	yuan-jiao	yüan-chiao	圓教
Four dharma realms	si-fa-jie	ssu-fa-chieh	四法界
Four moral sprouts (four beginnings)	si-duan	ssu-tuan	四端
Four transcendental wisdom			
Great mirror	da yuan jing zhi	ta yüan ching chih	大圓鏡智
Universal equality	ping deng xing zhi	p'ing teng hsing chih	平等性智
Profound contemplation	miao guan cha zhi	miao kuan ch'a chih	妙觀察智
Perfect achievement	cheng suo zuo zhi	ch'eng suo tso chih	成所作智
	Fu Xi	Fu-hsi	伏羲
	Gen	Ken	艮
God	shang-di	shang-ti	上帝
	Gongsun Long	Kung-sun Lung	公孫龍
Good	shan	shan	善
Great Calming and Contemplation	Mohe Zhiguan	Mo-ho Chih-kuan	摩訶止觀
Great Learning	Daxue	Ta-hsüeh	大學
Great Treatise	xi-zi-zhuan	hsi-tz'u-chuan	繫辭傳
Great Ultimate	Tai-ji	T'ai-chi	太極
	Guan-ding	Kuan-ting	灌頂
	Guo Xiang	Kuo Hsiang	郭象
	Han Yu	Han Yü	韓愈
Heart/mind	xin	hsin	心
Heaven	tian	t'ien	天
	He Lin	Ho Lin	賀林
	heng	heng	亨
Hexagram	gua	kua	卦
Historical records	Shi-ji	Shih Chi	史記
	Hong-ren	Hung-jen	弘忍

English	Pinyin	Wade/Giles	Chinese
	Hu Shi	Hu Shih	胡適
	Huang Bo	Huang Po	黃蘗
	Huang Zongxi	Huang Tsung-hsi	黃宗義
	Hui-ke	Hui-k'o	慧可
	Hui-neng	Hui-neng	慧能
	Hui Shi	Hui-shih	惠施
	Hui-si	Hui-ssu	慧思
	Hui-wen	Hui-wen	慧文
Humanity (benevolence) (kindness) (humaneness)	ren	jen	仁
Hundred Schools	bai-jia	pai-chia	百家
Illumination	ming	ming	明
Inactivity (non-action)	wu-wei	wu-wei	無為
	Ji-zang	Chi-tsang	吉藏
	Jie	Chieh	桀
	Jin Yuelin	Chin Yüeh-lin	金岳霖
Judgment on the classification of doctrines	pan jiao	p'an chiao	判教
	Kan	K'an	坎
	Kang Youwei	K'ang Yu-wei	康有為
Koan	gong-an	kung-an	公案
	Kuiji	K'uei-chi	窺基
	Kun	K'un	坤
	Lao Dan	Lao Tan	老聃
Law	fa	fa	法
Legalism	Fa-jia	Fa Chia	法家
	Li	Li	離
	Li Ao	Li Ao	李翱
	Li Er	Li Erh	李耳
Line	yao	yao	爻
	Li Si	Li Ssu	李斯
	Liang Qichao	Liang Ch'i-ch'ao	梁啟超
	Liang Shuming	Liang Sou-ming	梁漱溟
	Lin Ji	Lin Chi	臨濟
	Liu Zongzhou	Liu Tsung-chou	劉宗周
Lotus Sutra	Fahua Jing	Fa-hua Ching	法華經
Loyalty (conscientiousness)	zhong	chung	忠
	Lu Xiangshan	Lu Hsiang-shan	陸象山

English	Pinyin	Wade/Giles	Chinese
Mandate of Heaven	tian-ming	tian-ming	天命
Master Gao	Gaozi	Kao Tzu	告子
Master Han Fei	Hanfeizi	Han Fei Tzu	韓非子
Master Lao	Laozi	Lao Tzu	老子
Master Lie	Liezi	Lieh Tzu	列子
Master Mo	Mozi	Mo Tzu	墨子
Master Xun	Xunzi	Hsün Tzu	荀子
Master Zhuang	Zhuangzi	Chuang Tzu	莊子
Mencius	Mengzi	Meng Tzu	孟子
Mohism	Mo-jia	Mo Chia	墨家
	Mou Zongsan	Mou Tsung-san	牟宗三
Nature	xin	hsin	性
Nature (naturalness)	zi-ran	tzu-jan	自然
Nirvana	nie-pan	nieh-p'an	涅盤
Non-being (nothingness)	wu	wu	無
One thought contains three thousand worlds	yi nien san qian	i nian san ch'ien	一念三千
Platform Sutra	Liu-zu Tan-jing	Liu-tsu T'an-ching	六祖壇經
Political clout (power)	shi	shih	勢
Principle	li	li	理
Propriety (rites; rituals; social etiquettes)	li	li	禮
Pure	jing	ching	淨
Pure Land	Jing-tu	Ching-t'u	淨土
	Qian	Ch'ien	乾
	Qin	Ch'in	秦
	Qua-ci	kua-tz'u	卦辭
Realm of the noninterference between Principle and things			理事無礙法界
Realm of noninterference of all things			事事無礙法界
Realm of Principle			理法界
Realm of things			事法界
Rectification of names	zheng-ming	cheng-ming	正名

English	Pinyin	Wade/Giles	Chinese
Righteousness (uprightness)	yi	i	義
Sage	sheng	sheng	聖
	Seng-zhao	Seng-chao	僧肇
Shang Dynasty	Shang	Shang	商
	Shang-yang	Shang-yang	商鞅
	Shao Yong	Shao Yung	劭雍
	Shen-hui	Shen-hui	神會
	Shen-xiu	Shen-hsiu	神秀
	Shun	Shun	舜
	Si-ma Qian	Ssu-ma Ch'ien	司馬遷
Sincerity	cheng	ch'eng	誠
Six aspects in harmony	liu-xiang-yuan-rong	liu-hsiang-yüan-jung	六相圓融
Spring and autumn	Chun-qiu	Ch'un-Ch'iu	春秋
Statecraft	shu	shu	術
Subtle existence	miao-you	miao-yu	妙有
Suchness (Thusness)	ru	ju	如
Such-like characteristics	ru-shi-xiang	ju-shih-hsiang	如是相
Superior people (Gentlemen)	junzi	chün tzu	君子
Sutra of the Lotus Blossom of the Subtle Dharma	Miaofa Lianhua Jing	Miao-fa Lian-hua Ching	妙法蓮華經
	Tan Sitong	T'an Ssu-t'ung	譚嗣同
	Tang Junyi	T'ang Chün-i	唐君毅
Ten Wings	Shi-yi	Shih-i	十翼
Things (events)	shi	shih	事
	Tian-tai	T'ien-t'ai	天台
Threefold Truth	san-di	san-ti	三諦
Provisional existence	jia-di	jia-ti	假諦
Emptiness	kong-di	k'ung-ti	空諦
Middle-path	zhong-di	chung-ti	中諦
Threefold truth in unity	san-di-yuan-rong	san-ti-yüan-jung	三諦圓融
Time	shi	shih	時
Transforming consciousness into wisdom	zhuan shi cheng zhi	chuan shih ch'eng chih	轉識成智
True emptiness	zhen-kong	chen-k'ung	真空
True Thusness	zhen-ru	chen-ju	真如

English	Pinyin	Wade/Giles	Chinese
Universal love	jian-ai	chien-ai	兼愛
Virtue	de	te	德
	Wang Bi	Wang Pi	王弼
	Wang Chong	Wang Ch'ung	王充
	Wang Guowei	Wang Kuo-wei	王國維
	Wang Fuzhi	Wang Fu-chih	王夫之
	Wang Yangming	Wang Yang-ming	王陽明
Warring States	Zhan-guo	Chan-kuo	戰國
Way (the)	Dao	Tao	道
Will	zhi	chih	志
Wisdom	zhi	chih	智
Words and phrases of the Lotus Sutra	Fahua Wenju	Fa-hua Wen-chü	法華文句
	Xia	Hsia	夏
	Xiong Shili	Hsiung Shih-li	熊十力
	Xu Fuguan	Hsü Fu-kuan	徐復觀
	Xuan-zang	Hsüan-tsang	玄奘
	Yan Hui	Yen Hui	顏回
	yang	yang	陽
	Yang Xiong	Yang Hsiung	揚雄
	Yang Zhu	Yang Chu	楊朱
	Yao	Yao	堯
	yin	yin	陰
	Yu	Yü	禹
	yüan	yuan	元
Zen	Chan	Ch'an	禪
	Zhan-ran	Chan-jan	湛然
	Zhang Dongsun	Chang Tung-sun	張東蓀
	Zhang Junmai	Chang, (Carsun)	張君勱
	Zhang Zai	Chang Tsai	張載
	Zhi-yi	Chih-i	智顗
	Zhi-yan	Chih-yen	智儼
	Zhou Dunyi	Chou Tun-I	周敦頤
Zhou Dynasty	Zhou	Chou	周
	Zhen	Chen	震
	zhen	chen	貞
	Zhu Xi	Chu Hsi	朱熹

Index

Note: Page references in *italics* indicate tables and diagrams; those in **bold** type indicate main references to major topics.

Abe, Masao 210
acedia and *akrasia* 338 n.40
actuality, and names 51, 196–7, 201, 320, 324–5
afterlife
  and Tian-tai School 280
  and Xunzi 91
  and Zhuangzi 176
Ahern, Dennis M. 115, 145, 346–7 n.14
Alexander, G. G. 345 n.5
Allinson, Robert 53, 156
Altar Sutra see Platform Sutra
alterity, in Buddhism 237
altruism
  in Confucius 58
  in Mozi 110, 111, 115, 127
Ames, Roger 200, 336 n.4, 350 n.85
Analects see Confucius
anarchism, and Laozi 149
Annals of Spring and Autumn (Chun-qiu) 10
anti-rationalism, in Zhuangzi 156–7
arahat/arhat 218, 230, 281
Aristotle 154
Asanga 220
asceticism
  and bodhisattvas 272
  and Mozi 128

asuras 280, 369 n.12
atman 236, 237–9
atom
  in Indian materialism 233–4
  in pluralist view 234–5
attachments, and Buddhism 211–12, 217, 230, 272–3, 311, 316
attributes, artificial/natural 94–5
Austin, J. L. 326
authoritarianism, pragmatic 119–24

being and non-being 21–2
  in Buddhism 217–18
  in Chan School 318
  in Laozi 134–5, 140, 141, 150
  in Tian-tai School 291
benefit
  in Hanfeizi 183–5, 189, 195–6
  in Mozi 20, 115–19, 124–7, 129
  and religion 125–7
  in *Yijing* 36
benevolence
  in Confucius 56, 58
  in Hanfeizi 190
  in Mozi 110
  see also compassion
Berkeley, George, and idealism 364 n.41

Berkson, Mark 155, 158, 168, 351
    n.25
Bodde, Derk 7, 16, 219, 332 n.3,
    333 n.1a, 358 n.15, 360 n.27
Bodhi tree 307
Bodhidharma (patriarch of Chan
    Buddhism) 304, 373 n.11, 375
    n.50
bodhisattva 218–19, 230–1, 270–2,
    281, 293
Book of Changes see Yijing
Book of History (*Shu-jing*) 10–11, 125
Book of Odes (*Shi-jing*) 10–11, 68,
    125
Book of Rites (*Li-ji*) 10, 333 nn.3a,6
Brahmanism, and Vedanta School
    235–6, 237
Buddha
    meanings 268–9, 287–8, 319
    as Tathagata 310, 313
    see also Buddha-nature;
        Buddhahood; Gautama,
        Siddhartha
Buddha-nature 219
    in Chan School 305, 312, 314–15,
        319–23, 329, 330
    in Tian-tai School 270, 278–9,
        293, 298–9, 301, 302
Buddhahood 218–19
    in Chan School 315, 319–22,
        329–30
    in Consciousness-Only School 232
    in Hua-yan School 268–70
    in Tian-tai School 281, 287–9,
        293, 297–301, 302
Buddhism, Chinese
    and Daoism 209–10
    eightfold noble path 213
    evolution 209–10
    and Five Aggregates 213, 239–40
    schools 210, 217–19; *see also* Chan
        (Zen); Consciousness-Only;
        Hua-yan; Tian-tai
    and the soul 216
    and this-worldliness 219
    see also Four Noble Truths

Buddhism, Indian
    basic tenets **210–19**
    impact 209–10

Carus, Paul 345 n.5
Cârvâkas 233–4
categorical imperative 54
causality 214–17
    in Consciousness-Only School
        223–5, 227, 237
    in Hua-yan School 261, 273
    in Tian-tai School 286
    in Xunzi 88–9, 91
    in *Yijing* 42–5
Chan, Wing-tsit xii, 92, 94, 104,
    108, 233, 248, 253, 274, 278,
    308, 335 n.4, 344 n.57, 347
    n.23, 359 n.6, 363 nn.1,6,60
Chan (Zen) School 210, **304–30**
    as Chinese school 304, 305
    and education 325–9
    and enlightenment 268, 295, 305,
        306–7, 314–16, 319–22
    and ethics 322
    and language and knowledge 268,
        296, 306, 323–5
    and mind and nature 319–23
    and Mind-Only theory 309–11,
        316
    Northern and Southern Schools
        304–16, 323; beholding the
        mind/seeing one's nature
        311–12, 322; gradual/immediate
        enlightenment 306, 307–8,
        313–16; and Mind-Only thesis
        309–11; and self-realization
        314–16
    origins 304
    and pure mind 306, 307–8, 309,
        311–12, 313–14, 316, 317, 320
    and reality 308–11, 317–18,
        323–5, 329
    and Tian-tai School 301, 302, 316,
        318
    and Two Minds theory 309, 311,
        319–20

Chang, Garma C. C. 363 n.3, 364
  n.15, 365 n.34
change
  and periodicity 33
  and polar reversal 33, 37
  in *Yijing* 27–8, 29–34, 42, 43–4
Chappell, David 277, 278, 371 n.50
Chatterjee, Satischandra and Datta,
  Dhirendramohan 361 n.36
Chegwan, *Fourfold Teachings* 278
Cheng, Chung-ying 325, 352 n.44
Cheng-guan (patriarch of Hua-yan)
  249
  and noninterference of things 248,
    260
  and noumenon and phenomena
    263–4
Chinese philosophy
  description 1–12
  primary concerns 8–10
  and religion 1–4, 9, 20, 91–2, 329
Ching, Julia 110
Chuand Tzu *see* Zhuangzi
Cleary, Thomas 249, 258–9, 269,
  363 nn.1,6, 367 n.79, 375 n.34
cognition
  in Chan School 309
  in Laozi 137
  in Xunzi 90
  in Zhi-yi 301
  see also knowledge
Commentary on the Images (*Yijing*)
  28, 39–42
Commentary on the Judgment
  (*Yijing*) 28, 32, 36–7, 40–1
*Commentary on the Words of the
  Text* (*Yijing*) 29, 44
Commentary on Yi 47
Common Teaching 293, 296
compassion
  in Buddhism 217, 231, 271–2, 281
  in Mencius 73–6, 80, 81
  see also benevolence
conceptual relativism 154–5, 157–66
  in Hua-yan School 264, 265–7
  in Laozi 141

Confucianism 45
  and ethics 19–20, 23, 24–5, 34–5,
    37
  and the good 48, 62
  and Legalism 187–94
  and Mozi 108, 109, 112, 122, 128
  music 18–19, 21, 122
  and religion xii
  and rites 18, 20–1, 59–60, 105,
    122
  and Spring-Autumn period 16
  and Warring States period 17
  and *Yijing* 26, 28–9
  see also Confucius; *Doctrine of the
    Mean*; family; *Great Learning*;
    Mencius; Xunzi; *Yijing*
Confucius
  Analects 29, 43, **47–63**, 333 n.3a
  and *Dao* 6, 57, 59, 136
  and education 190, 332 n.14
  and empathy 53–6
  ethics 47–60, 63, 102, 168–9
  and fate 43
  and five classics 10–12
  and loyalty 48–53
  and Mencius 65, 83, 84
  and politics 16–19, 24, 47–8,
    49–56, 60–2, 63, 68, 82, 88,
    187
  and society 16–18, 48–56, 109,
    169
  as teacher 47, 191
  as Ultimate Sage 58
  and *Yijing* 4, 26, 28
  and Zhuangzi 168–9, 180
consciousness
  as creation of one mind 257–8
  discriminative 225–6, 228, 232,
    244
  eight forms 214, 221, 225–8, 229,
    231
  and external reality 222–3, 230,
    233–6, 240–2, 243, 250–5
  in Hua-yan School 252–4, 255–8
  intellective 225, 227–8, 230,
    231–2

and other minds 242–5
and plurality of phenomenal
  worlds 255–7, 261
and the self 236–40
storehouse (Alaya) 222, 223, 224,
  225–31, 242, 244, 255, 280,
  288, 310
transformation 222–3, 225–33,
  244, 254, 310
see also mind
Consciousness-Only (*Wei-shi*) School
  210, **220–46**
basic doctrine 222–33
and cause of consciousness 214,
  224
defense of 340–5
and dependent co-arising 223–5,
  242
origins 220–1
and other minds problem 242–5
and reality 222–3, 233–6, 240–2,
  243, 255, 280
and the self 236–40
transformation of consciousness
  222–3, 225–33
and wisdom 229–33
contemplation
and Realm of Principle 264
in Zhi-yi 301
Cook, Francis H. 253, 270, 366
  n.59
correspondence theory of truth 141,
  165, 290–2, 295
cosmogenesis, in Laozi 136, 138,
  150
cosmology 4, 5–8, 87
and interconnectedness of things
  258–60
and morality 34–5, 40, 42, 102
and *Yijing* 8, 26–9, 30, 40, 58
creation 2, 6, 22
and *Dao* 136, 139–40, 199
Creel, Herrlee G. 115, 123, 132–3,
  345 n.5, 346 n.13, 350 n.7
Cua, Antonio S. 48, 59, 97–8, 105,
  342 n.55

cultivation, moral
in Buddhism 231, 272, 301
in Confucius 17, 56, 57–8, 60,
  62–3, 84
in Mencius 65, 72–3, 76–9, 80–3
in Xunzi 86, 93, 104–6, 146
culture
in Laozi 146, 150
in Xunzi 146

Da-xue (*Great Learning*) 17, 333 n.3a
Danto, Arthur 346 n.13
Dao (Way) 8–9, 87
and change 135
in Confucius 6, 57, 59, 62, 63, 136
as constant/eternal 135, 139, 199
definition 5–6, 36, 132–4
as empty and inexhaustible 135,
  139
as female principle 138–9
as generative principle 5, 21, 136,
  139–40, 199
and goodness 36–7, 143
and Hanfeizi 199–200
and harmony and equilibrium 38
as imperceptible 136–7, 139, 142
as ineffable 133, 134, 137, 142
and Laozi 5–6, 21, 131–42, 166,
  200
and *li* 199–200
and morality 6, 8–10, 141, 142–4,
  168–9
as nameless 137–8, 141, 166
and Nature 138, 139, 150
as Non-being 21–2, 134–5, 140,
  141, 150
as pre-existent 135–6, 139, 142,
  199
as transcendent and immanent
  139–40
transmission 10–11
as undifferentiated 136
and virtue 142–3
and Zhuangzi 22, 23, 153–4, 155,
  157–8, 163–6, 167–71, 173,
  179, 268, 315

Dao-xin (patriarch of Chan
    Buddhism) 304
Daoism
    and Chan School 316, 330
    and human nature 22–3, 25
    and Indian Buddhism 209–10
    and individual deliverance 21
    and knowledge 268
    and Legalism 200–2
    and politics 22
    and religion xii
    and truth 22
    and *Yijing* 26, 138
    see also Laozi
Dawson, Raymond 60, 335 n.4
de see virtue
death
    in Xunzi 91
    in Zhuangzi 173–9
defilements 229–32, 262, 299, 307,
    309, 311–12, 313
democracy
    and Hanfeizi 198, 203
    and Mozi 121–2
deontology
    and Confucianism 52–5, 63, 193
    and Laozi 142–3
    and Mohism 115–19
dependent co-arising 214, 216, 217,
    293
    in Consciousness-Only School
    223–5, 242
    in Tian-tai School 284, 285
desire
    in Buddhism 211–13, 231, 272,
    317
    in Confucius 56
    in Daoism 23, 145
    in Laozi 23, 145, 147–8, 347 n.16
    in Mencius 71–2, 74–5, 76–7, 79,
    93
    in Xunzi 93–4, 96–8, 103–4
destiny *see* fatalism
detachment
    in Chan School 320
    in Daoism 23

determinism
    in Hua-yan School 273
    and *karma* 216
    and Mencius 68–9
    in Mozi 125–7
    in *Yijing* 26, 42–5
dharma
    Buddha-realm 288–9
    Chan School 309–10
    Consciousness-Only School 221,
    223, 224–5, 233–6
    four realms 249, 260, 282
    Hua-yan School 249, 254, 260,
    261
    and materialism 233–4
    "no dharma" thesis 213–14,
    233–6, 240–5, 272, 310
    reality 216, 217–18, 224
    six realms 279–80, 282, 302
    ten realms 279–82, *281*, 284, 287,
    288, 300, 302, 365 n.39
    two realms 249, 261–5, 279
    see also existence; reality
Dharma (Truth) 213
dhyana see meditation
dialogues (*mondo*), Chan 325–7
Diamond Sutra 306, 307, 308–9,
    310, 311–12, 317–18, 327
discrimination
    and bodhisattvas 272
    and Chan School 310, 311, 313,
    318, 320, 325
    and "True Thusness" 265, 266–8
divination 3–4, 28
    and *Yijing* 29–30, 31–2, 42, 43,
    91
Doctrine of the Mean (*Zhong-yong*)
    19, 38, 333 n.3a
Donner, Neal and Stevenson,
    Daniel B. 278, 370 n.44
Du-shun (patriarch of Hua-yan) 248,
    249, 259, 263, 267, 271
dualism
    in Brahmanism 236
    yin and *yang* 7, 27
Dumoulin, Heinrich 376 n.68

Earth (*di*)
  in ancient folk religion 2
  and Confucian ethics 34–5, 36
  in Xunzi 104–5
  in *Yijing* 40, 58
education
  in Chan School 325–9
  and five classics 10–11, 104
  moral 92–3, 203, 340–1 n.23
  and politics 47, 122, 190, 203
effort (*wei*) 94–6, 98–101, 103, 146
egoism, psychological 115, 184, 273,
  355 n.5
emotions
  in Buddhism 213, 246
  in Xunzi 93–4, 96–7, 105–6
  in Zhuangzi 170
empathy (*shu*)
  in Confucius 48, 53–6, 62, 112
  in Mencius 81
Emptiness (*kong, Sunyata*) 210–11,
  217–18
  in Consciousness-Only School
  224–5
  in Hua-yan School 250–3, 264,
  266, 271–2
  in Theravada Buddhism 290, 293
  in Tian-tai School 251, 282, 284,
  285–6, 289, 290–1
energy, cosmic, *see qi*
enlightenment 210, 212, 217–19
  in Chan School 268, 295, 305,
  306–8, 310, 313–16, 319–22
  in Consciousness-Only School 224,
  242
  gradual/immediate 306, 307–8,
  313–16
  in Hua-yan School 248, 255
  in Tian-tai School 293, 294, 296,
  299–301
epistemology
  and Buddhism 211
  and Chan School 311, 323–5
  and ethics 8–9
  and Hua-yan School 265–8
  in Zhuangzi 155–8

and other minds 242–5
  in Xunzi 89–90
equilibrium (*zhong*), and harmony
  19, 33, 37–9
ethics
  and categorical imperative 54
  and Chan School 322
  Christian 53–5, 102
  Confucian 19–20, 23, 24–5, 34–5,
  37, 48–60, 102, 168
  consequentialist 111
  and contextual prescriptivism
  39–42, 43
  and *Dao* 6, 8–10, 141, 142–4
  deontological 52–5, 63, 115–19,
  142–3, 193
  Divine Command theory 116–19
  and epistemology 9
  in Hanfeizi 187–94
  and Hua-yan School 268–74
  and Laozi 141, 142–6, 148
  and Mencius 9, 63, 69, 71–2,
  73–83, 102
  Mohist 110–19, 128–9
  and moral failure 76–80
  and moral ideal 56–60, 62,
  111–12, 167–73
  and moral realism 39, 80
  naturalistic 76, 87–92, 102
  and politics 17, 49–50, 146,
  187–94, 203
  and primary virtues 35–6
  situational 41, 48
  utilitarian 115–19, 122, 124, 127
  and Xunzi 92–106, 146, 184
  in *Yijing* 28, 34–9
  and Zhuangzi 144, 150, 153,
  167–73
evil
  in folk religion 2
  in Hua-yan School 273
  in Laozi 147
  in Mencius 72, 78, 80
  in Tian-tai School 298, 299–300, 302
  in Xunzi 93–4, 95–101, 104, 302,
  339–40 n.3

existence
  provisional 286, 290–1
  subtle 285–6
  threefold nature 224–5
  see also dharma
experience, and knowledge 267–8, 324
extension, moral (*tuei*) 80–1, 83

fa see Legalism
Fa-zang (patriarch of Hua-yan) 249,
  252–4, 257, 365 n.49
  and bodhisattvas 270
  and interconnectedness of things
  258–60
  and nirvana 271
  and Realm of Principle 261–4
  six aspects in harmony theory
  260–1
family
  and Confucianism 16, 17, 24–5,
  48, 49, 81
  and filial piety 49, 52–3, 112,
  113–14
  and hierarchy 48, 49
  and love with distinctions 16, 20,
  81, 112–13
  and Mohism 20, 112–13
  of ruler 195, 198
  in *Yijing* 40
Fang, Litian 358 n.1
fatalism
  and Chinese Buddhism 216
  and Confucianism 109
  in folk religion 87–8
  and Mozi 125–7
  in *Yijing* 42–5
  and Zhuangzi 153–4, 172–3, 180
Feng Shui 29, 88–9
feudalism
  and Confucianism 83
  and Mohism 122
filial piety, in Confucius 52–3, 112
Fingarette, Herbert 59
Five Hegemonies 15
folk religion, early 1–3, 9, 20, 87–8,
  91

Four Books 333 n.3a
Four Noble Truths 212–13, 299
free will, and determinism 42–5,
  273
Fu, Charles Wei-hsun 145, 344 n.3,
  345 n.9, 366 n.64
Fu Xi (legendary ruler) 27
funerals
  in Confucianism 123–4
  in Mozi 109, 122, 123–4
  in Xunzi 105
Fung, Yu-lan x, 138, 185, 188, 195,
  209, 253, 278, 346 n.12, 360
  n.27, 363 n.6

Gaozi, and human nature 70–2, 75
Garner, Richard 373 n.10
Gautama, Siddhartha 210–18, 238,
  240, 268–9, 297
ghosts
  in Mozi 20, 125–7
  in Xunzi 91
Gimello, Robert M. 266, 274
god, concept 87, 126
Golden Rule 53–5, 112
Goldin, Paul Rakita 88, 340 n.6
gong-an 325
Good, in *Yijing* 34, 35, 36–7, 42
Goodman, Russell 157
goodness, human
  in Buddhism 219, 302, 319
  in Confucius 56–7, 62
  in Hanfeizi 191, 192–3
  in Laozi 9, 143, 145–6, 150
  in Mencius 65, 67–8, 71–2, 73–6,
  77–80, 94–5, 319
  in Xunzi 86, 92–102
  in *Yijing* 9, 38
governance
  absolute 193–4
  authoritarian 119–24, 194, 202
  humane 82–3
  and Laozi 146–50
  see also law; punishment
Graham, A. C. 8–9, 50, 67–8, 83,
  93, 98, 110, 120–1, 126, 144,

156–7, 177, 336 n.4, 344–5 n.3, 346 nn.11,13, 350 n.4, 353 n.78
Great Learning (Da-xue) 17, 333 n.3a
Great Treatise (in *Yijing*) 5, 29, 30, 35, 36, 41–2
Guan-ding (student of Zhi-yi) 277, 280, 369 n.6

habituation
  in Confucius 56–7
  in Xunzi 94, 104
Hamilton, Clarence H. 359 nn.4,6, 361 n.35
Hanfeizi 183
Hanfeizi (Han Fei Tzu) 23–4, 110, 149, **182–204**
  and *Dao* 199–200
  and ethics 187–94
  and human nature 183–7, 191–3, 355–6 n.26
  and law, statecraft and power 194–8, 200–2
  and metaphysics 198–202
  and politics 182–3, 187–98, 200–4
Hansen, Chad 51, 86, 131–2, 144, 152, 154–5, 167, 334 n.16, 339 n.2, 349 n.49, 352 n.38
harmony
  and Confucian ethics 19, 55–6
  cosmic 2–3, 9, 32, 33, 37
  and equilibrium 19, 33, 37–9
  and goodness 94
  in Laozi 146
  in Mozi 120
  and music 19
  and six aspects theory 260–1
heart *see* mind
Heaven (*tian*)
  in ancient folk religion 2, 87–8
  and Confucianism 34–5, 87–8, 126
  in Mencius 87–8
  in Mozi 20, 116–19, 121, 125–7
  in Xunzi 87–92, 93, 104–5, 106
  in *Yijing* 34, 36, 40, 58
  in Zhuangzi 167–8

heng (penetration of *qi*) 36
hexagrams in *Yijing* 3–4, 26, 28–9
  and change 30–2
  Feng 34
  Kun 29, 35, 40, 44, 45
  and morality 34–6, 39–40
  and primary virtues 35–6
  Qian 29, 35, 38, 40, 45
  Return 37
  Song 39
  the Family 40
  and time 41
  Xiao Guo 42
  Xu 39
hierarchy, moral
  in Confucianism 19, 48–9, 49, 55, 119
  in Mencius 66
hierarchy, social
  in Confucius 48–9, 49
  in Mozi 119–20, 126
  in *Yijing* 40, 42
Hinayana ("Small Vehicle") School (Buddhist) *see* Theravada School
holism 6
  causal 214
  and Chan School 330
  and Hua-yan School 258–61, 274
Hon, Tze-ki 44
Hong-ren (patriarch of Chan Buddhism) 304–5, 306, 324, 373 n.11
Hsu, Sung-peng 345 n.10
Hsün Tzu *see* Xunzi
Hua-yan School 199, 210, **248–75**, 362 n.53
  and Buddhahood 268–9, 293
  as Chinese 248
  and classification of teachings 218
  and emptiness 250–3, 264, 266, 271
  and ethics 268–74
  and existence 249
  and external reality 250–5, 261–5, 274–5
  and four realms of dharma 249

Hua-yan School (*cont'd*)
impact 274
and interconnectedness of things
258–60
and language skepticism 265–8,
296
and *li* (principle) 248, 261–4,
274–5
metaphysics 250–65
and noninterference of things 248,
260
and the One Mind 257–8, 260,
274–5, 311, 316
origins 248–9
as pan-Buddhism 270
and plurality of phenomenal
worlds 255–7, 261
and self 272–3
six aspects in harmony theory
260–1
Ten Mysterious Gates 249
and "True Thusness" 261–5, 266,
287
Hua-yan Sutra 248, 249–53, 255–7,
261–5, 266, 269–73, 374 n.24
Hua-yen School *see* Hua-yan School
Huang, Alfred 36
Huang Bo (Huang Po) 306, 315,
319, 323, 326–8, 374 n.20, 376
n.81
Hui-ke (patriarch of Chan Buddhism)
304, 373 n.11
Hui-neng (leader of Southern Chan
School) 304–5, 306
and Buddha-nature 319, 321
and enlightenment 314–16
and knowledge and language 324,
326
and meditation 313–14
and mind and nature 320, 376
n.81
and Mind-Only thesis 310–11
and pure mind 307–8
and reality 317–18
and seeing one's nature 311–12
as teacher 327

Hui-si (teacher of Zhi-yi), *Method of
Cessation and Contemplation*
278, 287, 301
Hui-wen 369 n.6
human nature 9, 273
badness of 9, 68, 86, 92–102
in Chan School 312, 314–15,
319–23
in Confucius 56–8
containment in nature 300
in Daoism 21, 22
in Hanfeizi 183–7, 191–3, 355–6
n.26
and human mind 68–73, 76–80,
84
in Laozi 145–6
in Legalism 24
in Mencius 65, 66–80, 92–3,
94–101, 302
in Mohism 20, 24, 112
and morality 34–5
in Tian-tai School 298–300
in Xunzi 9, 68, 86, 92–102, 104,
106, 184, 302
in *Yijing* 9, 34–9
see also Buddha-nature; goodness
humanism, and Chinese philosophy
9, 22, 246, 270
humanity (*ren*)
in Confucianism 19, 48, 56, 57–8,
59–60, 62, 111
governance with 82–3, 191–2,
355–6 n.26
in Hanfeizi 191–2, 204, 355–6 n.26
in Laozi 147
in Mencius 71, 72, 73–6, 78, 81,
82–3
in Mozi 111
Hurvitz, Leon 283, 286, 300
Hutton, Eric L. 337 n.11

I Ching see Yijing
idealism
objective, and Consciousness-Only
Buddhism 223, 232–3, 255, 283,
367 n.92

subjective, and Hua-yan School 250, 252–6
illumination (*ming*), in Zhuangzi 165–6
impartiality
  in Chan School 322
  in Daoism 23, 202
  and Mencius 81
  and Mozi 109, 110
  and Zhuangzi 167, 170, 173
inactivity (*wu-wei*) 170, 200, 202
  in Laozi 22, 144–6, 150, 154
individual
  in Daoism 21
  in Hanfeizi 203
  in Hua-yan School 274
  in Xunzi 86
  in Yang Zhu 115
  in *Yijing* 41–2
intellectuals, in Hanfeizi 193, 201
interconnectedness of things 258–60
Ivanhoe, Philip J. 53–4, 69, 74, 155, 157, 167, 335 n.4, 337 n.12, 338–9 n.43, 347–8 nn.16,23,34
Ivanhoe, Philip J. and Van Norden, Bryan W. xii, 94,

Jainism school 238
Japan, and Zen School 304
junzi
  as government official 344 n.43
  see also superior person
just war, in Mencius 82–3, 150

Kaltenmark, Max 3
  and Laozi 138, 144, 345 n.10, 346 n.13, 348 n.44
Kalupahana, David J. 217, 358 n.10, 360 n.9
karma, and cause and effect 215–16
Kasulis, T. P. 145, 345–6 n.10
Kern, Iso 228
Kim, Ha-poong 326
Kjellburg, Paul 167
Kline, T. C. III 102, 104, 342 n.57

Kline, T. C. III and Ivanhoe, Philip J. 86, 339 n.1
knowledge
  in Chan School 268, 296, 306, 311, 322, 323–5
  in Hanfeizi 201, 203
  in Hua-yan School 265–8, 272
  intuitive 324
  and language 268, 296, 306, 323–5
  in Laozi 137, 147–8, 349 n.49
  of other minds 242–5, 323–4
  of own mind 323–4, 327, 329
  pursuit 8–9
  supreme 272
  in Tian-tai School 289
  in Xunzi 89–90
  in Zhuangzi 150, 154–8, 161–6
Koan 325, 327, 328
Kongzi *see* Confucius
Kuiji 221, 238–9, 361 nn.35,40
Kun (*Yijing* hexagram) 29, 35, 40, 44, 45

Lai, Whalen 274, 307, 316, 330, 366 n.70
language
  in Chan School 268, 296, 306, 323–9
  and Confucius 51
  deconstruction 154
  and education 325–9
  in Hua-yan School 265–8, 296
  in Laozi 6, 22, 132–42
  perlocutionary 326–7
  in Xinzi 90–1
  in Zhuangzi 22, 155, 157
Lankavatara Sutra 307, 308–10, 311, 312–13, 375–6 n.57
Lao Dan 131
Lao si-guan 343 n.18
Lao Tzu *see* Laozi
Laozi (Lao Tzu) **131–50**
  and Buddhism 210
  and *Dao* 5–6, 21, 132–42, 166, 169, 200

Laozi (Lao Tzu) (*cont'd*)
  Daodejing 6, 131–2, 133, 142, 143
  and ethics 141, 142–6, 148
  and gratification of senses 23
  and human goodness 9, 143, 145–6, 150
  and inactivity 22, 144–6, 150, 154
  and language 6, 22, 132–42
  and Legalism 149, 198–202
  and politics 22, 145, 146–50, 200
  reversal 33, 37
  and society 21, 23
  as teacher 11
  and virtue 139, 142–4, 149
Lau, D. C. 66, 94, 95, 131, 138, 146, 335 nn.4,8, 337 n.12, 341 n.24, 346 nn.11,14, 347 n.16
law
  in Confucius 61–2, 193
  in Laozi 149
  and Legalism 24, 68, 184–6, 188–90, 192–3, 194–5, 198, 201, 203
  and Mencius 68
  as public 194
  and Xunzi 86, 100–1, 104
Laycock, Steven W. 308
learning *see* knowledge
Lee, Jung H. 157, 352 n.37
Lee, K. K. 183, 188, 193, 201
Legalism 23–4, 25
  and Communist China 183
  and Confucianism 187–94
  and Daoism 200–2
  and Laozi 149, 198–202
  and Mohism 24, 110, 121, 128
  and realism 354–5 n.1
  see also Hanfeizi
Legge, James 36, 347 n.23
Legge, Russell D. 177
LePore, Ernest and Loewer, Barry 348 n.47, 349 n.48
li (as benefit) 36, 115–19, 124–7, 128

li (as principle) 5–6
  in Hanfeizi 199–200
  in Hua-yan School 248, 261–4, 274–5
li (as propriety) 188
  in Confucius 18, 48, 52, 59–60, 61–2
  in Laozi 147
  in Mencius 72, 75–6, 78
  in Mozi 123
  in Xunzi 96, 98–9, 101, 102–6
  see also benefit; music; rites
Li Er 131
Li Si 182, 194
Li-ji (*Book of Rites*) 10, 333 nn.3a,6
Lin Ji (Lin-Chi) 306, 315, 321–3, 328
Lin, Yih-jing 355 n.5
Liu, Xiaogan 348 n.37
Lotus Sutra
  and Buddhahood 297–8
  and Chan School 376 n.68
  and Perfect Teaching 295
  and truth 294, 295–6
  and Tian-tai School 277, 278, 279, 281–2, 287–8, 371 n.53
love
  in Confucius 81
  with distinctions 16, 20, 81, 108, 109, 110, 112
  extension 83, 113
  in Mohism 20, 22, 24, 108–9, 110–15, 116, 118
  selfish 114–15
Loy, David 351 n.25, 354 n.80
loyalty (*zhong*) 20, 48, 53
  and politics 49–50, 62
  see also piety, filial
Lum, Alice 128
Lusthaus, Dan 232–3, 237, 329, 359 nn.3,4,6, 360–1 n.27, 361 n.31

Machiavelli, Niccolò 62, 83, 189
Madhyamaka School (Buddhist) 217–18, 278, 293

Mahayana ("Great Vehicle") School
  (Buddhist)
  and bodhisattvas 281
  and Buddhahood 232
  and Common Teaching 293
  and enlightenment 218–19, 231,
    296
  and Middle Way 284, 285–6,
    290–1, 293, 295–6, 360 n.16
  and mind 309, 316
  and selflessness 273, 368 n.105
  and Special Teaching 293
  and truth 296
Major, John S. 172, 353 n.77
materialism, Indian 233–4, 237
matter, and *qi* 6
mean *see* equilibrium
meditation
  and Chan School 304, 305, 311,
    312–14
  sitting 313–14, 316
The Mencius (Mengzi) 65, 70–1, 82,
  333 n.3a
Mencius (Mengzi) **65–84**
  and agriculture 17, 82
  analogical reasoning 66, 69–71,
    78–9, 83, 338 n.43
  and Confucius 65, 83, 84
  and education 332 n.14
  and ethics 9, 63, 69, 71–2, 73–83,
    102
  and five classics 11
  and human nature 65, 66–80, 84,
    92–3, 302, 319, 330
  and Mozi 109
  political philosophy 66–7, 81,
    82–3, 84, 88, 187
  and Xunzi 86, 92–3, 94–102
meritocracy, in Mozi 121–2
Middle Way 284, 285–6, 290–1,
  293, 295–6, 360 n.16
mind (*xin*)
  in Chan School 309–14, 316,
    319–23, 327, 330
  conditioned 319–20
  in Mencius 68–73, 76–80, 84

Mind-Only thesis 257–8, 260,
  274–5, 309–11, 316
  original 319–20, 324, 327
  other minds problem 242–5
  Pure 301, 302, 306, 307–8, 309,
    311–12, 313–14, 316, 317, 320
  in Tian-tai School 282–5, 288–9,
    298–301
  as ultimate reality 308–11
  watchful 307
  in Xunzi 90, 93
  in Zhuangzi 177, 316
  see also consciousness
Mo Tzu *see* Mozi (Mo Tzu)
moderation, in Mozi 122
Mohism 25, 65
  dialectics 110
  and elimination of desire 23
  Grand Masters 108
  and human nature 20, 24, 112
  and society 20–1
  and universal love 20, 23, 108–9,
    110–15, 116, 118
  see also Legalism; Mozi
mondo (dialogues) 325–7
monism, and dharmas 235–6
Moody, Peter R. 202, 357 n.38
morality
  and Nature 28, 34, 36, 39
  origins 102, 106
  and *yin* and *yang* 35, 36, 40, 43,
    45
  see also ethics
Mou, Bo 345 n.10, 346–7 n.14
mourning 18, 20–1, 105, 109, 123
  and filial piety 52
The Mozi 109–10
Mozi (Mo Tzu) **108–29**
  and Confucianism 108–9, 112,
    122, 128
  and ethics 110–19, 128–9
  and love with distinctions 20, 81,
    108, 109, 110, 112
  and Mencius 109
  and music 21, 109, 122–3
  and politics 108, 119–24

Mozi (Mo Tzu) (*cont'd*)
and religion 20, 124–7
and rites 20–1, 109, 122–4
and social reform 20, 24, 108–9,
112–15, 128–9
as teacher 108
and universal love 20, 23, 24,
108–9, 110–15, 116, 118
and Upward Conformity 120–1
music
in Confucianism 18–19, 21, 122
in Mozi 21, 109, 122–3
in Xunzi 104
mysticism, in Zhuangzi 157

Nagarjuna, and Zhi-yi 278, 285
names
and actuality 51, 196–7, 201, 320,
324–5
rectification 51
and styles 137–8, 144, 347–8 n.34
naturalism, in Xunzi 87–92, 102,
106
Nature
in ancient folk religion 2–4, 9,
87
and *Dao* 138, 139, 150
in Laozi 138, 146
and morality 28, 34, 36, 39
in pre-Buddhist philosophy 9
in Xunzi 88
in *Yijing* 28, 34
in Zhuangzi 153
see also human nature
Neo-Confucianism x, 8
and *Dao* 5
and Hanfeizi 183, 199
and Hua-yan School 269, 274
and Laozi 150
and Mencius 86
and Tian-tai School 302
and Xunzi 106
and *Yijing* 29, 36
Ng, Yu-kwan 277, 278–9, 298–9
nihilism, epistemic 291, 351 n.18
Nirgrantha School 238

nirvana 210, 212, 213, 218
and Buddhahood 297
in Chan School 307, 310, 313–14,
316, 317–18, 329
and Common Teaching 293
in Consciousness-Only School 229,
230, 232, 246
in Hua-yan School 252, 264, 270–1
and Perfect Teaching 293, 295
and Special Teaching 293
in Tian-tai School 279–82, *280*,
284, 286, 289, 293, 294, 297–9,
302, 318
and Tripitaka Teaching 292–3
Nirvana Sutra 317
Nivison, David S. 50, 103, 338
nn.26,33,40, 338–9 n.43
noumenon and phenomena
in Hua-yan School 250–5, 261–5,
264, 265, 270
see also reality

One Mind
and Chan School 309, 327
in Hua-yan School 257–8, 260,
274–5
ontology
in Chan School 317–18
in Hanfeizi 199–200
in Laozi 134–6, 139–40
of other minds 242–5
in Xunzi 87
see also existence; reality
order, cosmic 5–9, 40–1
order, social
and Confucianism 16–17, 50–1
and Hanfeizi 184–7, 188, 194, 203
and Laozi 145
and Mohism 20, 117–18
and Xunzi 96, 103
in *Yijing* 40–1

parents *see* family; piety, filial
particularity, and universal love 20,
113
Pasupata School 239

perception
  in Chan School 311, 320
  and consciousness 228
  in Consciousness-Only School 230,
    236
  in Hua-yan School 250–4, 264,
    266–8
  as illusory 213, 230, 236, 250–4,
    266
  in Tian-tai School 284
perfectibility
  in Confucius 56
  in Mencius 65
perfuming of consciousness 222, 223,
    224, 227, 229, 231, 242
  and causation 214–16, 273–4
  and external reality 242, 255
personhood, ideal
  in Buddhism 218, 231
  in Confucianism 19–20, 62
  in Mozi 111–12
  in Zhuangzi 170–3, 174, 177
perspectivism, in Zhuangzi 154–66,
    167–8, 179
petty (inferior) person (*xiaoren*) 19,
    57, 79, 99, 175
phenomena *see* noumenon and
    phenomena; reality
philosophy, and religion xii, 1–4, 9,
    20, 124–7
physiognomy 91
piety, filial
  in Confucius 49, 52–3, 112
  and Mozi 112–13
Pinyin Romanization system x,
    407–13
Platform Sutra of the Sixth Patriarch
    304–6, 312, 324, 374 n.14, 376
    nn.68,80
Plato, *Republic* 50, 60–1, 113, 149
pleasure, as transient 211
pluralism, and dharmas 234–5, 238
politics
  and Confucius 16–19, 24, 47–8,
    49–56, 60–2, 63, 68, 82, 88
  and *Dao* 9

and Daoism 22
and ethically ideal state 168–70
and ethics 17, 49–50, 146,
    187–94, 203
and Hanfeizi 182–3, 187–98,
    200–4
and Laozi 22, 145, 146–50, 200
and Legalism 24, 68
and loyalty 49–51
and Mencius 66–7, 81, 82–3, 84,
    88, 187
and Mozi 108, 119–24
in Spring-Autumn and Warring
    States periods 16
and *Yijing* 40
and Zhuangzi 154, 168–70, 201–2
Poussin, Louis de La Vallée 359 n.4
power, political (*shi*), in Hanfeizi
    194, 195–8, 202
pragmatism
  and Chan School 329
  and Legalism 24, 25
  and Mohism 20–1, 122, 124–8, 129
  and truth 125, 127, 294–6
  and Zhuangzi 179
preferences, relativity 158–66
prescriptivism, moral 39–42, 43
present-awareness 323
principle *see li*
propriety *see li*
punishment
  in Confucius 61–2
  and Legalism 24, 68, 184–7,
    189–93, 194, 196–7, 201, 203
  in Mencius 68
  in Mozi 20, 126
  in Xunzi 86, 100–1, 104
Pure Land Buddhism 317, 358 n.3
Putnam, Hilary 142, 154, 348 n.47,
    352 n.31

qi (energy) 6–7
  in Mencius 77
  in *Yijing* 30, 32, 36, 37–8
  and *yin* and *yang* 8, 30
  in Zhuangzi 176–7

Qian (*Yijing* hexagram) 29, 35, 38, 40, 45
Qin (state)
  and book burning 201
  and reunification of China 15, 182

Radhakrishnan 358 n.7
Raju, P. T. 362 n.42
Raphals, Lisa 156
rationality
  in Hanfeizi 189
  in Mozi 121–2
  in Zhuangzi 156–7
realism 25, 90–1
  and Buddhism 210, 216, 217
  and Chan School 309–10, 318, 329
  and Hua-yan School 253, 255, 267
  and Legalism 354–5 n.1
  metaphysical 141–2, 348 n.46
  moral 39, 80
  pluralist 234–5
  scientific 348 n.46
  and Tian-tai School 283, 286, 329
  and Zhuangzi 156, 157–8, 166
reality
  as Buddha 269–70, 273, 284, 288–9, 319
  in Chan School 308–11, 317–18, 323–5, 329
  characteristics 241
  in Consciousness-Only School 222–3, 230, 232, 233–6, 240–2, 243, 255, 280
  in Hua-yan School 250–5, 261–5, 274–5
  and language 265–8, 326
  in Laozi 133
  and materialism 234
  and mind 282–5, 301, 309–11
  and monism 235–6
  as nirvana 297–8
  and pluralism 234–5, 261
  and ten dharma realms 279–82, *281*, 284, 287, 365 n.39

  in Tian-tai School 251, 279–89, 290–1, 297–8, 368–9 n.5
  in Zhuangzi 154–8, 165, 179
reasoning, analogical 66, 69–71, 78–9, 83, 338 n.43
rectification of names 51
reincarnation, in Buddhism 212, 224, 230
relativism
  asymmetrical 156
  ethical 143, 167
  perspectival 154–5, 157–66, 167–8, 179
  radical 154, 166
  soft/hard 167
  and truth 292–3, 295–6
religion
  and Buddhism 210, 270, 288, 329
  in Mozi 20, 124–7
  and philosophy xii, 1–4, 9, 20, 124–7
  in Xunzi 91–2
Rémusat, Jean Pierre Abel 345 n.5
ren see humanity
reversibility, and Golden Rule 53–4
revolution, in Mencius 83
righteousness (*yi*)
  in Confucius 48, 59, 115
  in Hanfeizi 191–2
  in Laozi 147
  in Mencius 71–2, 74–8
  in Mozi 117
  in Xunzi 94, 96, 98–9, 101
rites
  and Confucianism 18, 20–1, 59–60, 105, 122
  and Mozi 20–1, 109, 122–4
  and Xunzi 91–2, 94–5, 102–6, 184
Rorty, Richard 154
Rousseau, Jean-Jacques 73
ru see reality
Ru-ism *see* Confucianism
rule-utilitarianism 117–19
ruler
  and Confucianism 16–17, 35, 47, 50, 60–2, 63, 88, 202

and Daoism 22, 132
and Hanfeizi 182–3, 185–6,
  187–98, 200–2, 203
and Laozi 132, 145, 146–50, 200–2
and Legalism 24, 25
and Mencius 65, 66–7, 80, 81,
  82–3, 84, 88–9
and Mozi 119–24
and rites 103
in Xunzi 86, 100–1, 103
in *Yijing* 34, 40
in Zhuangzi 154

sage (*sheng*)
  in Confucius 19, 56, 58, 63, 82
  in Laozi 143, 145, 146–7, 149
sage king 17, 60–2, 82, 101, 109,
  125, 187–9
  in Xunzi 92, 93, 99–101, 102–4,
  106
  in Zhuangzi 156
salvation, in Buddhism 212, 217–18,
  231, 298–9
Samkhyas School 238
School of Being (Buddhist) 217, 225,
  286, 318
School of Emptiness (Buddhist) 217,
  225, 286, 318
School of Mind 302, 376
School of Nature 302, 376 n.80
Schwartz, Benjamin 6, 51, 56–7,
  100, 111, 114, 122, 143, 145,
  194, 343 n.19, 344 n.3, 345
  n.4, 346 nn.12,13,
Schwitzgabel, Eric 354 n.95
self
  in Brahmanism 236
  substantiality 236–40
self-denial, in Mencius 79–80
self-interest 273
  in Hanfeizi 24, 183–5, 189, 192–3
  in Mozi 20, 112–15, 122
self-realization, in Chan School
  314–16
selflessness, Buddhist 210, 211–12,
  213, 216–17

in Consciousness-Only School 221,
  224, 230, 236–40
in Hua-yan School 272–3
Seng-can (patriarch of Chan
  Buddhism) 304
senses
  in Buddhism 218
  in Chan School 311
  in Consciousness-Only School 228,
  234
  in Hua-yan School 252, 264,
  266–8, 272
  in Laozi 23, 136–7, 147–8
  in Mencius 76–7, 79
  in Xunzi 89–91, 93–4, 96
Seven Supremacies 15
Sextus Empiricus 154
Shakyamuni (Gautama Buddha)
  210–18, 238, 240, 268–9, 297
shan see goodness
Shang Yang 194
Shang-di (Supreme Being) 1
Shen-hui 305
Shen-xiu (leader of Northern Chan
  School) 304–5, 306, 307–8,
  309, 311–12, 313–14, 373 n.11
sheng see sage
Sheng-yan 300
shi (political power), in Hanfeizi 194,
  195–8
shi (things, events), in Hua-yan
  School 248
shi (time) *see* time
shu see empathy
Shun, Kwong-loi 338–9 n.43
Shun (sage king) 17, 58, 61, 109,
  187
skepticism
  in Hanfeizi 193
  language 6, 22, 154, 155, 157–8,
  265–8, 296
  radical 154–5
  soft 155
  therapeutic 155–6
  in Tian-tai School 289
  in Zhuangzi 154–6, 157, 161, 166

social control 18, 103–4, 185–93, 194, 202–3
society
  and Confucianism 16–18, 48–56, 109, 169
  and the family 16–17, 20, 112
  in Hanfeizi 184–93, 202, 203
  human 8–9, 12
  in Laozi 21, 23, 146–8
  in Mencius 68, 80
  in Mohism 20–1, 108–9, 112–15, 128–9
  in Spring-Autumn and Warring States periods 16
  in *Yijing* 40
  in Zhuangzi 168–70
Soles, David 341 n.24
Soles, David and Deborah 351 n.18
soul, in Buddhism 212, 216, 237
space, in Hua-yan School 262, 270
Special Teaching 293, 296
speech acts, perlocutionary 326–7
spirits, in Mozi 20, 125–7
Spring-Autumn period 15–16
state *see* politics
statecraft, in Hanfeizi 194, 195–8, 200, 202
Stoicism, and Zhuangzi 178–9
Strenski, Ivan 375 n.48
substance
  Mind as 284, 368–9 n.5
  noumenon as 262–5, 264, 265
  and pluralism 234–5, 238
  ultimate 229
suchness, Ten Suchnesses 287
suffering
  and bodhisattvas 271
  in Buddhism 211–13
  in Consciousness-Only School 230, 246
  in Daoism 23
  in Hua-yan School 271–3
  in Tian-tai School 284, 299
sun, in *Yijing* 34
Sun, Siao-Fang 157–8, 165, 279
Sunyata see Emptiness

superior person (*junzi*) 19
  in Confucius 49–50, 56, 57–8, 59, 60
  in Hanfeizi 190
  in Mencius 78
  in Mozi 120–1
  in Xunzi 99, 106
  in *Yijing* 39–42
superstition, and Xunzi 87–9, 91, 106
Supreme Being (*Shang-di*) 1
  Buddha as 269
  in Mozi 126
Suzuki, Daisetz Teitaro 304, 305, 312, 314, 320, 324, 328–9, 374 n.17
Swanson, Paul L. 278, 370–1 n.44

tai-ji (totality of *qi*) 32
Tathagata (Perfect One) 310, 313
Tathata (True Thusness)
  and Chan School 309, 313, 317
  in Consciousness-Only School 232–3
  in Hua-yan School 261–5, 266, 287
teachers
  and enlightenment 321
  as transmitters of *Dao* 10–12, 104, 166
Ten Wings (supplementary texts to *Yijing*) 27, 28–9, 333 n.2b
Theatetus 154
Theravada School (Buddhist)
  and Buddha-nature 302
  and Common Teaching 293, 296
  and emptiness 290
  and enlightenment 218–19
  and ethics 273
  and nirvana 260 n.24, 281
  and Tripitaka Teaching 292–3
Thompson, Kirill O. 149
Thucydides 101
tian see Heaven
Tian-tai School 210, **277–302**, 362 n.53

and Buddha-nature 269, 270,
278–9, 281, 287–9, 301, 302
and Chan School 301, 302, 316,
318
as Chinese 248, 277, 302
classic texts 277–8
and classification of teachings 218,
292, 295
and emptiness 251, 282, 284,
285–6, 289, 290–1
and external reality 251, 279–89,
297–8, 368–9 n.5
and mind and the world 282–5,
288–9, 298–301
and semantic truth 289–97
and subtle existence 285–6, 302
and Ten Suchnesses 287
and Threefold Truth 278–9,
285–7, 289, 290–2, 297
time (*shi*)
cyclical view 227, 229
and morality 41, 43
in *Yijing* 32, 33
timeline, comparative xiii–xvii
Tong, Lik Kuen 37
tortoise-shell divination 3, 29
totalitarianism, and Hanfeizi 202–3
transformation of things, in Zhuangzi
177–8
transmigration 212, 224, 230, 232,
241, 279
*Treatise on the Awakening of Faith
in the Mahayana* 309
trigrams, in *Yijing* 3–4, 27–8, 34, 39
Tripitaka Teaching 292–3, 295–6
True Thusness 232–3, 261–5, 266,
280, 287, 288, 313, 318
Truth (metaphysical)
in Buddhism 211
in Consciousness-Only School 225
in Hua-yan School 249, 263,
265–8, 293
ineffability 266
in Laozi 141
Threefold 278–9, 285–7, 289,
290–2, 297

in Tian-tai School 279–89
Two Truths theory 285
in Zhuangzi 22, 154–8, 159,
161–6
truth (semantic) 157–8, 265–8
in Chan School 325
correspondence theory 141, 165,
290–2, 295
as hierarchical 295–6
as ineffable 296–7
pragmatic theory 125, 127, 294–6
as relative to understanding and
intelligence 292–3, 295–6
in Tian-tai School 289–97
tyranny
and Confucianism 19
and Legalism 202–3

universe
as Buddha 269–70, 284, 288
and change 32–3
in Consciousness-Only Buddhism
228–9, 234
in folk religion 2–4
and harmony 2–3, 9, 32–3, 38,
146
in Laozi 136, 138, 150
and morality 34–5, 37–9, 42
see also cosmology
Upward Conformity, in Mozi 120–1
utilitarianism
and Legalism 193
and Mohism 115–19, 122, 124,
125–7

Vairocana, Buddha as 269–70
Vaisesika School 234, 238
Van Norden, Bryan W. 5, 79, 338–9
n.43
Vasubandhu 228, 235, 236, 360 n.9
*Thirty Stanzas of Consciousness-
Only* 220–1, 232, 240–2
*Twenty Stanzas of Consciousness-
Only* 220, 221, 225, 233,
240–2, 245, 361 n.34, 363 n.61
Vedas 235

Vendanta School 235–6
virtue (*de*)
  extension 80–1
  in Hanfeizi 190, 192
  in Laozi 139, 142–4, 147, 149
  in Mencius 69, 71–6, 80–1
  negative 144
  of rulers 16–17, 60–2, 63, 149
  in Xunzi 96, 104
  in *Yijing* 35–6
  see also loyalty
Vorenkamp, Dirck 117, 126

Wade-Giles Romanization system x,
  407–13
Waley, Arthur 354–5 n.1, 357 n.38
Wang, Hsiao-po 194
Wang, Qingjie 138, 144
Wang Yangming 268, 330
war
  in Confucianism 17–18
  in Laozi 149–50
  in Mencius 82–3, 150
  in Mozi 108, 124
  in Xunzi 150
Warring States period 15–17, 20,
  128, 150, 182
Watson, Burton 94, 126, 166, 183,
  277, 288, 296, 344 n.49, 357
  n.44
Watts, Alan 372 n.1
wealth
  in Confucius 57
  in Mencius 78
  in Mozi 122, 123
wei see effort; inactivity
Wei, Tat 359 n.6
Wen of Zhou, King 28
Wilhelm, Richard 27, 31, 32, 33, 34,
  41, 345 n.5
Wilhelm, Richard and Baynes,
  Cary F. 35–6
will (*zhi*)
  in Mencius 76–7, 79
  see also free will
Wing, R. L. 33

wisdom
  in ancient folk religion 3–4
  in Chan School 310, 314–15,
    320–3
  in Consciousness-Only Buddhism
    221, 229–33, 280
  Four Transcendental Wisdoms
    230–2
  in Hanfeizi 200–1
  in Laozi 147
  in Mencius 72, 75–6, 78
  in Tian-tai School 293
Wong, David B. 66, 74, 112–13,
  167, 338–9 n.43
Wright, Arthur F. 209
Wu, John C. H. 353 n.67
Wu, Kuang-ming 350 n.6
Wu Cheng-en 359 n.2
wu-wei see inactivity

Xia dynasty 342 n.2
xiao see piety, filial
xiaoren see petty person
Xie, Wenyu 354 n.93
xin see mind
Xuan-zang (Hsüan Tsang) 220–1,
  360 n.9
  Cheng Wei-Shi Lun (*Treatise*)
    221, 223, 225–9, 230, 238–9,
    240–5, 360 n.17, 361 n.34,
    362 n.45
The Xunzi 86, 104
Xunzi (Hsün Tzu) **86–106**
  and culture 145–6
  and ethics 92–106, 145–6, 184
  and Hanfeizi 182, 183
  and Heaven 87–92
  and human nature 9, 68, 86,
    92–102, 104, 106, 184, 302
  and Mencius 86, 92–3, 94–102
  and religion 91–2

Yampolsky, Philip 305, 373 n.7
Yan Hui (student of Confucius) 58
Yang, Huei-nan 373 n.3
Yang Zhu 65, 114

Yao (sage king) 17, 58, 61, 88, 99, 109, 187
Yearley, Lee 152, 168
Yen Hui (student of Confucius) 173
yi (change) 29–34
yi (righteousness)
  in Confucius 48, 59, 115
  in Hanfeizi 191–2
  and Laozi 147
  in Mencius 71–2, 74–8
  in Mozi 117
  in Xunzi 94, 96, 98–9, 101, 102
Yijing (*Book of Changes*) 26–45
  and change and non-change 27–8, 29–34, 42, 43–4
  Commentary on the Images 28, 39–42
  Commentary on the Judgment 28, 32, 36–7, 40–1
  Commentary on the Words of the Text 29, 44
  and Confucius 26, 28–9
  and cosmology 8, 26–9, 30, 40, 58
  and *Dao* 5, 138
  date 26
  and divination 3–4, 28, 29, 31–2, 42, 43, 91
  and ethics 28, 34–9
  and the Good 34, 35, 36–7, 42
  Great Treatise 5, 29, 30, 35, 36, 41–2
  hexagrams 3–4, 26, 28–9, 30–2, 34–6, 39–40
  and human goodness 9, 38
  influence 26, 45
  philosophy of action 42–5
  primary virtues 35–6
  role in education 10
  Ten Wings 27, 28–9, 333 n.2b
  trigrams 3–4, 27–8, 34, 39
yin and *yang* 7–8, 9
  and change 30–1, 33, 43
  and harmony 32, 37–8
  in Laozi 347 n.25
  and morality 35, 36, 40, 43, 45
  in *Yijing* 4, 26, 27, 30–1

Yogacara School 239–40
Yu (sage king) 99, 109
yuan (origin of life) 36

Zan-ran (student of Zhi-yi) 371 n.67
Zen Buddhism *see* Chan (Zen) School
Zengzi (Confucius' student) 48, 49
Zeuschner, Robert B. 215, 309, 311
zhen (correctness) 36
zhi see will
Zhi-yan (patriarch of Hua-yan) 248, 249, 252
Zhi-yi (Chih-i) 277–8
  and Buddha-nature 278–9, 288, 298–9, 301
  and classification of teaching 292, 295
  The Esoteric Meaning of the Lotus Sutra 277, 278
  and Fourfold Teaching 292–3
  The Great Calming and Contemplation 277–8, 291
  and hierarchy of truth 295–6
  and human nature 298–300
  and mind and the world 282–5
  and nirvana 294, 299
  and no-truth 296–7
  and reality 279, 280–2, 285–6, 288–9, 290–1
  and semantic truth 289–91
  and subtle existence 285–6, 302
  and ten dharma realms 280–2, 300
  and Threefold Truth 278–9, 285–7, 289, 290–2, 297
  The Words and Phrases of the Lotus Sutra 277–8
zhong see equilibrium; loyalty
Zhong-yong (*Doctrine of the Mean*) 19, 38, 333 n.3a
Zhou Dynasty 3,15, 28
Zhu, Bokun 346 n.11
Zhu Xi 333 n.3a
The Zhuangzi 152–3, 165
  Inner Chapters 152–4, 353 n.78
  Miscellaneous Chapters 152–3, 166, 169, 176

The Zhuangzi (*cont'd*)
  Outer Chapters 152–3, 159–60,
    172, 174
Zhuangzi (Chuang Tzu) **152–80**,
    210
  and Chan School 315, 316
  and Confucius 168–9, 180
  and *Dao* 22, 23, 153–4, 155,
    157–8, 163–6, 167–71, 173,
    179, 268, 315
  and ethics 144, 150, 153, 167–73
  and human goodness 9
  and language 22, 154, 155, 157–8
  and life and death 173–9
  and politics 154, 168–70, 201–2
  and transformation of things
    177–8
  and truth, reality and knowledge
    154–8
Zigong (Confucius' student) 335 n.25

Printed in the USA
CPSIA information can be obtained
at www.ICGtesting.com
JSHW010842181123
52044JS00016B/89